INVITATION
TO
LISTENING

INVITATION TO LISTENING

RICHARD L. WINK

LOIS G. WILLIAMS

An Introduction to Music

Houghton Mifflin Company
Boston
New York / Atlanta / Geneva, Illinois
Dallas / Palo Alto

MT
6
.W55

Library of Congress Catalog Card Number: 76-165037

ISBN: 0-395-12340-2

Contents

67701

Chapter 12

Musical Style: 1750 to the Present

Appendices

Preface

This text is designed for the general college student who is beginning a study of music as part of a liberal arts or teacher education program. For years, we have been faced with the problem of how to teach music to the student who has little or no musical background and whose formal study in music will be limited to one or two courses.

Music courses in the general college curriculum are commonly called music "appreciation." Webster defines appreciation as "sensitive awareness, especially recognition of esthetic values." However, this definition does not tell us how to approach the difficult task of teaching such courses.

The student should come away from a course in music appreciation with some idea of what the world of music has to offer and with the tools for understanding what he hears. But what kind of tools will be useful to him? Should he study the composers, their lives, loves, and libidos? Should he learn to read the musical score and follow it during the concert? Should he study a few select compositions by listening to them repeatedly and memorizing their themes? These traditional approaches to music appreciation are interesting and sometimes useful for the beginning student, but they are often irrelevant, unnecessary, or too limited.

The student should learn how to deal directly with any music he encounters. He should learn how to deal with musical *sound* itself, learn how to listen, how to make sense of what he hears, how to increase his perceptive powers. This book is designed with that purpose in mind: *to help the student learn how to listen to music.* The materials are organized so that he may identify the aural factors in music, discuss them, relate them to the other arts—poetry, painting, sculpture, and architecture—and experience them by listening to recorded excerpts of them. All this material is presented in non-technical language. The study begins with such elemental concepts as loud-soft and high-low, proceeds through repetition, contrast, and texture, and arrives at form, movement, and style.

Listening thus becomes both the means and the end; the student becomes a music listener by learning how to listen.

A number of friends and colleagues have offered immeasurable assistance in the preparation of this text. Special thanks are due to Richard Phipps, associate professor of art at Capital University, whose advice in the use of art examples was invaluable. We are grateful to the Boston Symphony Orchestra, who provided us with the photographs of the instruments of the orchestra in Chapter Two. Also, thanks go to three special music classes of "guinea pigs" who suffered through a trial run with the preliminary edition. Finally, our thanks to Arthur W. Hepner, of Houghton Mifflin Company, whose insight into music and faith in this project have made it all possible.

Lois G. Williams   Richard L. Wink
The Ohio State University
Mansfield, Ohio

Chapter 1

The Art of Listening

Nearly everyone likes music. Different as musical tastes may be, most people can find something to satisfy their listening preferences in the vast world of music: symphonies, operas, chamber music, or "popular" music such as jazz, folk, country-western, or rock. Of course, people do not all like the same kinds of music. Some prefer Bach, some the Beatles. Some like both. Unhappily, an imaginary dividing line separates "popular" from "serious" music, and too often those acquainted with one world are unwilling to cross over into the other.

Many people say they avoid so-called serious music because they do not like, or do not understand it. Even those who do listen to concert or recorded music may never have really learned *how* to listen or *what* to listen for. Even musical performers sometimes have difficulty in simply listening to music when they are not performing. So almost everyone, regardless of his musical background or tastes, can benefit from learning how to listen more carefully and more sensitively.

The quality of each musical experience depends on our ability to listen. The first step in developing the art of listening is learning to concentrate on the music. Here, modern man may be at a disadvantage. Technology offers us a mixed blessing. As an example, the electronic sound media of our society provide us with music instantly and constantly. The city is alive with music in stores, in professional offices, even on the street. But *background music* inhibits learning the art of listening because it is meant to be ignored rather than listened to. It actually trains us to be non-listeners. People who work all day in places where music is constantly droning in the background confess they no longer hear the music. They have tuned it out, much as people who live close to a noisy highway soon learn to tune out the noise.

The concert hall is different. There, we find the most effective situation for listening to music. Instead of being surrounded with and lulled into inattention by constant and subdued Muzak, we go to the concert hall for the express purpose of listening to a particular program. All other distractions are minimized; and there is even a suspenseful moment of silence before the conductor or performer enters which further heightens our anticipation and interest. The formal atmosphere forces us to focus our attention on the music; the lights are turned down; the audience is ready to listen. But effective listening depends on more than focusing attention. We must know what to listen *for*.

Listening has various dimensions. We first come to enjoy the sensuous effects of the musical sounds, primarily through the psychological associations which accompany various kinds of musical movement and sound. This is to be expected, since we are conditioned to associate specific kinds of music with specific types of dramatic action: the excited music of the chase; the soft, quiet music of the love scene; the mysterious sonorities which heighten moments of suspense.

The trained musician, on the other hand, listens to the changing plateaus of key centers, the subtle harmonic distinctions characteristic of various composers, or the unique ornamentation of a Mozart cadenza. This kind of listening is the result of extended music study and constitutes a highly specialized approach to the art of listening.

Although we need to go beyond the visceral level of musical experience to broaden our listening experience, we need not adopt the musician's highly technical approach to listening. We can cultivate the art of listening by learning to hear basic elements of musical expression which are understandable to everyone whether or not he is able to read music or play an instrument.

The material in this book is for you, designed to help you learn to listen to music, and arranged so that after reading about a musical element, you hear a recorded example of that element. You will thus *experience* the element by listening to it, much as you would experience it in the concert hall. In this manner, you can learn the basic aural elements of music. You will not need to learn to be a musician; you will simply learn how to listen to and enjoy music.

The Boundless Variety of Music

A rapid survey of music reveals such variety that the listener may be bewildered by it all. He is faced with a great mass of music literature —some historically significant, some esthetically pleasing, some acoustically interesting. Let us examine this "bewildering" variety. Our first encounter reveals that historical periods are partially responsible for the great variety in music. Examples 1.1–1.4 sound very different from one another, and were composed in distinctly different historical periods. Try to figure out what musical factors determine the differences you hear.

Example 1.1
Gregorian chant: *Easter Mass*

Example 1.2
Stravinsky: *Symphony of Psalms*

Example 1.3
Beethoven: *Symphony No. 3 in E-flat,* Op. 55 (*Eroica*)

Example 1.4
Couperin: Piece for Harpsichord, *La Galante*

You are immediately aware of major differences in the sounds, styles, and performance media of these pieces. By observing these differences, you can probably deduce which pieces are early and which are late. Relating these differences in sound to historical periods in music is one way you can make sense of what you hear. But it also helps to notice the similarities among the pieces. For example, in each pair of pieces, the medium of performance is the same: the first and second are performed by voices, the third and fourth by instruments. And in each pair, the composer's intent is the same: the first two pieces are sacred, the last two are secular. The first two have words, the last two have no words. Nevertheless, each piece sounds strikingly different from the others. You will encounter many more similarities and diversities as you explore other musical examples.

Example 1.5
Beethoven: *String Quartet,* Op. 132

Example 1.6
Ussachevsky: *Composition for Tape Recorder*

Example 1.7
Wagner: "Walther's Prize Song," from *Die Meistersinger,*
Act III, Scene 5

Example 1.8
Elgar: *Variations on an Original Theme*
(*Enigma Variations*)

Example 1.9
Dylan: "Mr. Tambourine Man"

These examples demonstrate the boundless variety in music. It is partly this variety that invites a deeper understanding and makes the study of music worth the effort. If we can make no sense of a particular piece of music on first hearing, we may not be moved to make further attempts at understanding or appreciating that piece. Good music, however, like all the other arts, deserves study. Great music can be microscopically examined, dissected, criticized, evaluated, reevaluated, and it will continue to offer something of interest. This does not mean that we will "like" all music generally conceded to be good. Some music will appeal to us immediately and will never cease to be appealing even after extensive study. Some will grow on us even if we did not like it on first hearing. Some will never interest us, even after extensive listening experience. But at that point the basis for our acceptance or rejection will be understanding of the art of music and a knowledge of its elements. At that point we will have developed discriminating tastes.

Thus, in summary, we must remember that a great deal is happening in a piece of music, much of which is not available to the un-skilled listener. But it is easy to become a skilled listener without being a musician. Anyone can develop the capacity to apprehend music more completely. The challenge for the beginner is to find some order in the boundless variety, a way to approach the diversity we have just heard. To do so, we concentrate on the listening process itself and defer anything that does not contribute to the task of listening. We shall always find variety in music, but we shall no longer find it overwhelming, because we shall be making constant attempts to synthesize, to find the unity that exists in it.

Abstract Media of Expression

Part of the problem in listening to music is that it is an *abstract* medium of expression. Music, by itself and without text, is not capable of communicating social, political, or moral "messages." Music merely *is;* the ideas communicated are musical. Let us draw an analogy with abstract art. Consider the painting in Plate 1,[1] an abstract work by Mondrian, *Composition with Red, Yellow, Blue and Black,* 1921. It may convey little meaning; in fact, this abstract work may seem bleak, or even repugnant. The absence of any reference to objects in the real world such as trees, mountains, or people makes the painting difficult to deal with; we are not sure what to look for. But perhaps if we view the stages of Mondrian's development toward that style, the new experience with abstract art might become more meaningful.

The picture painted in 1908 entitled *The Red Tree* (Plate 2) reveals Mondrian's early representational style. As he painted picture after picture of that same subject, Mondrian became fascinated with the possibility that his subject matter could be reduced to the essentials of shape, line, color, and texture. He was concerned with the shape of space rather than a literal translation of the object. He concentrated on the horizontal and vertical shapes *between* the branches of the tree (Plate 3).

The next stage in Mondrian's development was to distill from this subject the basic structure, which was a pure linear expression (Plate 4). By 1913, Mondrian was reaching the final stages in the development of his abstract style. Significantly, he began titling his paintings "composition" rather than "tree" or "sea" (Plate 5). Thus, when Mondrian's mature style evolved, all reference to the outside world had been eliminated. The painter was somehow able to ab-stract shape, line, and color from objects in the real world. The tree was no longer the object; in fact, it .was no longer important to refer to the tree. The shapes, lines, and colors now spoke for themselves.

[1] Plates 1–5 are reproduced on pages following p. 22.

The study of Mondrian's style development, even in this capsule form, improves our appreciation of the abstract. Abstract art is not more complex than representational art. It simply must be dealt with in different terms. We look to see what is in the painting itself—design, color, form—and do *not* try to think what it reminds us of, or become offended if we do not understand its "meaning." Similarly, in music, an abstract medium of expression akin to Mondrian's mature style of painting, we should look for what the music itself expresses—melody, color, form—and not merely search for "extramusical" meaning. Just as a painting need not look like a tree, so music need not sound like a chase to convey meaning. Because music is an abstract medium of expression, we must first learn to deal with abstract principles such as repetition, texture, tonality, design, and movement. When we understand the relationships among these musical elements, we will be experiencing musical meaning.

Chapter 2

The Elements of
Musical Sound

Music is made of sounds. They are high, low, long, short, loud, soft—qualities that can be measured. They are also dark, bright, strident, mellow—subjective qualities that can be described, but not measured. The various elements of sound can be classified into *pitch* (relative highness), *timbre* (quality), *duration* (relative length), and *dynamics* (relative loudness). These elements and the range of musical instruments available supply the composer with the materials necessary to express himself, much as line, shape, and a full palette of color supply the painter with the materials he needs for expression.

The Elements of Sound

Pitch

One of the first things we notice about a sound is that it is high or low. A flute produces higher sounds than a tuba, a soprano sings higher than a bass, and a boy sings lower as he matures. In perceiving relative highness and lowness in sounds, we are experiencing *pitch*.

Pitch is determined by the speed at which the sound object vibrates. This vibrating object can be a string, a bar, an enclosed column of air, a membrane, or, in fact, anything that can cause a disturbance in the air. Pitch is determined by a number of factors: length or size of the vibrating medium, amount of tension, composition of material. For example, the strings of a piano are drawn to various degrees of tautness, and they are of varying thicknesses and lengths. The string that produces the lowest sound on the piano is the longest and least taut, and it is wrapped in copper wire to make it the thickest. It vibrates about 30 times per second. The upper strings, which vibrate as fast as 4,000 times per second, are thin, short, and tightly drawn.

The principles for precise determination of pitch apply to other means of producing sound. The length of the column of air vibrating in a flute is altered as the player manipulates the keys and covers the finger holes. A short column of air vibrates more rapidly than a long one. The longest column of air in the flute is far shorter than the air column in a contrabassoon, with its great length of convoluted tubing. Likewise, the small drum with a tightly stretched drumhead is pitched higher than the larger drum with a thicker, more loosely-stretched head. It is logical, therefore, that the smallest instrument in the orchestra, the piccolo, also has the highest pitch. In the carillon, the bell with the highest pitch can fit in the palm of your hand; the one with the lowest pitch weighs several tons.

Instruments and voices vary in their pitch ranges. For example, the entire range of the flute is above any pitch in the usual range of the contrabassoon. Figure 2.1 gives the ranges of pitch for voices and for the standard instruments of the orchestra, and shows how these ranges compare with one another. Notice that the ranges of the human voices are much more limited than those of the instruments, and that the ranges of the instruments vary. For example, the range of the clarinet extends above and below that of the oboe; and the range of the French horn is much more extensive than that of the trumpet. It is significant to note the amount of overlap in the pitch ranges, indicating that many different instruments and voices are capable of producing the same pitches.

Timbre

The highness and lowness of sounds have implications far beyond pitch. A string stretched between two points seems to be producing a single pitch, but in reality is sounding *many* pitches at the same time. While the string vibrates along its full length, it also vibrates in halves, thirds, fourths, and so on. The listener "hears" a single pitch, though he is aware of the qualifying sounds produced by the other pitches. These subaudible pitches are called *overtones;* and it is the combination of all these pitches and the predominance of some which constitute the timbre, or tone quality, of the over-all sound. This is the primary reason why we can distinguish the sound of a flute from that of a clarinet; certain overtones in the clarinet tone set it apart from that of the flute. These overtones are produced by the structure of the instrument and by the nature of the vibrating medium.

The tone quality of certain instruments is so striking as to capture the attention of an audience and even distract from other features of a piece. Listen to Examples 2.1 and 2.2 which are actually the same composition, except that the first is arranged for two violins and orchestra and the second for two harpsichords and orchestra. The difference in total sound when harpsichords are substituted for violins is remarkable.

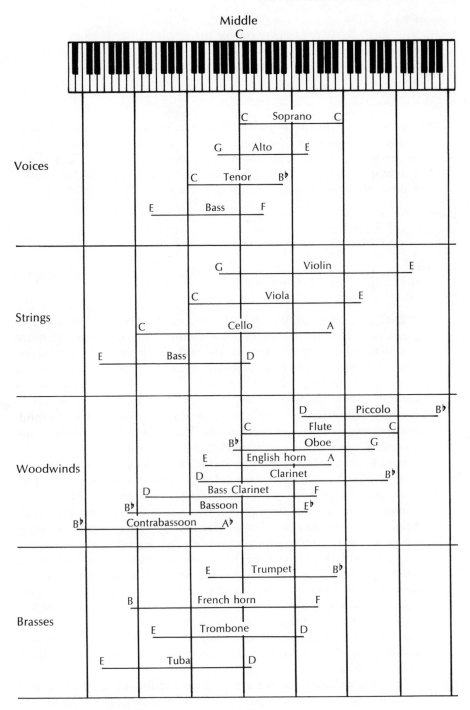

Figure 2.1 Pitch ranges of voices and instruments

Example 2.1

Bach: *Concerto for Two Violins and Orchestra
in D minor*

Example 2.2

Bach: *Concerto for Two Harpsichords and Orchestra
in C minor*

Listen now to the popular *Pictures at an Exhibition* written originally for piano by Moussorgsky and subsequently arranged for
orchestra by Ravel. The orchestral version, though faithful to the
original, is virtually a new composition because of the added dimension of the countless timbres of the symphony orchestra.

Example 2.3

Moussorgsky: "Great Gate at Kiev," from
Pictures at an Exhibition

Example 2.4

Moussorgsky-Ravel: "Great Gate at Kiev," from
Pictures at an Exhibition

Each instrument in the orchestra and each individual human voice
possesses its own timbre or tone quality, though some are more
distinctive than others. It may be difficult to distinguish a violin
from a viola, for example, because they are similarly constructed
and overlap in range. But it is easy to distinguish the violin from a
clarinet, oboe, flute, or trumpet, even if all play the same pitch,
because of the striking differences in timbres. Variations in timbre
are also possible in one instrument. Thus, the highest tones of the
clarinet have a quality different from the lowest, a trumpet can be
muted to change the tone color, and strings can be bowed or plucked.

A physicist can measure timbre objectively in terms of the over-
tone system, but his scientific measurement means little to the
listener who instead uses subjective, relative terms such as rich,
bright, dark, or thin to describe the quality of the sound he hears.
These terms, of course, are useful only when we come to understand
the experience they describe. We know the color yellow only as we
have experienced it individually; we know it collectively only as a
term which describes our common visual experience. We agree
that a canary is yellow, but we have no way of knowing whether
one person's perception of yellow is the same as another's. To say
that yellow is a rich color is a subjective statement, because each
person's experience with that color would dictate the quality of
yellow to him.

In music subjective terms are used to describe the quality of sound
in terms of the common experience of listeners. These terms are
useful in that they enable us to discuss music and its effect on us.
They should not be considered absolute measures and are not meant

to dictate your perception of the sounds to which they refer.

Timbre is as important to the composer as color is to the painter. Just as the painter decides which color should express certain shapes in his painting, the composer must decide which instruments shall play each part in his composition. The combinations of timbres play important roles in the expression of esthetic ideas much as combinations of colors express esthetic ideas in painting.

Duration

Besides pitch and timbre, each tone has the added dimension of length. This is called *duration*—the amount of time a musical sound is sustained. Sounds can be sustained for varying lengths of time, depending both on the means and the medium used for producing the sound. A singer or a flute player, for example, can sustain a sound for as long as his breath will support it. A violinist can sustain a tone as long as he continues to draw the bow across the string. An electronic instrument, such as an organ, can sustain a sound indefinitely (provided no one pulls the plug).

Composers use a system of notation to indicate the relative duration of sounds; for example, a half note ($\bd$) lasts twice as long as a quarter note ($\bd$). Appendix B illustrates the durational value of each note as it relates to other note values. The composer can indicate his intentions even more precisely in two ways: (1) he may use a *tempo* marking, or rate of speed, such as *allegro* (fast) or *lento* (slow)— Appendix C lists the most common of these terms; (2) he may use a timing device to measure precisely the durational value of each note. For example, a composer may indicate that there are to be sixty half notes per minute ($\bd$ = 60), meaning that each half note should last for one second. Sounds of varying durations are then combined to form *rhythm* in music. But rhythm is another story and we shall deal with that fascinating topic later.

Dynamics

Imagine what music would be like if it were all played at the same volume—dull and without expression. We hear variations in softness and loudness (dynamics) as components of musical expression. Everywhere in music we find changing levels of dynamics: the composer may write a part for a solo violin, for just a few violins, or for the entire violin section of the orchestra. The player can achieve further dynamic variation by increasing or decreasing the pressure of the bow on the strings. Decisions about dynamic level are made by both composer and performer. And how important these decisions are to the total effect of the music! The performer who is sensitive to appropriate dynamic levels can carry the listener to heightened esthetic enjoyment. The insensitive performer can bore or even offend his audience. Composers convey their wishes to performers through the use of symbols which indicate relative dynamic values (for example, *p = piano,* or soft; *f = forte,* or loud). Appendix C includes the most common of these dynamic symbols and terms. Although the loudness of any sound can be objectively measured in decibels, there is at present no way that a composer can express this exact measure in a musical score. The performer must decide just how softly to play "piano" or how loudly to play "forte."

Vehicles of Musical Sound

Voices

The first music ever produced was probably made by the human voice because it is part of man's physiology. Thus, music through the ages has developed with reference to the voice. It is not difficult to imagine that primitive man, discovering that his voice was capable of certain timbres and pitches, would have a natural interest in similar sounds discovered by accident: a plucked bow string, wind blowing across the reeds in a brook. This natural tendency to relate new sounds to the human voice makes the voice the most fundamental of musical sounds.

There are four basic classes or types of voice (Table 2.1, see pp. 14–15): high and low treble, usually female, called *soprano* and *alto;* and high and low bass, usually male, called *tenor* and *bass.* Much of the music in Western culture is based on these four classifications: the major choral literature is written for soprano, alto, tenor, and bass (SATB); and most of the instruments are classified and grouped with reference to these four types. However, there are subdivisions within each class. Among the sopranos, for example, we find a *coloratura* (specializing in florid ornaments and trills), *lyric* (a light, flexible voice), *dramatic* (given to heavier, usually serious music), and *mezzo* (overlapping the alto range). Between the tenor and bass lies the range of the *baritone* which overlaps the other two. The following table lists pitch ranges and qualities of the four basic voice types. Listen to the examples and study the relationships between the four vocal classes.

Instruments

Strings. Strings are not just the most important and largest section of the orchestra. They *are* the orchestra. The orchestra could survive —and has survived—without the other sections and retain its identity. Without strings, it may be a band, an ensemble, even a choir, but it is no longer an orchestra. In the early seventeenth century, a group of stringed instruments alone constituted the orchestra. Woodwinds, brasses, and percussion were gradually added as the technique of orchestration became more sophisticated and as these instruments were technically developed. But the strings have to the present remained the core of the orchestra, the center of musical action.

The instruments in the string family—violin, viola, cello, and double bass—are the counterparts of the soprano, alto, tenor, and bass voices, because their relative pitch ranges and their typical functions in the ensemble correspond roughly to those of the voices. However, each instrument has a greater pitch range than the corresponding voice, as indicated in Table 2.2 (pp. 16–17). All members of the string family are similar in shape and in the manner in which they are played: the sound is produced by drawing a bow across one or more of four strings, or, occasionally, by plucking the strings with the fingers. These instruments are extremely versatile and expressive and, because of their similarity, produce a relatively homogeneous sound. String players can play for a very long time without ceasing, in contrast with brass and wind players, whose lips and breathing need frequent rests. This is another reason why the strings have been historically the center or the foundation of the orchestra. The main function of the string section in the orchestra is to present the substance of the musical material. In the modern orchestra, we find two violin parts, high and low, or first and second. The melody is usually found in the first violins, the bass part in the cellos and double basses, and the harmony in the second violins and violas. Table 2.2 illustrates the relationship of the individual instruments in the string family. A picture of each instrument is included (Figure 2.2, p. 18) along with descriptions of the pitch range, timbre, and function of each. Examples for listening will help clarify their unique timbres and capabilities.

Woodwinds. Shepherds play the pipes, sailors pipe visitors aboard, soldiers march to fife and drum. All these pipes are woodwinds, an ancient family of musical instruments that has evolved into the sophisticated group found in today's orchestra.

The woodwind instruments are vastly outnumbered by the strings in the orchestra, but the woodwinds are more diverse in appearance, timbre, and means of sound production. There is deliberate competition between strings and woodwinds when a composer pits the two in what seems to be a battle or contest. The principal function of the woodwinds becomes one of *contrast* to the more homogeneous musical sound produced by the string section.

The woodwind sound is produced by a vibrating column of air enclosed in a tube, set in motion variously by blowing across an opening (flute), blowing against a single reed (clarinet), or blowing against a double reed (oboe, English horn, and bassoon). However, because these instruments have traditionally played together both as a section in the orchestra and in smaller ensembles, and because their timbres are compatible, they are considered a "family" of instruments.

Table 2.1

Voices	Pitch Range (see p. 9)
Soprano	**1.** High pitched **2.** Range narrow as compared with most instruments
Alto	**1.** Lower pitched than soprano **2.** Range narrow
Tenor	**1.** Higher pitched of the two male voices, lower than alto **2.** Range narrow
Bass	**1.** Lowest pitched of all voices **2.** Range narrow

Timbre and Technique	Typical Function in Ensemble	Solo Examples
1. Brilliant and clear **2.** Extremely agile	Usually performs melody in choral ensemble	**Example 2.5** Verdi: "Caro Nome," from *Rigoletto*
.1. Dark and rich **2.** Less agile than soprano	**1.** Usually performs close harmony with soprano **2.** Occasionally performs countermelody	**Example 2.6** Brahms: *Alto Rhapsody*, Op. 53
1. Brilliant and powerful **2.** More agile than bass	**1.** Although the counterpart of soprano in bass register, tenor rarely performs melody in ensemble **2.** Usually completes harmony with alto	**Example 2.7** Handel: "Every Valley Shall Be Exalted," from *Messiah*
1. Dark and rich **2.** Least agile of all voices	Provides harmonic foundation in choral ensemble	**Example 2.8** Mozart: "O Isis and Osiris," from *The Magic Flute*

Table 2.2

Instruments: Strings	Pitch Range (see p. 9)
Violin *Means of sound production:* Drawing a bow across strings, or plucking strings	**1.** Highest pitched of the stringed instruments **2.** Extremely wide range
Viola *Means of sound production:* Drawing a bow across strings, or plucking strings	**1.** Slightly lower pitched than violin **2.** Range narrower than violin
Cello *Means of sound production:* Drawing a bow across strings, or plucking strings	**1.** Range lower than violin and viola **2.** Ranges of all three overlap
Double Bass *Means of sound production:* Drawing a bow across strings, or plucking strings	**1.** Extremely low pitched **2.** Narrowest range of all stringed instruments **3.** Sounds one octave below the pitches shown on printed score

Timbre and Technique	Typical Function in Ensemble	Examples
1. Brilliant, clear; extremely agile **2.** Wide range of possible timbres, including rich, sonorous, harsh, strident, gentle, delicate, vibrant, and incisive	**1.** Two distinct violin sections. First violins provide melody, analogous to soprano voice. Second violins usually provide harmony, analogous to the alto voice **2.** Performs rapid, ornamental, virtuoso passages	**Example 2.9** Mendelssohn: *Violin Concerto in E minor,* Op. 64 **Example 2.10** **Sectional Passage:** Tchaikovsky: *Symphony No. 4 in F minor,* Op. 36, third movement "Pizzicato ostinato" (entire movement is played pizzicato)
1. Darker than violin; less agile **2.** Can be nasal, penetrating, rich, dark, gentle, lyric	**1.** Provides harmony; analogous to alto or tenor voice **2.** Sometimes doubles violin or cello part	**Example 2.11** Berlioz: *Harold in Italy,* Op. 16, first movement, Harold's theme **Example 2.12** **Sectional Passage:** Stravinsky: *The Rite of Spring,* "Mysterious Circle of the Adolescents"
1. Very strong and sonorous; more agile than double bass **2.** Can be warm, rich, full, intense, penetrating, lyric	**1.** Usually analogous to bass voice; provides foundation for harmony **2.** Sometimes analogous to tenor voice **3.** Occasionally performs melody	**Example 2.13** Schumann: *Concerto in A minor for Cello and Orchestra,* Op. 129 **Example 2.14** **Sectional Passage:** Schubert: *Symphony No. 8 in B minor (Unfinished),* principal theme
1. Strong, full, thick, and resonant **2.** Least agile of all stringed instruments; can be ponderous, even cumbersome	**1.** Provides foundation for harmony; analogous to bass voice, usually doubling cello part an octave lower **2.** Cumbersome technique makes solo passages rare, but section occasionally performs melody	**Sectional Passages:** **Example 2.15** Saint-Saëns: "V. The Elephant," from *Carnival of the Animals* **Example 2.16** Beethoven: *Symphony No. 5 in C minor,* Op. 67, third movement

Figure 2.2   Violin, viola, double bass and cello (John A. Wolters photos)

Figure 2.3   English horn, oboe, flute and piccolo

Figure 2.4   Clarinet, bass clarinet, bassoon and contrabassoon

Figure 2.5   French horn, tuba, trumpet and trombone

Table 2.3

Instruments: Woodwinds	Pitch Range (see p. 9)
Flute and Piccolo *Means of sound production:* Blowing across opening, causing vibrating air column	**Flute:** High-pitched; range comparable to violin, but narrower **Piccolo:** Highest-pitched of all instruments
Oboe and English Horn *Means of sound production:* Blowing against a double reed	**Oboe:** High-pitched; similar range to flute **English Horn:** Medium-pitched; more limited range than oboe
Clarinet and Bass Clarinet *Means of sound production:* Blowing against a single reed	Wide range in both **Clarinet:** High-pitched; similar range to flute, but range extends lower **Bass Clarinet:** Low-pitched
Bassoon and Contrabassoon *Means of sound production:* Blowing against a double reed	Lowest-pitched of woodwinds **Bassoon:** Very wide range **Contrabassoon:** Lowest-pitched of all instruments; sounds octave lower than written

Timbre and Technique	Typical Function in Ensemble	Examples
Flute: Brilliant, extremely agile; pure, clear sound; warm and rich in lower register to brilliant and piercing in upper register **Piccolo:** Agile, bright, penetrating, even shrill in upper tones	**1.** Flute is counterpart of soprano voice; piccolo extends range much higher **2.** Both instruments play rapid, ornamental, virtuoso passages **3.** Primarily melodic instruments, frequently solo **4.** Flutes usually in pairs in orchestra	**Example 2.17** **Flute** Debussy: *Prelude to the Afternoon of a Faun,* opening theme **Example 2.18** **Piccolo** Sousa: *The Stars and Stripes Forever,* final section
Oboe: Nasal, pungent, tangy, "reedy"; strident and piercing in upper register **English Horn:** Same as oboe in upper register; mellow, deep, and full in lower register	**1.** Oboe is counterpart of soprano, sometimes alto; English horn is counterpart of alto, sometimes tenor **2.** Both primarily melodic, frequently solo **3.** Both frequently play solo passages of quiet but penetrating quality **4.** Oboes usually in pairs	**Example 2.19** **Oboe** Schubert: *Symphony in C,* second movement **Example 2.20** **English Horn** Sibelius: "Swan of Tuonela"
Clarinet: Richer and fuller than flute or oboe; less agile than flute, but more agile than any other woodwind instrument. Wide range of color: bright, piercing in top register; rich, dark, and mellow in low register **Bass Clarinet:** Dark, rich, penetrating in low register	**1.** Clarinet can provide soprano or alto part; bass clarinet can provide tenor or bass **2.** Versatile instruments **3.** Virtuoso passages common for clarinet **4.** Both melodic, frequently solo **5.** Clarinets usually in pairs	**Example 2.21** **Clarinet** Mozart: *Clarinet Concerto in A,* K.622 **Example 2.22** **Bass Clarinet** Stravinsky: *The Rite of Spring,* "Evocation of the Ancestors"
Bassoon: Dark, pungent, reedy; similar to oboe because of double reed. Wide range of color possible, from sonorous to delicate to penetrating **Contrabassoon:** Deep, full, rich, with same reedy quality as bassoon and oboe	**1.** Counterpart of bass or of tenor **2.** Versatile instruments; wide range of technique **3.** Bassoon sometimes melodic, sometimes solo **4.** Contrabassoon markedly less agile, even cumbersome **5.** Bassoons usually in pairs	**Example 2.23** **Bassoon** Bartók: *Concerto for Orchestra,* opening of second movement **Example 2.24** **Contrabassoon** Ravel: *Mother Goose Suite,* "Beauty and the Beast"

The woodwinds are not nearly so homogeneous as the strings. Their characteristic timbres range from thin, piercing, high-pitched tones to nasal, exotic, low-pitched tones. Flute, oboe, clarinet, and bassoon constitute the standard instruments of the woodwind section (Figures 2.3 and 2.4) and correspond roughly to soprano, alto, tenor, and bass voice parts. The piccolo, English horn,[2] bass clarinet, and contrabassoon are auxiliary instruments, extending the range and timbre within the family. The total pitch range is even greater in the woodwinds than in the strings.

Woodwind instruments are frequently used for solo passages. Unlike the stringed instruments, the woodwinds are scored individually; for example, each oboe has its own part to play, different from the other oboe parts. Table 2.3 describes the woodwind family.

Brasses. The flourish of trumpets or horns brings to mind great diversity in human experience. For centuries, brass instruments have played a role in public ceremony: everything from crowning the king or pope to announcing the hunt or battle. We associate trumpets with chivalry, crusades, tournaments, war, and horse races. The sounding of "taps," which so strongly symbolizes death, is a brass sound; we cannot imagine it played on any other instrument.

Of course, the brasses play an important role in the orchestra as well. The brass section consists of a small group of instruments whose timbre is piercing and strident (see Table 2.4, pp. 24–25, and Figure 2.5). Our adjectives "brassy" and "brazen" suggest these qualities. The sound of brass instruments does not necessarily possess these unpleasant connotations, of course.

Like the woodwinds, the brasses produce their sound through a resonating air column within a tube. But in the brass instruments, a musician sets the air column in motion by vibrating his lips against a cupped mouthpiece. The highest-pitched brass instrument, counterpart to the soprano voice, is the trumpet. The French horn is related to the alto voice, the trombone to the tenor, and the tuba to the bass. A common role played by the brass section in the orchestra is that of powerful accent, or punctuation; for this reason, brass and percussion sections are often paired in the orchestra.

Until modern times, the French horn was the only brass instrument used extensively for solo passages in the orchestra because of its wide range and because its mellow timbre carries without being

---

[2] The English horn is neither English nor horn. Originally the barrel of this instrument was bent at an angle. Because of its angle and the need to blow through an opening to produce a sound, the French called it *cor anglais* (angled horn). *Cor anglais* became English horn. Although a horn is defined as a musical instrument originally made from an animal's horn, but today made of metal, the English horn is made of wood.

Plate 1. Mondrian, Piet, *Composition with Red, Yellow, Blue and Black,* 1921. Collection Haags Gemeentemuseum, The Hague. Lack of reference to objects in the real world makes it difficult to find meaning in this painting (see p. 5).

Plate 2. Mondrian, Piet, *The Red Tree,* 1908, Collection Haags Gemeente-museum, The Hague. Mondrian's early representational style (see p. 5).

Plate 3*:* Mondrian, Piet, *Horizontal Tree,* 1911, Collection of Munson-Williams-Proctor Institute, Utica, New York. The subject matter reduced to essentials of shape, line, color, texture (see p. 5).

Plate 4. Mondrian, Piet, *Tree*, Museum of Art, Carnegie Institute, Pittsburgh, Pennsylvania. The basic structure distilled into pure linear expression (see p. 5).

Plate 5. Mondrian, Piet, *Composition in Blue, Grey and Pink,* Rijksmuseum Kröller-Müller, Otterlo. The final stage of Mondrian's abstract style, in which the shapes, lines, colors now speak for themselves (see pp. 5–6).

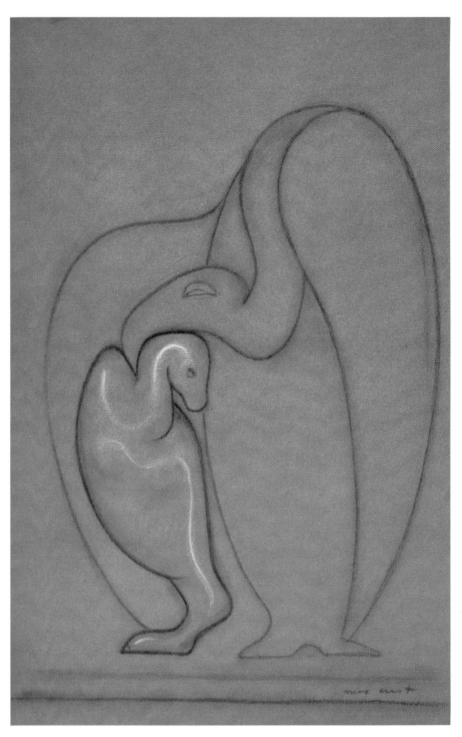

Plate 6. Ernst, Max, *Study for Surrealism and Painting,* 1942, Private Collection. Graphic line, like melodic line, can serve as the vehicle for the expression of an idea (see p. 41).

strident. In the nineteenth and twentieth centuries, composers have extensively explored the possibilities of the brass section for adding new tonal colors to the orchestra.

Percussion. Percussion, like brass, has long been associated with state occasions. In fact, in such ceremonies the percussion instruments almost always have been paired with the brass instruments. Likewise, as percussion instruments found their way into the orchestra, this pairing with brass instruments continued. Percussion instruments probably developed originally out of man's apparent need to "keep time." The urge to pick up a stick and beat when one is near a drum is almost irresistible both to children and to adults. Likewise, the composer "keeps time" in the orchestra by using percussion instruments.

It is always fun to watch the percussion section of an orchestra. The cymbal player often includes some theatrical movement in an exciting orchestral passage, crashing his cymbals with a flourish; the timpani player is dramatic as he plays, striking his instruments with sharp, springlike strokes; and they all seem so nonchalant, walking about in the rear of the orchestra, playing an instrument here and there, as if it were so easy that any of us could do it with only the slightest effort.

The percussion section contains a large number of diverse instruments, usually only one of each type, but all of whose sounds are produced by striking, rubbing, or shaking (see Table 2.5, pp. 26–27 and Figures 2.6, 2.7, and 2.8, pp. 28–29). Some percussion instruments are capable of producing definite pitches, but most of the members of this family have indefinite pitch; the composer notates only rhythmic values, with no pitch indication in the score. The composer seeks mainly the effect of striking. The main function of the percussion section, therefore, is *rhythmic accentuation.*

Probably the most important instruments of the percussion section are the timpani, or kettledrums, which are capable of definite pitch. The range of each instrument covers about five tones. But timpani come in different sizes, so the pitch range can be extended among several instruments. The technical process of changing the pitch does not allow the timpani to play elaborate melodies, but they are able to match and accentuate important tones played by other instruments. Timpani are standard components of all orchestras. Most orchestral music calls for at least one pair of them, sometimes many more.

Other instruments capable of producing definite pitches include the xylophone, celesta, chimes, and glockenspiel. These instruments are used not only for rhythmic accentuation, but also to add color to the melody.

Table 2.4

Instruments: Brasses	Pitch Range (see p. 9)
Trumpet *Means of sound production:* Blowing into a cupped mouthpiece	1. High-pitched 2. Range narrow
French Horn *Means of sound production:* Blowing into a cupped mouthpiece	1. Lower-pitched than trumpet 2. Extremely wide range, comparable in width to violin
Trombone *Means of sound production:* Blowing into a cupped mouthpiece	1. Low-pitched 2. Wider range than trumpet, narrower than French horn
Tuba *Means of sound production:* Blowing into a cupped mouthpiece	1. Lowest-pitched of brasses 2. Range width comparable to trombone, but lower, about the same as string double bass

Timbre and Technique	Typical Function in Ensemble	Examples
1. Powerful, brilliant, agile, penetrating, clear **2.** Capable of delicate tone when played softly or muted **3.** Full and rich in low register	**1.** Counterpart of soprano **2.** Often used for fanfares, flourishes **3.** Provides rhythmic accentuation **4.** Rarely used as a solo instrument in symphony orchestra until twentieth century; solo passages now quite common **5.** Usually in pairs	**Example 2.25** Tchaikovsky: *Capriccio Italien,* Op. 45, opening
1. Richer and less strident then trumpet **2.** Capable of considerable power **3.** Wide range of timbres from deep, mellow, rich to strong, bright, even blaring	**1.** Counterpart of alto or tenor **2.** Often scored with woodwinds because of mellow timbre **3.** Used for brilliant passages when played loudly **4.** Frequently melodic, often solo **5.** Usually in pairs or fours; often performs four-part harmonic background	**Example 2.26** Mendelssohn: "Nocturne," from *A Midsummer Night's Dream*
1. Powerful, usually dark and rich in low register and brilliant and penetrating in upper register **2.** More incisive than horn	**1.** Counterpart of tenor or bass **2.** Adds power, strength to total orchestral sound **3.** Occasionally supplies three-part harmonic background **4.** Occasionally used for solos **5.** Usually in pairs or threes	**Example 2.27** Mahler: *Symphony No. 3,* first movement
Full, rich, thick, dark; very powerful	**1.** Counterpart of bass **2.** Supplies large, solid foundation in the orchestra (or in the brass section) **3.** Occasionally melodic, rarely solo **4.** Usually only one tuba in the orchestra	**Example 2.28** Wagner: *Siegfried,* Fafner, the Dragon, Leitmotiv

Table 2.5

Instruments: Percussion	Pitch Range (see p. 9)
Timpani (kettledrums) *Means of sound production:* Striking	**1.** About a five-note range for each drum **2.** Ranges overlap; the smaller the drum, the higher the pitch
Celesta, Chimes (tubular bells), **Glockenspiel** (bells), **Xylophone** *Means of sound production:* Striking	**Celesta:** High-pitched, wide range **Chimes and Glockenspiel:** Middle range, narrower than celesta **Xylophone:** Similar to celesta range, but lower
Bass Drum, Snare Drum, Cymbals, Tam-Tam *(large gong),* **Tambourine, Triangle, Wood Block** *Means of sound production:* Striking, shaking	Indefinite
Folk Instruments: Claves, Maracas, Güiro, Castanets, Single-Headed Drums (e.g., **Bongo Drums** and **Tom-tom**) *Means of sound production:* Striking, rubbing (Güiro), shaking (Maracas)	Indefinite

Timbre and Technique	Typical Function in Ensemble	Examples
1. Resonant, pointed, intense 2. Wide dynamic range, partly controlled by use of various drumsticks, soft and hard; soft, delicate sounds to thunderous, penetrating sounds 3. Sustained by roll, or rapidly alternating strokes	1. Supplement low pitches in orchestra 2. Provide rhythmic, harmonic, and dynamic accentuation 3. One or two pair of timpani are standard in the orchestra	**Example 2.29** Bartók: *Music for Strings, Percussion, and Celesta,* second movement
All provide dramatic color **Celesta:** Bell-like (similar to glockenspiel), soft and delicate; keyboard instrument **Chimes:** Imitate church bells, deep, rich, resonant **Glockenspiel:** bell-like, bright, resonant **Xylophone:** Dry, brittle, clear, metallic Chimes, glockenspiel, and xylophone: All struck with hammers or sticks	1. Supplement melodic passages, making them more incisive 2. Provide special coloristic effects, sometimes dramatic or extramusical	**Example 2.30 Celesta** Bartók: *Music for Strings, Percussion, and Celesta,* third movement **Example 2.31 Xylophone** Saint-Saëns: *Danse Macabre,* Op. 40 **Example 2.32 Glockenspiel:** Wagner: "Dance of the Apprentices," from *Die Meistersinger*
Bass Drum: Resonant, powerful, incisive **Snare Drum:** Dry, brittle, rattle **Cymbals:** Bright, metallic, sharp, resonating **Tam-Tam:** Extremely resonant, metallic but mellow **Tambourine:** Rattling, jingling, metallic **Triangle:** Clear, bright, penetrating **Wood Block:** Resonant, hollow All sustained by roll	1. Augment rhythmic patterns, accent beats 2. Provide coloristic and dynamic effects	**Example 2.33** Britten: *The Young Person's Guide to the Orchestra,* Variation M
Claves: Hollow, resonant click **Maracas:** Dry rattle **Güiro:** Hollow scraping **Castanets:** Sharp, hollow click **Single-headed Drums:** Hollow thump or thud	1. Provide folk or exotic effects, especially Latin American 2. Augment rhythmic patterns 3. Provide coloristic and dynamic effects	**Example 2.34** de Falla: *The Three-Cornered Hat* (Suite), opening

Figure 2.6   Timpani (being played), snare drum, bass drum, and tam-tam (rear) (John A. Wolters photo)

Figure 2.7   Left to right: chimes (rear), glockenspiel, xylophone (being played), celesta (left foreground), wood block, tambourine, triangle (being played), cymbal (John A. Wolters photo)

The other individual percussion instruments have a limited, characteristic timbre, and are easily recognized by ear. The most common of these are snare and bass drums, cymbals, triangle, tambourine, wood block, and tam-tam (large gong). Composers often use these instruments prominently for special effects. Thunder of timpani, rattle of snare, thud of bass drum—all have become standard in the modern orchestra.

Figure 2.8   Bongo drums (being played), xylophone (left foreground), and (counterclockwise) two pairs of castanets, claves, maracas, güiro, bass drum (John A. Wolters photo)

Other Instruments. Other instruments often heard in the orchestra include the piano, harp, harpsichord, and organ (see Table 2.6). For the most part, these are solo instruments. Individually, they are capable of producing the full dimensions of music—that is, melody, rhythm, harmony, and tone color. The most popular of these instruments is the piano (Figure 2.9). To produce sounds on the piano, the player presses down keys which activate hammers that strike the strings inside the instrument. The action of the piano keyboard is constructed to allow the player through touch to produce variations in loudness and quality of sound. This was not possible on a keyboard instrument before the invention of the piano at the beginning of the eighteenth century. The meaning of *pianoforte,* the original name of the piano, indicated that it could be played both softly (*piano*) and loudly (*forte*). Although the piano has been popular as a featured solo instrument with the orchestra since its invention, it was not used as a regular member of the orchestra until the twentieth century.

The organ (Figure 2.10), the oldest keyboard instrument, is essentially a wind instrument. Its sound is made by columns of air vibrating in pipes of various sizes, controlled by valves operated by keyboard and pedals. A large bellows forces the air through the pipes. The organ is often heard as a solo instrument, but on occasion it has been scored with the orchestra. (Incidentally, the electronic organs

Figure 2.9   The piano (John A. Wolters photos)

Figure 2.10   The organ

found in many living rooms, rock and roll groups, and bars should never be equated with the pipe organ.)

The harpsichord (Figure 2.11) is a keyboard instrument whose design probably descended from the lute, an ancient guitar-like instrument. Many instruments which were plucked by the fingers, including the lute, guitar, and harp, were in common use immediately preceding the development of the harpsichord. It was natural, therefore, that the first stringed keyboard instrument be designed to pluck the strings. The strings are plucked by a mechanism operated by the keys. The timbre is similar to that of the guitar, small and delicate. Although the harpsichord enjoyed its greatest popularity

Table 2.6

Other Instruments	Pitch Range
Piano *Means of sound production:* Keys are struck, causing hammers to strike strings	Extensive range, encompassing pitches of all orchestral instruments and voices
Organ *Means of sound production:* Keys are pressed, controlling valves which regulate wind through pipes	Various ranges, but an even more extensive range than the piano
Harpsichord *Means of sound production:* Keys are struck, operating mechanism which plucks strings	Comparable to, but more limited than the piano
Harp *Means of sound production:* Strings are plucked by the fingers	About the same as the harpsichord

Timbre and Technique	Typical Function in Ensemble	Examples
1. Wide dynamic range and wide range of coloristic effects, from soft and delicate to loud and percussive **2.** Both short and sustained tones are possible (sustaining pedal makes longer tones possible)	**1.** Solo instrument able to supply melody, rhythm, and harmony, making it the most common solo concerto instrument **2.** Used extensively as accompanying instrument for solo voice and instruments **3.** In modern orchestra, occasionally used as a member of percussion ensemble	**Example 2.35** Beethoven: *Piano Sonata No. 27 in F minor*, Op. 57 (*Appassionata*)
1. Wide range of colors due to vast possibilities in combinations (coupling) of pipes (ranks) **2.** Great versatility in technique due to multiple keyboards, and relatively unlimited dynamic range **3.** Tones can be sustained indefinitely	**1.** Solo instrument; often used to accompany singers **2.** Occasionally used with orchestra for special effects, or as a solo concerto instrument	**Example 2.36** Bach: *Toccata and Fugue in D minor*
1. Tangy, lutelike, delicate **2.** Limited dynamic range; all tones have equal loudness; however, strings can be coupled so that more than one string is plucked by the action of a single key **3.** No way to sustain a tone except to hold down the key	**1.** Solo instrument **2.** Also used in the Baroque orchestra as continuo instrument, filling in harmonies	**Example 2.37** Scarlatti: *Harpsichord Sonata in D minor*
1. Crystalline in upper register; warm and sensuous in lower register **2.** Limited dynamic range	Most frequently used with orchestra to augment music with special effects; sometimes used as accompanying instrument for singers	**Example 2.38** Ravel: *Introduction and Allegro* (for harp, string quartet, flute, and clarinet)

Figure 2.11   The harpsichord (John A. Wolters photos)

in the seventeenth and eighteenth centuries, it has gained renewed importance in the twentieth, owing to the revival of interest in early music. It is even used by some rock and folk groups, though sometimes amplified electronically to match the other sounds of the group. In these situations the sound quality of the harpsichord is altered and sometimes distorted by amplification.

The harp (Figure 2.12) is often used with the orchestra, especially in music composed since 1800. Because of the size of the strings and because they are plucked with the fingers, the sound is warm and gentle, whether a melody, a simple accompaniment, or sweeping cascades of sounds.

Figure 2.12 The harp

The Conductor

The man who stands in front of the orchestra or chorus directing their activity holds our attention most of the time, and certainly the performers' attention, too. This is the conductor (Figure 2.13). Is he merely a glorified cheerleader, or do all those dancelike movements and gestures communicate specific meaning? To all competent conductors and performers, each gesture *does* have a meaning, and the conductor's function in the orchestra is vital.

His first duty is to keep everybody in the ensemble playing or singing together. He does this with his right hand, which usually wields a baton. He traces a pattern in the air which his performers

Figure 2.13 Conductor (John A. Wolters photo)

recognize as cues when to start, when to stop, and how fast to go. His left hand is used mainly to indicate emphasis, additional cues, and all other expressive qualities.

The most important function of the conductor, however, is interpretation of the music (see Figure 2.14, a page from an orchestral score). He spends long hours of study before the first rehearsal to determine exactly what the composer had in mind and how to perform his music. In rehearsal the conductor uses all his wiles, wit, and wisdom to prepare his ensemble for performance. At the performance, the conductor's hands, his face, and, in fact, his entire body work to remind, reinforce, and inspire his group to the highest possible response.

Figure 2.14   A page from the score of R. Strauss's *Ein Heldenleben,* Op. 40

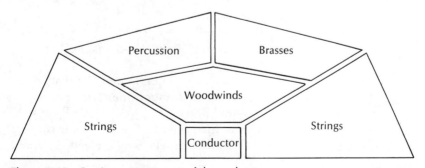

Figure 2.15   Seating arrangement of the orchestra

Summary

In this chapter we have examined four physical properties of musical sound—pitch, timbre, duration, and dynamics—as they relate to the human voice and the instruments of the orchestra.

We have found that musical sounds are produced by voices, instruments, or both, either alone or as part of a group or ensemble. These vehicles of musical sounds are classified idiomatically as follows:

I. Voices
    A. Soprano
    B. Alto
    C. Tenor
    D. Bass

II. Instruments
    A. Strings
        1. Violin
        2. Viola
        3. Cello
        4. Bass

    B. Woodwinds
        1. Piccolo
        2. Flute
        3. Oboe
        4. English Horn
        5. Clarinet
        6. Bass Clarinet
        7. Bassoon
        8. Contrabassoon

    C. Brasses
        1. Trumpet
        2. French Horn
        3. Trombone
        4. Tuba

    D. Percussion
        1. Timpani
        2. Celesta, Chimes, Glockenspiel, Xylophone
        3. Bass Drum, Snare Drum, Cymbals, Tam-Tam, Tambourine, Triangle, Wood Block
        4. Folk Instruments: Claves, Maracas, Güiro, Castanets, Single-Headed Drums

E. Other Instruments
    1. Piano
    2. Organ
    3. Harpsichord
    4. Harp

   Each professional orchestra has its own seating arrangement, but the strings are always at the front, the woodwinds in the middle, and the brasses and percussion at the back. This plan is standard because the winds and percussion have more carrying power than the strings. It is a matter of the balance within the entire ensemble. Identifying the instruments of the orchestra by listening can be frustrating or fun, depending on your point of view. But in the concert hall we have the distinct advantage of being able to *see* the instrument as it is played. If you should find the string basses on the right side of the seating plan in one orchestra and on the left side in another, do not be disturbed; each conductor has his own reasons (such as size of each section, stage area, or acoustics of the hall) for seating the orchestra as he does within the general plan in Figure 2.15.

Suggested Works for Additional Listening

Instrumental Identification

Britten: *The Young Person's Guide to the Orchestra*
Prokofiev: *Peter and the Wolf,* Op. 67
RCA: *Instruments of the Orchestra*
Saint-Saëns: *The Carnival of the Animals*
Tchaikovsky: *Nutcracker Suite*

The Baroque Orchestra

Bach: *Brandenburg Concerto No. 2*

The Modern Orchestra

Strauss: *Thus Spake Zarathustra*

Chapter 3

Tones in Combination

A composer creates music by combining tones. Of course, his task is not quite that simple. As we have seen from our brief examination of the elements of music, he is faced with infinite possibilities in the kinds of sounds available and in the ways they can be put together. Thus he selects and organizes sounds in a way that makes some kind of sense. By finding clues to the composer's choices of sounds and in beginning to see how he has combined them, we ourselves are able to make sense of what we hear.

There are three ways in which a composer may combine tones. Usually he does all three at once. When he combines tones in succession, or serially, he creates *melody*. When he combines them to sound simultaneously, he develops another kind of musical idea, *chords*. Imagine a melody as tones moving along a horizontal line and chords as a vertical arrangement of tones. It is helpful to establish these spatial relationships where none actually exists, in order to visualize the way tones are put together. Follow these artificial dimensions in Figure 3.1 as you listen to Chopin's *Prelude No. 25*.

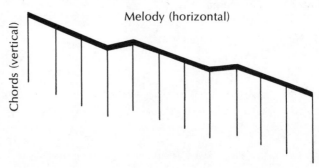

Figure 3.1　Spatial relationship of chords and melody

Example 3.1*
Chopin: *Prelude No. 25,* Op. 45

Time adds a third dimension to the relationship between tones. Both melody and chords exist within time, and we call this temporal framework *rhythm.*

Melody

Someone has said that melody is what music is all about. It is certainly the most familiar musical element and the easiest to identify. Melody is one of a child's first musical experiences. Remember "Happy Birthday" and "Jingle Bells"? Melody is the tune we whistle as we leave the theater; it is a musical theme repeated throughout a symphony. The casual listener usually listens for melody alone, never noticing other elements. He judges music by the quality of its melody—music with "good" melody is good music; music without recognizable melody is not music at all.

Melody is one of the most important vehicles for the expression of musical ideas. The composer combines tones successively in such a way that they are heard not individually but as a unit. Melody is heard as an entity; it gives a sense of completeness. Like a grammatical sentence, it is capable of standing alone. Tones, like words, are organized in a pattern which conveys a whole idea, and they mean little until ordered. Tones in a melody trace a line in our memory similar to the kind of line we see in the graphic arts. This melodic line is the entity, and just as the Max Ernst drawing in Plate 6[3] produces an idea through the use of line, melodic line produces a musical idea.

Melody comes in all manner of shapes, sizes, and movements. If we learn to recognize the various types, we can better follow melodic line. You are encouraged to refer often to the records which accompany this book and to the musical notation in Appendix D, because melodic line, chord types, and rhythmic concepts can be seen as well as heard. Certain musical concepts are visible on the printed page even if you do not read music.

Length

The simplest melodic concept is length. Some melodies are long, building slowly and deliberately; others are short, abrupt, and seem to be the kernel of an idea rather than a fully developed expression.

* Partial scores for Examples marked with an asterisk appear in Appendix D, beginning on p. 226.
[3] Plate 6 follows p. 22.

Although melodic length has historical implications (for example, Romantic melodies tend to be longer than Classical melodies), the most important thing for you to recognize is that there are differences in melodic length which have a great deal to do with the treatment a melody receives as it is developed. You should listen for the whole idea, the whole phrase, just as one listens for whole sentences.

A long theme is likely to be broken up in development; a short theme lends itself more to expansion and modification.[4] The melodies in Examples 3.2, 3.3, and 3.4 are complete ideas or phrases, though very short and abrupt. Each short theme is heard alone and then in its intended context. Listen to what happens to the theme after its initial statement. It is repeated in some way several times; in each case the composer has taken the melodic kernel and expanded it.

Example 3.2*
Bach: Prelude No. 2 in C minor, from Book I of
The Well-Tempered Clavier

Example 3.3*
Beethoven: *Symphony No. 5 in C minor,* Op. 67,
first movement, 1st and 2nd themes

Example 3.4*
Stravinsky: *The Rite of Spring,* opening theme

These short melodic ideas are extremely versatile; they can be kept in mind easily, and hence can be expanded, modified, transformed, or changed in other ways and still be recognizable. The melodies in Examples 3.5, 3.6, and 3.7 are longer. They seem to express a total unified musical idea—like a complex sentence rather than a simple one. It is more difficult to keep the whole idea in mind when a melody is long. We are more likely to hear it fragmented than expanded in development. Generally speaking, the difference between long and short melodies is one of function. The Bach "Air" in Example 3.5 is a fullblown idea, more complex and more self-contained than in the short examples above. As we listen to these three long melodies we sense a spinning out of complete ideas, a deliberate building within a framework, a total unit.

Example 3.5*
Bach: Air, from *Suite No. 3 in D*

Example 3.6*
Bach: *Brandenburg Concerto No. 5,* opening theme

Example 3.7*
Wagner: *Tannhäuser,* Overture, 1st theme

---

[4] A discussion of techniques of development is found in Chapter 5.

Movement

Melodies move in distinctive ways. The manner in which one tone follows another determines the movement of the melody, just as the manner in which a person places one foot ahead of the other determines his characteristic manner of walking or moving his body. Melody can move by step or by leap. (You will notice how different these two kinds of melody look on the printed page—see Appendix D.)

The following example contains one series of tones that move by step and one series of tones that move by leap.

Example 3.8*
Tones moving stepwise
Tones moving by leap

We can describe melodic movement even further. Some melodies are *lyric*, others are *angular*. The decision as to which description fits a particular melody is arbitrary, for no sharp line separates the two. The way in which a melody moves provides the clue to whether it is more lyric than angular.

Lyric melodies tend to be smooth and flowing. They move easily and freely, and usually rather slowly. For these reasons a lyric melody seems singable. This singability, or lyricism, generally results from a number of factors: the tones of the melody are close together in pitch, the range is limited, and the rhythm is simple, making the music relatively tuneful and easy to sing. The melodies in Examples 3.9 and 3.10, famous for their tunefulness, can be described as lyric.

Example 3.9*
Tchaikovsky: *Symphony No. 5 in E minor,*
Op. 64, second movement

Example 3.10*
Rachmaninoff: *Piano Concerto No. 2 in C minor,*
Op. 18, first movement, 2nd theme

Lyricism is often erroneously equated with melody itself. We sometimes think that melodies should be singable and pleasant, that melodies should be "melodious." But "lyric" does not mean pleasant or good, nor does "angular" mean unpleasant or bad. These two terms merely describe the ways melodies move.

The tones of an angular melody leap about in wide pitch ranges, and are rhythmically complex, making it relatively difficult to sing. The melody in Bach's *Concerto for Two Violins* contains several extremely wide leaps which would be a nightmare for singers.

Example 3.11*
Bach: *Concerto for Two Violins and Orchestra in
D minor,* first movement

Paganini's *Caprice* illustrates the angularity resulting from a complex rhythmic structure; it goes very fast and is constantly hesitating, stopping, and starting.

Example 3.12*
Paganini: *Caprice No. 24 in A minor*

The opening theme from Stravinsky's *Octet for Winds* is also angular. The elaborate trills and wide, melodic leaps are particularly suited to instruments.

Example 3.13*
Stravinsky: *Octet for Winds,* opening theme

Actually the differences between lyric and angular melodies are relative. Many melodies are combinations of the two and so are difficult to categorize. We might say that angularity and lyricism are opposite poles and the difference between them is one of degree. In the popular song by Burt Bacharach (Example 3.14), the melody seems lyric, with free, flowing motion and leisurely speed; but then, without warning, it makes wide leaps which are difficult to sing. The Strauss melody (Example 3.15) begins in lyric fashion, but it is played rather quickly, with separated, short tones, which tend to make it angular. In addition, of course, the wide range in pitch puts the music beyond the capabilities of most voices.

Example 3.14
Bacharach: "I Say a Little Prayer"

Example 3.15*
R. Strauss: *Till Eulenspiegel's Merry Pranks,*
Op. 28, 2nd theme

The rapid speed of these melodies contributes to their angularity. Singers find it difficult to manage rapid articulation of tones. In Handel's aria from *Messiah*, "Why Do the Nations," the movement of the melody is mostly flowing, but the rapid speed at which it must be sung makes it angular.

Example 3.16*
Handel: "Why Do the Nations," from *Messiah*

Lyricism has been an ideal in some historical style periods, and angularity an ideal in others. Composers can also be categorized in terms of the type of melody they choose to use. The style of one composer may be lyric, another angular.

Listen to the opening scene of Berg's opera, *Wozzeck,* and notice that this vocal music is pervasively angular, when compared with, say, Schubert's vocal music. Angularity seems to be as significant a part of Berg's esthetic ideal as lyricism is of Schubert's.

Example 3.17
Berg: *Wozzeck,* opening scene

Example 3.18
Schubert: *Frühlingstraum*

One last word of caution: lyric melodies are not meant only for voices nor are angular melodies meant only for instruments. Because the voice has physical limitations, lyric melodies are more common in vocal music than angular. However, an instrument can play both types with relative ease, and a great many lyric melodies have been designed for instruments.

Contour

Viewed as a whole unit, a melody has a distinctive shape or contour. It begins somewhere and goes somewhere, and it can travel by various routes. Some of the most basic routes, or contours, are *rising, falling, remaining on or about one pitch,* and *arch.*

The theme from the last movement of Mozart's *Fortieth Symphony* rises so rapidly that it and others like it have been labelled "rocket" themes. The melody in Verdi's "Celeste Aïda" also rises, but slowly and deliberately.

Example 3.19*
Mozart: *Symphony No. 40 in G minor,* K. 550, finale

Example 3.20*
Verdi: "Celeste Aïda," from *Aïda*

The famous romantic melody from Tchaikovsky's *Pathétique* symphony actually seems to fall. The opening theme of Brahms' *Third Symphony* descends also, but somewhat more forcefully.

Example 3.21*
Tchaikovsky: *Symphony No. 6 in B minor,* Op. 74
(*Pathétique*), first movement, 2nd theme

Example 3.22*
Brahms: *Symphony No. 3 in F,* Op. 90,
opening theme

The Schubert and Beethoven themes in Examples 3.23 and 3.24 appear to be weaving above and below one pitch, as if they cannot break away from that pitch range or from an important central tone.

Example 3.23*
Schubert: *Symphony No. 8 in B minor (Unfinished),*
first movement, 2nd theme

Example 3.24*
Beethoven: *Symphony No. 3 in E-flat,* Op. 55 (*Eroica*),
opening theme

The arch form is so named because the tones of the melody rise gradually to a peak and then move back down to the point of origin. The melody may also descend to and return from a low point. Notice the particular feeling of excitement this rising arch form brings to the first theme from "The Moldau." Rubinstein's melody from *Kamennoi-Ostrov* is an inverted arch. In both cases, whether the arch rises or descends, we sense movement toward the goal and the return.

Example 3.25*
Smetana: First theme of "The Moldau," from *My Country*
(Symphonic Cycle)

Example 3.26*
Rubinstein: *Kamennoi-Ostrov*, Op. 10, No. 22 (*Portraits*)

Recognizing these melodic contours will help us to focus attention more directly on the music we are hearing. As we extend our listening experience, it will soon become apparent that most music is made up of combinations of the lyric and angular types of melodies. The listener's first task is simply to recognize the different ways melodies move through time.

The next step is to understand the esthetic implications of melodic shape. Shapes in architecture are selected or devised by the architect for esthetic expression. For instance, those soaring shapes and lines in the design of the Air Force Academy Chapel (Figure 3.2) appropriately suggest flight. Similarly, some poets have used the shape of the printed poem itself to express an idea. The following poem by George Herbert is printed in the shape of an altar.

The Altar

A broken ALTAR, Lord, thy servant rears,
Made of a heart, and cemented with tears:
Whose parts are as thy hand did frame;
No workman's tool hath touched the same.
A   HEART   alone
Is   such   a   stone,
As   nothing   but
Thy power doth cut.
Wherefore each part
Of my hard heart
Meets in this frame,
To praise thy Name:
That, if I chance to hold my peace,
These stones to praise thee may not cease.
Oh let thy blessed SACRIFICE be mine,
And sanctify this ALTAR to be thine.

Melodic shape partially determines the esthetic message in music too. One manifestation of this principle is *pictorialism,* an attempt to express by musical means extramusical ideas such as sorrow and joy, bird songs, thunder, and battle. In Bach's *Mass in B minor,* the "Crucifixus" consists of melodic lines descending over an ever-descending bass figure in the orchestra. As you listen, notice the melodic pattern, sung first by the sopranos, and then descending in turn through the lower voices of the choir until it reaches the basses. What better way to express the sorrow and despair of the crucifixion?

Example 3.27*
Bach: "Crucifixus," from *Mass in B minor*

The music of the "Resurrexit," the next chorus in the same Mass, seems to burst forth with ascending melodic figures, bright tempos, colorful instrumentation, and elaborate ornamental passages depicting the excitement and joy of the Resurrection.

Example 3.28*
Bach: "Resurrexit," from *Mass in B minor*

Figure 3.2 Cadet Chapel, Air Force Academy, Colorado Springs, Colorado (Air Force Academy photo)

Rhythm

Music moves in more or less continuous motion. As it does, the sound ebbs and flows in a number of contrasts: sound and silence, long and short, fast and slow. This alternation in the continuum of sound is *rhythm*. The contrasts are provided when one tone is emphasized, or accented, more strongly than others so that it stands out, and this emphasis can be achieved by contrasts in volume, pitch, and duration. A tone stands out if it is louder, softer, higher, lower, longer, or shorter than the rest.

Almost all music, from the simplest to the most complex, is comprised of tones of specific duration. A series of pitches alone does not make a melody; it is only part of the total melody. Rhythmic, or durational, values complete the melodic idea. Occasionally, the rhythmic character is the most distinctive feature of a melody. The tune in Example 3.29 is made up of tones of equal durational values. We are not likely to recognize this tune until the durational values are assigned. Then the tune becomes familiar (Example 3.30). A slight rhythmic alteration in the same series of tones produces a completely different melody (Example 3.31).

Example 3.29*
Descending E major scale

Example 3.30*
Traditional carol: "Joy to the World"

Example 3.31*
Verdi: "Caro Nome," from *Rigoletto*

Because we are so oriented today to the "beat," we tend to associate rhythm with strong beat. We tend to think that music without heavy beat has no rhythm. Erroll Garner begins his jazz piano pieces with an improvised passage which seems to lack rhythm. When a contrasting section containing a strong beat follows we are inclined to say that the rhythm has finally begun.

Example 3.32
Garner: "Crème de Menthe"

But music need not have a heavy beat in order to be rhythmic. The alternation, the contrast in the flow which is rhythm, is always there. All music, like all language, has rhythm even in the absence of heavy, regular accent.

Music has not always been as oriented to regular accent as it is today. In some of the earliest music known in Western culture—plainsong or Gregorian chant—there were no assigned durational values. The melody was molded to fit the words of the liturgy; in performance the music took on the rhythmic quality of the text. Although these accents did not appear in any regular pattern, the music had the natural rise and fall of the language; it had rhythm.

Example 3.33*
Gregorian chant: *Dies irae*

In later music, specific durational values were assigned to tones, and accents came to be grouped into regular patterns. The repetition of these patterns was the beginning of what we call *meter*. In other words, the accents in metered music are spaced at regular intervals. Much the same thing happens when language, with its natural rhythmical rise and fall, is metered: prose becomes verse. The following lines are a paraphrase of a well-known poem.

> The cherry tree, which is the loveliest tree of all, standing along the woods trail, is now blooming white for Easter. I have now lived twenty years of my expected seventy, which leaves me only fifty. And since fifty years are very little to look at blooming things, I will go about the woodlands to see the cherry tree with snow hanging on it.

The poet A. E. Housman chose to express these ideas in metered lines grouped into stanzas. Of course this metric arrangement of lines of approximately equal length also allows for rhyme, which gives an added dimension to the poem.

Loveliest of Trees

Loveliest of trees, the cherry now
Is hung with bloom along the bough,
And stands about the woodland ride
Wearing white for Eastertide.

Now of my threescore years and ten,
Twenty will not come again,
And take from seventy springs a score,
It only leaves me fifty more.

And since to look at things in bloom
Fifty springs are little room,
About the woodlands I will go
To see the cherry hung with snow.

A. E. HOUSMAN*

* From "A Shropshire Lad" - Authorised Edition - from *The Collected Poems of A. E. Housman.* Copyright 1939, 1940, © 1959 by Holt, Rinehart and Winston, Inc. Copyright © 1967, 1968 by Robert E. Symons. Reprinted by permission of Holt, Rinehart and Winston, Inc., and The Society of Authors as the literary representative of the Estate of A. E. Housman, and Jonathan Cape Ltd., publishers of A. E. Housman's *Collected Poems.*

Doesn't the verse say it more beautifully and more memorably than the prose? Notice that almost every other syllable is accented, giving the lines a regularity that in itself is pleasing. The addition of meter has contributed to the total effect of the poem. The same result is achieved in music. The unmetered *Dies irae* of Example 3.33 is heard in metrical form in Example 3.34. Here the accents have been grouped into regular patterns and the listener becomes aware of the regularity.

Example 3.34*

Berlioz: *Symphonie Fantastique,* fifth movement

Meter, then, is patterned rhythm. Meter results from arranging rhythms in patterns to produce regular beat. The regularity of the pattern seems to appeal to us. We enjoy "feeling the beat," tapping our foot with the pattern. This physical reaction to meter is greatest in such activities as dancing and marching, which demand certain regular patterns, and which may account for the original incorporation of meter into our music. It has been said that man has a natural tendency to order things; it is really man who supplies the tick-tock to the ticking of the clock. When he hears steady, even beats, he soon begins to group them and even to hear accents where there are none.

Almost all of our music over the past eight centuries has been based on some kind of metrical pattern. The three pieces in Example 3.35 are of the type which marked the beginning of the use of regular accents, about 1200 A.D. The Gregorian chant, *Haec dies,* is heard first in its original form, and then as it is used with two different metrical patterns. The original chant is in the lower voice in the second and third settings.

Example 3.35*

Gregorian chant: *Haec dies*
Clausula for *Hec dies*
Motet for *Hec dies,* "Huic main"

Pulsations in music, or beats, are grouped into equal units, usually by twos or threes, and some beats are stressed more than others. In a musical score, these groupings of beats appear as measures, set off by bar lines. We say that one "feels" the beat in music because the tones are arranged in a way that causes pulse. In other words, the tones which are emphasized by length, pitch, volume, or orchestration are placed at regular intervals; that is why we feel a regular pulse. (It is *not* because a mystical beat exists somewhere in nature, and all we have to do is fit the music to it.) Also, this arrangement of tones in regular groups tends to give stress to the first tone in each group of beats. The pattern itself provides emphasis for the first beat.

Again, we can see a parallel in poetry. In the following lines by

Byron, words are arranged so that their natural stress recurs at regular intervals, and the groups form three-beat sets.

When a Man Hath No Freedom to Fight for at Home

When a man hath no freedom to fight for at home
Let him combat for that of his neighbors;
Let him think of the glories of Greece and of Rome,
And get knock'd on his head for his labors.

To do good to mankind is the chivalrous plan,
And is always as nobly requited;
Then battle for freedom wherever you can,
And, if not shot or hang'd, you'll get knighted.

LORD BYRON

Dances are especially useful to demonstrate beat groupings, because they are strongly accented to aid the dancers. Listen to the three-beat, or *triple,* groupings in the Tchaikovsky waltz in Example 3.36. It is easy to feel the triple meter because the first beat of each grouping is heavily stressed. The *oom* is heavier than the *pah, pah.* The dancers respond to the recurring three-beat pattern, because the melody and its accompaniment, no matter what else they do, continually stress the three-beat grouping.

Example 3.36*
Tchaikovsky: "Waltz of the Flowers," from
Nutcracker Suite

Two-beat groupings are perhaps more common, both in poetry and in music. Much of the finest English poetry, including the major works of Shakespeare, Milton, and all the writers of sonnets, is in two-beat, or *duple,* meter.

> If music be the food of love, play on!
> > SHAKESPEARE: *Twelfth Night,*
> > *Act I, scene 1*

> They also serve who only stand and wait.
> > MILTON: *When I consider how*
> > *my light is spent*

> When I have fears that I may cease to be
> Before my pen has gleaned my teeming brain,
> > KEATS: *When I have fears*

A musical example of two-beat grouping is heard in the "Dance of the Flutes."

Example 3.37*
Tchaikovsky: "Dance of the Flutes," from
Nutcracker Suite

The waltz in Example 3.36 has a graceful, lilting quality because of the typical waltz meter, easy tempo, and light instrumentation. The duple grouping in Example 3.37 lends a steady, even quality to the music. However, we should not expect every piece in triple meter to be graceful and lilting; nor should we look for a steadily driving quality in all music in duple meter. The rhythmic movement of any given musical passage depends upon the way duration, beat, accents, and tempo interact. Examples 3.38 and 3.39 reflect a rhythmic character much different from that of the Tchaikovsky pieces. The opening of Honegger's *Symphony No. 5* in triple meter moves in slow tempo, with long durational values and heavy accents, and is therefore solemn and ponderous. This quality of movement is further emphasized because all the parts are moving together. The "Gavotte" from Schoenberg's *Suite*, Op. 25, in duple meter is capricious and uneven because the rhythm is extremely irregular. At the beginning we hear two distinct parts moving individually.

Example 3.38*
Honegger: *Symphony No. 5,* opening

Example 3.39*
Schoenberg: "Gavotte," from *Suite,* Op. 25

The perception of rhythm involves much more than the recognition of whether or not a piece has a beat. It involves an increasing awareness of the way beat, accent, tempo, and durational values work together.

As listeners we should be able to distinguish between duple and triple meter. In the beginning, we may relate to metric stereotypes: marches for duple meter and waltzes for triple. But we must quickly move beyond these stereotypes, because they imply moods and tempos that are not always associated with duple and triple meters. A melody in duple meter may move in groups of twos or fours, and we may not be able to tell the difference; but in either case we should hear that the meter is duple. Listen now to the hymn, "O God Our Help in Ages Past," sung in duple meter. It is impossible to tell whether the hymn is notated in twos or fours. Had this tune been written in triple meter, we would hear a substantial difference. In Example 3.41 the durational values of the same hymn have been changed to express a triple-beat grouping. The second version is

Example 3.40*
Traditional hymn: "O God Our Help in Ages Past"
in duple meter

Example 3.41*
Traditional hymn: "O God Our Help in Ages Past"
in triple meter

just as true to the text as the first. The same words—God, help, ages, past, hope, years, come—are stressed in both metric settings. But the total effect has changed. If the duple setting seems more "correct," it may be because that is the familiar one, or because the meter actually contributes to the stateliness, the solemn dignity of the words.

Because of the substantial difference in aural effect between duple and triple meters, the composer carefully matches his meters with his esthetic intent. One meter is not more correct than another; it is simply more appropriate.

The alteration in meter in Example 3.41 was artificially contrived for the purpose of demonstration. Let us see what happens when a composer sets the same melody in two different meters. Bach set his original theme from *The Art of Fugue* in duple meter, and the eighteenth variation of that theme in triple meter.

Example 3.42*
Bach: Original theme from *The Art of Fugue*

Example 3.43*
Bach: Contrapunctus XVIII from *The Art of Fugue*

Changing the meter has altered the movement, and perhaps the total effect, of the original melodic statement.

Now listen to several examples taken from folk song and symphonic literature and determine whether the beat grouping is duple or triple. Remember that accents mark the beginning of each group. Tapping out the beat or moving with it will help to identify groupings.

Example 3.44
Dylan: "I Shall be Released"

Example 3.45
Traditional: "Scarborough Fair"

Example 3.46
Mahler: *Symphony No. 1 in D,* first movement,
1st and 2nd themes

Example 3.47
Mahler: *Symphony No. 1 in D,* second movement,
1st theme

Interesting disturbances in rhythmic flow occur when a duple-beat grouping is alternated with a triple-beat grouping. At first hearing, "Three to Get Ready" (Example 3.48) promises to be a simple waltz. But soon three- and four-beat groupings begin to alternate. The pattern, two groups of three followed by two groups of four, is established.

Example 3.48*
Brubeck: "Three to Get Ready"

The same disturbance in movement occurs when different rhythm patterns are placed side by side within the same meter. In the "Great Gate at Kiev" a two-note pattern alternates with a three-note pattern. The effect of including the three-note groupings among the two-note groups toward the close of this piece makes the ending more grandiose. The addition of more notes in the same unit of time also stretches out the movement.

Example 3.49*

Moussorgsky-Ravel: "Great Gate at Kiev," from *Pictures at an Exhibition*

These contrasting patterns can also be played simultaneously. This is a real challenge for pianists who must play three-note patterns in one hand against two-note patterns in the other. If you think it is easy, just try tapping two with one hand against three with the other.

Example 3.50*

Beethoven: *Piano Sonata*, Op. 14, No. 2

Another example of three against two appears in Gershwin's "It Ain't Necessarily So," from *Porgy and Bess*, where the voice sings in threes against twos in the instrumental accompaniment.

Although we as listeners are concerned primarily with duple and triple groupings, we should be aware that these basic groupings are sometimes regrouped into compound meters. *Simple meters* are those in which either two or three beats occur per measure. *Compound meters* contain multiples of two or three beats. In a compound meter, the first beat of the measure is accented most strongly. The first beat of the second grouping in the measure is a secondary accent. Thus, in the four-beat measure, probably the most common of all meters, the first beat receives the strongest accent; the third beat is accented too, but not as heavily: TA ta, Ta ta. The main theme from the fourth movement of Brahms' First Symphony is based on four-beat meter.

Example 3.51*

Brahms: *Symphony No. 1 in C minor*, Op. 68, fourth movement, main theme

In a six-beat measure, the first and fourth beats are accented, the first being the heaviest. Notice that there are two accents to the measure, just as in the four-beat example. This is a triple subdivision of the measure; the four-beat is a duple subdivision. Although both subdivisions have two accents per measure, note the different effect of the triple subdivision: TA ta ta, Ta ta ta.

Example 3.52

Mendelssohn: *Violin Concerto in E minor*, Op. 64, second movement

Plate 7. Miró, Joan, *The Beautiful Bird Revealing the Unknown to a Pair of Lovers,* 1941, gouache, 18 × 15″. Collection, The Museum of Modern Art, New York, acquired through the Lillie P. Bliss Bequest. Repetition of shapes and lines establishes an organic and coherent relationship between the parts and provides unity and balance, as does repetition in music (see pp. 64, 104).

Plate 8. Tintoretto (Jacopo Robusti), *The Finding of Moses,* The Metropolitan Museum of Art, Gwynne M. Andrews Fund, 1939. Repetition—here in the form of a mirror-image relationship between the left and the right halves of the painting—supplies symmetrical balance to a work of art (see pp. 65, 102).

Plate 9. Goya, Francisco de, *Majas on a Balcony,* The Metropolitan Museum of Art, bequest of Mrs. H. O. Havemeyer, 1929, The H. O. Havemeyer Collection. The use of contrast in the arts (here, between light values and styles of dress of the figures) relieves monotony and provides emphasis (see p. 71).

Plate 10. Ruisdael, Jacob Isaaksz van, *Wheatfields,* The Metropolitan Museum of Art, bequest of Benjamin Altman, 1913. Sequential repetition (here, of light and dark) provides a sense of movement in painting, as it does in music (see p. 73).

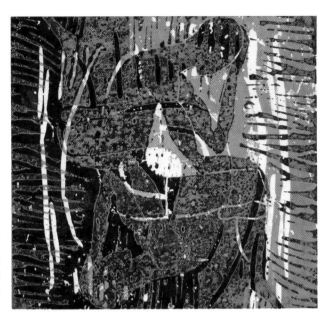

Plate 11. Wagoner, Robert E., *Untitled Print,* Private Collection. Inversion is one of the more subtle forms of repetition in the arts (see p. 74).

Plate 12. Courbet, Gustave, *Still Life: Apples and Pomegranates,* The National Gallery, London. The fruit dominates this painting because of the way the artist has chosen and arranged various elements. Similarly, the composer arranges musical elements to make one idea stand out, while maintaining, like the artist, a balanced and coherent relationship among all of them (see pp. 99, 102–103).

Whatever the meter, we are primarily concerned with recognizing basic groupings of twos and threes.

Occasionally, compound meters also include combinations of both beat groupings, such as a five-beat measure, which could be grouped into the combinations $3 + 2$, $2 + 3$, or $2 + 2 + 1$. In the Brubeck piece, "Take Five" (Example 3.53), the five beats are grouped $3 + 2$. Bartók does the same thing in his piano piece, *Mikrokosmos, No. 150* but groups his five beats in $2 + 3$.

Example 3.53*
Brubeck: "Take Five"

Let us take one more step. Consider the effects of regrouping beats within a nine-beat measure. Ordinarily, nine beats appear as three groups of three beats each: TA ta ta, Ta ta ta, Ta ta ta.

Example 3.54*
Bach: Prelude No. 20, from Book I of *The Well-Tempered Clavier*

Dave Brubeck, in his "Blue Rondo à la Turk" (Example 3.55) arranges his beats in three 2-beat groups and one 3-beat group: TA ta, Ta ta, Ta ta, Ta ta ta. Again, Bartók regroups his nine beats in identical fashion in *Mikrokosmos, No. 152*. Whereas Bach achieves a regular beat, Brubeck and Bartók achieve an irregular or uneven effect with the odd 3-beat group at the end of the measure.

Example 3.55*
Brubeck: "Blue Rondo à la Turk"

Modern music often reflects the attempt of composers to break down regularly recurring pulsations by displacing accents. They do this by using two or more meters at the same time, changing meters often, or even by using no meter at all. In Example 3.56 the first two measures represent "normal" beat patterns; the accent occurs on the first beat of the measure. But in the third measure, the accent is deliberately thrown off the regular pattern; the accent is now heard on beats other than the first one in a group. The deviation is effective because the regular pattern had already been established.

Example 3.56*
Stravinsky: *The Rite of Spring*, "Dance of the Adolescents"

Example 3.57 illustrates how two different meters are played at the same time. In this example, the composer has chosen to notate both meters within the context of one. The lower instruments continue a duple pattern while, at the same time, the higher instruments play a triple pattern.

Example 3.57*
Stravinsky: "Soldier's March," *L'histoire du Soldat*

Change of meter is common in twentieth century music. Notice how the beat is disturbed in Bartók's *Mikrokosmos, No. 140* (Example 3.58), because each beat grouping is followed by a different kind of grouping (see rhythm pattern in Appendix D). Even though you are aware of strong accent, you cannot pin it down to a regular pattern.

Example 3.58*
Bartók: *Mikrokosmos, No. 140*

Occasionally, a composer will choose to use no metrical indication at all for a free, unmetered rhythmic flow. This effect may also be achieved within a metric framework if the composer avoids strong, accented patterns. Bartók achieves this free-flowing effect in the opening passage of his *Music for Strings, Percussion, and Celesta* (Example 3.59). This quiet passage has four measures with the following meters: 8/8, 12/8, 8/8, 7/8 (see score in Appendix D). But to the listener, the passage seems rhythmically free, somewhat akin to the unmetered Gregorian chant.

Example 3.59*
Bartók: *Music for Strings, Percussion, and Celesta,*
opening theme

A particular rhythmic idea can be written in various ways, even in different meters, but it is the aural effect which is important. Metric effect can be manipulated in innumerable ways by careful arrangement of or avoidance of accents: by altering the customary beat pattern in a triple meter, the composer may produce a duple effect, or vice versa. A rapid 3/4 (triple) meter may sound like 6/8 (duple), and a complex metric arrangement may be impossible to analyze by ear.

Although attempts to destroy regular, recurring pulse have become standard in serious modern music, composers and performers of popular music continue to use it, accenting the beat to enhance the effects they wish to achieve.

The final element of rhythm to be considered is *tempo,* or the speed at which music moves. When considering the manner in which anything moves through time, one must take speed into account. Tempo and duration come together to provide the desired quality of movement. The casual listener is aware of differing speeds in music, but the experienced listener will attempt to apprehend the quality of movement through an understanding of the relationship between tempo and the other elements of rhythm. A more complete discussion of the way tempo relates to quality of movement is found in Chapter 8.

Chords

A *chord* may be defined as two or more tones sounded simultaneously. Although chords are commonly thought of as mere accompaniment to melody, like the chords which are played on a guitar to accompany a simple folk tune, their real function is to give depth to the esthetic expression of melody. One should recognize the difference between chords and harmony. A chord is a single instance of tones being sounded together; *harmony* results from several chords played in some intended order. A chord is to harmony as a tone is to melody; that is, one chord can no more express a harmonic idea than one tone can express a melodic idea. Harmony is formed when chords are placed in a series. (We reserve the discussion of harmony for Chapter 7.)

Tertian Chords

The *tertian chord* is called a *triad,* a simple three-note chord. The tones of a triad are three scale steps apart, for example *do, mi, sol.* These can be arranged in various ways. The triad is the heart of tertian harmony, a complex system of chord relationships growing out of the grouping of triads.

Tertian harmony is the basis of most music in Western civilization. Nearly all the examples in this text are in the tertian system, as is the great preponderance of music to which the average listener is exposed. Almost all music of the seventeenth through nineteenth centuries is tertian; so is most of the popular music of the twentieth century. Musical examples of tertian chords and harmony are therefore plentiful. Examples 3.60–3.63 were chosen for their simplicity; the sound of these chords is quite familiar to our ears.

Example 3.60*
Several chords played on piano

Example 3.61*
Beethoven: *Sonata No. 14 in C-sharp minor,* Op. 27,
No. 2 (*Moonlight*), second movement

Example 3.62
Beethoven: *Symphony No. 3 in E-flat,* Op. 55 (*Eroica*)

Example 3.63
Reynolds: "Little Boxes"

Tertian chords are not the only chords available to composers. In fact, many twentieth-century composers, feeling that the tertian system had been developed to its limits, sought other systems. One of the earliest attempts by modern composers to expand chordal materials was to use quartal chords, which are in fact not new at all.

Quartal Chords

Quartal chords are based on intervals of the fourth; that is, the tones of the chord are four scale steps apart instead of three.

Example 3.64*
Several quartal chords played on piano

The quartal chord produces a special kind of sound much different from the tertian chord to which we are so accustomed. The idea of quartal harmony is derived in part from the parallel *organum* of the ninth century. Organum, the earliest known example of music in parts, may be composed by the simple technique of adding a voice a fourth above the original voice so that the two voices move in parallel fourths.

Example 3.65*
Parallel organum in fourths

In an attempt to expand the tonal possibilities for composition, some twentieth-century composers use the quartal system instead of, or in addition to, the tertian system. The excerpt in Example 3.66 is taken from Hindemith's *Mathis der Maler*. This example demonstrates that the basic difference between the two systems is harmony. If you are unaccustomed to this quartal harmony, it may sound exotic, foreign, perhaps even archaic.

Example 3.66*
Hindemith: *Mathis der Maler,* Scene 7

Expanded Tertian Harmony

The quartal system in a pure form is not very common. What really occurs in much of the music of the twentieth century is an expansion of the tertian system to include what seem to be "foreign" tones—that is, extra tones added within, above, or below the basic triad to add harmonic color. The following are examples of *expanded tertian harmony.*

Example 3.67
Shostakovich: "Polka," *The Golden Age* (Ballet)

Example 3.68
Stravinsky: *The Rite of Spring,* "Rounds of Spring"

Example 3.69
Debussy: *Nuages*

There is another group of chords which does not belong to any of the above categories. These chords are named after the way the tones are arranged; they are "clustered" together.

Example 3.70*
Tone clusters played on piano

Tone Clusters

Tone clusters, like quartal chords, are used infrequently, usually for special effect. They do not constitute any kind of harmonic system as do tertian and quartal chords. Bartók uses clusters at the end of the third and fourth movements of his *Fourth String Quartet* (Example 3.71). He seems to be trying to obtain the most sound possible from the quartet; the tone clusters make the end forceful and climactic.

Example 3.71*
Bartók: *String Quartet No. 4,* final chords of third
and fourth movements

Example 3.72 from Ives' *Concord Sonata* is produced on the piano keyboard with a fourteen and three-fourths inch board. Ives even specifies the exact length of the board!

Example 3.72
Ives: *Concord Sonata,* second movement

Summary

Music is the result of combining tones. The elemental combinations of tones are called melody, rhythm, and chords. Melody results when one tone is placed after another, rhythm results when one tone is stressed more than another, and chords result when several tones are sounded at once. As musical tones are combined, melody takes on a distinctive length, movement, and contour. Rhythm provides a distinctive movement in terms of meter, beat, and tempo. Chords have distinctive sounds according to the manner in which their tones are combined.

Although we can analyze melody, rhythm, and chords separately, we must remember that the three are almost always found in combination. The simple piece in Example 3.73 consists of a *melody* with distinctive *rhythm* accompanied by appropriate *chords.*

Example 3.73*
Mozart: *Piano Sonata No. 11 in A,* K. 331

As listeners, our interest sometimes is drawn more to one element than another. But we are always concerned with the relationship among these three basic elements of music.

Suggested Works for Additional Listening

Short Melodic Idea

Strauss: *Thus Spake Zarathustra*

Bach: Fugue No. 4, from Book I of *The Well-Tempered Clavier*

Long Melodic Idea

Chopin: *Nocturne in E-flat,* Op. 9, No. 2.

Lyric Melody

Sibelius: *Finlandia,* Op. 26, No. 7

Angular Melody

Berg: *Lulu,* Act I

Schoenberg: *(String) Quartet No. 4,* Op. 37

Rising Contour

Beethoven: *Piano Sonata in C Minor,* Op. 13 (*Pathétique*), first movement

Falling Contour

Franck: *Symphony in D minor,* first movement, 2nd theme

Remaining On or About One Pitch

Schubert: *Symphony in C (Great),* first movement

Arch

Mozart: *Quartet in G,* K. 287 (andante cantabile)

Chapter 4

Repetition: Literal

Music is full of repetition. In some music, such as the popular *Bolero* by Ravel, both a pattern of rhythm and a melody are repeated throughout the piece; the entire piece, in fact, consists largely of simple melodic and rhythmic patterns repeated again and again. The repetition of the two patterns holds an engaging fascination for the listener.

Example 4.1*
Ravel: *Bolero*

Repetition is an essential part of music. Through its use, the composer supplies unity to his materials. He neatly ties his composition together by repeating fragments of melody, patterns of rhythm, and sequences of chords.

Repetition in the Arts

Repetition also plays a prominent role in all the other arts. The Greeks and Romans used it extensively in architecture, even when it was not structurally necessary, because of its great appeal to the eye. Repetition supplies a measure of security and satisfaction by producing familiar sights and sounds. We see extensive repetition in two famed landmarks, the columns of the Parthenon (Figure 4.1) and the arches of the Coliseum (Figure 4.2).

Repetition appears in oratory, poetry, dance, painting, music, not only because it appeals to the senses but also because it unifies a work of art by integrating its parts toward a central theme. When the orator repeats a phrase such as "I have a dream . . ." he sweeps the audience into litany-like response. When the dancer executes a complex series of movements, the audience expects to see the series repeated, perhaps with variation, and is somehow satisfied by the repetition.

When Poe in "The Raven" repeats the word, "Nevermore," he is emphasizing the theme of the poem. He unifies the structure of the

Figure 4.1   The Parthenon, Athens (Scala photo, New York)

poem by ending each stanza with "Nevermore." Poets repeat the sound and meaning of words to give sense to their poetry. Alexander Pope said,

> 'Tis not enough no harshness give offense
> The sound must seem an echo to the sense.

He was explaining the contribution which pure sound makes to the expression of an idea in poetry.

Melville's poem "The Bench of Boors," describing a group of beery bums gathered in the town square, appeals strongly to both visual and aural senses. The repetition of the *z* sound makes it seem as if the reader were actually looking at the scene and listening to its sounds.

> . . .
> Within low doors the slugs of boors
> Laze and yawn and doze again.
>
> In dreams they doze the drowzy boors,
> . . .

The repeated *z* sound describes perfectly the idea of lazy, drowsy bums. Likewise, in the poem "Upon Julia's Voice," Robert Herrick uses the repetition of sounds to enhance his poetic description. The *s* sound in the first line and the *l* and *m* sounds in the last line seem to express the quality of Julia's voice.

> So smooth, so sweet, so silv'ry is thy voice,
> As, could they hear, the Damned would make no noise,
> But listen to thee (walking in thy chamber)
> Melting melodious words to Lutes of Amber.

Figure 4.2 The Coliseum, Rome (Scala photo, New York)

The poet intends us to perceive such repetitions. We hear and re-member them, and our ear is satisfied. The poet may repeat words, phrases, or sometimes whole lines as refrains. He may repeat vowel and consonant sounds, or combinations of them, often forming rhymes. He may repeat metric patterns to shape the composition rhythmically.

In the following poem, repetition is used for emphasis of key words, for unity, and for pure pleasure of sound.

Counting-out Rhyme

Silver bark of beech, and sallow
Bark of yellow birch and yellow
　　Twig of willow.

Stripe of green in moosewood maple
Color seen in leaf of apple,
　　Bark of popple.

Wood of popple pale as moonbeam,
Wood of oak for yoke and barn-beam
　　Wood of hornbeam.

Silver bark of beech, and hollow
Stem of elder, tall and yellow
　　Twig of willow.

EDNA ST. VINCENT MILLAY*

In this splendid display of sound repetition, Millay emphasizes certain words by repeating them; she also repeats vowel sounds and initial, final, and internal consonant sounds. In particular she seems to enjoy using and repeating words that sound alike: beech–birch; sallow–yellow–willow–hollow; apple–popple. Try marking all such repetitions of sound in the poem and reading it again aloud.

The poet-philosopher Samuel Taylor Coleridge criticized empty and meaningless repetition in poetry. But he believed that there were some feelings or passions too great to be exhausted or satisfied by a single statement. He cited the following example of such an instance, and said of it, "Such repetitions I admit to be a beauty of the highest kind."

> At her feet he bowed, he fell, he lay down:
> at her feet he bowed, he fell: where he bowed,
> there he fell down dead.

> "SONG OF DEBORAH," JUDGES V. 27

In words, repetitions are easy to see. In painting, repetition is also obvious but is expressed differently. Miró repeats various shapes and lines over the entire canvas in *The Beautiful Bird Revealing the Unknown to a Pair of Lovers* (Plate 7),[5] providing an unmistakable unity to the painting. Indeed, those free-form, organic, small shapes connected by line seem to illustrate the principle of unity, literally tying the work together. They provide a coherence through their similarities in size, color, shape, and movement over the canvas.

In music, repetition can be exact or varied. Where the painter may repeat shapes, lines, brush strokes, and color, the poet and the musician repeat sounds, phrases, and rhythmic patterns. Repetition clarifies a musical passage by supplying a reference point for the listener; it helps him remember what he is hearing. As in all the other arts, repetition in music enables the composer to emphasize important elements and to unify, balance, and shape his work.

Our ear responds to *unity* in music. The parts of a musical piece are somehow related to one another, tied together organically. Repetition of elements in music, like the repetition in the Miró painting, enables us to perceive the organic relationship between parts.

Let us begin our listening for musical repetition with the Chopin *Prelude in E minor*, Op. 28, No. 4. The repetition of left-hand chords illustrates how a single element can provide artistic unity. The chords continue unobtrusively throughout beneath the melody. We feel, as listeners, a "oneness" in this composition which repetition of the chord figure reveals.

Example 4.2*
Chopin: *Prelude in E minor*, Op. 28, No. 4

---

[5] Plates 7–10 can be found following p. 54.

Balance, the state of equilibrium so important in a work of art, may also be supplied by repetition. Tintoretto's masterpiece, *The Finding of Moses* (Plate 8), illustrates a bisymmetrical balance in a near-perfect organization of shape and design. Notice how the women, trees, and background in the left half of the picture are almost a mirror-image of those in the right half. This could be contrasted to Mondrian (Plate 1) in which equilibrium was achieved through an asymmetrical arrangement of the parts, a balance of unequal but equivalent shapes and colors.

Surely the picture means more to us now. As we become familiar with the idea of repetition and balance in painting, we begin to find new meaning which may not have occurred to us before. We begin to understand that a painting may be more than a picture of something; factors other than photographic representation now contribute to our enjoyment of the work.

Let us see how balance is used in music. A section or musical idea is often repeated, sometimes with slight variation, to balance the original statement, much as the return swing of a pendulum "balances" the original movement. The imbalance at the end of the first part of a principal theme from Dvořák's *New World Symphony* (Example 4.3) is easily heard. It is as though we leaped into the air and remained there suspended. The second part is a repetition of the first, with slight variation.

Example 4.3*

Dvořák: *Symphony in E minor,* Op. 95 (*From the New World*), second movement, "Goin' Home" theme, first part

second part

The ear is now satisfied. We have returned to earth; the tune seems to be complete—balanced.

Repetition in music is sometimes obvious, other times subtle and elusive. Too much exact repetition would quickly bore the listener; too much obscure repetition would probably lose him too. It is even likely that we absorb some imperceptible repetitions which contribute to our sensing the unity of a piece. We have seen how much more is available in painting and poetry through an understanding of repetition. The same kind of expanded understanding is possible in music when we become aware of various types of repetitions.

We will be examining two basic kinds of repetition: literal (this chapter) and developmental (Chapter 5).

1. *Literal repetition* occurs when a musical fragment is presented more than once, *exactly* or with *slight* modification.
2. *Developmental repetition* begins with a musical fragment, but the repeated passages are *highly* modified, even transformed, until only the skeleton of the original idea remains.

Types of Melodic Repetition

Exact Repetition

The exact repetition of a simple musical idea, or phrase, is the easiest kind of repetition to hear. Note that in the familiar song, "Frère Jacques," the repetition can be heard in both the words and music. Each short phrase is repeated exactly before we hear the next.

Example 4.4*
French folk song: "Frère Jacques"

The immediate, short repetitions in "Frère Jacques" are matters of balance and symmetry. Each phrase is balanced by its repetition, and these pairs of phrases are symmetrical. Unity, on the other hand, is achieved in part by the recurrence of themes throughout a piece. We shall become more and more aware of repetition as a device for achieving balance and unity as we delve into other kinds of music.

Examples 4.5 and 4.6, both taken from the first section of Haydn's *Symphony No. 104 in D (London)*,[6] demonstrate the use of exact repetition in orchestral music. Notice in these examples the similarity to the kind of repetition in "Frère Jacques": short phrases repeated immediately and exactly.

Example 4.5*
Haydn: *Symphony No. 104 in D (London)*,
first movement

Example 4.6*
Haydn: *Symphony No. 104 in D (London)*,
first movement

Modified Repetition

The same feeling of balance and symmetry can be achieved even when the repetition is not exact. We hear the fundamental idea of the original, even though it is modified. Notice that in Examples 4.7–4.9, the last half has the same basic idea as the first; they balance each other in spite of the modification at the end. Repetition in the folk song, Example 4.7, is especially easy to hear because the words change when the music is modified.

Example 4.7
Seeger: "Where Have All the Flowers Gone?" based
on an old Ukrainian folk song

Example 4.8*
Bartók: *Mikrokosmos, No. 151*, opening

---

[6] Haydn's last twelve symphonies, composed in London under special arrangement with the impresario, Salomon, are sometimes called the *London Symphonies*. But the name *London* applied to a single symphony refers to the last, *No. 104 in D.*

Example 4.9*
Haydn: *Symphony No. 104 in D (London),*
first movement, opening

Thus far, the examples have been short and fairly easy to re-member. Distinguishing the repetitions of *long phrases* will not be as easy, but the principle is the same. In the popular song, "Both Sides Now," the second long phrase is an exact, balanced repetition of the first.

Example 4.10
Mitchell: "Both Sides Now"

The same technique occurs in symphonic music. Continuing with the *London Symphony,* we hear exact repetition in Example 4.11; there are slight differences only in terms of dynamics and orchestration.

Example 4.11*
Haydn: *Symphony No. 104 in D (London),*
third movement, opening

Even longer sections of music are often repeated exactly (the composer usually uses a symbol ‖: :‖ indicating to the performer that he should play that entire section again). In the third movement of Mozart's *Eine kleine Nachtmusik,* repeat symbols appear at the end of the first and second sections. Why did Mozart want those sections played twice? Did he believe the tunes to be so good that they must be heard more often? It was more likely that Mozart was concerned with form and shape. He balanced the first phrase against itself by repeating it exactly. He did the same with the second phrase, and because the second is merely a modification of the first, they balance each other. The resulting form is symmetrical.

Example 4.12*
Mozart: *Eine kleine Nachtmusik,* third
movement, opening

Antecedent-Consequent Phrases

Of course, long phrases, like short phrases, are frequently modified. They may be repeated intact, or with slight modifications. In the Rondo of the Clementi *Sonatina* (Op. 36, No. 6), we hear that the principal theme consists of two phrases. The balance achieved in this two-phrased theme is similar to that achieved in the theme from Dvořák's *New World Symphony* (Example 4.3). The first phrase seems to pose a question; the second seems to answer it.

Example 4.13*
Clementi: *Sonatina,* Op. 36, No. 6, Rondo, opening

This kind of repetition may be called antecedent-consequent, or statement-counterstatement. Similarly, we can return to the first movement of Haydn's *London Symphony* (Example 4.14) where a question is posed and subsequently answered in two relatively long phrases. The sense of repose felt at the end of the second phrase is called "resolution." We might say that the second phrase has "resolved" the question posed by the first. Haydn seemed to be especially fond of this type of repetition; for another example, listen to the opening of his *String Quartet* (Op. 64, No. 5, second movement).

Example 4.14*
Haydn: *Symphony No. 104 in D (London)*,
first movement, 1st theme

Functions of Repetition

Balance

The two-spired cathedral at Cologne reminds us that balance is a basic quality in all art. The use of two spires instead of one makes this balanced architectural design esthetically pleasing (Figure 4.3).

Intermittent Repetition

Examples 4.5–4.14 above illustrate how repetition can achieve balance when the phrases are juxtaposed. But repetition can serve other ends, and ideas are not always repeated immediately. Many times a repetition appears after intervening material. This treatment serves the architectural structure or design of the whole composition; that is, it serves the purpose of *unity*, more than of *balance*. Recognizing repetition after intervening material is somewhat more difficult than recognizing immediate repetition. It will be helpful if you listen carefully to the opening theme of Mozart's *Symphony No. 40 in G minor*, and then listen for its return.

Example 4.15*
Mozart: *Symphony No. 40 in G minor*, K. 550,
first movement, exposition

Another good example of intermittent repetition is the recurrence of the principal theme in the *London Symphony* (we hope by now you are becoming familiar with this work). This tuneful melody appears no less than four times in the opening section of the first movement.

Example 4.16
Haydn: *Symphony No. 104 in D (London)*,
first movement, exposition

Tonality

For an additional function of repetition, listen to the ending of Beethoven's *Fifth Symphony* (Example 4.17). We begin to wonder whether the piece will ever end; the final chord is repeated almost *ad absurdum*.

Example 4.17

Beethoven: *Symphony No. 5 in C minor,* Op. 67, fourth movement, ending

Was Beethoven trying to tell us something? He was attempting to establish beyond any doubt the tonal center of the symphony. The

Figure 4.3   Cologne Cathedral at night, Cologne, Germany (Lufthansa photo)

repetition of a single tone or chord establishes a *tonal center* in which a single pitch predominates, a center toward which all other tones gravitate. The composer wants us to anticipate that tone's return. When it does return, we feel that we have "arrived." This sense of arrival is especially strong when a tone or chord is repeated several times at the end of a musical passage. In Examples 4.18 and 4.19, the repetition at the end of a section reinforces the feeling of tonality. The silence at the end of the piece rings with the sound of a single tone strengthened by its repetition. That final tone is almost always the *key center* of the piece. Thus, we say that the Haydn Symphony is in the *key of D,* the Beethoven Sonata in the *key of G,* and the Beethoven Symphony in the *key of C minor.*

Example 4.18
Haydn: *Symphony No. 104 in D (London),*
first movement, ending

Example 4.19
Beethoven: *Sonata No. 16 in G,* Op. 31, No. 1, Rondo

Successive repetition of tones, then, serves to strengthen the feeling of tonality. This is true even when the repetition occurs intermittently as in the excerpt from Bach's *Brandenburg Concerto No. 3* (Example 4.20). Six of the first fifteen tones are *G;* it seems that Bach wished to establish firmly the key of G at the outset. Because Bach wrote his music at the time when the idea of tonality itself was emerging, it is logical to assume that he was deliberately establishing a tonal center partly through repetition.

Example 4.20*
Bach: *Brandenburg Concerto No. 3,*
first movement, opening

Debussy does the same thing in a different way. Where Bach repeated a single tone, Debussy outlined the notes in a single chord to establish tonality. The distinctive tonality of his piano piece *La Plus que lente* is strengthened by repetition of some of the tones in the initial chord (indicated in Appendix D by an *x* below the melody).

Example 4.21*
Debussy: *La Plus que lente,* opening

Contrast

Contrast is a necessary element of artistic expression. Elements are contrasted, or set in opposition to each other, partly to avoid monotony. They can also be contrasted to display one element in favor of another. In fiction and drama, writers use both techniques; the pairing of characters for contrast is common. Shakespeare sets off his hero, Prince Hal, by using Falstaff to provide "comic relief," and makes Othello more heroic by creating the evil Iago. In each instance, the monotony of goodness and nobility is relieved by the contrasting character. In each instance also, the character of the hero is strengthened by the contrast with the lesser figure.

Goya's painting, *Majas on a Balcony* (Plate 9, following p. 54), contrasts the two figures in light hues with those in dark hues. The contrasting light values emphasize the central figures in the painting.

In music, repetition of pitches often sets up situations for contrast. The composer prepares us for some kind of change by first presenting a momentary monotony of repeated pitches. A number of these repetitions makes us eager for a contrast, and we find the change satisfying. In the Beethoven and Bartók piano pieces presented in Examples 4.22 and 4.23, this kind of repetition occurs often.

Example 4.22*
Beethoven: *Piano Sonata,* Op. 53,
first movement, opening

Example 4.23*
Bartók: *Mikrokosmos, No. 149*

Contrasting elements sometimes occur simultaneously. The melodic line in Schubert's "Death and the Maiden" (Example 4.24) consists almost entirely of repeated tones, while the accompaniment consists of changing chords which provide necessary contrast with the melody. Imagine the boredom of this tune if it were performed without the accompaniment.

Example 4.24*
Schubert: "Death and the Maiden"

Again, in the third movement of Beethoven's *Piano Sonata (No. 12, Op. 26—*Example 4.25), the top voice consists of repeated, dronelike tones. In contrast, the lower voices are constantly changing, and that is where the main interest lies.

Example 4.25*
Beethoven: *Piano Sonata No. 12 in A-flat,* Op. 26,
third movement, opening

Contrast can also be achieved through the exact repetition of musical passages at different pitch levels. Imagine a man and a woman singing the same tune. The tune sounds the same, but the woman is singing it on a higher pitch level. In the Haydn excerpt in Example 4.26, the short statement is repeated exactly but on a higher pitch level.

Example 4.26*
Haydn: *Symphony No. 104 in D (London),*
first movement

In the fourth movement of the same symphony (Example 4.27), an entire theme is repeated on a higher pitch level.

Example 4.27*
Haydn: *Symphony No. 104 in D (London)*,
fourth movement, opening

Skillful orchestration can provide even more colorful contrasts in repeated passages. When a melodic idea is repeated by different instruments, even if the repetition is exact, the timbres are often so strikingly different that the character of the original is altered. In the excerpt from Schubert's *Symphony in C*, the clarinet and oboe repeat the opening horn melody. In Schubert's *Unfinished Symphony*, the violins repeat the cello theme. And in Mozart's *Piano Concerto No. 20*, the violins repeat the theme introduced by the piano.

Example 4.28
Schubert: *Symphony in C (Great)*,
first movement, opening

Example 4.29
Schubert: *Symphony No. 8 in B minor*
(*Unfinished*), first movement

Example 4.30
Mozart: *Piano Concerto No. 20 in D minor*, K. 466,
second movement, opening

Frequently, then, contrast is achieved when a passage is successively repeated by different instruments or voice parts: the clarinet repeats the melody the violin has played, the bass repeats the phrase the soprano has sung, the pianist's left hand repeats the passage his right hand has executed.

Techniques of Melodic Alteration

Contrast, as we have seen, is achieved through a distinct change in the mode of expression. Repetition can be both unifying and contrasting because it is in part the same and in part varied. This is particularly true of one type of repetition, *sequence.*

Sequence

The term *sequence* itself supplies a clue to its meaning: a sequence occurs when a melodic idea is repeated in a series, each time at a different level of pitch. Sequence has dual esthetic value: *unity,* through repetition, and *contrast,* through pitch modification.

The most common sequences consist of passages repeated one tone up or down from the original pitch level, such as the simple song fragment from "Westminster Carol" (Example 4.31). This example shows how a sequence can be used in descending patterns; each succeeding statement begins one tone lower than the last.

Example 4.31*
Traditional French-English carol:
"Westminster Carol"

Sequential patterns can also ascend, as in Mozart's *Piano Concerto No. 20* (Example 4.32). The ascending figures give us a feeling of building or moving.

Example 4.32*
Mozart: *Piano Concerto No. 20 in D minor, K̦. 466,*
first movement

Whether or not the sequence moves up or down, sequential repetition seems to provide a sense of movement to music, a sense of going somewhere. This sense of movement is somewhat akin to the movement in painting provided by contrasting light values. Consider the movement caused by contrasting light and dark colors in Ruisdael's *Wheatfields* (Plate 10, following p. 54). Our eye seems to move down the road from the dark section in the lower right corner of the painting through the light, back to dark, and finally back to light again, far in the distance.

The sequential passages in two inventions (Example 4.33) taken from Bach's keyboard literature consist of two short statements of the melodic idea. Even though both examples are descending passages, we seem to be moving toward some still undetermined goal.

Example 4.33*
Bach: *Two-Part Invention No. 8 in F*
Bach: *Two-Part Invention No. 10 in G*

A very elaborate sequence is found in the first movement of Bach's *Brandenburg Concerto No. 5*. This sequence comprises six statements, the treatment being exact in each instrumental part. If at first you have trouble hearing these patterns, concentrate on the lowest part, the harpsichord and cello, or on the highest part, the flute. These are the easiest to hear in the orchestral context; but be sure to listen to this excerpt several times—there is a great deal to hear.

Example 4.34*
Bach: *Brandenburg Concerto No. 5,* first movement

The sequence frequently consists of three or more statements of the melodic idea, as in Examples 4.33 and 4.34. Often, however, composers introduce modifications in the third statement. These unexpected changes relieve any temporary monotony that sequences might produce.

Composers often use the sequential technique as a unifying

device. In Wagner's Prelude to the opera *Tristan and Isolde,* the opening sequence contains a modified third statement, but the fundamental shape and sound of the original statement is retained. This is an excellent example of suspenseful building toward a climactic moment.

Example 4.35*

Wagner: Prelude, *Tristan and Isolde,* opening

Inversion

One of the more subtle devices of repetition is *inversion,* in which the melody is repeated upside down. Inversion is not unique to music. Artists continue to be intrigued by the possibilities of presenting an idea in unusual relationships—often by turning the image upside down. The print in Plate 11 (following p. 54) was made by applying the block once in a dark tint, and then upside down in a lighter color, superimposed.

The inversion technique in music is so subtle that repetition is often extremely difficult to hear; some inversions are easy to follow because they are short, have distinctive rhythm, or have a recognizable shape. However, it is likely that an inverted melody, even if it is not clear to the ear, contributes to the unity of the piece because the composer is working with the same notes and rhythm.

In the excerpt from Bach's *The Art of Fugue,* we first hear the theme, or subject, and then the countersubject in strict inversion (Example 4.36). The countersubject consists of the same melodic contour as the subject except that it is reversed, and the intervals now proceed in the opposite direction.

Example 4.36*

Bach: Subject, opening countersubject of
Contrapunctus IV, from *The Art of Fugue*

The excerpts from Brahms and Bartók (Examples 4.37 and 4.38) show a freer use of inversion. Although they are not as exactly inverse as the Bach illustration they retain the general idea of upsidedownness.

Example 4.37*

Brahms: *Symphony No. 3 in F,* Op. 90, first movement

Example 4.38*

Bartók: *Concerto for Orchestra,* first movement

In Bach's *Two-Part Invention* in Example 4.39, the melody and its inversion are played simultaneously. The top line moves down while the bottom line moves up.

Example 4.39*

Bach: *Two-Part Invention No. 6 in E,* opening

Retrograde

An even more subtle form of melodic repetition is called *retrograde* —the exact repetition of a melodic idea in reverse. Here, the repetition runs backwards; it begins with the last note of the original and ends with the first. The ability to hear a retrograde melody depends on a good memory. The longer the melody, the more difficult it is to recognize in retrograde form. Imagine reciting a sentence backwards; if it is short, the reverse form may be easy to recognize. "Pianos tuned by trained musicians are preferred." "Preferred are musicians trained by tuned pianos." As long as we can keep the whole sentence, or melody, in mind, the reverse form is discernible and can be related to the original.

The retrograde repetition of sentences and melodies is easier to hear if the original has unique features: a memorable word, a series of items, distinctive alliteration—or, in music, a striking leap, a series of patterns, or a distinctive rhythm. The tune in Example 4.40 is easy to follow in reverse because it is short and moves in stepwise manner. In the Beethoven piece (Example 4.41), though longer and more complicated, the retrograde is somewhat easier to hear because of the trill at the beginning of the original statement. Since the original *begins* with a trill, the retrograde naturally *ends* with it.

Example 4.40*

Eighteenth-century tune: Original and retrograde

Example 4.41*

Beethoven: *Piano Sonata No. 29 in B-flat,*
Op. 106, final fugue

A clever use of retrograde is found in the *Menuetto al Rovescio* of Haydn's *Sonata No. 4 in A for Violin and Piano.* In the repetition of the menuetto the performers are directed to play the entire section in reverse.

Retrograde Inversion

As if repeating an idea upside down or backwards were not confusing enough for us listeners, composers go one step further: they combine both techniques into what is called *retrograde inversion,* or upside down and backward. Suppose we invert the retrograde form of the tune in Example 4.40. The result, a retrograde inversion of the original, would sound like what is played in Example 4.42.

Example 4.42*

Eighteenth-century tune from Example 4.40:
Retrograde inversion

The melody has been turned upside down and backward. It has become extremely difficult to recognize, even if the original were familiar. Composers, however, are often intrigued by the challenge these techniques offer. By limiting himself to certain selected materials, a composer tries to create artistic unity within rigid confines. And, although the written results may be easy to see—and hence give academic delight to those who examine the score—they are usually not easy to hear. Nevertheless, the use of selected materials provides a unity, even though the elements creating the unity are not heard as an exact repetition of the original.

Example 4.43, taken from the beginning of the second movement of Honegger's *Fifth Symphony,* demonstrates the use of inversion, retrograde, and retrograde inversion. The original melody is stated by the first violins, accompanied by a clarinet, and is followed soon by a *retrograde inversion* in the bassoons, then by an *inversion* in the flutes, and then by a *retrograde* in the English horns and oboes. This ingenious manipulation of thematic material is prevalent throughout the movement. Even though we may not be able to identify each of these techniques without the score, we sense the unity throughout this passage because of the exclusive use of a single thematic idea. The music is a fine composition, one which deserves repeated hearing, not merely for the sake of mental exercise, but for an enjoyable musical experience.

Example 4.43*
Honegger: *Symphony No. 5* ("Di tre re"),
second movement

Motives

Up to now we have been concerned mainly with melodic repetition. But repetition is certainly not confined to melody alone. *Motives,* because they are short figures with distinctive rhythmic or melodic structure, lend themselves well to repetition. Motives are not substantially altered or developed when repeated, but usually occur incessantly or intermittently throughout a piece, contributing strongly to the sense of unity. The motive in Bach's *Prelude No. 1* (Example 4.44) is partly melodic, but its rhythm is its most identifiable characteristic. Bach uses very rapid notes throughout, all of the same, short duration. Beethoven applies the same technique in his *Piano Sonata,* Op. 31, No. 2 (Example 4.45); even when the melodic contour is changed slightly, the rhythmic motive is retained.

Example 4.44*
Bach: Prelude No. 1, from Book I of *The Well-Tempered
Clavier,* opening

Example 4.45*
Beethoven: *Piano Sonata in D minor,* Op. 31, No. 2,
third movement, opening

Rhythmic Repetition

The separation of rhythmic repetition from melodic repetition is arbitrary and academic. As we have seen, rhythm is an integral part of melody. Thus, when a melodic idea is repeated, the rhythm of that idea is usually repeated too, as you can see if you re-examine the examples of repetition in this chapter. For example, in Mozart's *Piano Concerto No. 20 in D minor* the rhythmic pattern as well as the melodic pattern is repeated. It is in part the rhythmic aspect of a melody that makes its repetition so easy to follow.

Indeed, a rhythmic structure can sometimes be more distinctive than the melody. Let us listen again to a section of Bartók's *Mikrokosmos* (Example 4.46). When the opening figure is repeated, we see how repetition of the rhythmic structure alone can be heard despite the changes in melodic contour (the melody now is played by the left hand).

Example 4.46*
Bartók: *Mikrokosmos, No. 151*

Augmentation and Diminution

Occasionally, a composer alters the rhythmic structure of the original. But if he retains enough of the original rhythmic idea, the repetition is easy to hear. Two very common rhythmic alterations which occur in repetitions are *augmentation* and *diminution*.

The term diminution means that a repetition is shorter than the original. When each tone is shortened, the result is a faster version. In his *Symphonie Fantastique*, Berlioz makes effective use of diminution. The original tune, which happens to be the Gregorian chant, *Dies irae*, is repeated with tones only half the original length.

Example 4.47*
Berlioz: *Symphonie Fantastique,* fifth movement

In the opposite technique, augmentation, the time values of the original melodic idea are extended, usually doubled. As a result, we hear a slowing or stretching-out of the original melodic idea.

Example 4.48*
Bach: Fugue No. 8, from Book I of *The Well-Tempered Clavier*

Summary

There is a bewildering amount of material available in repetition, and we have examined only half of it. Chapter 5 explores another kind of repetition—developmental. You may feel unsure of repetition from having heard only an example or two of each kind before moving to the next. But your skill will improve as you listen to more music, and particularly if you listen to entire pieces.

It may be wise to pause here and listen for literal repetition in a complete piece. In our discussion, we have often referred to Haydn's *London Symphony*, particularly the first movement. If you concentrate on the principal themes, you will hear them return, sometimes immediately and sometimes after intervening material. Do not worry about what else is going on, although you should always try to notice as much as you can. Just listen for those important themes. You will begin to notice your growing ability to recognize recurring themes and motives.

It is also important that you recognize that literal repetition in music serves the vital artistic functions of unity, contrast, balance, and symmetry.

Suggested Works for Additional Listening

Pieces Based on the Repetition of One or Two Simple Musical Ideas
Bach: *Two-Part Inventions*
Bartók: *Mikrokosmos,* Vol. VI
Chopin: *Preludes,* Op. 28

Pieces Based on the Repetition of Contrasting Musical Ideas
Brahms: *Piano Concerto No. 2 in B-flat,* Op. 83, first movement
Haydn: *String Quartet,* Op. 64, No. 5, second movement
Mozart: *Symphony No. 41 (Jupiter),* third movement

Chapter 5

Repetition: Developmental

The following recordings should be at hand for listening in connection with this chapter.

Mozart: *Symphony No. 40 in G minor,* K. 550, first movement
Bach: *Brandenburg Concerto No. 5,* first movement
Beethoven: *Symphony No. 5 in C minor,* Op. 67
Brahms: *Symphony No. 4 in E minor,* Op. 98, fourth movement
Wagner: *Siegfried Idyll*

The essence of almost any art work lies in its *theme,* or central idea. This idea is frequently simple but potent, and its continual repetition contributes to the unity of the piece. If the idea is substantially modified, we call the repetition developmental. Many works of architecture grow out of the development of some simple formal idea into a vast structure. The Guggenheim Museum (Figures 5.1, 5.2) designed by Frank Lloyd Wright, for example, springs from the development of so simple an idea as a curved line into a spiral shape. Everything in the building is circular in design, even the tiled floor and a spiraled ramp which curls from ceiling to ground level.

In the Van Gogh drawing, *The Bridge at Langlois* (Figure 5.3), the short, heavy strokes made with a reed pen are developed through repetition into a unified whole. Likewise, modest musical ideas are often developed into entire pieces of music. With the repetition of a few simple ideas, a composer may spin out a complete work. Some composers seem to enjoy economizing their material in exploiting an idea to the fullest. Music organized in this way, like the Guggenheim Museum and the Van Gogh drawing, is tightly unified.

But unity is not the only aim in art. Contrast, as we have seen, is equally important. Without it, repetition of unifying elements would be boring. Obviously, a composer with both unity and contrast in mind does not wish to simply repeat the same idea again and again, nor does he wish to constantly juxtapose entirely different ideas. Instead he frequently repeats a musical idea in varied form, achieving in the process both unity and contrast. We call this technique *developmental repetition*. By its use, a composer can fragment, extend, or modify a musical idea or combine it with other material in such a way that the new passage appears to evolve from the old. He may use a motive, a brief musical idea, as the basic material for an entire musical structure. Or he may build his structure from a theme, a longer idea, transforming it in a variety of ways.

Developmental repetition, therefore, functions like literal repetition: both supply unity and variety. They also differ: literal repetition merely *restates* a musical idea, whereas developmental repetition *reworks* the musical idea. The actual difference between the two is a matter of degree. At some point we go beyond the bounds of literal repetition into the realm of development. That occurs where the repeated musical idea is changed to rebuild the musical fabric, or to redirect the musical intention.

Development spins out the musical structure, extends a musical idea, and imprints form and design on the music. Composers use various developmental techniques to build and shape their compositions.

Figure 5.1   Exterior of the Guggenheim Museum, New York (The Solomon R. Guggenheim Museum photo)

Figure 5.2   Interior of the Guggenheim Museum, New York (The Solomon R. Guggenheim Museum photo)

Techniques of Development

The development of musical material involves the manipulation or modification of a musical idea. One way to develop musical material is to fragment the idea, to break it up and use the "pieces" in new ways.

Fragmentation

Fragmentation is the process of taking part of a musical idea, lifting it from its original context, and putting it in a new one. The fragment can then be repeated literally or developmentally in the

Figure 5.3   Van Gogh, Vincent, *The Bridge at Langlois,* Los Angeles County Museum of Art, The Mr. and Mrs. George Gard de Sylva Collection

new context. For example, in the first movement of Mozart's *Symphony No. 40 in G minor* (Example 5.1), the middle section begins with a fragment of the original theme, repeated literally in a sequence. The lower strings then extend the sequence through varied instrumentation.

Example 5.1*

Mozart: *Symphony No. 40 in G minor,* K. 550,
opening theme and middle section of first movement

The repetitions in Example 5.1 are more developmental than literal because the fragments of the theme are repeated so often and in such different ways that the result constitutes a *transformation* of the original theme.

Mozart based the middle section of this movement entirely on motives derived from the first part of the theme. Because this section develops the original theme, it is called the *development* section.[7] The opening bars of the development section (Example 5.2) reflect the same melodic and rhythmic ideas as the original theme, but in modified form. Mozart scored fragments for unusual combinations of instruments such as bassoon and double basses; he set fragments against contrasting thematic material, and he altered the melodic

---

[7] The entire structure of a movement which includes a development section is called *sonata form,* a topic discussed in Chapter 6, p. 111.

contour. In spite of these modifications, the fragments are clearly heard throughout the development section.

Example 5.2*
Mozart: *Symphony No. 40 in G minor, K. 550,*
first movement

Example 5.3 illustrates what can be done with the smallest of fragments. Here the fragments are only three notes long, yet they retain the essence of the original idea.

Example 5.3*
Mozart: *Symphony No. 40 in G minor, K. 550,*
first movement

Observe the technique of fragmentation in Mozart's *Symphony No. 40* as you listen to the entire first movement.

In Bach's *Brandenburg Concerto No. 5,* the main theme in the opening passage is relatively long and is in a state of continuous movement. You may notice that the theme seems about to end at several midpoints, but instead continues moving through those points, driving on to the end. It is as though Bach designed the theme to be fragmented.

Example 5.4*
Bach: *Brandenburg Concerto No. 5,*
first movement
Three fragments played separately

The fragments of the theme appear throughout the piece, sometimes in new form, sometimes as accompaniment to prominent solo parts. In addition, each section of the movement is set off by a return of a portion of the original theme. The result is a tightly woven movement that begins, ends, and depends throughout on one eight-measure musical idea. The theme and its parts are distinctive; Bach has seen to it that we have no trouble recognizing them as they return throughout the movement. Follow this versatile theme in the score (Appendix D) and note the fragments most often used. Then listen to the whole movement, concentrating on the thematic fragments.

Examples 5.1–5.4, above, involve both melody and rhythm. We have learned that rhythm is as vital as contour to the nature of a theme. In fact, a theme at times has far more distinctive rhythm than melodic contour and development sometimes consists of rhythmic patterns alone. Examine once again the small three-note fragments in the Mozart symphony in Example 5.3. Some are inverted melodically; some are changed in contour. The only remaining identifying feature of these fragments is the rhythmic pattern of the first three notes of the original theme: two short tones and one long (♫ ♩).

Modification

Some themes are developed by a process known as *modification,* in which the theme is substantially altered, or transformed, while still maintaining its original identity. It may take some practice before you can easily identify modifications of themes, but remember that a composer usually makes his modification similar enough to the original to allow us to recognize it as repetition. Composers achieve this kind of development by modifying motive, melodic contour, rhythm, key and mode, or harmonic progression.

Motives. As we have seen in Bach's *Brandenburg Concerto No. 5,* first movement (Example 5.4), the fragments of a theme can, through development, become the basis for a whole composition. But a composer does not need to begin with fragments of a long theme; he may create a motive, which is itself a complete though terse musical idea, and build long sections from the smallest of these. The motives can be developed rhythmically, melodically, or both. In Mozart's *Symphony No. 40 in G minor,* we saw an example of a motive whose melodic contour changed while its rhythm remained the same. One of the finest examples of the use of rhythmic motives is found in Beethoven's *Symphony No. 5 in C minor.* The first four notes of the symphony announce the rhythmic motive which appears in various forms in all four movements (Figure 5.4). This pattern, comprising three short tones and one long one, occurs frequently in the opening bars of the first movement and reappears throughout (Example 5.5).

Figure 5.4   Opening bars of Beethoven's *Symphony No. 5 in C minor*

Example 5.5*
Beethoven: *Symphony No. 5 in C minor,* Op. 67,
first movement, four-note motive
Opening section

In the second movement the motive appears again, but in different form. Now the meter is triple instead of duple and the tempo is slower. However, the three short notes and a long note are un-mistakable.

Example 5.6*
Beethoven: *Symphony No. 5 in C minor,* Op. 67,
second movement

The third movement is based on a fast, rollicking triple meter where, again, the rhythmic motive appears, but this time on a single pitch.

Example 5.7*
Beethoven: *Symphony No. 5 in C minor,* Op. 67,
third movement

Finally, in the fourth movement, the rhythmic motive appears in the original duple pattern, but in still another form. Here, the three-note rhythmic groupings, called triplets, supply a unique variety to the three-shorts-and-one-long pattern heard in the opening bars of the first movement.

Example 5.8*
Beethoven: *Symphony No. 5 in C minor,* Op. 67,
fourth movement

These four excerpts from Beethoven's *Symphony No. 5* illustrate not only the possibilities for expansion and variety that rhythmic motives provide, but also the unity that development produces. The three-shorts-and-one-long rhythmic figure unifies the entire symphony. Prior to the composition of this work, about 1807, the four movements of a symphony contained little organic relationship. Each movement was an entity. Beethoven's treatment of the entire symphony as an organic unit is one reason why his *Fifth Symphony* is an important work historically. At this point, we suggest that you listen to the entire symphony, identifying the rhythmic motive and concentrating on its structural importance.

Melodic Contour. A musical idea can also be developed by the altering of its melodic contour. In the chorus, "And with His Stripes" from the oratorio *Messiah,* Handel repeats one basic theme throughout the piece. He modifies the melodic contour of each new thematic statement, but maintains close relationship with the original statement. With each new statement he repeats the text, "And with His stripes we are healed." Also, each return of the theme begins with the same rhythm and the same basic shape, with a striking leap on the word "stripes." This wide angular leap, which is out of character with the general lyricism of the melody, is a pictorial reference to pain.

The most significant modifications do not occur until enunciation of the last word of the text, "healed." But these modifications are extensive; in each repetition the musical material is completely transformed. Both melodic contour and rhythm are affected. The length of time given to the word "healed," for example, varies greatly (in the first statement, it is two measures; in the last, nine). Thus, after the composer has firmly established the repetition of the theme in the listener's mind, he makes dramatic modifications of the ending portion, providing both unity and contrast. The entire piece evolves from one basic thematic idea.

Example 5.9*
Handel: "And with His Stripes," from *Messiah,*
five separate excerpts
Entire piece

Rhythm. An idea can also be developed by the modifying of its rhythmic pattern. Berlioz demonstrates how this may be done. In his *Symphonie Fantastique* he develops the main theme of the work by presenting it in various movements with changed rhythmic values. After initially stating it in one meter in the opening movement, he sets it in a different meter in the second movement. Thus Berlioz changes the character of the melody without substantially altering the melodic contour. In the fifth movement, he repeats the melody again, this time in still another meter, with ornamentation and an unusual accompaniment consisting mostly of timpani and bass drum.

Example 5.10*
Berlioz: *Symphonie Fantastique,* first movement
Second movement
Fifth movement

Key and Mode. One characteristic of developmental passages in music is that they frequently move from key to key. *Key* in music refers to a family of tones whose special relationship to each other establishes a center of tonality. It is not really important for the listener to be able to identify each key by name, but it is useful to recognize that changes in key are taking place. The process of moving from one key to another is called *modulation.*

A modulatory passage conveys a feeling of vague or transitory tonality. Some sections are more modulatory, more transitory, than others, and music of certain periods (for example, the nineteenth century) is more modulatory than that of other periods (the eighteenth century). The process of modulation is easier to hear when the change of key is abrupt than when it is gradual. Sometimes the modulation is subtle, as if to conceal the change of key; other times it is obvious, as if to draw our attention to the change. In Example 5.11, an excerpt from the second movement of Mahler's *Symphony No. 1 in D,* when the bass starts to move downward, we have a feeling that we are heading somewhere, that we are making a change. In fact, we are moving toward a different key. We may even recognize the destination as "home," the tonal center of the piece. This homeward modulation is relatively easy to hear, causing us to wonder how we got away from home in the first place. The modulation away from the tonal center is much more subtle than the returning one. After hearing the first excerpt in Example 5.11, listen to the entire movement up to that point, to see if you can hear both the departure from and return to the tonal center. Certain changes of key are easy to hear, whereas others are extremely difficult. With practice you can hear the activity involved in modulation; you will become sensitive to the process of change and aware that some sections in music reflect constant shifts of key.

Example 5.11

Mahler: *Symphony No. 1 in D,* second movement

The reasons that some passages of music appear to be more transitory than others are: (1) the relative frequency of key changes; (2) the relative use of many different keys; and (3) the relative subtlety with which the changes are made. The manipulation of these three factors results in a certain style of developmental repetition unique to each composer and period. Compared with the development section of the first movement of Mozart's *Symphony No. 40* (Example 5.1), Chopin's *Prelude No. 25,* Op. 45 (Example 5.12), is much more transitory. Mozart moves from one key to another smoothly and unobtrusively. He begins with a sequence, for example, which takes us so subtly through a modulation that we hardly notice the change. Chopin, on the other hand, makes his changes so abrupt and striking that our attention is called to the changes themselves. Since the Mozart symphony has a stable opening section, the departure of the development section appears to be a kind of temporary wandering. The Chopin prelude has no such opening—we seem to begin wandering at the very start of the piece. We soon learn to expect abrupt changes in the prelude, and the modulatory process itself becomes a strong unifying feature. Thus, the interest is not so much in the theme as in the harmonic process of modulation; therein lies the substance of the piece.

Example 5.12

Chopin: *Prelude No. 25,* Op. 45

Although it is sometimes difficult to distinguish one key from another, it is usually much easier to hear a change of *mode.* The modes most often used in Western music are *major* and *minor.* Each is a succession of tones, or a scale, within which a melody may be organized. Example 5.13 begins with the C major scale, starting and ending on C. The tune following is in the key of C major; it utilizes the tones of the C major scale, and a sense of repose is felt on the final tone, C.

Example 5.13*

C major scale
Folk tune: "Country Gardens"

The minor mode also starts and ends on C, but certain tones within the key have been altered. This is called the C minor scale (Example 5.14). Listen to the same folk tune played in the minor mode. The appropriate tones have been altered. Note the difference in the character of the melody in these two versions.

Example 5.14*
C minor scale
"Country Gardens" in C minor

You may have been told that major and minor modes evoke different moods or feelings. The minor mode, for example, has been said to be sad, pensive, or melancholy. It is interesting to note, in this respect, that funeral dirges (such as the second movement of Beethoven's *Symphony No. 3 in E-flat*, known as the *Eroica*) are almost always in the minor mode. However, such stereotypes are dangerous because emotional associations are highly individual matters. What seems sad or melancholy to one listener may seem stately or proud to another. Other factors, such as tempo, play an important role in the evocation of feeling. If a tune in the minor mode is played rapidly with a bouncing accompaniment, like the song "When Johnny Comes Marching Home," it probably sounds as "happy" as any other tune.

Example 5.15
Beethoven: *Symphony No. 3 in E-flat*, Op. 55
(*Eroica*), second movement

Example 5.16
Folk song: "When Johnny Comes Marching Home"

Composers often repeat a major mode theme in the minor mode, or vice versa. The reason for these shifts of mode is again to provide contrast while maintaining unity. This kind of repetition offers a near-perfect balance of unity and variety. Mozart, in his *Variations in C*, K. 265, uses a theme in the major mode and then presents one of his variations in the minor mode. In Example 5.17 we hear first the original theme in C major and then Variation 8 in C minor. Note the shift in mood or character in the change from major to minor.

Example 5.17
Mozart: *Variations in C*, K. 265, Theme and
Variation 8

A heightened use of contrast between major and minor modes occurs in the solo and chorus entitled "Balulalow" from Benjamin Britten's *Ceremony of Carols* (Example 5.18). In this piece, major and minor are alternated in close succession.

Example 5.18
Britten: "Balulalow," from *Ceremony of Carols*

Harmonic Progressions. The term musical "theme" or musical "idea," usually refers to a melody. It can also indicate harmonic progressions, or the distinctive manner in which one chord follows another. Sometimes a chord progression, instead of a melody, is repeated and used as the basis for development. This repetition can more easily be heard in the bass line than in the melody. It can also be seen in the score. The *foundation* of the music seems to be repeated.

Most students are familiar with this technique in popular music and jazz. Many of us have discovered the fun of playing a piano duet in which a series of chords, a "formula," is repeated continuously, while different melodies are played above it. A simple chord pattern repeated again and again fits many tunes. While the melody changes several times, the chord pattern remains the same.

Sometimes in the repetition of a musical idea, the melody is completely modified, and only the basic harmony remains intact. The variation differs so much from the original that the listener is only vaguely aware of the relationship between the two. In Brahms' *Variations on a Theme of Haydn,* the original simple tune is never simple again after the initial statement; in fact, some of the variations display entirely new themes. Brahms uses the harmonic pattern, rather than the tune, to build his variations. This movement of the harmonic foundation can thus be seen and heard best in the bass line. Note the similarity of the bass line in the original and Variation 6 in Example 5.19.

Example 5.19*
Brahms: Original theme and Variation 6 from
Variations on a Theme of Haydn

A similar effect is produced in a rigid formal structure called the *passacaglia,* a set of variations on a theme in the bass line. Here the composer presents his theme in a series of tones in the bass voice instead of the usual melody found in the higher voices. Brahms uses this technique in the last movement of his *Fourth Symphony,* in which he has composed thirty-four variations on the "theme" presented in Example 5.20. Remember that this theme is the harmonic foundation, and although it is heard first in the upper voices, it is played later by the low voices in the orchestra.

Example 5.20*
Brahms: *Symphony No. 4 in E minor,* Op. 98, fourth
movement, Passacaglia theme and opening passage

Monotony, a dangerous possibility with thirty-four variations on a short theme, is never a problem here. Each variation is different, with new instrumentation and inventive developmental techniques, such as adding new melodies to the original passacaglia theme. Often the theme is masked by brilliant activity in the upper voices, and is difficult to recognize. In fact, we are not even aware of thirty-four distinct sections in the movement, since each variation is tied to the preceding and following ones, all of them building to a high point in the movement. Listen to the entire movement, concentrating on the repetition of the theme which is almost entirely obscured at times, and blatantly obvious in the horns and the double basses at other times. Note both the unity the theme provides and the variety it permits.

Combinations

Composers often develop their material by combining it with new material in orchestration, harmony, or accompaniment. As we discovered with fragmentation, applying an idea to a new context yields an entirely new piece of music. This technique turns up frequently in literature where an old plot appears in a new setting. For example, the classic love story, *Romeo and Juliet,* provided the basic plot for the musical, *West Side Story.*

One musical structure that embodies combinations is *theme and variations.* Here a theme is repeated several times, each time in a new setting. The two examples cited in this chapter, Mozart's *Variations in C,* K. 265, and Brahms' *Variations on a Theme of Haydn,* illustrate this technique. The composer may choose to combine new material with an original theme, or new material with an original bass line.

Another example of the combination of a theme with new material occurs in Berlioz' *Symphonie Fantastique* (Example 5.10). In addition to being presented in different meters, the theme is fused with new material. Violins and flutes play the theme in the first movement; the tempo is fast and the theme stands out because it has virtually no accompaniment. In the second movement, solo flute and oboe, alternating with clarinet, play the theme softly to the accompaniment of quiet strings. In the fifth movement, a solo clarinet, accompanied by timpani and bass drum, plays the theme softly and rapidly. The original melodic material has thus been developed with different instruments and accompaniment.

Medieval music was often based on a pre-existing, familiar tune which, in order to be prominent, was typically placed in the highest voice. However, the tune may also have appeared in an inner voice where it could not easily be distinguished. It is possible that the practice of "hiding" a tune somewhere in the fabric of the music was common because the tune was secular and therefore unacceptable in the church. The Mass *L'Homme armé,* by Dufay (Example 5.21), was based on the popular folk tune of the same name. Listen first to the original folk tune and then to the treatment given it by Guillaume Dufay. If you have difficulty in hearing the tune in the Mass setting, remember that Dufay did not intend for it to be obvious; he deliberately "cloistered" that tune from the ears of the clergy.

Example 5.21*
Folk tune: *L'Homme armé*
Dufay: "Agnus Dei" from *L'Homme armé* (Mass)

In Baroque and later music (eighteenth century), the use of a pre-existing tune in combination with new material was still common. In the Baroque period, chorales, or familiar hymn tunes, were frequently the basis for new compositions. Such hymn tunes are usually found in the upper voice where they are more recognizable than in an inner voice. In Example 5.22, the chorale sung by the soprano continues to be prominent even when the other three voices accompany it, each entering separately in a counterpoint of shorter tones. The tune is thereby developed through the complex movement of the other voices transforming the original into a completely new musical statement.

Example 5.22*
Bach: *Cantata No. 140* (*Wachet auf*)

Summary

Let us examine an entire piece of music in terms of developmental repetition. Wagner's *Siegfried Idyll* is a one-movement composition based largely on themes from his opera, *Siegfried.* The principal theme is distinctive, pleasing, and easy to recognize, and it is developed by all the techniques we have described: fragmentation, modification, and combination with other material. After the theme is presented and repeated several times, new material is introduced and combined with the original theme or fragments of it. Although there are two or three things happening at once, we do not really encounter much difficulty in listening to them because the themes are not significantly changed.

The piece consists of six prominent themes which are presented in the order of their appearance in Example 5.23. The first theme is the main theme because of its frequent return and constant combination with the other themes.

Example 5.23*
Wagner: *Siegfried Idyll,* six themes, played separately

Table 5.1 which illustrates the thematic sections of *Siegfried Idyll* may help you keep track of where you are as you read and listen. The combinations are shown graphically in proportion to the length of time required to perform each section. For example, the main theme is heard alone first, and is then joined by the second theme; the third theme is then heard alone, and so on.

Table 5.1 Thematic chart, *Siegfried Idyll*

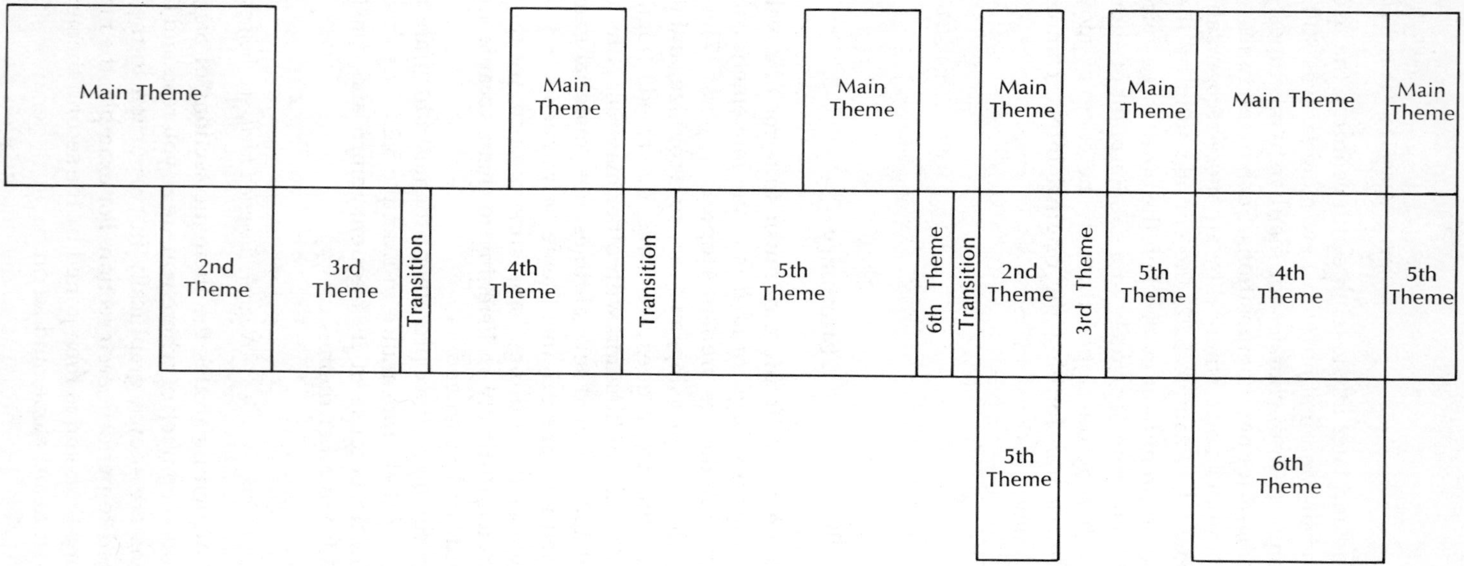

The best way to approach this exercise in listening is to refer to the chart while reading the following discussion. Then use the chart while listening to a recording of *Siegfried Idyll*.

Siegfried Idyll opens with an introductory section composed of fragments of the main theme. This rather unusual practice of beginning with fragments of a theme before the theme is actually stated occurs several times in this piece. Note also that the main theme is usually played by the strings, particularly the violins.

Soon after the statement of the main theme, the theme reappears as though it were beginning again in imitation of itself. But this is only a fragment of the main theme, and instead of going on, it introduces the second theme, a short descending passage played by the flutes.

The third theme is stated briefly by the clarinets. A transitional section of material derived from this theme leads to a contrasting section which features the rather long fourth theme played by the oboe. Fragments of the smooth, connected main theme and the short, light fourth theme are then combined, which heightens the contrast between the two.

After another transition section, which contains several trills and obvious changes in key, we hear fragments of the fifth theme before it is fully stated; this is the same technique that introduced the main theme. Soon after the introduction of the fifth theme, Wagner combines it with the main theme, and extends the combination to some length. The compatibility of these two musical ideas allows for this extended development.

The presentation of the sixth theme by the horns is striking because of its contrast with the preceding material, both in dynamic level and general character.

After a brief transition, we reach the area of climax in which *three* themes, the main, second, and fifth themes, are combined. We have now reached the most intense point of Wagner's discourse. From here on, we can expect and we hear a decline, a tapering off from the high point. This decline is accomplished through a return of the third theme, and continues with another combination of fragments of the main theme with the fifth theme.

The concluding section begins with a combination of the main, fourth, and sixth themes, all fragmented. Finally, the fifth theme returns briefly, leads to the main theme, and brings the piece to a quiet close. Note that all six themes return during the decline.

The developmental repetition in this piece revolves essentially around a single theme, repeated several times throughout the work. The remaining musical material consists of several subsidiary themes which are developed along with the main theme. One technique of development is to repeat musical ideas in rather free modulations in various keys. In most cases the modulation is accomplished subtly. You may have to listen several times before you hear these changes.

Wagner also used the technique of repeating an idea in a different orchestral setting. This technique is especially effective when a composer has conceived a musical idea idiomatically, that is, with a particular instrument in mind. If he designs the idea for the oboe, for example, a substantial alteration takes place when the brass section picks up that idea. The predominant technique of developmental repetition in the *Siegfried Idyll* is combination: the main theme is combined with each of the other themes and, in places, is even combined with fragments of itself. Repetition of the main theme provides the unity, and the combination with many other themes contributes to the music's variety.

Because each repetition of the main theme is so similar to the original, the question might arise, why is this called developmental, and not literal, repetition? As we have said, the difference between the two is a matter of degree and the answer to the question is therefore arbitrary: we must decide whether the repetition has been altered sufficiently to make the music appear to be taking a new direction, to be evolving or growing. Literal repetition does not effect this evolution; it is static by nature. Developmental repetition, though substantially different from the original, is recognized by the listener as repetition even though the changes are substantial.

There would be no reason to examine developmental repetition in this detail, except for its vital function in music. It is more than the application of a mechanical technique to provide variety in an otherwise dull piece; it is a basic building block in the structure of music. The organic whole grows out of and by means of the developmental repetition of musical ideas.

Suggested Works for Additional Listening

Fragmentation:
Beethoven: *Piano Sonata in C minor,* Op. 10, No. 1, finale
Bach: *Brandenburg Concerto No. 3,* first movement
Bartók: *Mikrokosmos, No. 145*

Modification:
Mahler: *Symphony No. 9 in D minor,* first movement
Schubert: *Die Post* (The second section is in the minor mode to express sadness when no letter arrives)
Mozart: *Piano Sonata in A,* K. 331, first movement

Combination:
Reger: *Variations on a Theme by Mozart*
Haydn: *String Quartet in C (Emperor),* Op. 76, No. 3, first movement
Beethoven: *Piano Sonata in A,* Op. 2, No. 2, first movement

Chapter 6

Form and Design

The following recordings should be at hand for listening in connection with this chapter.

Mozart: *Symphony No. 40 in G minor*
Mozart: Variations on "Ah, vous dirai-je, Maman," K. 265
Haydn: *Symphony No. 104 in D* (*London*)
Tchaikovsky: *1812 Overture*

Every work of art has a unique design which results from the selection and arrangement of elements by the artist. To perceive this design, we examine the relationship of the parts to one another and to the whole. It is like looking at a blueprint; we perceive the essence of structure. Just as a tone has no meaning until used with other tones to form melodies and chords, or as a chord has no meaning until joined with other chords, so themes and motives derive their meaning from the relationship "formed" with all other elements in the piece. Formal design in music is the manner in which the musical elements are put together.

When we speak of musical form we are really talking about two different things: *form,* the total, over-all structure, and *design,* the inner structure, the relationship of all elements—themes, motives, harmonic progressions, rhythm patterns—to the total structure. We might say that over-all structure is the result of design. In our discussion we are concerned with (1) those elements that constitute the design of a piece, (2) how they are organized, and (3) the kinds of design that result when certain relationships exist among these elements. An acquaintance with design in music provides us with an opportunity for "significant hearing."

Every artist arranges the parts of his composition in a certain *design.* As he places them in a particular order, a pattern, he is guided by certain principles of design. A painter or sculptor organizes his materials *in space* in order to create visual effectiveness. A poet or musician organizes his materials *in time* to create aural effectiveness. Anyone interested in viewing or hearing a work of art, then, should be concerned with understanding the inner design of the work. As we begin to distinguish the relationship of the parts to the whole, we learn to see or hear significantly.

Let us consider a work with which you are already familiar: Haydn's *Symphony No. 104 in D (London)*. As you recall, Haydn used three important thematic ideas: a slow, stately theme played by the full orchestra, a sprightly folk melody played by the violins, and a vigorous theme which features an interplay between the first and second violins (see Examples 4.9, 4.14, and 4.6). When Haydn decided to use the slow theme as an introduction and the folk tune as the principal theme, he was making basic design decisions. Another basic decision which determined the design of the entire movement was that there would be three large sections, each set off by a long pause, and each contrasting in character with the previous section. The first and last sections are similar in design, and the middle section is largely a development of the principal theme. Listen to the entire movement with the over-all design in mind; in noticing these elements of design, you are apprehending Haydn's blueprint, his plan for the movement.

In painting, "composition" comprises the arrangement of objects, lines, and shapes on canvas to form the total work. One of the first things a young artist learns is to get a feel for the size of his canvas as he begins to place lines and shapes in his picture. The musician, likewise, must have a feel for the scope of his projected composition. He must decide whether a piece should be large in scope, such as a symphony or an opera, or small, such as a sonata or an art song. He may have specific themes in mind, or he may wish to write a composition for specific instruments. He must make several decisions about the design of the piece: he must decide how its parts should fit together, where each theme goes, and how it will be used. Both painter and composer are concerned with design—both are "composing" their work.

A sculptor may decide to carve the figure of a man. Or he may choose to carve just the head or bust of a man, or a group of several men. Whichever choice he makes, the resulting sculpture, if successful, would be a complete unit. The *Venus de Milo* (Figure 6.1), a sculpture of an armless figure, contains an artistic integration of parts to the whole, as does Michelangelo's *Pietà* (Figure 6.2, p. 98), a sculpture in which two figures produce a single, cohesive statement.

Anyone who wishes to write a narrative short story concerning the events of a single day does not write a diary or a newspaper account, but carefully chooses incidents which contribute to his theme. He

Figure 6.1   *The Venus de Milo,* Musée du Louvre, Paris (Scala photo, New York)

may be dealing with love, hate, fear, loneliness, meaninglessness, or any other subject. He selects and organizes his materials in order to present a distilled, directed account of life. This intention to offer a unified impression is one of the things that make the art object "truer than real life."

The poet organizes his materials—meter, images, sound devices, rhyme—to express a unified theme. To perceive the inner structure of his poem, we look for the main parts and how they relate to one another. "The Eagle" by Tennyson is made up of two main parts, or

Figure 6.2 Michelangelo, *Pietà,* The Vatican, Rome (Scala photo, New York)

stanzas. These stanzas are alike in structure, rhyme scheme, and meter. They are also alike in theme: both describe the eagle. They are separated, however, because there is a separation in thought. The poet makes two different comments about the eagle: in the first stanza the eagle stands atop the cliff; in the second he falls "like a thunderbolt." Thus, the design consists of a unique arrangement of material within stanzas, and this design contributes directly to the statement of theme.

The Eagle

He clasps the crag with crooked hands;
Close to the sun in lonely lands,
Ring'd with the azure world, he stands.

The wrinkled sea beneath him crawls;
He watches from his mountain walls,
And like a thunderbolt he falls.

ALFRED, LORD TENNYSON

An artist who works from a scene in nature, or a photograph, frequently makes significant changes in the arrangement of elements to improve the design. By emphasizing one element over others or balancing elements against each other, he is, in a sense, improving on nature's design. Ordinarily, photography is a representation of real life. Painting is a representation of an *idea* about real life. We are afforded the opportunity to make such a comparison from the works of Paul Cézanne. Notice the improvement in design as Cézanne selected and rearranged elements in the natural setting pictured in Figure 6.4 for his painting *View of Gardanne* in Figure 6.3 (pp. 100, 101).

Principles of Design

Artists and musicians, then, select their materials and arrange them in a design. It might be fun and useful to compare a painting and a musical piece in terms of their design alone. We have chosen *Still Life: Apples and Pomegranates* by Courbet, and the second movement of Bach's *Brandenburg Concerto No. 6*. Although both of these well-known works have much to recommend them, we will limit our discussion here to principles of design.

As we examine the relationships of elements, visual or musical, we see that some elements *predominate* over others, while *balance* and *coherence* prevail among all. Design supports and enhances these basic principles. That is, elements are arranged in such a way that the principles become evident.

Predominance

In the painting by Courbet, Plate 12 (following p. 54), the plate of fruit dominates the picture because of its size, intensity of color, bright light values, and central location. The fruit stands out; it is what the painting is all about; our attention focuses on it. Everything else in the painting exists only to enhance the predominance of this central idea.

Predominance is a factor in the relationship between musical elements too. The composer provides one element (or a few elements) for us to concentrate on. This idea stands out. It may be any musical

Figure 6.3 Cézanne, Paul, *The Village of Gardanne,* courtesy of The Brooklyn Museum, Ella T. Woodward Fund

idea—a melody, a rhythmic pattern, a harmonic progression (for example, a modulation), an orchestral effect. The idea can dominate at one given time in a composition, or it can dominate throughout.

A particular theme can dominate a composition by its "size," instrumentation, or location in the piece. A melody that is long and loud can dominate. It can also dominate by frequent recurrences. The little motive in Beethoven's *Fifth Symphony*   is important, not because it is large, but because it is omnipresent. A theme can also predominate through instrumentation. A theme played by many instruments usually predominates over one played

Figure 6.4   Photograph of the village of Gardanne (Rapho photo, Paris)

by few instruments. Also, the timbre of certain instruments gives them natural predominance over others; for example, a theme played by the oboe can be heard above all the strings. Finally, the location of a theme may give it predominance. The first and last positions in both music and literature are positions of greatest emphasis. The first theme is often the most important, and it frequently returns at the end.

In the second movement of *Brandenburg Concerto No. 6* (Example 6.1), the main theme predominates because it is long, because it is always being heard, and because of its instrumentation; that is, the melody is played on a high instrument, whereas the accompaniment is played on low instruments. Listen to a few of the opening bars long enough to be convinced that the first theme played by a viola is a predominant element.

Example 6.1
Bach: *Brandenburg Concerto No. 6,*
second movement

Balance

We have observed the principle of balance at work before, both in painting and music. Unlike Tintoretto's painting (Plate 8) the balance in Courbet's painting is not symmetrical. Tintoretto proved that balance can be achieved by similarity and repetition of visual elements. Courbet, like Mondrian, proves that balance can also be achieved by contrast—call it asymmetrical balance. Here factors other than size and shape come into play, such as contrasting location, light, and color, a balance of equal but opposing forces. Courbet achieved balance through equalizing the bright light values and intense colors with the opposing dark background. The warm colors of the fruit are balanced by the cool color of the stein, even though their sizes and shapes are quite dissimilar.

Balance in music can also be achieved in numerous ways, in either simultaneous or successive combinations of voices. A melody may be balanced by a chordal accompaniment or by another melody. Frequently balance is accomplished orchestrally, where a solo instrument is set against a section, or sections against each other. And frequently balance in music is successive; one section balances the next. Predominance and balance can both be seen in music where one voice predominates in one section, and another voice takes over in the balancing section.

There is a degree of what might be called asymmetrical balance in the instrumentation used by Bach in *Brandenburg Concerto No. 6.* Listen to the opening passage again and notice that high instruments (violas) are balanced against lower instruments (cello and harpsichord). Symmetrical balance is established by consecutive arrangement of phrases: there are six phrases fairly equal in length, each marked off by a distinctive close. A trill played by the violas will help you recognize the ending of each phrase. But as in painting, balance in music need not consist of the symmetrical arrangement of themes. Musical forces can be equalized in numerous ways; dynamics, timbre, length, weight of themes—all can affect balance.

Coherence

No matter how the predominant elements are arranged or how the elements balance one another, they all have coherence, a sense of belonging together. They seem to fit, to make sense in the compositional arrangement. In painting, we think of elements as cohering, even attaching themselves to one another. There is no empty space on the canvas. In the Courbet painting there would be an obvious coherence in the pieces of fruit caused by the clustering and over-lapping of shapes, even if nothing else were happening.

A direct parallel can be made in music. The overlapping shapes in the Courbet painting are directly analogous to the overlapping themes in the Bach concerto we just heard. The result in both cases is coherence. Listen again to the beginning of the movement. The theme is stated first by one viola, but before that theme is finished, the other viola begins its statement of the theme, so that the two statements overlap.

But in music the concept of coherence is one of *time,* not space. And so we think of coherence as bringing order and transition to ideas. The elements are coherent because the composer arranges his ideas successively and logically, and makes smooth transitions be-tween them. He repeats various elements to emphasize similarity and compatibility of ideas. He can even achieve coherence as the painter does, by clustering or overlapping themes. Some composers use the technique of "dovetailing," in which the end of one theme is actually the beginning of the next.

Coherence can also be achieved by tonality, a term which both musicians and painters use. In painting, cohesiveness is achieved partly by the use of compatible colors. The color of each object is complementary to the other colors; they blend and seem to exude a unified effect. In other words, Courbet's plate of fruit exhibits a single color, a kind of orange, even though there are greens, reds, yellows, and browns also scattered in the group. All colors in the painting seem to enhance the predominant color, orange, thus pro-ducing a *color tonality.* The use of color tonality is really what finally brings the visual elements together in this painting.

In music, tonality is a total unified perception of key. Just as the painting is particularly coherent because one color tonality pre-dominates, the Bach concerto is coherent because one key predom-inates. Like the painting, the piece exhibits a single key sound, even though other keys appear throughout. And the more you listen to this piece, the more you realize the strength of that central key.

We have been talking about principles of design—dominance, coherence, and balance—which mainly concern *proportion,* that is, the arrangement of shapes on the canvas and themes in a composi-tion. One of the most important means of supplying a work with these principles is *repetition,* which we have already seen at work in music.

The Bach concerto contains both literal and developmental rep-etition. The main theme is repeated literally many times and is also developed by fragmentation and modulation. The fragmentation occurs midway in the piece; the cello and harpsichord repeat only the first four notes of the theme several times. The theme modulates every time the four-note phrase is repeated. A somewhat "flowing" repetition, analogous to line in painting, appears in the bass part, which Bach keeps in motion even through the ends of phrases.

Repetition in painting can be *literal* (ooooo); it can consist of *alternating* (oOoOoO) shapes, colors, or light values; it can be *progressive* (ooooO), when the element is changed gradually in volume, shape, or color. It can also be *flowing,* which usually appears as a line or something that represents a line. The Miró painting (Plate 7) illustrates all four types of repetition.

Our continual reference to other arts is quite deliberate because their similarities with music in terms of the perceiver are remarkable. For example, the four types of repetition in painting are analogous to the types of musical repetition discussed earlier: *literal* (our exact word in Chapter 6), *alternating* (we called it "intermittent"), *progressive* ("developmental" in Chapter 5), and *flowing* (which could be "rhythm," "melody," or "tempo"). These are parallel design elements; they are designated differently in painting and music because in painting we are dealing with space and in music with time. In relating the design elements of art to music we will be talking about themes, pitch, timbre, and dynamics rather than shapes, color, and light.

Musical Structure

To perceive musical design, or the basic structure of a composition, we try to see how ideas are arranged. To do so, we examine the whole piece, looking for its major divisions. We determine how many parts or sections it has, and how these sections fit together.

The first step in analyzing musical structure is to consider the total composition, its size and scope. Some compositions, usually small in scope, consist of a single, indivisible unit, played without interruption. These are *simple* forms, such as art songs, piano character pieces and most tone poems. Compositions of larger scope which are divided into separate sections are called *composite* forms. These sections are customarily separated by a pause. A composition which is made up of movements, such as a piano sonata, a concerto, or a symphony, is composite. So is the opera with its acts and scenes, the suite with its various dances, and the Mass with its liturgical sections. You may notice that the divisions in a composite form are organized to provide contrast in tempo, mood, or media. For example, the movements of a concerto are fast, slow, fast; the opera and oratorio often alternate solos with choruses.

The next step in analyzing design is to examine the inner structure of each movement. Even though a movement is played without interruption, it usually has discernible sections. A section is a part of the total composition which is typically dominated by one basic musical idea and generally has a discernible ending, called a *cadence*. A cadence may bring a phrase, a melody, a section, or an entire composition to a close. Some cadences are strong and final; others are only momentary hesitations. But the strongest ones usually mark the ends of sections and of the piece itself.[8]

Examining the design of a piece of music is like examining the outline of an essay. It is useful for the reader to understand the outline in order to master the material of the essay and to follow the logical arrangement and development of ideas. The musical theme is similar to a topic sentence and the musical sections resemble paragraphs. Both themes and sections can end in cadences, but the stronger cadences occur at the end of sections, just as the strong divisions in an essay separate paragraphs.

Any distinctive musical idea—melodic, rhythmic, harmonic, orchestral—may be the agent of design, the "theme" we have been talking about. Hence, to discern the design of a movement, we look for (1) the major themes; (2) the number of major sections; and (3) the arrangement of the sections.

The design of any given piece of music begins to take shape as soon as the composer makes a musical statement. He may decide that a *single statement* is adequate to express his idea. If so, the result would be a short piece consisting of essentially one musical idea, or theme. The design of such a piece would be very simple, and easy for the listener to understand. Example 6.2 illustrates just such a piece, a simple, single statement—one musical idea, undeveloped, but repeated as many times as there are verses.

Example 6.2*
Folk song: "On Top of Old Smoky"

However, few pieces are that simple, even the short ones. More often the composer elects to introduce more than a single statement; and frequently the second statement is a contrasting one. He makes a statement and may repeat it in any of the ways we have examined earlier, or he may introduce a new idea. The techniques of repetition and contrast provide distinctive design to a musical piece. And this can be said of all art forms.

The repetition and contrast of themes and motives constitute the main framework of compositional design. All music from the simplest songs to the most grandiose symphonies and operas is designed this way. Let us take a careful look at a few simple songs to illustrate the principle of *thematic* design.

We should always keep in mind that just as no two paintings are exactly alike in their design, no two musical compositions are alike. There are many portraits, many sonnets, and many sonatas. But each consists of its own unique relationship of elements, even though

---

[8] Various types and functions of cadences are discussed in Chapter 7, pp. 127–28.

the over-all general scheme may be classified along with hundreds of others. There are thousands of statues of women, even some without arms, but the *Venus de Milo* is unique because of the distinctive way its parts fit together (Figure 6.1). In music, too, we must do more than simply determine that this piece is a symphony or that one is an oratorio; that information is frequently on the record jacket. In other words, each composition should be examined for its unique inner structure.

We have already heard an example of the simplest type of design—a single thematic statement (Example 6.2). Obviously, the next step is either to repeat that single statement literally or with modification, or to add another theme, different and contrasting. Whereas we had a one-part design in Example 6.2, if we add another theme, we would then have a two-part design. Musicians commonly label parts of their musical design with letters of the alphabet. Thus, a single statement would be simply A or AA if repeated. A single statement repeated with modification would then be AA', and two different themes would be labelled AB, etc. We shall be using these letter designations from here on.

A two-part design can be achieved by repeating the original statement, either literally (AA) or with variation (AA') as in the Scottish folk song, "Ca' the Yowes."

Example 6.3*
Scottish folk song: "Ca' the Yowes"

Composers often introduce a contrasting theme to establish some kind of balance with the original statement, a balance of equal but opposing forces, AB. In the tune, "Liverpool Lullaby," we find the song made up of two slightly different themes. As we examine more complex designs, we shall see that the principle found in these simple tunes is basically the same in complex pieces.

Example 6.4
Kelly: "Liverpool Lullaby"

The following brief outline of available types of thematic design will clarify the ensuing material.

    I. Standard forms
        A. Single themes (monothematic—A, AA')
        B. Multiple themes (polythematic)
            1. two themes
                a. two parts (AB)
                b. three parts (ABA)
            2. more than two themes (ABC, ABCD, ABCBA, or any combination)
    II. Free forms

Single Themes

A single-theme composition will almost always include more than one statement of that theme; otherwise it would either require a very long theme or result in a very short piece. So most such designs are based primarily on a single theme repeated and varied in a number of ways. Chopin's *Prelude in A,* Op. 28, No. 7, is a short and simple piano piece in which theme A is repeated with slight alteration. The structure of this piece, then, is AA'. In listening for formal design, it is always a good idea to listen first to the entire section or composition. It is difficult to detect form without first gaining a concept of the scope of the piece.

Example 6.5*
Chopin: *Prelude in A,* Op. 28, No. 7

Bach's Prelude No. 1 and Fugue No. 1 from *The Well-Tempered Clavier,* Book I, are both monothematic pieces, but each is relatively lengthy. The prelude consists merely of a series of broken chords all played in identical fashion. We have, in effect, one theme.

Example 6.6*
Bach: Prelude No. 1, from Book I of
The Well-Tempered Clavier

The fugue is also based on a single theme, a melody which is repeated through the technique of imitation. Each repetition of the theme in this fugue is easy to hear because of its distinctive contour. Here is an excellent example of coherence in music achieved by "overlapping" themes. The design consists of a series of overlapping repetitions of a single theme.

Example 6.7*
Bach: Fugue No. 1, from Book I of
The Well-Tempered Clavier

In the attempt to exploit all the possibilities presented by a single theme, composers set for themselves a kind of compositional game, in which they repeat the theme in many different settings. They may alter the accompaniment or change the key, tempo, dynamics, or rhythm, while retaining enough of the original theme to keep it recognizable. Thus, the composer is able to present variety while maintaining a basic unity of structure. Composers have called this "game" *theme and variations,* a type of composition with which we are now familiar. Its scheme is labelled AA'A''A''', etc. The original theme is A and the variations begin with A'. One of the simplest examples of this design is Mozart's charming *Ah, vous dirai-je, Maman* (you may recognize the tune as "Twinkle, Twinkle, Little Star"). Notice the variety when Mozart places the theme in a different setting with each variation.

Multiple Themes—Two-Part Form

Most music is made up of at least two different contrasting themes. The composer is more likely to keep interest alive by introducing a contrasting theme than by repeating the same theme. And, curiously, we do not usually find too many more themes, as if the composer were reluctant to have us wander through a myriad of different tunes and lose our sense of unity and our perception of the inter-relationship of design elements.

The contrasting theme often consists of a different rhythm pattern, contour, or movement. The simplest method of stating two themes, AB, is illustrated in the Schubert song, "Am Meer" (Example 6.8). Notice the striking contrast between the two themes: the first theme is quiet and lyric; the second theme is louder and more dramatic, and the accompaniment more agitated. The AB design is repeated, so the final design of this song is ABAB. The Scarlatti sonata (Example 6.9) is an instrumental piece in AB design, but here the A theme is repeated before B begins; the resulting scheme would be AABB.

Example 6.8
Schubert: "Am Meer"

Example 6.9
Scarlatti: *Sonata No. 11 in C minor*

Three-Part Form

We have been talking about two-part pieces, that is, two themes symmetrically balanced. It should be pointed out that, like the A or AA' design, the AB design by itself is relatively rare both in music and in architecture (Figure 6.5). The most frequent type of design is three-part, ABA, which can be found in some form in many types of musical compositions, ranging from short, simple pieces to extremely long, complex ones. The odd thing about the three-part design is that we are not really dealing with three themes, but have instead two statements of the original, with a contrasting theme between: ABA.

We find the three-part design in most of the other arts as well. Architects place a door between two windows, a gable between two spires, or an arch between two columns. Painters place a brook between two trees. Musicians place a slow theme between two fast ones. This ABA structure exemplifies the principles of balance and cohesiveness, and also the continuing reverence of artists for unity and variety.

We can see at a glance the three-part design of a gable between two spires, as in Figure 6.6 (p. 110), but we can hear the three-part structure of music only one part at a time. Because of the time element, we refer to ABA as a *statement* (A), *departure* (B), and *return* (A). The

Figure 6.5   Perisphere and Trylon, New York, 1939 (Museum of the City of New York)

repetition of the A theme at the end heightens the contrast of the B theme. We hear the "clash" of these two themes twice, once when we depart and again when we return. Another reason for the prevalent use of the ABA design could be that the principal theme (A) predominates by its location—it is both first and last. Most folk songs and popular tunes consist of three-part structure with this slight modification: the first theme is often repeated before the second theme is introduced, thus giving an AA'BA. This does not

Figure 6.6   St. Paul's Cathedral, London (BOAC photo)

destroy the three-part character of the structure. The folk song, Example 6.10, is ABA, and each section is relatively short. The Chopin *Prelude* in Example 6.11, is AA'BA, and each section is relatively long.

Example 6.10
Seeger: "Turn, Turn, Turn"

Example 6.11
Chopin: *Prelude in D-flat,* Op. 28, No. 15

Three-part form can also be found in elaborate, extended designs. The minuet and trio from Mozart's *Symphony No. 40 in G minor* is a three-part design akin to the AA'BA structure of the folk song, although you are going to have to wait longer to hear the B theme in the Mozart. You may have to listen to it more than once to catch it. Notice that A and A' are played loudly by the full orchestra. You will recognize the entrance of the B theme because it is performed by fewer instruments and played more softly.

Sonata Form

The most elaborate three-part scheme is the *sonata form*. This design consists of three long sections, each based on the same thematic material:

1. The first section, called *exposition,* consists of the original theme and a contrasting one. This section is usually repeated.
2. The second section consists of a *development* of these same two themes. (Recall the discussion of developmental repetition in Chapter 5.) This is a contrasting section because, even though the composer is using the same themes, they are altered so much that they seem to be transformed. The total effect of this section is therefore quite different from the first.
3. The last section is an almost literal *recapitulation* of the first. This time the section is not repeated.

The development section is freer than the other two in its inner design: either one or both themes may be exploited, more modulations occur, and it is more developmental. The total sonata form design looks something like this:

(Introduction)   ‖ : A : ‖   B   A   (Coda)

	Exposition (Statement)	Development (Departure)	Recapitulation (Return)
	Theme 1	Theme 1 or	Theme 1
	Theme 2	Theme 2 or both	Theme 2

This basic pattern allows for many slight deviations. Frequently, there is introductory material that is not properly called "theme" because it is not treated like a theme. Similarly, and even more frequently, "ending" material (coda) is added to the design. Occasionally, there are more than two themes in the exposition, and new thematic material may be found in the development section.

You may recall the introduction of the *London Symphony* as something which draws your attention, which sets a kind of mood and introduces you to the main thematic material. The coda, on the other hand, gives you a feeling of finality. Here, by the way, is a good point for you to listen once more to the first movement of this work and observe the effects of the introduction and coda.

Because of the complexity of the sonata design, it would be helpful for us to hear the two principal themes alone. Theme 1 of Mozart's *Symphony No. 40 in G minor* is fast and active; Theme 2 is slower and quieter, more lyrical (Example 6.12). The B section consists of a development of Theme 1, which has been reduced to fragments and developed. The recapitulation is almost a literal restatement of the exposition.

Example 6.12*
Mozart: *Symphony No. 40 in G minor,* K. 550,
first movement, 1st and 2nd themes

Notice that the plan which constitutes the entire first movement of this symphony is structured around only two themes. This is evidence that the sonata design is a means of extending and expanding simple musical material into a large, complex composition. This design also represents the epitome of unity within a large, extended framework. You should listen to the entire first movement before going on.

Multiple Themes

In addition to the occasional occurrence of more than two themes in the sonata form, there are a few other designs that use three or more themes. The listener is likely to have difficulty perceiving the design of a piece based on three or more themes. Fortunately, most music contains some sort of return, either of a principal theme, or of other themes, to help our musical memory and therefore enhance our ability to follow the music. The song by Schubert, "Frühlingstraum," for instance, is based on three entirely different themes, ABC. As we listen for the appearance of each theme, we begin to suspect that the song is wandering, that a different theme is added to what has gone before, that there is no real conscious attempt to construct a logical pattern. But before long we realize that the entire ABC structure is repeated, giving us a chance to hear each theme once again. This reinforcement is satisfying. We welcome the chance to tie things together, to sense the unity and balance of this art song.

Example 6.13
Schubert: "Frühlingstraum"

Another design in which the original theme returns several times after contrasting material is called *rondo,* which implies that the original theme keeps coming "round" again and again. The scheme can appear in any of several patterns, as long as the original theme appears at least three times in its original state. Here is one of the most common patterns: *ABACABA.* An audience can become quite familiar with a rondo upon first hearing, because the principal theme reappears several times. This exact repetition is appealing to the listener primarily because the principal theme has become familiar, thus reinforcing the design. We become increasingly satisfied with the fact that we can hear the underlying structure of the composition. Listen, for example, to the Mozart piece (Example 6.14) which is based on ABACA.

Example 6.14

Mozart: *Sonata in C,* K. 545, Rondo

Non-Schematic Designs

There are literally thousands of rondos in the world of music, which is true of most of the other designs we have talked about. However, composers need not follow these popular designs. They can invent or develop their own, and frequently do. They can lay out a unique design for a given piece. Tchaikovsky has done so in his *1812 Overture,* an example of that kind of free design called *free form.* There are several themes, several sections; some themes return, some do not. This is a more or less unrestricted form, where the composer has allowed himself the freedom to design his composition anew, instead of imposing upon himself the rules and limitations of a pre-existing design.

Some of the themes in the *1812 Overture* are familiar tunes, including the French and Russian national anthems, but this particular arrangement of tunes is not found anywhere else in music; its design is unique. You will enjoy the return of these familiar themes and the design into which they are woven. You might allow yourself the luxury of listening also to the extravagant effects in this piece produced by real cannons and carillon bells.

A composer must choose whether to write in a pre-existing form or to make up his own form for the occasion. A poet faces a similar choice. Poetry also has certain prescribed forms with rigid "rules." The most important types in English probably are *blank verse* and *sonnet.* Blank verse is unrhymed iambic pentameter (lines of duple meter, with ten syllables and five accents each). The sonnet is also composed in iambic pentameter, but rhymes in fairly rigidly prescribed ways, and always has fourteen lines. It is probably the structure of the English language that makes duple meter so appropriate for poetry, but how do we explain the decision of such great poets as Shakespeare, Milton, Wordsworth, and Keats to write a poem with precisely fourteen lines?

Why do intelligent people choose a rule-oriented art form, job, religion, or government? Is it lack of imagination, insecurity, basic conservatism? Apparently, many people find a certain freedom in rules. We often point to the paradox that absolute liberty of self expression, such as anarchy, does not provide absolute freedom. We can choose a pre-existing form, and we need not be bothered with establishing workable principles; those already established have, after all, worked for others. There is a certain discipline and a certain challenge about working within established rules or designs. On the other hand, some people prefer the discipline and challenge of establishing their own rules for each occasion. They feel that establishing the form is a part of their self-expression—to them, establishing unique principles is part of freedom.

Becoming familiar with basic designs in music will help you to listen more efficiently to the musical material. You will be better prepared to listen because you will know what to expect. As you learn to listen for the entrance of new themes and the repetition of old ones, you will probably want to sketch out a thematic scheme of what you are hearing. This is good practice for perceiving form. As you listen, jot down patterns of AB, ABA, or whatever, remembering that the end of this study is not simply to "schematize" every piece of music, but to hear the music itself more significantly. In fact, it is difficult to imagine anything more useful in listening to music than perceiving form.

Summary

Formal design is determined by the manner in which the elements in a work of art or music relate to one another in achieving a unified impression. Principles of design in both art and music include predominance, coherence, balance, repetition, and contrast. One element may predominate in a painting by its size, color intensity, light or dark values, or location in the painting. In music, a theme predominates by its size, instrumentation, and location in the piece. Elements in painting, sculpture, or architecture may cohere if they are clustered or overlapped or if they are portrayed in compatible colors. Coherence in music is achieved by logical progression of ideas, by overlapping and dovetailing themes, and by tonality, a unified perception of key. Balance in art is achieved symmetrically by similarity and repetition of visual elements. It can also be achieved asymmetrically by contrast in size, light value, location, and color. In music, instead of light, color, and shapes, balance is achieved with themes, instrumentation, and key changes.

A composer may choose for his composition a standard design which other composers have used, or he may construct a unique design. Basic design types in music include single themes (monothematic) and multiple themes (polythematic). The latter may use two themes (AB—two-part, or ABA—three-part), or more than two themes (ABC, ABCD, ABCBA, or any combination).

Understanding design facilitates the task of listening to music. The listener will be better able to place meat on the bones, that is, to relate content to structure. And it is only in this way that he can retain what he has heard.

Suggested Works for Additional Listening

Single Theme Form

Bach: *The Art of Fugue*

Mozart: *Piano Sonata in A,* K. 331

Multiple Theme Form

Mozart: *String Quintet in G Minor,* K. 516, last movement (Rondo)

Beethoven: *Symphony No. 3 in E-flat,* Op. 55, second movement (ABA)

Debussy: *Prelude to the Afternoon of a Faun* (ABA)

Free Form

Stravinsky: *Petrouchka*

R. Strauss: *Death and Transfiguration*

Tchaikovsky: *1812 Overture*

Chapter 7

Other Combinations:
Texture and Tonality

We have only begun to explore the many ways in which sounds are combined to make music. We have seen that sounds combine to form melodies and chords. In this chapter we shall see what happens when melodies are combined with melodies, chords with chords, and melodies with chords. We shall be talking about *texture* and *tonality*, two basic musical concepts resulting from these combinations.

Texture

Music flows along, one sound tumbling after another, sometimes exciting, sometimes relaxing, sometimes triggering momentary flights of fancy. What we are hearing are many sounds in succession, a thread of sound flowing through time. But we should remember that sounds are also occurring simultaneously. Both the simultaneous and successive combinations of tones are of interest to us as listeners. Music consists of these two distinct dimensions, successive and simultaneous—sometimes called horizontal and vertical, respectively, because of the way the tones appear in the musical score. The horizontal dimension we have loosely defined as melody and the vertical dimension as chord (see Figure 7.1).

Figure 7.1 Chopin, *Waltz in C-sharp minor*, Op. 64, No. 2

With the exception of unaccompanied melody, all music has both horizontal and vertical dimensions, and the particular manner in which these dimensions relate to each other is called *texture*. Texture in music has to do with the ways in which melodies and chords can be combined. It is similar to the idea of texture in textiles, which results from a weave of vertical and horizontal threads. The texture of each fabric depends on the unique manner in which the vertical and horizontal relate.

We use sensory images, especially tactile ones, to describe texture in an art work—rough, slippery, lacy, massive, dense. And we can actually feel the texture of some art works—a tactile texture. A painting or a piece of sculpture may have a surface which is smooth or rough to the touch. But more important in these arts is the visual aspect of texture, the *effect* we perceive with our eyes. The painting may look rough, for example, even if the surface of the canvas is smooth. Objects may seem to stand out from the background, giving the flat smooth painting a three-dimensional effect. A piece of sculpture may appear massive and heavy, but may be made of very light-weight materials. The artist is concerned, however, only with our visual perception of texture.

Sometimes texture in painting is determined by the manner in which the paint is applied to the canvas. A painting rendered with a palette knife may have a texture much rougher than a painting rendered with a brush. The canvas not only looks rougher, but feels rougher to the touch. Texture in painting depends on the materials and method of application, the techniques, and the use of visual elements such as line, light, color. The impressionistic painting *Water-Lilies: Giverny*, by Monet (Plate 13, following p. 134) has a soft, lacy texture because of the absence of heavy line, the use of small, interwoven shapes, and the delicate play of light against a dark background. The Pollock painting *One* (Plate 14) has a rough, heavy texture because the distinct lines cross over one another and because the paint was applied heavily to the canvas by dripping.

We respond to the texture of a painting or sculpture by an almost irresistible urge to touch it or feel it—witness the "Do Not Touch" signs all over art galleries. Although we may not touch the painting, we still imagine how it would feel if we did. To describe the texture, we use adjectives that relate to the tactile sense. In music we go one step further: we imagine what sound would "feel" like. We use many of the same tactile adjectives to describe what we hear: thick, thin, rough, smooth, heavy, light. Thus actual touch is not involved in either music or the visual arts, although both make reference to tactile images to describe texture.

The following musical combinations contribute most strongly to musical texture:

1. Orchestration
2. Angularity–Lyricism
3. Rhythmic Complexity
4. Homophony–Polyphony

Keep in mind that texture results when tones are combined. The foregoing list represents various ways of combining tones. Textures that result from these combinations are difficult to categorize, and perhaps classification is unnecessary. The important task for the listener is to describe the texture as he perceives it. Some examples illustrating different ways to achieve various kinds of musical texture should prove helpful.

Orchestration

Recall the entirely new effect created in the "Great Gate at Kiev" when Ravel scored Moussorgsky's piano piece for full orchestra. The orchestra achieves a much thicker, more massive, more monumental sound than a pianist's two hands can produce.

Tone color makes a difference in effect, too. Different textures can be achieved in fabric with different kinds of yarn or thread even if the same pattern of weave is used. A painting in pastel colors seems to be lighter, more transparent, more delicate than a similar painting using deeper, brighter colors. Remember the contrasting timbres of the flute and the tuba, and imagine the same passage played by four flutes and then by four tubas. The musical ideas here are the same, but the texture becomes heavy, thick, even fuzzy. The choice of instruments, that is, orchestration, clearly contributes to texture.

But there is more to texture than the mere selection of the most appropriate instruments. The composer can choose to present many tones at once, or he can choose to economize. Here we are considering the total amount of sound. The texture of a piece composed for seven instruments will be somewhat different from one composed for one hundred instruments. Thus, the texture of Stravinsky's *L'histoire du Soldat* is thin compared to, say, the opening of Brahms' *First Symphony* which is thick.

Example 7.1
Stravinsky: *L'histoire du Soldat*

Example 7.2
Brahms: *Symphony No. 1 in C minor,* Op. 68, opening

Angularity-Lyricism

A string quartet will produce a comparatively thin texture because there are only four instruments involved. In the Haydn *String Quartet,* Op. 33, No. 1, the texture is indeed thin, but when compared to Stravinsky's piece, other textural qualities are apparent. We might say that the Haydn piece is smooth, and that the Stravinsky is rough.

Example 7.3

Haydn: *String Quartet in B minor,* Op. 33, No. 1,
third movement

Part of the reason for the difference in texture is that Haydn's piece is more lyric and Stravinsky's more angular. These qualities also play a role in musical texture and are closely related to a broader concept which we might call "rhythmic complexity."

Rhythmic Complexity

Rhythms become complex when there is a great deal of activity: when there are a great many notes; when the tempo is rapid; when the durational values of tones are irregular, that is, when tones do not coincide with the beat; and when the voices move at different times. Generally speaking, the more complex the rhythm, the more intricate the texture becomes—sometimes thick, sometimes dense, sometimes rough. *L'histoire* is denser and rougher than the Haydn quartet for all of the reasons having to do with rhythmic complexity: activity, tempo, irregular rhythm, and independently-moving voices.

Homophony-Polyphony

Texture in music is usually defined exclusively in terms of *homophony* and *polyphony*. But musical texture is much more than that; it involves every aspect of the combination and relationship of tones. Homophony and polyphony, along with the other factors we have discussed, contribute importantly to the nature of texture. If homophony and polyphony are the most important considerations, it is because they most clearly exploit the interweaving of horizontal and vertical dimensions in music.

All music possesses a horizontal dimension, because all music is made of successive sounds. And music that has more than one voice or part (which includes almost all Western music) has a vertical dimension as well, because those parts are sounding simultaneously. In some music, horizontal considerations predominate, whereas in other music, vertical considerations predominate. These differing emphases provide the basis for determining whether a given piece is homophonic or polyphonic.

Melody is the most horizontally conceived of musical ideas. So the music with the most horizontal emphasis is that which consists entirely of melody in all voices. Such music, consisting of two or more melodic voices, is called *polyphony*. In music with polyphonic texture, the voices are independent and equally balanced; no one voice predominates.

A chord is the most vertically conceived of musical ideas, so music with the most vertical emphasis is that which is made up mostly of chords. Such music, in which only one voice, or in which no voice is melodic, is called *homophony*. In music with homophonic texture, either one melodic voice predominates, or the harmonic progression itself is of primary interest.

A simple tune with accompaniment is homophonic because the simultaneous sounds exist only to support the melody. The homophonic texture exists mainly to supply the melody with a harmonic foundation. The chorale tune "Wachet Auf" with simple accompaniment is an example of homophonic texture, vertically conceived; it consists of a simple tune with chordal accompaniment.

Example 7.4*
Bach: "Wachet Auf," Chorale

Now let us take a look at polyphonic texture which is primarily horizontally conceived and is sometimes called *counterpoint*. Counterpoint is a combination of *two* or more melodic lines. Although the composer is concerned with how the melodies fit together, he is mainly interested in the integrity of each voice part as a melody and the balance between them, which means he is more concerned with the horizontal than the vertical dimension. In Example 7.5 we hear the voice parts entering at different times, each maintaining a melodic integrity.[9]

Example 7.5*
Bach: "Wachet Auf," *Cantata No. 140,*
opening choral section

The chorale tune is heard clearly in each setting (Examples 7.4 and 7.5), but in the first setting, the three lower voices support the tune in the upper voice, whereas in the second setting, all voices sing independently. In the homophonic setting the sopranos enjoy their usual monopoly of melody; in the polyphonic setting all the voices sing parts with melodic integrity. Notice that the texture of the homophonic setting is solid and simple, whereas the polyphonic texture is complex and intricately woven.

Thus, some musical textures consist of a melody with chords, some of chords alone, and some of two or more melodies. No type appears in its pure form for very long. Most musical texture is some combination of types; in fact, composers frequently balance polyphony and homophony as a means of contrast. In the madrigal in Example 7.6 a polyphonic section follows a homophonic section.

Example 7.6
Morley: (Madrigal) "My bonny lass she smileth"

[9] See Example 5.22 in Appendix D for score.

In some music it is difficult to determine whether the musical texture has greater vertical or horizontal emphasis. The chorale tune "Wachet Auf" was harmonized by Bach in the final chorus of his *Cantata No. 140* in what seems to be a homophonic setting with the tune in the upper voice. Yet each voice part has a certain melodic integrity—there is an attempt to make each part rhythmically and melodically important. Of course, the chorale tune is still in the soprano voice and still predominates, so the piece is basically homophonic. But the polyphonic tendencies are more pronounced than in Example 7.4.

Example 7.7

Bach: "Wachet Auf," *Cantata No. 140,* final chorale

All qualities of texture are matters of degree, as are designations such as light and dark, hot and cold, large and small. We may therefore differ in our perceptions of texture. If you perceive musical texture to be smooth in a given spot and your friend perceives it to be rough, it does not necessarily mean that one of you is wrong. It simply means that your background, experience, and associations cause you to respond to textures in a unique way.

Polyphony and homophony are extremely important concepts in the study of music history because some style periods have tended more toward polyphony, some toward homophony. But apart from style, the concepts themselves also provide valuable tools for the apprehension of any music. Homophony and polyphony come in all manner of shape and form; here are some of the most interesting:

Homophony. Homophonic music consists of two or more voices moving together in time with an interdependence between the voices. One voice usually presents a predominant melody to which the other voices are subservient, as we found in Example 7.7. The composer arrives at a musical idea through the *harmonic* process. He may place a melody over a series of chords; he may present a series of chords and derive from them an appropriate melody; or he may present a series of chords which seem to support no melody at all, simply a harmonic progression. In all cases, the harmonic process is itself of interest, whether it supports a melody or not.

Examples 7.8 and 7.9 are based on the same tune. Both treatments are homophonic. Example 7.8 moves in chords, like a hymn, and is *isometric* because all the voices are rhythmically concurrent. This is homophony in the strictest sense, with both rhythm and harmony contributing to the vertical conception. Example 7.9 is also homophonic because there is one predominant melodic line. The other voices, although they are rhythmically independent, merely provide ornamental manipulations of chords and remain subservient to the melody.

Example 7.8*
Mozart: *Sonata in G,* K. 283, second movement
(first four measures melody with block chords)

Example 7.9*
Mozart: Same as above—as written

In these two examples, the composer probably began with a melody and used various harmonic settings to accompany it. In Example 7.10, also homophonic, the interest is primarily in the harmonic process. The listener is not aware of any melody.

Example 7.10
Debussy: *Nuages*

In the fourth movement of Brahms' *Symphony No. 4 in E minor* (Example 5.20), it is apparent that the composer began with a series of chords and subsequently derived from them appropriate melodies. But in all the foregoing homophonic excerpts, the strong relationship between melody and chords emphasizes the vertical dimension of texture.

Polyphony. Polyphonic music is also made up of two or more voices moving together in time, a combination of melodies. But instead of interdependence or subservience between voices, we find *equality.* Each voice is melodic; each has individuality. The voices seem to move independently of one another, even though the tones of the melodies frequently sound simultaneously and seem to be "harmonious." Thus, the interplay among voices, both the independent movement and the coincidence of tones, is of primary interest. One voice may seem to be superior for a time, and then another takes over. A balance of importance is thus maintained among the voices. The challenge for the composer is to make two or more independent voices fit together and still maintain the individuality of each. It is our challenge as listeners to apprehend this process. Notice the equality and individuality of the voice parts in the Palestrina Mass in Example 7.11.

Example 7.11*
Palestrina: "Agnus Dei," *Pope Marcellus Mass*

Though counterpoint has been used freely in many style periods, the technique seems to have been most prevalent before 1750. But the art of counterpoint has become so sophisticated that various contrapuntal techniques have developed and have been widely used in all style periods in Western music.

The most elemental concept of melodic combination is *descant,* a countermelody usually written higher in pitch and designed to complement the main melody. The simple song in Example 7.12 illustrates the relative independence of the two melodies in descant. Notice that when more than one melody appears at one time, the music becomes more complex and the texture more intricate.

Example 7.12*
Song: "Now the Day Is Over"

Descant frequently appears in concert music as well. For example, Wagner's *Siegfried Idyll* was developed throughout by combining melodies in a descant-like fashion.

Most of the music of the Renaissance period, 1450–1600, and much music since then, was composed on the principle of *imitative counterpoint*. Imitation means that the melody in one voice is repeated and overlapped by another voice, usually at a different level of pitch, such as in the Bach setting of "Wachet Auf" (Example 7.5). Imitative counterpoint, then, is a technique of composition in which a melody is set against itself at slightly different time intervals. Composers seem to enjoy manipulating melody contrapuntally because the technique imposes challenging restrictions; a melody must be constructed so that it will fit "with itself." At the same time, the technique provides for great versatility. This technique has been an important tool for composers since the fifteenth century. Styles for composing melodies have changed through the centuries, but the technique of imitation has thrived in all of them, and has become especially important in twentieth-century music. Examples 7.13–7.17 illustrate the use of imitative counterpoint in each of the important style periods from 1450 on.

Example 7.13
Josquin des Prez (Renaissance): *Ave Maria*

Example 7.14
Bach (Baroque): "Gloria," *Mass in B minor,* opening

Example 7.15
Beethoven (Classic): *Symphony No. 5 in C minor,*
Op. 67, third movement

Example 7.16
Wagner (Romantic): *Die Meistersinger,* Prelude

Example 7.17
Bartók (Modern): *Music for Strings, Percussion, and
Celesta,* first movement

One specific type of imitative counterpoint is *canon,* a strict device in which an entire melody sung by one voice is imitated by another. The rounds sung by children in grade school, such as "Row, Row, Row Your Boat," are examples of canon. The composition, *Sumer is icumen in,* is a famous example of canon which dates from the Medieval period (*c.* thirteenth century).

Example 7.18
Sumer is icumen in

Again, many composers seem to enjoy the intellectual exercise of working within the restrictions which the canon imposes. Bach, for example, used the canon frequently in his keyboard works. A well-known instance is the collection of ten canons found in his *Goldberg Variations.*

Example 7.19*
Bach: *Goldberg Variations,* Variation 18

The most elaborate technique of imitative counterpoint is *fugue,* a form that begins with a theme (subject) in one voice which is imitated by another voice in close succession (answer). Whereas the canon is restricted to the exact imitation of the entire melody, the fugue is freer in form. The subject recurs many times, episodes appear which may or may not be related to the subject, and the fabric of the entire piece reflects a complex, intricately woven texture. In the *Little Fugue in G minor,* Bach begins his long subject with three relatively long tones, making each return of the theme easy to hear.

Example 7.20*
Bach: *Little Fugue in G minor*

In some fugal settings the answer appears in close succession to the subject, entering soon after the subject begins. This device, called *stretto,* results in even more complex texture and an intensified feeling of movement. At one point in the *Fugue No. 1* from Bach's *The Well-Tempered Clavier* (Example 7.21), the answer appears in stretto, trailing the subject by only one beat.

Example 7.21*
Bach: Fugue No. 1, from Book I of
The Well-Tempered Clavier

Tonality

We have seen that combinations of tones produce various kinds of texture. Another dimension in the combinations of tones is represented by *tonality.*

We have spoken of tonality in painting as the predominance of one color over the whole art work. We use the same term in music to apply to the predominance of one tone over a whole composition. The selection of the tone, like the selection of the color, is a purely arbitrary matter; it depends on what the composer or painter wants to say and how he wants to say it. Like the painter, the composer uses tonality to organize his materials—to give the listener a reference point, a focus, an aid to making sense of what he hears. Some music contains a strong central tone toward which all other tones gravitate. Other music avoids such clearly distinguishable tonal centers. And, in some instances, the tonal center shifts constantly so that we feel not one tone center, but many.

Sometimes the degree of tonality which a composer uses is determined by the period in which he lives, much as the language he speaks is largely determined by where he lives. A twentieth-century composer has a greater range of choices in the degree of tonality he can use than earlier composers because of the additional degrees that have evolved. Thus a composer is either born into or chooses a system of organizing his tonal materials. He usually writes within one system, or tonal language, for most of his musical life, although there are many notable exceptions of composers who use several different languages. Even the exceptions are likely to use just one language at a time, however, going through various languages at different stages in their lifetimes. Examples 7.22–7.24 are, surprisingly, all written by the same composer, Stravinsky, at three different stages of his life. The first is strongly tonal, the second much more vague, and the last atonal.

Example 7.22
Stravinsky: *Pulcinella,* opening

Example 7.23
Stravinsky: *Symphony in Three Movements,*
first movement

Example 7.24
Stravinsky: *Agon,* opening

At one time in the development of music, composers seemed to be determined to express the strongest feeling of tonality possible. Composers in the Classical period, particularly Haydn and Mozart, presented their musical ideas with economy, faithful to the Classical ideal of simplicity. In a simple statement, it is easy for us to hear the strong tonality inherent in the music. The Haydn piece in Example 7.25 repeats a central tone many times. Haydn constructed the music to accent and lead to that central tone, building phrases around it, and frequently ending with it. We cannot escape that tone because we are constantly reminded of it and referred back to it. As we listen, we are able to hear which tone is the tonic, and can easily remember it when the music is finished. Try humming the tonic when Example 7.25 has ended.

Example 7.25
Haydn: *Symphony No. 101 in D (Clock),*
fourth movement, opening

The tonality in the Strauss piece, on the other hand (Example 7.26), does not seem as strong. Strauss, like Haydn, repeats the tonic, refers to it, even ends with it. What causes the difference in the strength of the tonal center? The feeling of tonality is more vague in the Strauss piece because of his freer use of all the tones available. He emphasizes not one tonal center, but many. Composers in the late nineteenth century were, as a rule, interested in extending the possibilities within the range of tonality by exploring a variety of different and distant keys.

Example 7.26
R. Strauss: *Don Juan,* opening

Establishing a Tonal Center

How does a composer go about organizing his composition around a central tone? Basically he does it by utilizing all the techniques we have discussed for emphasizing tones. If he wants a particularly strong tonal center, he emphasizes one tone extensively. If he wants a shifting or a weak tonal center, he avoids repeated emphasis of one tone, or he emphasizes several tones. Thus anything that makes one tone stand out from its context renders that tone important, and causes us to hear it as a center. The most basic techniques for establishing a tonal center are: (1) repeating the tone, (2) accenting the tone, (3) melodic movement toward and away from the tone, (4) formal design, (5) harmonic organization around the tone.

We saw in Chapter 4 how repeating a tone a number of times may emphasize it as a tonal center. If you emphasize one tone often enough and long enough, it begins to sound like home. The same is true of accenting the tone by placing it on the first beat, by holding it longer than the others, or by beginning and ending a phrase or section with it. Rising or descending movement toward a tone or away from it also tends to emphasize that tone. Usually, all of these techniques occur together: a tone is repeated a number of times on the accented beat, it is held longer than the others, and it is emphasized by rising and descending melody. Listen to the clarity and strength of the central tone in ·the Mahler excerpt in Example 7.27.

Example 7.27
Mahler: *Symphony No. 1 in D,* second movement

Formal design can also emphasize and help establish tonality. In an ABA design, for example, not only does the original melody return after the contrasting melody, but it returns in the same key, or tonal center. It is common for the B section to move to a new tonal center or centers, which makes the sense of A's return even stronger, and emphasizes the original tonal center more than if we had not departed from it. In the Brahms piece (Example 7.28), the B section is in a different key. In addition, you may notice several other contrasting factors in the B section, including tempo, meter, and mood.

Example 7.28
Brahms: *Romanze No. 5,* from
Sechs Klavier-Stücke, Op. 118

Finally, and most important, the tonal center can be emphasized by placing it in a context of chord relationships usually called *functional harmony.* The system of functional harmony is the basis for most of the music we know—most seventeenth-, eighteenth-, and nineteenth-century music, and most of the popular music of the twentieth century. The system is highly organized and complex, a fascinating study in itself, but far too broad in scope to undertake here. However, the listener should be aware that functional harmony exists to emphasize tonality—and it does so by arranging chords so that one chord, the one built on the tonic, is heard as the tonal center. Some chords in context have a built-in tension which *requires* another chord to follow and resolve that tension. These "resolutions" constantly reinforce the feeling of tonality. We hear them as arrivals, as resting places or releases. So the important thing to listen for is the movement of chords to and from the tonic chord. Chord progression is akin to melodic progression in that both can lead us from and back to the tonal center, and both strongly influence the degree of tonality present in any given piece of music.

Remember that an easy way to hear chord progression is to concentrate on the bass line. Listen again to the Mahler *Ländler* from his *First Symphony* (Example 7.27), and note how the bass line emphasizes the central tone of that piece. The tonal center is repeated, held longer than other tones, and heavily accented even more in the bass line than in the melody.

In the system of functional harmony, there are many standard progressions, and these change from one era to another. But we will deal only with the most important of these progressions—those that end phrases or sections. These "ending" progressions, or *cadences,* are important in the consideration of tonality because they involve a strong pull toward the tonic and because endings are natural positions of emphasis. Here the need for resolution is strongest. Cadence leaves us with a feeling of finality when the tonic is reached. Examples 7.29 and 7.30 are two of the simplest cadence formulas. The second of these is sometimes called an "amen" cadence, the familiar hymn ending.

Example 7.29*
Cadence: (Dominant-Tonic)

Example 7.30*
Cadence: (Subdominant-Tonic)

A cadence can be elaborated limitlessly, but it is common to hear progressions like those in Examples 7.31 and 7.32 at the end of a piece:

Example 7.31*
Cadence elaborated: (Tonic-Subdominant-
Dominant-Tonic)

Example 7.32*
Cadence elaborated: (Dominant-[Pedal]-Tonic)

These simple, basic progressions are pervasive throughout the history of tonal music. Usually they are extended, repeated, elaborated upon, as in Examples 7.33 and 7.34, and these elaborations tend to enhance the anticipation of the tonic. If we wait for it, all the while knowing it is coming, but not knowing exactly when, its final arrival is thus strengthened.

Example 7.33
Bach: Prelude No. 12, from Book I of *The Well-Tempered Clavier*

Example 7.34
Beethoven: *Piano Sonata*, Op. 14, No. 2,
second movement

Cadences are found not only at the end, but also throughout a composition. Any resolution at the end of a phrase is a cadence, but a cadence does not always involve resolution to the tonic. Those cadences that do resolve to the tonic are the strongest. Nor is the resolution always to the same tonic; various tonal centers may be emphasized. Thus a piece of music containing frequent cadences that resolve into one tonic is more tonal than a piece that has infrequent tonic cadences, or in which several tonal centers are emphasized.

Recall the Haydn and Strauss excerpts used at the beginning of this discussion (Examples 7.25 and 7.26). Haydn's music sounds more tonal to us than Strauss' because his cadences occur more frequently and they more often follow simple cadential formulas. In the Haydn excerpt, we hear two distinct cadences in only eight measures. In the Strauss excerpt, we hear no distinct cadences at all.

We can also hear a difference in the strength of the ending cadence in each of these pieces. At the end of the Haydn symphony we feel sure of the tonic (Example 7.35); we can hum or remember it easily. Through a series of chord progressions, Haydn brings us directly to the tonic so we are able to anticipate its arrival. At the end of the Strauss piece, on the other hand, we are uncertain about the tonic until the very end (Example 7.36). Strauss takes us through a circuitous series of chord progressions only remotely related to the tonic. The feeling of tonality is so tentative at the end that Strauss sounds the final tone twice, just to be sure the tonic is established.

Example 7.35
Haydn: *Symphony No. 101 in D (Clock),*
fourth movement, coda

Example 7.36
Strauss: *Don Juan,* coda

Although we find varying degrees of tonality in music, it is important to stress that almost all music has a tonal center or centers. Tonality seems to be a natural thing, for both composers and listeners. Perhaps it arises out of man's need to organize. Or perhaps it occurs naturally because tonality is difficult for a composer to avoid and unless he makes a conscious effort to avoid a tone center, one or more may appear in his music. More likely, however, tonality is exploited by the composer and perceived by the listener because of man's need to reduce the complex to essences for easy comprehension. Out of all the tonal possibilities, a composer chooses a limited system of composition in order to communicate with his listeners, much as the writer chooses one language for his communication.

Atonality

Let us take a look at the other extreme: non-tonality. The technical term is *atonality,* which means that no feeling of tonality exists. The interesting thing about a lack of tonality is that you can think of it in two different ways, and either way is correct. You can think of atonality, by which we mean that no tone is emphasized over the others, or you can think of *pantonality,* by which we mean that all tones are emphasized equally. The two concepts mean literally the same thing—no tonal center is heard. But Schoenberg, its inventor, preferred the latter definition because he considered it more positive.

Schoenberg developed a system of composing music called *twelve-tone,* or *dodecaphonic,* or *serial,* which would emphasize the equality of each tone. In serial music, the composer makes a systematic attempt to treat all twelve tones equally.[10] He does this by arranging the twelve tones in a certain order, called a *tone row.* He then composes a piece of music based on that row, using the following general principles: the row is repeated throughout the piece; it is always complete and always in order; extra tones are never added. Some composers follow these rules to the letter while others adapt them freely. You might think that the constant repetition of this row would be monotonous, but in fact it is nearly impossible to recognize the row as it is repeated. The entire row is rarely performed by one voice, so it is not usually heard as a melody. Also, the rhythms are constantly changing, and any number or all of the tones may be sounded at once. The premise is that even though the row is not

[10] In Western music, only twelve different tones are available. See keyboard, p. 9.

clearly distinguishable, it acts to unify the music in much the same way as a conventional key does.

Křenek uses this system in his piano piece, *Dancing Toys* (Example 7.37). As you listen, try to find the tonic and hum it, as you did with the Haydn piece. You should find it impossible, because there is no tonic. The tone row used for this piece is found in Appendix D, p. 226.

Example 7.37*
Křenek: *Dancing Toys*

Composers like Křenek or Schoenberg who wish to avoid a feeling of tonality, must make a conscious, systematic effort to do so because a sense of tonal center is so easily established. Tones must be repeated in any system—after all, only twelve are available—and music is full of natural points of emphasis, accents, or starts and stops, each of which is heard as "important" in its context. The ending note is likely to be thought of as a tonic because the composer has chosen to leave us with that final sound.

Scales

We have seen that atonal composition is an organization of tones to *avoid* tonality. But the great bulk of music we know is composed within a system that organizes tones to *emphasize* tonality.

The tonal languages thus far evolved are largely based on a patterned arrangement of tones called a *scale*. Some scales used in the past have been discarded. Some have been standard in Western music for at least three centuries. And some are made for the occasion —they are used as the basis for only one composition.

We should notice two important features of a scale: how many tones it utilizes, and the order in which they are placed.

Most of our music is based on the familiar *diatonic* scale that we all remember as *do, re, mi, fa, sol, la, ti, do.* This scale uses eight tones (the second *do* being a repetition of the initial *do*). The pattern is such that if you begin on the piano tone *C*, every white key is sounded in succession until you reach the next *C*. You may begin this diatonic scale on any piano key you wish, making twelve different scales possible. They all sound the same; only the pitch level has changed. But if you begin anywhere other than *C*, you will have to use some black keys in place of some white in order to keep the pattern intact.

Diatonic scales are of two types: *major* and *minor*. The minor scale is simply an alteration in the pattern of the major scale. If you begin on the piano tone *A* and play all white keys to the next *A*, you have played an A-minor scale.

Largely because of its harmonic implications, music based on the diatonic scale system is the most tonal of all music. This probably explains why the major and minor scales, established as early as the mid-fifteenth century, have served as the basis for musical composition to the present. Other systems of scales produce music that is less tonal.

In the Middle Ages, a series of scales called church *modes* served as the basis of Medieval music. Like the diatonic scales, they consisted of eight tones. You can construct a mode by beginning on any one of the piano's white keys and playing eight white keys in succession, the eighth being the same note as the first. Thus, there are seven basic model patterns possible. The plainsong in Example 7.38 is based on the *dorian* mode, the mode which begins and ends on *D*, and which is sometimes called Mode I. The mode is heard first.

Example 7.38

Dorian mode. Gregorian chant: *Salve Regina*

Notice that two of these modes, the one beginning on *C*, and the one beginning on *A*, coincide with the diatonic scales and thus sound the most familiar to us. It can be seen that the major and minor diatonic system grew out of the church modes. The modes other than major and minor survived past the Middle Ages only in terms of occasional use in melodic passages and certain modal cadences, especially in the twentieth century. The cadences in the following examples are modal; the sound is probably quite familiar, as it is heard frequently in folk and popular music.

Example 7.39

Folk song: "Follow the Drinking Gourd"

Example 7.40

Orff: "Veris leta facies," *Carmina Burana*

In the early days of tonality, composers usually made use of a limited number of key centers in one piece, and then used only the scales that had most tones in common with the tonic scale. For example, the G-major scale is more closely related to the C-major scale than is the D-flat-major scale, because G and C have more tones in common. In the G-major scale, all tones are the same as in the C-major except for one, *F#*. The D-flat-major scale, however, has only two tones in common with the C-major, *F* and *C* (Figure 7.2, p. 132).

This practice of using only closely-related keys began to change in the late nineteenth century. Late in the century, composers began to explore the full range of possibilities within the confines of tonality by adding "foreign," or non-scale, tones; by shifting frequently and abruptly to new keys; and by using more and more remote keys (that is, keys using fewer common scale tones). The Strauss piece in Example 7.26 is a typical example of this trend. In the last 100 years, several new systems have been employed by composers in the attempt to exploit all the possibilities within the range of tonality.

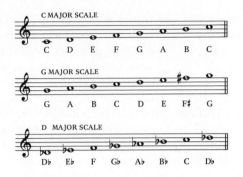

Figure 7.2 Scales

The *chromatic* scale, a scale made of all twelve tones in order, is one such system.

Example 7.41*
Chromatic Scale

> This scale has never been extensively used as the basis for composition, but it is frequently used melodically, and it has implications within the diatonic system of harmony as well. If a piece uses nine different key centers, it sounds more "chromatic" than one that uses only four because more of the twelve tones are in use more often.
>
> Another scale which exploits a different sound within a tonal framework is called the *whole-tone* scale, of which Debussy and others made extensive use. This scale is made up of only six tones in the arrangement heard in Example 7.42. Debussy's music is identifiable partly because much of it is based on this system.

Example 7.42*
Whole-tone scale
Debussy: *Estampes II,* "La Soirée dans Grenade"

Polytonality

> Other composers experimented with the idea of using more than one diatonic scale at once, a system which has been called *polytonality*. If each scale were played separately, the tonality of each would be clear. But the use of two different scales at once tends to mask the tonality of both, resulting in only a vague sense of tonal center. The Stravinsky excerpt in Example 7.43 is almost percussive because two different keys are used at once, and neither is distinctly heard. In Example 7.44, Ives scores the violins in one key as accompaniment to melodic fragments by the oboe and the French horn in a different key.

Example 7.43*
Stravinsky: *The Rite of Spring*

Example 7.44
Ives: "The Housatonic at Stockbridge,"
A New England Symphony (Third Symphony)

Finally, complete atonality was achieved by Schoenberg's twelve-tone system. The tone row might itself be considered a scale: it is a patterned arrangement of tones. One crucial difference between the row and other scales is that a new row is designed for each composition. The row may be carefully designed as to contour, with wide leaps, few leaps, or other distinctive features, or it may be a completely random placement of tones. The row also differs from traditional scales in that Schoenberg established rigid rules for its use and in that it has no harmonic implications.

Although Schoenberg's activity may signify the end of traditional tonality for all those who would adopt his method of composition, it really set the stage for all tonal activity to come. Tonal activity still exists, but within a more liberal framework, because it has been released from the confines of key. Composers now frequently base their tonal composition on considerations other than key—repetition, accent, melodic movement, and formal design—thus expanding infinitely the range of tonal possibilities.

Summary

Texture and tonality result when certain combinations of tones occur. Texture in music is determined by the relationship between horizontal and vertical dimensions, called melody and chords. Texture depends on orchestration, angularity and lyricism, rhythmic complexity, and homophony and polyphony. Music is homophonic when vertical considerations predominate and polyphonic when horizontal considerations predominate.

Tonality, the predominance of one tone over all the others in a given context, is also a result of combining tones. The degree of tonality establishes a kind of tonal language which helps to identify a composer's style. Tonal centers are established by repetition or accentuation of a tone, melodic movement toward and away from the tone, formal design, and harmonic organization around the tone. Within the tonal spectrum we find the extremes of strong tonality in functional harmony, and absence of tonality in serial composition. Various degrees of tonality can be attained with different kinds of scales: diatonic, modal, chromatic, whole-tone. A system which obscures tonality and uses many keys at once is called polytonality.

Suggested Works for Additional Listening

Homophonic Texture

Mendelssohn: *Violin Concerto in E Minor,* Op. 64

Moussorgsky: *Pictures at an Exhibition,* opening

Polyphonic Texture

Hindemith: *String Quartet No. 3,* Op. 22, first movement

Monteverdi: "Alas! if you love so much" (Madrigal)

Strong Tonality

Beethoven: *Symphony No. 1 in C,* Op. 21

Haydn: *String Quartets,* Op. 33

Vague Tonality

Schoenberg: *Verklärte Nacht*

Stravinsky: *The Firebird*

Atonality

Schoenberg: *Pierrot Lunaire*

Webern: *Six Pieces for Orchestra*

Plate 13. Monet, Claude, *Waterlilies: Giverny,* Musée du Louvre, Paris. The sense of texture in a work of art, although expressed in terms of tactile images, is a visual or aural effect. Here, the absence of heavy line, use of small, interwoven shapes, and the delicate play of light against a dark background, create a soft and lacy texture (see pp. 117, 148).

Plate 14. Pollock, Jackson, *One (Number 31, 1950),* oil and enamel on canvas, 8' 10" × 17' 5⅝". Collection, The Museum of Modern Art, New York, gift of Sidney Janis. Frequently-crossing heavy lines and thick encrustations of paint create here a rough, heavy texture (see p. 117).

Plate 15. After Rubens, Peter Paul, *The Horrors of War,* The National Gallery, London. A sense of movement can be created both in a kinetic art, such as music, and in static forms of art such as painting, photography, or sculpture. Here it is achieved by the use of contrasting light values and colors, curved, intertwining lines, and figures in poses of arrested action (see pp. 135, 186).

Plate 16. *A multiple-image photograph of Marcel Duchamp descending a staircase.* Eliot Elisofon, *Life,* © 1952, Time Inc. (see p. 135).

Plate 17. Duchamp, Marcel, *Nude Descending a Staircase, No. 2,* Philadelphia Museum of Art, Louise and Walter Arensberg Collection, '50–134–59. Many attempts have been made to create the sensation of movement in art. Real movement is portrayed in this painting by overlapping transparent figures (see pp. 135, 138).

Plate 18. Pollock, Jackson, *Number 12*, 1949, oil on paper mounted on composition board, 31 × 22½". Collection, The Museum of Modern Art, New York, gift of Edgar Kaufmann, Jr. The quality of movement in this painting reflects the technique with which the paint was applied, much as the sense of movement in a musical composition is shaped by the composer's technique in selecting his musical materials (see p. 149).

Chapter 8

Movement

Music is a kinetic art. Movement is its very essence. Without movement, the art form could not exist. Paradoxically, real movement is not involved. The movement in music and in most of the other arts is really only a sensation, that is, a *feeling* of movement. This sensation of movement in art forms like music and poetry concerns the manner in which the art work moves through time, and not just the time required for its rendition. A sensation of movement can be created in many ways, and can even exist in static forms such as painting, photography, or sculpture.

In the painting, *The Horrors of War* (Plate 15),[11] a sense of movement is created through use of contrasting light values and colors; curved, intertwining lines; and representational elements such as leaning figures poised in the midst of physical movement. Diagonal lines seem to suggest more movement than either vertical or horizontal lines. Apparently we associate vertical and horizontal lines with familiar, static objects: walls, trees, posts, buildings, horizon. Anything that is diagonal appears to be leaning toward the horizontal or the vertical, thus creating a dynamic sense of tension, or potential movement. Most of the curved lines in Plate 15 are diagonal from the lower-left corner to the upper-right corner. Compare this painting with Courbet's *Still Life,* Plate 12 (following p. 54), and note the dominant influence of line over shape in creating a sense of movement.

In the last fifty years, there have been many attempts by artists to create the sensation of movement by representing actual movement in painting, sculpture, and architecture. Duchamp revolutionized the ideas of movement in art with his painting, *Nude Descending a Staircase* (Plate 17). Influenced by stroboscopic motion studies in photography, Duchamp portrays real movement by overlapping transparent figures on his canvas. The multi-exposed picture in Plate 16 illustrates the parallel technique in photography.

[11] Plates 15–18 follow p. 134.

There are two types of movement—*activity* and *drive*. Activity in this sense is agitation about a central axis. Drive is that movement which leads purposefully toward a goal. The earth rotates about its axis (activity) while heading in an elliptical path around the sun (drive). Another example of both types of movement is the walking racer. He is executing a complex series of movements, involving both a twisting activity around his own spinal axis and a driving movement toward the finish line. If we could take one of those fellows out of the race and put him on a treadmill, we would have pure activity-type movement; we will have taken away the drive. Or, if we could put him on a forward-moving belt, we would drive him along to the goal without twisting physical activity. Thus, for study and examination, we have arbitrarily separated the two types of movement involved in walking races; we can do the same thing with art.

In José de Rivera's *Construction 8* (Figure 8.1), activity and drive can be examined separately. Drive movement is suggested by smooth, curved, continuous line; and activity movement is provided by placing the entire sculpture on a rotating base so that it moves at all times.

Activity

Both activity and drive are evident in music. Here, too, they are easily separated for purposes of study and examination. Musical movement of the activity type is caused by rhythmic agitation, fast tempos, and polyphonic textures.

Agitation

Agitation is brought about by repetition of a rhythmic motive. Exciting scenes in a movie are almost always accompanied by rapid rhythmic figures or motives in the musical score. Listen to Paganini's *Moto Perpetuo* (Example 8.1), based on fast rhythmic figures. Apart from any other consideration, we can hear a great deal of activity— that is, movement that is not going anywhere.

Example 8.1
Paganini: *Moto Perpetuo*, Op. 11

Another type of "static" movement is created by a rapid repetition of the same tone, or by rapid alternation of a single chord figure (*tremolo*). This music is not going anywhere either; it is simply standing still, quivering, often giving the listener a feeling of suspense or anticipation. In Example 8.2, the tremolo begins in the high strings and descends gradually throughout the string family.

Example 8.2
Debussy: *La Mer*, first movement, opening

Figure 8.1   de Rivera, José, *Construction 8,* 1954. Forged rod, stainless steel, 9⅜″ high. Collection, The Museum of Modern Art, New York. Gift of Mrs. Heinz Schultz in memory of her husband.

Tempo

Directly related to the sense of movement is tempo. A fast tempo significantly influences the quality of musical movement. Generally speaking, increased tempo augments the sense of both activity and drive. "Zorba's Dance" (Example 8.3) begins slowly, but steadily increases in tempo. The momentum gathers, producing much more excitement than if the tempo were rapid throughout.

Example 8.3

Theodorakis: "Zorba's Dance"

Discrepancies in tempo sometimes exist in the interpretations of a piece of music by various performers, partly because of indefinite, relative tempo indications given by its composer. For example, the composer might indicate that a piece should be played "slowly," or "brightly," or even "in the manner of a funeral march."[12] Because these indications are imprecise, performers perceive a piece of music in different ways. By altering the speed at which a piece is played, a performer can change the character of the music. Notice the distinct change in the character of Example 8.4 when it is played considerably slower than usual. The traditional tempo provides a light,

[12] Common tempo markings with their meanings are listed in Appendix C, p. 225.

lilting character; played at a slow tempo, the music becomes deliberate, even ponderous.

Example 8.4
Beethoven: *Piano Sonata No. 14 in C-sharp minor, Op. 27,*
No. 2 (Moonlight Sonata), second movement. Played at two
different tempos

Texture

Look at Duchamp's painting again (Plate 17). What causes the sense of movement? We have already mentioned the effects of overlapping shapes and diagonal and curved lines. The manner in which these elements are woven together creates texture; in this painting opposing lines and shapes provide an active and complex texture. In other words, the *texture* of the painting contributes to the sense of movement. In general, the more complicated the texture, the more active the movement.

As we discovered in Chapter 7, polyphonic textures in music are created by independent melodic lines. Imitative counterpoint and overlapping melodies create a polyphonic texture comparable to that in Duchamp's painting. In the painting, overlapping, transparent shapes and diagonal lines cause the activity; and in the polyphonic pieces in Examples 8.5 and 8.6, the independent, overlapping melodies in a polyphonic texture cause active movement.

Example 8.5*
Bach: *Brandenburg Concerto No. 5*, third movement

Example 8.6
Bartók: *String Quartet No. 4*, first movement

If melodic lines are brought together, overlapped, and placed in opposition, the music is concise. The more concise the music, the more agitated it appears to be, and the more the sense of movement increases. We find evidence of this in Bach's Fugue No. 1 from Book I of *The Well-Tempered Clavier* (Examples 6.7 and 7.21) in which the concise stretto expresses more movement than the original statement.

Drive

Because of associations in our experience, activity is the more obvious kind of movement. The movement we have described as "driving toward a goal" is much more subtle and elusive, more likely to carry us along than to agitate us. But driving movement is far more important, because it is more closely related to the substance of music, including melodic direction, harmonic structure, and formal design. Drive is caused by regular accent, by functional harmony, and by melodic contour. We will call these three types of movement *metric drive*, *harmonic drive*, and *melodic drive*.

Metric Drive

Metric drive, the simplest of the three, is caused by regular accent. It is especially noticeable in pieces with heavy accent, such as marches, waltzes, and other dances. The regularity of accent itself supplies a sense of inexorable movement toward a goal. It creates in us a feeling that we are going somewhere.

Once established, the beat tends to perpetuate itself and strengthen the drive. Perhaps association with actual marching or dancing has something to do with this sense or feeling. The "Triumphal March" from *Aïda* (Example 8.7) is not as fast as Sousa's marches, but the sense of purpose is just as strong. It may be even stronger, particularly if we happen to be viewing the triumphal scene in the opera with scores of men, women, and beasts trooping across the stage.

Example 8.7

Verdi: *Aïda,* "Triumphal March" from Act II

Harmonic Drive

A very powerful type of movement in music is that which is caused by harmonic drive. The term "harmonic progression," as we have said before, implies a relationship between chords that results in progress or movement toward a goal. The best way to describe this progression is that the music seems to be pulling toward the tonic, or key center, of the piece. This gravitational pull propels us through the musical fabric, whether the music be agitated or placid. The harmonic pull is almost always there to some degree. When the pull toward the tonic is strong, the movement is more evident. When this pull is vague or diverted, the movement is less evident, even elusive and deceptive.

We have chosen two examples which will demonstrate the aural effect of lack of harmonic pull. The Wagner Prelude to *Das Rheingold* (Example 8.8) is based entirely on a single chord. This music lacks harmonic drive because there are no chord changes. Movement in this piece is merely languid activity about a central axis—the three notes of the E-flat chord. Wagner sets the scene for the opera by portraying the swirling movement of an underwater world. In Monteverdi's Prelude to *Orfeo* (Example 8.9) the opening passage is also based entirely on one chord. The movement is not progressive; we seem to be running in place, marking time. But after a slight pause, the second section, obviously based on more frequent chord changes, possesses a strong driving movement.

Example 8.8

Wagner: *Das Rheingold,* Prelude

Example 8.9

Monteverdi: *Orfeo,* Prelude

Harmonic drive, then, is strong when the chords change frequently. It is strongest as we approach the end of a harmonic progression, and we sense a gravitational pull toward the tonic. When the music comes to rest, we have a *cadence*. The gravitational pull to a cadence and the eventual fulfillment create within the listener a feeling of *tension* followed by *release*. Music is full of these tensions and releases. The tension created by harmonic considerations supplies us with a strong sense of musical movement. The following excerpts contain harmonic tension followed by a release. In each the release, or cadence, consists of the tonic chord. Haydn builds tension just before the final chord in the second movement of his *Sonata No. 2* (Example 8.10). Beethoven uses harmonic tension to create suspenseful anticipation of the active main theme in the introduction of his *Pathétique Sonata* (Example 8.11). Hindemith creates tension with his unique, new harmonies, and releases the tension suddenly with a very conventional triad (Example 8.12).

Example 8.10*
Haydn: *Sonata No. 2 in E-flat,* second movement, ending

Example 8.11*
Beethoven: *Piano Sonata No. 8 in C minor,* Op. 13
(*Pathétique*), opening

Example 8.12
Hindemith: *Ludus Tonalis,* Postludium, ending

Neither tension nor release occurs alone because one is not perceived without the other. There can be no release without tension, nor can there be tension unrelieved. Here the harmonic context is important; if a chord of tension is followed by a series of similar chords rather than chords of release, we no longer perceive tension. The use of such a chord series, called *non-functional harmony,* produces coloristic, often exotic, harmonic effects.

If the music heads toward a cadence, but does not end as expected, the sense of movement continues and is heightened. This surprise continuation is aptly called a *deceptive cadence*. The listener is deceived into thinking the movement is going to end and the tension be relieved. Instead, he is actually propelled onward and new tension is created; the movement has been prolonged by the sidestepping of the expected end. In Example 8.13, the pianist plays the second half of the now-familiar Chopin *Prelude,* Op. 28, No. 4 which contains a prominent deceptive cadence. You can even feel the performer making an effort to emphasize it. Chopin apparently believed that the expected cadence would be too abrupt; he evidently thought that he should come down gradually from the climax, extend the closing passage, and provide a satisfying balance to the total effect.

Fauré in his *Fourth Barcarolle* (Example 8.14) uses deceptive cadences to sidestep into different keys (modulation). The slight shock of the unexpected change after the original key is well established creates a pleasant harmonic color which is characteristic of Fauré's music.

Beethoven supplies us with a "classic" example of deceptive cadence in the fourth movement of his *Ninth Symphony* (Example 8.15). In one of the grandest moments of this, his grandest symphony, the entire orchestra and chorus singing and playing at the top of their lungs come to the end of a section, where we hear what seems to be a definite ending on a tonic cadence. We hear the chorus sing the phrase "vor Gott" three times, apparently reinforcing this ending on the tonic. But the final cadence is deceptive, and the movement resumes. Beethoven used this grand deceptive cadence to halt the momentum of that large section before going on to the next, a little German band tune, completely different from what had gone before. He chose to end with a mighty chord which would still maintain a strong feeling that more was to come.

Example 8.13*
Chopin: *Prelude in E minor,* Op. 28, No. 4

Example 8.14*
Fauré: *Fourth Barcarolle in A-flat,* Op. 44

Example 8.15*
Beethoven: *Symphony No. 9 in D minor,* Op. 125,
fourth movement

Melodic Drive

Movement in music depends to a certain extent on the shape or contour of a melodic line. We hear melody as a unit; it has a beginning and an end, and is therefore goal-oriented. A melody becomes an entity as it flows toward its goal. The inner movement it possesses determines the manner of reaching its goal. This inner movement can be *chromatic, diatonic,* or *chord-built.*

Chromatic movement develops the tightest or most closely-knit association between tones. When every tone on the piano keyboard is played in succession, including both black and white keys, the movement is chromatic. When tones are selected and placed in the familiar do-re-mi arrangement, the movement is diatonic. Even in these simple scales, the difference in movement is quite obvious. If we consider that both scales begin and end on the same tones, we might say that the chromatic scale makes more fuss about reaching its goal, utilizing all the tones *possible;* the diatonic scale is more direct; more driving. The chromatic scale then contains more potential for activity-type movement than the diatonic scale.

Example 8.16
Chromatic scale C to C
Diatonic scale C major

The melodies in Examples 8.17 and 8.18 are based on the chromatic scale. Their tones are closer together than tones in the diatonic scales, and so the movement is more active.

Example 8.17*
Bach: *Chromatic Fantasy and Fugue,* fugue theme

Example 8.18*
Rimsky-Korsakof: *Le Coq d'or,* first movement, 1st theme

Diatonic contour is the most familiar to us because it is the basis of our traditional harmonic system. A diatonic melody is based primarily on the tones of the major and minor scales. Diatonic melodies usually drive toward a goal, because the system itself contains and glorifies the idea of the tonic, which is always thought of as a goal. The theme from the final movement of Beethoven's *Ninth Symphony* (Example 8.19) is a diatonic melody; the first long phrase is made up entirely of adjacent scale tones, and it ends on the tonic, the goal. The Tchaikovsky theme (Example 8.20) moves upward following closely, but not exactly, the diatonic scale. Each of these melodies possesses intrinsic driving movement, because each has the tonic as its goal.

Example 8.19*
Beethoven: *Symphony No. 9 in D minor,* Op. 125,
fourth movement

Example 8.20*
Tchaikovsky: *Symphony No. 6 in B minor,* Op. 74
(*Pathétique*), second movement, 1st theme

Chord-built melodic contour is constructed primarily with the tones of a chord. The movement tends to be static because the harmonic progression is retarded to give the melody a chance to move about within one chord before moving on to the next. When the chords do change, movement toward the goal is provided, whereas the melody provides activity-type movement within each chord.

In Example 8.21 we hear first the chord upon which the melody is built. Beethoven sounds this chord twice before presenting the melody. Haydn's piece (Example 8.22) is a perfect example of what we have been talking about. As the harmony changes, each chord is clearly outlined by the melodic contour.

Example 8.21*
Beethoven: *Symphony No. 3 in E-flat,* Op. 55 (*Eroica*),
first movement, 1st theme

Example 8.22*
Haydn: *Symphony No. 94 in G (Surprise),*
second movement

Continuous and Intermittent Movement

Apart from activity and drive there is a dimension of movement which describes the actual continuity of sound. Some music moves along continuously whereas other music stops and starts. We can classify these two broad categories of movement as *continuous* and *intermittent.* Continuous music may sometimes draw back and build again; but forward, uninterrupted motion predominates. In intermittent movement, small sections and short phrases are balanced against one another. Although these sections and phrases move toward a long-range goal, they proceed through a series of steps rather than extended sweeps.

These characteristics of movement can be seen in poetry as well. Some poetry moves in a continuous manner. Other poetry moves in stops and starts. Read aloud the following lines by Dickinson, Pope, and Browning, and see the different degrees of movement. Note where the important pauses occur. Periods, colons, and semicolons set up the strongest pauses, but commas also break the movement. Note in each piece the frequency and strength of the cadences and their effect on movement. In order to comprehend the full meaning of a poem, you pause where the punctuation indicates and not necessarily at the end of each line.

The simple poem, *I Never Saw a Moor,* by Emily Dickinson, is made up of two sentences. Each line is short, and there is a pause at the end of nearly every one; the resulting movement is intermittent and choppy. Note also that the third line of each stanza has an extra beat which tends to propel us on to the end of the stanza.

> ### I Never Saw a Moor
> I never saw a moor—
> I never saw the sea—
> Yet know I how the heather looks
> And what a billow be.
>
> I never spoke with God
> Nor visited in Heaven—
> Yet certain am I of the spot
> As if the checks were given.
>
> EMILY DICKINSON*

* Reprinted by permission of the publishers and the Trustees of Amherst College from Thomas H. Johnson, Editor, *The Poems of Emily Dickinson,* Cambridge, Mass.: The Belknap Press of Harvard University Press, Copyright, 1951, 1955, by The President and Fellows of Harvard College.

The excerpt from Alexander Pope's *Essay on Criticism* represents a different kind of movement. Here again, each line is end-stopped, as in the Dickinson poem. But the lines in Pope's poem are longer, and the movement is more flowing and continuous than choppy and intermittent.

Excerpt from *An Essay on Criticism*

True ease in writing comes from art, not chance,
As those move easiest who have learned to dance.
'Tis not enough no harshness gives offense,
The sound must seem an echo to the sense:
Soft is the strain when Zephyr gently blows,
And the smooth stream in smoother number flows;
But when loud surges lash the sounding shore,
The hoarse, rough verse should like the torrent roar;

ALEXANDER POPE

Finally, in Robert Browning's famous poem, *My Last Duchess*, we see even more continuous movement. Browning seems deliberately to avoid placing strong punctuation at the ends of lines. Several lines have no end punctuation at all (these are called run-on lines), and several contain inner periods, semicolons, or question marks. The irregular distances between cadences and the relatively long phrases give this poem the most flowing and continuous movement of the three. Notice that the lines of Browning and Pope are of the same length—approximately ten syllables each—and yet the feeling of movement is quite different.

Excerpt from *My Last Duchess*

That's my last Duchess painted on the wall,
Looking as if she were alive. I call
That piece a wonder, now; Fra Pandolf's hands
Worked busily a day, and there she stands.
Will 't please you sit and look at her? I said
"Fra Pandolf" by design, for never read
Strangers like you that pictured countenance,
The depth and passion of its earnest glance,
But to myself they turned (since none puts by
The curtain I have drawn for you, but I)
And seemed as they would ask me, if they durst,
How such a glance came there; so, not the first
Are you to turn and ask thus. . . .

ROBERT BROWNING

Likewise in music, the frequency of cadences affects the movement. We know, for example, that Haydn's music contains more frequent cadences than Bach's music. We can expect, therefore, that movement in Haydn's music is going to be more intermittent and in Bach's more continuous. Music like Haydn's with frequent cadences has short, motivic phrases which emphasize stop-start, intermittent movement. Music like Bach's with infrequent cadences has long, sweeping phrases and more continuous movement.

Haydn adds to the feeling of intermittent movement by frequent rests or momentary silences. Bach seems to be interested in keeping the sound going all the time; when one part has a rest, another part is playing. Haydn stops the movement in every part. When he comes to a cadence, he organizes his entire musical context to emphasize the halting of movement. Bach seems reluctant to stop the movement altogether at a cadence. He frequently disguises the cadence in some way; he will make it deceptive, or he will tumble right through it, bringing rhythmic agitation into play to de-emphasize it.

It may be hard for listeners to tell when Bach's cadences occur. The only ones he strongly emphasizes are those at the end of a section or entire piece when the tempo is drastically reduced or the harmonic drive increased. His textures are more polyphonic, where Haydn's are more homophonic. The overlapping, independent melodic lines of Bach's piece create an endless fabric, so that even as one melodic line comes to an end, another continues on. Because of this overlap, the movement is continuous.

Example 8.23*

Bach: *Brandenburg Concerto No. 2,* second movement

Example 8.24*

Haydn: *Symphony No. 94 in G (Surprise),*
third movement

Because the Bach and Haydn examples so distinctly exemplify continuous and intermittent movement, we may be inclined to think that all polyphonic music is continuous and all homophonic music is intermittent. However, *melodic length* may determine the continuity of movement. The longer the melody, the more continuous the movement. The main theme in Schubert's *Unfinished Symphony* (Example 4.29) is a long melodic idea; the texture is clearly homophonic, yet the movement is continuous. It is the length of the melody that causes continuous movement. Stravinsky's *L'histoire du Soldat* (Example 7.1) consists mainly of short phrases in basically polyphonic texture. In this case, the short phrases cause intermittent movement.

Even though the Bach and Stravinsky compositions are both polyphonic, the movement in Bach is continuous whereas the movement in Stravinsky is intermittent. The same contrast in movement is evident in the homophonic music of Schubert and Haydn.

Movement in Form

We have talked about movement in music, both as activity and as drive toward a goal. But we have not said anything about that goal.

All music seems to be going somewhere, but of course there is no physical "destination" to which it goes. However, in most music there is an area in which we sense a feeling of arrival. We call this area the climax—and its high point represents the destination in our musical journey. It is the moment we have been waiting for. This is where design and movement come together. When we speak of "goal," we are talking about the *shape* of movement in a composition. We move toward the goal, arrive at it, and sometimes move away from it, all a part of the formal design of the piece.

The specific forms we have discussed all have implications for movement. For example, when a section is repeated, any movement which has started to build by the end of the section recedes at the end of that section. But when we start over, and repeat the section, we have increased the momentum—we are now more ready to go on than we were the first time.

We have spoken of a contrasting section or development section as "departure," implying movement away from something. This principle of movement with reference to a goal may be another reason for the prevalence of the ABA form: the B section may contain a climactic area or it may build to a climactic return of A.

The Rondo form, ABACABA, continually moves us back to the starting point. This ever-circular return to the beginning may appear to be static; but usually we see an over-all buildup in the rondo which takes place in the contrasting B and C sections. The C section is likely to be the longest and most prominent of all, the high point of the piece. And the fact that we keep returning to A gives added impetus to the contrasting material.

Theme and Variations has been described as numerous repetitions of the same theme: A A'A''A''', etc. But this form tells us nothing about the movement of the music. Most theme and variation compositions are constructed as a unit, with each variation more complex, more varied than the last. Here, too, we see an over-all building to a high point.

The Sonata form usually rises to a climax which is carefully built into the design of the piece. The development section, transitory in nature, freely wanders through various key centers, exploiting and expanding the material laid out in the opening section. Usually, the development (or departure) section involves building to a climax, which comes somewhere between the end of the development and the end of the movement. Frequently the return of the opening theme is a dynamic high point, but sometimes the return of the second theme near the end is even more climactic. And sometimes the movement comes to a crashing climax at the very end.

In addition to seeing movement as activity and drive, we should think of the path of movement as progressing toward a goal, arriving, and receding. We should be listening to the whole composition —listening for its movement, as expressed in the *shape* of the piece. There are many rises and falls, ebbs and flows within a composition, but usually over-all, there is a building to a high point and a receding from it. The buildup may be gradual or rapid, direct or roundabout; it may rise to a limited plane or to a towering height. It may rise and then fall and rise again, as if to take two steps forward and one step back. The descent from the climax may be slow or sudden—or there may be no descent. It is almost certain to be more rapid than the rise. But the shape of an entire movement is usually some sort of lopsided arch such as those shown graphically in Figure 8.2. This arch of movement can be heard in most music, no matter what design or form the composer uses. It is vital to the sensing of movement as progress toward something.

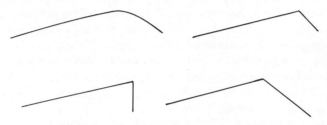

Figure 8.2   The "shape" of a piece

This arch is also an ideal of movement in literature. A play or a short story usually has an opening section in which the characters and themes are all introduced and the situation established. This section is followed by a large and complex one in which the themes or characters are developed, and in which the situation grows very complicated, building and increasing in complexity and tension. At the height of the complexity, things begin to resolve. Sometimes they fall into place suddenly, sometimes they work out slowly. That height of complexity and beginning of resolution, also called *climax*, usually occurs in the last third of the play. If we were to draw an arch representing the dramatic movement in a play or story, it would resemble the arch of musical movement in most compositions.

Summary

Here is a sampling of various types of movement found in musical literature.

The polyphonic texture of Palestrina's sixteenth-century style is an excellent example of both activity and drive. The most significant movement is activity, caused by a texture of continually overlapping voice parts. But driving movement is also present, caused by melodic direction and, to a lesser degree, harmonic pull.

Example 8.25
Palestrina: "Agnus Dei," from *Veni Sponsa Christi* (Mass)

In the madrigal, "Now is the month of Maying," by Thomas Morley, the movement is sporadic. A chordal, isometric phrase—everyone singing together—is followed by a polyphonic phrase—each voice singing an individual part. The result is an alternation between two qualities of movement, one primarily drive, the other activity.

Example 8.26
Morley: "Now is the month of Maying"

The long, sweeping melodies and phrases common to nineteenth-century music supply us with many examples of complex rhythmic texture within basic homophonic structures, where we have prominent melodic lines with many subservient but active accompanying parts. The result is purposeful, driving music consisting of grand, sweeping melodies spiced with rhythmic activity among the other voice parts. We have chosen the first movement of Brahms' *Symphony No. 4* to illustrate this driving movement. The second theme is preceded by a short, excited passage played by the woodwinds. The cellos play the theme first, which the violins repeat.

Example 8.27
Brahms: *Symphony No. 4 in E minor,* Op. 98,
first movement, 2nd theme

The Impressionistic music of Debussy generally lacks drive and instead seems to hang in mid-air and shimmer like a Monet painting. As we learned in Chapter 7, Debussy discovered the whole-tone scale and used it as a basis for his style. By eliminating the half tones found in conventional diatonic scales, Debussy lessened both melodic and harmonic pull.

Example 8.28
Debussy: *Pelléas et Mélisande,* Act I,
near opening

Thus, most of Debussy's compositions lack the harmonic drive of earlier music and concentrate on coloristic effects of non-functional harmony and exotic instrumentation. Impressionistic painters were similarly preoccupied with the effects of light to the near exclusion of heavy line and pure representation. Their paintings, like Debussy's music, seem to stand still and shimmer with inner light (see the Monet painting, Plate 13).

Movement in Example 8.29 is different from the movement in any of the previous four examples. Anton Webern, a modern German composer, preferred to use as few tones as possible, playing as much on the effects of silence as those of sound. The result is stark "points" of sound placed on a canvas of silence. With the fantastic leaps and the tossing of tones sparsely from one instrument to another, we sense a movement that can best be described as "pointillistic." Such techniques are comparable to Pollock's painting technique (Plate 18, following p. 134). Here droplets of paint appear on a canvas and remain mere patterns of "drippings," never making a picture of recognizable objects, but expressing a unique quality of movement reflecting the very manner in which the paint was applied.

Example 8.29

Webern: *Symphonie,* Op. 21

Chapter 9

Combinations:
Instrumental Ensembles
and Forms

The following recordings should be at hand for listening in connection with this chapter.

Haydn: *Symphony No. 104 in D (London)*
Mozart: *Symphony No. 40 in G minor, K. 550*
Beethoven: *Symphony No. 3 in E-flat, Op. 55 (Eroica)*
Tchaikovsky: *Symphony No. 5 in E minor, Op. 64*
Mozart: *Piano Concerto No. 21 in C, K. 467*
Berlioz: *Roman Carnival Overture, Op. 9*
Strauss: *Thus Spake Zarathustra*
Mendelssohn: *A Midsummer Night's Dream, Op. 61a (incidental music)*
Beethoven: *Sonata No. 6 for Violin and Piano in A, Op. 30, No. 1*
Schumann: *Papillons, Op. 2*
Haydn: *String Quartet in G minor, Op. 74, No. 3*
Schoenberg: *String Quartet No. 4, Op. 37*
Beethoven: *Piano Trio No. 6 in B-flat, Op. 97 (Archduke)*

Up to this point, we have dealt with basic principles which help us approach the task of listening to music. From now on, we will examine the broader aspects of musical experience: the types of performing ensembles, the kinds of compositions they perform, and the characteristics of various historical styles in music.

Orchestral Ensembles and Forms

If music were played by only one instrument or sung by only one voice, it would soon become tiresome. Most of us enjoy and are capable of hearing complex combinations of sounds; in fact, when different instruments play together or when several voices sing together, we can hear and appreciate the dimension of movement within music, because the distinctive timbre of each helps to distinguish it from the others. In ancient times, instruments began to "accompany" the voice. At first they probably played the same melody the voice was singing; they later provided contrasting or supporting parts. Composers in their search for variety have long experimented with combinations of instrumental and vocal timbres. Any combination is of course possible, but certain ones seem to be more appropriate to the musical expression of a given era than others and so become standard ensembles with which composers of that era work. We shall discuss these standard ensembles in both instrumental and vocal music.

Because we wish to relate our knowledge of formal design to our experiences in the concert hall or with records, let us first examine the performing media as they relate to form. In many instances, the performing ensemble bears the same name as the form it is playing: symphony orchestras play symphonies, string quartets play string quartets, piano trios play trios, electronic equipment plays electronic music. Our discussion covers the most important performing media along with the types of compositions each performs.

Symphony Orchestra

Among all musical media, the symphony orchestra has been the most popular for two hundred years. Most large cities and many small ones have their own resident symphony orchestras. During these two hundred years, the orchestra has evolved to a large ensemble numbering approximately one hundred instruments grouped into four individually homogeneous families: strings, woodwinds, brass, and percussion. Each group maintains a balance of pitch among its own members, both high and low voices being represented. Each also balances the timbre and volume of sound of the other families in the orchestra. For example, the brass section, which usually contains no more than fifteen players, balances the string section, often composed of sixty players. This arrangement allows contrast between the timbres of the lyric string section and those of the penetrating, powerful brass section. The variety of timbres available in the orchestra makes possible a wide range of contrasts, both between families and between individual instruments. The composer may also write solo passages, especially for woodwind and brass instruments, to provide varieties of color in the total ensemble.

A good example of modern orchestral sound is found in the opening bars of Britten's *The Young Person's Guide to the Orchestra,* based on a seventeenth-century tune by Purcell. Britten presents first the full orchestra, then each of the four families separately.

Example 9.1

Britten: *The Young Person's Guide to the Orchestra,*
Themes A (full ensemble), B (woodwinds), C (brass),
D (strings), E (percussion), and F (full ensemble)

When instrumental music was first written, in the late fifteenth century, composers did not designate which instruments were to play each part. But by the seventeenth century, the art of *orchestration,* or writing music with specific instruments in mind for each part, was well established. Composers began to score parts according to differences in instrumental capability. For example, even though the pitch range of the trombone overlaps the pitch range of the flute, the trombone is not capable of playing these common tones with the agility of the flute. The usual result is that the flute part is more elaborate and ornamental than the trombone part, as evidenced in Example 9.2.

Example 9.2*

Britten: *The Young Person's Guide to the Orchestra,*
Variations A and L (flute and trombone)

In modern times, the use of specified instruments and combinations has become a most important factor in the composition of orchestral music. It is almost as important for the composer to be familiar with the timbres and capabilities of each instrument as to know all the intricacies of rhythm, harmony, counterpoint, form, or any other musical element. If the composer is especially skillful in the craft of orchestration, or in choosing those instruments and combinations which best express his musical ideas, the result can be an infinitely more interesting piece of music. We discovered as much in listening to Moussorgsky's *Pictures at an Exhibition,* first as it was originally composed for solo piano (Example 2.3), and then as orchestrated by Ravel (Example 2.4). The musical ideas originally expressed in the piano version seem more vivid when played by the orchestra. The range of timbres is extended to encompass a greater variety of possibilities for esthetic expression. A great measure of the success of the orchestrated version of *Pictures* must be attributed to Ravel, the orchestrator.

After hearing such a contrast, we may well ask why composers bother to write for the piano when they have the resources of the orchestra at hand. The reason is that not all music is appropriate for orchestra. Many composers feel that if a piece is truly "pianistic," that is, if it is artfully designed for the scope and capabilities of the piano, it would lose its appeal if transcribed to the orchestral medium. Therefore, we must conclude that Moussorgsky's composition did indeed possess the capacity for an orchestral setting. But many pieces written for piano neither need nor benefit from the expanded orchestral setting. Most of the piano works of Chopin and Debussy are cases in point. It may be appropriate to produce a large copy of a small painting if the subject such as a battle scene or a landscape demands a large scope. But the artistic merit of a small painting whose subject is a flower or a portrait would be lost if its proportions were greatly expanded.

Another example illustrating the possibilities available through orchestration, even when using limited thematic material, is the prelude to Wagner's opera, *Das Rheingold* (Example 8.8). As you will recall, the entire composition consists of only one three-note chord, which is sustained throughout. The prelude begins modestly with the lowest voices in the orchestra and, without changing the chord, builds to a climax with the gradual addition of voices, exploring a wide range of tone colors.

In early experiments with orchestration, a great variety of wind and stringed instruments were used. Gradually, many of these instruments were discarded in favor of the most versatile. Thus, the symphony orchestra of today had its origins in the late seventeenth and early eighteenth centuries as a small string ensemble which was often accompanied by harpsichord or organ, and which made only occasional use of winds, brass, and percussion. In this Baroque orchestra, the brass and percussion usually played together to accentuate rhythmic patterns. Table 9.1 (p. 154) demonstrates how the orchestra has grown in numbers and variety of instruments used. Although there has been a great deal of variation in all eras, the compositions cited are reasonably representative of the seventeenth-, eighteenth-, nineteenth-, and twentieth-century orchestras.

Bach's scoring in the early eighteenth century depended a great deal on the availability of players in the church or court where he was employed. For the most part, his orchestra included flutes, oboes, bassoons, horns, and about ten strings, plus harpsichord or organ—all in various combinations. This precursor to the modern orchestral sound is illustrated in Bach's *Brandenburg Concerto No. 2* (see Table 9.1 for exact instrumentation). Here Bach uses the trumpet in addition to the usual winds.

Example 9.3

Bach: *Brandenburg Concerto No. 2,* first movement

Gradually, other instruments were added until, by the time of Haydn and Mozart in the last half of the eighteenth century, the woodwind, brass, and percussion sections were of sufficient size to be prominent and independent. Haydn used almost a standard formula for instrumentation in his late symphonies. These symphonies called for pairs of flutes, oboes, clarinets, bassoons, horns, trumpets, timpani, and a string section containing approximately thirty players. His last symphony (*Symphony No. 104 in D*), written about 1800, illustrates Classical balance between sections. In this

Table 9.1 Development of Instrumentation

Instrumental Family	Bach: Brandenburg Concerto No. 2	Haydn: Symphony No. 104 in D (London)	Berlioz: Symphonie Fantastique	Stravinsky: The Rite of Spring
Woodwind	1 flute 1 oboe	2 flutes 2 oboes 2 clarinets 2 bassoons	1 piccolo 2 flutes 2 oboes 4 clarinets 4 bassoons	2 piccolos 3 flutes 1 alto flute 4 oboes 2 English horns 2 clarinets piccolo 5 clarinets 2 bass clarinets 4 bassoons 2 contrabassoons
Brass	1 trumpet	2 horns 2 trumpets	4 horns 2 trumpets 2 cornets 3 trombones 2 tubas	8 horns 1 trumpet piccolo 4 trumpets 1 bass trumpet 3 trombones 2 tenor tubas 2 bass tubas
Percussion		2 timpani	4 timpani bass drum chimes cymbals	6 timpani bass drum triangle antique cymbals tam-tam tambourine cymbals güiro
Strings	strings (10–20) 1 solo violin	strings (30–35)	strings (60)	strings (60)
Other	harpsichord		2 harps	

music the woodwind and brass sections play prominent roles, and the orchestra consists of four well-defined groups. Bach and Handel used the woodwinds and brasses either as solo instruments or to play the same parts as the strings, whereas Mozart and Haydn scored the winds as full-fledged sections playing in contrast to the string section. Note in Table 9.1 that as more wind instruments are added, the numbers of strings are increased to maintain balance between sections.

The main thing to remember when comparing Bach with Haydn is that Haydn was interested in contrasting individual timbres and balance between sections, whereas Bach was interested in balance between voice parts in the polyphonic texture. Thus, in the music of Bach and his predecessors, you are likely to hear a violin and a flute playing one part and another violin and flute playing a contrasting part. Here the timbres of violin and flute are unimportant; rather it is the balance of the voice parts which is important. Though we may find more wind instruments of greater variety in Bach than in Haydn, Bach's ensemble never became standardized. Its makeup was unique to every composition, whereas Haydn's orchestra became reasonably standard in terms of size and instrumentation. It is because of his standard formula that Haydn is considered the father of the modern orchestra. The development of the orchestra since his time has been largely an expansion of Haydn's basic formula.

In Berlioz' nineteenth-century orchestra, the sections are all larger than before, but the striking difference is in the greater size and prominence of the wind sections, especially the brass (see Table 9.1). Now all sections are more closely balanced in terms of the importance of their respective roles. The woodwinds and brasses perform passages with the strength and individuality of the strings. The capabilities of the wind instruments are more fully exploited to compete, in a sense, with the strings. Berlioz in his *Symphonie Fantastique,* produces a sound typical of the nineteenth-century orchestra; the winds and percussion play longer and more important passages than ever before.

Example 9.4

Berlioz: *Symphonie Fantastique,* fourth movement

Did you ever attend a concert and wonder why part of the orchestra leaves the stage for certain compositions and returns for others? We can now see reasons for this practice. If the large ensemble required for a Berlioz symphony were to play a Haydn symphony, the balance would be disturbed.

The modern orchestra is a huge ensemble whose instrumental variety allows the composer great freedom in the choice of combinations. The result is that the orchestra's character may alter with each of his compositions. Stravinsky, in *The Rite of Spring,* calls for a very large orchestra with great variety of instrumental color, particularly in the brass and woodwinds (see Table 9.1). But in his *Pulcinella* he calls for a smaller, more Classical orchestra.

Example 9.5
Stravinsky: *The Rite of Spring,* "Dance of the Earth,"
end of Part I

Example 9.6
Stravinsky: *Pulcinella*

We must remember that the modern orchestra consists of great numbers of instruments which do not necessarily all play at once. The large composite sound is indeed heard, but modern composers are also interested in balance between sections, in unique combinations of instruments, and in the use of solo instruments to provide additional possibilities for tone color. For example, Mahler, in his *First Symphony,* exploits the unique timbre of the trumpet in an unusual solo passage (Example 9.7).

Example 9.7
Mahler: *Symphony No. 1 in D,* "second" movement

The outcome of all these developments is the large orchestra of today whose timbre depends on numerous small ensemble combinations and solo instruments within the context of the total ensemble. The whole orchestra seldom plays at once; that special effect is usually reserved for great climactic moments, such as the ending of *The Rite of Spring.*

In all the metamorphoses of the orchestra, balance in instrumentation has been an ideal. The strings have been gradually increased in number to balance the expanded wind sections. When the entire orchestra plays in unison (plays the same thing at the same time), the sections are balanced *simultaneously;* the strings do not predominate over the horns, or vice versa. In the opening bars of Haydn's *London Symphony* (Example 4.5) this simultaneous balance, or homogeneity of sound, is clearly heard.

Composers also balance one instrumental group against another *consecutively.* For example, in the development section of the same movement of the *London Symphony,* the woodwinds repeat the string melody, thus achieving consecutive balance between sections.

Orchestral Forms

Symphony. "Symphony" is the name of the most popular performing ensemble today. It is also the name for the most frequently performed orchestral form. A symphony is a large-scale composition for orchestra, usually containing four movements, one or more of which is typically in sonata form. Stemming from the opera overtures of the early eighteenth century, the symphony developed as an independent composition about a half-century later. It gained immediate popularity and continues to be the hallmark of the concert hall. The orchestra normally pauses between movements, promoting the integrity of each. The movements, with their stopping and starting within the bounds of a single composition, can be compared loosely with the acts of a play. The first act comprises a unit, but it is somehow incomplete by itself. Occasionally, we hear orchestras perform a single movement, much to the consternation of the avid concert-goer. Imagine seeing only the first act of Shakespeare's *A Midsummer Night's Dream.* As in theater, the whole story in a symphony is not told until the final curtain.

The four movements of the symphony are even more formal than the acts of a play because the movements are usually of a specified order and design. The following plan of movements, called the *sonata cycle,* is fairly typical:

First Movement	(fast) Sonata Form
Second Movement	(slow) Sonata Form or ABA (ternary), Rondo, Theme and Variations
Third Movement	(fast, usually triple) Minuet and Trio (ABA), or Scherzo
Fourth Movement	(fast) Rondo, Theme and Variations, or Sonata Form

Many variations are possible within this design, but the contrasting tempo arrangement, fast, slow, fast (triple), fast, is common. It is impossible to supply a neat, standard formula for the movements of a symphony because none exists. But it is useful to recognize the general scheme of movements that applies to most symphonies. There are symphonies with three movements or five movements; symphonies whose tempo arrangement places the fast (triple) movement ahead of the slow movement; and symphonies whose formal structure resembles the "standard" only remotely. Considering the variety possible within the loose definition of "symphony," it is remarkable that composers have been so consistent in their treatment of this popular form, especially in the four-movement structure and the use of the sonata design.

Sonata form is so often used for the first movement of symphonies, concertos, string quartets, and other compositions, that it is sometimes referred to as "first movement" form. The other movements are less likely to follow standard rules. The second movement, usually in slow tempo, may be rondo, sonata form, or ternary. The third movement is usually in fast triple meter, either a minuet and trio or a scherzo and trio. The dancelike character of the third movement adds another dimension to the contrast between the second and fourth movements which are commonly in duple meter. The scherzo is different from the minuet only in terms of a supposed character of whim and humor. It is generally agreed that Beethoven was the first to establish the scherzo in the symphony. The character of the scherzo is implied in the meaning of the word in Italian: joke. The fourth movement is usually fast and may be in sonata form, theme and variations, rondo, or even passacaglia as we found in Brahms' *Fourth Symphony* (Example 5.20). Also, the final movement is usually a climax to the entire symphony; thus the dramatic arch which we have seen within each movement also extends over the whole work.

The following symphonies are suggested for listening. The structures of movements shown are typical.

Haydn: *Symphony No. 94 in F (Surprise)*
First Movement	Sonata Form
Second Movement	Theme and Variations
Third Movement	Minuet and Trio
Fourth Movement	Rondo

Mozart: *Symphony No. 40 in G minor, K. 550*
First Movement	Sonata Form
Second Movement	Sonata Form
Third Movement	Minuet and Trio
Fourth Movement	Sonata Form

Beethoven: *Symphony No. 3 in E-flat (Eroica)*
First Movement	Sonata Form
Second Movement	Sonata Form (Funeral March)
Third Movement	Scherzo and Trio
Fourth Movement	Theme and Variations

Tchaikovsky: *Symphony No. 5 in E minor, Op. 64*
First Movement	Sonata Form
Second Movement	Ternary (ABA)
Third Movement	Ternary (Waltz)
Fourth Movement	Sonata Form

Concerto. Another prominent form played by the orchestra is the concerto, a composition for solo instrument and orchestra. In the concerto, the solo instrument and the orchestra perform as equals, balancing each other. Sometimes the solo instrument is accompanied by the orchestra; sometimes their equality is emphasized when they play the same themes alternately. In the typical concerto, the opening theme or even the entire exposition is played first by the orchestra and then by the solo instrument. In this way, the timbres of the solo instrument and ensemble are strikingly contrasted. Listen to the first movement of Mozart's *Piano Concerto No. 21 in C*, K. 467 for this contrast between soloist and orchestra.

Besides featuring the solo instrument, the concerto differs from the symphony in two other important ways. There are usually only three movements; the minuet or scherzo is omitted, and the first movement contains a double exposition—one for the orchestra and one for the solo instrument. Another slight difference is that somewhere along the way, usually near the end of the first movement (sometimes in the second or third movements as well), everything pauses while the soloist plays a brilliant virtuoso passage without accompaniment. This passage, called a *cadenza,* is usually written out by the composer, but often in the early concertos was left to the performer to improvise according to the limits of his ability. Whenever a particularly dazzling display of technique has been performed in a cadenza, audiences are moved to break tradition and applaud at the end of the first movement. Indeed, we often encounter first movements of concertos performed alone, owing perhaps to their length and the unusual feeling of finality.

In a concerto, the first movement is extremely important because of its length and climactic treatment of material. The pattern of movements is fast, slow, fast, an arrangement that dates back to the concertos of Vivaldi in the early eighteenth century. As in the symphony, the first movement of the concerto is most often sonata form; the second and third movements can be sonata form, theme and variations, or ternary. Occasionally there is no pause between movements, perhaps because of the desire for closer unity throughout, or better balance between movements of different lengths (that is, the second and third movements when run together function as one movement to balance the first). Additional examples of the solo concerto include Beethoven's *Piano Concerto No. 3 in C minor,* Op. 37, and Mendelssohn's *Violin Concerto in E minor,* Op. 64.

Our definition of concerto would not be complete without the mention of double and triple concertos. These concertos feature more than one solo instrument, but in addition to virtuoso performance, the soloists must work together as a group. So in the multiple concerto, we hear the large ensemble balanced against and contrasted with the small group. The composition follows the same general lines as the more common solo concerto. Examples of these multiple concertos are Mozart's *Concerto for Two Pianos in E-flat,* K. 365, and Beethoven's *Triple Concerto in C,* Op. 56, for piano, violin, and cello.

Concert Overture. The concert overture, as distinguished from the opera overture, is an independent, single-movement orchestral composition which flourished in the nineteenth century. It may be freely designed, like Tchaikovsky's *1812 Overture,* or it may utilize one of the standard forms. Overtures are often used to open a concert program because they are flashy and relatively short (usually not more than fifteen minutes long). An exciting example is the well-known *Roman Carnival Overture* by Berlioz.

Tone Poem. The tone poem, or symphonic poem, is closely related to the concert overture in that both consist of a single movement and are similar in design, but the tone poem is more *programmatic.* Program music is meant to convey extramusical ideas such as a story line, sounds of nature, or the aura of a geographical locale. The difficulty with program music is that the listener cannot be certain what the music is meant to convey unless the composer supplies him with a printed "program." Even with a detailed story line such as is available with Strauss' *Till Eulenspiegel,* we are never quite sure which musical passage goes with which episode in the story. Nevertheless, the use of extramusical elements supplies the music with added interest, and helps us understand the sensuous Romanticism of the nineteenth century. Of the many tone poems available, Strauss' *Death and Transfiguration* and *Thus Spake Zarathustra,* Debussy's *Prelude to the Afternoon of a Faun,* and Respighi's *Pines of Rome,* are outstanding examples.

Concerto Grosso. The concerto grosso is one of the most important types of instrumental composition of the Baroque period, 1600–1750. It is scored for orchestra, called *tutti,* and a small group of solo instruments, called *concertino.* The small group often consists of two or three high-pitched instruments, such as flutes, oboes, or violins, and a low-pitched instrument with keyboard accompaniment, such as cello with harpsichord. This is the same ensemble that constitutes the trio sonata, a separate chamber music form to be discussed later. The function of the concertino may be compared with that of the solo instrument in the concerto, in that each is contrasted with the rest of the orchestra. However, where the solo instrument is concerned with virtuosity, the concertino is more apt to mirror the effects of the tutti; it functions as a group. This contrast and alternation between the large and small ensembles is called *concertato.* We have seen this principle at work in the multiple concertos. It is also evident in the works of many modern composers, some of whom have actually adopted the Baroque concerto grosso form.

The concerto grosso usually contains three movements arranged in a fast, slow, fast pattern. The six *Brandenburg Concertos* by J. S. Bach are outstanding examples of the concerto grosso form. We have heard parts of Nos. 2, 3, 5, and 6. Listen to an excerpt from the first movement of *Brandenburg Concerto No. 2* (Example 9.8) and notice the concertato effect of alternating groups.

Example 9.8

Bach: *Brandenburg Concerto No. 2,* first movement

Another example of the concerto grosso form is Handel's *Concertante*, scored for two violins and cello as concertino, and strings and two oboes as tutti.

Suite. There are two distinct types of suite: Baroque (eighteenth century), and Modern (nineteenth and twentieth centuries). Both are sets of dances. There were numerous dance forms available in the Baroque period, many of which date back to the beginning of instrumental ensemble music. These dances, usually binary (AB) in form, are characterized by varying meters, tempos, and modes. They include the allemande, courante, sarabande, minuet, gigue, gavotte, bourrée. Any of the existing dance forms may be included in the suite. They are usually in the same key (though sometimes in contrasting mode), and ordered so that tempo and meter contrast. The Baroque suite, developed and refined by Bach, and hence sometimes called the Bach suite, frequently displays the following order of dances: prelude, allemande, courante, sarabande, minuet (or another dance form), and gigue. The Baroque suite was scored either for keyboard instrument or instrumental ensemble—any of Bach's four orchestral suites are especially recommended for listening.

The Modern suite consists of a series of movements, freely designed and freely ordered. These suites are programmatic because they are selected from music written for plays (Mendelssohn's incidental music to *A Midsummer Night's Dream*) and ballets. The ballet is an important, independent musical form of the nineteenth and twentieth centuries. The composition of a ballet involves collaboration between a composer and a choreographer, and the result is a unique combination of two art forms, music and dance. However, because the music is itself a valid art form, it is often performed in concert without dancers. Two important composers of ballet are Tchaikovsky (*Swan Lake, Nutcracker Suite,* and *Sleeping Beauty*) and Stravinsky (*Petrushka, The Firebird,* and *The Rite of Spring*).

Chamber Ensembles and Forms

Chamber ensembles are smaller than the symphony orchestra and play works of small dimensions. Although the scope of the ensemble is intimate enough for performance in a chamber or room rather than in the concert hall, chamber music is now common fare for concert halls. Chamber music is played by a soloist, or by a small ensemble. Usually it is meant to be performed one player to a part, in contrast to the symphony orchestra where there are many players to a part. The ensembles are named according to the number of players: a string quartet consists of two violins, viola, and cello; a piano trio has a piano, violin, and cello; a woodwind quintet has a flute, oboe, clarinet, bassoon, and French horn. These are the most common groups, although the chamber music label can apply to any small combination of instruments—even to a small orchestra.

Solo Forms

Sonata. Perhaps the simplest and most familiar kind of instrumental chamber music is the sonata, a composition for solo instrument either accompanied by a keyboard instrument or performing alone. Sonatas have been popular for about three centuries, and have been written for nearly every instrument. The most popular are those written for piano or for violin, flute, cello, or oboe with piano. The versatility of these instruments makes them the most capable of achieving equal status with the piano. The most successful sonatas are really duets in which the piano takes on a solo character of its own, rather than playing a completely subordinate role. Beethoven, for example, preferred to think of the piano in this way as you will hear in his *Sonata for Violin and Piano No. 6 in A,* Op. 30, No. 1. Note that the title of the work verifies the equality of the two instruments.

The double use of the term *sonata* may prove confusing. Remember that sonata is both a type of composition and a design common to many types. If we had to choose the most important form in all of music it would probably be the sonata. The similarity in structure of the solo sonata to the symphony, string quartet, concerto, and trio is certainly no accident; all are based on sonata form and the sonata cycle of movements. In fact, the symphony is really a sonata for orchestra, the string quartet a sonata for four strings, and so on. Likewise, the solo sonata usually has four movements in the traditional order: fast, slow, fast (triple), fast. The first movement is in sonata form and the other movements follow the same general scheme as those of the symphony.

Of particular interest will be Mozart's *Piano Sonata in A minor,* K. 310, Beethoven's *Piano Sonata in C minor,* Op. 13 (*Pathétique*), and Brahms' *Violin Sonata in G,* Op. 78.

Character Piece. In the early part of the nineteenth century, composers began to write short piano compositions designed to express a definite mood or character. Character pieces, as they have been aptly labelled, consist of a single movement either in free form or, more often, ABA or ternary design. The three-part design is well suited to expressing two contrasting moods within a single character. They are named according to the mood or character of the piece: Chopin's *Nocturne in E-flat,* Op. 9, No. 2 (*Night Song*), Mendelssohn's *On Wings of Song,* Schumann's *Papillons,* Op. 2 (*Butterflies*), Debussy's *Reflets dans l'eau (Reflections on the Water).*

Ensemble Forms

String Quartet. The string quartet, which comprises two violins, viola, and cello, is the most important chamber group. It has been a standard ensemble for two centuries, developed and exploited by many great composers, especially Haydn, Beethoven, Bartók, Schoenberg, and, to a lesser extent, Mozart, Schubert, and Brahms. The string quartet is considered by many to be the ideal medium of musical expression. The instruments correspond directly to the soprano, alto, tenor, and bass voice classifications, providing an exquisite balance of voicing and timbre; the quartet employs the essentials for pure musical expression. As we mentioned, the form consists of the same basic four-movement structure as the symphony and the sonata. Haydn's quartets are among the first and remain some of the finest examples of string quartet literature. Listen to the first movement of his Op. 74, No. 3.

The music of Arnold Schoenberg, a twentieth-century composer, is organized around completely different principles from those of Haydn. Both composers, however, utilized the string quartet as a suitable ensemble for musical expression. Both composers were interested in the individuality of each instrument in the ensemble, but their quartets sound drastically different because Schoenberg greatly extended the virtuoso limits of each instrument. Schoenberg created new timbres and stretched each instrument's capability by the use of mutes, playing with the back of the bow, glissandos, harmonics, and other virtuoso techniques. For Schoenberg's treatment of the quartet, listen to his *String Quartet No. 4*, Op. 37.

Other chamber ensembles are important, although none is as standard as the string quartet. Other combinations of stringed instruments include the *string quintet* (an extra viola or cello added to the quartet) and the *string orchestra*.

Trio Sonata. Worth special mention is the trio sonata, popular in the seventeenth and eighteenth centuries. This Baroque form consists of two high-pitched instruments and *continuo*. The high instruments are often violins, flutes, or oboes, and the continuo is the combination of a bass-line instrument (usually the cello) and a keyboard instrument (usually the harpsichord). Hence, in performance, the trio sonata requires four players who play three parts. The harpsichordist was obliged to improvise an accompaniment from chord symbols supplied by the composer rather than playing chords written out (Figure 9.1, p. 164). This bass part with chord numbers or figures is called "figured bass." You recall from our discussion of concerto grosso, page 160, that the trio sonata ensemble frequently constitutes the smaller group, or concertino, which contrasts with the large group, or tutti (Example 9.9).

Figure 9.1   Figured bass

Example 9.9
Corelli: *Sonata da chiesa in E minor,* Op. 3, No. 7,
first movement

    Piano Trio. The piano is frequently added to string groups to extend the range of possible timbres. The piano trio, consisting of violin, cello, and piano, is the most popular of this type of ensemble. The piano trio probably developed from the trio sonata; however, the cello has a great deal more independence in the piano trio than in the trio sonata, because in the latter it played only a bass line in the continuo part. Also, the piano is capable of greater ranges of tone color and dynamics than the harpsichord.

    The four-movement sonata cycle of the symphony and string quartet prevails in the piano trio. The artistic worth of the piano trio depends on the composer's ability to maintain the integrity of each instrument, rather than mirroring the piano part in the strings. Beethoven's *Piano Trio in B-flat,* Op. 97 (*Archduke*), and Ravel's *Piano Trio in A minor* are fine examples of this form.

    Other Ensembles. The *piano quartet* and *quintet,* consisting of trio or quartet of strings plus piano, are also popular chamber groups: for example, Mozart's *Piano Quartet in E-flat,* K. 493; Schubert's *Quintet in A,* Op. 114 (*Trout*).

    Other instruments, such as clarinet, flute, or oboe, are sometimes used with the string groups. The term "clarinet quintet" thus refers to string quartet plus clarinet, as in Mozart's famous *Clarinet Quintet in A,* K. 581.

    Other popular chamber ensembles are made up of groups of instruments within families, such as brass, string, woodwind, even percussion choirs. The *woodwind quintet,* comprising flute, oboe, clarinet, French horn, and bassoon, is especially common. A good twentieth-century example of this ensemble is Hindemith's *Kleine Kammermusik,* Op. 25.

Modern Chamber Music

    Twentieth-century composers appear to be as interested in chamber groups as in large orchestras. There are many twentieth-century compositions for the standard chamber ensembles. But the modern composer also seeks variety in unusual combinations of instrumental color. The result is a large collection of works for unique chamber groups. Here is a sampling of these new scorings:

Stravinsky: *L'histoire du Soldat (The Soldier's Tale)*, 1918

violin, double bass, clarinet, bassoon, cornet, trombone, and battery of percussion (7 players in all)

Les Noces (The Wedding), 1917–23

four pianos and percussion

Septet, 1953

clarinet, horn, bassoon, piano, violin, viola, and cello

Schoenberg: *Pierrot Lunaire (Moonstruck Pierrot)*, 1912

contralto soloist, flute (piccolo), clarinet (bass clarinet), violin (viola), cello, and piano (5 players, 8 instruments)

Berg: *Chamber Concerto*, 1923–25

violin, piano, and thirteen other instruments

Summary

As we encounter more and more live and recorded music, we begin to realize that the vast majority of it is performed by standard ensembles. By far the most important and the most popular instrumental ensemble is the symphony orchestra, an ensemble of approximately one hundred players, which is the most versatile of all musical performance media. The makeup of the orchestra has changed considerably in its four-hundred-year development. At first composed mainly of strings, the orchestra gradually developed into a large, balanced ensemble of four individually homogeneous sections: strings, woodwinds, brass, and percussion.

The symphony orchestra performs standard forms, the most important being the symphony, a four-movement work based on the sonata form. Other forms written for the orchestra include concerto, concert overture, tone poem, concerto grosso, and suite.

Smaller instrumental ensembles are categorized as chamber music and, like the symphony, many are standard in their makeup. Frequently the form and the performance ensemble bear the same title. Solo forms include sonata for any solo instrument and character piece for piano. Chamber ensembles include the string quartet, trio sonata, piano trio, woodwind quintet, and a variety of others.

Suggested Works for Additional Listening

Solo Concerto

Beethoven: *Piano Concerto No. 3 in C minor*, Op. 37

Mendelssohn: *Violin Concerto in E minor*, Op. 64

Multiple Concertos
Beethoven: *Triple Concerto in C, Op. 56, for piano, violin, cello, and orchestra*
Mozart: *Concerto in E-flat (for Two Pianos and Orchestra), K. 365*

Tone Poem
Debussy: *Prelude to the Afternoon of a Faun*
Respighi: *The Pines of Rome*
R. Strauss: *Till Eulenspiegel's Merry Pranks*
          Death and Transfiguration

Concerto Grosso
Handel: *Concertante in C*

Suite
Bach: *Four Orchestral Suites*
Stravinsky: *Petroushka*
Tchaikovsky: *Nutcracker Suite*

Sonata
Beethoven: *Piano Sonata in C minor, Op. 13 (Pathétique)*
Brahms: *Violin Sonata in G, Op. 78*
Mozart: *Sonata in A minor, K. 310*

Character Piece
Chopin: *Nocturne in E-flat, Op. 9, No. 2*
Debussy: *Reflets dans l'eau (Reflections on the Water)*

Orchestra and String Quintet
Barber: *Adagio for Strings, Op. 11*
Schubert: *String Quintet in C, Op. 163*

Piano Trio
Ravel: *Piano Trio*

Piano Quartet and Quintet
Mozart: *Piano Quartet in E-flat, K. 493*
Schubert: *Quintet in A, Op. 114 (Trout)*

Clarinet Quintet
Mozart: *Clarinet Quintet in A, K. 581*

Woodwind Quintet
Hindemith: *Kleine Kammermusik, Op. 25*

Modern Chamber Groups
Berg: *Chamber Concerto*
Schoenberg: *Pierrot Lunaire*
Stravinsky: *L'histoire du Soldat, Les Noces, Septet*

Plate 19. Martini, Simone, *Christ Carrying the Cross,* Musée du Louvre, Paris. This fourteenth-century painting lacks a strong feeling of depth since the figures in the foreground and the background are the same size (see p. 183).

Plate 20. Fra Angelico and Fra Filippo Lippi, *The Adoration of the Magi,* National Gallery of Art, Washington, D. C., Samuel H. Kress Collection. Discovery of the principles of perspective added depth to Renaissance paintings, just as the consistent use of triadic harmony added harmonic depth to Renaissance music (see pp. 183, 186).

Plate 21. David, Jacques Louis, *The Oath of the Horatii,* The Toledo Museum of Art, Toledo, Ohio, gift of Edward Drummond Libbey, 1950. Order, balance, simplicity, and symmetry—here achieved by the symmetrical arrangement of the figures—facilitate precise expression of meaning and are characteristic of the Classical period in music and art (see p. 194).

Plate 22. Goya, Francisco de, *El Aquelarre (The Witches' Sabbath),* Museo del Prado, Madrid. Ambiguous, personal symbolism, the sense of the "strangeness of beauty," and the visionary quality apparent in this work are often characteristic of Romantic music and art (see p. 201).

Plate 23. Monet, Claude, *Rouen Cathedral, Tour d'Albane: Early Morning,* Museum of Fine Arts, Boston, Massachusetts. The style characteristics of Impressionist art—lack of strong line and specific detail, subdued and subtle language, creation of a total impression rather than a direct statement—parallel those of Impressionist music (see p. 211).

Plate 24. Van Gogh, Vincent, *Road with Cypress and Stars,* Rijksmuseum Kröller-Müller, Otterlo. The intensity achieved in this Expressionist painting by the rough texture, strong colors, and violent movement is also characteristic of Expressionist music, which often takes as its subject the nightmarish world of the subconscious or supernatural (see p. 212).

Chapter 10

Combinations:
Vocal and Experimental

The following recordings should be at hand for listening in connection with this chapter.

Mahler: *Symphony No. 2 in C minor*
Schubert: *Der Erlkönig*
Mozart: *Ave Verum Corpus,* motet
Morley: "Sing we and chant it," madrigal
Wagner: Prelude to *Die Meistersinger von Nürnberg*
Mendelssohn: *Elijah*
Bach: *Cantata No. 4 (Christ lag in Todesbanden)*
Palestrina: *Pope Marcellus Mass*
Varèse: *Poème Electronique*
Stockhausen: *Zyklus*

Vocal music dominated most of music history, from antiquity to the mid-eighteenth century. Yet, when you go to concerts or listen to records today, most of what you hear is instrumental music. It was only after 1600 that instruments were developed to the high level of sophistication which enabled composers to experiment with the idiomatic possibilities of their individual timbres. Instrumental music thus rose to a position of prominence equal to vocal music in the Baroque period, 1600–1750. Then, after 1750, instrumental music eclipsed vocal music, which never has regained its former prominent position.

Vocal music did not really suffer a decline after 1750; it was simply overshadowed by the remarkable growth of instrumental music. During the eighteenth century, instruments were technically developed and standardized, and instrumental music was composed largely under court patronage. By the end of the eighteenth century, musical performance was shifting from the court to the public concert hall. Vocal music had always been composed primarily for the opera or for the church. With the decline of the church as a political and social force, and the consequent decline of sacred music, composers turned their attention to the new demands for music in the public concert hall.

Opera, on the other hand, has held its ground as a prominent form since its inception in 1600. Although modern composers have concentrated on instrumental music, operas continue to be written and performed today. However, the operas performed today are mainly those written in the nineteenth century.

A number of compositions for chorus and orchestra have appeared since Beethoven's *Symphony No. 9 in D minor,* Op. 125 (*Choral Symphony*) and, happily, are finding a place in today's concert halls. For example, Mahler's *Symphonies No. 2 in C minor, No. 3 in D minor,* and *No. 8 in E-flat* are choral symphonies.

Vocal Forms

We shall examine the common vocal ensembles and their forms as they are encountered in the concert hall, the opera house, the church, or the recital hall.

Solo Voice

Art Song. The simplest and most familiar type of vocal music is the solo voice, usually combined with an accompanying instrument or group of instruments. Compositions for solo voice, written to be performed in the concert or recital hall, are called art songs. A great deal of song literature is available in each voice range. Accompaniment is occasionally orchestral, but is usually provided by the piano which, as in the instrumental sonata, achieves considerable individuality and independence. Rather than merely supporting the voice, the piano "cooperates" with it.

Song has been present in all recorded history of music, but never with such splendid treatment and never so popular as in the nineteenth century, the Romantic period. The time was right for the intimate, personal quality characteristic of the art song. Selecting the most elegant and expressive poetry of the period, including that of Shelley, Keats, Goethe, and Heine, composers attempted to wed their music to the words in order to intensify poetic meaning. One of the most successful attempts is *Der Erlkönig* by Schubert. The effort is so successful, in fact, that if we are given the basic plot of the poem we can follow the story line even when the song is sung in an unfamiliar language. The poem tells of a father riding home through a storm and carrying his dying son. Death, in pursuit, plies the youth with promises and gifts and finally wins him at the journey's end. The singer portrays all four characters: the narrator, the father, the son, and the Erlking who is the symbol of Death.

Der Erlkönig is an example of a *through-composed* song; that is, it is composed straight through without repetition of stanzas. The other type of art song is *strophic,* which repeats the same music for each stanza of the poem. An example of strophic art song is Schubert's *Der Wegweiser.*

An excellent example of art song written for solo voice with orchestral accompaniment is Mahler's *Songs of a Wayfarer,* No. 2.

Aria. The aria is an elaborate, dramatic piece for solo voice incorporated in such large choral forms as opera, oratorio, and cantata. The aria is usually in three-part, ABA form. Its function in each of the larger forms will be discussed later in the chapter.

The aria is usually characterized by lyric contours and dramatic treatment. Most composers have designed their arias as independent compositions with their own integrity, which allows for performance outside the original context. The aria "O Patria Mia," from the opera *Aïda* (Example 10.1) is often performed separately in recital.

Example 10.1

Verdi: "O Patria Mia," from *Aïda*

Recitative. The solo voice also performs the recitative, an episode in free form commonly used in conjunction with the aria. The character of the recitative is declamatory: it is very close to speech, partly because the function is to convey extended text. The result is a relatively rapid articulation of words over a simple skeleton accompaniment. For an example of recitative look ahead to Mozart's recitative and aria from *Don Giovanni* (Example 10.4).

Vocal Ensemble

Chorus. Composers have long experimented with combinations of voices and of voices with instruments. The most important vocal ensemble is the *chorus* or *choir,* a large group, normally twenty to eighty singers, in which the voice parts (usually four) are equally balanced. Though the orchestra possesses great variety of timbre, it cannot produce the special timbre of the chorus. In addition, the chorus is capable of providing text. So there is a great body of music that combines chorus and orchestra, thereby giving a special, added dimension to each.

Voices, like instruments, can be combined in many ways; there are choruses for women, for men, for children, for mixed voices. A chorus frequently performs with piano or organ accompaniment, though it can also perform *a cappella* (without accompaniment), or with an instrumental ensemble or even a full orchestra. The chorus performs *a cappella* the opening bars of the excerpt from *Messiah* in Example 10.2 and is then joined by the orchestra, providing us with the opportunity to compare the difference in tone color.

Example 10.2

Handel: "Since by Man Came Death," from *Messiah*

> *Small Ensembles.* Small vocal ensembles consisting of solo voices,
> that is, one voice singing each part, take on a character different from
> the chorus in which a large number of voices sing each part, just as
> chamber music differs from orchestral music. The individual voices
> are more agile and independent, and the combination of voices is
> more intricate. Although the large chorus can produce a massive
> sound, the ensemble is capable of much more complicated textures.
> Opera contains many examples of these brilliant solo ensembles.
> Example 10.3 is one of the most famous.

Example 10.3

Bizet: "Écoute, écoute, compagnon," from *Carmen*

Simple Forms

There are at least two standard forms performed by chamber ensembles which usually employ one voice (or very few voices) to a
part—the *motet* and the *madrigal.* Both therefore fall into a category
of vocal music similar to instrumental chamber music.

Motet. The motet was an extremely important form in the thirteenth through the eighteenth centuries; indeed, motets are still
being composed and performed today. Although the term is applied
to various types of composition, in general, *motet* can be defined as
an unaccompanied, religious choral composition either of single
movement design such as Mozart's *Ave Verum,* or of a larger, composite form such as Bach's *Jesu, meine Freude.* The motet is usually
polyphonic in texture, and in some early motets each voice sang a
different text.

Madrigal. Madrigal, a secular part song for unaccompanied mixed
voices, may be considered the secular counterpart of the motet. The
madrigal, an important form in sixteenth- and seventeenth-century
music, has received renewed interest in twentieth-century performance. The character of a madrigal is typically light, the text frequently depicting idyllic themes.

Most madrigals heard in concert today are scored for four to six
voice parts. They are free in design, containing both homophonic
and polyphonic passages which usually alternate. The intricate polyphonic textures and the articulation of the poetic text call for performance by a small group. In fact, some of the finest recordings of madrigals are performed with one voice for each voice part. Each part
has independence and agility comparable to the parts in the string
quartet. The madrigal is thus challenging and rewarding to sing.

In many madrigals, such as Morley's "Sing we and chant it," the poetic text is set in homophonic sections. The polyphonic sections, where text is more difficult to understand, are devoted to mere syllables—fa la la. When the voices sing syllables instead of words, they function almost instrumentally.

Composite Forms

Most of the important vocal forms are combinations of various smaller ones in which solo voice, chorus, and vocal and instrumental timbres are combined into large composite forms. The most important of these standard composite types are the *opera, oratorio, cantata,* and *Mass.*

Opera. The opera is the most prodigious art form ever to be developed anywhere. It is an extended dramatic musical work employing singers, orchestra, dancers, scenery, lighting, staging, costumes. It has been called by some a bizarre, monstrous conglomeration of various art forms, the result of which is far from artful. It has been called by others the most perfect of art forms because it successfully combines many different art forms. It has been called any number of things, even by those who have never seen one. Opera remains, nevertheless, the most important vocal composite form of all time.

The design of opera varies somewhat from one style period to the next, but a special kind of dramatic flow is characteristic in all. When drama is set to music, an ebb and flow of dramatic action is created through *recitative* and *aria,* two distinct forms within the larger operatic framework. Most of the dramatic action takes place during the recitative, when an extraordinary amount of text or *libretto* is delivered, accompanied by very simple musical background. The aria is more reflective than active. It usually follows the recitative and is quite the opposite in character: the dramatic action pauses while the singer or singers perform the elaborate three-part song. After the aria, customary applause and polite bows interrupt before the action resumes. And so the dramatic flow continues: recitative followed by aria, action followed by reflection.

Example 10.4

Mozart: Recitative and aria "Il mio tesoro," from
Don Giovanni

Many ensembles appear throughout opera to enhance the mood or provide musical contrast. The chorus in the opening of Act IV in *Carmen,* for example, presents the hubbub in the square in Seville before the bullfight.

Example 10.5

Bizet: *Carmen,* Act IV, opening

The famous quartet from Verdi's *Rigoletto* illustrates one of the more fascinating examples of solo ensembles performed by leading characters. It typifies the fantastic drama which frequents the world of opera. The quartet is divided in half—the two groups, one outside a tavern and the other inside the tavern, sing about altogether different things. Totally unrealistic, the musical result is nevertheless a masterpiece.

Example 10.6
Verdi: *Rigoletto*, Quartet, Act IV

The operatic orchestra is more than mere accompaniment to the singers; it cooperates with the voices, but it also supplies a good deal of the musical material on its own. This is particularly evident in the overtures, dances, and instrumental passages between acts. Indeed, opera composers usually display great interest in the art of orchestration. Wagner, an opera composer also known as an orchestral innovator, calls for a full symphonic orchestra in his operas. The overture to *Die Meistersinger von Nürnberg* is one of the best examples of the full opera orchestra in the literature.

The best way to learn about opera is to listen to one, perhaps *Carmen*, by Bizet. The dramatic content in *Carmen* is as strong as the music; it has good plot and character development, excellent music and, furthermore, drama and music that are well suited to each other. Because the form is conceived both as a visual and aural art, merely listening to a recording does not do justice to opera. If it is at all possible, try to *see* it. Also, it is a good idea to read the story beforehand, even if the opera is performed in English. Then you will be able to follow the dramatic action despite its intermittent dramatic flow.

In most operas the music is continuous, and there is little, if any, spoken dialogue. This calls for a great deal of stamina on the part of the singers and players, but it also has important implications for drama. Spoken dialogue tends to make the drama more realistic, but composers were interested in maintaining the dramatic content through musical means. In the past century, beginning with Wagner and Verdi's late operas, there has been increasing interest in this wedding of drama and music. Composers began to deal with the question of how to keep the opera a musical form and at the same time make it dramatically plausible. They have tried to make the opera as realistic as possible, despite the improbability in real life, for example, of a dying woman bursting into song. Consequently, there has been a tendency toward more continuous flow of music in opera, and less stopping and starting with detachable show pieces for accomplished singers. Wagner's ideal, that music should serve the drama, still reigns.

Oratorio. The oratorio holds second rank to the opera in its importance as a vocal form. It is usually based on a religious libretto, whereas the opera is usually secular. The oratorio has the recitatives, arias, ensembles, and choruses of opera without the dramatic trappings such as scenery, staging, costumes. That is probably the reason for the more limited appeal of oratorio. There is one exception: every December an ever-recurring, ubiquitous phenomenon, Handel's *Messiah,* is performed in every city, village, and hamlet from Bangor to Berkeley, in concert halls, schools, churches, and gymnasiums. One can only guess at the reasons for such a strong tradition— perhaps it is due to the stirring "Hallelujah" Chorus alone. Other excellent oratorios whose performance is less frequent include Bach's *Christmas Oratorio,* Haydn's *The Creation,* Mendelssohn's *Elijah,* and Honegger's *King David.*

Cantata. Like the oratorio, the cantata is largely a sacred form; but because of its wide appeal and artistic merit it has found its way into the concert hall. The cantata is shorter than the oratorio, and most cantatas, especially Bach's, have a somewhat standard order of sections. Among composers of cantatas, J. S. Bach is the most successful. A typical Bach cantata begins with an orchestral prelude and polyphonic *chorale* (a choral piece based on a familiar hymn tune), continues with a number of recitatives, arias, and choruses, and ends with a harmonized chorale. Bach's *Christ lag in Todesbanden* is an excellent example of sacred cantata.

Mass. The Mass is the oldest surviving composite vocal form, dating from about 1300. Its text is taken from the Ordinary of the Roman Catholic liturgy and appears in five parts or movements: Kyrie, Gloria, Credo, Sanctus, Agnus Dei. Even today, composers are setting the Mass to music but its performance is no longer restricted to the church. In fact, most Romantic Masses are meant for performance in the concert hall. Verdi's *Requiem*[13] is operatic in style; the orchestra is scored fully and the arias are as lyric and sweeping as those of his operas. In addition to Bach's *B-Minor Mass,* whose proportions are gigantic, you may wish to listen to Palestrina's *Pope Marcellus Mass,* Mozart's *Requiem,* Schubert's *Mass in G,* and Brahms' *A German Requiem.* The Brahms work is not properly a Mass because the text is freely adapted from the scriptures and sung in German rather than the usual Latin. This excellent work exemplifies late tendencies to secularize the Mass. Recently, the text of the Mass has even been treated to jazz and rock settings.

---

[13] The *Requiem* is a Mass for the dead from which the joyful sections (Gloria and Credo) are omitted and other appropriate texts are added.

Popular Music. The popular songs of today are not so different from art songs. Who is to say that Schubert's songs are more artistic than Lennon's and McCartney's? Except for 150 years or so, probably very little difference exists between the two, either in intent or artistic merit. The earlier music has the advantage of history; the chaff has been winnowed. Only the best examples of song remain in the art song repertoire.

Many popular songs are called "folk" music, a term which has come to mean composed songs, usually ballads or songs of social comment. But the term has historically referred to songs handed down through oral tradition, frequently with national or regional characteristics. They usually deal with elemental human experience, such as love and death, or sometimes with mythical or legendary material. Today, both scholars and performers have taken an interest in preserving the folk tradition by notating and recording the folk music of both the recent and distant past.

In the same vein, we should also mention the comparison between opera, on the one hand, and Broadway musical and operetta, vigorous mutations of opera, on the other. The crucial difference is that the musical is lighter in character, usually comic. It consists mainly of spoken dialogue which takes the place of recitative except where there are brief musical introductions to songs. So the music takes the form of set pieces, usually simple songs and dances, within the context of a play. In opera, the music is more or less continuous and is a major component of the drama.

Experimental Combinations

If you were asked to encapsulate into one word the efforts of twentieth-century composers, it would have to be "experimentalism." And since 1950, composers have experimented with perhaps the most revolutionary medium of expression since the birth of instruments: electronic music.

Electronic Music

Electronic sound generators and magnetic tape rather than conventional instruments are utilized as the media of sound in electronic music. These experiments have resulted in a dramatic expansion of available timbres. Whereas composers of conventional music experiment with musical elements such as melody, harmony, rhythm, and form, composers of electronic music experiment primarily with new timbres. The composer freely manipulates sounds made with electronic equipment, capturing those recorded sounds that he feels are especially appropriate for the work at hand.

At least two subdivisions of electronic music can be delineated: (1) *electronic sounds* devoid of overtones, produced by tone generators, and (2) *musique concrète,* consisting of natural sounds of many types, recorded and manipulated by magnetic tape. Many examples of electronic music contain both electronic sounds and *musique concrète.*

The simpler, and in many ways more fascinating, technique of composing electronic music is the manipulation of recorded sounds. For example, any given sound may be transposed to a different frequency (or pitch) simply by increasing or decreasing the speed of the tape. Ussachevsky illustrates this principle in Example 10.7 by using a single tone, the lowest note on the piano. Notice that as the pitch changes, the duration or length also changes because the tape is moving half as rapidly with each manipulation.

Example 10.7
Ussachevsky: *Transposition*

Ussachevsky also illustrates another technique of electronic tape manipulation called reverberation, by which a sound is repeated several times at decreasing levels of loudness producing an echolike effect. This effect is achieved mechanically by recording the same sound again and again at close time intervals.

Example 10.8
Ussachevsky: *Reverberation*

Composers of electronic music are fascinated by any new kind of sound. One composition by Ussachevsky was inspired by the reverberating click of a switch on a tape recorder. Thus the act of composing electronic music itself perpetrates new discoveries in that realm.

One of the most intriguing examples of electronic music, employing both electronic sounds and *musique concrète,* is *Gesang der Jünglinge,* by Karlheinz Stockhausen. Children's voices were recorded and manipulated and subsequently combined with patterns of pure electronic sounds in the composition of this piece.

Example 10.9
Stockhausen: *Gesang der Jünglinge*

Electronic music composers have begun to deal with the problem of concertizing the new medium by combining electronic sounds with conventional instruments and ensembles. In their attempt to reconcile public taste with the striking sonorities of electronic music, Luening and Ussachevsky have composed a piece for orchestra and tape recorder called *A Poem in Cycles and Bells.* Although not specifically meant to be performed in the concert hall, this piece and others like it have paved the way toward concertizing electronic music in the conventional orchestral setting.

Example 10.10
Luening and Ussachevsky: *A Poem in
Cycles and Bells*

Because it is so new, so radically different from conventional
music in sound, sound production, and composition, electronic
music is best associated with its pioneers: Stockhausen, Varèse, and
Ussachevsky. Electronic music most frequently takes the form of a
single movement. In the interest of unity, a limited range of sound
material is used (one electronic composition was made solely from
the sound of water dripping into a glass). The result resembles the
tone poem discussed in Chapter 9. One of the best examples of this
type of composition is Varèse's *Poème Électronique* composed for
continuous performance at the 1958 World's Fair in Brussels. Careful
and repeated listening will reveal returning motives and consequently concern for formal design and unity.

Electronic music has matured well beyond the primitive experimental stages, and, despite predicted reaction against it, continues
to enchant and intrigue those of us who are receptive to its possibilities.

Chance Music

Chance music (*aleatory*) is that in which some or all of the elements
are undetermined by the composer; something is left to chance.
Chance music, which may use either electronic sounds or conventional instruments, has influenced many areas of contemporary composition. Its most avid exponent, John Cage, has composed his
Imaginary Landscape No. 4 for twelve radios to be switched on or off
according to specified directions. In a piano piece by Cage, the performer may shuffle the pages of music and play them in any order.
Still another of his pieces for piano consists of four minutes and
thirty-three seconds of utter silence. *Zyklus,* by Stockhausen, calls
for a lone performer standing within a ring of percussion instruments with instructions to begin at any point in the circle and continue several times in either direction around the ring.

Film Music

Film music poses unique problems for the composer. Because of
the nature of film, the music which serves it is usually in brief seg-
ments without significant transition from one to another. There can
be no sustained passages unless appropriate to the film. The standard
forms described in Chapter 6 are thus rarely appropriate to film;
except for returning themes or motives, the design of the music
parallels the story line of the film.

Aaron Copland is a successful composer of both concert and film
music. Instead of echoing the scenes, providing mood music, as it
were, Copland supplies vital elements of the film's message. Without

his music, much of the meaning in "Of Mice and Men" and "The Red Pony" would be lost. Also, the music is capable of standing alone, apart from the film.

The most successful film music is that which contributes measurably to the effect of the film. Both film and television music today is in a high state of sophistication in that it appropriately enhances the theme or contributes to the atmosphere. Examples of films in which the music is deliberately appropriate to the geography, atmosphere, and era of the story include "The Man with the Golden Arm," "Bonnie and Clyde," and "The Graduate." We have certainly come a long way since the silent movie theater, when the piano player breathed life into the silent, ghostly figures on the screen. Because of the recent experimental endeavors in film-making, electronic music has proved especially effective for use in both movie and television films.

Even though film music may be performed on record or in concert as distinctive individual compositions, its total artistic merit can be measured only in the movie theater where both visual and aural elements are experienced together as originally intended.

Summary

Although vocal music forms no longer predominate over instrumental forms, many important vocal compositions appear regularly in concert halls or on recordings. Nothing has ever taken the place of vocal music because composers and audiences continue to enjoy both the setting of texts and the special, inimitable timbre of the voice.

Vocal music is easily classified into solo forms and ensemble forms. Solo voice is heard in the art song, aria, and recitative. The vocal ensemble appears in two different forms: the solo ensemble, where one voice sings each part (duets, trios, quartets, and the like, and motet and madrigal), and the large vocal ensemble, where many voices sing each part. More frequently, we encounter the large ensemble, the chorus or choir, which performs composite vocal forms: opera, oratorio, cantata, and the Mass. Of all the vocal forms, opera has always been the most venerable, beginning in 1600 and continuing to the present.

Certain experimental combinations are difficult to classify in a discussion such as this, not only because they are new, but because they are so radically different from what has gone before. Since 1900, composers have been experimenting with every kind of sound medium available to them. Experiments since 1950 have brought about an exciting discovery of musical expression called electronic music. Although the direction of these new discoveries has not yet been determined, it is fairly certain that electronic music has found a place in our world.

Suggested Works for Additional Listening

Choral Symphonies
Mahler: *Symphony No. 3 in D minor,* and *Symphony No. 8 in E-flat*

Art Song
Schumann: "Seit ich ihn gesehen," *Frauenliebe und Leben*

Art Song with Orchestral Accompaniment
Mahler: "Ging heut' morgen über's Feld," *Songs of a Wayfarer,* No. 2

Motet
Bach: *Jesu, Meine Freude*

Madrigal
di Lasso: "My heart doth beg you'll not forget"

Opera
Britten: *Peter Grimes*
Donizetti: *Lucia di Lammermoor*
Puccini: *La Bohème,* Act I
Purcell: *Dido and Aeneas*
Wagner: *Lohengrin*

Oratorio
Bach: *Christmas Oratorio*
Haydn: *The Creation*
Honegger: *King David*

Mass
Brahms: *A German Requiem*
Mozart: *Requiem*
Schubert: *Mass in G*

Electronic Music
Varèse: *Poème Électronique*

Chance Music
Stockhausen: *Zyklus*

Film Music
Copland: "The Red Pony"

Chapter 11

Musical Style:
1450–1750

The following recordings should be at hand for listening in connection with this chapter.

Renaissance

Machaut: *Messe de Nostre Dame*
A madrigal by Morley, Byrd, or Lassus
Josquin des Prez: *Pange Lingua* Mass
Palestrina: "Agnus Dei," from *Missa in festis Apostolorum*
G. Gabrieli: *Ricercare*

Baroque

Handel: *Water Music*
Purcell: *Dido and Aeneas*
Bach: *The Art of Fugue*
      The Well-Tempered Clavier
      B-Minor Mass
Gibbons: "The Silver Swan"
Vivaldi: *Concerto in C for Two Oboes and Two Clarinets*, P. 74
Corelli: *Sonata da Chiesa in E Minor*, Op. 3, No. 7, second movement
Haydn: *String Quartet in D*, Op. 64, No. 5 *(The Lark)*, third movement (Classic)

Musical style is a characteristic and distinctive manner of composing and performing music. Each composer has a relatively consistent style of composition, and so the music of each composer is identifiable—we should be able to tell the difference between music composed by Bach and music composed by Mozart by listening to it. We can do this if we learn to identify the basic, distinctive characteristics of each style.

Difficulty in identification arises when we attempt to discern differences between the styles of, say, Mozart and Haydn, because their music is so similar. This brings us to the problem and peculiarity of style in music and the other arts. Although each composer's style is unique, there exists a decided similarity in the music of composers living and working at the same time. For example, this means that all the music composed from 1750 to 1820 sounds alike when compared to music written at any other time. Consequently, eras in music history are set apart and given names which serve to identify their style. These *style periods* are:

Renaissance	1450–1600
Baroque	1600–1750
Classical	1750–1820
Romantic	1820–1900
Modern	1900–The Present

Each style period begins at a time in history when significant changes in the manner of composing music are taking place. Old styles end, important composers die, and new composers come to prominence because their style is appealing, thus setting new trends and influencing generations of composers to follow.

Although in retrospect some style periods seem to have sprung up overnight, style actually develops slowly and deliberately over a long period of time. There is always a period of transition in which both old and new styles coexist; for this reason, the selection of a style period's beginning or ending date must be arbitrary. For example, the death of Bach (1750) furnishes us with a convenient date on which to end the Baroque period; however, a great many composers during Bach's lifetime were already writing in the radically new mode which was to become the Classical style of Haydn and Mozart. Likewise, the beginning of the Romantic period was marked by a gradual growth of many slightly different musical characteristics resulting in an overlapping of Classical and Romantic styles for several decades.

Historical sociologists could certainly help us with clues to the extramusical factors that influence musical style, because the tenor of society, political structures, and activity in the other arts all greatly affect composers. These combined factors are part of the reason for the similarity of style within one period of time. We shall see evidence of this as we examine each style period.

One more thing: it is said that history repeats itself. In a sense, this can also be said of music history. Musical style seems to alternate in ever-returning cycles around two basic esthetic philosophies, Classical and Romantic. Classical art involves an intellectual approach: controlled, balanced, formal, logical. Romantic art, almost the opposite, involves an emotional approach: free, limitless, ethereal, intuitive.

If we assign one of these basic esthetic philosophies to each style period, we discover that they appear to alternate. The alternation in styles is like a swinging pendulum. When the pendulum swings back, we have entered another style period. In a way, *because* one age is Classical, the next is Romantic and vice versa, each age living in reaction to the previous one.

Keep in mind that this cyclic idea of musical style involves only a basic attitude toward art and not specific style traits. The following list shows the basic esthetic philosophy of each style period:

Renaissance	(Classical)
Baroque	(Romantic)
Classical	(Classical)
Romantic	(Romantic)
Modern	(Classical)

Historians look back, analyze, and designate style periods according to these two classifications. The designations of style periods were all applied artificially, long after the composers shaping them were dead. We know very little about how music historians will evaluate and categorize the music being written at this very moment. They must have the perspective of time and trends in order to assess accurately our present direction. It is a matter of looking back to see where we have been; nobody knows exactly where we are going, but we can speculate that if we are now in a Classical period, we can look forward to a Romantic period.

Renaissance (1450–1600)

The Renaissance movement began in Italy in the fourteenth century and in the next three hundred years spread over the entire European continent. It was preceded by the Medieval period, which lasted roughly from the beginning of polyphony in the ninth century up to 1450. The music of this period was characterized by a lack of harmonic depth and open, stark chords. A representative example is the liturgical drama, *The Play of Daniel*. For the most part, medieval composers were under the control of the Roman Catholic Church; their music was largely sacred and did not reflect much individuality.

The Renaissance, on the other hand, was a time of revival of ancient Roman and Greek culture, especially art and philosophy. Although "Classical" in the sense of the interest in and imitation of an earlier age, practically speaking, the Renaissance represented a great new flowering of the arts. Man found a belief in himself and in the beauty of earthly things in alliance with his still profound religious belief. Art was man's own creation of beauty, visible evidence of his loftiest capabilities.

The nobility, such as the Florentine Medici family, passionately patronized artists and musicians. Artists therefore enjoyed a new position and leisure in society which enabled them to concentrate on their art.

Although we know a good deal about music written before 1450, we rarely encounter it in the concert hall or on recordings. It is for this reason that we begin our chronological discussion of musical style with the Renaissance period.

If we assume that music began with primitive man, it is obvious that today's music—that composed since 1450—represents a relatively brief span in time. Basic musical principles developed in the Renaissance have endured through all style periods to the present; thus, we might say that modern music began in the fifteenth century. One of these principles is the tendency of Renaissance composers to write for four or more balanced voices. Earlier, the common texture was based on three voices without regard for balance. Not only did the voices sing different tunes, they sometimes sang in different languages, occasionally mixing sacred with secular texts. This practice of obscuring texts and tunes within the fabric of a composition fell into disfavor in the Renaissance. Renaissance composers continued to use polyphonic textures, but their polyphony was primarily imitative. Hence, the total sound was more homogeneous than in previous styles because the voices were singing the same text and tunes.

Another reason for calling Renaissance music "modern" is that composers began consistently to base their harmonies on the triad rather than on the open fourth or fifth. Try it on the piano—play first a triad—that is, any three white keys, every other one in succession as in Figure 11.1.

Figure 11.1   Triad (John A. Wolters photos)

Then play a fourth or a fifth—that is, two white keys four or five tones away from each other as in Figures 11.2 and 11.3.

The triad is immediately familiar and full-sounding. The fourth and fifth, especially if they are played in a series, are stark, open, and generally unfamiliar, although they are occasionally heard in modern works. Compare the degree of harmonic depth in Machaut's *Messe de Nostre Dame* (14th c.)[14] with any of the sixteenth-century English

[14] See *Masterpieces of Music Before 1750,* Carl Parrish and John F. Ohl, W. W. Norton, 1951, pp. 38–39.

madrigals. Machaut's music lacks harmonic depth because it is based on the open fourth and fifth instead of the triad heard in the sixteenth-century madrigal. This new harmonic depth in the Renaissance might be compared to a parallel development in art called *perspective*. The two paintings in Plate 19 and Plate 20 (following p. 166) illustrate the difference in perspective between fourteenth- and fifteenth-century art.

Both paintings show figures coming through an archway, but the later work achieves more depth by using principles of perspective such as smaller figures in the background and lines converging to a point in the distance. The earlier work reveals less depth because the figures in the distance are the same size as those in the foreground. Both perspective in art and triadic harmony in music have been dominant forces from the Renaissance through the Romantic eras. Although modern painters and composers have experimented in new directions, these basic principles exist in much art and music still enjoyed by the general public.

As in the Middle Ages, the church remained a dominant force in the Renaissance. Although a great many artists worked under court patronage, their subject matter continued to be primarily religious. Most of the music of this period was written for voices with sacred text. But the Renaissance also marked the beginning of the Protestant Reformation under the leadership of Martin Luther in the second decade of the sixteenth century. The influence on music, although its full impact was not felt until the Baroque period, was much the

Figure 11.2 Fourth   **Figure 11.3** Fifth

same as that on general practices in the church. Latin began to be discarded in favor of the vernacular. The music was simplified so that it could be sung by the congregation, and it became somewhat less liturgical. The result was the development in the Protestant church of hymns, simple tunes based on scriptural texts sung in the vernacular by the congregation.

The Reformation sparked the Counter Reformation in Rome, a move by the Catholic Church to strengthen itself by reaffirming and reforming traditional practices. Hence, there were two trends: the

Reformation which paved the way for the Baroque style, and the Counter Reformation which shaped the style of Renaissance music until the death of Palestrina in 1594.

Performance Practices

Much of the Renaissance music surviving today was written to be sung in the church as part of the service. But in addition to Masses and sacred motets, there were secular part songs composed in the motet style (called motets or madrigals) and secular songs (usually French chansons) performed at court. Public concerts as we know them today were unknown. Instruments were used to accompany voices in the church and dances outside the church. Because of the predominance of church music, the organ is considered the principal instrument of the period.

Instruments were used primarily to double voice parts. And since composers did not designate which instruments were to be used for each part, instruments were employed whenever and wherever performers desired. The keyboard instruments, the harpsichord and clavichord, were developed during this period and became very popular, as did the lute. Occasionally, music was written for undesignated instruments and performed without voices. Some instrumental forms of the period include *ricercar, canzona,* and dance music. Giovanni Gabrieli, Merulo, and Bull were among the composers of instrumental music.

Style Characteristics

We can identify Renaissance music easily by simply remembering that most of it is four- or five-part, unaccompanied, sacred vocal music. It also helps to know that Renaissance composers were interested in fine *balance* between voices and *clarity* of sound.

More prominent than anything else in the musical style is the relentless use of *imitation*. Except for temporary contrasting sections of isometric, or chordal, scoring, the voices forever chase one another, each independent, each bearing strong melodic integrity. For the most part the beat is steady. The total resulting sound is an intricately woven fabric of fine, almost transparent, polyphonic texture marked by the unmistakable clarity of human voices, expressive in religious conviction but controlled in emotional outcry. This is, after all, a "Classical" period.

In the high Renaissance (sixteenth century), the secular madrigal fully matured. The compositional style was basically the same as that of sacred music, but a notable stylistic feature of these madrigals was that they relied heavily on pictorialism, or word painting. Madrigal composers used musical imitation of nature or animal sounds, or strikingly discordant intervals on words like "death," "Hell," or "despair" to give what they felt was a highly expressive enrichment of the text.

The following compositions represent some of the most important Renaissance composers: *Pange Lingua* Mass, by Josquin des Prez, "Agnus Dei," from *Missa in festis Apostolorum*, by Palestrina, and *Ricercare*, by Gabrieli.

Even though the music of the Renaissance is considered to be "modern," it still may sound archaic, unfamiliar. Part of the reason for this difference is that the *church modes* had not completely faded from use. Further justification for designating the Renaissance as the beginning of modern music is the gradual selection of two modes, the Aeolian (minor) and the Ionian (major), as the basis for our system of tonality. If we remember that the minor scale is derived from the same succession of tones found in the major scale, we can see that the whole of Western music is actually composed after a system of a single set of tones, a system which lasted from 1450 to the present and which, although threatened in the last seventy years, has never been totally replaced by other systems.

Summary

In short, we can expect music of the Renaissance period to be sacred, imitative, vocal music based on modal scales. Additional spice was provided by instruments, most of which were not technically perfected as we know them today, especially in the dynamic sense; the instruments were not yet capable of the intensity of sound to which we are accustomed in music today. This contributes to the characteristically subdued sound of Renaissance music.

The Renaissance period was a time when the Mass, motet, and madrigal enjoyed their most fruitful period of development and performance. Principal composers of Masses and motets were Dufay, Josquin, Lassus, and Palestrina. Some important composers of madrigals were Morley, Byrd, Marenzio, and Gesualdo, but they enjoyed a large company of colleagues in madrigal composition; in fact, all of the noted composers of the sixteenth century wrote madrigals.

Suggested Works for Listening That Typify Renaissance Music

Josquin: *Missa Hercules dux Ferrariae*
Dufay: *Se la face ay pale* (Mass)
Gabrieli: *Aria della battaglia*
Lassus: *Requiem*, Madrigals
Palestrina: "Adoramus te, Christe," from *Missa sine nomine*

Baroque Period (1600–1750)

A hundred and fifty years is a long time for one style of music to hold sway. Both the Renaissance and Baroque periods extended for that amount of time. Indeed, there are some who assert that the Baroque period should be divided into three style periods, early, middle, and late, each with its unique characteristics. Yet these divisions are all a part of the larger designation, Baroque—with all the differences, one style prevails. It was during these hundred and fifty years that the basic musical principles which began in the previous era were fully established. It was during this time also that instruments as we know them were fully developed, that the major-minor system of tonality was completely adopted, and that instrumental and vocal music attained equal stature. Opera began and flowered, opening the door to public concerts for the first time.

The feudal system of land ownership continued to wane as did the influence of the Roman Catholic Church. Both factors contributed to the growing importance, power, and liberty of the common man. All along the social ladder from serf to king, social forces were contributing to man's growing sense of individualism. The Protestant Reformation gave each person responsibility for his own salvation; here started a long, gradual rise in the importance and power of the individual.

The rise of the individual has implications for the composition of music. Art in all forms began to express the individual artist's feelings about his world instead of reflecting conventional attitudes imposed by the Establishment, Church and State. It makes sense, therefore, for the Baroque period to be called a "Romantic" period—one in which expression in art is tempered by feelings and strong emotions, inspired by spiritual experience.

The word "Baroque" was applied (derogatorily at first) to the music of the 1600–1750 period because of its lavish, highly decorative treatment. It was ornamental, full-sounding, and grandiose. The Baroque era in architecture and painting extends through the same time period as music and can be described in the same terms. The interior of the pilgrimage church Vierzehnheiligen is highly decorative, ornamental and grandiose (Figure 11.4). If only we could hear a performance of Bach's *B-Minor Mass* in this church, how appropriately the music would parallel the architecture! The painting, *The Horrors of War* (Plate 15, following p. 134), illustrates the Baroque spirit in its lavish, extravagant treatment. Compare it with the Renaissance painting in Plate 20; the Baroque painting expresses strong feeling through its symbolism and turbulent movement. The Renaissance painting reflects a control of emotion through its statue-like figures and peaceful subject matter.

Figure 11.4 Vierzehnheiligen, a pilgrimage church near Bamberg, Germany (Marburg photo)

Performance Practices

Probably the most significant change in performance practice in the Baroque period is the pervasive use of the figured bass. A more descriptive term is *basso continuo*, which indicates the practice of improvising over a "continuous bass" line. Although the technique of improvisation varied within the period and from country to country, it was a highly developed art and an essential feature of instrumental and vocal music.

Although the first public opera house was built in Venice in 1637, and some attempts were made later in the seventeenth century to bring music into the concert hall for the public, Baroque music remained essentially a product for the consumption of the nobility and the church. Composers made their living through aristocratic patronage and as church musicians.

Music was almost always performed in conjunction with social events, such as dining, dancing, worshipping, ceremonies, and festivals. Once in a while, the lowly serf had a taste of concert music. When George I took a long trip up the Thames River accompanied by his entire court entourage, one barge in the splendid flotilla contained an orchestra conducted by Georg Friedrich Handel himself. His new composition, *Water Music,* was heard all the way from London to Chelsea and back by the people lining the banks.

The only other chance for the common man to encounter concert music might have been the opera. It is doubtful however that he ever got to the opera house. After all, it was not free, and because it was totally out of his realm of experience, he would not be inclined to go there in the first place. The idea that music is meant to be enjoyed only by the upper classes has never really died out completely. Attending an opera today is tantamount to attending a gathering of the elite, with its parade of furs, diamonds, and fine clothes.

Style Characteristics

Polyphony, in a highly refined state, continued to be the predominant texture throughout the Baroque period. However, in 1600, monodic music had its beginnings with the rise of opera. As the term suggests, *monody* is a single voice with simple accompaniment, such as an aria, recitative, or art song. The mother of this invention was the necessity of declamation. The treatment of text is one of the most startling reversals in style between the Renaissance and Baroque periods. In the Renaissance, music was the master of the word; in the Baroque, the word became master of the music. Of course, in both eras the text was extremely important, but the early Baroque theorists rejected polyphony altogether on the grounds that it hampered the understanding of the text. They created opera as an art form which would support the theory that it was essential to make the text or libretto understandable. Monody provides listeners with the most understandable musical method of textual declamation. Compare the simple statement of the aria, "When I am laid in earth" from Purcell's opera *Dido and Aeneas* with the madrigal "The Silver Swan" by Gibbons. Although both are in English, the text in Purcell's aria is easily understood whereas the text in Gibbons' madrigal is complicated by the polyphonic textures of five voices moving along at different time intervals.

Early Baroque composers, intent on making the text as clear as possible, reduced the performing medium to one voice and simplified the accompanying textures so that nothing in the musical structure would stand in the way of the words.

But polyphony was not to die. Although it may have lost its prominence to the early monodists, it soon regained its stature to the extent that the Baroque period is now thought of as a great polyphonic era whose greatest composers, Bach and Handel, were masters of the art of counterpoint. In any case, all the Baroque composers retained a reverence for the word, and even the best counterpoint of the age reveals the intent to express the text above all.

Imitative counterpoint continued to be a favorite compositional device throughout the Baroque period. It culminated in the refined instrumental form, fugue, which found an appropriate medium of expression in the organ and harpsichord. These two instruments are constructed in such a manner that the manuals (harpsichord) or ranks of pipes (organ) provide the symmetrical balance required between voices in imitative counterpoint. Unsurpassed examples of fugue may be found in *The Art of Fugue*[15] and in *The Well-Tempered Clavier*,[16] both composed by J. S. Bach, the most revered composer of fugue in the history of music.

Doctrine of the Affections. In spite of differences in style found in Baroque music the unanimity that exists was due in part to a commonly accepted theory known as the "doctrine of the affections." Where Renaissance composers treated words and phrases pictorially, Baroque composers felt that entire sections or even entire pieces should express one idea, that is, one emotion or "affect." The code dictated that each feeling to be expressed should be represented by a specific, stereotyped musical figure. Musical ideas, such as melodic contours, rhythmic agitation, harmony, even intervals, were categorized according to the emotion or feeling to be depicted. For example, descending figures depict grief and ascending figures depict joy, and either one may serve as basic material for an entire piece. Recall the "Crucifixus" and "Et Resurrexit" from Bach's *B-Minor Mass* (Examples 3.27 and 3.28). These pieces reflect the moods of grief and joy by means of descending and ascending figures, respectively.

Another factor which contributes to the single affect in a passage of music is *terraced dynamics*, where the changes in dynamic level are abrupt rather than gradual and the loudness does not vary within a section. Terraced dynamics with their sudden changes in loudness reflect the mechanical limitations of the harpsichord and Baroque organ in which dynamic level is determined by the number of tones sounding rather than by the force with which the keys are struck, as is the case with the piano.

Terraced dynamics are expressed in *concertato,* the alternation of large and small instrumental groups. If everyone plays with the same intensity there will be a dynamically terraced contrast between large and small groups. The terraced treatment of dynamics, mainly in the form of concertato, is found everywhere in Baroque music. The final movement of Vivaldi's *Concerto in C for Two Oboes and Two Clarinets* well illustrates the concertato principle.[17] You may also have noticed concertato effect between the orchestra and chorus in "Et Resurrexit" from Bach's *B-Minor Mass* (Example 3.28).

Movement. The figured bass, or basso continuo, had implications beyond improvisation. The constant motion from pitch to pitch in

[15] Examples 3.42, 3.43, and 4.36.
[16] Examples 4.48, 6.7, 7.21, and 7.33.
[17] See also Example 9.3.

the bass line provides an aurally distinguishable symbol of Baroque music. Compare Corelli's *Sonata da chiesa in E minor,* Op. 3, No. 7, second movement, with Haydn's *String Quartet in D,* Op. 64, No. 5 *(The Lark),* third movement, in terms of the bass line and resulting harmonic movement. It is partly because of the movement of the bass line that Corelli's Baroque music appears to be in continuous driving motion, changing chords sometimes with every beat. The bass line in the Classical example by Haydn exhibits considerable repetition of single tones, causing activity-type movement in a static state. Driving movement is delayed until the bass line changes pitch.[18]

Instrumental Music. By the end of the Renaissance, vocal music had evolved to a state of relative refinement, both in performance and in forms. Instruments were used sparingly in performance, limited to playing occasional vocal parts, and used without regard to timbre. The important thing was the musical line; it did not matter who or what performed it.

In the Baroque period, especially in opera, instruments were called more and more into use as pure accompaniment rather than to double the voice parts. They had parts of their own to play. Accordingly, more and more demands were made upon instruments— brilliance of tone, sustained playing, and virtuoso performance to match that of the voices. As old instruments were refined and new ones developed, composers began writing for specific instrumental ensembles. We referred to this activity earlier as "idiomatic" writing. As music was composed with specific instrumental timbres in mind, it marked the beginning of the art of orchestration. The most important outcome of this activity was the homogeneous grouping of instruments into families and the development of specific performing ensembles and forms. Among the best known of these Baroque forms are the trio sonata, the concerto, and the suite.

Vocal Music. The Renaissance vocal forms, the Mass, motet, and madrigal, continued their popularity through most of the Baroque period. New vocal forms gained favor and were more frequently composed and performed. Opera, the first of these new forms, gained immediate popularity, as evidenced by the considerable number of compositions to appear throughout the period. Opera houses sprang up everywhere—from Italy to France, Germany, and England. Monteverdi was the foremost composer of early Baroque opera, and Handel the foremost of the late Baroque. Some of the best operas of the period include Monteverdi's *Orfeo,* Purcell's *Dido and Aeneas,* Handel's *Rinaldo,* and Pergolesi's *La serva padrona,* a comic opera in

---

[18] See also Examples 9.9 and 7.3.

two acts designed to appear in the intermissions of a three-act serious opera. By Handel's time (1685–1759) the opera was firmly established as a three-act form and as a popular medium of musical entertainment.

The oratorio developed in conjunction with the operas, as evidenced by its similar form. Although oratorios usually have sacred subjects, they are not liturgical music; they are intended to be performed in the concert hall. They are "theatrical" in the sense that they generally have a plot and dramatic music similar to opera. As we noted before, in performance the oratorio differs from the opera in that there are no costumes, special effects, or dramatic action. Handel is known as a prominent composer both of operas and of oratorios. His oratorios include *Messiah* (Example 5.9), *Judas Maccabaeus,* and *Israel in Egypt.* Bach, who never wrote an opera, composed the *Christmas Oratorio.*

Influenced largely by the monodic style of the early operas, the cantata appeared first in secular form, essentially replacing the Renaissance madrigal. It was in the hands of J. S. Bach that the sacred cantata as we know and hear it today was fully developed. Bach's nearly three hundred cantatas contain the same basic forms as opera and oratorio, namely, recitatives, arias, and choruses. But a cantata is much shorter than an oratorio and has a more standard arrangement of individual pieces. Almost all of Bach's cantatas open with a polyphonic chorale and close with a homophonic chorale (Examples 7.5 and 7.7).

Rise of Tonality. During the Baroque period, tonality was firmly established. The modes were abandoned in favor of the major and minor system, and the idea of "key" was formulated. That the key of C major is exactly like the keys of D major, E major, and so on, in relationship of tones within each scale, is not so important in itself; the most startling innovation resulting from this new conception was the idea of modulation. Beginning a composition in the key of C major and modulating briefly into related keys such as G major, C minor, or D major, widened the spectrum of harmonic possibilities. This expanded harmonic universe made it possible for a composer to provide much greater variety while still maintaining thematic unity. This idea provides us with at least one clue to explain the dearth of pre-Baroque music in today's concert repertory.

Bach's *Well-Tempered Clavier,* examples of which we have heard in previous chapters, represents one of the first attempts to experiment with a systematic approach to key. Bach included in this collection a prelude and a fugue in every key, major and minor, making twenty-four preludes and twenty-four fugues in all.[19]

[19] Examples 3.2, 3.54, 4.44, 4.48, 6.6, 6.7, 7.21, and 7.33.

Summary

In the concert hall, you may recognize a Baroque piece by its polyphonic textures, imitative counterpoint, and terraced dynamics manifest in concertato, a give-and-take between large and small ensembles. The continuous motion of Baroque music is caused by long melodic lines, infrequent cadences, and active basso continuo. We should also expect each section, either an entire piece, an entire movement, or a given passage, to express a single mood or affect in accordance with the commonly accepted theory of the doctrine of the affections.

Although there is not an overabundance of Baroque music on concert programs today, a number of concertos, suites, operas, oratorios, cantatas, or organ pieces are performed in concert halls or in church. Concern for lack of concert performance of Baroque music (and of Renaissance music) has resulted in the formation of numerous societies devoted to the researching and performing of early music. Part of the reason that early music has been relegated to special societies is because of the need for instruments not found in the modern symphony orchestra, including the viols, recorders, harpsichord, and a variety of other wind instruments. But recorders and harpsichords are now being manufactured and played, indicating that Baroque music indeed appeals more and more to twentieth-century audiences.

Suggested Works for Listening That Typify Baroque Music

Concerto Grosso
Vivaldi: *Four Seasons*, Op. 8

Opera
Handel: *Rinaldo*
Monteverdi: *Incoronazione di Poppea*

Oratorio
Bach: *Christmas Oratorio*
Schütz: *The Seven Last Words of Jesus Christ on the Cross*

Organ Works
Buxtehude: Organ works

Pieces for Instruments and Voices
G. Gabrieli: *Sacred Symphonies*

Trio Sonata
Corelli: *Trio Sonata in A*, Op. 4, No. 3

Chapter 12

Musical Style:
1750 to the Present

The following should be at hand for listening in connection with this chapter.

Classical
Mozart: *String Quartet in C, K. 465*
   Symphony No. 41 in G minor
Bach: *Brandenburg Concerto No. 3* (Baroque)

Romantic
Beethoven: *Symphony No. 6 (Pastoral)*
Berlioz: *Symphonie Fantastique*
Liszt: *Les Préludes*
Tchaikovsky: Overture, *Romeo and Juliet*

Modern
Stravinsky: *L'histoire du Soldat*
    Ragtime for Eleven Instruments
    Octet for Wind Instruments
Debussy: *La Mer*
Schoenberg: *Pierrot Lunaire*
    Variations for Orchestra, Op. 31
Berg: *Wozzeck*
Ives: *Symphony No. 4*
Webern: *Symphonie,* Op. 21

Classical Period (1750–1820)

As important as Classical music is today in the concert hall and on recordings, the Classical period lasted for a surprisingly short time. The style spans roughly the time from the death of Bach (1750) to the end of Beethoven's productive output (1820). One reason for its tremendous importance is that the Classical period boasts three towering musical geniuses—Haydn, Mozart, and Beethoven. Part of the reason that the period was so short is that the Classical period in music was out of phase with the Classical period in other art forms. This is not unusual, because musical style ordinarily develops later than the similar style in other art forms.

By 1750, when Classical music was beginning to evolve, Neo-Classical painting—"Neo-Classical" because it recalled the Classical age in Greece and Rome—was already fully established. The philosphers Descartes, Spinoza, Locke, Leibnitz, and Hume, whose ideas set the scene for the Neo-Classical age, dated from the last half of the seventeenth century and the first half of the eighteenth. The major portion of Neo-Classical literature and poetry had already been written. The Neo-Classicists, Swift and Pope, both died before Bach, and Samuel Johnson died in 1784.

By the last half of the eighteenth century, Romantic tendencies were beginning to flower in all the other arts; but, in music, the Classical period was at its zenith. Beethoven (b. 1770) is considered a transitional figure grounded in the Classical tradition but displaying Romantic tendencies in his *Second Symphony*, composed in 1802.

In other arts the Classical period is referred to as the "Age of Reason," or the "Enlightenment." It was the age of Newton, when the great thinkers believed that the universe operated in accordance with a divinely-instituted plan made evident by clearly discernible natural laws. The ultimate judge of what was right and wrong, real or unreal, was man himself. Reason asserted itself over faith, and the age was an eminently *rational* one. The Classicist's approach to art could be described as restrained, orderly, intellectual, formalistic. We find in Classical art, therefore, emphasis on form and symmetrical balance; ideals were economy of means, simplicity, and clarity.

The Classicist believed in the capabilities of man's intellectual prowess. There was a great emphasis on science which fostered such inventions as the steam engine (1760's) and the cotton gin (1795), and such discoveries as electricity (1752) and oxygen (1774). These accomplishments convinced eighteenth-century man that he could accomplish almost anything by the use of his mind, his reason.

Classical art displays the kind of order that is necessary to the scientist and philosopher. The painting by David, Plate 21 (following p. 166) illustrates this order and balance in the symmetrical arrangement of figures—three women on the right, three sons on the left, father in the middle, each group framed by identical arches in the background squarely in the center of the picture. Simplicity is expressed by static figures at rest. The subject matter is typically Neo-Classical harking back to the Classical age of ancient Rome. These characteristics—order, balance, and simplicity—can be found in the music of Haydn and Mozart and Beethoven.

We read and hear a great deal about "form" being a Classical ideal in music. It would almost lead us to think that form or design was not an ideal in other periods of music history, which of course is not true. Baroque composers were concerned with form too, as composers have been in every other style period. The difference in the treatment of form is a matter of emphasis and attitude. The Classical composer was concerned with balance and symmetry between phrases and sections, whereas the Baroque composer was concerned with balance between voices and the way they move. Classical composers emphasized form by simple treatment, transparent homophonic textures, and short phrases. The Classicists saw form itself as beauty, reflecting the beauty of design in Nature. To them the orderly life or work of art was the most beautiful, the most to be admired. On the other hand, the Baroque composer saw form only as a means of presenting other musical ideas. He may have had a text to convey, or he may have been interested in a particular concertato balance. Design merely facilitated that expression. The Classicist was concerned with developing and refining form itself. He concentrated on the design process as an artistic goal.

Remember that one of the most obvious differences between the Classical and Baroque periods is that vocal music was eclipsed by instrumental music. In fact, many of the great works of the Baroque period—its oratorios, cantatas, and operas—are vocal, and most of the great works of the Classical period—its symphonies, chamber music, and concertos—are instrumental. In an age of instrumental music, composers must rely upon something other than text for unity. Classical form supplied music with the unity that text or texture gave to Baroque music. The result was *absolute music*. It was not to tell a story, not for worship, not to accompany a dance, not to praise a king, but music to be heard just for itself.

The symphony is the great symbol of this difference between the Classical and Baroque periods. It is absolute music in its most highly-developed form. It has an orderly pattern involving logical key relationships. Finally, it is pervasive throughout the period; all of the Classicists wrote symphonies for a standard orchestra. In contrast, there was no such predominant standard ensemble or form with which to work in the Baroque period.

The Classical composers' concern for form resulted in standard types of composition. Haydn, Mozart and Beethoven wrote a considerable number of symphonies, concertos, string quartets, piano trios, and sonatas. All of these forms are based on sonata design, the most complex and formal of all. Thus, when we speak of Classical form, we should keep in mind that the term refers to a special kind of balanced, symmetrical form, and to an attitude which treats form as the highest artistic ideal. All other elements of the composer's art must serve its purpose.

The symphony did not suddenly spring up overnight in Mozart's and Haydn's day. There was a period of transition between Baroque and Classical music beginning before Bach died; in fact, Bach's own sons, C. P. E. Bach and W. F. Bach, played a role in this transition. During this transition, the sonata form and the symphony were developed. As the symphony replaced the concerto as the most prominent form, the Classical ideal of balance and contrasting phrases superseded the Baroque concertato principle.

By the time Haydn and Mozart began composing, symphonies, sonatas, and string quartets were already the important musical forms. All that remained for them was to refine and perfect these Classical forms. Haydn (1732–1809) contributed a great deal to this refinement. Although he wrote oratorios and Masses and a few chamber operas, Haydn is known primarily as an instrumental composer. Many of his one hundred four symphonies and eighty-three string quartets are standard fare for today's concert programs. These compositions reveal Haydn as a master craftsman in Classical treatment both of formal design and performing ensembles. They also reveal a coolness and a sense of humor which today is greatly admired.

Mozart (1756–1791) wrote a great deal of important music, both instrumental and vocal, in his short lifetime. It was well-known and influential in his own time, and is flourishing on today's concert and opera programs. Significant as his forty-one symphonies and several string quartets are, probably his most distinctive contributions were his many piano concertos and numerous operas. Mozart's piano concertos, in which he treats the piano and orchestra as equals, were the first of their kind and remain among the most important in the great piano concerto tradition which continues to the present. His operas are frequently performed today and are thought by many to contain Mozart's most delightfully lyric music and perhaps his most inventive orchestration. The most important of these were *Don Giovanni, The Marriage of Figaro, The Abduction from the Seraglio, Così fan tutte,* and *The Magic Flute.*

Haydn and Mozart wrote a great deal more music than is treated here—piano sonatas, other chamber music, songs, Masses, cantatas, and more. By comparison, Beethoven's (1770–1827) creative output may seem small. He too has a long list of miscellaneous works, but he wrote only five piano concertos, twenty-seven string quartets, and nine symphonies. However, all of these works are exceedingly significant, both for the influence they held over the entire nineteenth century and for their frequent concert performance today. Beethoven significantly expanded each Classical form he worked with—each is larger, more intense, and technically more complex than it had ever been before. The late string quartets are extremely difficult to play; the piano concertos are a challenge to any modern pianist; the gigantic *Ninth Symphony* is argued by some to be too difficult to be performed well by anyone, but is admired by all in its noble aspiration. It is easy to see why Beethoven's music and his dynamic personality established him as a hero to the Romantic age.

Performance Practices

The patronage system which had provided a livelihood for composers came to an end during the Classical period. Haydn was the last of the great composers to work exclusively for an aristocratic patron. Both Mozart and Beethoven were themselves concert artists who composed for the public. It makes a good deal of difference in the music whether a composer writes for a select group of court musicians, or whether he composes his work according to an ideal and then finds the musicians required to play it.

It also makes a difference in the music whether he composes to please a patron, a concert audience, or, indeed, an entire nation. Music in the court was often part of a larger social function and so was likely to be subdued and unobtrusive. When music moved to the concert hall, it became the center of attention, the orchestras grew larger, and the music became more exciting, more intense. We can easily follow this development in the symphonies of Beethoven. His *First Symphony,* completely in the Classical tradition, could be performed by a small court orchestra and is a relatively short piece in the restrained Classical mode. By the time we come to his later symphonies, we find the scoring for larger orchestras, the music more passionate in intensity and extramusical intent, and the scope much more expanded; for example, his lengthy *Ninth Symphony* includes a chorus and four vocal soloists.

An important change both in style and performance practices occurred after 1750. The performance of Baroque music was dependent upon improvisation. Baroque composers would typically sketch out a melodic pattern or a harmonic pattern (figured bass) and allow the keyboard performers to elaborate on these according to their judgment, skill, and caprice. An outstanding example of this practice is found in Bach's *Brandenburg Concerto No. 3,* where the second movement consists only of a few chords and instructions for the harpsichordist to improvise a passage modulating to the key of the next movement. Indeed, improvisation is important in all Baroque music: instrumentalists improvised ornaments and cadenzas, and opera singers improvised extensively in arias. However, after 1750, improvisation was practically nonexistent. The notable exception is the cadenza found in the Classical concerto, whose function is to display the performer's virtuosity.

Style Characteristics

Striking changes are found in the music composed after Bach's death. *Homophonic texture,* which had begun with the monodic style in opera as early as 1600, had fully matured and become the predominant texture of the Classical period. There is a definite polarity between the two outer voices in Classical music, a tendency which had begun to show itself early in the Baroque period but which had never before replaced polyphony. The upper voice sustains the melody in a much freer way than imitative counterpoint allows, and the bass supplies the harmonic foundation. Polyphonic textures, of course, continued to be used after 1750, but primarily as contrasts to homophonic textures. In the Classical style, the two textures come to be known as *learned style* (polyphonic) and *galant style* (homophonic). Excellent use of both is exploited in the finale of Mozart's *String Quartet in C,* K. 465.

Textures are generally more spare in Classical music than in Baroque, *economy of means* being a Classical ideal. Although the orchestra grew larger during this period, the increasing interest in instrumental timbres made it necessary for individual instruments to be heard within the total ensemble. This idiomatic scoring, along with homophonic textures, resulted in a clean, transparent quality.

Another important feature of Classical music is its intermittent movement. The continuous movement found in Baroque music is caused by polyphonic textures, infrequent or disguised cadences, and a constantly moving bass part. In contrast, Classical intermittent movement is caused by homophonic texture, frequent cadences, and a bass part which punctuates rather than predominates. Bass lines are likely to have as many rests as notes, and often a single tone is repeated many times before the pitch changes. The Baroque bass is likely to be constantly moving, with a different pitch for every beat, rarely stopping or pausing. Homophonic textures call for more frequent cadences which cause stop-and-start movement, and result in short, balanced phrases. Compare the intermittent movement of Mozart's *Symphony No. 41*[20] with any of the Bach *Brandenburg Concertos.*[21]

The Mozart symphony also illustrates the new dynamics of gradual building and diminishing of loudness, called *crescendo* and *diminuendo,* which replaced the terraced dynamics of the Baroque period. The new dynamics were influenced by the development of the piano in the early part of the eighteenth century. The original name "pianoforte" means soft-loud in Italian, a designation indicating that the performer can vary the loudness by keyboard touch, which he could not do on the harpsichord or organ. A typical passage in Baroque harpsichord music would thus be performed in the terraced dynamic style; contrasts in volume are produced by couplings, a mechanical device which allows for several strings to be played at once by pressing one key. In a typical passage in Classical piano music the com-

[20] See also Examples 7.25 and 8.24.
[21] Examples 8.5, 8.23, and 9.8.

poser would include dynamic markings, crescendo and diminuendo, to indicate that the performer should make gradual rather than sudden changes of loudness.

The development and widespread use of the piano has implications for homophonic texture as well. Because the pianist is able to play one musical figure louder and more expressively than another, he can easily render a melody with one hand which predominates over accompanying harmonic figures in the other hand.

The Classical composer's concern for balance led to the maturing of the orchestra. During the Classical period, the orchestra developed into the balanced ensemble of four individually homogeneous groups that we have previously discussed. Because Baroque composers were concerned primarily with balance between voice parts, their orchestras were not divided into separate functioning families of instruments. Contrasts were achieved mainly through the concertato technique. Contrasts in Classical music were achieved between families of instruments rather than between tutti and concertino. Balance in the Classical orchestra is maintained primarily between the strings and woodwinds. Although the percussion and brass sections also achieved considerable stature in this period, they were not fully employed as independent families of instruments until the Romantic age.

The new orchestra was also exploited more fully in terms of its higher and lower ranges. Generally speaking, a Baroque melody is likely to be played within the range of the human voice. The separation between vocal and instrumental idioms was not yet complete. The Classical composers, however, exploited pitches much greater than the human voice. They used the full range of each instrument, often writing parts for flutes or violins in high registers and bassoons or double basses in low registers.

The results of all these developments are thinner textures, wider pitch ranges, brighter timbres, and an orchestral balance between groups of instruments. The basic function of each group of instruments within the symphony orchestra was established during the Classical period. The strings present the bulk of the musical material, melody and harmony; the woodwinds provide contrasting material; the brasses add power to climactic moments; and the percussion accentuate the rhythm.[22]

Suggested Works for Listening That Typify Classical Music

Symphony
Beethoven: *Symphonies No. 1* and *No. 9*
Haydn: *Symphony No. 103 (Drum Roll)*

[22] See Examples 1.3 and 5.1.

Piano Concerto
Beethoven: *Piano Concerto No. 4*

String Quartet
Mozart: *String Quartet, K. 465*

Opera
Mozart: *Così fan tutte*

Oratorio
Haydn: *The Creation*

Piano Trio
Beethoven: *Trio No. 6 in B-flat, Op. 97 (Archduke)*

Serenade
Mozart: *Eine kleine Nachtmusik*

Romantic Period (1820–1900)

As we move from one style period to the next, we see that each new period comes about partly as a result of a reaction against existing practices. We might wonder whether the Romantic age is an exception, because the Classical forms were never abandoned or called into disfavor. On the contrary, Classical forms remained the basis for composition in the Romantic period. The great difference between the eighteenth and nineteenth centuries is not in the forms used, but in the attitudes toward those forms and indeed toward art itself. The design was no longer of crucial importance; self-expression became the primary goal. The Romanticist merely used existing forms or found new ones to express his musical ideas.

The Romantic period could properly be called an age of expansion. The political climate was changing rapidly. The middle class was on the rise, largely as a result of the French and American Revolutions and growing free enterprise. The power of the aristocracy was eclipsed by that of the industrial middle class. The common man had risen to a position of importance unequalled in all previous history.

Art, literature, and music reflected this new emphasis on the individual. The man is more important than society. In fact, whereas the Rationalists believed in the civilizing influence of institutions, many Romanticists believed that society corrupted the natural goodness of man. Wordsworth saw the child as perfect and innocent, "trailing clouds of glory" as he entered life, but gradually being corrupted by society.

Neo-Classical poetry was rational and its main vehicle was satire—an attempt to point out society's faults so that they could be corrected. But Romantic poetry emphasized the intimate, personal expression which evokes a private, unique feeling in the reader. This intimacy is best expressed in lyric poetry, an ideal derived from music. There was a reaction against the eighteenth-century faith in intellectual judgment in favor of a belief in the power of the imagination. Art began to be seen mainly as an outlet for personal feelings, as a mode for creative self-expression; these ideas never existed in art before Romanticism. Poets, artists, and musicians wrote philosophical treatises revealing an interest in the creative process itself.

The Romanticist searches endlessly for the unattainable. The poetry of Shelley, Keats, Byron, and Goethe embodies this theme. The Neo-Classical ideal of perfection within well-defined limits is rejected. It is better to aim for the stars, to try to accomplish the impossible; even if we fail, there is something noble in the attempt. This straining for the infinite may be heard in Beethoven's *Ninth Symphony,* and in the works of Berlioz, Wagner, and Mahler.

The Romanticist stresses the imagination, the emotions, the private instead of the public side of life. Wordsworth's definition of poetry as "the spontaneous overflow of powerful feelings" might be used to define all Romantic art. The Romanticist is preoccupied with beauty, strangeness, vision, fancy, mystery, magic, love. Interest in superstition, ancient or Medieval folklore, demonology, and the exotic or far away, can be seen in Coleridge's *The Ancient Mariner* and *Kubla Khan,* Keats' *Eve of St. Agnes* and *Lamia,* Tennyson's *Ulysses,* and Sir Walter Scott's poetry and novels about Medieval England and Scotland. Emphasis on the dark side of the human spirit, with special use of symbol, allegory, and deliberate ambiguity can be seen in the works of the Americans, Hawthorne and Poe.

Symbolism, often ambiguous in meaning, is used in some Romantic painting as well. Nobody really knows exactly what the floating figures symbolize in Goya's painting, *El Aquelarre* (Plate 22, following p. 166). The Romantic ideal, because it emphasizes emotion, involves ambiguity, in contrast with the Classical concept of total, restrained control and precise meaning. Symbolism, with its inherent ambiguity, allows the perceiver to participate in the creative process.

Frequently, these symbols involve mystical, mysterious, or terrifying experiences. The "strangeness of beauty" seen in the Goya painting is also revealed in Weber's opera, *Der Freischütz,* particularly in the Wolf Glen scene where, amidst the eerie backdrop of a mystical night, the Devil casts magic bullets which will enable the hero to win his lady love. Both the painting and the music portray the broad sweep of gesture characteristic of Romantic art.

Romantic painters are sometimes brutal in their symbolic representation of ideas. Goya in his painting, *Saturn Devouring One of His Children,* symbolizes time as a ravenous evil, and in his *Execution of the Rioters, May 3, 1808,* portrays the bloody execution of citizens of Madrid by Napoleon's soldiers. Shelley is just as brutally descriptive in his allegorical representation of British Foreign Secretary Castlereagh in *The Mask of Anarchy:*

> I met Murder on the way—
> He had a mask like Castlereagh;
> Very smooth he looked, yet grim;
> Seven bloodhounds followed him.
>
> All were fat; and well they might
> Be in admirable plight,
> For one by one, and two by two,
> He tossed them human hearts to chew,
> Which from his wide cloak he drew.

A more positive side of Romantic symbolism is its treatment of nature, which represented the simple, elemental life, and therefore man's purest side. If man was corrupted by civilization, society, or science, then perhaps his salvation lay in a return to nature. Nature also represented communion with the eternal, with infinity. Rarely did the Romanticist merely describe nature; rather, he regarded nature as a resource for meditation and for the renewal of a sense of awe and wonder. It is what nature *represents* that made it important to the Romanticist. The Romantic composer used nature as subject matter in a significant and symbolic way. Beethoven's *Symphony No. 6 (Pastoral)*, one of the first examples of this use of nature, does not stop with imitating natural sounds; it evokes a series of moods. There followed a great many Romantic operas, symphonies, tone poems, and other compositions which used nature as subject matter, such as Schumann's *Spring* and *Rhenish* symphonies, Mendelssohn's *The Hebrides,* and Smetana's *The Moldau.*

The Romantic scope was both larger and smaller than that of the Classical. The Romanticist concentrated on the extremes: small, intimate forms of expression, including art songs, character pieces, and lyric poetry, and grandiose forms of expression, including huge orchestras, lengthy symphonies, large canvases, and sweeping gestures and ideas. The paintings by J. M. W. Turner, such as *Valley of Aosta—Snowstorm, Avalanche and Thunderstorm,* illustrate the opening up of space, the quest for the extravagant and unattainable.

The music is much more diverse, more difficult to encapsulate, than the Classical. In this age of extremes which emphasized personal freedom and individual expression, the music is difficult to categorize. It was natural that the music of the age should be filled with crosscurrents, even contradictions. Another reason for the diversity of style is that although there were many outstanding musicians in the nineteenth century, there was no one individual who set the style for all composers. Again, in this age of individualism, each composer contributed according to his own special interest. Some were innovative, some followed the example of others; hence we find both radical and conservative composers. The conservatives worked within the Classical models, whereas the radicals experimented more with new forms, program music, and new orchestral timbres.

Most of the great music of the Romantic era was composed for orchestra or for soloist, in accord with the Romantic propensity for the immense or the intimate. This age of extremes was not conducive to chamber music, which falls somewhere between. It is interesting, therefore, to note that the most successful composers of chamber music, Schubert, Mendelssohn, and Brahms, were the most "Classical" of the Romantics.

The early symphonists of the Romantic period were Schubert (1797–1808), Mendelssohn (1809–1847), and Schumann (1810–1856), of whom Schumann was the most Romantic because of his programmatic piano music. Two of Schubert's symphonies, *No. 8 in B Minor (Unfinished)* and *No. 9 in C (The Great)*, are frequently performed today. Schubert retained the Classical form of the symphony but his use of orchestral color and his lyric melodies classify him as a Romantic. Mendelssohn, also espousing Classical form, used the Romantic technique of scene painting in two of his symphonies, the *Italian* and the *Scotch*. Schumann's *Spring* and *Rhenish* symphonies modeled after Beethoven's *Pastoral Symphony* are specifically programmatic.

In the mid-nineteenth century, there were two important composers who represented a radical wing of Romanticism: Berlioz and Liszt. Both men were more consciously and deliberately programmatic than the early symphonists. Because of their orchestral innovations, both had an important influence on later symphonic writing. Berlioz (1803–1869), a genius of orchestration, wrote a number of program symphonies: *Symphonie Fantastique* (Example 9.4), *Harold in Italy*, *Damnation of Faust*, *Romeo and Juliet*. There is also a program accompanying each of these works, far more detailed than Beethoven's. In the last, which he called a "dramatic symphony" in seven movements, Berlioz follows Beethoven's example by adding vocal soloists and chorus to the symphony orchestra, a practice which several Romantic composers subsequently followed. Also noteworthy is Berlioz' *Grande Messe des Morts (Requiem)*, which is not really liturgical music, but another dramatic symphony of vast proportions, utilizing an orchestra of one hundred forty players, large chorus, four brass choirs, four tam-tams, ten pairs of cymbals, and sixteen timpani. The orchestral effects are dazzling.

Liszt (1811–1886), too, was an inventive orchestrator, but wrote only two symphonies, *Faust Symphony*, and *Dante Symphony*. Liszt's most important contribution was his development of the tone poem, of which he composed more than a dozen. These were shorter than symphonies and were usually of one movement with contrasting sections. Although Liszt's tone poems are not frequently played today, the form was imitated by numerous other composers including Tchaikovsky, Smetana, Franck, and Strauss. The highly emotional programs, idealistic philosophy, and typically Romantic subjects such as Dante and Faust make Liszt one of the most Romantic in spirit of all composers.

The third generation of important Romantic composers most clearly represents the two trends—Brahms (1833–1897), the conservative, and Wagner (1813–1883), the radical. Brahms wrote four symphonies, all still frequently played. They are absolute music, not programmatic in any sense. Although Classical in form, they are Romantic in their treatment of expanded harmonies and orchestral color. Brahms was one of the few Romanticists who was interested in and wrote good chamber music.

Wagner's only important music is opera, but these operas were influential in later opera and in symphonic music. He was a brilliant orchestrator, master of an infinite variety of instrumental effects; his operas are just as interesting orchestrally as vocally or dramatically. In addition, his chromatic harmonies and use of folklore material (*The Ring of the Nibelungen*) and medieval legend (*Parsifal, Die Meistersinger von Nürnberg, Tristan und Isolde*) place him on the ultra-Romantic side of the spectrum.

The last generation of symphonic composers include Tchaikovsky (1840–1893), Bruckner (1824–1896), Mahler (1860–1911), and Richard Strauss (1864–1949). Another group of composers, some of whom lived well into the twentieth century, treated nationalistic material in their music and remained Romantic in the midst of modern trends and experiments. Hence the radical became conservative: Moussorgsky (1839–1881), Rimsky-Korsakof (1844–1903), Rachmaninov (1873–1943), Smetana (1824–1884), Dvořak (1841–1904), Grieg (1843–1907), Elgar (1859–1934), and Sibelius (1865–1957). All drew heavily on folk tunes, rhythms, and harmonies, and used national subject material in the attempt to establish a national idiom, according to the Romantic ideal. Nationalism is largely a matter of the composer's deliberate attempt to enshrine his national affiliation by establishing a national musical dialect.

The symphonists represent the expansive side of Romanticism, the reaching for the unattainable. The other important side is the intimate, the personal, the communication among composer, performer, and listener. This intimacy found expression most commonly in the art song (in German, *Lied*) and in piano music. The most important composers of art song were Schubert, Schumann, Brahms, Mahler, Strauss, and Wolf (1860–1903). The conservative Romanticists, Schubert and Brahms, showed their most Romantic side in their art songs. Schubert's songs cover the entire gamut of human emotions, some quiet and introspective, some dramatic and thunderous. Brahms' songs (especially the *Vier Ernste Gesang*) tend to be serious, with controlled emotional expression. All these composers were interested in setting Romantic poetry to music, and all display great lyrical quality in the wedding of piano and voice, and of poetry and music.

The nineteenth century was a great age of piano music. The piano was technically perfected early in the century and was capable of a wide range of expressive and dynamic quality. It is no accident that the men who wrote the most expressive, virtuoso, and popular piano music of the day were themselves pianists, some highly gifted and technically accomplished musicians. The most important of these were Chopin (1810–1849), Liszt, Schumann, Rubinstein (1829–1894), and Rachmaninov. All combined lyricism with technical virtuosity and usually programmatic content or mood. Chopin's piano music is probably the most lasting in significance. He concentrated on piano music and was responsible for exploring early in the century the particular technical problems and possibilities which the piano presents, especially in his *Études* and *Préludes*.

Performance Practices

Public concerts, as we know them today, with all the decorum, propriety, and trappings were molded during the nineteenth century. Music moved into the concert hall and recital hall and became part of the social activity of the middle and upper classes. Having been an integral part of the education of the upper classes in the eighteenth century, music now became everybody's ideal. There was a piano in virtually every living room or parlor. The virtuoso performers became international figures, almost of heroic proportions, as symbolic of the "Romantic" spirit. The concert hall of the nineteenth century became an exciting arena of entertainment. For the first time in history, concert music was enjoyed by all classes. Music became a medium of artistic communication between the individual artist and the individual listener. Music grew into an art for everyman.

Style Characteristics

Beethoven began the age of expansion. Composers, in their quest for opening up space and reaching for the infinite, gradually extended Classical forms and modified Classical design to enlarge the scope of musical composition. Pieces became longer and larger. Increasing interest in the art of orchestration resulted in larger orchestras and wider dynamic range. Chromatic harmonies and constantly shifting tonalities fostered the expansion and ultimate breakdown of Classical tonality.

Textures grew rich and lush with the addition of more instruments to the orchestra, more chromaticism in the harmonies, and thicker scoring. Textures continued to be predominantly homophonic, but were fuller sounding and more polyphonic than Classical ones. The intermittent movement of the Classical period gave way to more continuous movement in the Romantic period. It was primarily Romantic melody and harmony that supplied continuous movement to nineteenth-century music. Chromaticism and modulation, both of which expand harmonies, also defer cadences and extend movement. Romantic melody, characterized by great length, predominance, and lyricism, may be compared with the broad sweeping gestures in Romantic painting.

Although the Romantic period in music was in some ways an extension and expansion of the Classical period, several important innovations occurred in direct contradiction to Classical ideals. One of the most startling of these innovations was *program music,* as opposed to *absolute music.* Program music is instrumental and suggests an extramusical idea indicated in the title or by elaborate explanation supplied by the composer. All music is capable of extramusical meaning to some degree, depending on the listener, but in the strictest sense, program music is a matter of the composer's intent. A composer of program music wants to express an idea, evoke a mood, or tell a story.

One of the earliest examples of programmatic content in music is Beethoven's *Sixth Symphony,* in which each of the five movements is named according to the scene that it portrays. The symphony itself is called the *Pastoral* and the movements are: I. The awakening of serene feelings on arrival in the country; II. Scene by the brook; III. A merry meeting of country folk; IV. Thunderstorm and tempest; V. Song of the shepherds, glad and thankful after the storm. Listen to the fourth movement in particular, in which Beethoven displays his most programmatic music in his vivid portrayal of nature. This symphony was emulated by a great many Romantic composers.

The tendency to give compositions names other than formal designations became standard practice throughout the nineteenth century: Berlioz' *Symphonie Fantastique;* Mendelssohn's *Symphony No. 3 (Scotch), Symphony No. 4 (Italian), Symphony No. 5 (Reformation),* Dvořák's *Symphony No. 5 (New World),* Tchaikovsky's *Symphony No. 6 (Pathétique).* Incidentally, notice the extension of Classical form to five movements in Beethoven's *Symphony No. 6* and Berlioz' *Symphonie Fantastique.*

Symphonic program music appeared in four guises: the *program symphony,* the *tone poem,* the *concert overture,* and *incidental music* to plays. The program symphony came first, beginning with Beethoven's *Sixth* and fully developed as a consummate form in Berlioz' *Symphonie Fantastique.* The program for Berlioz' work is thought to be autobiographical, portraying his own dreams and love life.

The *program symphony* led to Liszt's creation of the tone poem. One of the first examples is his *Les Préludes*. The tone poem was brought to full maturity by Richard Strauss in his *Thus Spake Zarathustra, Till Eulenspiegel, Don Juan,* and *Death and Transfiguration*. The tone poem is a one-movement composition often in free form. Programs for tone poems range from the vague description of life in *Les Préludes* to the elaborate and detailed story in *Till Eulenspiegel*.

The *concert overture* closely resembles the tone poem. Descended from the opera overture, it was composed as a separate entity in the nineteenth century. Like the tone poem, the concert overture is a one-movement form. Tchaikovsky's *Romeo and Juliet* is a typical example.

Incidental music is meant to accompany plays, and the program is based on the content of the play for which it is composed and performed. However, incidental music which stands well by itself is often performed in concert. Grieg's *Peer Gynt Suite* is a popular example.

The emphasis on the intimate is exemplified in two forms, the *art song* and the *character piece*. Each is extremely small and is performed best in a room rather than in a large hall. Probably because of this intimate communication among performer, composer, and audience, art songs and character pieces gained considerable popularity and became two of the most important forms of the Romantic period. The art song's artistic validity is found in the successful union of music and poetry. Composers were enamored of the Romantic poets and attempted to enhance the meaning of the poetry in their music. The heightened feeling or mood created in the union of poetry and music made the performance of art songs popular fare for the Romantic soul. Schubert, who wrote more than six hundred *Lieder,* is considered by many to be the most successful composer of art songs. Evidence of this can be found in his collections, *Die schöne Müllerin* and *Die Winterreise*.

Character pieces, composed for the piano, are the short, lyric instrumental counterpart of the art song. Based on a single mood, these program pieces often bear titles such as "Butterflies," "Albumleaf," "Nocturne," "Song Without Words," "Dream-Visions," or "Soaring." Schumann's *Phantasiestücke,* Op. 12 (*Fantasy Pieces*), is a collection of eight character pieces that are typical of the simple structure, usually ABA, and program titles found in character pieces.

New Attempts at Unity

As we discovered in Chapter 5, Beethoven used a single rhythmic figure throughout the four movements of his *Fifth Symphony*. This attempt to supply unity through an entire symphony was the beginning of the Romantic notion of *cyclic* treatment of themes. A great many Romantic composers, especially the late Romantics, used themes related to the program which recur throughout a symphony or opera. Berlioz called his theme an *idée fixe,* or fixed idea, which in his *Symphonie Fantastique* returns in each movement as a symbol of his sweetheart. Wagner used a motive called *Leitmotiv* to represent important characters or ideas in his operas. In Bizet's *Carmen,* it is called the "fate motive," and we hear it every time Carmen comes on stage, presumably foretelling her tragic destiny.

Romantic Opera

The world of opera as we know it today is largely a product of the Romantic period. It was during the nineteenth century that grand opera rose to full maturity, but it was largely through the efforts of Richard Wagner that dramatic emphasis in opera was changed drastically. In the early 1800's, in the operas of Rossini, Bellini, Meyerbeer, and Donizetti, the emphasis was on vocal virtuosity and on orchestral polish. Wagner in his music and writings placed greater emphasis on dramatic action; the purpose of the music was to serve the drama. He even called his operas music-dramas. This tendency toward dramatically strong opera exists in the operas of Wagner's contemporaries and successors to the present: late Verdi (*Otello*), Puccini (*La Bohème*), R. Strauss (*Elektra*), Berg (*Wozzeck*).

Suggested Works for Listening That Typify Romantic Music

Art Song
Schubert: *Die Winterreise*

Character Pieces
Schumann: *Phantasiestücke*

Concerto
Grieg: *Piano Concerto in A minor*

Opera
Bizet: *Carmen*
Wagner: *Die Walküre,* Act IV

Symphony
Brahms: *Symphony No. 2*
Bruckner: *Symphony No. 6*
Mahler: *Das Lied von der Erde*
Schumann: *Symphony No. 1 (Spring)*
Tchaikovsky: *Symphony No. 6 (Pathétique)*

Tone Poem
Smetana: *The Moldau*

Modern Period (1900–the Present)

The term "modern" is relative, and we have used it to refer to many trends throughout the history of music. We have called all music since 1450 "modern," and we have discussed the "modern" orchestra as that which was developed in the Classical period. Although it seems appropriate to apply the term to music of the twentieth century, it does not adequately describe emerging styles and their great diversity.

Perhaps more than ever before, twentieth-century composers have shown an adverse reaction to the preceding period. In the early 1900's the spirit of Romanticism dried up. World Wars and depressions brought disillusionment and cynicism to many people. Science and technology became dominant forces. Man was drawing away from nature and back to civilization. But most of all, in reaction to the extravagance of Romanticism, twentieth-century man came to find beauty in economy and in the new and different.

The first few decades of the century made up an age of experimentation resulting in diversity and plurality of style. There developed, in effect, a number of "isms"—Impressionism, Expressionism, Primitivism, Experimentalism, Neo-Classicism. Tonal harmony was thought to have reached its limit in the chromaticism of Wagner and Strauss. Thus, many new systems of tonal organization were developed which expanded Romantic harmony until it burst, leading to the eventual breakdown of Classical tonality. Other systems were developed to take its place, including the whole-tone scale, expanded tertian harmony, polytonality, serial music, and electronic music.

America was enjoying increasing prestige in the field of music, partly because eminent composers, conductors, and performers were coming to this country to practice their craft. Some of the most important included Bartók, Dvořák, Schoenberg, Stravinsky, Ussachevsky, Toscanini, Koussevitsky, Munch, and Szell. Even more important to the country's prestige were increasing numbers of American-born composers: Ives, Piston, Copland, Hanson, Virgil Thomson, Randall Thompson, Barber, Harris, Gershwin, William Schuman, and Bernstein.

The tenor of society in the twentieth century has been conducive to experimental activity in music. A society where a plurality of life styles coexist, and where change is the mode, is amenable to new and different ideas and is likely to be in a state of flux. The advance of technology has supplied the world of music with an expanded universe, both in composition and performance.

Performance Practices

Performance practices in the concert hall have not changed radically since they were established in the Romantic period. We still follow the procedures and etiquette of the earlier period: the orchestra is seated on stage, the conductor enters when all are ready, the audience applauds in the correct places, the performers bow in recognition of the applause, and so on. However, some important changes occurred both in the orchestra and in the style of composition. World War I left Europe in a serious economic condition affecting considerably the status of orchestras. Composers began writing for smaller ensembles and smaller forms, in order to make concert tours economically feasible. It was because of this economic situation that Stravinsky, after the extravagance of his ballets, came to write *L'histoire du Soldat* for seven instruments, two dancer-pantomimists, and a narrator (Example 7.1).

In the 1920's, the influence of American jazz began to be felt in concert music both in Europe and America. Composers like Milhaud, Gershwin, Copland, Hindemith, and Stravinsky began incorporating jazz rhythms and improvisations in their music. Significant compositions containing jazz elements include Stravinsky's *Ragtime for Eleven Instruments*, Milhaud's *La Création du monde*, Gershwin's *Rhapsody in Blue*, and Copland's *Concerto for Piano*.

We cannot ignore the fact that the manufacture and sale of recordings have had an influence on the musical scene. Music of all kinds is now available to anybody at a very low cost. Owing to this availability, people have become much more knowledgeable about music; through recordings they are able to listen to any given composition as many times as they wish. Although audiences may be diminishing in size these days, they are probably more discriminating. The effect has been to upgrade the quality of musical performances. Recordings also make the serious study of music more feasible, and the science of musicology has flourished. If a group in New York researches Renaissance music, for example, and collects the instruments to play it, that group can make a recording, and people all over the world can benefit from that study.

The story of performance in the twentieth century does not yet have an ending. With the advent of electronic music since 1950, new problems must be solved in terms of standard performance practice. Some composers have dealt with the problem of live performance by combining conventional instruments with recorded music, as in Ussachevsky and Luening's *A Poem in Cycles and Bells* (Example 10.10). The problems can be resolved only when the direction of electronic music is well established.

Style Characteristics

Impressionism began in the 1870's with Claude Monet. His painting, *Impression: Rising Sun* (1874), provided the name and impetus for the movement. The technique of the Impressionist painters centered on their fascination with light. Monet was known for painting the same subject at different times of the day in order to capture the various effects of sunlight on that subject. This experimentation illustrated the importance of light in changing the appearance of a subject from one time of day to the next.

Monet's painting, *Rouen Cathedral, Tour d'Albane: Early Morning,* Plate 23 (following p. 166), illustrates the Impressionist's technique: concentration on effects of light so that movement is reduced to a shimmer; lack of strong line in favor of patches of color and total impression rather than detail; subdued colors tending toward the pastel. The result is a direct reflection of reality in subtle, subdued language, most often set in the outdoors.

Style characteristics in Impressionist music closely parallel those of Impressionist painting. It was for this reason that the music of Debussy (1862–1918) and Ravel (1875–1937) has been called Impressionist. Debussy's composition, *La Mer* (Example 8.2), contains musical effects of orchestral color, eliminates strong metric beat and accented rhythms so that movement is reduced to a shimmer, lacks strong melodic line in favor of harmonic color and total impression, subdues dynamic quality—no emotional outcry. It is still program music, but the attempt here is to evoke the atmosphere of the sea by subtle suggestion, by impression rather than direct statement.

This comparison is purely artificial and academic. Debussy never labelled his music "Impressionist." He, like most of the other twentieth-century composers, was experimenting with new techniques of musical composition. His use of whole-tone, pentatonic, and modal scales together with expanded harmonies satisfied his desire for a tonal organization different from that used by the Romantic and Classical composers. Although the whole-tone, pentatonic, and modal scales are rarely heard intact, they are important as a basis for tonal organization.

One of the most revolutionary innovations of Impressionist music, particularly Debussy's, is the absence of literal and developmental repetition of themes. This is not to say that repetition does not exist in Impressionist music—Debussy's *Prelude to the Afternoon of a Faun* (Example 2.17) is a large ABA design—but the Impressionists deliberately avoided the kind of thematic repetitions, extensions, and developments found in Classical and Romantic music. Impressionists achieved unity through texture, motives, tonal language, and harmonic and orchestral colors.

Another technique used by the Impressionists was nonfunctional harmony with its lack of inexorable drive toward a cadence. Instead of resolving a chord of tension, the Impressionists preferred to follow it with another chord of tension, and another, and another, so that all of them cease to be heard as chords of tension, and begin to add a new color to the harmony. Movement in Impressionist music is not driving or purposeful, like that of Classical and Romantic music, but vague, suggestive, and shimmering. We call this principle "parallel harmonic movement," and it may be found throughout Debussy's music; a good example of this kind of movement is his opera, *Pelléas et Mélisande* (Example 8.28).

Whether the Impressionist painters actually influenced Debussy, Ravel, and others toward their form of musical composition is not certain. But they are all products of the same age, and noting the striking similarity of their techniques helps us to comprehend Impressionist music.

Impressionist composers were the first to turn their backs on conventional tonality, and thus the modern period began. This was a period which was to witness the complete disintegration of the major-minor system. And that brings us to the man who was finally responsible for this iconoclastic development, Arnold Schoenberg (1874–1951), leading exponent of the school of Expressionism.

Expressionism, in contrast to Impressionism which portrays the outer world, portrays the inner world of the subconscious. Expressionism is named after a school of painting led by Kandinsky and Beckmann, who attempted to depict the artist's inner self, particularly the dark side. The subject matter in Expressionist painting is often brutal, ugly, and distorted. Likewise, *Pierrot Lunaire,* one of Schoenberg's early works, exaggerates this violent and distorted side of human personality. The subject matter here is lunacy, which, along with depravity and ugliness, are common Expressionist themes. At the time Schoenberg composed this work, he was interested in exploring atonal music, and made a deliberate attempt to avoid conventional tonality. He had not yet worked out his highly formal serial technique.

The painting by Van Gogh (Plate 24, following p. 166) also expresses the savage violence of an artist who paints the world as it affects him. He pictures reality in harsh, rough textures; the colors are raw and deep; the movement is violent, seeming to swirl up through the painting, turning trees into distorted flames which melt into unending movement in the sky.

The important characteristic of Expressionist music is its treatment of extramusical subject matter, particularly the supernatural, the brutal, the fatalistic, and the nightmarish world of the subconscious. Berg's opera, *Wozzeck,* is a prime example. Wozzeck represents the "arme Leut," the poor or common folk who have no control over their fate. He is taken advantage of by his superiors, a Captain and a Doctor, who use him as a virtual slave. The only bright spot in his life is his mistress, Marie, and their child. Marie is unfaithful to Wozzeck, who is taunted by the Captain and the Doctor. Later he is beaten by the seducer, a Drum Major. Finally, by a lake, Wozzeck kills Marie with a knife and later returns to get rid of the murder weapon. He wanders into the lake in a dazed frenzy, imagines that the lake itself is blood, and drowns. In the last scene, all the neighborhood children run down to the lakeside to see what has happened, with the young, uncomprehending son of Marie and Wozzeck wandering curiously after them. Grim fatalism pervades the entire opera through the suffering of the "arme Leut."

Primitivism refers to an interest in primitive cultures which manifests itself largely in the new treatment of rhythm and polytonality in Stravinsky's work and, to a degree, in Bartók's. In *The Rite of Spring,* one of the most revolutionary works of the twentieth century, Stravinsky eliminated the regular recurring accent common in Classical and Romantic music. He discovered that by alternating and juxtaposing different metric patterns and occasionally throwing the accent off the first beat of a measure, he could prevent the listener from anticipating regular accent. A frenzied, driving movement results. In the same work, in the "Dance of the Adolescents" (Example 3.56) Stravinsky achieves a violently percussive quality even in the string section by presenting sets of chords in two different keys at the same time. This produces a thud similar to the sound of a drum rather than discernible pitches; the percussive effect is enhanced by repetition of these chords.

Primitivism is an unfortunate name for the new treatment of rhythm in Stravinsky's *Rite.* To relate it to primitive cultures is artificial and inaccurate, except that rhythm is a dominant element in both. The important difference is that rhythms in twentieth-century music are very sophisticated, extremely complicated, and difficult to play, not at all primitive in any other sense of the word.

Polytonality represents modern composers' attempts to experiment and deal with new tonal organization. The twentieth century was the time to explore beyond the confines of Classical tonality. One of the most interesting experiments in polytonality may be found in Ives' *Fourth Symphony* composed for two orchestras, two conductors, and chorus. The two orchestras are actually heard playing two different pieces at the same time, not to mention the fact that the pieces are in different keys. Although you may not hear entire compositions written in a polytonal framework, almost all twentieth-century composers use polytonality for special effects—Hindemith, Bartók, Stravinsky, Milhaud, Honegger, and a great many others.

As time passes, we may come to know the music of the first half of the twentieth century as *Neo-Classicism.* This designation signifies a revival of old forms and compositional techniques as a framework for expression in terms of new tonal organization. Neo-Classicism followed in the wake of early twentieth-century composers' rejection of extravagant Romantic principles. Neo-Classical principles became standard among many composers in the 1920's and 1930's: thin, polyphonic textures; the typical Classical clarity and simplicity; and a return to absolute music (in reaction to Romantic program music). The old forms include the suite, concerto grosso, passacaglia, and fugue. Stravinsky began experimenting with smaller forms after World War I and discovered in 1923 that the Baroque suite, polyphonic textures, and concertato procedures were appropriate media for his new form of expression. His outstanding Neo-Classical works are *Octet for Wind Instruments* (Example 3.13); *Pulcinella* (Example 7.22), based on melodies by Baroque composer Pergolesi; and *Mass* for mixed chorus and double wind quintet.

Webern, also a Neo-Classicist, is known for the extreme in sparse scoring. In his *Symphonie,* Op. 21 (Example 8.29), Webern replaces entire sections of the traditional orchestra with only one or two instruments; it is scored for clarinet, bass clarinet, two horns, harp, and string quartet.

Other Neo-Classical composers and works include Bartók's *Concerto for Orchestra* and *Mikrokosmos;* Hindemith's *Kleine Kammermusik, Symphonic Metamorphoses on a Theme of Weber,* and *Ludus Tonalis;* and Poulenc's *Pastoral Concerto* for harpsichord and orchestra.

Serial Music is the name of Schoenberg's tonal system of arranging the available twelve tones in a series. The result, a tone row, serves as the basic material for composition, and ordinarily, a new tone row is created for each composition. Because the tone row is a melodic concept with no harmonic considerations, serial music is almost totally polyphonic. The music is difficult to comprehend because of its fantastic complexity. The row, even if we memorize it, is almost never recognizable in the context of the music. Twelve-tone music has suffered from charges of being too cerebral, academic, and esoteric, lacking all the familiar characteristics of Classical and Romantic music, namely, lyric melody, rich harmony, and steady rhythm. Of course, that is exactly what Schoenberg was trying to do, eliminate those characteristics of Classical and Romantic music and create new systems appropriate to the age. His principal serial compositions include *Variations for Orchestra,* Op. 31; *String Quartet No. 4,* Op. 37; and *Dreimal Tausend Jahre* for chorus.

Other composers of serial music are Berg (*Lyric Suite*) and Webern (*Concerto for Nine Instruments,* Op. 24). The influence of serial technique is found in the works of many composers not ordinarily considered serialists such as Stravinsky (*Agon*) and Copland (*Fantasy* for piano).

Although Webern and Berg were both pupils of Schoenberg and composers in the twelve-tone tradition, the style of each is unique. Webern's is angular, stark, and thinly textured. Berg's is lyric, full-scored, and richly textured. Webern is thus the more Classical and Berg the more Romantic.

Webern is thought to have exerted a strong, direct influence on *electronic music* and the electronic experiments beginning in 1950. His sparse textures, points of sound, were appropriate predecessors to the snippets of electronic sounds which are characteristic of the first experiments in the new idiom.

Electronic devices seemed to be at their best producing blips and bleeps rather than lyric melodies. Perhaps the composer felt that these kinds of sounds more properly reflected our new mechanistic society. Electronic music has met with more adverse criticism than any of the previous experiments in music, probably because it does not utilize conventional instruments, and therefore is more threatening to music as we know it than any other *avant-garde* movement. Its influence is nevertheless profound, and it will undoubtedly play an important role in the shaping of the music of the future. Important composers are Stockhausen (*Elektronische Studien II*), Ussachevsky (*Composition for Tape Recorder*—Example 1.6), Varèse (*Poème Électronique*), and Babbitt (*Philomel* for voice and electronic sound).

A number of twentieth-century composers, the *Traditionalists*, have written and are continuing to write mainly in earlier styles, particularly the Romantic style. Although these composers have not essentially been innovators, their music is frequently more popular with concert audiences than experimental music. They include Ralph Vaughn Williams (*Fantasia on a Theme of Thomas Tallis*) and Prokofiev (*Piano Concerto No. 3*), whose music reflects a highly personalized style of momentary flights into unexpected keys. Copland's *Symphony No. 3* is especially popular because of the incorporation of the "Fanfare for the Common Man" in the Fourth Movement. The symphonies of Shostakovich have gained popularity around the world. Benjamin Britten is now established as one of the leading composers of our time; his works include several operas (*Peter Grimes, Billy Budd, The Turn of the Screw*) and the *War Requiem*. Hanson, Sessions, Thomson, Harris, Carter, Bernstein, and Barber are prominent American composers. These composers properly belong to the twentieth century, not simply because they have lived in it, but because their tonal language ranges beyond the bounds of Classical-Romantic harmonies. They are close enough to the Romantics to remain popular with concert audiences, but distant enough to be captivating to an age which restlessly seeks the new.

Suggested Works for Listening That Typify Modern Music

Impressionism

Debussy: *Prelude to the Afternoon of a Faun*
          Pelléas et Mélisande

Expressionism

Schoenberg: *Erwartung*

Neo-Classicism
Bloch: *Concerto Grosso No. 1*
Stravinsky: *Three Pieces for String Quartet*

Jazz
Copland: *Concerto for Piano*

Traditionalists
Bernstein: *Jeremiah Symphony*
Harris: *Symphony No. 3*
Shostakovich: *Symphony No. 5,* Op. 47

Electronic Music
Boulez: *Poésie pour Pouvoir*

Chance Music
Boulez: *Piano Sonata No. 3*

Appendices

Appendix A

The following charts are designed to provide a concise summary of certain concepts discussed in the text. Because they cover large spans of time, the brief descriptions are necessarily oversimplified. The charts simply give an overview of various aspects of historical style.

Renaissance	Baroque	Classic	Romantic	Modern
1. Clarity of sound	1. Doctrine of the Affections	1. Balance, clarity, and economy of means	1. Powerful, exaggerated expression	1. Diversity and experimentation prevail: new rhythms, harmony, tonal systems, timbres
2. Balance between four or more homogeneous voices	2. Terraced dynamics, concertato, figured bass	2. Short phrases; intermittent movement	2. Intimate, personal expression	2. Impressionism
3. Imitative counterpoint	3. Imitative counterpoint	3. New dynamics: crescendo and diminuendo	3. Long, lyric melodies; chromaticism and expanded tertian harmony	3. Expressionism, Primitivism, Polytonality
4. Vocal, sacred music	4. Continuous movement; long, overlapping melodies	4. Emphasis on formal design and tonal relationships	4. Extended Classical form	4. Neo-Classicism
				5. Serial music
				6. Electronic and aleatoric music
				7. Neo-Romantic tendencies

Renaissance	Baroque	Classic	Romantic	Modern
(Ricercare)	Concerto grosso	Symphony	Symphony	Symphony
	Concerto	Concerto	Concerto	'Concerto
(Canzona)	Sonata	Sonata	Sonata	Sonata
	Trio Sonata	String Quartet	String Quartet	String Quartet
		Piano Trio	Piano Trio	Piano Trio
(Dances)	Suite		Suite	Suite
			Tone Poem	Tone Poem
			Overture	Overture
			Character Piece	Character Piece
				Electronic Music
	Opera	Opera	Opera	Opera
Mass	Mass	Mass	Mass	Mass
	Oratorio	Oratorio	Oratorio	Oratorio
	Cantata	Cantata	Cantata	Cantata
Madrigal			Art Song	Art Song
Motet	Motet			

Renaissance	Baroque	Classic	Romantic	Modern
Dufay, 1400–1474	Monteverdi, 1567–1643	Haydn, 1732–1809	Schubert, 1797–1828	Debussy, 1862–1918
Ockeghem, 1430–1495	Frescobaldi, 1583–1643	Mozart, 1756–1791	Berlioz, 1803–1869	Vaughan Williams, 1872–1958
Josquin des Prez, 1440–1521	Schütz, 1585–1672	Beethoven, 1770–1827	Mendelssohn, 1809–1847	Ives, 1874–1954
Obrecht, 1452–1505	Corelli, 1653–1713	Gluck, 1714–1787	Chopin, 1810–1849	Schoenberg, 1874–1951
Gabrieli, A., 1520–1586	Purcell, 1659–1695		Schumann, 1810–1856	Bartok, 1881–1945
Palestrina, 1525–1594	Couperin, 1668–1733		Liszt, 1811–1886	Stravinsky, 1882–1971
Lassus, 1532–1594	Vivaldi, 1678–1741		Verdi, 1813–1901	Webern, 1883–1945
Byrd, 1543–1623	Rameau, 1683–1764		Wagner, 1813–1883	Berg, 1885–1935
Gabrieli, G., 1557–1612	Bach, 1685–1750		Bruckner, 1824–1896	Varese, 1885–1965
	Handel, 1685–1759		Brahms, 1833–1897	Hindemith, 1895–1963
	Scarlatti, D., 1685–1757		Tchaikovsky, 1840–1893	Harris, 1898–
			Puccini, 1858–1924	Copland, 1900–
			Mahler, 1860–1911	Ussachevsky, 1911–
			Strauss, R., 1864–1949	Cage, 1912–
				Britten, 1913–
				Boulez, 1925–

	Renaissance	Baroque
Tonality	Modal systems of organization.	Tonal system emerges. All keys possible with even temperament. Tonality firmly established in late Baroque.
Orchestra	Great diversity of instruments, but no idiomatic writing.	Beginning of idiomatic writing for instruments. No standard ensemble in the period.
Opera		First operas were monodic with text all-important. Public opera houses begin. Aria-recitative develops. Venetian opera emerges, where text is subordinated to music. Neapolitan opera develops, with da capo aria and rigid alternation of recitative and aria. Aria becomes the most important feature, highly ornamental and improvisatory.
Vocal and Instrumental; Absolute and Program Music	Music is primarily vocal. Pictorialism in word painting.	Both vocal and instrumental music are important. "Affect" controls entire sections. Absolute music develops with the rise of instrumental idioms.
Homophony vs. Polyphony	Polyphony (thin texture)	Two styles: homophony in monody (thin) and polyphony (thick)

Classic	Romantic	Modern
Tonality becomes basis for formal organization. Classical music is the most highly tonal.	Tonality expands. Distant keys, unusual juxtapositions explored. Shifting tonalities, highly modulatory.	Tonality breaks down. New systems explored, including atonality, polytonality, quartal harmony, aleatory relationships.
Standard, modern orchestra develops with four homogeneous families. Art of orchestration emerging.	Orchestra grows to very large ensemble (about 100 players) still in four families. Brass and percussion more prominent than before. Art of orchestration highly developed.	Very large orchestra continues but there are many experiments with new, smaller combinations. Electronic music develops.
Neapolitan opera fades. Opera is "reformed" to be more realistic dramatically. Chorus and orchestra become more important. Comic opera emerges; Mozart develops it to highly polished art form.	Opera becomes public entertainment: grand opera results, an exciting spectacle. Lyric and comic opera also important, with typically Romantic and Nationalistic themes. Height of dramatic opera in Verdi and music-drama of Wagner. Increasing interest in the drama, especially in Puccini and "verismo" school.	As in all 20th century music, experimentalism prevails in opera, beginning with Debussy and Strauss. Expressionist themes sometimes used. One-act operas and smaller dimensions are common. Public performance centers mainly around 19th-century grand opera.
Most of the important music of this period is instrumental. Absolute music prevails.	Both vocal and instrumental music important, from large, grand forms to small, intimate forms. Program music prevails.	Both vocal and instrumental are important, but there is a return to emphasis on absolute music with Neo-Classicism. Instrumental forms are more prominent than vocal.
Homophony (thin)	Homophony (full, rich, thick)	Polyphony (thin, except in Neo-Romantic music; rhythmically complex)

Appendix B
Relative Note Values

Note Name   **Relative Value**

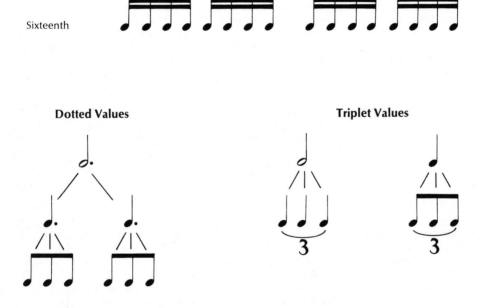

Whole

Half

Quarter

Eighth

Sixteenth

Dotted Values   **Triplet Values**

Appendix C
Tempo Indications

Largo Lento Adagio	very slow tempo
Andante Moderato	moderate tempo
Allegro Vivace Presto	very fast tempo

Dynamic Indications

pp (pianissimo)	very soft
p (piano)	soft
mp (mezzo-piano)	medium soft
mf (mezzo-forte)	medium loud
f (forte)	loud
ff (fortissimo)	very loud

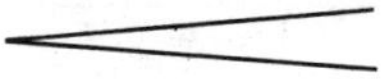 (crescendo) becoming louder

 (diminuendo) becoming softer

Appendix D
Examples

Example 3.1 Chopin: *Prelude No. 25*

Example 3.2 Bach: Prelude No. 2, from Book I of *The Well-Tempered Clavier*

Example 3.3 Beethoven: *Symphony No. 5,* first movement

Example 3.4 Stravinsky: *The Rite of Spring,* opening theme. Copyright 1921 by Edition Russe de Musique (Russicher Musikverlag). Copyright assigned 1947 to Boosey & Hawkes, Inc., for all countries. Reprinted by permission.

Example 3.5 Bach: Air, from *Suite No. 3*

Example 3.6 Bach: *Brandenburg Concerto No. 5*, opening theme

Example 3.7 Wagner: *Tannhäuser*, Overture, 1st theme

Example 3.8 Tones moving stepwise

Tones moving by leap

Example 3.9 Tchaikovsky: *Symphony No. 5*, second movement

Example 3.10   Rachmaninoff: *Piano Concerto No. 2,* first movement, 2nd theme

Example 3.11   Bach: *Concerto for Two Violins and Orchestra,* first movement

Example 3.12   Paganini: *Caprice No. 24*

Example 3.13   Stravinsky: *Octet for Winds,* opening theme. Copyright 1942 by Edition Russe de Musique; Renewed 1952. Copyright and renewal assigned 1951 to Boosey and Hawkes, Inc. Revised version Copyright 1952 by Boosey and Hawkes, Inc. Reprinted by permission.

Example 3.15   R. Strauss: *Till Eulenspiegel's Merry Pranks,* 2nd theme

Example 3.16   Handel: "Why Do the Nations," from *Messiah*

Why   do   the na-tions rage - - - - - - - - - - - - - -

Example 3.19   Mozart: *Symphony No. 40,* finale

Example 3.20   Verdi: "Celeste Aïda," from *Aïda*

Example 3.21   Tchaikovsky: *Symphony No. 6* (Pathétique), first movement, 2nd theme

Example 3.22   Brahms: *Symphony No. 3,* opening theme

Example 3.23   Schubert: *Symphony No. 8 (Unfinished),* first movement, 2nd theme

Example 3.24   Beethoven: *Symphony No. 3 (Eroica),* opening theme

Example 3.25   Smetana: First theme of "The Moldau" from *My Country*

Example 3.26 Rubinstein: *Kamennoi-Ostrov*, No. 22 *(Portraits)*

Example 3.27 Bach: "Crucifixus," from *Mass in B minor*

Example 3.28 Bach: "Resurrexit," from *Mass in B minor*

Example 3.29 Descending E major scale

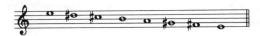

Example 3.30 Traditional carol: "Joy to the World"

Example 3.31 Verdi: "Caro Nome," from *Rigoletto*

Example 3.33 Gregorian chant: *Dies irae*

Di-es i-rae di-es il-la, Sol-vet saec - lum in fa-vil-la, Tes-te Da-vid cum Si-bil-la.

Example 3.34 Berlioz: *Symphonie Fantastique,* fifth movement

Example 3.35 Gregorian chant: *Haec dies*

Haec di - es,

Clausula for *Hec dies*

Haec

di -

Example 3.35 Motet for *Hec dies,* "Huic main"

Huic main au doz mois de mai De - souz le so - lau le - vant,

A.

En un ver - gier m'en en - trai. De - souz un pin ver - doi - ant

A.

U - ne pu - cele i tro - vai Ro - ses coil - lant. Lors me trais vers

A.

li De fine a - mour la pri. E - le me res pon - dit: A

B.

moi n'a - tou - che - res vos j'a Qar j'ai mi - gnot a - mi.

A.

Example 3.36 Tchaikovsky: "Waltz of the Flowers," from *Nutcracker Suite*

Continued on next page

Example 3.36 (continued)

Example 3.37 Tchaikovsky: "Dance of the Flutes," from *Nutcracker Suite*

Example 3.38 Honegger: *Symphony No. 5,* opening. Copyright 1951 Editions Salabert International. Copyright secured. All rights reserved. Editions Salabert 22, rue Chauchat Paris 9e France. Reprinted by permission.

Example 3.39 Schoenberg, "Gavotte," *Suite,* Op. 25. Copyright Wilhelm Hansen, Copenhagen. Used by permission of Belmont Music Publishers, Los Angeles, California 90049.

Example 3.40   Traditional hymn: "O God Our Help in Ages Past" in duple meter

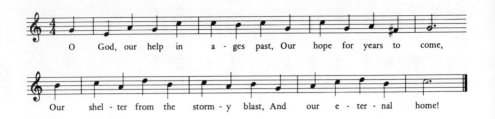

O   God, our help in   a - ges past, Our   hope for years to   come,

Our   shel - ter from the   storm - y blast, And   our   e - ter - nal   home!

Traditional hymn: "O God Our Help in Ages Past" in duple meter

Example 3.41   Traditional hymn: "O God Our Help in Ages Past" in triple meter

Example 3.42   Bach: Original theme from *The Art of Fugue*

Example 3.43   Bach: Contrapunctus XVIII from *The Art of Fugue*

Example 3.48   Brubeck: "Three to Get Ready" (rhythmic pattern only)

Example 3.49   Moussorgsky-Ravel: "Great Gate at Kiev," from *Pictures at an Exhibition* (rhythmic pattern only)

Example 3.50   Beethoven: *Piano Sonata,* Op. 14, No. 2

Example 3.51   Brahms: *Symphony No. 1,* fourth movement, main theme

Example 3.53   Brubeck: "Take Five" (rhythmic pattern only)

Example 3.54   Bach: Prelude No. 20, from Book I of *The Well-Tempered Clavier*

Example 3.55   Brubeck: "Blue Rondo à la Turk" (rhythmic pattern only)

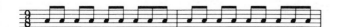

Example 3.56 Stravinsky: *The Rite of Spring,* "Dance of the Adolescents" (rhythmic pattern only)

Example 3.57 Stravinsky: "Soldier's March," *L'histoire du Soldat.* Copyright by J. & W. Chester Ltd. Reprinted by permission.

Example 3.58 Bartók: *Mikrokosmos, No. 140* (rhythmic pattern only)

Example 3.59 Bartók: *Music for Strings, Percussion, and Celesta,* opening theme. Copyright 1937 by Universal Edition; Renewed 1964. Copyright and Renewal assigned to Boosey & Hawkes, Inc., for the U.S.A. Reprinted by permission. Permission for Canada from Universal Edition through their agent, the Theodore Presser Company.

Example 3.60   Tertian chords

Example 3.61   Beethoven: *Sonata No. 14 (Moonlight),* second movement

Example 3.64   Quartal chords

Example 3.65   Parallel organum in fourths

Sit glo - ri - a Do-mi - ni,   in sae-cu - la lae -ta - bi-tur Do-mi-nus in o - pe - ri - bus su - is.

Example 3.66   Hindemith: *Mathis der Maler,* Scene 7. © Copyright 1934 by B. Schott's Söhne. © Copyright renewed 1962 by B. Schott's Söhne. Used by permission of Bellwin-Mills Publishing Corp. and Leeds Music, a Division of MCA Canada Ltd.

Example 3.70   Tone clusters

Example 3.71   Bartók: *String Quartet No. 4*, final chords of third and fourth movements. Copyright 1929 by Universal Edition. Renewed 1956. Copyright and Renewal assigned to Boosey & Hawkes, Inc., for the U.S.A. Reprinted by permission. Permission for Canada from Universal Edition through their agent, the Theodore Presser Company.

Example 3.73   Mozart: *Piano Sonata No. 11*

Example 4.1   Ravel: *Bolero* (rhythmic pattern only)

Example 4.2   Chopin: *Prelude in E minor*

Continued on next page

Example 4.2 (continued)

Example 4.3 Dvořák: *Symphony in E minor*, "Goin' Home" theme, 1st and 2nd parts

Example 4.4 French folk song: "Frère Jacques"

Frè - re Jac - ques, Frè - re Jac - ques. Dor - mez vous? Dor - mez vous?

Son-nez les ma-tin - es, son-nez les ma-tin - es, din, din, don, din, din, don.

Example 4.5 Haydn: *Symphony No. 104*, first movement

Example 4.6 Haydn: *Symphony No. 104*, first movement

Example 4.8 Bartók: *Mikrokosmos, No. 151*, opening. Copyright 1940 by Hawkes & Son (London) Ltd. Renewed 1967. Reprinted by permission of Boosey & Hawkes, Inc.

Example 4.9 Haydn: *Symphony No. 104,* first movement, opening

Example 4.11 Haydn: *Symphony No. 104,* third movement, opening

Example 4.12 Mozart: *Eine kleine Nachtmusik,* third movement, opening

Example 4.13 Clementi: *Sonatina,* Op. 36, No. 6, Rondo, opening

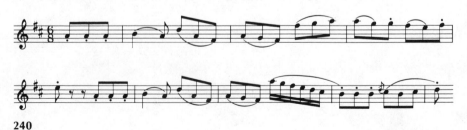

Example 4.14   Haydn: *Symphony No. 104,* first movement, 1st theme

Example 4.15   Mozart: *Symphony No. 40,* first movement, opening

Example 4.20   Bach: *Brandenburg Concerto No. 3,* first movement, opening

Example 4.21   Debussy: *La Plus que lente,* opening. © Copyright 1910 Durand et Cie. Used by permission of the publisher. Elkan-Vogel, Inc., sole representative in the United States.

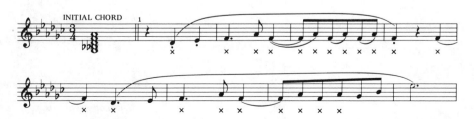

Example 4.22 Beethoven: *Piano Sonata,* Op. 53, first movement, opening

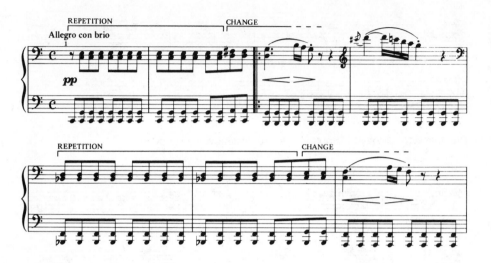

Example 4.23 Bartók: *Mikrokosmos, No. 149.* Copyright 1940 by Hawkes & Son (London) Ltd. Renewed 1967. Reprinted by permission of Boosey & Hawkes, Inc.

Example 4.24 Schubert: "Death and the Maiden"

Gib dei - ne Hand, du schön und zart Ge - bild! bin Freund und

Continued on next page

242

Example 4.24 (continued)

kom - me nicht zu___ stra - fen. Sei gut - es Muts! ich

bin nicht wild, sollst sanft in mein - en ar - men schla - fen!

Example 4.25 Beethoven: *Piano Sonata No. 12,* third movement, opening

Example 4.26 Haydn: *Symphony No. 104,* first movement

ORIGINAL   REPETITION

Example 4.27   Haydn: *Symphony No. 104,* fourth movement, opening

Example 4.31   Traditional French-English carol: "Westminster Carol"

Glo - ri - a.

Example 4.32   Mozart: *Piano Concerto No. 20,* first movement

Example 4.33   Bach: *Two-Part Invention No. 8*

Bach: *Two-Part Invention No. 10*

Example 4.34   Bach: *Brandenburg Concerto No. 5*, first movement

Example 4.35 Wagner: Prelude, *Tristan and Isolde,* opening

Example 4.36 Bach: *The Art of Fugue*

Example 4.37 Brahms: *Symphony No. 3,* first movement

Example 4.38 Bartók: *Concerto for Orchestra,* first movement. Copyright 1946 by Hawkes & Son (London) Ltd. Reprinted by permission of Boosey & Hawkes, Inc.

Example 4.39 Bach: *Two-Part Invention No. 6*, opening

Example 4.40 Eighteenth-century tune

Example 4.41 Beethoven: *Piano Sonata No. 29*, final fugue

Example 4.42 Eighteenth-century tune from Example 4.40: Retrograde inversion

Example 4.43 Honegger, *Symphony No. 5*, second movement. Copyright 1951 Editions Salabert International. Copyright secured. All rights reserved. Editions Salabert 22, rue Chauchat Paris 9e France. Reprinted by permission.

Example 4.44 Bach: Prelude No. 1, from Book I of *The Well-Tempered Clavier,* opening

Example 4.45 Beethoven: *Piano Sonata in D minor*, Op. 31, No. 2, third movement, opening

Example 4.46 Bartók: *Mikrokosmos, No. 151.* Copyright 1940 by Hawkes & Son (London) Ltd. Renewed 1967. Reprinted by permission of Boosey & Hawkes, Inc.

Example 4.47 Berlioz: *Symphonie Fantastique,* fifth movement

Example 4.48 Bach: Fugue No. 8, from Book I of *The Well-Tempered Clavier*

Example 5.1 Mozart: *Symphony No. 40,* first movement

Mozart: *Symphony No. 40,* first movement

Example 5.2 Mozart: *Symphony No. 40,* first movement

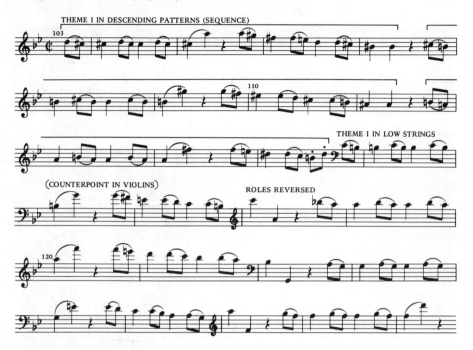

Example 5.3 Mozart: *Symphony No. 40,* first movement

Example 5.4 Bach: *Brandenburg Concerto No. 5,* first movement

Example 5.5 Beethoven: *Symphony No. 5,* first movement, opening section

Example 5.6 Beethoven: *Symphony No. 5,* second movement

Example 5.7 Beethoven: *Symphony No. 5,* third movement

Example 5.8 Beethoven: *Symphony No. 5,* fourth movement

Example 5.9   Handel: "And with His Stripes," from *Messiah*

Example 5.10   Berlioz: *Symphonie Fantastique,* first movement

Berlioz: *Symphonie Fantastique,* second movement

Example 5.10   Berlioz: *Symphonie Fantastique,* fifth movement

Example 5.13   C major scale

Folk tune: "Country Gardens"

Example 5.14   C minor scale

"Country Gardens" in C minor

Example 5.19   Brahms: *Variations on a Theme of Haydn*

Brahms: *Variations on a Theme of Haydn*

Example 5.20 Brahms: *Symphony No. 4,* fourth movement, Passacaglia theme and opening passage

Example 5.21 Folk tune: *L'Homme armé*

L'hom - me, l'hom - me, l'homme ar - mé,

Dufay: "Agnus Dei" from *L'Homme armé* (Mass)

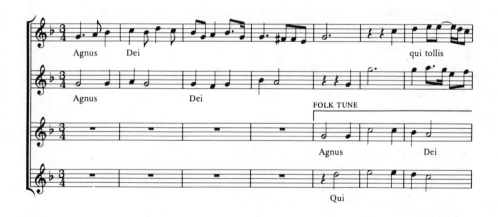

FOLK TUNE

Agnus   Dei   qui tollis

Agnus   Dei

Agnus   Dei

Qui

tollis

255

Example 5.22 Bach: *Cantata No. 140 (Wachet Auf)*

Example 5.23 Wagner: *Siegfried Idyll*

Continued on next page

Example 5.23 (continued)

4th THEME

5th THEME

6th THEME

Example 6.2 Folk song: "On Top of Old Smoky"

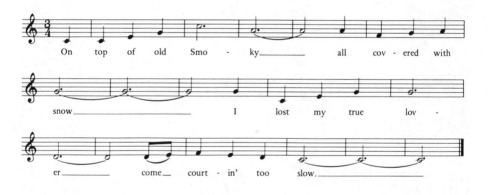

On top of old Smo - ky_____ all cov - ered with

snow_____ I lost my true lov -

er____ come_ court - in' too slow._____

Example 6.3 Scottish folk song: "Ca' the Yowes"

Example 6.5   Chopin: *Prelude in A*, Op. 28, No. 7

Example 6.6   Bach: Prelude No. 1, from Book I of *The Well-Tempered Clavier*

Example 6.7   Bach: Fugue No. 1, from Book I of *The Well-Tempered Clavier*

Example 6.12   Mozart: *Symphony No. 40*, first movement, 1st theme

Example 6.12 Mozart: *Symphony No. 40,* first movement, 2nd theme

Example 7.4 Bach: Chorale, "Wachet Auf"

Example 7.5 Bach: *Cantata No. 140 (Wachet Auf),* opening choral section

Example 7.8 Mozart: *Sonata in G,* second movement (first four measures melody with block chords)

Example 7.9 Mozart: *Sonata in G,* second movement (first four measures melody as written)

Example 7.11 Palestrina: "Agnus Dei," *Pope Marcellus Mass*

Continued on next page

Example 7.11   (continued)

Example 7.12   Song: "Now the Day is Over"

Example 7.19   Bach: *Goldberg Variations,* Variation 18

Example 7.20   Bach: *Little Fugue in G minor*

Example 7.21   Bach: Fugue No. 1, from Book I of *The Well-Tempered Clavier*

Example 7.29   Cadence: (Dominant-Tonic)

V   I

Example 7.30   Cadence: (Subdominant-Tonic)

IV   I

Example 7.31   Cadence elaborated: (Tonic-Subdominant-Dominant-Tonic)

I   IV   V   I

Example 7.32   Cadence elaborated: (Dominant- [Pedal] -Tonic)

I$_4^6$ V   I

Example 7.37   Křenek: *Dancing Toys.* © 1939, 1966 by G. Schirmer, Inc. Reprinted by permission.

Example 7.41   Chromatic Scale

Example 7.42   Whole-tone Scale

Debussy: *Estampes II*, ''La Soirée dans Grenade

Example 7.43 Polytonality in Stravinsky: *The Rite of Spring*

Example 8.5 Bach: *Brandenburg Concerto No. 5*, third movement

Example 8.10 Haydn: *Sonata No. 2*, second movement, ending

Example 8.11 Beethoven: *Piano Sonata No. 8 (Pathétique)*, opening

Example 8.13 Chopin: *Prelude,* Op. 28, No. 4

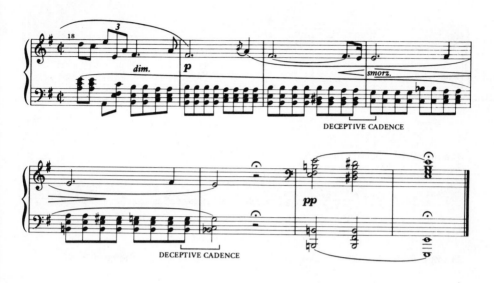

DECEPTIVE CADENCE

DECEPTIVE CADENCE

Example 8.14 Fauré: *Fourth Barcarolle in A-flat*

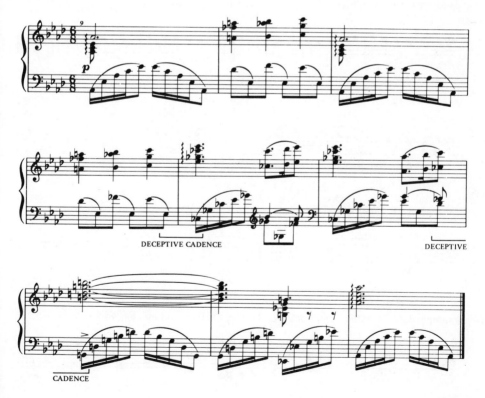

DECEPTIVE CADENCE

DECEPTIVE

CADENCE

Example 8.15 Beethoven: *Symphony No. 9,* fourth movement

vor   Gott   vor   Gott   vor   Gott

DECEPTIVE
CADENCE

Example 8.17 Bach: *Chromatic Fantasy and Fugue,* fugue theme

Example 8.18 Rimsky-Korsakof: *Le Coq d'or,* first movement, 1st theme

Example 8.19 Beethoven: *Symphony No. 9,* fourth movement

Example 8.20 Tchaikovsky: *Symphony No. 6 (Pathétique),* second movement, 1st theme

Example 8.21 Beethoven: *Symphony No. 3 (Eroica),* first movement, 1st theme

Example 8.22 Haydn: *Symphony No. 94 (Surprise),* second movement

Example 8.23 Bach: *Brandenburg Concerto No. 2*, second movement

Example 8.24 Haydn: *Symphony No. 94 (Surprise)*, third movement

Example 9.2 Britten: *The Young Person's Guide to the Orchestra*, Variation A. Copyright 1947 by Hawkes & Son (London) Ltd. Reprinted by permission of Boosey & Hawkes, Inc.

Britten: *The Young Person's Guide to the Orchestra*, Variation L

Index

The symbol (R) indicates selections which are included in the set of records accompanying this text. These selections are also listed separately, by composer. in the Index of Recorded Examples, p. 285. The numbers in boldface type indicate pages containing illustrations.

Index of Recorded Examples

ABCDEFGHIJ— VB —7654321

A BRIEF GUIDE TO WRITING ACADEMIC ARGUMENTS

Stephen Wilhoit
University of Dayton

Longman

New York   San Francisco   Boston
London   Toronto   Sydney   Tokyo   Singapore   Madrid
Mexico City   Munich   Paris   Cape Town   Hong Kong   Montreal

Acquisitions Editor: Lauren Finn
Senior Marketing Manager: Sandra McGuire
Production Manager: Denise Phillip
Project Coordination, Text Design, and Electronic Page Makeup: Electronic Publishing Services
   Inc., NYC
Cover Design Manager: John Callahan
Cover Design: Base Art Co.
Photo Researcher: Rona Tuccillo
Senior Manufacturing Manager: Roy Pickering
Printer and Binder: R. R. Donnelley & Sons/Crawfordsville
Cover Printer: Phoenix Color Corporation

For permission to use copyrighted material, grateful acknowledgment is made to the copyright
holders on pp. 325, which is hereby made part of this copyright page.

Library of Congress Cataloging-in-Publication Data

A brief guide to academic arguments / Stephen Wilhoit.
   p. cm.
   Includes bibliographical references and index.
   ISBN-13: 978-0-205-56861-1 (alk. paper)
   ISBN-10 : 0-205-56861-0 (alk. paper)
   1. English language—Rhetoric—problems, exercises, etc. 2. Persuasion (Rhetoric)—
Problems, exercises, etc. 3. Critical thinking—Problems, exercises, etc. 4. Report writing—
Problems, exercises, etc. 5. Academic writing—Problems, exercises, etc. I. Title.

PE1431.W64 2009
808'.0427—dc22   200848777

Copyright © 2009 by Pearson Education Inc.

Longman
is an imprint of

12345678910—DOC—11 10 09 08

www.pearsonhighered.com/wilhoit

ISBN-13: 978-0-205-56861-1
ISBN-10:   0-205-56861-0

CONTENTS

■ CHAPTER 6

EXPLAINING YOUR ARGUMENT   74

■ CHAPTER 7

QUALIFYING CLAIMS AND REBUTTING OPPOSITION IN ACADEMIC ARGUMENTS   88

■ CHAPTER 8

WORKING WITH SOURCES IN ACADEMIC ARGUMENTS   97

■ CHAPTER 9

WORKING WITH THE VISUAL ELEMENTS OF ACADEMIC ARGUMENTS   114

■ CHAPTER 10

WRITING ARGUMENTS: AN OVERVIEW   123

■ CHAPTER 11

WRITING DEFINITION ARGUMENTS   154

■ CHAPTER 12

WRITING CAUSAL ARGUMENTS   201

■ CHAPTER 13

WRITING PROPOSAL ARGUMENTS   240

CHAPTER 14

WRITING EVALUATION ARGUMENTS   277

PREFACE

THE APPROACH OF THE TEXT

A Brief Guide to Writing Academic Arguments is designed to help prepare students to write the types of argument-based assignments they are likely to encounter in college, especially during their first few years of class work. Published surveys of writing assignments required across the curriculum, longitudinal studies of student writing, and my own experience as a composition instructor and writing-across-the-curriculum consultant confirm the ubiquity of college assignments that ask students to marshal source texts in support of an argumentative thesis. These assignments ask students to form and defend assertions in arguments that meet the specific rhetorical context of the course they are taking and that adhere to discipline-specific conventions.

To help students write these types of essays, *A Brief Guide* offers an introduction to argumentation, critical reading, and argument-related source-based writing. The instruction is firmly based in both writing process and rhetorical theory, offering step-by-step advice on producing effective, persuasive, conventionally sound arguments for academic audiences and purposes.

When discussing the nature and elements of arguments, the text draws on the work of Stephen Toulmin. Those familiar with Toulmin argumentation will recognize much of the terminology I use in the text—e.g., *claims, grounds, qualifiers.* However, *A Brief Guide* departs from Toulmin and many other argument texts on the market in its treatment of warrants. Instead of viewing warrants strictly as underlying assumptions that link grounds to a claim, it discusses the need for writers to *explain* how grounds support a claim. In my experience as a classroom teacher, students can easily learn how and why writers must explain their line of thought in an academic argument, how the grounds they offer actually support the claim they are making. Also, instead of trying to differentiate between "argument" and "persuasion," which almost always co-exist in practice, I offer instruction on how to write persuasive academic arguments, examining how logos, pathos, and ethos tend to function in academic discourse communities.

As the instruction and advice offered in the text makes clear, my approach to teaching academic argumentation is informed by a number of composition theories—expressive, cognitive, social, and rhetorical. Expressive theories help us understand the importance of the writer's commitment to his or her thesis, the mysterious and generative nature of writing, and the importance of establishing and maintaining one's voice in academic writing; cognitive theories help us see writing as a problem-solving and problem-posing activity that can be analyzed and understood; social theories help us understand how writing is always a communal activity, how writers always write in a social context, and how knowledge in the academy is generated and disseminated; and rhetorical theories help us produce persuasive texts that meet the unique demands of every context in which we write.

My goal was to produce a text students will find informative, helpful, and accessible, a text instructors will find easy to teach in class and students will find easy to use on their own. Toward this end, I address student writers from two related perspectives—as an experienced teacher offering instruction to novice students and as a more experienced writer sharing tips and insights.

STRUCTURE OF THE TEXT

A brief overview of the book will help you understand its coverage and organization. The first three chapters cover some basics of academic arguments: what they are, what goes into them, and how to read them.

- **Chapter 1** offers a definition of "academic" arguments in terms of their unique qualities, features, and rhetorical elements.
- **Chapter 2** provides an overview of the elements of persuasive academic arguments, including claims, grounds, explanations, and rebuttals. It also examines the roles logos, pathos, and ethos play in arguments.
- **Chapter 3** discusses the role critical reading plays in academic arguments. It includes instruction on how to understand, analyze, and critique arguments.

The next four chapters examine the elements of academic arguments in greater detail.

- **Chapter 4** examines the role claims play in academic arguments and includes instruction on how to write effective claims.
- **Chapter 5** examines the role reasons and evidence play in supporting claims.
- **Chapter 6** redefines "warrants" as the term is commonly used in approaches to argumentation that draw on the work of Stephen Toulmin. It stresses the importance of explaining the link between claims and grounds in academic arguments.
- **Chapter 7** offers instruction on how to qualify academic arguments and rebut possible opposing views.

The following chapters offer instruction on how to work with source material and visuals when writing academic arguments.

- **Chapter 8** provides instruction on how to quote, paraphrase, and document source material in academic arguments and closes with advice on how to avoid plagiarism.
- **Chapter 9** addresses the visual elements of academic arguments. It offers guidance on how to understand and evaluate the visual elements of arguments, how to incorporate pictures, drawings, diagrams, tables, and graphs into arguments, and how to manipulate the typographical features in texts.
- **Chapter 10** offers students a step-by-step process for writing arguments they can modify to suit their own composing practices and particular demands of whatever assignment they are working on.

The final four chapters offer detailed instruction on four common aims of argumentation: to define some term or idea, to examine causes and/or effects, to propose some kind of action, or to evaluate something. The text's appendix includes a series of checklists students can use as they revise and proofread their work.

- **Chapter 11** offers instruction on writing proposal arguments.
- **Chapter 12** offers instruction on writing causal arguments.
- **Chapter 13** offers instruction on writing proposal arguments.
- **Chapter 14** offers instruction on writing evaluation arguments.
- **Appendix 1** offers guides for revising the argumentative essays discussed in the text.
- **Appendix 2** offers instruction on writing annotated bibliographies.

Though the text suggests a series of steps students can follow to develop, draft, and revise various types of academic arguments and related writing assignments (such as annotated bibliographies), it also encourages students to adapt the instruction to meet the needs of the assignment they are writing.

FEATURES OF THE TEXT
Readings

The text contains 19 professional and student essays and one sample annotated bibliography. Professional readings drawn from disciplines across the curriculum are included to help students understand the nature of academic arguments; how academic writers produce persuasive arguments; how they form, support, and explain claims; and how they use source material as evidence. Additional readings help students learn how to analyze and evaluate academic arguments.

The readings included at the end of chapters 11–14 also differ from those found in many other texts: they tend to be longer than the readings found in many other textbooks and are drawn from academic sources. These readings may prove challenging for some students. However, given that this textbook focuses on writing *academic* arguments, I wanted the additional readings to come from academic sources. I also wanted to include challenging readings, the "real stuff" so many first-year college students are ready and eager to tackle. The two or three additional readings found at the end of each chapter address a common topic:

- Chapter 11: Defining "spirituality"
- Chapter 12: Exploring the causes and effects of bullying
- Chapter 13: Examining various proposals to address the problem of binge drinking
- Chapter 14: Evaluating the effectiveness of and justification for campus speech codes

Should teachers choose to use these additional readings in their classes, they can ask their students to analyze or evaluate them in light of the instruction offered in each chapter or can ask students to use them as source texts for arguments or other essays they write. Additional sample assignments are included in the Instructors Manual that accompanies this textbook.

Sample Student Essays

As with many other textbooks, sample student argumentative essays are provided as well. These sample essays, located in Chapters 11–14, are purposefully varied to reflect the types of texts students may be asked to write in college:

- Chapter 11, "Writing Definition Arguments," offers a sample stipulative definition argument on global warming and a sample categorical definition argument on whether cheerleading is a sport. The first essay incorporates all documentation within the text while the second is written and documented according to MLA guidelines. Both arguments are based on secondary sources.
- Chapter 12, "Writing Causal Arguments," offers an essay on the cause of the last great dinosaur extinction written and documented according to APA guidelines. The argument is based on secondary sources.
- Chapter 13 "Writing Proposal Arguments," offers an essay examining efforts at a fictional university to increase its student retention rate. The writer explores several possible solutions to the problem and offers an argument supporting a particular course of action. The argument is based on *primary research*—interviews and a writer-generated survey.
- Chapter 14, "Writing Evaluation Arguments," offers a sample essay examining an advertisement that appeared in a popular magazine. The writer critiques the advertisement and offers an argument concerning its effectiveness, given the rhetorical context in which it appeared. The argument is based on primary research—analysis and evaluation of the advertisement's visual and graphical elements.

Instructors and students should understand how these sample arguments vary from those found in other argument textbooks. While they are model texts in terms of their structure, use of source material, and documentation practices, *each of the arguments could be improved*. Students are encouraged to read the sample arguments critically, to evaluate and critique the essays by applying lessons learned earlier in the text. The textbook provides questions before each sample essay to guide their critiques. My goal here is simple: discourage students from reading arguments passively—any arguments—and encourage them to actively employ the instruction offered throughout the textbook. Class discussions of these sample arguments can focus on their strengths and their limitations, and students can be encouraged to identify how each might be improved.

Critical Reading Questions

Extensive sets of questions accompany most of the readings, questions designed to help students understand, analyze, and evaluate the additional readings. Some questions, which students consider prior to reading the texts, ask them to reflect on the topic the readings address and form predictions about the texts' content. Other questions guide them through the texts themselves. Still others encourage them to analyze and critique the texts after they've read them, establishing for themselves each reading's value and worth.

Something to write about . . .

Brief writing-to-learn exercises are located at strategic points throughout the text. These exercises are designed to help students understand, critique, or apply the instruction being offered at that point in the text. Some are collaborative in nature, some are not; some ask the students to share their insights with their peers; some do not. Instructors can easily modify these assignments as needed. The text also includes many formal writing assignments. Additional formal and informal writing exercises and assignments can be found in the text's Instructors Manual.

Something to talk about . . .

The text also includes a wide variety of discussion prompts. These "talk-to-learn" activities ask students to discuss issues or questions raised by the text in pairs or larger groups. Students are often asked to share their insights with the rest of their peers to prompt class discussions. Instructors who wish could easily modify these activities to include writing.

Something to think about . . .

Finally, the text also includes a wide variety of critical thinking or reflection exercises. These activities serve a wide range of purposes: to help students reflect on and evaluate their own reading, writing, and thinking processes; to help them better understand the conventions of academic argumentation; to help them apply the material covered in the text to their own lives, interests, and education. Again, instructors who wish to could easily develop writing activities to accompany these exercises and prompts.

Writing Process

As pointed out above, Chapters 1–7 examine the elements of academic arguments and offer instruction on how to read them critically. Chapters 8–10 offer students detailed instruction on writing academic arguments, including how to work with both visual and print source texts. These chapters are firmly rooted in writing process theory and pedagogy, instructing students how to plan, draft, and revise their work effectively and reflectively. Chapters 11–14 offer even more detailed instruction on how to write four commonly assigned types of academic arguments: definition, causal, proposal, and evaluative. These chapters include various heuristics to help students select appropriate topics and generate material for their arguments, paradigms they can use to help them structure their work, and extensive revision guides and checklists (found in the appendix) to help them revise and proofread their work. Numerous model texts are also provided in each chapter, by both student and professional writers.

ACKNOWLEDGMENTS

The author would like to thank Amy Krug, who read and responded to earlier drafts of this manuscript, and his family for their patience. Thanks also to the reviewers for their valuable input. They are: Jeffrey Andelora, Mesa Community College; Bill Bolin, Texas A&M University—Commerce; Kelly Ritter, Southern Connecticut State University; Kevin Ball, Youngstown State University; Tommy Kim, Highline Community College; Susanmarie Harrington, University of Vermont; Kate Kiefer, Colorado State University; Linda Macri, University of Maryland; Patricia Webb Boyd, Arizona State University; Chitralekha Duttagupta, Arizona State University; Dominic Delli Carpini, York College of Pennsylvania; Donna Strickland, University of Missouri—Columbia; Michelle Sidler, Auburn University; Kevin Ball, Youngstown State University; and Tim N. Taylor, Eastern Illinois University.

WHAT MAKES AN ACADEMIC ARGUMENT "ACADEMIC"?

THE GOAL OF THIS TEXTBOOK is to help you learn how to compose effective, persuasive academic arguments, the kinds of arguments you commonly write in high school and college. As a first step toward that goal, it is important to define some terms, to explore the various meanings of "argument," to examine what makes an academic argument "academic," and to describe the qualities that tend to make these arguments effective and persuasive.

WHAT "ARGUMENT" MEANS IN AN ACADEMIC SETTING

For many people, "argue" is synonymous with "fight," as in, "I argued with my parents the other night, and now I'm not speaking to them." In this context, argument has only negative connotations; it is an emotional and hostile exchange that tears people apart and results only in rancor and hurt feelings. Thanks largely to popular radio and television news and talk shows, this view of argument has come to dominate the public sphere as well. On these shows, people "argue" by shouting at each other. Instead of offering considered rationales for the positions they hold, listening carefully to what others have to say, and responding in measured ways, they rely on sound bites and accusations to make their case. In these combative settings, the goal is to "win" the argument, even if it not clear what, exactly, is won.

In academic settings, to "argue" a point typically means something different. Typically, people engage in academic arguments to accomplish one of three goals: (1) to *explain* positions or ideas to readers; (2) to *persuade* readers to change what they think, what they believe, or how they act; or (3) to help *mediate or reconcile* disputes that exist among readers, positions, or ideas (these three purposes for academic arguments are examined more closely below). To achieve these ends, in their arguments writers offer a series of claims which they support with appropriate reasons, evidence, and appeals.

Of course, the key word here is "appropriate." When you write an argument for an academic audience, readers expect the claims, reasons, evidence, and appeals you employ to meet certain standards and to adhere to certain conventions. Learning these standards and conventions is one of the primary purposes of your education. What makes academic writing especially challenging, though, is the fact that while disciplines share certain expectations regarding academic arguments, each has its own set of standards and conventions as well. For example, academic readers across the curriculum expect writers to support claims with appropriate evidence. However, the way readers define "appropriate" evidence can vary among disciplines: what counts as appropriate evidence for an argument you write in a biology class may not be considered appropriate for an argument you write in a religious studies or management class. Understanding and negotiating these different expectations is essential to producing effective academic arguments.

In college, these expectations become more specific as you advance in your major. While introductory college writing courses may help you learn general academic writing skills, many of the classes you take in your major will be designed to help you learn discipline-specific skills. Course assignments and projects will help you learn how to read, write, and think like a member of your future profession, how to conduct research and generate knowledge in discipline-specific ways, and how to construct and present convincing arguments based on that research.

Something to think about . . .

Why do you think there is such variety in the way disciplines define "appropriate" claims, reasons, evidence, and appeals in academic writing? Why might teachers in one class expect you to organize the arguments you write differently than you might organize them in some other class you are taking? Why might the teachers and researchers in one field of study have different expectations for the content, structure, style, and tone of the academic arguments you write than the teachers and researchers in another field of study? Why aren't they all the same?

Something to write about . . .

Make a list of the major writing assignments you have written in high school and/or college, including the topic you wrote about and the class you were taking at the time. Using that information, fill out the *first three* columns of a chart like the one below:

Class	Grade/Year in School	Topic	Qualities

Now, consider the teacher's evaluation of your work in that class. What qualities do you think your teachers looked for when they graded your writing in each class? Summarize your conclusions in the fourth column. Based on your experience, what are the defining characteristics or features of effective writing in each class? How did they vary by discipline? Briefly summarize your conclusions in a few paragraphs citing specific examples from the chart.

CONTEXT IS EVERYTHING: UNDERSTANDING THE RHETORICAL SITUATION OF ACADEMIC ARGUMENTS

Many students come to college believing that good writing results from following a set of rules and formulas that they can memorize and apply to assignments they receive in any class. When they write a paper, they simply need to gather the relevant information and put it together according to some preexisting formula (i.e., the five-paragraph essay) and make sure they follow all the rules in their handbooks (i.e., commas in the right place, no misspelled words). Writing effective academic essays is actually more complicated than that. Formulas and rules certainly have their place: formulas often provide helpful frameworks around which to build a paper, and you lose credibility as a writer in academic settings if your writing is full of errors. However, understanding the rhetoric of academic writing is more important than simply memorizing and following a set of predetermined formulas and rules.

Rhetoric, simply, is the study of effective language use. For centuries, rhetoricians have paid particular attention to the role language plays in argument and persuasion; therefore, gaining some knowledge of basic rhetorical principles and effective rhetorical practices will help you write stronger academic arguments. For example, every assignment you write in college presents you with a unique rhetorical problem to solve—to write a successful paper, you need to determine the most effective way to develop and structure your argument given the topic you are examining, the audience you are addressing, and goals you are trying to accomplish. These various elements of the writing task—writer, audience, topic, purpose, and occasion—make up the assignment's *rhetorical situation.* Learning how to critique or write an argument based on its unique rhetorical situation is one of the keys to succeeding in college and beyond.

Elements of the Rhetorical Situation

The various elements of an argument's rhetorical situation might be summarized this way.

Writer:	The role, stance, or persona the writer is expected to assume when he or she writes an argument
Audience:	The person or people the writer is addressing in his or her argument or the type of person the writer expects will read the argument
Topic:	The subject the writer is addressing in his or her argument
Occasion:	What compels the writer to write the argument, what gives rise to the argument, what the argument is responding to
Purpose:	What the writer is supposed to accomplish by writing the argument or why the writer is writing it

Understanding how the elements of the rhetorical situation interact with, influence, and shape one another is central to evaluating or writing academic arguments. Each of these elements is explained more fully below.

Writer

In rhetorical terms, understanding the role the writer plans in an argument is more complex than simply knowing his or her name or identity. Answering questions such as these can help you determine how the writer's background, attitudes, and goals might shape the argument he or she writes.

- What is the author's expertise?
- What qualifies the author to write about this topic?
- Is the author writing as an expert or a novice?
- In terms of the topic he or she is addressing, is the author writing as a believer or as a skeptic?
- What does the author reveal about his or her feelings regarding the topic?
- Has the writer collaborated with others to write the argument?
- Has the author written anything else about this topic? If so, what?

Audience

Think of audience in two closely related ways: in terms of specific people and in terms of traits and predispositions. Some arguments are written with specific readers in mind: an argument written to a university president, one written to the mayor of a city, one written to a classmate. Others are written to certain *types* of readers: to readers who are likely to be skeptical of the author's thesis, readers who know little about the topic he or she is addressing, readers who will likely sympathize with the writer's assertions. Answering the following questions can help you better understand the role audience may play in shaping an argument.

- What specific audience, if any, is the writer addressing?
- What does the writer assume about his or her reader's attitudes toward the topic of the essay or knowledge of the subject?
- Is the writer assuming a skeptical or accepting audience?
- Is the writer assuming a friendly or hostile audience?
- How has the writer adjusted the content, organization, or style of his or her argument to better sway his or her audience?

Topic

What is the writer writing about? This may seem like a fairly straightforward question to answer, but it is often complicated by the other elements of an argument's rhetorical situation. To better understand the role topic plays in an argument, consider the following questions.

- How broadly or narrowly does the writer define the topic he or she is addressing? Why?
- Which elements of the topic receive the most attention? Which are downplayed? Why?
- How might the writer's background and/or intended audience influence the way he or she addresses the argument's topic?

- How does the writer shape, explain, and defend his or her claims concerning the argument's topic? What informs or guides the writer's decisions in these areas?

Occasion

Occasion can be captured in one question: What moved or compelled the writer to compose this argument? Answering these questions can help you better understand the role occasion plays in academic arguments.

- What gave rise to the argument?
- Why did the writer compose this argument?
- How does the writer indicate what prompted him or her to write the piece?
- Does the writer place his or her argument in the context of other argument? If so, what is that context?
- Does the writer indicate how his or her argument questions or advances arguments other writers have produced? If so, what are those other arguments?

Purpose

Assuming you are reading an academic argument, the writer's purpose may seem clear: convince readers of the veracity of his or her position on the topic or persuade readers to change the way they think, believe, feel, or act. However, writers may have several purposes or goals in mind when writing an argument, including these.

- Writing an argument to persuade readers: writers want to sway their readers' opinions by offering logical, properly qualified assertions in support of a thesis and supporting those claims with evidence that both establishes the writers' authority and appeals to their readers' reason and emotions
- Writing an argument to gain a better understanding of the topic: writers want to learn more about the topic they are addressing in their essay
- Writing an argument to learn about oneself: writers hope to gain a better understanding of what they truly think, feel, or believe about the topic they are addressing in their essay
- Writing an argument to reconcile or mediate: writers hope to synthesize a conflicting point of view into a more comprehensive whole
- Writing an argument to determine what is true: writers challenge current thought to determine what is right or true

Answering the following questions will help you determine the purpose(s) underlying the academic arguments you read.

- Has the writer stated his or her purpose for writing the argument, either in the body of the essay or in an abstract of the piece?
- If the writer does not state the purpose, what purpose is implied by his or her thesis or argument?
- If there appear to be two or more purposes, what are they? Do they complement one another or do they conflict with each other? Does one purpose seem dominant and another secondary? If so, which is which?

■ How has the writer's purpose influenced the content, organization, or style of his or her argument?

How the Elements of the Rhetorical Situation Are Interconnected

Though the various elements of the rhetorical situation were just examined in isolation, in practice they are always intimately connected. Each element affects and is affected by the others. Figure 1 offers a better way to think about the relationship that exists among the various elements of the rhetorical situation.

Consider, for example, possible relationships between the intended audience of an argument and the other elements of the rhetorical situation. What the writer knows, learns, or assumes about the audience will impact how he or she addresses the topic. Likewise, the writer needs to assess the audience's knowledge of and attitude toward the exigency which compelled the writer to compose the argument. Finally, the writer must consider his or her purpose in light of the intended audience: what effect does the writer want to have on those reading his or her argument? What is he or she hoping to accomplish by addressing this audience with this argument? Learning how to successfully balance and manipulate the various elements of the rhetorical situation when writing academic arguments takes time and practice, but becomes easier with experience: the more you read, analyze, and discuss academic arguments, the easier it becomes to write them yourself.

Something to talk about . . .

Read the following essay by columnist Thomas L. Friedman, "Generation Q." In this piece, Friedman argues that the current generation of college students may be too quiet and too politically passive for its (and America's) own good. Analyze the essay in terms of its rhetorical situation and discuss it with other students in class, focusing on questions such as these:

1. What are Friedman's primary claims? How does he support his argument?
2. Who is the intended audience of the piece? What does Friedman assume about his audience?
3. What is the occasion for the piece? What prompted Friedman to write it?
4. What is the purpose of the piece? What does Friedman hope to accomplish by writing it?
5. How might Friedman's own beliefs, values, and politics seem to influence his argument?
6. How do the various elements of the rhetorical situation interact to influence one another? For example, how does the occasion for the piece influence the way Friedman addresses the topic and conceives of his audience? How does the writer's purpose arise from the occasion of the piece?

Finally, discuss whether you agree or disagree with Friedman's assertions, explaining why.

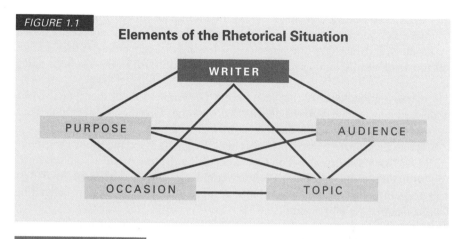

FIGURE 1.1
Elements of the Rhetorical Situation

SAMPLE READING

"Generation Q"

Thomas L. Friedman

Thomas Friedman is foreign affairs columnist for the New York Times *and winner of the 2002 Pulitzer Prize for his commentaries. He is the author of numerous award-winning books that often address issues of politics, culture, and technology.*

I just spent the past week visiting several colleges—Auburn, the University of Mississippi, Lake Forest and Williams—and I can report that the more I am around this generation of college students, the more I am both baffled and impressed.

I am impressed because they are so much more optimistic and idealistic than they should be. I am baffled because they are so much less radical and politically engaged than they need to be.

One of the things I feared most after 9/11—that my daughters would not be able to travel the world with the same carefree attitude my wife and I did at their age—has not come to pass.

Whether it was at Ole Miss or Williams or my alma mater, Brandeis, college students today are not only going abroad to study in record numbers, but they are also going abroad to build homes for the poor in El Salvador in record numbers or volunteering at AIDS clinics in record numbers. Not only has terrorism not deterred them from traveling, they are rolling up their sleeves and diving in deeper than ever.

The Iraq war may be a mess, but I noticed at Auburn and Ole Miss more than a few young men and women proudly wearing their R.O.T.C. uniforms. Many of those not going abroad have channeled their national service impulses into increasingly popular programs at home like "Teach for America," which has become to this generation what the Peace Corps was to mine.

It's for all these reasons that I've been calling them "Generation Q"—the Quiet Americans, in the best sense of that term, quietly pursuing their idealism, at home and abroad.

But Generation Q may be too quiet, too online, for its own good, and for the country's own good. When I think of the huge budget deficit, Social Security deficit and ecological deficit that our generation is leaving this generation, if they are not spitting mad, well, then they're just not paying attention. And we'll just keep piling it on them.

There is a good chance that members of Generation Q will spend their entire adult lives digging out from the deficits that we—the "Greediest Generation," epitomized by George W. Bush—are leaving them.

When I was visiting my daughter at her college, she asked me about a terrifying story that ran in this newspaper on Oct. 2, reporting that the Arctic ice cap was melting "to an extent unparalleled in a century or more"—and that the entire Arctic system appears to be "heading toward a new, more watery state" likely triggered by "human-caused global warming."

"What happened to that Arctic story, Dad?" my daughter asked me. How could the news media just report one day that the Arctic ice was melting far faster than any models predicted "and then the story just disappeared?" Why weren't any of the candidates talking about it? Didn't they understand: this has become the big issue on campuses?

No, they don't seem to understand. They seem to be too busy raising money or buying votes with subsidies for ethanol farmers in Iowa. The candidates could actually use a good kick in the pants on this point. But where is it going to come from?

Generation Q would be doing itself a favor, and America a favor, if it demanded from every candidate who comes on campus answers to three questions: What is your plan for mitigating climate change? What is your plan for reforming Social Security? What is your plan for dealing with the deficit—so we all won't be working for China in 20 years?

America needs a jolt of the idealism, activism and outrage (it must be in there) of Generation Q. That's what twentysomethings are for—to light a fire under the country. But they can't e-mail it in, and an online petition or a mouse click for carbon neutrality won't cut it. They have to get organized in a way that will force politicians to pay attention rather than just patronize them.

Martin Luther King and Bobby Kennedy didn't change the world by asking people to join their Facebook crusades or to download their platforms. Activism can only be uploaded, the old-fashioned way—by young voters speaking truth to power, face to face, in big numbers, on campuses or the Washington Mall. Virtual politics is just that—virtual.

Maybe that's why what impressed me most on my brief college swing was actually a statue—the life-size statue of James Meredith at the University of Mississippi. Meredith was the first African-American to be admitted to Ole Miss in 1962. The Meredith bronze is posed as if he is striding toward a tall limestone archway, re-enacting his fateful step onto the then-segregated campus—defying a violent, angry mob and protected by the National Guard.

Above the archway, carved into the stone, is the word "Courage." That is what real activism looks like. There is no substitute.

QUALITIES OF EFFECTIVE ACADEMIC ARGUMENTS

As mentioned at the beginning of this chapter, academic arguments adhere to discipline-specific standards and conventions. These standards and conventions help to define each discipline; knowing and using them helps to establish you as an insider in that field of study. However, regardless of the course for which they are written, all effective academic arguments share certain characteristics: they are clear and precise, well supported, properly qualified, adequately contextualized, stylistically appropriate, conventionally sound, and sensitive to audience needs.

Effective Academic Arguments Are Clear and Precise

In an effective academic argument, claims are unambiguous and evidence is exact; the link between the writer's claims and evidence is explained; language is precise; and syntax aids rather than hinders comprehension. Key terms are defined, quoted and paraphrased material is properly documented, and all source material is effectively integrated into the writer's own prose.

Effective Academic Arguments Are Well Supported

In an effective academic argument, the writer supports all of his or her claims with reasons, evidence, and explanations. Academic audiences expect writers to support the claims they make; few claims are taken on faith alone. Sometimes inexperienced college writers believe incorrectly that a claim speaks for itself, that readers will accept it without any support or explanation. Though what counts as appropriate evidence may vary by discipline, academic audiences tend to discount unsupported claims in arguments.

Effective Academic Arguments Are Properly Qualified

In academic writing, most claims are qualified in some way (for example, note the word "most" in this sentence). Writers tend to avoid words such as "every," "all," "none," and "always." Sweeping claims such as "It is always the case that . . ." or "Every person would agree that . . ." are typically easy to dismiss: a critical reader need only cite one counterexample to dispute the claim. However, a more fundamental reason writers qualify claims involves the pursuit of truth. In *most* cases, assertions of truth in academic writing are provisional and contextual; they are based on the current state of knowledge. Effective academic writers qualify their arguments because they understand the tentative nature of their assertions and have learned when and how to acknowledge the limitations of the claims they make.

Effective Academic Arguments Are Placed in Context

Effective academic writers know how to contextualize their arguments, to establish how their argument contributes to an ongoing conversation or debate in their discipline. For example, academic arguments frequently begin with a "survey of the literature," a summary of what others have written on the topic the writer is addressing to help clarify what the writer is contributing to the debate he or she is joining. Academic arguments do not exist in a vacuum; they relate in some way to what has been said and written about the topic in the past. Establishing the context of an argument helps writers establish its value and readers assess its worth. In fact, writers often conclude an academic argument by examining the implications of the claims they have made, explaining how their argument recasts, clarifies, or advances research or thought in the field.

Effective Academic Arguments Employ an Appropriate Voice and Tone

Academic arguments are often accused of being overly dry and scholarly, a recitation of facts and findings that comes across as impersonal and mechanical. This characterization still holds true for many academic arguments today; however, stylistic conventions change over time, and academic writing is currently in a state of flux. The desire to be "objective" or "scholarly" has often led to dry and impersonal writing; any sense of individuality or personality in academic writing was considered to be at best unnecessary and at worst inappropriate. Many college professors still believe this to be the case; others, however, prefer their students employ a less formal style of writing in their arguments. For example, while many readers still object to the use of first person in academic writing, it is becoming increasingly acceptable in professional publications across the curriculum. That being said, though a range of stylistic conventions govern writing across the curriculum, most academic audiences still expect writers to adopt a voice and tone that do not distract from an essay's argument.

Effective Academic Arguments Follow Established Conventions

Academic writing is expected to adhere to discipline-specific writing and research conventions. Over time, you will learn these conventions by reading widely in your field or receiving instruction on them from your teachers. Conventions can govern how you format a paper, what kinds of material you include and exclude in your argument, what you need to document, and how you should cite it.

Sometimes there are logical reasons for a discipline's writing conventions. For example, consider differences in documentation practices for classes in the humanities that follow guidelines advocated by the Modern Language Association (MLA) and those in the social sciences that follow guidelines advocated by the American Psychological Association (APA). APA guidelines stipulate that when writers cite material parenthetically in their texts, they include the date of publication for that information; MLA in-text documentation does not include dates. Because employing the most recent research is crucial to academic arguments in many of the social sciences, APA conventions stipulate including the year of publication in the documentation. Because the humanities frequently do not share the social sciences' emphasis on citing the most recent research on a topic, MLA documentation practices exclude the date. Other times there may not be a clear explanation for why a text is expected to be written, formatted, or documented in a particular way. You will simply be expected to adhere to long-established discipline-specific textual conventions. When you ask, "Why do I have to say it like this?" or "Why is it written like that?" the answer may be a less than satisfying, "Just because that's the way we do it."

Effective Academic Arguments Are Sensitive to Audience Needs

Effective academic arguments are written with an audience clearly in mind; they are intended to have some effect on their readers. To achieve this effect, writers manipulate their argument's content, structure, and style. Successful academic writers make a conscious effort to anticipate what their readers need to know—what assertions need to be explained more thoroughly, what terms need to be defined, what lines of reasoning need to be explicated more fully, what word choice or punctuation might be confusing. The organizational strategy they employ will help readers move easily through their essay, removing distractions and establishing clear links among their claims. However, knowing they can never anticipate all of their readers' needs, successful academic writers usually make sure that someone they trust responds to drafts of their work. As they revise their papers, they ask other readers to critique their writing, using the response they receive to clarify and strengthen their arguments. The more experience you gain writing academic arguments, the easier it becomes to anticipate the way readers are likely to respond to your work.

Something to talk about . . .

Carefully examine the qualities of effective academic arguments listed above. What does this list tell you about the values and expectations academic readers bring to the texts they read? What are they looking for when they read academic arguments? What standards of writing and reasoning do they reflect?

Share your thoughts with someone else in class then together rank order the qualities you think characterize academic writing from most important to least important. Your teacher might ask you to share the results of your discussion with the class.

Something to write about . . .

1. Choose any of the sample readings included in this textbook for analysis and identify the elements of its rhetorical situation. Briefly summarize the reading then answer the following questions:
   a. Who is its writer?
   b. Who is its intended audience?
   c. What topics does it address?
   d. What is the purpose of the text?
   e. What is the occasion for the text?

2. In the section on rhetorical context, the elements are examined in isolation so you can see each one more clearly. However, in actual arguments, the elements always influence one another: the writer's audience influences how he or she addresses the topic, the occasion for the piece may dictate the purpose, and so

on. To better understand these connections, write out your answers to the following questions. Your teacher may want you to share your responses with other students in the class.

a. How might a writer's purpose influence his or her treatment of an argument's topic?

b. How might a writer's intended audience influence his or her treatment of an argument's topic?

c. How might a writer's treatment of the topic change if his or her audience changed?

d. How might an argument's purpose and audience be related? What range of purposes might a writer have for his or her argument, and how might those purposes be related to his or her intended audience?

e. How might occasion and writer be connected? In school writing, what range of occasions are writers most likely to encounter?

f. Is it possible to separate occasion and purpose? Can the occasion for an argument generate multiple purposes?

3. Carefully examine the wording of an argumentative assignment you have been asked to write in one of your classes (or that your teacher has given you to study). Based on the wording of that assignment, write your answers to the following questions then share your responses with other students in class.

a. What role are you being asked to assume as the person writing this assignment?

b. Who is the intended audience for the assignment?

c. What topics does the assignment ask you to address?

d. What is the stated or implied purpose of the assignment?

e. What is the stated or implied occasion for the argument?

THE ELEMENTS OF PERSUASIVE ACADEMIC ARGUMENTS

WHAT MAKES ACADEMIC ARGUMENTS PERSUASIVE?

Persuasive academic arguments present a logical, compelling case for a thesis, appeal to the reader's emotions or values, and establish and maintain the writer's credibility. Since antiquity, these elements of persuasion have been known as *logos* (persuading through appeals to logic or reason), *pathos* (persuading through appeals to emotion or values), and *ethos* (persuading through appeals to the writer's credibility and character). Though logos dominates academic writing (academic arguments are unlikely to persuade readers if significant problems exist in their logic or reasoning), understanding how to appeal to your readers' emotions and values and to establish your own credibility as a writer will help you produce persuasive arguments in college.

For reasons of discussion and instruction, teachers often draw a distinction between argument, with its emphasis on logos, and persuasion, with its added emphasis on pathos and ethos. In practice, though, writers usually draw on all three appeals when writing academic arguments. Producing an effective academic argument is not just a matter of logos, of explaining logically how the well-chosen evidence you include in your essay supports your claims. Though many academic arguments attempt to rely on logos alone to make their case, they usually prove less persuasive than arguments that purposefully employ appeals to pathos and ethos as well.

Suppose, for example, that you are writing an argument and have several examples you can offer as evidence in support of a particular claim. How can you choose which one to include in your essay if your intended audience is likely to view them all as equally reasonable? To make this decision, you need to consider not just logic but emotion as well. Given the choices you have before you, what evidence is most likely to appeal to your reader's values or desires? Which is likely to have the most emotional impact? To make this decision, you will need to employ the analytical skills and empathy typically associated with pathos, not logos.

Ethos is an inevitable part of every academic argument as well. Consciously or unconsciously, when people read a text, they form judgments about the credibility and, perhaps, character of the author. Sometimes these judgments are correct, and sometimes they are wrong, but people make them nonetheless. From a writer's perspective, you can influence how your readers view you through the decisions you make concerning your argument's content, structure, and style.

For example, fairness and balance are generally valued in academic writing, and writers who exhibit these traits are usually more persuasive than writers who do not. Will choosing one example over another to include in an essay make you appear more authoritative because it comes from a publication that your readers value and trust? You can't avoid making an impression on your reader—you always will every time you write an essay. How you present yourself in an academic argument—and how readers perceive you—are important aspects of ethos.

In summary then, academic readers expect writers to produce logical and reasonable arguments—logos is a given. Persuasive academic arguments do more. Through their use of pathos and ethos, they move readers to agree with or act on their assertions. The role of logos, pathos, and ethos in academic arguments is described in more detail below. With practice, you will learn how to employ all three elements of persuasion effectively in your writing.

Something to write about . . .

In your own words, briefly explain the meaning of "logos," "pathos," and "ethos." Save these definitions—you will be asked to write about them again at the end of this chapter.

LOGOS: THE ROLE OF LOGIC AND REASON IN ACADEMIC ARGUMENTS

At the heart of any academic argument is a claim supported by reasons and evidence, an explanation of the link between that claim and its support, and an acknowledgement of the claim's limitations. British philosopher Stephen Toulmin used many of these terms in his book *The Uses of Argument*, a work that has had a profound effect on how argument is taught in writing and communication courses. The elements that make up Toulmin's model of argumentation are usually portrayed something like this:

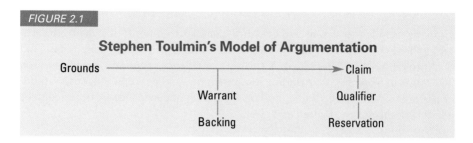

FIGURE 2.1

Stephen Toulmin's Model of Argumentation

Grounds ————————————————→ Claim

Warrant   Qualifier

Backing   Reservation

According to Toulmin, the basic elements of an argument include its claim, grounds, and warrant, plus its qualifiers, backing, and reservations. In an argument, a writer offers grounds or evidence in support of a claim or assertion. This claim is often qualified or limited in some way, while reservations acknowledge conditions under which the claim might not be true.

The most difficult part of Toulmin's model to understand is the warrant. For Toulmin, a warrant is an assumption that allows someone to assert a claim from the given evidence. Sometimes the warrant must be defended (the role of backing); other times, it can simply be stated without explanation; and still other times, it will be assumed and go unstated. In most academic arguments, readers expect writers to *explain* their warrants, to make explicit and if necessary defend the link they see between a claim and the grounds they provide to support it. Using Toulmin's terms, academic audiences expect writers to explain and defend their warrants.

Simplifying Toulmin's terms a bit (Figure 2.2), the core of an academic argument consists of a *claim, grounds,* and the *explanation* that links them. Writers are also expected to *qualify* these claims when necessary and to examine possible *rebuttals* to their assertions—alternative points of view or objections that might be raised against their claim. While each of these elements will be defined more fully below, Chapters 4 and 7 explains in detail how to develop effective claims, qualifications, and rebuttals; Chapter 5 examines grounds; and Chapter 6 addresses explanations or warrants.

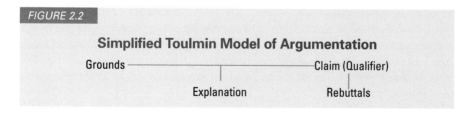

FIGURE 2.2

Simplified Toulmin Model of Argumentation

Grounds ————————————————Claim (Qualifier)

Explanation   Rebuttals

Claims

Claims are the assertions you make in an argument. Effective claims are clear, limited, and logical. They arise from and add to some ongoing conversation concerning the topic of your essay. Your primary claim in an argument is your thesis.

Grounds

Grounds include the reasons and evidence you offer in support of a claim. Reasons are explicitly or implicitly linked to a claim through a "because" statement: "You ought to do X (claim) because of Y (reason)." Evidence supports a claim or reason and comes in many forms, including research findings, expert opinion, observations, or personal experience. In academic writing, reasons and evidence are expected to be relevant, authoritative, logical, and clear.

Explanations

Explanations make explicit the connection that exists between your argument's grounds and claims. When writing an academic argument, do not assume that this connection is self-evident, that your readers will understand without explanation how the grounds you provide justify, support, or lead to the claim you are making. Instead, you need to explain the connection, as you perceive it. This explanation will answer two questions central to any argument: (1) How, exactly, do the grounds you provide support the claim you are making? and (2) What justifies the move from your grounds to your claim? In academic arguments, a great deal of attention is devoted to these explanations.

Qualifications

What are the limitations of the claims you make? With what degree of certainty can you maintain them? Is the claim true all of the time and under all circumstances or only some of the time and under some circumstances? Will it hold true for everyone or just for some people? These questions concern a claim's qualifications. As explained in the previous chapter, academic writers are usually careful to acknowledge the limitations of their assertions.

Rebuttals

In academic writing, few claims can or will go unchallenged. Questioning assertions or offering opposing arguments is one of the ways the academic community tests the validity, accuracy, and strength of claims. When writing an academic argument, you have three ways to address possible rebuttals to your claims: refute them, concede to them, or accommodate them. When you refute an opposing view, you explain how it is flawed, wrong, or irrelevant to your assertion; when you concede to it, you acknowledge its legitimacy but explain why your assertion still holds; when you accommodate it, you acknowledge its legitimacy and explain how it is or can be made compatible with your own assertion.

Logos in Action: A Sample Argument

Imagine you are a student taking an introductory college writing course at a school whose administration has decided to pave over a popular playing field on campus to provide faculty additional parking (arguments that address specific proposals such as this are discussed in much more detail in Chapter 13). Because this decision has angered many students (and keeps coming up for discussion in your writing class), your teacher has decided to ask every student to write a letter to the campus newspaper arguing in favor or against the administration's proposal. You plan to argue against the decision to put in the new parking lot.

One of the benefits of understanding Toulmin's approach to argumentation is that along with helping you analyze arguments, it can also serve as a tool to help you develop material for the papers you write in school. If you know that most academic arguments are built around claims, grounds, explanations, and rebuttals, you can carefully consider how you might address each element in your essay.

Turning to the hypothetical assignment described above, you already have the primary claim or thesis of your letter—the administration should not pave over the playing field. Let's assume that you feel pretty adamant about this claim and do not want to qualify it. Using Toulmin's scheme, your essay begins to look like this:

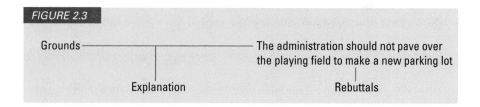

FIGURE 2.3

Grounds —————————————— The administration should not pave over
the playing field to make a new parking lot

Explanation   Rebuttals

Next, you will want to generate grounds to support your claim. Remember, grounds are reasons and evidence you provide to support the assertions you make. After thinking about the issue, listening to your classmates discuss it in class, and talking about the issue with your roommate, you come up with several reasons to support your claim. The administration should not pave over the playing fields because

1. it would interfere with student intramural sports;
2. it would destroy the only green space in the western end of the campus; and
3. it would be more practical to simply expand two existing lots close to the playing field.

Because you are writing a letter to your campus newspaper, you believe that space restrictions will likely keep you from including all three reasons in your response, especially if you develop them in any detail. So you decide to concentrate on the first reason you listed for now. Using Toulmin's scheme, your plan now looks like this:

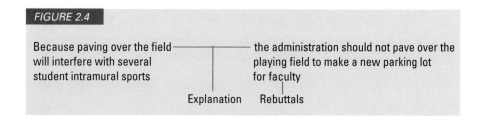

FIGURE 2.4

Because paving over the field ————————— the administration should not pave over the
will interfere with several   playing field to make a new parking lot
student intramural sports   for faculty

Explanation   Rebuttals

So far, your argument looks fine, but you begin to worry that readers unfamiliar with the intramural sports program might not understand how they are connected to the proposed parking lot. Because you work at the student recreation center, you know that the field the administration is planning to asphalt is the only one on campus big enough to accommodate intramural flag football, rugby, and ultimate Frisbee, all popular sports. You figure that you ought to explain this connection between your claim and grounds. Now, the outline of your argument looks like this:

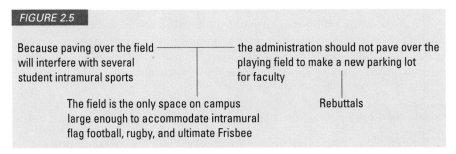

FIGURE 2.5

Because paving over the field — the administration should not pave over the playing field to make a new parking lot for faculty

will interfere with several student intramural sports

The field is the only space on campus large enough to accommodate intramural flag football, rugby, and ultimate Frisbee

Rebuttals

When you show this plan to several of your classmates, one of them suggests that you need more of an explanation. For example, she wonders why it's a problem if students can't play these sports on campus and suggests that you consider why you believe losing these sports matters. Thinking about it, you realize that you need to state in your letter that these are all popular sports. By paving over the field, the administration will deny a large number of students their favorite recreational activity, thus violating its stated commitment to promoting student health. Now, your outline might look like this:

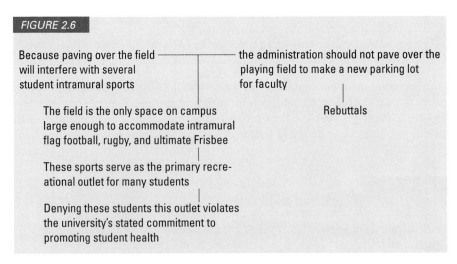

FIGURE 2.6

Because paving over the field — the administration should not pave over the playing field to make a new parking lot for faculty

will interfere with several student intramural sports

The field is the only space on campus large enough to accommodate intramural flag football, rugby, and ultimate Frisbee

Rebuttals

These sports serve as the primary recreational outlet for many students

Denying these students this outlet violates the university's stated commitment to promoting student health

Finally, you need to consider why someone might object to your argument. Suppose your roommate points out that the university owns a large parcel of land a short drive off campus and suggests that students could play intramural flag football, rugby, and ultimate Frisbee there. While it is true that the school owns that land, you point out that it would greatly inconvenience students to drive there; that students participate in all of these sports late in the evening, making it impractical to hold the matches off campus; and that because freshmen and sophomores are not allowed to have cars on campus, transportation issues make the move unwise. You are now in a position to add and answer a possible rebuttal to your argument. Now, your outline looks like this:

FIGURE 2.7

Because paving over the field will interfere with several student intramural sports ──────── the administration should not pave over the playing field to make a new parking lot for faculty

The field is the only space on campus large enough to accommodate intramural flag football, rugby, and ultimate Frisbee

These sports serve as the primary recreational outlet for many students

Denying these students this outlet violates the university's stated commitment to promoting student health

The intramural sports could be moved to a large field the school owns off campus

This is not a good plan: (a) the location is inconvenient, (b) holding evening matches there is impractical, (c) first- and second-year students have no cars to drive there

---

When you use the Toulmin framework as a tool to help you develop material for an argument, consider filling out a grid such as the one below (Figure 2.8). You will be generating the same material but may find the grid an easier format to employ.

Now that you have worked through the various elements of your argument concerning the administration's plans for a new parking lot on campus, you are ready to write the first draft of your letter. As you write, other ideas and insights will likely arise. When this occurs, make note of them and decide where and how they might be incorporated into the piece. Using the outline you generated as a guide to get started, your draft letter might look like the one below.

FIGURE 2.8

Claim	Grounds	Explanation	Rebuttal
The administration should not pave over the playing field to make a new parking lot for faculty	Because paving over the field will interfere with several student intramural sports	The field is the only space on campus large enough to accommodate intramural flag football, rugby, and ultimate Frisbee	The intramural sports could be moved to a large field the school owns off campus
	These sports serve as the primary recreational outlet for many students	Denying these violates the university's stated commitment to promoting student health	This is not a good plan: (a) the location is inconvenient, (b) holding evening matches there is impractical, (c) first- and second-year students have no cars to drive there

---

SAMPLE READING

Dear Editor:

Last week the administration announced plans to pave over Founders Field in order to provide more parking for faculty. While it is true that faculty need more parking spaces, sacrificing Founders to provide it is not a good idea. As some may already know, Founders is the only field on campus large enough to accommodate intramural flag football, rugby, and ultimate Frisbee matches. I've worked in the Recreation Complex for two years and know from experience just how popular these sports are—every fall and spring the fields are in constant use during the evening hours.

Denying students the opportunity to participate in these sports by demolishing Founders would be both unfair and unwise. These sports represent the only athletic outlet for many students on campus and for others serve as an important leisure activity. Denying them the opportunity to play might adversely affect both their health and their academic success. In addition, the friendships formed during the matches is one of the things that makes our school unique. On our school's Web site, the administration states that it is committed to promoting student health. By paving over Founders Field, the administration would be violating commitments it has made to every student on campus.

Some may argue that intramural sports teams could just use the newly purchased fields near the river. However, they are several miles away from campus, making this solution impractical. Students have a difficult enough time as it is setting aside time for intramural sports. Having to travel that distance to participate is impractical. Because so many of the matches take place at night, asking students to walk to and from the site in the evening would not be safe. Finally, because first- and second-year students are not allowed to have cars on campus, the university would have to provide transportation to the fields, which would be very expensive.

Instead of paving over Founders Field, the administration should consider just expanding both "J" and "K" lots to provide more parking for faculty. Doing so would accommodate the faculty while preserving Founders.

Something to talk about . . .

Assume the student who wrote the letter above is one of your classmates. Your teacher has asked you to look over this draft and make recommendations for improving it. What suggestions would you offer?

Something to write about . . .

To get a better sense of how claims, grounds, and explanations form the core of most academic arguments, work through this exercise. Below you will find a series of claims. For each one, write out grounds you might offer to support each one plus a few sentences explaining how the grounds and claims are connected (you can argue the opposite position on each claim if you like).

1. Baseball is no longer "America's sport," football is.
2. Radio stations should not broadcast songs with racist, sexist, or homophobic lyrics.
3. Each year, the Academy Award for best picture should go to the movie that brought in the most money at the theaters.
4. All illegal drugs in America should be legalized to reduce crime.
5. Students should be required to declare a major before they are admitted to college.
6. Though people do not like to fight wars, sometimes they are necessary and justified.
7. This generation of students holds fewer prejudices than did earlier generations.

Common Logos-Related Fallacies

Over time, certain types of claims have been identified by logicians and rhetoricians as false or misleading. These logical fallacies usually involve questionable links between claims and grounds. Because academic audiences are familiar with these logical fallacies, avoiding them will strengthen the arguments you write. Also, be on the watch for them in the arguments you read for class. You need to question seriously any argument that rests upon or employs any of these fallacies. Some of the more common are defined below.

1. Hasty Generalization

Basing a broad claim on too little evidence.

> *Because John took the pencil from class, the teacher can't trust any of the boys.*

The fact that John is dishonest does not mean that other boys can't be trusted. The other boys will not necessarily behave the same way John behaved.

2. False Cause

Claiming a causal relationship between events only related in time.

> *Of course it's going to rain—I washed my car today. It rains every time I wash my car.*

Simply because it rains after someone washes his or her car does not mean that washing the car caused it to rain.

3. Appeal to Ignorance

Claiming an assertion is true because it has not or cannot be disproved.

> *Martians must have built the pyramids because no one can prove they didn't.*

To prove this argument, you would need evidence that Martians *did* build the pyramids.

4. Non Sequitur

Making a claim that does not follow from the evidence given.

> *Beth will be a successful painter because she has blue eyes.*

The fact that someone has blue eyes has no impact on whether he or she will be a successful painter—one has nothing to do with the other.

5. Begging the Question

Arguing in circles—using aspects of the claim itself as evidence.

> *Joan is always going to be late because she's never on time.*

This argument simply says the same thing twice. Instead of advancing an argument, it simply repeats its assertion.

6. Straw Man

Oversimplifying or misrepresenting opposing views in order to discredit them.

People who support legalizing marijuana really want to legalize all drugs.

While some who support legalizing marijuana may want to legalize all drugs, it is wrong to assume this position applies to everyone who does. The aim is to discredit their position on one issue by attaching it to another, likely more unpopular, position.

7. False Dilemma

Claiming that there are only two options to pursue: either do this or do that.

America, love it or leave it.

This type of argument oversimplifies issues and ignores other possibilities.

Something to talk about . . .

With one or two other students in your class, discuss why you think each of the logical fallacies described above represents a faulty form of reasoning. Using the samples provided for each type of logical fallacy as models, develop additional examples of your own. Be ready to share your examples with the rest of the class.

PATHOS: THE ROLE OF EMOTION IN ACADEMIC ARGUMENTS

Many academic writers and readers approach pathos cautiously and skeptically, perhaps for good reason. While logos appeals to readers' intellect and reason, pathos appeals to their values and emotions, and emotions (skeptics believe) are more easily manipulated than reason. Politicians and advertising executives have long understood that they can avoid the intellectual scrutiny of their claims by appealing directly to and playing upon people's emotions. However, properly and ethically employed, emotional appeals can work with logical appeals to enhance the persuasive power of your academic arguments. Pathos can help you decide which claims and evidence to include in your essay, help you shape the language you employ, and help you communicate your own emotional commitment to the arguments you explore. It can also help readers understand how your arguments are relevant to their lives.

Pathos in Action: A Sample Essay

Few issues are more emotionally charged than the debate over embryonic stem cell research. Almost all scientists agree that stem cell research holds great promise, especially in treating cancer and paralysis. However, major controversies have emerged: whether scientists should use embryonic or adult stem cells for research purposes and whether the federal government should fund research that uses embryonic stem cells.

The following essay by Republican Congressman Christopher Smith argues against embryonic stem cell research. Pay close attention to how Congressman Smith uses appeals to emotion and values to bolster his argument.

Perils and Promise: Destroy an Embryo, Waste a Life

Christopher H. Smith

U.S. Representative Christopher H. Smith (R, New Jersey) is the senior member of the House Foreign Affairs Committee and has authored numerous bills addressing issues of human rights and ethics.

The debate over stem-cell research has a face and a name.

Hannah Strege is a happy 2½-year-old girl. By all accounts, she is a normal, healthy toddler discovering the joy of life. In a few days I hope to meet Hannah, and when I do, I will reassure her that there is no such thing as a spare or leftover person.

Although she may not yet understand what that means, her parents sure do. They understand perfectly because Hannah used to be a frozen embryo in an in vitro fertilization (IVF) clinic. She was what those who support embryonic stem-cell research—research that destroys such human embryos—callously call spare and leftover.

But Hannah is neither spare nor leftover, even though she spent a considerable time in a deep-freeze tank that served as her frozen orphanage. She could have been fodder for researchers, but instead today she is talking a blue streak. And according to the Snowflakes program, which arranged for Hannah to be adopted as an embryo, there are between 11,000 and 22,000 similar children today who could be placed for adoption with any one of the 2 million infertile couples waiting to begin families of their own.

The story of Hannah and other adopted embryos underscores why we should not spend federal taxpayer dollars to destroy human embryos to steal their precious stem cells. These cells are not ours to take. And given the breathtaking discoveries from adult stem-cell research, which does not rely on destroying human embryos, arguments for federally funding embryonic stem-cell research are less persuasive than ever.

In just the past few months, several dramatic breakthroughs have been reported by the *New England Journal of Medicine* and others validating the promise of adult stem-cell research. Donald Orlic of the National Human Genome Research Institute recently said that "we are currently finding that these adult stem cells can function as well, perhaps even better than, embryonic stem cells."

Unlike embryonic stem cells, which have never been used in any clinical applications, adult stem cells are today helping to treat numerous conditions, including brain tumors, ovarian cancer, leukemia, breast cancer, non-Hodgkin's lymphoma, autoimmune diseases, stroke, anemia, blood and liver disease. I have introduced legislation to expand federal funding for adult stem-cell research because it already holds the promise of saving lives without destroying lives.

Recent studies have shown, furthermore, that adult stem cells have the exciting potential to treat diabetes, spinal cord injuries, muscular dystrophy, blindness, Parkinson's, Alzheimer's, and glaucoma, as well as to repair or replace organs and tissues.

In view of this growing body of evidence supporting adult stem-cell research, the only way to justify federal funding for embryonic stem-cell research is to take the position that a human embryo has no value—none, zero, less than the dot above the i on this piece of paper. Now that medical advances have clearly demonstrated that adult stem cells are a legitimate alternative to research that destroys human embryos, the only way to justify embryo-destructive work is to assert that Hannah has no value at all.

For all of our sakes, I hope that ethics do matter in this debate. I hope that we can all agree that human embryos have innate value. Once we determine that any human life can be destroyed in the name of science, all life is devalued.

Too many cultures and societies have believed it acceptable to sacrifice the few, the weak, and the vulnerable for the benefit of the strong and the many. But experience and ethics dictate that it is unacceptable to destroy one life for the potential benefit of others, particularly when there are legitimate alternatives.

Adult stem-cell research is scientifically justified, ethically responsible and morally acceptable. Embryonic stem cell research is not.

No child is spare or leftover, and the weak and the vulnerable will always need someone to speak for them. We must speak for them, and for Hannah.

How Pathos Can Help You Develop Content and Choose Language

For better or worse, readers will respond emotionally to the arguments you put forward. While you cannot dictate anyone's emotional response to your writing, you do have the ability to influence it, primarily through the material you choose to include in your essay and the language you choose to employ.

Consider Smith's essay. As Smith thought about the content of his argument, why do you think he chose to focus on Hannah Strege, the "happy 2½-year-old girl"? Why characterize Hannah as a "spare" or a "leftover"? Why do you think he included such a long list of diseases and ailments adult stem cell research might help cure? Why end the piece by appealing to his readers' values: "I hope that we can all agree that human embryos have innate value." Smith could have focused the entire editorial on the scientific issues involved in adult and embryonic stem cell research—the relative strengths and limitations of both protocols—but he chose instead to focus on Hannah, to use this language, and to make these appeals. Smith does not rely entirely on pathos to make his case, but his desire to appeal to his readers' emotions and values clearly influenced the content and language of his editorial.

As you consider the emotional impact of your argument's content and language, ask yourself the following questions.

- Given what I know about my intended audience, what is likely to be their emotional predisposition toward the argument I am advancing?
- How are members of my intended audience likely to respond emotionally to each claim I make, the evidence I provide to support these claims, and the language I use to communicate my ideas?
- How might my argument's content and language appeal to some readers and alienate others?
- What claims, support, and language most accurately reflect my feelings toward the topic of my essay and my thesis?

How Pathos Can Help You Create a Bond with Your Audience

Readers will find your writing more persuasive if your arguments are relevant to their lives or experience. If your readers believe that you understand their values or concerns, they are more likely to consider and perhaps accept your assertions. In this way, imagination and empathy play a vital role in producing persuasive academic arguments. As you write your essay, you need to ask yourself the following questions: Given my intended audience, what claims, evidence, or language will have the greatest emotional impact on my readers? Can I create emotional bonds with my audience by appealing to their feelings and values, fears and concerns, or needs and desire for self-esteem?

Appealing to Your Readers' Feelings and Values

Successful appeals to your readers' feelings and values require both sophisticated analytical skills and empathy. You need to anticipate how your readers are likely to respond emotionally to your essay's claims, evidence, and language and how your argument might support or challenge their values. You will never be able to identify your readers' feelings and values with absolute certainty, but you are more likely to succeed if you know your intended audience well, are a member of that audience yourself, or have written effective arguments for similar audiences in the past.

Turn again to Smith's editorial. Hannah's story is clearly intended to pull at the readers' heartstrings—what reader wants to see a little girl as a "spare" or a "leftover"? As he states in his opening line, Smith wants to put a "face and a name" on the issue. Instead of thinking about embryonic stem cell research in abstract terms, he wants readers to think about it in human terms, specifically the fate of the human embryos that are destroyed by researchers (of course, there are counterarguments to Smith's assertions, but we are just examining his persuasive strategies at this point). Examine the various appeals Smith makes to his readers' values as well. With statements such as "I hope that ethics do matter in this debate" or "too many cultures and societies have believed it acceptable to sacrifice the few, the weak, and the vulnerable for the benefit of the strong and the many," Smith directly appeals to his readers' values. He believes he can persuade his readers that supporting research on adult rather than embryonic stem cell research is more in line with their values. Look at the language Smith uses in these sentences: "The story of Hannah and other adopted embryos underscores why we should not spend federal taxpayer dollars to destroy human embryos to *steal* their precious stem cells. *These cells are not ours to take*" (emphasis added). Here Smith is appealing to his readers' sense of justice—what reader would want to be complicit in theft?

Answering the questions below will help you identify and address your readers' feelings and values as you develop and draft arguments of your own.

- How are my readers likely to feel about the topic of my essay?
- How are they likely to feel about each of my claims?
- What is the relationship between my readers' likely emotional responses to my claims and the language I use to communicate them?
- Which aspects of my argument are likely to evoke positive feelings in my readers and which are likely to invoke negative responses?
- How can I best mitigate those negative responses without compromising my own argument?
- What are my readers' dominant values?
- How are my readers' values likely to influence their response to my argument?
- What content and language do I need to include in my essay to appeal to my readers' values?
- How should I present claims that I believe will conflict with my audience's values?

As you appeal to your readers' feelings and values, do not pander. Do not abandon your own position on the topic in an effort to sway your readers. Instead, consider which emotional appeals will best persuade readers to accept and perhaps act on the argument you are presenting.

Appealing to Your Readers' Fears and Concerns

Appealing to your readers' fears or concerns can greatly increase their interest in your argument. However, it is easy to overplay such appeals and produce heavy-handed, overly emotional arguments. You do not want to manipulate and unfairly play on your readers' emotions. Instead, your goal is to demonstrate how the positions you promote in your argument can assuage their concerns or address their fears.

Smith makes an interesting appeal to his readers' fears and concerns in his opinion piece. He knows that for many years scientists and researchers have been pointing out the potential benefits of embryonic stem cell research. Readers know that they, too, may someday need the kinds of medical treatments that embryonic stem cell research promises. Notice how Smith devotes several paragraphs to explaining how adult stem cell research may also help scientists develop treatments for these ailments. In fact, he suggests that adult stem cell research is clinically preferable when developing treatments: "Unlike embryonic stem cells, which have never been used in any clinical applications, adult stem cells are today helping to treat numerous conditions . . . ." Smith wants to persuade his readers to oppose federally funded embryonic stem cell research and instead support adult stem cell research by demonstrating, in part, how such a change in position addresses some of the fears and concerns they may have regarding their health or the health of their loved ones.

Because readers' fears and concerns can be wide ranging, they can be difficult to determine. Answering the following questions might help:

- What might my audience's fears or concerns be concerning the topic of my paper? Does it raise concerns about their safety, well-being, or happiness?
- What might be the basis for those fears or concerns?
- Might readers be unconcerned about the topic of my essay but worried about some of the claims I make?
- Will they be worried about the impact my assertions or ideas might have on them, their families, or their way of life?
- Might they be worried about the ethical, religious, or social implications of my argument?
- Are my readers' fears and concerns legitimate? If so, what do I need to change in my argument to address them?

Appealing to Your Readers' Emotional Needs and Self-esteem

This type of emotional appeal is more subtle than the others and employing it successfully requires a close and accurate analysis of your reader's psychological state. Human behavior is driven by a complex set of needs and a desire for self-esteem. Humans need to feel loved, safe, and valued; they need to feel a sense of self-worth and pride. They are more likely to find your argument persuasive if they believe it addresses these needs, contributes to their self-esteem, or validates their sense of self-worth.

One way you can appeal to your readers' desire for self-esteem is through the claims or assertions you make. Do your assertions address your readers' needs or promote their sense of worth? What are you asking your readers to think or do? Will such thought or action make them feel better about themselves? How do you make this clear in your essay? Another way you can appeal to your readers' needs and desire for self-esteem is through the tone you adopt in your argument. Do you treat your readers with respect? Do you honor their values? Insulting or demeaning academic arguments are unlikely to be persuasive.

To persuade readers to accept or act on your thesis, you could also appeal to their lesser angels, to their greed, pride, or prejudices. While such appeals might prove persuasive for some readers, most critical academic audiences will reject them. Such appeals stand in direct opposition to the academic values of honesty, fairness, and even-handedness.

The primary way Smith appeals to his readers' emotional needs and desires involves his use of the first person plural point of view: "we" and "our." Look at his closing sentences: "No child is spare or leftover, and the weak and the vulnerable will always need someone to speak for them. We must speak for them, and for Hannah." Here Smith invites his readers to join him in a heroic action—together, "we" can save the weak and the vulnerable, we can speak for powerless kids like Hannah, we can fight the oppression and misuse of the children. Some readers may see this appeal as a little over the top emotionally, but Smith's strategy is clear. He is assuming that his readers will be swayed to his position if, in doing so, they feel better about themselves or can see themselves working with others on a noble cause.

Below are some questions that will help you develop or refine appeals to your readers' needs and desire for self-esteem when you write arguments of your own.

- What are my readers' emotional needs?
- How might I address these needs effectively in my essay?
- How might my claims, evidence, or language conflict with my readers' emotional needs or desire for self-esteem? How can I mitigate this conflict while remaining true to my own argument?
- Is my essay likely to be read by some readers as an attack on their self-esteem? If so, how can I avoid this problem without compromising my argument?
- Will any of my readers find my ideas, arguments, or language in any way demeaning or insulting? If so, what revisions can I make to avoid this problem?

Something to think about . . .

While persuading someone to adopt your point of view or to act in a particular way by appealing to their feelings, values, fears, concerns, needs, and self-esteem can be very effective, when might it not be fair or ethical? What role does fairness or ethics play in persuasion? How do you balance appeals such as these with the pursuit of truth? Is it fair or ethical to use these persuasive techniques for less than noble ends? Can you think of times when this has happened? Can you find examples in Smith's editorial that you think cross the line, appeals to emotions and values that are unfair or unethical? Which ones? What makes them unfair or unethical?

How Pathos Can Help You Communicate Your Own Emotional Investment in Your Argument

While emotional appeals can help you persuade readers to accept or act on your arguments, they can also communicate your own emotional investment in the assertions you put forward. You will produce your best arguments when you care deeply about them, when they mean something to you emotionally, not just intellectually. Your argument will likely be more persuasive when you genuinely want your readers to care about an issue the way you care about it, to support positions you strongly endorse, to act in ways you think are right and just. Through the claims, grounds, and language you include in your essay, you communicate to your readers the emotional investment you have in your argument and produce the kinds of passionate, engaged prose that academic audiences find most persuasive.

Something to write about . . .

Describe how you might use pathos to compose persuasive arguments on each of the topics listed below. If you were addressing each topic in an argument, how might you appeal to your readers' emotions, values, fears, needs, and self-esteem? What examples and language might you include in your essay? Explain why you think each appeal would be successful.

1. An argument in favor of the city funding a center to care for stray dogs and cats.
2. An argument in favor of instituting a minute of silence at the start of classes in your city's public schools.
3. An argument in favor of banning smoking in all public spaces.
4. An argument against raising the age for obtaining a driver's license to 18.
5. An argument in favor of abolishing all required courses at your school, allowing students to take whatever classes interest them.

Common Pathos-Related Fallacies

Just as there are well-established logical fallacies, so are there lines of fallacious reasoning associated with emotional appeals. Employing these pathos-related fallacies in your arguments will damage your credibility. Some of the more common are described below.

1. Bandwagon

Trying to sway people to adopt a position because it happens to be popular.

> *We need to move to this new software program because all the other schools in the region have moved to it.*

Just because other schools have acted in a particular way does not mean it's the best policy for this school—being like everyone else is not necessarily desirable.

2. Slippery Slope

Assuming that a series of undesirable consequences will necessarily follow from a decision, often appealing to the readers' fears.

> *If we discuss contraception in the public schools, students will become more sexually active, we'll see an increase in teen pregnancy rates, venereal disease will become epidemic, and many more children will die.*

There is no guarantee that all of the bad consequences listed will result from discussing contraception in public schools. Arguing that they will is misleading.

3. Scare Tactics

Predicting horrible consequences will necessarily follow from a decision when they may not.

> *If we don't change our current gun laws, criminals will be rampaging through every neighborhood.*

Appealing to readers' need for security is an accepted persuasive tool; trying to frighten them needlessly and illogically is not.

4. Appeals to Sentiment

Trying to sway opinion by attaching it to unrelated emotions.

If you don't support the park levy, you don't love little puppies or baby ducks.

Playing on a reader's emotions can be effective, but the appeal must be fair and relevant. Overplaying this type of appeal often results in bathos, not pathos.

5. Appeals to Tradition

Arguing for a course of action because it has always been done that way.

We can't change the course requirements for the major because we've always required the current courses.

Just because something has always been done one way does not mean it is still the best way to do it.

> **Something to talk about . . .**
>
> With one or two other students in your class, discuss why you think each of the pathos-related fallacies described above represent faulty forms of reasoning. Using the samples provided for each type of pathos-related fallacy as models, develop additional examples of your own.

ETHOS: THE ROLE OF THE WRITER'S AUTHORITY AND CREDIBILITY IN ACADEMIC ARGUMENTS

Establishing your credibility is essential when writing academic arguments. To be taken seriously as an academic writer, you need to learn and adhere to accepted standards of content, structure, and form. Writers who routinely fail to meet these expectations lose their credibility and alienate readers, and once you have lost your readers' trust, you will not be able to persuade them to accept or act on your argument. Academic writers generally establish their authority, or ethos, by producing arguments that are knowledgeable, accurate, and fair and that adhere to established disciplinary conventions.

Establishing Ethos Through Your Knowledge of the Topic

Academic readers tend to trust writers they believe to be authoritative and knowledgeable. One of the best ways to improve your ethos as an author is to present yourself as fully informed, as someone who thoroughly understands the topic you are addressing. This knowledge typically arises from some combination of research, reflection, and personal experience. You will demonstrate your knowledge of the topic through the types and numbers of sources you use to support your claims and by fully and carefully explaining your line of reasoning. Academic readers will also expect you to examine alternative points of view in the arguments you write. If you do not address possible opposition to your claims, your readers will simply assume that you either overlooked them or are purposefully ignoring them because you believe your claims will not withstand scrutiny. In either case, your ethos suffers.

Establishing Ethos Through Accurate Writing

Being accurate in what you write is another way to establish your credibility among academic audiences. Unfortunately, many beginning college writers severely damage their credibility by turning in argumentative essays filled with inaccuracies and errors. Fallacious claims, misquoted material, faulty documentation, even sentence-level errors involving spelling or punctuation can damage your credibility and your essay's ability to persuade readers.

Clear and Qualified Claims

First, be sure that all of the claims you make in your essay are clear, properly qualified, and accurate. If readers feel that your claims are unclear or can demonstrate that they are inaccurate or too sweeping, they will likely reject your entire argument. Carefully choose the language you use to state your claims and clarify any ambiguous terms. Most importantly, though, be sure your claims are factually accurate. Misrepresenting facts in a claim damages your credibility, whether that misrepresentation is intentional or not. If your claims are inaccurate, no amount of supporting evidence will convince readers to accept your argument.

Accurate Use of Source Material

One of the primary ways you support claims in academic writing is by quoting or paraphrasing material from source texts, such as books, articles, newspapers, and Web sites. This source material must be accurate and accurately presented. Inexperienced college writers often misuse source material when writing academic arguments. Avoiding the errors described below can improve your credibility as a writer (for a fuller discussion of using source material in academic arguments, see Chapter 8).

Using Inaccurate Source Material

Be sure the source material you use to support a claim is itself accurate. Simply because something is in print does not mean it is correct or true. When possible, verify information you decide to include in your essay. One reason academic audiences prefer scholarly sources of information over popular sources relates directly to this issue—articles in scholarly journals have undergone peer review to ensure their accuracy; those in non-scholarly journals generally have not.

Misquoting or Unethically Manipulating Source Material

Sometimes inexperienced student writers do not understand how crucial it is to quote source material accurately in their arguments. Quoted material has to exactly match the writing in the source text—any changes need to be indicated with the correct punctuation. Inadvertently misquoting source material will cause readers to question your competence and fairness as a writer. (See Chapter 8 for advice on how to quote material properly.)

A more serious problem involves purposefully changing quoted material to misrepresent what an author has written. Suppose, for example, an author has written the following sentence:

> **"There is no evidence to show that the vice president was involved in the president's death."**

but a student quotes the sentence in his paper as follows:

> **"There is . . . evidence to show that the vice president was involved in the president's death."**

Without question, the writer here has misrepresented the author's position by manipulating the quotation, a practice that is unethical and unacceptable.

Misrepresenting Evidence

Misrepresenting evidence is sometimes more difficult to avoid than the other errors: a writer cites evidence to support a claim that, in the source text, was used to support a different, unrelated claim. Suppose, for example, that an author has produced a study showing that single-sex education drastically improved the math scores of the fourth grade girls he studied, but a writer uses that information to support a claim that single-sex education improves math scores of boys or of high school girls. The author of the source text based his study on fourth grade girls—asserting that his results apply to other types of students is misleading and likely inaccurate. Misrepresenting evidence like this compromises your credibility as an academic writer.

Accurate Documentation

Proper documentation of source material is also essential in academic writing. Readers expect writers to document all quoted and paraphrased material in their arguments properly and accurately. Providing proper documentation demonstrates that you have researched your topic, that your argument contributes to an ongoing conversation on the topic, and that you understand the writing conventions of your discipline. Failing to document material that needs to be documented or documenting material inaccurately detracts from your credibility. (See Chapter 8 for more information on documentation.)

Accurate Language, Grammar, Mechanics, and Punctuation

If the language you use in your argument is inaccurate or vague, your readers may believe that your thinking is equally inaccurate or vague. These problems are often related to word choice: in any argument, you must choose your words carefully, understanding both their connotative and denotative meanings. Even errors involving grammar, mechanics, punctuation, and spelling can damage your credibility and your argument's effectiveness. Again, some readers will believe that if your prose is full of sentence-level errors, your reasoning might be flawed as well.

Something to think about . . .

Why do you think that accuracy is so valued in academic writing? What is it about the rhetorical situation of academic writing that makes accuracy so important? Think back to the purposes of academic writing discussed in Chapter 1 of this text—how might accuracy be central to achieving each of those purposes?

Establishing Ethos by Being Open-minded, Honest, and Fair

Academic audiences expect writers to be open-minded, honest, and fair. Being open-minded means, in part, that you are willing to examine multiple points of view on an issue and that you openly acknowledge the limitations of your own claims, data, and findings. Basic fairness in academic writing involves treating alternative points of view accurately and respectfully, even if you strongly disagree with them. Being honest includes acknowledging the limitations of your own argument. Inexperienced college writers sometimes make the mistake of sounding arrogant, refusing to qualify their claims or findings or to address the limitations of their research method-ologies. However, your ethos is actually enhanced when you are open-minded and honest enough to offer your arguments with humility and circumspection.

Establishing Ethos by Following Conventions

As mentioned in Chapter 1, academic writing follows a number of disciplinary con-ventions that will impact the content, structure, and style of the arguments you write. Academic audiences tend to consider writers who properly adhere to these conven-tions as more authoritative than those who do not. This generalization is especially true in more advanced courses. First-year students or those just entering a major may not be expected to understand all of the writing conventions governing a particular discipline. However, as you move toward graduation, you will be expected to know and follow them. In fact, learning these conventions will be an important part of your professional training. Mastering discipline-specific writing and research con-ventions increases your ethos among academic readers, conferring on you an "insider" status other writers may lack.

Ethos in Action: A Sample Reading

Below you will find an article on embryonic stem cell research originally published in the *New England Journal of Medicine.* The article's author, Michael J. Sandel, is a pro-fessor of ethics and justice at Harvard University who has published widely on the ethics of medical research and at one time served on the President's Council on Bioethics. Following the reading, you will be asked to consider a number of questions concerning the role ethos plays in Dr. Sandel's argument, but as you read the piece for the first time, pay close attention to the way he addresses counterarguments, the tone he establishes, and his efforts to reach a compromise position on the use of human embryos for stem cell research.

`SAMPLE READING`

Embryo Ethics: The Moral Logic of Stem-cell Research

Michael J. Sandel

Michael J. Sandel is Anne T. and Robert M. Bass Professor of Government at Harvard University.

At first glance, the case for federal funding of embryonic stem-cell research seems too obvious to need defending. Why should the government refuse to support research that holds promise for the treatment and cure of devastating conditions such as Parkinson's disease, Alzheimer's disease, diabetes, and spinal cord injury? Critics of stem-cell research offer two main objections: some hold that despite its worthy ends, stem-cell research is wrong because it involves the destruction of human embryos; others worry that even if research on embryos is not wrong in itself, it will open the way to a slippery slope of dehumanizing practices, such as embryo farms, cloned babies, the use of fetuses for spare parts, and the commodification of human life.

Neither objection is ultimately persuasive, though each raises questions that proponents of stem-cell research should take seriously. Consider the first objection. Those who make it begin by arguing, rightly, that biomedical ethics is not only about ends but also about means; even research that achieves great good is unjustified if it comes at the price of violating fundamental human rights. For example, the ghoulish experiments of Nazi doctors would not be morally justified even if they resulted in discoveries that alleviated human suffering.

Few would dispute the idea that respect for human dignity imposes certain moral constraints on medical research. The question is whether the destruction of human embryos in stem-cell research amounts to the killing of human beings. The "embryo objection" insists that it does. For those who adhere to this view, extracting stem cells from a blastocyst is morally equivalent to yanking organs from a baby to save other people's lives.

Some base this conclusion on the religious belief that ensoulment occurs at conception. Others try to defend it without recourse to religion, by the following line of reasoning: Each of us began life as an embryo. If our lives are worthy of respect, and hence inviolable, simply by virtue of our humanity, one would be mistaken to think that at some younger age or earlier stage of development we were not worthy of respect. Unless we can point to a definitive moment in the passage from conception to birth that marks the emergence of the human person, this argument claims, we must regard embryos as possessing the same inviolability as fully developed human beings.

But this argument is flawed. The fact that every person began life as an embryo does not prove that embryos are persons. Consider an analogy: although every oak tree was once an acorn, it does not follow that acorns are oak trees, or that I should treat the loss of an acorn eaten by a squirrel in my front yard as the same kind of loss as the death of an oak tree felled by a storm. Despite their developmental continuity, acorns and oak trees are different kinds of things. So are human embryos and human beings. Sentient creatures make claims on us that nonsentient ones do not; beings capable of experience and consciousness make higher claims still. Human life develops by degrees.

Those who view embryos as persons often assume that the only alternative is to treat them with moral indifference. But one need not regard the embryo as a full human being in order to accord it a certain respect. To regard an embryo as a mere thing, open to any use we desire or devise, does, it seems to me, miss its significance as potential human life. Few would favor the wanton destruction of embryos or the use of embryos for the purpose of developing a new line of cosmetics. Personhood is not the only warrant for respect. For example, we consider it an act of disrespect when a hiker carves his initials in an ancient sequoia, not because we regard the sequoia as a person, but because we regard it as a natural wonder worthy of appreciation and awe. To respect the old-growth forest does not mean that no tree may ever be felled or harvested for human purposes. Respecting the forest may be consistent with using it. But the purposes should be weighty and appropriate to the wondrous nature of the thing.

The notion that an embryo in a petri dish has the same moral status as a person can be challenged on further grounds. Perhaps the best way to see its implausibility is to play out its full implications. First, if harvesting stem cells from a blastocyst were truly on a par with harvesting organs from a baby, then the morally responsible policy would be to ban it, not merely deny it federal funding. If some doctors made a practice of killing children to get organs for transplantation, no one would take the position that the infanticide should be ineligible for federal funding but allowed to continue in the private sector. If we were persuaded that embryonic stem-cell research were tantamount to infanticide, we would not only ban it but treat it as a grisly form of murder and subject scientists who performed it to criminal punishment.

Second, viewing the embryo as a person rules out not only stem-cell research, but all fertility treatments that involve the creation and discarding of excess embryos. In order to increase pregnancy rates and spare women the ordeal of repeated attempts, most in vitro fertilization clinics create more fertilized eggs than are ultimately implanted. Excess embryos are typically frozen indefinitely or discarded. (A small number are donated for stem-cell research.) But if it is immoral to sacrifice embryos for the sake of curing or treating devastating diseases, it is also immoral to sacrifice them for the sake of treating infertility.

Third, defenders of in vitro fertilization point out that embryo loss in assisted reproduction is less frequent than in natural pregnancy, in which more than half of all fertilized eggs either fail to implant or are otherwise lost. This fact highlights a further difficulty with the view that equates embryos and persons. If natural procreation entails the loss of some embryos for every successful birth, perhaps we should worry less about the loss of embryos that occurs in in vitro fertilization and stem-cell research. Those who view embryos as persons might reply that high infant mortality would not justify infanticide. But the way we respond to the natural loss of embryos suggests that we do not regard this event as the moral or religious equivalent of the death of infants. Even those religious traditions that are the most solicitous of nascent human life do not mandate the same burial rituals and mourning rites for the loss of an embryo as for the death of a child. Moreover, if the embryo loss that accompanies natural procreation were the moral equivalent of infant death, then pregnancy would have to be regarded as a public health crisis of epidemic proportions; alleviating natural embryo loss would be a more urgent moral cause than abortion, in vitro fertilization, and stem-cell research combined.

Even critics of stem-cell research hesitate to embrace the full implications of the embryo objection. President George W. Bush has prohibited federal funding for research on embryonic stem-cell lines derived after August 9, 2001, but has not sought to ban such research, nor has he called on scientists to desist from it. And as the stem-cell debate heats up in Congress, even outspoken opponents of embryo research have not mounted a national campaign to ban in vitro fertilization or to prohibit fertility clinics from creating and discarding excess embryos. This does not mean that their positions are unprincipled, only that their positions cannot rest on the principle that embryos are inviolable.

What else could justify restricting federal funding for stem-cell research? It might be the worry, mentioned above, that embryo research will lead down a slippery slope of exploitation and abuse. This objection raises legitimate concerns, but curtailing stem-cell research is the wrong way to address them. Congress can stave off the slippery slope by enacting sensible regulations, beginning with a simple ban on human reproductive cloning. Following the approach adopted by the United Kingdom, Congress might also require that research embryos not be allowed to develop beyond 14 days, restrict the commodification of embryos and gametes, and establish a stem-cell bank to prevent proprietary interests from monopolizing access to stem-cell lines. Regulations such as these could save us from slouching toward a brave new world as we seek to redeem the great biomedical promise of our time.

Note how Sandel enhances his credibility by demonstrating his expert knowledge of the topic and by being open minded, honest, and fair. Sandel states that advocates of embryonic stem cell research should "take seriously" the primary arguments opponents raise against the procedure. He then fairly and accurately summarizes the primary arguments opponents raise against the procedure before carefully explaining why he finds each unpersuasive. Also note how in the last two paragraphs Sandel attempts to find common ground with those who oppose embryonic stem cell research. Overall, most people reading Sandel's article would agree that he presents a knowledgeable, accurate, and fair argument on the topic. Though they might disagree with his thesis, they would have to concede that he offers an effective argument in support of his case, one greatly enhanced by his ethos.

Common Ethos-Related Fallacies

Certain types of reasoning errors are particularly damaging to a writer's efforts to establish his or her authority or credibility. Avoiding them will help increase your ethos when writing academic arguments. Some of the more common ethos-related fallacies are described below.

1. Ad hominem *Attacks*

Attacking someone personally instead of addressing his or her argument.

> *You can't take Joe's argument seriously—the guy's a communist.*

Whether or not Joe is a communist may have nothing to do with the quality of his argument; the aim is to attack him personally, not to address his ideas. Such an argument is unfair and damages your ethos.

2. Poisoning the Well

Casting doubt on someone's argument even before they offer it.

> *You can listen to Senator Thompson's ideas on global warming if you want to, but she drives an SUV at home.*

The aim here is to discredit the senator's ideas even before she offers them by discrediting her or the arguments she is about to make. She may drive an SUV and still have ideas regarding global warming that are worth considering. Again, such an argument is unfair.

3. False Authority

Basing a claim on the authority of someone unqualified to offer it or placing too much trust in the authority of one source.

> *You should purchase that car because two or three athletes say they drive it.*

How is an athlete qualified to offer opinions on cars? If you base a claim on false authority, readers may question your own judgment and credibility.

4. Dogmatism

Maintaining that there is just one correct position on an issue and dismissing all others.

> *Welfare reform will never work, and time for debate on the issue is over.*

Being dogmatic is the opposite of being open-minded and fair, key qualities of mind that are valued in academics.

Something to talk about . . .

With one or two other students in your class, discuss why you think each of the ethos-related fallacies described above represent faulty forms of reasoning. Are there any you think are not fallacies? Why is that? Under what circumstances might that form of reasoning be valid? Using the samples provided for each type of ethos-related fallacy as models, develop additional examples of your own.

THE INTERRELATEDNESS OF LOGOS, PATHOS, AND ETHOS

Though logos, pathos, and ethos have been dealt with individually in this chapter, in academic arguments all three frequently work together to make your writing persuasive. Sound reasoning helps you appeal to your readers' intellect; careful attention to pathos helps you appeal to their emotions, needs, and desires; establishing your credibility and authority as a writer increases their confidence in your argument.

Something to write about . . .

Review the definitions of "logos," "pathos," and "ethos" you wrote as you began to read this chapter. In light of what you have now read, written, and discussed, how accurate and comprehensive are they? Revise your definition of each term to make it more accurate and comprehensive.

3

READING ACADEMIC ARGUMENTS CRITICALLY

WHEN YOU READ AN ARGUMENT CRITICALLY, you determine its meaning and value in light of its rhetorical context. Your goal is to understand what the argument is actually saying, examine how it is put together, and establish its worth. Because critical reading involves individual interpretations of texts, readers can honestly reach different conclusions about an argument's validity or strength. Also complicating critical reading is the fact that every argument exists in a certain rhetorical context. Whether an argument is "good" or "bad," "effective" or "ineffective" largely depends on its intended audience and purpose. An argument intended for one audience may be very persuasive, but the same argument presented to a different audience may prove ineffective.

Learning how to critique an argument is closely related to learning how to write one. The criteria and standards you use to evaluate someone's argument are the same criteria and standards readers will likely use to evaluate the arguments you write. Some of the defining criteria for an effective argument are shared by scholars across the curriculum; for example, most would agree that an argument's claims should be clear, precise, and supported by appropriate evidence. However, the exact definition of "clear," "precise," and "appropriate" will vary by discipline. As you study and critique texts in classes across the curriculum, you will learn how to apply these evaluative criteria and standards in a wide range of disciplines. To succeed in college, you need to know which questions to ask when you evaluate arguments and which questions your teachers will ask when they evaluate the arguments you write.

A PROCESS APPROACH TO CRITICAL READING

When you read an argument critically, you determine its meaning and evaluate its value and/or effectiveness. To accomplish these goals, you need to summarize what you read (determine what it actually says), analyze it (determine how the text says it), and critique it (determine how well the text says it). Successful college writers understand that critical reading is a complex endeavor best approached through a multistep process that involves prereading, reading for comprehension, reading for analysis, and reading for evaluation. Each of these steps is examined below. You will practice your critical reading skills by examining David Leonhardt's essay, "Rank Colleges, But Rank Them Right." Leonhardt, a *New York Times* columnist, examines a number of controversies concerning the way colleges and universities are ranked in the United States, focusing on the highly influential rankings published by *U.S. News & World Report.*

PREREADING STRATEGIES

Before you read a text, you should consider a number of questions that will help you approach the piece more critically. For example, devote some time to an examination of the reading's author, answering questions such as these:

- Who wrote the piece?
- What is the author's background or credentials?
- What else has the author written on the topic?
- What biases or perspectives might the author bring to the text and how might they influence what he or she writes?

If you are reading a journal article, you can usually find biographical information at the beginning or end of the piece or in a section of the journal called "Contributors" or "Contributor Notes." If you are reading a book, you can often find this information at the beginning or end of the book or inside the dust jacket. You can also search the author's name online to gather additional information.

The argument an author forwards in a text is often influenced by his or her background, prejudices, or professional affiliations. To say that authors bring certain prejudices to their work is not to discount their arguments; all authors have certain predispositions toward the topic they are addressing. When you critically read a text, you simply take these prejudices into account. Being aware of these possible biases and preferences as you read a text will help you assess the reading's value or worth.

Next, examine the text's publication information, considering questions such as these:

- Who published the work? Was the work published by an academic press, political party, or advocacy group?
- When was it published? How might the place or date of publication influence the reading's content or argument?
- Judging by the date of publication, how recent is the information the work contains?

The place of publication can also influence your understanding of a text. Certain journals or magazines have identifiable political, ideological, theoretical, or methodological biases. Again, knowing and recognizing this fact can help you understand why a text is written a particular way or why it advances certain arguments over others. Knowing the year of publication can also help you evaluate an argument's credibility or worth. Generally speaking, basing an argument on recent research is preferable to basing it on research that is dated.

Finally, consider the title and topic of the essay. Ask yourself questions such as these:

- Given the title of the piece, what information or arguments might the reading address?
- What do I know about the topic? What is my position on these arguments?
- How might my own biases and preferences influence my reading of the text?

Titles serve as an author's first opportunity to introduce his or her argument and influence the way you read the text. They serve the significant purpose of orienting readers to the writer's argument, so consider them carefully. Also, just as authors bring their own biases and preferences to the texts they write, so too do readers. Consequently, before you read a text, consider what you expect the reading to contain or to accomplish, what you already know and think about the topic, and how those predispositions might influence your understanding of the text.

Now, before you read "Rank Colleges, But Rank Them Right," consider the following questions. (*Note:* Superscript numbers have been added to the paragraphs to make it easier for you to discuss the essay in class.)

- The headnote to the reading states that Leonhardt is a reporter for the *New York Times*. What kind of text would you expect a reporter to write? What, in your mind, is the purpose of most work that reporters publish?
- Look at the title of the piece, "Rank Colleges, But Rank Them Right." What do you think the author's argument is likely to be? Do you think he will endorse or criticize current ranking systems? Do you think he will offer an alternative approach to ranking colleges, something different from current ranking systems?
- Does the fact that the piece was published in the *New York Times* signify anything to you? Can you make any judgments concerning the argument's credibility or possible bias based on its place of publication?
- Have you ever read or used one of the many rankings of American colleges and universities that are published annually?
- Have you ever read or used the rankings published by *U.S. News & World Report*, which Leonhardt addresses in this argument? If so, what did you think of it?
- In your view, what are the primary purposes of such rankings?
- What do you think the rankings are based on?
- Who do you think is the primary audience for these rankings? Prospective students? Their parents? The colleges and universities themselves?

Rank Colleges, But Rank Them Right

David Leonhardt

David Leonhardt is a columnist for the New York Times *who specializes in economics and business.*

[1]Early this morning, *U.S. News & World Report* will send e-mail messages to hundreds of college administrators, giving them an advance peek at the magazine's annual college ranking. They will find out whether Princeton will be at the top of the list for the seventh straight year, whether Emory can break into the top 15 and where their own university ranks. The administrators must agree to keep the information to themselves until Friday at midnight, when the list goes live on the *U.S. News* Web site, but the e-mail message gives them a couple of days to prepare a response.

[2]By now, 23 years after *U.S. News* got into this game, the responses have become pretty predictable. Disappointed college officials dismiss the ranking as being beneath the lofty aims of a university, while administrators pleased with their status order new marketing materials bragging about it—and then tell anyone who asks that, obviously, they realize the ranking is beneath the lofty aims of a university.

[3]There are indeed some silly aspects to the *U.S. News* franchise and its many imitators. The largest part of a university's *U.S. News* score, for instance, is based on a survey of presidents, provosts and admissions deans, most of whom have never sat in a class at the colleges they're judging.

[4]That's made it easy to dismiss all the efforts to rate colleges as the product of a status-obsessed society with a need to turn everything, even learning, into a competition. As Richard R. Beeman, a historian and former dean at the University of Pennsylvania, has argued, "The very idea that universities with very different institutional cultures and program priorities can be compared, and that the resulting rankings can be useful to students, is highly problematic."

[5]Of course, the same argument could be made about students. They come from different cultures, they learn in different ways and no one-dimensional scoring system can ever fully capture how well they have mastered a subject. Yet colleges go on giving grades, drawing fine lines that determine who is *summa cum laude* and bestowing graduation prizes—all for good reason.

[6]Human beings do a better job of just about anything when their performance is evaluated and they are held accountable for it. You can't manage what you don't measure, as the management adage says, and because higher education is by all accounts critical to the country's economic future, it sure seems to be deserving of rigorous measurement.

[7]So do we spend too much time worrying about college rankings? Or not nearly enough?

[8]Not so long ago, college administrators could respond that they seemed to be doing just fine. American universities have long attracted talented students

from other continents, and this country's population was once the most educated in the world.

[9]But it isn't anymore. Today the United States ranks ninth among industrialized nations in higher-education attainment, in large measure because only 53 percent of students who enter college emerge with a bachelor's degree, according to census data. And those who don't finish pay an enormous price. For every $1 earned by a college graduate, someone leaving before obtaining a four-year degree earns only 67 cents.

[10]Last week, in a report to the Education Department, a group called the Commission on the Future of Higher Education bluntly pointed out the economic dangers of these trends. "What we have learned over the last year makes clear that American higher education has become what, in the business world, would be called a mature enterprise: increasingly risk-averse, at times self-satisfied, and unduly expensive," it said. "To meet the challenges of the 21st century, higher education must change from a system primarily based on reputation to one based on performance."

[11]The report comes with a handful of recommendations—simplify financial aid, give more of it to low-income students, control university costs—but says they all depend on universities becoming more accountable. Tellingly, only one of the commission's 19 members, who included executives from Boeing, I.B.M. and Microsoft and former university presidents, refused to sign the report: David Ward, president of the nation's largest association of colleges and universities, the American Council on Education. But that's to be expected. Many students don't enjoy being graded, either. The task of grading colleges will fall to the federal government, which gives enough money to universities to demand accountability, and to private groups outside higher education.

[12]"The degree of defensiveness that colleges have is unreasonable," said Michael S. McPherson, a former president of Macalester College in Minnesota who now runs the Spencer Foundation in Chicago. "It's just the usual resistance to having someone interfere with their own marketing efforts."

[13]The commission urged the Education Department to create an easily navigable Web site that allows comparisons of colleges based on their actual cost (not just list price), admissions data and meaningful graduation rates. (Right now, the statistics don't distinguish between students who transfer and true dropouts.) Eventually, it said, the site should include data on "learning outcomes."

[14]Measuring how well students learn is incredibly difficult, but there are some worthy efforts being made. Researchers at Indiana University ask students around the country how they spend their time and how engaged they are in their education, while another group is measuring whether students become better writers and problem solvers during their college years.

[15]As Mr. McPherson points out, all the yardsticks for universities have their drawbacks. Yet parents and students are clearly desperate for information. Without it, they turn to *U.S. News*, causing applications to jump at colleges that move up the ranking, even though some colleges that are highly ranked may not actually excel at making

students smarter than they were upon arrival. To take one small example that's highlighted in the current issue of *Washington Monthly*, Emory has an unimpressive graduation rate given the affluence and S.A.T. scores of its incoming freshmen.

[16]When *U.S. News* started its ranking back in the 1980s, universities released even less information about themselves than they do today. But the attention that the project received forced colleges to become a little more open. Imagine, then, what might happen if a big foundation or another magazine—or *U.S. News*—announced that it would rank schools based on how well they did on measures like the Indiana survey.

[17]The elite universities would surely skip it, confident that they had nothing to gain, but there is a much larger group of colleges that can't rest on a brand name. The ones that did well would be rewarded with applications from just the sort of students universities supposedly want—ones who are willing to keep an open mind and be persuaded by evidence.

Something to think about . . .

How did "Rank Colleges, But Rank Them Right" meet your expectations, based on the questions you asked yourself before you read the piece? What, if anything, did you learn? What did you find surprising or unexpected?

COMPREHENDING ARGUMENTS

The first few times you read through an argument, your primary goal is to form a clear, literal understanding of the text. The material you read in college is often so complicated you need to read it several times just to comprehend its meaning, to understand what it says. Devote as much time to re-reading a text as you need to form a clear understanding of the information and arguments it contains. You can't critically analyze and evaluate a reading if you do not first clearly understand what it says.

If the text provides an abstract, read it. The abstract will explain the author's primary assertions or findings, research methodologies, purpose or aim, and line of argument.

Next, read the opening section of the text, identifying the thesis if there is one. Stating a thesis in the opening section of an argument is a common practice among academic writers, though you will find many exceptions to this convention. After reading the opening section of the text, read the rest of the argument carefully, paying close attention to any headings or subheadings—these structural elements will help you locate the author's primary assertions and better understand how the author develops his or her thesis.

When you read an argument critically, you need to have a pencil in your hand to highlight and annotate the text. Though readers routinely develop individualized systems for annotating and highlighting texts, here are a few practices many writers have found helpful to aid their understanding of arguments.

- Underline the text's thesis statement and place a checkmark next to it in the margin of the page. If the author does not state a thesis in the piece, determine the implied thesis and write it somewhere near the reading's title.
- Underline every primary assertion that the author makes and summarize it in two or three words in the margin of the page.
- Bracket sections of the text where the author develops one idea or argument and summarize that idea or argument in the margin of the page.
- Circle key words or phrases.
- Look up the definitions of any words unfamiliar to you.
- Write any questions that come to mind as you read the text in the margin of the page or at the bottom of the page.
- Write out any reactions you have to the author's argument in the margin or at the bottom of the page.
- Note any contradictions you see in the author's argument in the margin of the page.
- Underline then highlight with a check mark information or quotations you think you might like to include in an argument of your own.
- Place check marks next to citations in the author's bibliography or works cited list that you would like to read yourself to better understand the topic you are studying.

Below is an annotated passage from "Rank Colleges, But Rank Them Right." Note how the person annotating highlights and comments on the text.

READING FOR COMPREHENSION: SAMPLE ANNOTATED TEXT

There are indeed some silly aspects to the *U.S. News* franchise and its many imitators. The largest part of a university's *U.S. News* score, for instance, is based on a survey of presidents, provosts and admissions deans, most of whom have never sat in a class at the colleges they're judging.

    That's made it easy to dismiss all the efforts to rate colleges as the product of a status-obsessed society with a need to turn everything, even learning, into a competition. As Richard R. Beeman, a historian and former dean at the University of Pennsylvania, has argued, "The very idea that universities with very different institutional cultures and program priorities can be compared, and that the resulting rankings can be useful to students, is highly problematic."

    Of course, the same argument could be made about students. They come from different cultures, they learn in different ways and no one-dimensional

Note word

Is this correct?

Credentials

Rejects idea that evaluations can be made (analogy with evaluating students at beginning of next paragraph)

scoring system can ever fully capture how well they have mastered a subject. Yet colleges go on giving grades, drawing fine lines that determine who is *summa cum laude* and bestowing graduation prizes—all for good reason. <u>Human beings do a better job of just about anything when their performance is evaluated and they are held accountable for it.</u>

Why accountability is good

You can't manage what you don't measure, as the management adage says, and because higher education is by all accounts critical to the country's economic future, it sure seems to be deserving of rigorous measurement.

<u>So do we spend too much time worrying about college rankings? Or not nearly enough?</u>

A key question in this reading

Something to write about . . .

With pencil in hand, highlight and annotate Leonhardt's essay yourself then write out your answers to the following questions:

1. What is Leonhardt's thesis? If he states it, which sentence is it? If he implies it, paraphrase what you think it is.
2. What are the primary claims Leonhardt makes in his argument? Write them out, indicating the paragraph numbers in which they are found.
3. How does Leonhardt support each claim he makes? Summarize the primary means of support he offers for each of the claims he makes.
4. Write out any questions you have concerning Leonhardt's argument, questions you would like to ask your teacher or other students in class.
5. Write a summary of Leonhardt's essay.

ANALYZING ARGUMENTS

When reading for comprehension, your primary concern is to determine *what* a text says. Your goal is to identify a reading's thesis, its primary claims, the support the author offers for those claims, along with any rebuttals or qualifications the author offers. When you analyze a text, your primary concern is to determine *how* the various parts of the argument work together to support the writer's thesis, to speculate on *why* the text is written as it is.

These can be difficult questions to answer and require you to consider carefully the text's rhetorical situation. Given the author's purpose and audience along with the occasion for or context of the piece, why does the writer include certain information and arguments, structure the piece a particular way, or employ a particular style? To help you analyze an argument, consider the following questions:

Analytical Questions Regarding an Argument's Author
- How does the author's background influence his or her argument?
- How does the author's relationship to his or her audience influence his or her argument?
- What is the relationship between the author and the occasion for the argument?

Analytical Questions Regarding an Argument's Topic

■ How is the topic defined in the argument? How is this definition related to the argument's intended audience and purpose?

■ Which aspects of the topic get emphasized over other aspects? How is this focus related to the argument's occasion, intended audience, and purpose?

■ How might the occasion of the argument have influenced the writer's choice of topics?

Analytical Questions Regarding an Argument's Audience

■ Who is the intended audience for the argument?

■ What characteristics of the audience influenced the author's argument?

■ What is the relationship between the audience and the occasion for the argument?

■ How does the intended audience influence the way the author defines or addresses the topic of the argument?

Analytical Questions Regarding an Argument's Purpose

■ What is the argument's purpose and how is that purpose related to its occasion and intended audience?

■ How does the argument's purpose influence the way the author addresses its topic?

Analytical Questions Regarding an Argument's Occasion

■ What aspects of the argument's occasion most impact its purpose?

■ What is the relationship between the intended audience and the occasion for the argument?

Analytical Questions Regarding an Argument's Claims

■ What reasons and evidence does the writer offer to support his or her claims? Given the argument's rhetorical context, why might the writer have chosen to use these reasons and evidence?

■ Does the writer examine alternative points of view in the argument? If so, what are they? Why would the writer bring up these opposing views? Where in the argument are opposing views introduced? Why might they be placed there?

Analytical Questions Regarding an Argument's Structure

■ Examine the argument's opening paragraphs. What strategy does the writer employ to capture his or her readers' interest? Why do you think the writer employs this strategy?

■ Examine each section of the writer's argument. In what order are the claims presented? Why are they presented in this order?

■ How does the writer conclude the argument? What strategy does the writer employ? How might the rhetorical situation have influenced his or her choice of strategy for concluding the argument?

Analytical Questions Regarding an Argument's Language

■ Examine the writer's language throughout the argument. What level of diction does the writer employ? How might the writer's intended purpose and audience have influenced his or her choice of language?

To practice analyzing an argument, return to "Rank Colleges, but Rank Them Right" and answer the following questions:

1. What purpose is served by the opening three paragraphs' focus on the *U.S. News & World Report* ranking of American colleges?
2. In paragraph 4, Leonhardt uses comments by the former dean at the University of Pennsylvania to cast doubt on the utility of college rankings, but then in paragraphs 5 and 6, he seems to justify them by drawing an analogy between ranking colleges and grading student work. What is the purpose of these two paragraphs?
3. Look at paragraph 7, which contains just two short sentences. What purpose does this paragraph serve given its placement in the argument?
4. In paragraphs 8 and 9, Leonhardt introduces a new assertion—that the quality of American higher education is in decline—an assertion he supports in paragraphs 10, 11, and 12 with evidence from a report produced by the Education Department's Commission on the Future of Higher Education. How does this assertion further his argument?
5. Paragraph 14 raises the issue of measuring the quality of student learning. Why does Leonhardt refer to the surveys of student engagement conducted by Indiana University?
6. Leonhardt's argument takes an interesting turn in paragraph 15. Is he endorsing or criticizing the *U.S. News* ranking in this paragraph? How do you know?
7. Again, in paragraph 16 is Leonhardt supporting or criticizing the *U.S. News* ranking? What connection is he drawing between that ranking and the surveys conducted by Indiana University first mentioned in paragraph 14?
8. In the closing paragraph, Leonhardt draws a distinction between elite universities and the larger number of colleges "that can't rest on a brand name." Why does he believe these schools would be rewarded if they ranked highly on a survey that measured student learning and engagement?
9. What does the final sentence of the piece tell you about Leonhardt's intended audience and purpose?
10. What might have motivated Leonhardt to write this piece? What is he responding to?

Something to talk about . . .

Discuss your analysis of "Rank Colleges, But Rank Them Right" with someone else in class, comparing your answers to the questions listed above. Where do you agree? Where do you disagree? What can account for these differences? Your teacher may want you to share the results of your discussion with the rest of the class.

EVALUATING ARGUMENTS

Once you have carefully read and analyzed an argument, you will be in a better position to evaluate how effectively the author makes his or her case. When you evaluate an argument, you form, explain, and defend a judgment concerning its quality or worth: Given its rhetorical context, how effective is the argument? To evaluate an argument, consider the strength and limitations of its claims, grounds, explanations, and rebuttals in light of its rhetorical situation. Not every element of an argument will be equally strong or weak—for example, an argument can have strong claims but weak support, strong support but weak or missing explanations.

Answering the following questions will help you form a judgment concerning the quality of the arguments you read.

Evaluating the Quality of an Argument's Claims

- How clearly stated are the claims? Which of the claims, if any, are ambiguous or lend themselves to multiple readings? Which contain unexplained terms?
- Given the intended audience, which of the claims (if any) are likely to be challenged? Has the author recognized these likely challenges? Has the author taken steps to address these challenges?
- Given the argument's rhetorical situation, how well has the author acknowledged and, if necessary, explained and defended any assumptions upon which his or her claims are based?
- Given the grounds provided, are all the claims equally reasonable? Which are more reasonable than others?
- Given the argument's rhetorical situation, are the claims adequately qualified? Which claims, if any, might be seen as too sweeping?
- How well has the author explained how the argument's various claims are connected to one another and to the author's thesis?

Evaluating the Quality of an Argument's Grounds

- Given the argument's rhetorical situation, how clear, credible, and authoritative is the support offered for each of the claims?
- How adequately is each claim supported, including the quality and quantity of the grounds provided?

- How effective are the steps the writer has taken to establish the quality of the support he or she provides in the argument?
- How does the writer demonstrate that the support is current and trustworthy?
- Which claims, if any, lack adequate support? How so? Which claims receive too much support? How so?
- How well does the writer document the support he or she provides? How does the quality of the documentation add to or detract from the argument's effectiveness, given its rhetorical situation?

Evaluating the Quality of an Argument's Explanations

- How clear are links the writer draws between each of his or her claims and their support? Which claims are adequately explained and which are not?
- Given the argument's rhetorical situation, which claims or assumptions need to be more fully explained?
- Which explanations are logical, clear, and thorough and which are not?

Evaluating the Quality of an Argument's Rebuttals

- Does the writer acknowledge any counterarguments to his or her thesis?
- Given the argument's rhetorical situation, how effective are the rebuttals?
- How well does the writer refute possible objections to his or her assertions?

To practice evaluating arguments, turn again to "Rank Colleges, But Rank Them Right." First, to clarify the rhetorical situation of Leonhardt's essay, fill in the following prompts:

a. The argument's topic is: _____.
b. The argument's primary audience is: _____.
c. The argument's primary purpose is: _____.
d. The occasion for writing the argument is: _____.
e. The author's stance in this argument is: _____.

Next, *given the argument's rhetorical situation,* consider your answers to the following questions:

- How successful is Leonhardt's decision to open his essay with a discussion of the *U.S. News & World Report's* annual college ranking?
- How effective was Leonhardt's decision to leave his thesis out of the opening paragraph?
- Is it a good idea for Leonhardt to acknowledge in paragraph 4 that people find it easy to dismiss all college rankings? How effective is it to quote a former dean from the University of Pennsylvania in that paragraph? Why?
- Leonhardt opens paragraph 6 by stating an assumption about the relationship between motivation and evaluation. Is it wise to leave that assumption unexplained and unsupported?

■ Paragraph 7 serves as a transition from the first part of Leonhardt's argument to the second. How effective is it?

■ In paragraph 9, Leonhardt brings in an economic argument concerning the value of a college education. How effective is that choice?

■ Paragraphs 10–13 focus on a report issued by the Commission on the Future of Higher Education. Is this report adequately explained? Does this report add credibility to Leonhardt's argument?

■ In paragraph 11, Leonhardt implicitly endorses the idea of rating colleges, stating that the government is justified in demanding accountability. Would his argument be strengthened or weakened if he stated rather than implied this endorsement?

■ In paragraph 13, Leonhardt mentions a growing move to measure student learning outcomes when ranking colleges and in paragraph 14 cites work completed by researchers at Indiana University along these lines. In paragraph 16 he cites the Indiana survey instrument as an alternative to the *U.S. News* ranking. Does Leonhardt adequately explain the nature of the Indiana survey?

■ In the concluding paragraph, who is Leonhardt addressing: colleges that participate in ranking services, students and parents who use them, the general public? Is this an effective closing strategy?

Something to write about . . .

Write an evaluation of the argument David Leonhardt presents in "Rank Colleges, But Rank Them Right." Prior to your evaluation, carefully read and analyze the piece. Assume that you are writing your evaluation for readers who are familiar with Leonhardt's essay and with the material you have covered in your composition course.

THE ROLE OF CLAIMS IN ACADEMIC ARGUMENTS

WHAT CLAIMS ARE AND WHAT THEY AREN'T

A claim is an assertion you want your readers to accept and perhaps act on. In an argument, the primary claim you make is your thesis, an assertion you develop and support in the body of your essay. Consider these two claims taken from a pair of readings found in Chapter 2 of this text that address the question of whether the federal government should fund embryonic stem cell research:

> . . . given the breathtaking discoveries from adult stem-cell research, which does not rely on destroying human embryos, arguments for federally funding embryonic stem-cell research are less persuasive than ever.

> Charles Smith, "Perils and Promise: Destroy an Embryo, Waste a Life"

> At first glance, the case for federal funding of embryonic stem-cell research seems too obvious to need defending. Why should the government refuse to support research that holds promise for the treatment and cure of devastating conditions such as Parkinson's disease, Alzheimer's disease, diabetes, and spinal cord injury?

> Michael Sandel, "Embryo Ethics: The Moral Logic of Stem-cell Research"

These writers are making very different claims: one asserts that the federal government should not fund embryonic stem cell research and the other that arguments against such funding seem misguided.

In college, as you investigate topics you will consistently run across conflicting claims such as these. While your first impulse might be to assume that one author is right and the other is wrong, usually this is not the case. Instead, the authors have simply reached different conclusions based on their own research and reflection, conclusions that lead them to assert different claims. More often than not, authors will attempt to persuade you to accept their claims—to view the topic they way they view it, to accept their assertions. While some claims may be shown to be factually true or false, usually they are neither—they are opinions, interpretations, or positions an author wants to explain and defend. To read and write academic arguments effectively, you need to understand what claims are and what makes them effective.

Claims Are Debatable

A claim is debatable when reasonable people might disagree with it. For example, when writing an academic argument, statements of personal preference or taste cannot serve as claims because they are not contestable. If I state, "*The Godfather* is my favorite movie," no one is likely to argue the point with me. What would they say, "No, that's not your favorite movie. Your favorite movie is *Caddyshack*." They may want to claim that some other movie is better than *The Godfather*, but that is a different discussion.

Likewise, statements of established fact typically cannot function as claims, again because they are not debatable. For example, most people today would not argue with the following statement: "The Earth revolves around the Sun." That the Earth revolves around the Sun is a fact and for most people would not constitute a debatable claim. However, in the past it was contestable. Scientists such as Galileo placed themselves in considerable jeopardy by arguing in favor of a heliocentric universe. What is considered established fact changes over time, usually as a result of argument. If you question an accepted fact in an argument—if you treat it as a debatable claim—you need to explain what makes it contestable.

Consider current arguments over the topic of global warming. Which of the following claims do you think are debatable and which are not?

A. Over the past century, the Earth's temperature has been rising.
B. Human activity is one of the causes of global warming.
C. Human activity may be one of the causes of global warming.
D. Human activity is the primary cause of global warming.
E. Global warming, if unchecked, will result in massive coastal flooding around the Earth.
F. Human beings have a moral obligation to reduce global warming.

Are they all debatable? For years, various authorities have debated the first assertion, many saying that global warming is an observable, recordable fact and therefore beyond debate. Others argued either that efforts to take the Earth's temperature were flawed or that research findings did not support the general conclusion that the temperature of the entire Earth was rising. More recently, it appears that this debate has been settled and most authorities agree that the Earth is getting hotter. However, debate still rages over the role human activity plays in global warming (claims B, C, and D), what the results of global warming might be (claim E), and the extent to which humans are obliged to address the issue (claim F).

Something to talk about . . .

What is your position on each of the claims concerning global warming stated in A–F above? Discuss them with other students in your class. In your view, how debatable is each claim? How settled or certain is each one? Finally, how are the claims different from one another? Claim A seems to be a different sort of claim than E or F. Talk about these differences and explain them in your own words.

Claims Are Substantive

A claim you make in an academic argument should also be substantive; it should be serious, significant, and informed, not frivolous, simplistic, or self-evidently true. For several reasons, inexperienced college writers often have a difficult time meeting this standard. First, what counts as a substantive claim in college often differs from what counts as a substantive claim in high school. Second, what counts as a substantive claim in one course may not in another. Third, an argument may be considered substantive if offered by a first-year student but not if offered by a graduating senior. In each of these cases, context determines whether an academic audience is likely to consider a claim to be substantive.

Consider the following claims:

A. Shakespeare was a great writer.
B. The dialogue and structure of Shakespeare's plays set new standards of excellence in Elizabethan drama.
C. The dialogue and structure of Shakespeare's history plays, particularly *Henry IV Part One*, *Henry IV Part Two*, and *Henry V*, demonstrate both the continuing influence of patronage on Elizabethan theatre and the changing tastes of Elizabethan audiences.

How is this final claim more substantial than the first? How do you think a professor might react if a senior English major submitted an essay with the first claim serving as its thesis? Remember: as you gain expertise in a discipline, your teachers will expect you to make increasingly more substantial claims in the arguments you write.

Claims Are Sincere

Finally, in an academic argument, claims should be sincere; they should reflect what you truly think or believe, not what you think your teacher wants you to think or believe. Unfortunately, some college professors would disagree with this statement—they want and expect their students' arguments to reflect or echo positions the teacher has advocated in class. However, you will find that most college teachers prefer that you form your own positions on issues and argue forcefully for them in your essays. In the long run, the best course to follow when writing academic arguments is to articulate and defend claims you sincerely endorse—your writing will be stronger and more persuasive if you do.

> ### Something to write about . . .
>
> Work with a classmate or two to identify a topic that interests you and generate three claims about it that are debatable and three claims that are not debatable. Next, exchange your list of claims with another group of students in class and decide which of the claims produced by the other group are substantive and which are not. Finally, join the members of the other group to discuss your conclusions. If the members of the other group thought that one or more of your "debatable" claims were not debatable, decide how you might change the wording to make it contestable.

STATING CLAIMS EFFECTIVELY

Because claims in academic arguments are often complex and highly qualified or conditional, finding just the right language to communicate them can be difficult. Below are some criteria you can use to help you draft, revise, and refine the claims you make in your arguments. The most effective claims are stated in language that is precise, clear, qualified, and affirmative.

Effective Claims Are Precise

Claims should be precise; they should state exactly what you want to assert. Academic audiences tend to assume that you have chosen your words carefully and mean precisely what you have written. Sometimes the best way to check for precision is to ask friends to read your claims and to paraphrase them for you. If their understanding of your claims does not match your intentions, revise them until they do. For example, consider the following claim concerning the treatment of depression:

> **In treating depression, combining psychological counseling and medication is more effective.**

This claim is not precise—it leaves too much room for misinterpretation because it leaves unanswered too many questions:

- In treating what type(s) of depression?
- What type of counseling?
- What types of medication?
- The treatment is more effective *at* what?
- The treatment is more effective *than* what?

A more precise claim might read something like this:

> **In treating major depression, combining short-term talk therapy with antidepressive medications such as selective serotonin reuptake inhibitors tends to be more effective at relieving symptoms than using either treatment alone.**

This revised claim answers many of the questions critical readers might raise.

Effective Claims Are Clear

When stating a claim, your language and syntax should be clear. Pay particular attention to any technical terms you use in a claim. Readers unfamiliar with these terms might find your claim difficult to read or even understand if you do not define them. Overly complicated sentence structure can also make a claim unclear. Because academic writing tends to be highly qualified, writers sometimes produce overly complicated claims. Consider this example:

> **Taking advantage of prior research and current research methods, one may question assertions (made by archaeologists who worked primarily in the nineteenth century) concerning the trade routes established by the pre-Columbian inhabitants of North America, especially those living in the Scioto River Valley, who maintained there was limited contact with the civilizations of Central America and the Pacific Northwest.**

Such a claim needs to be revised to improve and simplify the syntax and to eliminate wordiness. A clearer revision could read something like this:

> **Due to recent archaeological discoveries, prior claims that the pre-Columbian inhabitants of the Scioto River Valley had limited trade contacts with the people of Central America and the Pacific Northwest can now be seriously questioned.**

Even this version could be revised further, perhaps to eliminate passive voice.

> **Due to recent archaeological discoveries, scientists are now questioning prior claims that the pre-Columbian inhabitants of the Scioto River Valley had limited trade contact with the people of Central America and the Pacific Northwest.**

Effective Claims Are Properly Qualified

Claims in academic arguments tend to be qualified. As you write an argument, consider how general or sweeping your claims can be. Do they always hold true? Do they hold true among all people? With what degree of certainty do you hold them? Sweeping claims tend to be unpersuasive because they are easy to refute—a skeptical reader needs to cite just one counterexample and the claim does not hold. Determine your claims' limitations and employ language that precisely reflects your conclusions. (See Chapter 7 for more advice on how to qualify claims.)

Effective Claims Are Affirmative

Generally speaking, affirmative claims are clearer, more precise, more economical, and more effective than negative claims. Consider these two examples:

A. It is not the case that Thomas Jefferson's writings show him to be a traditional Christian but rather a Deist.

B. Thomas Jefferson's writings show him to be a Deist rather than a traditional Christian.

Most readers would find the second claim clearer and more direct than the first. Whenever possible, state your claims affirmatively, but if you must state them negatively, be sure your writing remains clear and precise.

Something to think about . . .

Why do you think academic audiences value claims that are precise, clear, qualified, and affirmative? What is it about the nature of academic work that makes these qualities so important?

Something to talk about . . .

With one or two other students in class, discuss the claims below, deciding how each could be made more precise or clear, better qualified, or affirmative. Be ready to share your conclusions with the other students in class if your teacher asks you to.

a. Our school really ought to do something to improve safety.
b. Practicing yoga might help athletes improve.
c. Some have claimed that there are health benefits to drinking green tea.
d. Popular television shows today are nothing like popular shows used to be.
e. For some reason or the other, horror films are always popular.

Something to write about . . .

Read though your local newspaper, school newspaper, a news magazine, or a political Web site and make a list of ten claims you find. State whether each of these claims is (a) precise, (b) clear, and (c) qualified. Explain each of your judgments.

THE STRUCTURE OF CLAIMS IN ACADEMIC ARGUMENTS

Structurally, your claim should reflect the nature of your assertion, identifying whether you are forwarding one assertion, more than one assertion, or a particular relationship between or among assertions. Though claims can be stated in a wide variety of ways, three constructions are common in academic writing: simple, compound, and complex claims.

Simple Claims

Suppose you are writing an argumentative essay concerning the purpose of the prehistoric earthworks located at Fort Ancient in Ohio. Archaeologists, historians, and anthropologists are still debating the purpose this huge enclosure served. Based on your research, you are ready to write the thesis for your paper, a claim you will develop and defend in the body of your essay. Your paper might focus on a single, simple claim:

> **The earthworks at Fort Ancient likely served as a seasonal calendar.**

With this statement you have a single assertion to support, that the Fort Ancient people used the site to track the seasons.

Compound Claims

Perhaps you want to develop more than one claim in your essay. In this case, you might consider using a compound claim, one that lists the various assertions you will explore and defend:

> **The earthworks at Fort Ancient likely served as both a seasonal calendar and a ceremonial center.**

If you included this claim in your essay, your readers would expect you to explain and defend two primary assertions: that the earthworks served as a seasonal calendar and as a ceremonial site.

Complex Claims

Sometimes you might want to argue a more complex relationship among multiple assertions in a claim. These complex claims can assume many forms, depending on the assertions' logical relationship. For example, academic arguments often claim a *causal* relationship between assertions: *A caused or was caused by B*. If this is the case with the paper on Fort Ancient, your claim might read like this:

> **The need to accurately predict seasonal changes likely motivated the ancient inhabitants of the Scioto River Valley to build Fort Ancient.**

This sentence actually presents two claims you would develop in your essay: that the Fort Ancient people needed to accurately predict the seasons and that this need dictated the construction of the earthworks. You would first establish why the builders of the site were motivated to predict seasonal changes, and then argue that these needs determined how and why they constructed the site.

Other times, you may want to establish a *conditional* relationship among the assertions in a claim: *if A is the case, then B follows*. If this is the type of claim you want to make regarding the Fort Ancient earthworks, your thesis might read something like this:

> **If recent astronomical studies at the Fort Ancient site are correct, the earthworks likely served as a seasonal calendar, not as a defensive fortification.**

To develop this conditional claim, you would first examine the veracity of recent studies concerning the Fort Ancient peoples' knowledge of astronomy, and then you would argue that these findings lead to a particular conclusion: the earthworks served as a seasonal calendar, not as a defensive fortification.

A final commonly employed complex claim in academic writing involves *rebuttal: while most scholars think A, B is actually the case.* If you wanted to assert this type of claim in your argument, it would read something like this:

> **While most early scholars believed that the earthworks at Fort Ancient served as fortifications, recent examinations of the site support the contention that they functioned as a seasonal calendar and ceremonial center.**

With this type of claim, you would first establish that past scholars believed that the earthworks at Fort Ancient served as fortifications, and then critique this argument, explaining how it is wrong, misguided, or limited. Next, you would argue that more recent research offers a better explanation of the site's purpose: helping the Fort Ancient people predict the seasons and providing them a location to hold important ceremonies.

Whatever type of claim you employ—simple, compound, or complex—understand its predictive purpose: readers will expect you to develop and defend that claim in a manner consistent with its wording. Be sure you use the type of claim that most accurately captures and communicates the relationship you see existing among the assertions you want to make.

Something to write about . . .

With a classmate, choose one of the following topics to write about:

  a. The best place to relax on campus
  b. The most important social issue confronting college students today
  c. The most popular television shows on campus

Together, write six claims about your topic, two that are simple, two that are compound, and two that are complex.

THE PROCESS OF CRAFTING CLAIMS

As you develop and draft the claims you assert in an argument, keep in mind these five Rs: research, reflection, rebuttal, rehearsal, and revision (Figure 4.1). First, academic readers will expect you to explain the relationship between your claim and what others have written or said on the topic. You cannot adequately contextualize your claim if you have not completed the necessary **research**. Research will help you write claims that are precise, clear, substantive, and properly qualified. (See Chapter 10 for more advice on how to conduct research.)

Second, be sure you **reflect** carefully on the claims you make. Reflection gives you the opportunity to examine, critique, and weigh information you gather for your essay; to consider carefully the argument you would like to develop; and to craft language that effectively communicates your assertions. As you draft your essay, pause on occasion to reflect on the accuracy, clarity, and appropriateness of your essay's claims, making necessary changes along the way.

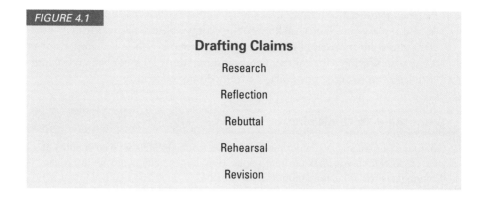

FIGURE 4.1

Drafting Claims

Research

Reflection

Rebuttal

Rehearsal

Revision

As you reflect on your argument, the third R becomes very important: **rebuttal**. As you form claims, consider alternative points of view. What are the strengths and weaknesses of your position? What other positions on this issue should you be investigating? What objections might readers raise to your arguments? How would you answer them? Anticipating and addressing possible questions and objections is crucial to developing effective academic claims.

Next comes **rehearsal**: write out the first draft of your claim. You will often be unhappy with the way a claim first sounds—most writers are. Just remember that this is only rehearsal. If you get started writing your essays early enough, you should have plenty of time to work on your claims before you present them to an audience. As you draft your claim, you may need to return to some of the earlier Rs.

Few writers, even the most experienced, are able to produce effective claims in just one draft. Most writers have to carefully **revise** their claims to make them clear, precise, and properly qualified. Though every writer's revision process is unique in some ways, here are a few suggestions you might follow to help you revise claims more effectively:

- Start with the words
  Once you have written out a claim, consider the words you have used. Are the words as *precise, specific,* and *concrete* as they can be? Might some of the words be easily misinterpreted or misunderstood by people who read your essay? Take the time to consider alternative ways to articulate each of your claims. Is your writing as economical as it can be?
- Move on to the syntax
  Does each sentence read clearly and smoothly? Can readers follow your train of thought in each sentence, clearly understanding how one idea leads to the next? Could a claim be easier to read and understand if you reorganized the sentence, shifting the order of the words or ideas?
- Consider qualifications
  As discussed earlier, effective claims in academic arguments are properly qualified. General, sweeping claims are frequently difficult to defend. Check each claim you write to be sure it is properly and effectively qualified.

■ Be true to yourself

As you revise your claims, make sure the claims reflect what you truly believe, what you want to assert, the case you want to make. While it is important to revise your writing with your audience in mind, don't let that concern for audience lead you to argue positions you really do not endorse.

Something to think about . . .

Carefully examine any academic essay you have written in the past year. Identify at least three claims you make in that paper. How might each claim be improved through research, reflection, rebuttal, and revision?

Something to write about . . .

1. Assume you are an English instructor teaching a class in academic writing. Produce a set of instructions your students might follow to write effective claims. These instructions should help your students form, articulate, and revise claims that would prove effective in academic settings. Write out your instructions using language you think would be clear to the students in your class.

2. Choose for study any three or four paragraph passage from any of the readings included in this textbook. List each claim the author makes in this passage then evaluate each one. What are the strengths and limitations of each claim, according to the criteria established in this chapter?

CHAPTER 5

SUPPORTING CLAIMS

IN AN ACADEMIC ARGUMENT, you support claims with reasons, evidence, and appeals to values. To get a sense of how these three elements function in an argument, suppose the following exchange occurs between the professor and a student in a political science class.

Professor: Who do you think is the best announced candidate for the U.S. Senate from our state?

Student: Probably Congressman Brown.

Professor: Why's that?

Student: I guess because I trust the guy.

Professor: Why do you trust him?

Student: No one's dug up any dirt on him yet that I can see.

Professor: So the lack of a scandal proves he's trustworthy?

Student: Well, not by itself, I suppose. The last time he ran for office, he made a series of promises, and I know he kept most of them. The guy has a track record of following through on what he says. Plus, he's the only one of the candidates to release his tax returns, and they at least show he's honest.

Professor: Okay, let's grant that he's trustworthy—why do you think being trustworthy is an important quality for a politician to possess? Why is it one of the key qualifications for someone running for office?

Student: I guess because like we discussed last week, in a representative democracy like ours, we elect leaders to enact our will. We vote for them based on what they say they'll do in office—we vote for people who will act in ways we endorse. If we can't trust them to keep their word, the system breaks down, representative democracy fails because the politicians can't be trusted to act in ways the voters expect them to act. That would be bad for every American citizen.

In this dialogue, the student supports her claims with reasons, evidence, and appeals to certain values. Her primary claim is that Congressman Brown is the best candidate to be senator. Her primary reason for this claim is that Congressman Brown is trustworthy, and when pressed by the professor, she provides some evidence to back up this position—Congressman Brown's clean political record, his success in fulfilling prior campaign promises, and his willingness to make his tax returns public—and an explanation supporting her view that the ability to trust politicians is important in a representative democracy. The student further supports this claim by appealing to values she assumes others share—that the country's form of government is good and that citizens should vote for politicians whose actions uphold its principles. The rest of this chapter will discuss how reasons, evidence, and values work together to support academic arguments.

Something to think about . . .

Before you read the rest of this chapter, consider these terms: reasons, evidence, and values. In your view, how do they differ from one another? What do you think it means to support a claim with a reason? How is that different than supporting it with evidence or through an appeal to some value? Do you think one type of support would be more persuasive than the others in an academic argument? Why? Which type of support do you find most persuasive in the arguments you read and hear? Why?

THE ROLE OF REASONS IN SUPPORTING ARGUMENTS

In and out of the classroom, we usually have reasons for the claims we make. Understanding how to support claims with reasons that academic audiences find persuasive is central to composing effective arguments in college.

The Relationship Between Claims and Reasons

Reasons are linked to claims through "because" statements: *X (the claim) is the case because of Y (a reason)*. Because academic readers expect you to offer substantive reasons in support of the claims you make, they should be based on more than just a personal preference. Suppose in the example above that when the professor asked the student why she thought Congressman Brown was the best senatorial candidate that the student simply replied, "I don't know. I just think he is." The discussion would have stopped at this point—"I just think he is" is not a substantial reason for a claim. If you can't offer a substantive reason to support a claim, you should reconsider your argument.

Choosing Which Reasons to Include in an Argument

Through research and reflection, you may develop a number of reasons to support the claims you make in an argument. Choosing which ones to actually include in your essay takes some planning and careful thought. Your primary concern is rhetorical: which of these reasons is likely to be most persuasive given the assignment's audience and purpose? To answer this question, you need to shift roles as you plan and draft your essay, viewing your claims and reasons as if you were one of your intended readers, not the person writing the essay. If you were a member of your intended audience reading this argument, which of the reasons would you find most persuasive? These are the reasons you should consider using to support your argument's claims.

Instead of selecting reasons based on the rhetorical context of the assignment, sometimes writers rely on reasons they are most familiar with, that come quickly to mind, or that reflect their own prejudices and life experience. Through research and reflection, identify the most rhetorical effective reasons to support the arguments you make in college, even if they are not the first ones you think of.

Something to think about . . .

Why might it be a bad idea to support arguments with reasons that come to mind quickly, regardless of the rhetorical situation of an assignment? How might the rhetorical situation of the assignment help you determine which reasons might best support a claim? Teachers often tell students to write about what they know. When might this not be good advice when developing reasons to support an academic argument?

Something to talk about . . .

With one or two other students in class, discuss why the reasons offered for each claim below might or might not be effective given the rhetorical context.

1. In an introductory sociology course, a student is arguing that women should stay at home to raise their children, at least until the children are old enough to go to school.

   Reason 1:   Mothers are best suited to raise children successfully.

   Reason 2:   Many mothers want to return to the workforce just because they want the money to purchase luxury items, live in larger homes, or have more lavish vacations. They should stay home instead.

   Reason 3:   Wanting to return to the workforce after having a child is essentially selfish.

   Reason 4:   Children raised by stay-at-home mothers are inevitably better adjusted adults than are children raised in homes where the mother and father both work outside the house.

2. In an introductory music class, a student is arguing that rap music is a legitimate art form.

   Reason 1:   Rapping is difficult, successfully achieved by only a few people.

   Reason 2:   Rap music is enormously popular.

   Reason 3:   Several rap genres have emerged, each unique.

   Reason 4:   Rap music often offers sophisticated political commentary on contemporary society.

Choosing How Many Reasons to Include in an Argument

Another question every writer has to address is how many reasons to offer in support of a claim. The answer, again, is a matter of rhetoric: given your audience and purpose, how many reasons are enough? Sometimes just one truly persuasive reason will suffice; other times more may be required. Often the only way you can determine if you have sufficiently supported your claims with reasons is to ask someone to read a draft of your argument and tell you.

Organizing Reasons in Support of a Thesis

If you use multiple reasons to support a thesis, you will present them in your essay one of two ways, as *independent* or *interdependent*. Either structure can persuasively support a thesis; which one you use depends on the nature of your argument.

Supporting a Thesis with a Series of Independent Reasons

You may decide to support your thesis with a series of independent reasons. Consider the scenario presented earlier in the chapter, a professor and group of students discussing an upcoming senate election. Suppose the professor asked another student the same question.

> **Professor:** Who do you think is the best candidate for the U.S. Senate?
> **Student:** I think State Senator Perez is the best candidate.
> **Professor:** Why is that?
> **Student:** Well, she has the best experience of anyone in the field—she's served for twelve years in the state senate and successfully run two major corporations. She also supports several issues I think are important, especially expanding federal support for higher education. Finally, she already has a good working relationship with the state's other senator. Together, they could make a powerful team in Washington.

This student offers three independent reasons supporting his assertion that Perez is the best senate candidate: Perez's experience, her stand on higher education funding, and her relationship with the state's other senator. These reasons are all related in that they support the same claim, but each can be presented and discussed on its own—accepting one does not depend on accepting the others.

If you decide that you will support your thesis with a series of independent reasons, you need to decide how to order them in your essay. One strategy is to open with the strongest reason you have and move sequentially to the weakest. This strategy gets your argument off to a fast start and assumes that the first reason you present in support of your thesis has the greatest impact on readers. You have to be sure, though, that even your weakest reason is still legitimate, even if it might not be the most persuasive. Alternatively, you could begin your essay with the weakest reason and build sequentially to your strongest. This strategy has the advantage of allowing you to end on a strong note; however, you also run the risk of alienating your readers early in your essay if they find the opening reasons so weak that you damage your credibility.

A compromise strategy is to open with a reason that is neither the strongest nor weakest but somewhere in the middle. You then offer your weaker reasons and close with your strongest. In an argument, the first and last reasons you provide to support your thesis enjoy privileged positions; these are the reasons readers tend to remember most. This third strategy enables you to offer strong reasons in both of these positions while placing your weakest reasons in the middle of the essay, reducing the attention they get from readers.

Supporting a Thesis with Interdependent Reasons

Interdependent reasons work together like a chain to support a thesis. Instead of functioning independently, they are linked, each one leading to or arising from another. Here's an example. Suppose in our fictive senatorial race that a student supports the candidacy of the current governor. The student's argument might sound something like this:

> At this point in our country's history, we need leaders who are decisive and coura-
> geous. Governor Shelby will be just that kind of senator. During the Vietnam War,
> he demonstrated the ability to be decisive and courageous in some of the most
> difficult circumstances it is possible to imagine. These experiences have shaped
> his personality and leadership style. When he assumes office, he will bring these
> leadership skills with him, making him the kind of courageous and decisive sen-
> ator we need today.

The chain of reasons offered here in support of Governor Shelby's candidacy looks something like this:

1. Our country needs leaders who are decisive and courageous.
2. Governor Shelby was decisive and courageous in combat.
3. Governor Shelby retains the ability to be courageous and decisive that he developed in combat.
4. As a senator, Governor Shelby will exhibit the courage and decisiveness our country needs.

These linked reasons rest upon several assumptions about the current state of the country and the nature of leadership, as well as Governor Shelby's experience, personality, and leadership style, all of which would need to be further explained and supported with evidence or explanations. It is easy to see, however, how the reasons are all connected. An argument structured this way can be quite compelling but may fail if readers reject the legitimacy of any reason or its logical connection to the others. Supporting a thesis with a series of linked, interdependent reasons requires you to explain the links clearly and convincingly, anticipating and addressing possible questions or objections.

Something to talk about . . .

What are the strengths and limitations of supporting an academic argument with a series of independent reasons? What are the strengths and limitations of supporting it with a series of interdependent reasons?

Note: Using First-person Point of View When Stating Reasons

Students often ask, "Is it okay if I use 'I' in this paper when stating and supporting a claim?" The answer you get will vary by discipline and even by teacher within a discipline. In some fields of study, using first person to present reasons in support of a claim is generally accepted; in other fields of study, it is not. Teachers who object to the use of first person when offering reasons in an argument usually focus on expressions such as "I think," "I feel," or "I believe." They maintain that a student's writing is more forceful and direct without them. If you use these expressions in your essay, they are easy to revise if necessary.

> **I think people should vote for Governor Shelby because he is a true leader.**
> *People should vote for Governor Shelby because he is a true leader.*
> **I believe the best reason to vote for Senator Perez is her experience.**
> *The best reason to vote for Senator Perez is her experience.*

Conventions governing the role of first person in arguments are changing; disciplines that used to discourage its use are now allowing it. Your best course of action when writing an academic paper is simply to check with your teacher about whether and how to use first person in your essay.

THE ROLE OF EVIDENCE IN SUPPORTING ARGUMENTS

In academic writing, you will support reasons with evidence. What counts as appropriate evidence for an argument varies by discipline in college. Over the years, you will learn these discipline-specific standards of evidence, what sorts of information are considered authoritative, and what sources of information are valued.

Types of Evidence Commonly Employed in Academic Arguments

Below is a brief description of several forms of evidence commonly employed in academic arguments.

Facts

Facts are well-established, generally unquestioned statements about reality: $2 + 2 = 4$; George Washington was the first president of the United States; water is composed of hydrogen and oxygen atoms. Of course, what we accept as fact can change over time.

Statements about reality that were once considered factual, may not be today, and what we consider to be a fact today, may not be thought so in the future.

Examples

In academic arguments, you will frequently use examples to support claims and reasons. Examples can be drawn from academic and nonacademic sources, depending on their purpose and the argument's rhetorical situation. Sometimes, you will provide examples to illustrate or explain assertions; at other times, you will provide them to examine possible objections to an assertion.

Statistics

Many readers find statistics highly persuasive in an argument. However, statistics are also easy to manipulate—they can be partially reported, skewed, or biased. When you use statistics to support an academic argument, you need to be especially scrupulous about selecting and reporting them. Employ statistics generated by reputable researchers, and do not use statistics without understanding the research that produced them. Make sure you can identify who the researchers are, what sample or population the statistics are based on, and how recent they are.

Expert Opinion

In college you will frequently write about other people's opinions, ideas, and arguments. Academic audiences value expert opinion, so long as they recognize and accept the authority of the source. Consequently, when you cite expert opinion to support a claim or reason, let your readers know the person's credentials and where the information was published.

Interviews

You may also support the claims you make with information garnered from published interviews or from interviews you conduct yourself. If you use information drawn from published interviews, be sure to tell your reader when the interview took place and who was involved. If you conduct an interview yourself and use the results in your essay, explain when and under what conditions the interview took place.

Survey Results

Instead of interviewing a few people to gather information for your essay, you might want to develop, distribute, and analyze the results of a survey. If you conduct a survey, be sure you explain how it was administered, who was surveyed, and when the survey took place. Also, include in your paper a copy of the survey instrument itself, perhaps as an appendix. If you are reporting on a survey conducted by someone else, include similar information in your essay: who conducted the survey, when it was conducted, who was surveyed, and where was it published.

Observations

Sometimes you will gather evidence for an argument through close observation of your subject. Suppose, for example, that for a psychology class you are writing a paper on the way men and women interact in groups. To gather evidence for your essay, you could spend time carefully observing how students interact in your school cafeteria or at sporting events, or watching people interact with one another at a shopping mall. When you use this type of evidence in an argument, you need to establish the nature of your study; how, when, and where the observations took place; any behavior you observed that did not fit your thesis; and any limitations to your study.

Experiments

In some courses—most notably the natural sciences, social sciences, and education— the arguments you write will be based on the results of experiments you conduct. When setting up and reporting on an experiment, be sure to follow disciplinary conventions. Every field of study has its own guidelines for designing experiments and reporting the results. These conventions can dictate what you write about, how you structure your essay, even the language you use.

Personal Experience

Whether you should use personal experience as evidence in an academic argument depends largely on the nature of the assignment. The acceptability of personal experience as evidence in an academic argument varies widely across courses and instructors. In many fields of study, using relevant personal experience as evidence in an argument is perfectly acceptable; in other fields of study, it is not. Even within particular fields of study, some instructors will accept personal experience as valid evidence while others won't. The best practice is to simply ask your teachers if personal experience can be used as evidence in arguments you write in their courses. If you do use personal experiences as evidence, you must clearly explain its relevancy to your claim and acknowledge its limitations. In most cases, making personal experience the sole support you offer for an argument is unwise, unless the rhetorical context of the assignment makes it acceptable (for example, if the assignment asks you to base an argument on your own experience and observations).

Something to talk about . . .

Discuss with a classmate the relative strength of each type of evidence described above. Do you think any particular type of evidence would carry more weight in an academic argument than the others? Why? Do you think any type of evidence listed above does not belong in an academic argument? Why?

What Makes Evidence Persuasive

For evidence to be persuasive, readers need to accept it as valid, relevant, and sufficient. **Valid** evidence can be trusted—it comes from an authoritative source and has been gathered or generated appropriately. You can help establish the validity of your evidence by explaining the source of any statistics or survey results you use as evidence or by establishing the authority of any experts you cite.

For evidence to be **relevant**, it has to be linked directly and clearly to a claim or reason. Suppose, for example, you are examining whether standardized test scores are good predictors of success in college. As part of your argument you cite statistics on how well standardized test scores predict high school achievement. A critical reader might well reject this evidence on the grounds of relevancy: a study of high school student success is quite different than a study of college success. As you write an academic argument, you need to consider when skeptical readers might question the relevancy of the evidence you employ in your essay.

Whether the evidence a writer provides is **sufficient** to support a claim has to do with how much is presented. Sometimes supplying one or two examples or citing one or two experts might be enough to support a claim; other times, you will need to supply more evidence. Sufficiency depends on the nature of the audience you are addressing and the quality of the evidence itself. For example, readers who agree with your claim will tend to need less evidence to be persuaded than will readers who likely disagree with it. Readers who are unfamiliar with your topic might need more evidence than readers who are familiar with it. The best way to determine if you have supplied a sufficient amount of evidence to persuade your audience is to ask people to respond to a draft of your work and let you know.

THE ROLE OF BELIEFS AND VALUES IN SUPPORTING ARGUMENTS

Every assertion we make is based on certain values or beliefs, what we hold to be good, right, or true. Sometimes these values or beliefs serve as the sole basis for the claims we make or the reasons we offer in support of an argument. When writing academic arguments, you will frequently need to state, explain, and defend these values or beliefs; other times, you may not—the values and beliefs will be so widely accepted that you can simply assume that your audience accepts them. Yet, even if you do not have to explain or defend these values or beliefs, you should understand how they support the claims or reasons you put forward in an argument. You should be able to explain or defend them if needed. In college, you will frequently be asked to question what you value and believe and what you have always assumed to be true. Sometimes this questioning will lead you to change your beliefs and values; other times it will reaffirm them.

Consider the arguments below. Each rests upon certain unstated beliefs or values. What are they? In each case, what is the person assuming to be right, good, or true? How do you know? How can you know if you have misinterpreted them?

- **That politician can't be elected to congress because he smoked marijuana in college.**
  Is the person assuming that smoking marijuana disqualifies a candidate for Congress or that people won't vote for a candidate who smoked marijuana in college, thus making him unelectable?

- **Helen would be the best person to hire as a teacher because she's a mother with kids of her own.**
  What link is this person making between being a mother and being a teacher? What is this person assuming about the nature of teaching and the nature of parenting? What is the person assuming about the quality of Helen's skills as a

mother? What assumptions is the person making about differences between mothers and fathers as parents?

▪ **Tom and Brad can't be married because they are gay.**

What is the person here assuming about marriage—that marriage is never an option for gays, that marriage as a concept does not apply to gays, or that the state in which he or she lives does not recognize gay marriages? Can Tom and Brad already be married, a fact the person is simply trying to deny with this argument?

Something to talk about . . .

How can understanding the rhetorical situation of an argument help you determine when you might need to explain and/or defend beliefs and values?

Stating Beliefs and Values in Support of an Argument

Knowing when you have to articulate the beliefs and values underlying an academic argument and when you do not can be difficult to determine. In the end, though, the decision comes down to effective rhetorical practice. When making that decision, consider the following questions.

▪ Given your assignment's audience, topic, and purpose, which beliefs and values should you state and defend because doing so will enhance your ethos? Will your audience see you as a more credible writer if you demonstrate that you share certain beliefs or values with them? Likewise, will possibly antagonistic audiences grant you more credibility if you clearly state the beliefs and values underlying your argument even if they disagree with them, giving you credit for your candor and honesty?

▪ When might stating the beliefs and values underlying your argument help to clarify the source or impetus for your argument? Your writing will be less persuasive than it might otherwise be if readers are unsure "where you are coming from" in an argument because you do not articulate the beliefs and values underlying your assertions.

▪ When might stating your beliefs and values give you the opportunity to address questions or concerns that are central to your argument? Academic arguments often center on disputes over beliefs and values. You will not be able to join such debates and discussions without stating and defending your own.

▪ When might stating your beliefs and values help you bridge gaps that exist between you and your audience? If you think you are addressing a hostile audience, open your argument by stressing the beliefs and values you share with your readers. Doing so will put you in a better position to present the arguments you think they might disagree with because you have already begun to establish the common ground you share with them.

Leaving Beliefs and Values Unstated in an Argument

In everyday arguments, most beliefs and values remain unstated and operate as assumptions. We tend to assume that our beliefs and values are clear and do not need to be stated or defended. When writing an academic argument, you can sometimes leave unstated the beliefs and values underlying your argument. However, just be sure you *decide* to do so after careful consideration. Know and understand the beliefs and values you are relying on to support your claims and reasons and determine when you need to state and defend them and when you don't based on the rhetorical situation of the argument you are making.

Something to write about . . .

1. To help you get a better sense of how academic writers support arguments with reasons, evidence, and appeals to values, complete a "support outline" of any argument included in this textbook. Write down the author's thesis then note, in order, every reason, all evidence, and each appeal to values he or she offers in support of that assertion. Though such an outline can be formatted any number of ways, you might consider employing this template:

   Title: _____

   Author: _____

   Thesis: _____

   Reason 1: _____

        Support:_____

   Reason 2: _____

        Support:_____

   Reason X: _____

        Support:_____

2. Collect two newspaper editorials to study. In an essay, analyze them in terms of the support they offer for the claims they make: what reasons do they offer to support their claims, what kinds of evidence do they provide to back up their assertions, what beliefs or values do they invoke? Be sure to support your own analysis with specific examples from the editorials. In the second half of your essay, evaluate the support offered in each editorial. What are the strengths and limitations of the support each writer provides?

3. Analyze and evaluate one of your own argumentative essays in terms of the support you offer for your claims. What types of support did you offer and how effective was it? What was it about your own preferences or the rhetorical situation of the assignment that led you to use that type of support?

EXPLAINING YOUR ARGUMENT

CONNECTING CLAIMS, REASONS, AND EVIDENCE

In academic arguments, readers will expect you to explain how the reasons and evidence you provide actually support the claim you are making. You cannot expect your readers to draw connections between the two on their own—that leaves too much room for misinterpretation. Professors who read your arguments will want to know both what you think and why you think it. They will expect you to explain your reasoning on the page, to lay out for them how you move logically from one assertion to the next in your argument and how the grounds you provide actually support the claim you are making. Most of the writing you include in an academic argument serves just this purpose—explaining your reasoning process, justifying your assertions, elaborating on your evidence, explicating your thoughts, and addressing possible exceptions to your claims. How you accomplish these goals will make your argument uniquely yours. While any number of writers may support a claim with similar reasons and evidence, how they explain and justify their arguments will vary—the reasoning process each writer follows to reach that claim will differ.

Case in Point: The TV Courtroom Drama

One way to understand the role explanations play in arguments is to consider one of the most popular genres on television-the courtroom drama. Most everyone has seen shows like this: a crime has been committed and a defendant is brought to trial. The prosecution and the defense present their cases then square off during the closing arguments. At this point in the trial, the District Attorney (D.A.) and defense attorney try one last time to persuade the jury to accept their arguments: for the D.A., that the defendant is guilty of the charge; for the defense attorney, that the defendant is not guilty. When presenting closing arguments to the jury, these two people carefully explain how the evidence that has been presented at trial supports his or her argument. The D.A. and defense attorney argue from the same set of evidence, but each explains how that evidence supports a different claim. This explanation—the connections each person draws between the claim he or she is making and the evidence that has been presented—will largely determine whether the defendant is convicted.

In the academic arguments you write, you too will need to explain the connections you see between the claims you make and the support you offer for them. Like the D.A. and defense attorney, you cannot simply believe that the reasons and evidence you provide for a claim will speak for themselves, that your readers will understand how they support or justify the claim you are asserting. When you explain your argument, you lay out your thinking processes for others to study and understand. The clarity, logic, thoroughness, and ethics of your explanation will play a major role in persuading your readers to accept your argument.

Something to think about . . .

Why do you think explanations play such an important role in academic writing? Why would academic readers be so interested in knowing not just what a writer thinks but why he or she thinks it?

Explaining Your Argument: An Exercise

Laying out your line of thought on the page for examination and debate is a central feature of academic writing. The following exercise may help you understand why. Assume the following facts about the fictional city of Springfield are correct:

- Three major interstate highways run through or near Springfield.
- Close to 50 percent of the country's population lives within an eight-hour drive of Springfield.
- The cost of housing in Springfield is 12 percent lower than in cities of comparable size.
- Springfield's tax laws favor corporate development in the city.
- Springfield's city and county governments are merged.

Now, assume you are working on the following assignment:

> In a well-developed paragraph, use the facts provided to argue the following position: Springfield is an attractive place to locate a manufacturing business.

After you think through the assignment and review the facts you have to work with, suppose you open your paragraph with the following claim:

Springfield is an attractive place to locate a manufacturing business for two reasons: its proximity to interstate highways and its tax laws.

You now need to provide evidence to support these reasons, which you will draw from the list of facts you have been provided:

> **Springfield is an attractive place to locate a manufacturing business for two reasons: its proximity to interstate highways and its tax laws. Three major interstate highways run through or near Springfield and the city's tax laws favor corporate development in the city.**

Your argument now consists of a claim supported by reasons and evidence. So are you finished with your paragraph? Not really because two fundamental questions are left unanswered:

1. *Why* is being near three interstate highways good for a manufacturing business?
2. *Why* do favorable tax laws make Springfield an attractive site for a new manufacturing business?

You may assume that your readers will understand the connections between your claim and the support you offer without any explanation. However, when writing an academic argument, making such an assumption is generally not a good idea. First, you cannot count on your readers to make the connections between your claim and the support you provide, no matter how clear and obvious the connections seem to you. Second, the connection between a claim you make and the support you offer for it may not be clear in your own mind until you put it in writing. Explaining the link forces you to clarify your own thinking. Third, the academic arguments you write in college will usually be graded on more than just the quality of your claims and support. In most of your classes, your teachers are also going to evaluate the quality of the thinking and reasoning skills you employ to explain your assertions.

Returning to the assignment described above, you might answer these two questions this way:

Question 1: Why is being near three interstate highways good for a manufacturing business?
- The interstate highways provide reliable transportation.
- A manufacturing business needs reliable transportation to bring in raw materials and to distribute its manufactured goods.

Question 2: Why do favorable tax laws make Springfield an attractive site for a new manufacturing business?

- Opening a new business is terribly expensive—tax breaks will reduce costs.
- A city that offers tax breaks is more attractive than one that does not offer them.

Now, you are in a position to elaborate on your original argument by explaining the connections between the claims you are making and the support you provide for them. Your paragraph may read something like this:

> **Springfield is an attractive place to locate a manufacturing business for two reasons: its proximity to interstate highways and its tax laws. Three major interstate highways run through or near Springfield and the city's tax laws favor corporate development in the city. Having access to several interstate highways will provide**

the business with the reliable, quality transportation system it needs. The business will find it more affordable to ship in needed raw materials and parts and ship out its manufactured goods with such easy access to these highways. In addition, favorable tax laws will enable the business to reduce costs involved in establishing a new manufacturing site. Not every city has tax laws that favor the kinds of capital investments required to establish a new business. Springfield's tax laws will allow a business to locate more cheaply in that city than in other locations, enabling it to invest more capital in its plant and personnel.

At this point, you would review your argument to see if you need to clarify any other assertions, provide additional examples, address any likely counterarguments, define any terms, or offer any additional reasons or evidence to support your claims. Whatever changes or additions you make to your argument, however, you still need to lay before your readers the reasoning process you employ to connect your claims and grounds.

Something to write about . . .

Assume the following facts are true about the city of Franklin:

- Franklin city schools are consistently ranked among the best in the state academically.
- Franklin is within a two-hour drive of two state parks.
- Franklin's crime rate, though higher than other cities' in the county, has been falling for the past four years.
- Franklin has recently established a series of parks and bicycle trails across the city.
- The price of housing in the city is about average for the region.

Write your response to this assignment:

In a well-developed paragraph, use the facts provided to argue the following position: Franklin would be a good place to raise a family.

WHAT TO EXPLAIN AND HOW TO EXPLAIN IT

Learning what to explain in an academic argument and how to explain it takes practice. Unfortunately, there are no rules for you to follow when deciding when and how to explain your reasoning; instead, your decisions need to be guided by your argument's rhetorical context. Given your topic, audience, and purpose, what aspects of your argument do you need to explain and how can you best clarify your reasoning process?

What Typically Needs Explanation

When they write academic arguments, students frequently fail to explain the assumptions they make, the link they're drawing between a claim and its support, and the reasons they reached one conclusion and not another.

Explaining Assumptions

Every argument rests upon certain assumptions about what is right, good, real, or true (see Chapter 5 for a discussion of the role beliefs and values play in academic arguments). In everyday arguments, you may not need to explain these assumptions. When writing academic arguments, however, you frequently have to state—and often defend—them. When you do not clearly articulate the assumptions underlying your claims, readers can misinterpret your argument. For example, consider an assertion which appears in Thomas Freidman's essay "Generation Q" (pp. 7-8. In this piece, Friedman comments on the nature of today's college students (which he terms "Generation Q"), writing at one point:

> But Generation Q may be too quiet, too online, for its own good, and for the country's own good.

What assumption is Friedman making here about the relationship between being "quiet" or "online" and the students' and the nation's welfare? Clearly, he is assuming something about the negative consequences of certain behavior—being quiet and being online—and about the way college students ought to behave. Toward the end of his essay, Friedman examples what he means in this passage, clarifying his underlying certain assumptions:

> America needs a jolt of the idealism, activism and outrage (it must be in there) of Generation Q. That's what twentysomethings are for—to light a fire under the country. But they can't e-mail it in, and an online petition or a mouse click for carbon neutrality won't cut it. They have to get organized in a way that will force politicians to pay attention rather than just patronize them.
>
> Martin Luther King and Bobby Kennedy didn't change the world by asking people to join their Facebook crusades or to download their platforms. Activism can only be uploaded, the old-fashioned way—by young voters speaking truth to power, face to face, in big numbers, on campuses or the Washington Mall. Virtual politics is just that—virtual.

Friedman states his belief that as "twentysomethings," members of Generation Q are obligated to be activists—remaining quiet is not what they "are for"—and that being an activist requires personal, not virtual involvement in political or social causes. If you wanted to disagree with Friedman's argument, here is where you could focus your attention. Once he explains the reasoning underlying his earlier assumption-based claim, you can begin to critique his position.

When you write an argument, asking yourself these questions might help you identify when you should state and defend assumptions:

1. What assumptions underlie the claim I am making?
2. Is my intended audience likely to share these assumptions?
3. To produce a persuasive argument, do I need to state the underlying assumptions?
4. Do I need to defend or explain these assumptions because my readers might be unaware of them or might question them?

5. What assumptions connect the claims I make and the support I offer for each of them?

6. What is the clearest and most effective way for me to explain these assertions?

Remember, you may need to explain assumptions at any point in your essay: not just at the beginning or at the end, but wherever you think your argument would be clearer and more persuasive if you do, given its rhetorical situation.

Something to talk about . . .

Divide into groups of three or four and discuss the assumptions that seem to underlie the following arguments. Which assumptions would you likely have to explain and defend if you were presenting these arguments to an academic audience?

a. The conflict in Vietnam was immoral because Congress never declared war against that country.

b. Movies such as *Ghostbusters* or *Stripes* will never win Academy Awards as best picture because they are comedies and because they are so popular.

c. Fraternities and sororities should be banned from campus if the University is serious about combating binge drinking.

d. The United States should have socialized health care because it is the only major Western industrial nation without it.

e. Based on game attendance, football, not baseball, is now America's real pastime.

Explaining the Link between Claims and Their Support

As the Springfield exercise above illustrates, in academic arguments, writers usually have to explain the link between claims and support, but this is not always the case. Consider this argument:

Look at the smoke and flames coming out of that roof—the house must be on fire!

The claim (the house must be on fire) is supported by two pieces of evidence (smoke and flames coming out of the roof). Most readers would likely understand and accept the link between the claim and its grounds here. How about this argument:

Tom might make a good basketball player—he's almost seven feet tall.

Again, if a reader understands the relationship between height and success at basketball, no further explanation would be necessary. If, however, someone is unfamiliar with the sport, you might need to explain the link between your claim (that Tom could make a good basketball player) and the support you offer (his height).

Here is another example—decide if you think the argument is clear as it stands or if the writer needs to explain the link made between the claim and grounds.

Student cheating has increased because of the Internet.

The student supports the claim that cheating has increased with one reason: "because of the Internet." You will likely agree that as it's written, this argument is vague and unsubstantiated. Suppose the student revised the argument to make it more precise:

> **Student cheating in college—especially plagiarism—has increased over the past decade because of the easier access students have to papers on the Internet.**

The nature of the argument is now clearer: the claim concerns not just students, but college students; not just cheating, but plagiarism; not just the Internet, but easier access to papers through that technology. But is the argument really clear now? What is the connection between easier access to papers via the Internet and a rise in cheating among college students? As a reader, you might assume you understand this writer's argument—that with easier access to the Internet, students can download papers and turn them in as their own (one form of plagiarism) or perhaps exchange papers with another student at the school (another form of plagiarism). Which of these arguments is the writer making? Both? Neither? Without even further explanation of the writer's reasoning, readers can't know.

Something to talk about . . .

Suppose each of the following arguments is intended for an academic audience. Why does each need further explanation? What explanation is called for in each case?

1. College athletes should be paid because of all the money they generate for their schools.
2. The sustained popularity of horror movies demonstrates society's long-standing hostility toward women.
3. The fall of the Soviet Union is sufficient proof that communism is a fatally flawed economic theory.
4. Printed books will soon be obsolete because of laptops and the environmental movement.
5. Downloading music should not be illegal because it is convenient, fair, and economical.

Explaining Why You Reach One Conclusion and Not Another

Academic readers are active readers—they question texts. Knowing this, you should anticipate that readers may not always draw the same conclusions you draw in your essay or connect claims and grounds the way you connect them.

Suppose, for example, that you have been asked to write an argument concerning whether Acme Inc. should expand its corporate headquarters in the fictional city of Hamilton. Your teacher has given you several facts regarding Hamilton to help you form and defend your thesis:

- Hamilton's economy has been in a decade-long decline.
- Over the past five years, four businesses in the area around the current corporate headquarters have closed.

- Hamilton's city government has recently passed tax breaks aimed at supporting business expansion.
- Acme Inc. has long-established ties to several existing Hamilton companies.

Looking over this information, you decide to argue in favor of expanding the business, but you are confident that many readers presented with these facts would decide otherwise. As you explain your position, you decide to also examine the alternative position. The beginning of your argument may look something like this:

> **Given the facts presented in the case, Acme should expand its corporate headquarters in Hamilton. Even though Hamilton's economy is suffering, Acme can actually benefit from the current situation and play an important role in revitalizing the city. Hamilton's economy has been in a decade-long decline and several businesses around Acme's headquarters have already closed. Understandably, many people would question the decision to expand Acme's headquarters when Hamilton's economy is so depressed, supposing that if other businesses have failed, Acme might face difficult times as well if it stays in the city. Expanding at this time may actually put Acme in financial jeopardy. However, Acme may be in a position to actually profit from the depressed economy. Expansion will require land, and the closed properties surrounding Acme's headquarters might be acquired at a cheaper price than would otherwise be expected. Land acquisition is one of the largest inhibiting factors for corporate expansion. If the land can be purchased more cheaply in the area around Acme's headquarters, then one of the primary impediments to expansion will have been addressed.**
>
> **In fact, expansion makes excellent business sense now that the city government has passed pro-growth tax incentives . . .**

In this argument, you not only explain the reasons for your claim (that Acme should expand its corporate headquarters) but also addresses why you do not agree with a likely alternative position (that expansion at this time is not wise).

Something to think about . . .

Some students have a difficult time understanding why, in an academic argument, a writer might need to explain why he or she rejects certain claims, interpretations, or lines of reasoning. Why do you think academic readers might find an argument more persuasive if the writer provides explanations such as these?

Common Methods Used to Explain Arguments

Described below are some of the more common methods academic writers employ to clarify and defend arguments across the disciplines. As you write arguments of your own, consider which of these methods best suits the claims you are advancing.

Explain and Defend Assumptions

When you write an academic argument, which assumptions you need to state and which can go unstated depends on the assignment's rhetorical situation. Given your thesis and purpose, which assumptions are most crucial to your argument? Which assumptions underpin your primary assertions? What assumptions link your claims and grounds? All of these are assumptions you should consider explaining and defending. At a minimum, you should consider explicitly address- ing any assumptions your intended audience is likely to question. Critical readers may reject your argument if those assumptions are not clearly stated, fully explained, and carefully defended.

Explain How Reasons Are Connected

When you support a claim with more than one reason, you will need to explain how these reasons are connected. Depending on the argument, you might need to explain how the reasons independently support a central claim or how one reason arises from or gives rise to another (see Chapter 5).

Paraphrase and Restate

Another way to clarify your argument is to paraphrase and restate your claims and support. If you believe readers may have a difficult time understanding what you write, restate it using slightly different words. Offering multiple versions of your claims and support can help make both clearer and more persuasive. Note, however, that too much repetition may damage your argument by making your writing seem redundant and padded.

Note Exceptions

As you explain your argument, note any exceptions to your line of reasoning. Explain what the exceptions are and how they impact your argument. What are the limita- tions of your claims and support? What alternative positions or interpretations are likely? What makes your position or interpretation preferable? Noting exceptions can help clarify your line of thought and enhance your credibility.

Note Implications

Sometimes a claim or its support has implications beyond the thesis you are support- ing. Recognizing and addressing these implications—both positive and negative— can help you anticipate your readers' questions or concerns and clarify your argu- ment. For example, suppose that you are arguing in favor of embryonic stem cell research because you think it could lead to cures for many diseases and greatly enhance human life expectancy. What are the ethical implications of this type of research? What are the social and economic implications of extending life expectancy? Answering questions such as these will help you explain your argument and perhaps better persuade skeptical readers.

Note Precedent

Explain any precedent that serves as a basis of your argument. What is the precedent for the position you are arguing, for the interpretation of evidence you are provid- ing, or for the approach to the topic you have adopted? Remember that when you write an argument, you are joining an ongoing conversation concerning the topic of your essay. Noting how your argument builds on previous research and thought strengthens your position.

Establish the Authority of Source Material You Use

To establish the authority of the source material you use in your argument, explain where it came from—who authored it, what the author's credentials are, when and where it was published. Once you establish the source text's authority, explain its relationship to the argument you are advancing. Does it bolster your position? How so? Does it call your thesis into question? If so, how can you reconcile the two?

Explaining Arguments: An Example

In the following article, "Student Cheating," Professor Bill Puka offers an unusual argument on the topic of cheating, asserting that it is sometimes justified at school and perhaps even obligatory. He even asserts that at times teachers themselves are responsible for student cheating. As you read Puka's argument, identify the claims he makes, the types of support he offers for each one, and the various ways he explains his assertions.

SAMPLE READING

Student Cheating

Bill Puka

Bill Puka is a professor of philosophy and psychology at Rensselaer Polytechnic Institute.

In social perspective, the ethical problems of college life are small. One billion of our six billion fellow humans are apparently ill or dying in pain of unnecessary deprivation at this moment. We live with a democratic government that pays mostly lip service to democracy. College students cause smaller problems. Typically, they do not form violent street gangs or crime syndicates that threaten the life, health, or safety of others; they rarely engage in wholesale fraud or embezzlement.

Date rape is likely the most serious campus ethics problem; it stands alone as a perennial capital crime. But, fortunately, there is little left to debate here ethically—date rape is rape, and rape is horribly wrong for readily statable reasons. Colleges are "on the case" here, focusing now on the attitude change needed to prevent the offense, with effective programs for undermining its mindset. After date rape, perhaps, come racism, homophobia, and sexism on the campus list of shame. Next comes reckless drug use (from cocaine to alcohol and tobacco), then suicide and serious theft and vandalism in the dorms, where some violence also is reported. Academic dishonesty—student cheating and plagiarism—may come even farther down the list, though some would order matters differently.

Most faculty and administrators, however, rate academic dishonesty a high crime, fatal to education. Obviously cheating is wrong: an affront to learning and self-integrity. But even where cheating is widespread, seeming to threaten the educational mission of a university, its touted harms do not stand scrutiny. Cheating need not decrease overall learning at college. Largely this is because learning and test-achievement do not correlate well; tests are not very good measures of the learning process. Thus, to cheat on tests also is not automatically to cheat oneself as a learner. Only rarely does cheating undermine the trust required by teaching-learning relationships—a trust that, in most cases, was long eroded by the authoritarian qualities of pre-college education. Such trust is required less for learning than for grading anyway, as government intelligence agents, and especially double-agents, have shown in spades.

Cheating is not especially unfair to other students, but for the questionably comparative grading curves that some faculty employ in courses. The "stealing others' ideas" that occurs in plagiarizing typical classroom assignments visits no harms on their supposed victims, who, along with their descendants, are usually long dead. Only a single professor or teaching assistant reads the course paper involved anyway, which is not made public.

What cheating shows that merits strong opposition is a student's pride in deceptively "getting over" on professors and "the system," even where both are recognized as fair. This affection for injustice and casual disregard for honest dealings must be trained out of students along with the jaded immaturity involved. Accompanying rationalizations must also be confronted—rationalizations that mask to the cheater how pathetic, embarrassing, childish, sleazy, and incompetent it is to steal others' answers because one couldn't even think up one's own. That's kindergarten.

By contrast, there are important situations where cheating or plagiarism is not only justified, but de facto obligatory. If I had to cite a single regret of my own student history, it would be failing to cheat when I was being victimized by unfair testing and grading, not to mention abusive teaching overall. In submitting to this treatment, I showed undue conventionalism and acquiescence in petty tyranny, both of which are toxic to ethical integrity.

True, I often protested such unfair treatment. But this invariably worked to my detriment and that of my peers. (No de facto, due-process option is available for winning such protests.) Worse, my protest was viewed as courageous, as properly standing up for principle. The courage I really needed to learn was that of dirtying one's hands a bit, adjusting my general principles to the specific context of unjust treatment. I needed the distinctive moral courage to besmirch my personal virtue in hopes of subverting injustice and its harms.

One comes to learn that those willing to sully their purity to fight wrongs show a level of moral commitment that rises well above nobility. After all, nobility normally requires conspiring, if not purposely, in the oppressive practices of others. In the present case, it means failing to expose poor teaching and its misrepresentation as students' failure to learn. Adult morality demands "principled" flexibility, not personal consistency masquerading as character. At the college level especially, ethics education can cleave toward the adult, though it presently does not, transcending childhood devices like codes of conduct or "do-and-don't" rules.

Faculty Ethics

Some faculty actually boast about their bad teaching behavior, and they are admired for it by their colleagues. They proudly depict themselves as "hard-nosed graders" who give "killer exams," which many fail and almost all do poorly on. This is a self-indicting outrage. A competent teacher makes course material sing and partners with students in skill development. If students do not do top-notch work, then either they are not functioning primarily as students in the course or the teaching approach taken needs radical change.

With a little thought and effort, most faculty can make it well-nigh impossible for students to cheat or plagiarize. One way is by not giving the same exams repeatedly. Another is by not using multiple-choice or other mechanical examination formats. A third is by asking students to do several drafts of a paper, illustrating the developing process of their work on each task, and integrating progressive drafts incrementally. (One searches the Web in vain for papers satisfying these requirements.) Add an oral, face-to-face component to the drafting process and the learning involved simply can't be faked or simulated.

Such "progressive" measures can take more faculty effort and time than do standard tests. But isn't that what "hard-headed teachers and graders" expect of their students? Why not of themselves also? Measurement batteries that get at the full variety of student learning and effort have long been available. Why then do faculty cling to the long outmoded and discredited in their course practices? (Unfortunately, this rhetorical question has an all-too-pragmatic answer: college faculty must decrease teaching and grading time relative to research and grant-making activities. This response is ethically self-indicting as well—for faculty and administrators.)

Isn't such negligent or disingenuous teaching more ethically problematic than student cheating? What of its compounding with institutional evaluation criteria that rate faculty publications and grant dollars over teaching competence? Doesn't another whole set of more serious problems emanate from the professionalization and corporatization of academe? This, after all, pressures faculty into compliance with these evaluation measures. And how rates the timid and cowardly submission of faculty to these measures?

Administrator Ethics

College administrators routinely tout their faculty's dedication to personalized teaching, especially in official materials sent to applicants and their parents. Simultaneously, they push reward structures that punish such dedication. Official publications reinterpret the array of college assets and foci so that they appear to match student interests. The aim here is to meet admissions quotas, not to model truth in advertising. And advertising is the name of the game, after all; "information technology" is the ad slogan of the moment. How does orienting to the student pool as market shares, or enticing applicants through false advertising, size up as an academic integrity issue? Is there a single college ethics initiative that addresses it?

One looks in vain through college brochures or catalogs for even the slightest hint that most professors receive zero teaching instruction before going to the head of the classroom. Nor do most colleges train professors during their teaching careers. This news would surprise prospective students, I'd bet, not to mention their check-toting parents. But paradoxically, it might improve student course evaluations: "for someone who never took a course in teaching, the professor isn't that bad."

It has become a common practice for faculty to comb calls for grant proposals, see what topics granting agencies want researched, and then skew their research direction accordingly. Often, faculty do not take this direction because they believe it is worthwhile or because they feel qualified in the area. Rather, they do it to bring in the funding with overhead their administrative "overlords" demand. What level of fraudulence and deception does such collusion reach? Never have I heard faculty even hush their tones when discussing research opportunities of this sort, nor have I heard administrators caution against such chicanery.

The Academic Integrity Movement

I cite these examples in "honor" of the growing academic integrity movement, which somehow sees the ethical splinters in students' eyes without seeing the beam in its own. Consider the following succinct summary of the movement's aims taken from one of its leading Web sites. "Academic Integrity is a fundamental value of teaching, learning, and scholarship. Yet, there is growing evidence that students cheat and plagiarize. Assess your climate of learning. Evaluate current academic programs and policies by purchasing the Academic Integrity Assessment Guide." While "teaching, learning, and scholarship" are all mentioned here, only the learning or student cheating focus is followed up. No mention is made of cheating, plagiarizing, and other forms of academic dishonesty by faculty-scholars. And when "learning climate" is noted, nothing untoward about college administration or institutional structure is so much as hinted at.

It is puzzling that the faculty involved in the academic integrity movement equate dishonesty with lack of integrity, or pose dishonesty as the negative pole on a continuum with positive integrity. The former involves a trait or vice—dishonesty and principled inconsistency; the latter concerns overall character and life orientation.

Ethicists who are incensed by student cheating show no similar concern for the rampant disrespect shown students, nor for the extreme anxiety caused them when inflexible deadlines are mandated for class assignments or when faculty assign exams and papers that are all due at the same time. A complete lack of coordination is clear here among faculty in different courses and departments, with a lack of concern even to try. Students suffer prolonged and painful loneliness at college, especially at first, and periods of isolating alienation from peers. They anguish alone with crises of identity and the loss of spiritual orientation, personal meaning, and self-worth. Conflicts with parents and the breakup of love relationships often rob them of interest and motivation, sapping the power to concentrate on studies. The real harm, the real suffering involved here often gets recorded as poor classroom achievement. Were institutions actually fostering the kind of community and the sense of belonging they advertise, along with the social skills mentioned in descriptions of campus "leadership" programs, these evils could be mitigated. Yet instead of addressing such institutional failings openly and responsibly, the blame is shifted to the emotional problems of particular students. And these problems are treated confidentially through individual counseling outside the curriculum.

A last puzzler: at most universities, students are banished from their learning community for cheating and plagiarism. The unwitting ethical lesson taught here is that enlightened and reflective communities handle internal messes by sweeping them outside. They handle rule violations and significant faults in their members by changing the locks on the doors. If the student offense is small, expulsion is replaced by "hard labor," usually in the form of assigned research on academic honesty. Here the ideals of inquiry are portrayed as a form of punishment, and student suspicions about the real nature of "school work" are affirmed.

Notwithstanding the above tally, some colleges and universities show that higher education can get serious about ethics education. All can do so, potentially, by putting their own houses in order as an example to their students. Coming full circle, we also must recognize that, in social context, even the worst ethical offenses just attributed to academe are small potatoes. Even the ethics codes aspired to in business and most other professions are themselves more ethically problematic than the misbehavior of faculty. Most college professors approach teaching as a mission, conscientiously dedicating their lives to the highest benefit of others' children, with little external reward.

Something to write about . . .

1. Watch a television show that centers on a legal case argued in court (some version of *Law and Order*, for example). In an essay, summarize the case then analyze the closing arguments of both the prosecutor and defense attorney. How does each person explain the relationship between the evidence presented in the case and the verdict he or she would like the jury to reach? How does each person try to convince the jury that the facts of the case support his or her argument?

2. Analyze two of the readings included in this textbook. How often do the writers explain the connection between the claims they are making and the support they offer for these assertions? What methods of explanation do they employ?

3. With a partner from class, write a paragraph in which you support a claim with some combination of reasons, evidence, beliefs, or values. In your first version of this paragraph, do not provide any explanations. In a second version, supply them. Identify and discuss any difficulties you faced providing these explanations for your argument.

7

QUALIFYING CLAIMS AND REBUTTING OPPOSITION IN ACADEMIC ARGUMENTS

EFFECTIVE ACADEMIC ARGUMENTS are properly qualified and, when necessary, address opposing points of view. To qualify a claim is to recognize its limitations. Qualified claims tend to be more difficult to refute than unqualified claims and more credible among academic readers. Acknowledging and rebutting opposing points of view in your argument also improves your credibility. As you research and reflect on the topic of your essay, seek out alternative points of view and decide how you will address them in your argument. You cannot simply ignore them.

WHY YOU NEED TO QUALIFY YOUR CLAIMS IN ACADEMIC ARGUMENTS

Qualifying your claims in an academic argument may strike you as the wrong move to make. After all, aren't grand, sweeping claims more impressive than limited, qualified ones? Not really. Remember, academic audiences tend to be skeptical readers; they approach arguments critically, assessing every assertion's strengths and weaknesses by identifying when, why, and how it might not hold. In academic arguments, carefully qualified claims are more persuasive than broad, unqualified assertions because they tend to be more honest, easier to support, more immune to rebuttal, and more in line with accepted practice.

Qualified Claims Tend to Be More Honest Than Unqualified Claims

Sometimes unscrupulous writers try to persuade readers that their claims apply to everyone and in all circumstances. Think about advertisers who claim that their product can make anyone slimmer or more attractive, can help anyone become a millionaire, or will improve anyone's health. In almost all cases, such sweeping claims are not honest. In fact, if you look carefully at the ad's fine print, you will see the qualifications; the advertiser has to admit that "results may vary." In academic writing you need to acknowledge the limitations of your claims straightforwardly and honestly. In the end, dishonest writing is not persuasive.

Qualified Claims Are Easier to Support Than Are Unqualified Claims

In academic arguments, adequately supporting unqualified claims is difficult. First, the sheer *amount* of evidence needed to support sweeping claims makes them impractical to assert. Consider the number of examples you would need to provide to support a claim such as "The only way to eliminate hunger in every nation across the globe is to promote hydroponic farming." Is it possible to eliminate hunger in *every* nation? Would it be possible to examine the causes of and solutions to hunger in every country? Is hydroponic farming the *only* way to do this? How many other types of farming would you have to examine to support this claim? Second, as you gather material for your essay you will find that most previous research on your topic addresses specific cases or claims—using this material to support a more sweeping claim is a questionable academic practice. In an academic argument, the more precise and qualified the claim, the easier it is to provide precise, effective support.

Qualified Claims Are More Difficult to Refute Than Are Unqualified Claims

When reading arguments, academic audiences tend to be on the lookout for weak, poorly supported assertions. Unqualified claims are easy targets. To refute an unqualified claim, a reader needs to cite only one instance when the assertion will not hold. Properly qualified claims are more difficult to refute.

Qualified Claims Conform to the Conventions of Academic Writing

Properly qualifying claims is one of the conventions of academic writing. Knowing how and when to qualify claims marks you as an insider when writing academic papers, enhancing your ethos; failing to do so marks you as a novice. Academic readers tend to lend more credence to claims made by writers who

---

Something to talk about . . .

With one or two other students in class, discuss each of the four reasons writers need to qualify claims in academic writing, as outlined above. Which of the reasons, if any, do you question? Which ones seem to make the most sense to you? Which, if any, do you have a difficult time understanding?

understand and follow the conventions of academic writing than to writers who do not.

LANGUAGE COMMONLY USED TO QUALIFY CLAIMS

To qualify your claims, add language that acknowledges their limitations. Below you will find some terms academic writers commonly employ to quality the claims they make. Choose language that accurately captures the nature of the claim you are making and that suits your essay's tone and diction.

To indicate that your claim does not apply to everyone

some	almost everyone
many	a majority
most	almost all
a few	hardly any

To indicate that your claim does not apply in all cases

usually	routinely
commonly	for the most part
rarely	under certain conditions
sometimes	it may be that
tends to	likely
in some cases/ instances	normally
in most cases	inclined to
frequently	almost always

To indicate the uncertainty of your claim

possibly	perhaps
it is possible that	suggests that
it would seem that	it may be that
it seems	probably
might be the case that	seems to indicate that

To indicate that not everyone agrees with your claim

it is commonly	recent research shows
one could/might argue that	though some disagree

Something to think about . . .

Carefully examine the list of frequently employed qualifying terms provided above. To what degree are these terms interchangeable? How would you know when to use one of them and not another if they mean roughly the same thing and qualify a claim in roughly the same way? On what basis could you decide which one to use in an argument you are writing?

Something to talk about . . .

With one or two classmates, discuss each set of claims below. Sweeping claims are in bold; more qualified claims follow. How does the meaning and scope of each claim change with the change in wording? Which versions strike you as most honest, easiest to support, and harder to refute? Why?

The only way to eliminate hunger in every nation across the globe is to promote hydroponic farming.

- **One way to help eliminate world hunger is to promote hydroponic farming.**
- Perhaps the best way to help relieve world hunger is to promote hydroponic farming.
- **First-year students are always completely lost when it comes to deciding on a major.**
- First-year students are often lost when it comes to deciding on a major.
- Some first-year students are completely lost when it comes to deciding on a major.
- **Everyone agrees that medicine is the best profession for university students to consider.**
- Recent research seems to suggest that medicine is one of the best professions for university students to consider.
- Many analysts agree that medicine is the best profession for university students to consider if they are interested in both service and financial security.

ADDRESSING OPPOSITION IN ACADEMIC ARGUMENTS

When you write academic arguments, besides properly qualifying your claims, you also need to address possible opposition to your assertions. Investigating opposing views begins early in the writing process, as you gather and reflect on information related to your essay topic. It continues as you draft and revise your essay. Addressing possible rebuttals to your argument improves your credibility and authority; it shows you have taken steps to inform yourself fully on the issue, that you are open-minded, and that you feel strongly enough about your position that you believe it can stand up to critical scrutiny.

Why It Is Important to Research and Address Opposing Views in Academic Arguments

One of the key differences between academic and nonacademic writing involves the way writers address opposing points of view in their arguments. When you write an academic argument, your readers expect that your positions are based on a thorough understanding of the topic. When they read your paper, they will look for evidence that you have examined multiple points of view before forming your own opinions and claims. However, addressing opposing points of view has more than just a rhetorical value. It will, in fact, make you better informed on the topic and put you in a better position to write an effective argument.

Examining Opposing Views Will Help You Generate Material for Your Argument

In purely practical terms, expanding your research agenda to include opposing views will give you more material to write about in your paper. Examining alternative points of view helps you generate the material you need to write a richer, fuller, more persuasive essay.

Examining Opposing Views Will Help You Develop New Ideas

Students frequently make the mistake of deciding on their thesis relatively early in the writing process and limit their research to that point of view alone. They only look for and examine sources of information that support the position they want to advance in their argument. While this strategy saves time, it results in a weaker argument. An academic argument should reflect a thorough understanding of the topic you are addressing. You should be able to explain why your position is better or stronger than the alternatives. In fact, writers sometimes change their position on a topic as they research and write an essay. They begin to question what they believe and alter or refine their argument. This type of intellectual development is one of the great benefits of writing academic arguments.

Examining Opposing Views Will Help You Demonstrate Your Critical Thinking Skills

Academic audiences value critical thinking, and one fundamental critical thinking skill is the ability to examine multiple points of view before reaching a conclusion. One of the primary ways you will demonstrate that you have thought critically about your topic is by examining the strengths and limitations of multiple positions on the topic you are addressing. After researching alternative perspectives on or arguments concerning your topic, carefully and critically critique them in your essay, demonstrating the superior nature of the position you endorse in your thesis.

Examining Opposing Views Will Improve Your Ethos

In the end, examining alternative points of view will improve your credibility as an academic writer. Academic audiences are more likely to be persuaded by writers they believe to be informed, open-minded, and fair. Examining alternative points of view and possible opposition in your argument helps you accomplish all three goals. Addressing possible opposition to your argument is particularly important when you believe readers are likely to question your thesis. Critical readers are going to be more open to your ideas if they see that you have carefully considered positions they endorse instead of just ignoring them or dismissing them out of hand.

Anticipating Opposition

Anticipating possible opposition to your argument becomes easier with experience—you learn the kinds of questions readers typically raise and develop strategies for addressing them. Below are some questions you can ask as you develop material for your argument that may help you identify possible opposing points of view. While it is impossible to anticipate all the objections or questions readers might raise about your assertions, answering these questions will serve as a good start.

1. **Why might readers disagree with my position on the topic?**
   What position might they endorse instead? What questions might readers have about the position I assume in my argument? How might I better explain or defend my assertions against the kinds of objections readers might raise?
2. **Why might readers disagree with any of my claims?**
   Why might readers agree with my thesis but question or disagree with some of my claims? Might readers disagree with any of my claims because they are not clearly worded, adequately supported, or properly qualified? If so, how do I strengthen or clarify them?
3. **Why might readers disagree with any of the reasons or evidence I offer to support a claim?**
   How might a reader misunderstand any of the reasons I offer in support of my claims? Are there ambiguities in wording of any reasons or evidence I need to address? If so, how do I correct the problem? How can I most clearly explain the link between my claims and the reasons or evidence I provide to support them? How do I establish that the evidence I use to support my claims comes from legitimate sources? Where might I need to provide more support for my claims?
4. **How might readers interpret the evidence I provide differently than I do?**
   Might readers think that the evidence I offer comes from legitimate sources but disagree with the way I interpret it? If so, how many alternative interpretations of the evidence should I address in my paper?
5. **Why might readers approach the topic with a different set of values than mine?**
   What set of values have I brought to my argument? What set of values might readers bring? How might my argument look to someone who approaches the topic with a set of values different than mine? How can I best acknowledge and/or address a variety of value systems as I develop my argument? How well do the qualifications I provide for my claims take into account readers who approach the argument with a set of values different than mine?
6. **Why might readers emphasize or value various aspects of my argument differently than I do?**

Which aspects of my argument do I take for granted that readers might question or find objectionable? Which possible objections do I treat too lightly? Which do I need to take more seriously? Looked at objectively, what aspects of my argument receive the most emphasis or support? Is this emphasis appropriate given my intended audience and given possible alternative approaches to my topic?

Rebutting Opposition

While acknowledging opposing points of view in your argument is important, simply including them in your essay is not sufficient—you have to find ways to integrate them into your own argument. There are three effective ways to rebut opposing points of view in an academic argument: refute them, concede to them, or accommodate them.

Refute

When you refute an opposing point of view in your argument, you first summarize it clearly and impartially. You then explain why or how this argument is flawed or incorrect. When refuting an argument, you must be fair and open-minded. Avoid ridicule, name calling, or *ad hominem* attacks when refuting opposing positions in an academic argument. Instead, demonstrate that you have carefully considered an alternative point of view, explain why it is flawed or inadequate, and demonstrate why the argument you support is better. Consider this example:

> **In his 2001 study, Jones determined that very few students read for pleasure outside of class. However, he did not include in his study students who read material online, including those who regularly read web sites, emails, and blogs; he only examined whether students read novels outside of class. When all student reading in taken into account, a clear majority read for pleasure outside of class and the number is increasing (Smith 2002).**

Here the writer refutes a study completed by Jones in 2001 by pointing out a flaw in his research methodology and by citing the work of another researcher, Smith.

Concede

When you concede to an opposing point of view, you acknowledge its legitimacy in part or in whole. As you develop material for your essay and study alternative positions on the topic, you may find yourself agreeing with some of the claims other authors make even though you ultimately reject their thesis. When you present your own argument, you can acknowledge the strength of those claims but explain how your thesis still holds, how those claims, though legitimate, do not invalidate your argument. Consider this example:

> **Over the past few years, the amount of reading students complete outside of class has actually increased, though a few studies seem to call this claim into question. For example, Jones (2001) found that only 45% of students read novels outside of class for pleasure. While his findings may be true, they tell only part of the story. Taking into account the amount of reading students complete online—including web pages, emails, and blogs—reading rates have, in fact, increased over the past decade (Smith 2002).**

Here the writer concedes that Jones's findings are valid but points out that his results do not invalidate her claim that student reading outside of class has recently increased.

Accommodate

When you accommodate opposing points of view, you explain how they can be reconciled with your own argument—you grant a certain amount of legitimacy to an opposing point of view, but explain how it is compatible with your own. When you *concede* to an opposing view, you maintain that your argument holds even if that alternative view is true or valid as well; when you *accommodate* an opposing view, you demonstrate how it can be reconciled or combined with your own. In effect, you are using your opponents' positions to further your own argument. By accommodating an opposing point of view, you show the strength of your own position; you demonstrate that your claim is strong or broad enough to be reconciled with opposing positions. Consider this example:

> **Over the past few years, the amount of reading students complete outside of class has increased. Not everyone agrees, however. For example, Jones has argued forcefully that just the opposite is true, stating in his 2001 study that only 45% of students read novels outside of class for pleasure. Yet in her 1995 study, Harvey found that just 39% of students read novels for pleasure, and in his 1999 report, Juarez stated that 40% did so. Taking those earlier studies into account, Jones's results only confirm that the amount of reading students complete outside of class is on the *increase*, even without taking into account all the reading students complete online today (i.e., reading web sites, emails, and blogs) (Smith 2002).**

The writer uses Jones's results to support her wider claim concerning the amount of reading students complete outside of class. Instead of refuting Jones's findings or just conceding them, she uses them to bolster her own assertions.

Finally, as you research or reflect upon your topic, if you encounter truly superior arguments, you may need to seriously question your own assertions. As an academic writer, remain open to the possibility that your argument is wrong or flawed. Only through research and reflection can you make this determination and change your position if necessary.

Something to talk about . . .

Carefully study the way Michael Sandel addresses opposing views in his article, "Embryo Ethics: The Moral Logic of Stem-cell Research" (pp. 35–37). Throughout his article, Sandel acknowledges and rebuts a range of arguments raised against embryonic stem cell research. As you review his essay, note which techniques he employs to counter these arguments. Also pay attention to his tone. Though Sandel rejects many of the arguments raised against this type of research, he remains fair and respectful. How does this tone contribute to Sandel's ethos?

Something to write about . . .

1. Collect several newspaper editorials or other short arguments for study. Draw a line down the middle of a sheet of paper and on the left side list the primary claims made in each reading. Opposite each of those claims indicate on the right side of the paper how you might refute, concede to, or accommodate each of those claims if you had to rebut them in an argument you were writing.
2. In one or two concise paragraphs explain to someone who has not read this textbook why it is important to properly qualify academic arguments. Be sure to provide examples to illustrate and support your explanation.

WORKING WITH SOURCES IN ACADEMIC ARGUMENTS

MANY OF THE ARGUMENTS you write in college will be based on readings. Because you can expect to draw material from a wide variety of books, journals, and Web sites to develop and support the arguments you write, mastering certain source-based writing skills is essential to your success in college. In classes across the curriculum, you will be summarizing, paraphrasing, and quoting material from readings to support the arguments you write. This chapter offers advice on how to incorporate source-based material into your essays and how to avoid plagiarism, an important issue for all academic writers.

ROLES SOURCES COMMONLY PLAY IN ACADEMIC ARGUMENTS

Provide Background Information

When you write academic arguments, you will frequently summarize, paraphrase, and quote material to provide your readers with necessary background information. How much background information you need to provide depends entirely on the topic you are addressing, your intended audience, and your purpose. The more you can safely assume that your readers know about the topic you are addressing in your argument, the less background information you will likely need to provide. If you believe, however, that your readers will be unfamiliar with the topic, then you will need to provide them enough background information to enable them to follow your argument.

Where in your essay you provide this background information will vary assignment to assignment. Sometimes you will open your argument with a summary of what has already been written about your topic (what scholars in many disciplines call a "survey of the literature"). This summary helps your readers understand the ongoing debate or discussion you are joining. You will continue to provide background information as needed throughout your essay, wherever you believe your readers need it.

Support Claims

You will also summarize, paraphrase, and quote material from readings to support the claims you make in your argument. As will be discussed below, you enhance your credibility as an academic writer if you can demonstrate support for your claims from legitimate, recognized authorities. In most cases, you will accomplish this goal by summarizing, paraphrasing, and quoting their work.

Present Opposing Views

For a number of reasons, you will want to include opposing views in your argument, views that counter your own thesis. Addressing opposing views adds depth to your argument, demonstrates your knowledge of the topic, and enhances your credibility. One of the best ways to incorporate opposing views into your argument is to quote or paraphrase them.

Improve Ethos

Summarizing, quoting, and paraphrasing source material is one of the primary ways you will enhance your ethos or credibility and authority as an academic writer. Citing authorities who support the claims you make adds weight and credibility to those assertions. Citing opposing views demonstrates your sense of fairness and the faith you have in your thesis by showing that it can stand up to criticism. Citing the work of other writers also places your argument in context. As an academic, you need to demonstrate your familiarity with what has already been written on the topic you are addressing and explain how your argument contributes to, advances, or critiques that discussion. You will accomplish these goals largely by drawing on the work of previous writers.

TECHNIQUES COMMONLY USED TO INTEGRATE SOURCE MATERIAL INTO ACADEMIC ARGUMENTS

To incorporate source material into the academic arguments you write, you will usually summarize, paraphrase, or quote from readings. When you summarize a text, you restate its main ideas, findings, or information in your own words, leaving out what is not important. When you paraphrase a text, you restate all of the ideas, findings, or information it contains in your own words. When you quote material, you copy passages word-for-word into your own essay, placing the material in quotation marks or otherwise letting your readers know that it is a *verbatim* copy of the text. In most cases, you will be expected to properly document all of the source material you incorporate into your essay, whether it is summarized, paraphrased, or quoted.

Before moving on with an examination of how to integrated source material you use in an essay argument, first read this short essay: "Regular Exercise and Weight Management: Myths and Reality" by Steven Jonas.

SAMPLE READING

Regular Exercise and Weight Management: Myths and Reality

Steven Jonas

Steven Jonas is a professor of Preventive Medicine at Stony Brook University (NY) School of Medicine and editor-in-chief of the American Medical Athletic Association Journal.

It is so easy to set up straw men and then knock them down. And so comes along journalist Gary Taubes. These days he is best known for being, in his book *Good Calories, Bad Calories* (New York City: Knopf, 2007), the latest promoter of eating lots of fat to lose weight. On October 1, 2007, he furthered his crusade against nutrition and exercise science in *New York* magazine by proclaiming "Why Most of Us Believe that Exercise Makes Us Thinner—and Why We're Wrong." Boy that is a mouthful. And talk about wrong—but not in the way he makes use of the word. Rather he is wrong because he spends most of his article misinterpreting the studies of a variety of scientists. Additionally, his opening reveals just how little he actually knows about regular exercise, regular exercisers, and the scientists who promote it.

The message that Taubes tells us "we" the people are getting about exercise and weight loss is easy to see in the pulp fiction at supermarket check-out counters and the misleading ads for exercise equipment sold on TV. For example, a variety of such ads tell the viewer that if they work out on *their* machine for 30 minutes twice a week they can lose a significant amount of weight, and quickly too. But I have never read anything by a *responsible* scientist that says "working out by itself will make a fat person lean," or, for that matter, that "sitting around by itself will make a lean person fat." Yet on the subject of weight management, Taubes goes after the scientists, not the sellers of that pulp fiction and TV-advertised exercise equipment. I have worked in the exercise/weight management field for a long time and many other scientists I know and know of have worked in it even longer. I don't know of any who would hold that exercise alone, without engaging in healthy eating as well, can lead to weight loss.

Trying to make his case that "scientists" now fold in exercise when talking about healthy eating, he refers to the most recent USDHHS/Department of Agriculture "food pyramid." It introduced, for the first time, a recommendation for regular exercise alongside the "healthy eating pyramid." Taubes cites it as evidence of the "ubiquity of the message" that "burn calories, lose weight" "will keep us from fattening further." What Taubes did not report, and perhaps didn't know, is that: a) the pyramid also increased the previous recommendations for the amount of fat and protein considered to be part of a healthy diet; b) many professional nutritionists and exercise scientists have taken great exception to it; and c) it just happened to have been written by a former lobbyist for the food industry.

Taubes reveals that he knows little about why most people who regularly exercise actually do it. A major reason, Taubes claims, is that they feel guilty if they don't. I guess he doesn't hang around with too many regular exercisers (and by "regular" I mean engaging in the activity several times a week for more than a year). Anyone who knows anything about exercise knows that guilt is a lousy motivator: it almost invariably leads to frustration, anger, possible injury, and quitting. Therefore, guilt cannot be a major motivating factor for the vast majority of long-term regular exercisers.

Taubes also claims that most of the non-guilt-driven regular exercisers do it primarily for weight management but anyone who has lost a significant amount of weight and kept it off—and there are plenty of us—will tell you that the key to doing so is healthy eating. Sorry Mr. Taubes (and Dr. Atkins), this does mean high-carb/low fat/low protein eating, in the *appropriate* types and amounts. Of course, regular exercise is a very helpful adjunct for weight loss; however, both experience and science tell us that exercise by itself will not do the trick.

So why do we do it? I'll bet that every reader of this column who is a regular exerciser knows the answer to that one. We do it primarily because it makes us look good, feel good, feel good about ourselves, and for a great many of us it's just plain fun. Of course, it also offers risk reduction for a wide variety of diseases down the road. And it does help in weight management. But the regular exercisers who do it for those reasons are few and far between.

Since it was discovered about 50 years ago that exercise can play a role in weight management, the health professional, scientific recommendation has always been that weight loss is achieved by a combination of healthy eating *and* exercise, never by exercise alone. The claim that there are scientific recommendations stating that exercise alone can do the trick is a straw man. Yes, regular exercise does offer an assist for weight loss but, contrary to Taubes' claims, no responsible authorities will tell you that exercise alone will do the trick. And yet Taubes claims, "Despite a half a century of effort to prove otherwise, scientists still can't say that exercise [alone] will help keep the pounds off." Ah those straw men. I wonder how much exercise Taubes had to engage in to be able to knock that one down.

SUMMARIZING MATERIAL

To summarize a text or passage, you must read the material carefully, identify the most important or significant information it contains, then restate that information in your own words. Sometimes you will summarize an entire reading in your argument; other times, you will summarize only passages from readings. Your summaries will vary in length, from a single sentence to several paragraphs. The key is to summarize only what you need to in order to advance your argument—do not try to pad your essay by needlessly summarizing other texts.

Qualities of a Good Summary

A good summary of a source text is brief, comprehensive, objective, accurate, and independent First, summaries are **brief**: they should include only the most essential content of a reading. Though a summary is brief, it should still be **comprehensive**. It should include all of the reading's relevant assertions, arguments, findings, or information. Third, when you summarize material, stay **objective**—do not comment on the material or try to sway reader opinion with loaded terms or jargon. Fairness dictates that your summary also be **accurate**—you need to work diligently when writing and revising your summary to accurately reflect the source text's content and intention. Finally, your summary has to be **independent**; it has to make sense to someone who has not read the source text.

Something to talk about . . .

Reread "Regular Exercise and Weight Management: Myths and Reality." In this essay, Jonas frequently summarizes the work of Gary Taubes. What purposes do these summarized passages serve?

Writing a Summary

If you are asked to summarize a text, use the following steps as a guide. You can modify them to suit your own composing style.

1. *Read, reread, and annotate the source text.*
   Read the source text with a pencil or pen in hand. On a first read, identify and mark the text's thesis, along with its primary claims and grounds. Get a sense of how the reading is structured. Also, identify the text's rhetorical situation. What seems to be the author's goal in the piece, what occasion prompted its writing, what audience is being addressed, how does the rhetorical situation shape the content, structure, and tone of the piece?

   Consider Steven Jonas's "Regular Exercise and Weight Management." As I read the text, Jonas's primary goal is to refute the argument Gary Taubes presented in *Good Calories, Bad Calories* concerning the relationship between exercise and weight loss. What prompted him to write the piece was dissatisfaction with Taubes's book. He seems to be addressing people who know something about exercise and weight loss but who may not have read Taubes's book.

2. *Write out the author's thesis and primary claims in your own words, either in the text's margins or on a separate sheet of paper.*
   I would summarize Jonas's thesis this way: in *Good Calories, Bad Calories*, Gary Taubes falsely claims that science supports the idea that exercise alone is the key to weight loss; Jonas's primary claims are as follows:

   - Taubes's claims concerning the relationship between weight loss and exercise are unfounded because they misrepresent scientific literature on the question.
   - No responsible scientist has claimed that exercise alone will help someone reduce weight.
   - Reputable scientists have long argued that weight loss depends on a combination of exercise and proper diet.

- People who exercise regularly do so because it makes them feel and look good, not because they feel guilty if they do not.
- Some scientists have questioned the most recent version of the Department of Agriculture food pyramid which recommends an increased intake of fat and protein coupled with regular exercise.

3. *Write a rough draft of your summary.*
    Using your summaries of the source text's thesis and primary assertions, write your rough draft. Summarize the text's grounds as needed and provide transitions to make the piece easier to read. You may also want to include the author's name, his or her credentials, and the place of publication.

    Here is my rough draft summary of Jonas's essay. As you read it, consider whether I am exhibiting the qualities of a good summary discussed earlier in this chapter.

> In **"Regular Exercise and Weight Management: Myths and Realities,"** Steven Jonas, editor-in-chief of the *American Medical Athletic Association Journal,* refutes several claims made by author Gary Taubes in his recent book *Good Calories, Bad Calories.* Specifically, Jonas criticizes Taubes's assertion that scientists have concluded that exercise alone is sufficient for weight loss. Jonas maintains that Taubes's claim is unsupported by scholarship on the issue. First, Jonas points out that, despite Taubes's claims to the contrary, no reputable scientist that he knows of supports the idea that exercise without healthy eating will result in weight loss. Second, he asserts that Taubes's use of the most recent Department of Agriculture's version of the food pyramid to support his claims is misleading because Taubes fails to point out that many scientists and nutritionists have criticized the Department's recent changes to the pyramid. Jonas further questions Taubes's assertion that most people who exercise regularly are driven by guilt. Instead, Jonas asserts that the desire to look and feel good motivate those who exercise regularly. Finally, Jonas returns to his primary criticism of Taubes's book, pointing out that fifty years of research supports the idea that weight loss is best achieved by a combination of exercise and healthy eating.

4. *Revise your rough draft using the qualities of a good summary as a guide.*
    When you revise summarized material, first reread the source text then check to see if your summary is brief, comprehensive, objective, accurate, and independent. Use questions such as these to guide your revision:

- Have I addressed all of the primary assertions in the reading that I identified when I annotated the text? Did my initial readings capture all the main ideas?
- Which words might not be seen as objective? How can I revise them?
- How accurate is my summary? How might I be misrepresenting the source text though my summary's language or content?
- What background information have I provided as context for my summary? How have I tried to help my reader understand the intention of the source text and why it was written?
- Where can I cut words or combine sentences to make the summary more concise?

Something to write about . . .

Using the guidelines and questions provided above, revise my rough draft summary of "Regular Exercise and Weight Management." Be ready to explain and defend each of the changes you would make to improve the summary.

---

5. *Integrate the summary into your argument.*

As you integrate summarized material into your argument, pay close attention to how you introduce and respond to it. The material should be a vital part of your argument, clearly contributing to whatever claim you are developing in that part of your essay. Do not assume that your readers will understand how the summarized material relates to your argument—explain its importance, react to it, critique it, demonstrate how it furthers your argument. Finally, document the passage according to the guidelines your teacher wants you to follow.

Something to write about . . .

Write your own summary of "Regular Exercise and Weight Management: Myths and Reality" by Steven Jonas.

PARAPHRASING MATERIAL

When you paraphrase material, you restate another person's ideas, findings, or arguments in your own words, just as you would in a summary. However, when you summarize a passage you are more selective than you are when you paraphrase the same material. When you paraphrase a source text, you try to capture all its important ideas, arguments, or findings. Because you are restating someone else's work, be sure to document all paraphrased material.

When and Why to Paraphrase Material

In classes across the curriculum, when you write academic arguments you will paraphrase source texts to accomplish several goals.

To Support Assertions You Are Making

One of the primary reasons to paraphrase material in an academic argument is to support the claims you are making. Paraphrasing the work of experts who agree with the position you are putting forward can persuade readers to accept your argument. Remember, though, that paraphrased material won't "speak for itself." In other words, when you paraphrase source material to support one of your claims, you need to explain how that material adds credence to your assertion.

To Introduce Opposing Points of View

You can also paraphrase material to introduce opposing points of view into your paper. As when summarizing material for this same purpose, you have to paraphrase texts fairly and accurately; you cannot misrepresent an author's ideas, findings, or arguments when you paraphrase his or her work. Once you introduce an opposing point of view by paraphrasing it, you need to explain the relationship between any opposing views you introduce and your overall thesis or the assertions you are making at that point in your essay.

To Provide Background Information

One of the most effective ways to provide readers background information on the subject of your argument is to paraphrase the work of other authors. This background information can establish the context for your own argument or provide readers information they need to better understand your claims.

Qualities of a Good Paraphrase

In academic writing, a paraphrased passage ought to be comprehensive, accurate, clear, and integrated. First, a paraphrase of a passage ought to include all of the important information found in the source text. When you revise a paraphrased passage, always check it against the original to be sure it is **comprehensive**. Because you are substituting your words for the author's to communicate the same ideas, findings, or arguments, make every effort to be **accurate**. Likewise, be sure your paraphrase is **fair**, that you are not misrepresenting the source text, even if you disagree with the author. A paraphrase must also be **clear**; it must make sense to someone who has not read the source text and needs to be written in the same style as the rest of your argument. Finally, a well-**integrated** paraphrase reads smoothly with the text around it.

How to Paraphrase Material

Too often, inexperienced college writers think that paraphrasing simply means substituting one or two words in the passage for other words with roughly the same meaning. Almost all of the source text remains unchanged, except for those one or two words. Material paraphrased this poorly often results in plagiarism. Below are several techniques writers frequently use in combination to paraphrase material properly.

Rephrase Passages

When you paraphrase material, you restate the entire passage in your own words, preserving its essential meaning. However, because words have both denotative and connotative meanings, finding language that communicates a passage's meaning accurately and fairly can take considerable effort. In most cases, you will have to revise paraphrased passages several times before you find the right language. Sometimes a passage will include a key word or phase that simply can't be rephrased. When this is the case, quote that language in your paraphrase.

Suppose, for example, I wanted to paraphrase the following material from Steven Jonas's "Regular Exercise and Weight Management" primarily by rephrasing the passage:

> Since it was discovered about 50 years ago that exercise can play a role in weight management, the health professional, scientific recommendation has always been

that weight loss is achieved by a combination of healthy eating *and* exercise, never by exercise alone.

Rephrasing the passage, my first draft might look like this:

> **For 50 years, health professionals and scientists, knowing the link between exercise and weight control, have recommended that people lose weight by eating well and exercising, not just by exercising alone.**

In my paraphrase of the passage, I changed a lot of the language. I think I've captured the main points of the passage and communicated them pretty clearly in my own words, but I'm not happy with the last phrase: "not just by exercising alone" strikes me as too close to the original "never by exercising alone." Were I to revise this paraphrase, I might focus my attention there.

Alter Syntax

Besides rephrasing passages, another commonly employed method to paraphrase material is to alter the source text's sentence structure. With this technique, writers alter not only the reading's language but also the order in which the ideas, arguments, or findings are presented. Assume I want to paraphrase the following passage from Jonas's argument:

> Yes, regular exercise does offer an assist for weight loss but, contrary to Taubes' claims, no responsible authorities will tell you that exercise alone will do the trick.

By altering both the syntax and the words, I would paraphrase it this way:

> **Taubes mistakenly claims that scientists and nutritionists maintain that people can reduce their weight solely through exercise, those exercising regularly can help them lose pounds.**

In this paraphrase, I flip-flopped the order of the ideas presented in the original, moving the last part of the original sentence to the opening of my paraphrase. I also substituted words, for example changing "responsible authorities" to "scientists and nutritionists" and "regular exercise" to "exercising regularly."

Combine and Synthesize Material

When you paraphrase material, you often work with passages that may be several sentences long in the source text. Using this technique, you recast the entire passage in your paraphrase, combining and reorganizing material as needed. Your paraphrase may be longer or shorter than the source text. Again, suppose I wanted to paraphrase this material from "Regular Exercise and Weight Management":

> So why do we do it? I'll bet that every reader of this column who is a regular exerciser knows the answer to that one. We do it primarily because it makes us look good, feel good, feel good about ourselves, and for a great many of us it's just plain fun. Of course, it also offers risk reduction for a wide variety of diseases down the road. And it does help in weight management. But the regular exercisers who do it for those reasons are few and far between.

My goal in paraphrasing this passage is to capture the gist of Jonas's argument, rear-ranging material as needed. I might end up with a paraphrase that reads like this:

> **According to Jonas, people who exercise regularly are motivated by a desire to look good, to feel good, and to have fun. While most know that physical activity can reduce the risk of some diseases and help control weight, these are not the primary reasons they exercise.**

While this paraphrase is much shorter than the original passage, I have tried to ensure that it is still comprehensive. You can see that I have tried to identify the essential information found in the source text then restate it using my own words and sentences.

Something to write about . . .

1. Revise any of the examples of paraphrased passages I have included above to make them more comprehensive, accurate, fair, and clear. Be ready to explain and defend any changes you propose.
2. Paraphrase the following passages taken from "Regular Exercise and Weight Management: Myths and Reality":
   a. I have worked in the exercise/weight management field for a long time and many other scientists I know and know of have worked in it even longer. I don't know of any who would hold that exercise alone, without engaging in healthy eating as well, can lead to weight loss.
   b. But I have never read anything by a *responsible* scientist that says "working out by itself will make a fat person lean," or, for that matter, that "sitting around by itself will make a lean person fat."
   c. Anyone who knows anything about exercise knows that guilt is a lousy motivator: it almost invariably leads to frustration, anger, possible injury, and quitting.

QUOTING MATERIAL

When you quote material in academic arguments, accuracy and integrity are vital considerations. By placing material in quotation mark, you are assuring your readers that if they examine the source text, they will find the same material exactly as you quoted it. Through proper punctuation, you need to indicate if you make any substantive changes to material you quote—leaving words out, putting words in, or changing words or punctuation. Quoting material properly can enhance your ethos, enliven your writing, and advance your argument; misusing or overusing quotations can seriously damage your authority. Learning how to use quoted material effectively and judiciously in academic writing takes practice and some familiarity with discipline-specific conventions.

When and Why to Quote Material

Unfortunately, too many students quote material in their essays just to take up space—their papers are filled with long block quotes that fail to advance the argument they are making in any meaningful way. When you quote material, do so purposefully and judiciously to accomplish a specific goal. When writing an academic argument, you should consider quoting material for any of the following reasons.

To Capture Interesting or Provocative Language

One of the best reasons to quote a passage is that its author has stated something in an especially interesting or provocative manner. You quote it because, in your mind, there just is not a better way to say it or because you believe the passage will capture your reader's attention or move them in some way.

To Support an Assertion

Authors of academic arguments often quote authorities to support an assertion they are advancing in their essay. Proving that experts in the field agree with your argument or some aspect of it by quoting them enhances your credibility. However, be sure you fully integrate all quoted material with your own prose. Explain the connection you see between any material you quote and any claim you are advancing.

To Introduce Opposing Points of View

Another way you improve your ethos in academic writing is by addressing opposing points of view in your argument. A favored way to do this among academic writers is to quote authorities who question the position they are advancing or who offer alternative points of view. Quoting your opposition—and then addressing their arguments or concerns—demonstrates the conviction you have in your own position as well as your willingness to be fair and open-minded.

Something to talk about . . .

With another student in your class, choose any of the "Additional Readings" included in this textbook for study. Examine how the author of that reading uses quoted material to advance his or her argument. Make a list of the various uses to which he or she puts quoted material and come up with a specific example of each one drawn from the reading. Be ready to share the results of your discussion with the other students in class if asked to do so by your instructor.

How to Quote Material

Any examination of academic arguments will reveal a wide range of methods authors employ to incorporate quoted material into their writing. Below are some of the more common.

Introduce with a Verb

With this method, you use a verb of saying to introduce the quoted material, inserting a comma after the verb. Commonly used verbs include:

states	claims	writes	asserts	argues
says	maintains	finds	concludes	objects

When you introduce quoted material with a verb of saying, consider including the full name of the source text's author, his or her credentials, and perhaps even the title of the piece the first time you refer to that reading.

Source Text

> Anyone who knows anything about exercise knows that guilt is a lousy motivator: it almost invariably leads to frustration, anger, possible injury, and quitting.

Quoted Passage

> **In "Regular Exercise and Weight Management: Myths and Reality," Dr. Steven Jonas argues, "Anyone who knows anything about exercise knows that guilt is a lousy motivator: it almost invariably leads to frustration, anger, possible injury, and quitting."**

In this example, I use the title of the source text and the author's name to help introduce the quoted material. Here is another way to convey the same information:

> **In his essay "Regular Exercise and Weight Management: Myths and Reality," Steven Jonas, professor of Preventive Medicine at Stony Brook University School of Medicine, argues, "Anyone who knows anything about exercise knows that guilt is a lousy motivator: it almost invariably leads to frustration, anger, possible injury, and quitting."**

By providing the title of the source text, the author's name, and his credentials, I hope to enhance the authority of the quoted material.

Incorporate without a Verb

Sometimes you may want to incorporate quoted material into your argument without using a verb of saying. In these cases, the quoted material should flow naturally from the sentence preceding it.

Source Text

> Anyone who knows anything about exercise knows that guilt is a lousy motivator: it almost invariably leads to frustration, anger, possible injury, and quitting.

Quoted Passage

> **According to Jonas, guilt rarely motivates people to exercise: "Anyone who knows anything about exercise knows that guilt is a lousy motivator: it almost invariably leads to frustration, anger, possible injury, and quitting."**

Notice how the sentence leads to the quote and how I used a colon to mark the transition to the quoted material.

Blend Quoted Material with Your Own Writing

A more sophisticated way to incorporate quoted material into your essay is to blend your writing seamlessly with the quoted material. When done correctly, the sentence reads smoothly and naturally; punctuation and documentation indicates which material is quoted.

Source Text

> Anyone who knows anything about exercise knows that guilt is a lousy motivator: it almost invariably leads to frustration, anger, possible injury, and quitting.

Quoted Passage

> **According to Jonas, most people are not motivated to exercise out of guilt because "it almost invariably leads to frustration, anger, possible injury, and quitting."**

When you read the quoted passage aloud, you would not be able to tell where my writing ended and the quoted material begins. On the page, though, quote marks indicate which words were lifted from the source text. If you use this technique to integrate quoted material into your argument, make every effort to revise your writing to fit the quoted passage.

Quote Selected Words or Passages

You do not have to limit yourself to quoting entire sentences when you incorporate source material into your arguments. In fact, you may decide that you only need to quote one or two key words or phrases. In an academic argument, most of the language should be yours, not someone else's. One way to cut back on quoted material in an essay is to selectively quote only the words or passages you need to pull from a source text.

Source Text

> Anyone who knows anything about exercise knows that guilt is a lousy motivator: it almost invariably leads to frustration, anger, possible injury, and quitting.

Quoted Passage

> **According to Jonas, when it comes to exercise, "guilt is a lousy motivator" because, among other things, it can lead to "frustration, anger, [and] possible injury."**

Note how I quoted just two passages from the source text and integrated them into my own sentence. At the end of my sentence, I had to add the word "and" to the passage so it would read smoothly (because I added that word to the quoted passage, I had to place it in brackets).

Adding Material to a Quoted Passage

If you need to *add* information inside a quoted passage in order for it to make sense, place that information in squared brackets (not in parentheses).

Source Text

> I don't know of any who would hold that exercise alone, without engaging in healthy eating as well, can lead to weight loss.

Quoted Passage

> Jonas concludes, "I don't know of any [scientists] who would hold that exercise alone, without engaging in healthy eating as well, can lead to weight loss."

In the context of the source text, Jonas is clearly referring to scientists when he writes to "any"; however, someone who had not read his essay would not know this, which is why I add "scientists" to the quote I use, placing it in brackets.

Leaving Material Out of a Quoted Passage

If you leave out information from a quoted passage, use ellipses (. . .) to indicate where the words were removed. Be careful not to change the meaning or intent of any passage you quote by leaving out words.

Source Text

> Yes, regular exercise does offer an assist for weight loss but, contrary to Taubes' claims, no responsible authorities will tell you that exercise alone will do the trick.

Quoted Passage

> Jonas argues, ". . . regular exercise does offer an assist for weight loss but . . . no responsible authorities will tell you that exercise alone will do the trick."

Note which words I left out of the source text and how I used ellipses to indicate that they are missing. If you leave off words at the end of a sentence in a quote, you will add a fourth dot to serve as the period.

Retaining Original Punctuation in Quoted Passages

When you quote material, retain the punctuation and other typographical features in the source text, including any material that is underlined or italicized.

Source Text

> Since it was discovered about 50 years ago that exercise can play a role in weight management, the health professional, scientific recommendation has always been that weight loss is achieved by a combination of healthy eating *and* exercise, never by exercise alone.

Quoted Passage

> Jonas suggests that for the past fifty years ". . .the health professional, scientific recommendation has always been that weight loss is achieved by a combination of healthy eating *and* exercise, never by exercise alone."

If you want to add italics to a quoted passage, you can. You simply have to indicate parenthetically that you have done so following the passage with a phrase such as "italics added" or "emphasis added."

Source Text

> Anyone who knows anything about exercise knows that guilt is a lousy motivator: it almost invariably leads to frustration, anger, possible injury, and quitting.

Quoted Passage

> **Jonas clarifies one point in his essay: "Anyone who knows anything about exercise knows that guilt is a *lousy* motivator: it almost invariably leads to frustration, anger, possible injury, and quitting" (emphasis added).**

Quoting Material That Contains Quoted Material

Sometimes you will quote material that already contains quoted material. When you incorporate this material into your argument, you add quote marks around the passage and change to single quote marks any quote marks found in the source text.

Source Text

> But I have never read anything by a *responsible* scientist that says "working out by itself will make a fat person lean," or, for that matter, that "sitting around by itself will make a lean person fat."

Quoted Passage

> **Jonas states that he has "never read anything by a *responsible* scientist that says 'working out by itself will make a fat person lean,' or, for that matter, that 'sitting around by itself will make a lean person fat.'"**

Note how I placed quote marks around the material I copied from the source text. Next, I replaced the regular quote marks found in the reading with single quote marks. Finally, note that the word "responsible" is in italics in the quoted passage because it was italicized in the source text.

Longer Quotes

In academic writing, longer quoted passages are frequently formatted differently than shorter quoted passages, but what counts as a "longer" passage and how writers are supposed to format it vary by field of study. In most disciplines, longer quoted passages are set off from the rest of the essay by changes in indentation and perhaps line spacing. To learn how to quote longer passages correctly when writing a paper in a class, consult the appropriate style manual. If you are unsure what style manual to follow, ask your teacher for advice.

Something to write about . . .

Gather three academic arguments for study (you can use readings found in this text or collect them on your own). Carefully study how the author of each text integrates quoted material in his or her argument. Note each time each technique is used in each reading. What conclusions can you draw from your analysis?

AVOIDING PLAGIARISM

Though the term "plagiarism" covers a wide range of academic transgressions, it generally refers to writers failing to give proper credit in their essays to the work of others. Academic audiences react strongly to plagiarism, and the penalties for turning in plagiarized work can be severe. The best way to avoid problems with plagiarism is to understand why and how it commonly occurs.

Something to talk about . . .

With one or two classmates, develop a definition of plagiarism. Once you agree on a definition, write it down then share it with another group. Compare the definitions the groups developed then work with those other students to reconcile any differences. When you are finished, share your revised definition with the class, then as a class, develop a single definition of the term.

Common Forms of Plagiarism in Academic Writing

Plagiarism can assume many forms in academic writing. Some of the more common ones are listed below.

Knowingly Turning in Work You Did Not Write

This form of plagiarism occurs when students turn in work they did not write themselves. They may have purchased the paper on the Internet, paid or asked someone to write the paper for them, or even "borrowed" the paper from a friend or roommate. Regardless, they knowingly turn in for a grade work they did not write themselves.

Improperly Paraphrasing Material

This form of plagiarism occurs when students retain too much of an author's language in a paraphrased passage—they have changed some of the language found in the source text, but have kept significant passages unchanged. Even if this passage is documented, the writer would still be guilty of plagiarism. The documentation the writer provides credits the author for his or her ideas, but without placing in quote marks the passage lifted directly from the source text; the writer fails to credit the author for his or her language.

Improperly Documenting Paraphrased Material

This form of plagiarism occurs when writers properly paraphrase material from a source text but fail to document it. Though they have rephrased the material in their own words, without proper documentation the original author does not receive credit for his or her ideas, arguments, or findings.

Avoiding Problems with Plagiarism

Academic writers can take several steps to avoid problems with plagiarism. None of the steps is especially difficult, but inexperienced college writers frequently fail to follow them.

Proper Note Taking and Proofreading

Two of the main sources of plagiarism are faulty note taking and poor proofreading. As they gather material for their paper, students often copy passages word for word in their notes without putting that material in quotation marks. When they copy that material from their notes into their papers, they forget that the language was lifted directly from the source text. They document that material in their paper, but because it also needs to be placed in quotation marks, plagiarism occurs.

Inadvertent plagiarism also occurs when writers fail to properly proofread their work. Many inexperienced college writers fall into the bad habit of writing early drafts of their papers without any documentation. They believe that in later drafts they can go back and add it. Unfortunately, they sometimes end up plagiarizing material because as they revise and proofread their essays they overlook passages that need to be documented.

Documentation Conventions

Another common source of plagiarism among inexperienced college writers is simply failing to understand what material needs to be documented and what does not. They often fall back on the old adage that "common knowledge" does not need to be documented, but what counts as common knowledge varies widely field to field. For example, some students mistakenly believe that any information found on the Internet or in an encyclopedia is common knowledge. If you ever have a question about whether something should or should not be documented, ask your teacher for advice. Generally speaking, if the material you are working with comes from a source text and is new to you—you didn't know it before you read the material—you should consider documenting it in your paper.

Personal Ethics

A final source of plagiarism in academic writing involves personal ethics. More often than not, plagiarism in academic papers is unintentional. It results from students not understanding particular rules and conventions of academic writing, from faulty note taking, poor proofreading, or from carelessness. Other times, however, it results from a decision to cheat, to deceive, and to earn good grades without doing the required work.

Something to write about . . .

Get a copy of your school's student handbook or pull up a copy online. Paraphrase one of the following policy statements:

 a. your school's definition of and policy concerning plagiarism
 b. your school's definition of and policy concerning academic honesty

Something to write about . . .

On your own or with a classmate, write your own set of directions for avoiding plagiarism in academic writing. Assume you are writing these directions for a group of first-year college students, so use language and examples that they would likely understand and might find interesting.

9

WORKING WITH THE VISUAL ELEMENTS OF ACADEMIC ARGUMENTS

WHY IT'S IMPORTANT TO UNDERSTAND THE VISUAL ELEMENTS OF ARGUMENTS

Some visual elements of arguments are so common, they go unnoticed. However, the way you present words on the page and the graphics you use can be an important part of the academic arguments you write. As a writer, you need to decide how you will use headings and subheadings, font size, typeface, and other typographical features of your essay to highlight your argument and influence the way your audience reads your text. In classes across the curriculum, you might also need to decide how best to use pictures, drawings, diagrams, tables, and graphs in your arguments.

Until recently, few argument textbooks would have included a chapter such as this one; now, they are common. This change has come about for several reasons. First, increasing numbers of writers and readers today are "visual learners." Much more than earlier generations, students today understand and are comfortable working with the visual elements of communication.

Second, modern computer technology has made it increasingly easy to incorporate visual elements into written arguments. With just a few keystrokes, you can accomplish in seconds what it used to take writers hours to accomplish—create tables and graphs, draw or download diagrams, edit pictures, or format text. Because it has become so easy to include visuals in arguments, readers increasingly expect to see them used.

Third, the wise use of visuals can make your writing more persuasive and easier to read. Visual images often capture and convey emotional appeals more effectively and efficiently than words alone can. Visuals can add humor to your writing, increase reader interest, and even enhance your ethos—supporting a claim with a picture or graphic, for example, can help you sway readers for whom seeing is believing.

Finally, you need to understand how writers use visuals in arguments to sway *your* opinion or change *your* behavior. For example, how much do advertisers depend on visual images to sell their products? How often do politicians use visuals in their campaign ads to persuade you to vote for them or against their opponents? You need to be a critical consumer of visual arguments the same way you are of written or oral arguments.

HOW VISUALS FUNCTION IN ACADEMIC ARGUMENTS

The roles visuals play in academic arguments vary by discipline. In some fields of study—business, engineering, the fine arts, and some social sciences—they are common. Many of the arguments you write in these classes will include charts, diagrams, pictures, and drawings. In other fields of studies—most notably the humanities—you will use fewer visuals in your arguments, though nothing prohibits you from incorporating them into your essays when appropriate. In academic writing, visuals often assert an argument, support an argument, or make an argument easier to read.

Using Visuals to Make an Argument

Sometimes a picture, diagram, image, or symbol alone will make an argument. Consider the way political cartoonists often assert an argument through the pictures they draw, even without captions. Sometimes photographs serve the same purpose. Think about the famous picture of the lone student standing in front of a Chinese tank in Tiananmen Square, the crying student kneeling beside her stricken friend at Kent State, Tommie Smith and John Carlos standing with raised fists at their medal ceremony during the 1968 Summer Olympics. All of these images portray powerful arguments.

Using Visuals to Support an Argument

While in college you may not be asked to produce an argument that relies on visuals alone; you will frequently have the opportunity to use them to support the arguments you write. Consider how visuals—especially pictures, photographs, or illustrations—can make your arguments more persuasive than they might otherwise be and how they can enhance your credibility or appeal to your readers' emotions and values.

Using Visuals to Make an Argument Easier to Understand

As will be discussed below, sometimes visuals—especially charts and graphs—represent the most effective and efficient way to present information in an argument. When this is the case, using the graphic will make your argument easier to follow, so long as the graphic is clearly written and integrated into the rest of your argument. When you use graphics to provide information in your essay, do not assume that it speaks for itself, that your reader will readily understand it and its relationship to your argument. Instead, refer to the visual in the body of your essay, guiding your reader through the information it contains.

Something to talk about . . .

As a class, develop a list of the most common visual elements of the texts you routinely read inside and outside of school. What are they and what is their function? Do you see a difference in the types of visuals found in academic and nonacademic texts? What types of visuals are most commonly found in the academic texts you read?

READING VISUAL TEXTS CRITICALLY

It may seem odd to talk about "reading" the graphic elements of texts, but you need to approach them the same way you would written elements—you should read both carefully and critically. Assume that authors place visuals in their texts for specific reasons, to help them accomplish particular goals. When you examine Web sites, the visual elements of the text take on even more importance—to a great degree, these sites are built around the graphics they contain.

Below are a series of questions that help you "read" the visual elements of arguments more effectively.

Reading Pictures and Drawings

To critically read the pictures or drawings a text contains, examine them carefully then answer the following questions.

What does the picture or drawing contain?

This may seem like a simple question, but you would be surprised how casually students often approach pictures and diagrams included in academic texts, paying them very little attention. Just as you should be able to summarize a reading accurately, you should also be able to summarize a visual it contains. You should be able to describe it in exact detail, noting both what it contains (including its visual and textual elements) and how it is structured (how these elements are arranged on the page or on the screen).

What is the intended purpose of the picture or drawing?

Why do you think the author included this visual in his or her text? Is it intended to help readers better understand the text's argument? Is it intended to appeal to readers' emotions? Is it supposed to help enhance the writer's credibility? To support your interpretation, you need to cite specific elements of the picture or drawing. In other words, if you think the visual is intended to appeal to readers' emotions, you need to point out which elements of the visual contribute to this effect and how.

What is the source of the picture or drawing?

As with every element of a text, try to identify the source of the picture or drawing an author includes. Just as written texts reflect the writer's biases, so too do visual texts. To accurately interpret a picture or drawing, you need to know its source and determine how that information should influence your reading.

Reading Diagrams, Tables, and Graphs

Authors frequently include diagrams, tables, and graphs in their texts to summarize information. However, they can serve other purposes as well. As with the other visual elements of arguments, you should not just "skip over" the diagrams, tables, and graphs authors include in their texts. Instead, you should examine them carefully to determine their purpose, utility, and effectiveness. Answering questions such as these should help.

What information does the diagram, table, or graph contain?

As always, start your analysis with the literal—what information does the diagram, table, or graph contain? Sometimes answering this seemingly simple question can prove difficult. If the diagram, table, or graph is poorly constructed or inadequately labeled, it may take you awhile to figure out what it's communicating. Pay attention to any labels, legends, or captions that accompany the diagram, table, or graph.

How clearly does the diagram, table, or graph communicate information?

How difficult is it to read the diagram, table, or graph? Is it labeled well? Does the legend provide enough guidance? Is the diagram, table, or graph so poorly constructed that reading it is difficult? Does it contain too much information? Too little information? Contradictory information?

What is the purpose of the diagram, table, or graph?

As stated earlier, most readers assume that the primary purpose of the diagrams, tables, or graphs authors include in their texts is to summarize information. In many cases, this will be true. However, understand that as with any other element of an argument, authors can manipulate diagrams, tables, or graphs for specific rhetorical purposes. Authors make purposeful decisions regarding what to put into a visual and what to leave out, guided by their rhetorical goals. Do not read diagrams, tables, or graphs naively; always try to determine the purpose behind every visual an author includes in a text.

What is the source of the diagram, table, or graph?

Did the author create the diagram, table, or graph him- or herself or does it come from some other source? If it comes from another text, what is that source? Who put together the diagram, table, or graph? What are that person's credentials or possible biases? Where and when was it published? Answering these questions will help you read the diagram, table, or graph more critically.

WORKING WITH PICTURES, DRAWINGS, AND DIAGRAMS

As with other visual elements of an argument, pictures, drawings, and diagrams are intended to support, clarify, advance, or enhance a claim. Pictures and drawings are especially effective at appealing to readers' emotions while diagrams are especially effective at helping readers identify how various parts of something relate to one another.

Qualities of Effective Pictures, Drawings, and Diagrams

Effective pictures, drawings, and diagrams are purposeful, appropriate, and integrated. First, you should have a clear **purpose** for adding any picture, drawing, or diagram to your argument. Adding them just because you can isn't a good enough reason. If you can't articulate a clear reason to include the visual, leave it out. Second, as you think about adding a picture, drawing, or diagram to your argument, consider your intended audience and purpose. Is the visual rhetorically **appropriate** for this audience? Might the picture or drawing offend some readers? Is the diagram too simple or too complicated? Third, when you use a picture, drawing, or diagram in your argument, be sure you **integrate** it with the rest of your argument. Introduce it in the body of your essay and comment on its meaning or significance. Don't just place it in your essay without commentary. *Note:* Any picture, drawing, or diagram that you copy from a source text needs to be documented. You should give credit to the person who created the image and indicate where it was posted or published. This information is usually included beneath the image in your essay and may be included in your works cited list or bibliography. Consult the appropriate style manual for directions on how to write these types of entries. If you do not document a picture, drawing, or diagram, readers will assume that you created it yourself.

WORKING WITH TABLES

Tables enable you to summarize information effectively and depict how findings or data relate to one another. Sometimes presenting information in a table is the most effective way to advance your argument. For example, suppose in an essay you are examining the number of doctoral degrees earned by men and women in the United States in 2005, focusing on a few specific areas of study. In the body of your essay, you might summarize some of the statistics this way:

> **According to the National Opinion Research Center at the University of Chicago, in 2005, 620 students received doctoral degrees in civil engineering, 502 men and 118 women; 1,158 in clinical psychology, 317 men and 841 women; 953 in computer science, 796 men and 157 women; 1,435 in educational leadership, 532 men and 903 women; 902 in music, 483 men and 419 women; 279 in public health, 80 men and 199 women; and 369 in religion, 246 men and 123 women.**

Table 9.1 presents the same information.

Table 9.1 Doctoral Degrees Earned in U.S. Universities in 2005

	Men	Women	Total
Civil Engineering	502	118	620
Clinical Psychology	317	841	1,158
Computer Science	796	157	953
Educational Leadership	532	903	1,435
Music	483	419	902
Public Health	80	199	279
Religion	246	123	369

Data obtained from the National Opinion Research Center, University of Chicago, 2005, 10 June 2007, /http://www.norc.org/projects+2/SED+Tables.htm.

The information is much more clearly presented in the table than it is in the paragraph. The table not only makes it easier to understand the number of degrees men and women obtained in each field of study but also to compare these numbers. Sometimes the best course of action is to present the material in a table and analyze it in the body of your argument.

Qualities of Effective Tables

Effective tables are clear and integrated. Be sure the data presented in a table is **clear**, including any labels, titles, and legends. To **integrate** a table into the body of your essay, first introduce it then comment on it—do not expect the data contained in the table to speak for itself. Number tables consecutively in the body of your essay. If you copy a table another writer created, document its source. Likewise, if the data you use in a table comes from a source text, document it as well.

WORKING WITH GRAPHS

Graphs effectively portray trends and relationships that exist among data. In some disciplines—notably the natural sciences, social sciences, engineering, and business—portraying research findings in graphs is a common practice.

Common Types of Graphs

Bar, line, and pie—these are the most common forms of graphs you will use in your college courses. Which you ultimately decide to use in an argument depends on the nature of the data, the audience you are addressing, the course you are taking, and your personal preferences.

Bar Graphs

As Figure 9.1 shows, bar graphs make it easy to conduct side-by-side comparisons of data. Notice how the legend identifies the color code used in the graph and how the various disciplines are labeled along the bottom. I chose to include the

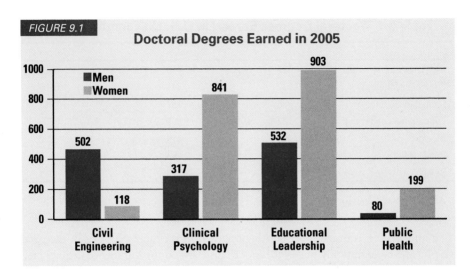

FIGURE 9.1

Doctoral Degrees Earned in 2005

exact number of degrees earned in each field of study to make it easier to read the graph. You may also decide to include relative percentages as well.

Pie Graphs

Pie graphs are a helpful way to depict numbers or percentages of a whole. For example, if I wanted to show the number and percentage of women earning doctorates in each field of study in 2005, I could do it with a pie graph (see Figure 9.2). I could do the same thing with men (see Figure 9.3). You have the option of labeling each

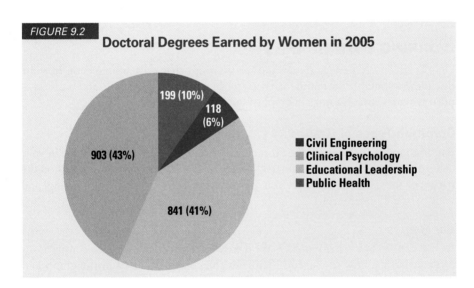

FIGURE 9.2

Doctoral Degrees Earned by Women in 2005

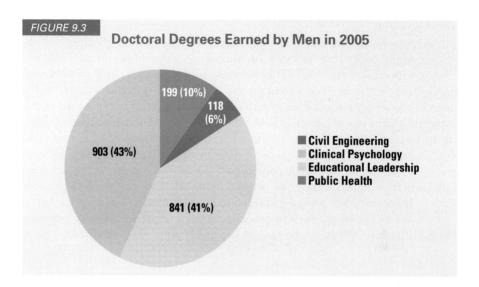

FIGURE 9.3

Doctoral Degrees Earned by Men in 2005

199 (10%)
118 (6%)
903 (43%)
841 (41%)

■ Civil Engineering
  Clinical Psychology
  Educational Leadership
■ Public Health

slice of the pie with total numbers and/or percentages. Again, note the legend identifying sectors of the graph.

Line Graphs

Figure 9.4 depicts the same information regarding the number of men and women obtaining doctoral degrees in the form of a line graph. Note how easy it is to see distinct similarities and differences between the number of men and women earning degrees in each field of study.

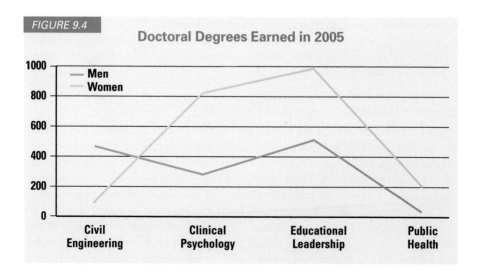

FIGURE 9.4

Doctoral Degrees Earned in 2005

— Men
— Women

1000
800
600
400
200
0

Civil Engineering   Clinical Psychology   Educational Leadership   Public Health

Qualities of Effective Graphs

Effective graphs are clear and integrated. Graphs should be intuitively **clear**. That is, readers should understand how they are constructed and read the information they contain with relative ease. Instead of enhancing your argument, overly complicated, poorly constructed, or ill-conceived graphs call into question your mastery of the material you are presenting. Also, as with all other visual elements of your argument, **integrate** graphs into the body of your essay by introducing then discussing them. In the body of your essay, refer to the information contained in your graph and explain its relevance to your argument. Also, provide a label or heading for each graph you use and number them consecutively in the body of your essay. Label the information contained in the graph as needed, provide a comprehensive legend for readers, and if you are copying a graph another writer created, document its source. If the data you are using comes from a source text, document it as well, following the guidelines established by the appropriate style manual for your course.

WORKING WITH TYPOGRAPHICAL FEATURES OF A TEXT

As you write an argument, among the typographical features you can manipulate are headings, fonts, and spacing. Through the use of headings and subheadings, you can create a visual outline of your argument on the page, helping your readers understand how you have structured your argument. You can also draw attention to particular words, passages, or ideas in your text by writing them in unusually large type, underlining or italicizing them, placing them in boldface, or even making them a different color.

Word processing programs make it easy to change these elements of your text, but be sure you employ them effectively and purposefully, not just because they are easy to add. Overusing such features can damage your ethos, creating a cartoon-like document that many critical academic readers will dismiss. Also be aware of disciplinary conventions governing the use of typographical features. For example, the APA style manual specifies a specific format for headings and subheadings writers are expected to follow.

Effective Use of Typographical Features

Typographical features should be purposeful, systematic, functional, and conventional. **Purposeful** means that there should be a good reason for all the typographical changes you make in a manuscript—don't make them just because you can. You do not enhance your credibility among academic readers by randomly adding multicolored typefaces or long, italicized passages. Second, employ typographical features in a text **systematically**. That is, establish and maintain a consistent pattern of use in your argument. Typographical features should be **functional** as well—they should aid comprehension. Finally, they should be **conventional**. If the stylebook you follow for a particular discipline dictates how to use particular typographical features in an essay, adhere to those conventions.

WRITING ARGUMENTS: AN OVERVIEW

WRITING SUCCESSFUL ACADEMIC ARGUMENTS IN college can be extremely challenging—they tend to be longer than the essays you wrote in high school, the grading standards tend to be higher, and the topics tend to be more difficult. The best way to approach these assignments is one step at a time—to follow a process that breaks complicated writing tasks into a series of more manageable steps. If you procrastinate and put off writing an assignment until the last possible moment, you will likely be unhappy with the results. The better approach is to get started early so you have time to plan, research, draft, and revise the arguments you write.

This chapter offers a three-stage process you can adopt or modify when you write academic arguments in college:

1. choosing and investigating a topic,
2. forming a position, crafting a thesis statement, and developing an organizational plan,
3. drafting and revising

Though the instruction is presented in a step-by-step manner, writing rarely follows such a neat, sequential process. While you will likely engage in each of the activities described in this chapter as you write an academic argument, the order in which you attend to them and the attention you give to each will vary by assignment. Through experience and the responses you receive from your readers, you will develop a set of practices that works best for you when writing arguments in college.

UNDERSTANDING THE RHETORICAL SITUATION OF AN ASSIGNMENT

Chapter 1 identified five central elements of any argument's rhetorical situation: writer, audience, topic, occasion, and purpose. Answering the questions below will help you understand an assignment's rhetorical situation and determine the most effective way to develop, structure, and support any argumentative essay you write, whether the topic is assigned or open.

Writer

These questions will help you determine the role or persona you are to assume when you write an academic argument.

- Am I expected to write as an expert or a novice? How well am I expected to know the topic I'm addressing?
- Am I expected to write as a believer or as a skeptic?
- Am I expected to write as myself (a student in this class) or am I being asked to assume or play some other role?
- Am I supposed to write this assignment on my own or collaborate with others?
- What do I already know about the topic?
- What would I like to find out about the topic?
- What are my feelings about the topic?
- When have I ever written anything like this before?

Audience

To better understand the intended audience of an academic argument assignment, consider these questions:

- Does the teacher specify an audience? If so, who are my intended readers? If not, what is the best way for me to clarify the assignment's intended audience?
- What do I know about the intended audience? What do I need to find out about this audience? Where can I gather this information?
- Have I written for this audience or similar audiences in the past? If so, what did I do to shape my argument for this audience? What worked and what did not work?
- What are my intended readers likely to know, think, or feel about the topic?
- How open will my intended readers be to what I have to say?
- What might they want to learn about my topic?
- What arguments, ideas, or positions might they find convincing? Which arguments, ideas, or positions might they seriously question or reject?

Topic

Teachers may assign you a specific topic to address, a list of possible topics, or leave the choice of topics completely open. To better understand how the choice of topic may influence the argument you write, consider these questions:

- Has the teacher specified a topic for my paper? If so, what is it?
- Does the teacher offer several possible topics for the paper? If so, which do I find most interesting or challenging? Which one would I like to write about?
- What topics would be most appropriate to address in this class?

- What topics might appeal most to my intended audience?
- Is the topic I am considering too broad or too narrow? How can I clarify the topic?
- What resources are available on campus for me to use as I learn about the topic, including faculty members and library holdings?

Occasion

Occasion can be captured in one question: What gives rise to your need to write this argument? As a student, the answer to this question might seem obvious—you are writing it because your teacher assigned it. However, the role occasion plays in the rhetorical situation of an assignment is more complicated than it might appear. Answering these questions may help you better understand the role occasion plays in the arguments you write:

- How does this assignment fit into the structure of the course I am taking?
- How is this assignment related to other course assignments and requirements?
- How does this assignment fit into the goals of the course I am taking?
- Why do I feel a need to write about this topic?
- Why do I feel a need to argue a particular thesis?
- How is this need to write related to my own interests, my intended audience, and my purpose?
- How does completing this assignment fit into my goals for the course?

Purpose

Answering the following questions will help you determine the purpose or purposes underlying the academic arguments you write:

- Has the teacher specified a purpose for this paper? If so, what is it?
- If a purpose is not stated, is one implied? If so, what is it?
- What am I trying to achieve by writing this paper? Does it match the teacher's stated or implied purpose? If not, how can I reconcile the conflict?
- How can I manipulate the various elements of my argument—for example, content, structure, style, voice—to help me achieve my purpose(s)?
- Given the paper's topic, audience, and my own knowledge and preferences, what obstacles am I likely to face as I try to achieve my purpose in this paper? How might I address and overcome those obstacles?

WORKING WITH ASSIGNED TOPICS

One of the biggest problems college writer's face is misinterpreting writing assignments. Here are a few steps you can take to help ensure that you understand an assignment:

1. Ask about any element of the rhetorical situation that is missing from the assignment or that puzzles you.

If any element of the rhetorical situation is missing from the assignment, or if an element is worded unclearly, ask the teacher for a fuller explanation of the task. Don't just *assume* that you know your teacher's intentions or that you are reading the assignment correctly—ask.

2. Paraphrase the assignment
   Using your own words, state what you think the assignment is asking you do. Share your paraphrase with your teacher to see if he or she agrees that you are interpreting the assignment correctly. If the teacher does not think you fully understand the assignment, paraphrase it again until you and your teacher agree that you have captured its intention.

3. Share an early draft with your teacher
   If your teacher does not routinely collect and respond to drafts of your work, ask him or her to read an early version of your paper to see if you are on the right track. You may feel you understand an assignment until you begin to write it. If thus happens, ask your teacher to look at an early draft of your work.

Something to talk about . . .

With one or two classmates, use the rhetorical situation questions provided above to generate specific assignments for argumentative essays out of each subject listed below. Use your imagination and experience to generate interesting, detailed assignments.

1. American horror films
2. human cloning
3. prayer in public high schools
4. 9/11

Be ready to share the results of your discussion with the other students in class should your teacher ask you to.

WORKING WITH OPEN TOPICS

Sometimes your teachers will leave the choice of topic up to you. The freedom inherent in open topics, however, can come at a price. Many writers find open topic assignments too challenging and have a difficult time deciding what to write about. One way to identify a topic to address is to employ a heuristic, a set of reflective questions that helps you think through a problem. Below are two heuristics you might employ if you need help generating or choosing a topic for an argumentative essay.

Choosing a Topic for an Argumentative Essay: A General Heuristic

This heuristic helps you choose a topic for your essay by answering a number of questions related to what you feel, think, and know. Writing down your answers to these questions is the most effective way to work through them.

What aspects of the course interest you?

What subjects do you feel passionately about?

What interesting topics emerge from your preliminary research?

How is common thought about a topic wrong?

Examine your answers to these questions to see if an interesting topic emerges for your argument.

Choosing a Topic for an Argumentative Essay: A Stasis-Based Heuristic

Another method of identifying a topic for an argument has roots in classical rhetoric. In ancient Greece, rhetoricians developed a series of questions to determine the exact nature of a dispute. Answering these questions will help you explore an issue and identify a topic for your essay. Not every set of questions will be appropriate for every argument you are assigned to write. Work with the set that most closely matches the purpose of the assignment.

Questions of Fact

These questions explore whether something is true or factual:

- As you review issues related to the course, is there some factual dispute that interests you, an ongoing conversation or debate over the factual status of some claim or assertion you would like to explore more fully?
- Has the instructor assumed something to be factual that you would like to dispute?
- Has the factual status of some claim or assertion been established in a way you think needs to be questioned or further examined?

Questions of Definition

These questions explore how something has been defined or ought to be defined:

- Has some important term in the course been defined incorrectly or insufficiently?
- Is there some dispute over the definition of a term that you would like to investigate?
- Is there some dispute over whether a definition fits a particular instance or case?
- Has sufficient attention been paid to the effects of defining something in a particular way?

Questions of Cause and Effect

These questions explore the cause and/or effect of some event or phenomenon:

- Is there some dispute over the cause of some event or phenomenon you would like to explore?
- Is there some dispute over the possible or actual effects brought about by some event or phenomenon that interests you?
- In your view, have experts mistakenly identified a particular cause or effect of some historical event or cultural phenomenon?
- What causes or effects of some historical event or cultural phenomenon have been overlooked or undervalued?

Questions of Evaluation

These questions explore how something is, has been, or should be evaluated, judged, or assessed:

- Do experts disagree on how to evaluate something that interests you?
- Has something been evaluated incorrectly and needs to be reexamined?
- Will evaluating something in a particular way lead to particular results?
- Have the moral, religious, political, or practical implications of a particular evaluation been sufficiently or accurately acknowledged?

Questions of Recommendation

These questions explore particular policies or courses of action that have been taken, are being taken, or might be taken:

- Is there a dispute over which course of action to take in a particular case?
- Is there a dispute over whether a particular course of action has been effective?
- Is there a dispute over the value and efficacy of a course of action taken in the past?
- Is there a dispute over the implications of a current or proposed course of action?
- Is there a problem that needs to be solved? If so, why and how?

Something to write about . . .

Alone or with a classmate, use the stasis-based questions discussed above to develop possible essay topics related to the following topics:

a. the Iraq War
   possible topics related to questions of fact
   possible topics related to questions of definition
   possible topics related to questions of cause or effect
   possible topics related to questions of evaluation
   possible topics related to questions of recommendation
b. high school pregnancy prevention programs
   possible topics related to questions of fact
   possible topics related to questions of definition
   possible topics related to questions of cause or effect
   possible topics related to questions of evaluation
   possible topics related to questions of recommendation

Narrowing and Focusing a Topic

Once you have identified a possible topic for your essay, you may need to narrow and focus it. The more focused your topic, the easier it is to conduct research and write an effective argument. One of the major hurdles inexperienced writers have to overcome is the tendency to tackle topics that are too broad. Below are some strategies you might use to narrow a topic for an academic argument.

Subdivide the Topic

Identify various aspects of the topic you might want to investigate. For example, instead of examining all solutions to world hunger, identify one to investigate. Instead of defending all of Nietzsche's aesthetics, identify a single aesthetic principle to examine. You will likely find that even these topics can be subdivided to further focus your argument.

Identify an Aspect of the Topic That Is Easier to Understand or Research than Others

This practical approach to the narrowing the focus of an argument reflects one of the realities of academic writing: some aspects of a topic will be easier to write about than others. There might be some aspects of the topic you understand better than others or might have an easier time researching.

Identify an Aspect of the Topic That Will Be More Challenging to Investigate

The flip side of the previous strategy can also be effective: identify an aspect of the topic you think will be more difficult to write about than others. Though the topic may be harder to understand and write about, in the end you stand the chance of growing more significantly as a scholar by working on the project.

Determine What Interests You

Identify one aspect of the topic you find particularly interesting and write about it. It might interest you because it has some special connection to your life, because you have studied it before, or because it appeals to your imagination.

Something to write about . . .

With one or two classmates, generate several ways you might narrow the following topics if you had to write about them in an academic argument:

1. recycling
2. college drinking
3. the benefits of exercising
4. the impact of technology on people's lives
5. the best way to choose a college

INVESTIGATING THE TOPIC

Once you have identified a topic for your essay, you should investigate it carefully through some combination of reflection and research before deciding on a position you would like to argue. Don't be too eager to form a thesis for your argument; your thesis should emerge from a thoughtful consideration of your topic and assignment.

Investigating a Topic through Reflection

Reflection and introspection will sometimes serve as the primary means of investigating a topic; other times they will aid or guide other research activities, helping you to determine the types of information you need to gather and to evaluate what you find.

Reflection as the Primary Means of Investigating a Topic

In college, some of the arguments you write will be based on what you already know, what you have come to believe, or what you feel. No outside research will be required. Instead, you will be expected to think deeply about the assignment's topic and generate appropriate, effective arguments. When you encounter assignments such as these, the following steps will help you reflect productively on the topic and generate material for your essay.

Step 1: Determine the exact nature of the assignment

Identify what you are expected to write about, who your audience is, and what your writing is expected to accomplish. Does the assignment ask you to generate material from your personal experience, to explore what you already know about the topic, to examine your beliefs and feelings, or some combination of these? If you are unsure about any aspect of the assignment, ask your teacher for help.

Step 2: Begin to generate material for your argument

Because writing frequently generates ideas, free writing and listing activities might help you develop material for your argument. Write your topic on a piece of paper and just begin to list ideas as they come to you. At this point, do not worry about whether you might actually write about these ideas in your paper or how you might organize them, just allow your mind to work.

Another way to generate material for your essay is to answer questions like these:

- What do I already know about X (the topic of your paper)?
- How and when did I learn this? How trustworthy or authoritative are my sources of information?
- What are the limitations of my knowledge?
- Which aspects of the topic do I know the most about? Which do I know the least about?
- What have I heard or read about X?
- What do other people think about X?
- How do I feel about X? Why do I feel this way?
- What do I believe about X? What is the basis for these beliefs?
- How would I explain these feelings or beliefs to someone else?
- What would it take to change my feelings or beliefs?
- How might my feelings or beliefs be misguided?
- What personal experience is relevant to the topic? How is it relevant?

- How might I explain to someone else how my experience is relevant to the topic?
- How might my experience hinder my understanding of the topic?

Reflection as an Aid to Primary and Secondary Research

While some of the academic arguments you write will be based on reflection, many others will be based on information you obtain through primary or secondary research. However, even when writing these types of arguments, reflection can play an important role in your research. As you engage in research, you will reflect on the information you gather, carefully determining its credibility, value, and worth by comparing it to what you already know about the topic, what others have written or said about it, and its relationship to your topic or thesis. Through reflection, you will decide when you have gathered enough information to begin your paper or when you need to research a topic further as you write your essay. Research involves more than just a mechanical process of gathering information; it also serves as an occasion for you to reflect on and improve the way you learn.

Investigating a Topic through Research

With research-based assignments, the quality of your argument will largely depend of the quality of the material you collect and examine. Writing a persuasive academic argument may be impossible unless you have thoroughly researched the topic and offer convincing support for your assertions. Your teacher may instruct you on how to conduct research using the resources available at your school, but the information provided below will also help make the research process more productive.

Types of Research

Primary research involves first-hand investigations of a topic or subject, such as conducting laboratory experiments, carrying out a survey, or analyzing a work of art. **Secondary research** involves reporting on information generated by others. Most of the arguments you write in your first few years of college will involve secondary research, though some courses may require primary research as well.

> **Something to write about . . .**
>
> Before you read the next section of this text, write a brief summary of the steps you usually follow when you write an essay that requires secondary research. From the day that you get the assignment, write out in order the steps you typically take to research your topic.

Developing a Research Strategy

One of the keys to successful research is being organized and purposeful. Developing a research strategy can help. The exact research strategy you employ will vary depending on the nature of each assignment you write, but a few of the practices employed by most successful college writers are explained below.

Form a Set of Research Questions

Begin by writing out a few questions to guide your research process, questions related to the topic you are investigating or to the argument you plan to advance. Research is more productive if it is focused on finding answers to specific questions. For example, if you are writing an argument on whether cheerleading is a sport, you might ask these research questions: What are the defining characteristics of a sport? Does cheerleading share these characteristics? How have various experts already answered these questions?

Identify What You Already Know About the Topic

Reflect on and write down what you already know about the topic and your research questions. If possible, determine where you learned it and assess its authority or credibility.

Identify What You Need to Find Out about the Topic

The next step is vital: identify the information you need to collect in order to answer your research questions and construct a persuasive argument given your purpose, assignment, and intended audience. As you write your argument, you should continuously reassess the information you need to collect and formulate new research questions to answer.

Identify Potential Sources Of Information

Once you have identified the information you need to collect, determine where and how you can locate it. Do not fall into the trap of believing that only one source exists for the information you need. In most cases, you can gather useful information from several sources. Be open to investigating sources of information that are new to you. Ask your teacher or a librarian for suggestions—they will frequently point you in directions you never would have thought of.

Set Goals and Deadlines

This step is complex and requires almost continual reassessment, but most scholars find it invaluable: establish a set of goals and deadlines that will enable you to complete the project in the allotted time. List the tasks you need to complete and set a specific deadline for each one (see Figure 10.1 for a sample list). Check off tasks as you complete them and add new ones as they arise.

Begin the Process of Collecting Material

Having identified the information you need to collect, possible sources for that information, and a set of deadlines to meet, begin to gather material for your essay. You should start this process early because the material you want can sometimes be difficult to locate. Understand, too, that research continues throughout the drafting process. As you write your essay, you will likely discover new research questions to investigate.

FIGURE 10.1

Sample List of Goals and Deadlines
Assignment: Is Cheerleading a Sport?

Activity	Due Date	Done
Read and reread assignment/ask teacher questions	———	———
Write out my initial position	———	———
Write out what I need to find out	———	———
Conduct some preliminary research	———	———
Check Internet sources	———	———
Ask my sister for ideas (a current cheerleader)	———	———
See if there's anything at the library on it	———	———
Come up with an initial stand	———	———
Write out a thesis statement	———	———
Get teacher to look at it	———	———
Write out a block outline of the paper	———	———
Thesis (+) reasons	———	———
Indication of sources I can use in each section	———	———
Get teacher to look at it	———	———
Initial draft	———	———
Write opening section	———	———
Write body	———	———
Write conclusion (if possible)	———	———
Let my mother look at it to see if it makes sense	———	———
Second draft	———	———
Let someone from class look at it for response	———	———
Time out (get away from it)	———	———
Final draft	———	———
Proofread for content and structure	———	———
Proofread for quotes and documentation	———	———
Turn in paper	———	———

Something to think about . . .

How could you change your typical research process to make it more efficient and effective? What changes can you make to how you research a topic, organize the tasks you need to complete, and manage your time?

Evaluating Source Material

Evaluating the source material you use in an academic argument is central to producing a persuasive essay. You cannot expect to write an effective argument if you are drawing on faulty or suspect sources of information to form, explain, and defend your claims. The following evaluative criteria will help you select effective sources of information when you are writing arguments for an academic audience.

Authorial Credibility

When evaluating source material, a good place to start is with the author. Answering the questions below will help you determine an author's credibility.

- Who is the author?
- What are his or her credentials? What establishes him or her as an expert on this particular topic?
- Who employs the author? Is the author affiliated with an academic institution?
- What else has the author written on the topic or on related topics?
- What possible biases might the author bring to his or her work?
- How reliable are the author's sources of information?

Publication Credibility

Another way to evaluate a source text is to examine where it was published. Some publications are going to be more authoritative and reliable than others, particularly when writing for academic audiences. The following questions will help you determine whether the information you have gathered comes from a reliable publication.

Questions regarding the credibility of print sources

- What company, institution, or organization published the journal or book?
- When was it published?
- What possible biases might the publisher have? What biases has the publication exhibited in the past?
- With what regard is the publication held by members of the academic community?

Questions regarding the credibility of online sources

- Is the site signed or unsigned? Is it attributed to a particular organization or institution? Is there any contact information provided?
- In what regard is the author, organization, or institution held in the academic community?
- When was the information posted? When was it last updated?
- Did the person or organization creating the Web site use credible sources?
- What is the overall quality of writing on the Web site? Does the site appear to be professionally developed or amateurish?

Possible Bias

While some sources of information or authors are more blatantly slanted than others, totally avoiding bias is impossible. Books, articles, and Web sites are written by people, and people have biases which color their writing even when they try to remain neutral. The better course of action is to acknowledge certain bias exists in what we read and make efforts to weigh the information we use in our arguments accordingly.

You can use biased information in your papers so long as you recognize and address that bias, balancing it with other sources of information when necessary. To uncover bias in the sources you use, you might consider evaluating them with the following questions:

- Does the information come from an author who is known for maintaining a particular bias? How might this bias have influenced what he or she has written?
- Does the information come from a publication that is known to maintain a particular bias? How might this bias have influenced the text's content or tone?
- Does the author reveal any particular ideological or methodological bias or preference?
- Does the author's language, graphics, sources, research questions, or thesis reveal any particular bias? How might that bias have influenced what he or she has written?

Something to talk about . . .

In small groups, discuss how you could determine each of the following when researching a topic for an argumentative essay:

1. the credibility of a source's author
2. the credibility of a publication's credibility
3. possible biases in a source
4. the appropriateness of a source
5. whether the source would be considered academic or popular

Academic vs. Popular Sources of Information

Most college teachers will expect you to base the arguments you write on academic sources of information rather than on popular sources. Sometimes the dividing line between academic and popular sources of information can be difficult to determine, but generally the differences are these: Academic sources of information tend to be written by experts in the discipline who publish their work in peer-reviewed venues, document their findings and claims, and provide bibliographies or works cited lists; popular sources of information tend to be written by reporters or people who are not experts in the discipline, who support their claims through secondary research, publish their work in venues that are not peer-reviewed, do not document their assertions, and typically do not provide bibliographies or a works cited lists (see Figure 2).

FIGURE 10.1
Academic vs. Popular Sources of Information

	Academic	Popular
Sources of Information	Scholars, academics	Reporters, nonexperts
Genesis of Information	Largely primary research	Largely secondary research
Review of Information	Reviewed by experts in the field	Not reviewed by experts in the field
Documentation	Documentation common	Documentation uncommon
Bibliographies	Usually included	Usually not included

Whether a source is authoritative and therefore appropriate for an academic paper depends more on the writer's expertise rather than on the type of journal or Web site publishing his or her work. For example, most teachers would see *Sports Illustrated* as a popular rather than an academic source of information. However, suppose you are writing a paper on Title IX and find in *Sports Illustrated* a narrative written by a student athlete who benefited from the legislation, a critique of the law written by a college administrator who had to oversee its implementation at his or her institution, or an analysis of the regulations written by a legislator who helped craft the bill in Congress. Would these sources of information be appropriate to include in your essay? Most teachers would say they are because they are authoritative and relevant, even though they appear in a popular magazine. If you ever have a question about whether a publication is academic or whether certain sources of information are appropriate to cite in an academic argument, ask your teacher for guidance.

UNDERSTANDING THE ROLE OF THESIS STATEMENTS IN ACADEMIC WRITING

In academic writing, a thesis statement serves at least three important functions. First, it articulates the primary claim or set of claims you intend to develop and defend in your argument. Second, the thesis helps guide your writing as you draft your argument. Once you have articulated a thesis, you are in a better position to draft and revise your paper—the thesis will help you structure your argument and make decisions regarding your essay's content and language. Finally, a thesis statement guides your readers through your essay when they read it. It forecasts the content and structure of your essay, raising certain expectations in your readers' minds. Meeting these expectations makes the essay easier to read, gives readers a sense of satisfaction, and improves your ethos.

Choosing Among Possible Positions

Sometimes your teacher will assign you a position to argue in your paper. More frequently, though, you will form a thesis of your own. As you formulate a thesis for your argument, the following guidelines might prove helpful:

- Base your thesis on your preliminary research; do not base your preliminary research on your thesis. Conduct some research on the topic of your essay before you form a thesis. If you form your thesis first, you are likely to investigate that position alone, limiting what you learn about the topic. Your thesis should be informed; it should reflect the breadth of your research and relevant experience.
- Play devil's advocate and generate one or two alternative or even contradictory positions. Consider their strengths and weaknesses. How is your thesis in some way preferable to the alternative positions? Are there aspects of the

other positions that are worth combining with your own? Is it possible to reconcile conflicting positions into a single new thesis that is more comprehensive and complex?

After you form an idea of what your argument's thesis will likely be, you will need to determine its exact wording and structure.

Common Types of Thesis Statements in Academic Writing

In academic writing, thesis statements can be *implied* or *stated*. An implied thesis guides the argument's development but is never written out—readers come to understand what it is as they make their way through your argument. Stated theses, which are more common in academic writing, can be either *open* or *closed*. An open thesis statement indicates the primary assertion of an argument; a closed thesis also indicates how the writer plans to develop that argument. Compare these two thesis statements:

> Open thesis:
> **Picasso was the most influential visual artist of the twentieth century.**
> Closed thesis:
> **Picasso was the most influential visual artist of the twentieth century due to his radical rejection of photographic realism and his ability to synthesize in his work such a wide range of artistic movements.**

The first thesis indicates the primary argument the writer will make in her paper: that Picasso was the most influential visual artist of the twentieth century. The second thesis indicates that the writer will offer two reasons in support of her claim: Picasso was the most influential visual artist of the twentieth century because of his radical rejection of photographic realism and his ability to combine in his work a range of artistic movements.

Neither type of thesis is inherently better than the other. Generally, the shorter the essay, the easier and more effective it is to use a closed thesis. If you are writing a longer, more complex argument, including all of your supporting reasons in your thesis will make it too cumbersome. Longer arguments tend to employ an open thesis and topic sentences that introduce each supporting reason.

Qualities of Effective Thesis Statements

In academic writing, the qualities that define an effective thesis statement vary by discipline. For example, some disciplines accept or even encourage declaratory thesis statements ("In this paper I will argue that Picasso was the most influential visual artist of the twentieth century" or "This paper argues that Picasso was the most influential visual artist of the twentieth century"). In other fields of study, such wording is discouraged. You will begin to see many of these differences as you complete your general education courses in college—the "rules" governing academic writing in one class will not necessary be the same as those governing academic writing in other classes. Regardless of which class you are taking, though, effective thesis statements in academic arguments tend to be assertive, conventionally correct, clear, predictive, and original.

Assertive

Too often, the thesis statements students include in an academic *argument* is not assertive—it is not argumentative. Often, it is merely a statement of fact or personal preference. Consider these statements. Which are truly arguments? Which are merely statements of fact or personal preference?

- Picasso was a painter.
- Picasso was an important twentieth century painter.
- Picasso is my favorite twentieth century painter.
- Picasso is the most important painter of the twentieth century.
- At his death, Picasso was mourned as one of the greatest painters of the twentieth century.
- Most art historians would agree that Picasso stands alone as the greatest painter of the twentieth century.

As explained in Chapter 1, statements of fact or of personal preference are not arguments. Therefore, be sure your thesis communicates clearly and directly the *argument* you will develop in your essay.

Conventionally Correct

You should follow the conventions of the field in which you are writing when wording your thesis. As you read work produced in a discipline, pay attention to how the authors word and structure their thesis statements and follow their lead. If you are not sure how to properly present a thesis statement, ask your teacher for help.

Clear

The language you use in your thesis has to be clear. Consider carefully how you use technical terms or jargon in a thesis statement: would your intended audience understand this language? Your thesis announces your primary argument and perhaps how you plan on developing and defending it. Consequently, your thesis must be worded as clearly as possible.

Predictive

In a sense, a thesis statement is a promise. Your thesis declares that you will develop a particular argument in a particular way. Readers will expect your paper to adhere to your thesis; they will expect you to keep your promise. If it does not, your argument is unlikely to be persuasive. This is particularly true if you employ a closed thesis.

Original

Your thesis should announce a position you have developed through careful research and reflection. It should not be a paraphrase of someone else's argument or a quotation from someone else's work.

Crafting a Thesis Statement: A Process Approach

While everyone's composing process is unique, employing the following steps may help you construct an effective thesis statement for an argumentative essay. As always, modify these steps as needed to better suit the way you write. Also note that these suggestions presuppose that you will write your thesis statement before you write the first draft of your argument. However, some writers have to complete the first draft of their argument before they compose their thesis.

Step 1: Determine the position you want to argue in your paper

In many ways, of course, this can be the hardest step: what position will you assume in the argument you are writing? As you try to decide, take comfort knowing that as you gather additional information, continue to think about the topic, and draft your essay, you can change your position. For the sake of drafting a thesis statement, however, you need to decide where you stand for now.

Step 2: Determine how you will develop, explain, or defend that position

You can skip this step if you plan on employing an open thesis statement. If, however, you want to draft a closed thesis, then you do need to decide how you will develop, explain, or defend your position in the body of your essay.

Step 3: Draft your thesis

Once you know the position you plan to address and (perhaps) how you will organize your supporting reasons and claims, you are ready to draft your thesis statement. For some writers, this is a trying process. Writers are rarely happy with the first draft of thesis statements. As you work to find more precise and clear language for your thesis, you are fine tuning your argument.

Step 4: Take a break and/or let someone else read your thesis before you revise it

When you think you have the thesis worded about right, take a break. Spend some time away from your thesis. When you return to it, you will be able to see it with fresh eyes which will help you revise it more effectively. Some writers like to share their thesis statement with a trusted reader at this point in the process, asking that person to give them an honest assessment of the writing.

Step 5: If needed, revise your thesis as and after you draft your argument

As you write the rough draft of your argument, the essay may not unfold as you planned. This is normal—academic writers often restructure their arguments, change the content of their essays, even alter their positions as they compose. If you make substantial changes to your argument, be sure you revise your thesis accordingly.

Thesis Placement

True or false: an argument's thesis statement is *always* the last sentence of the opening paragraph? Placing the thesis statement at the end of an essay's first paragraph is a prevalent convention in academic writing but is not a rule. Your thesis can be placed elsewhere in your essay and still be effective. For example, you may open your essay with an overview of your topic, a brief survey of what is commonly believed about the issue you are addressing, or an interesting anecdote to capture reader interest. Placing your thesis at the end of this introduction usually works well, even if that means it appears on the second page of your essay. If you are addressing a hostile audience, you may delay your thesis even longer, perhaps even holding it until the end of your essay.

ORGANIZING AN ARGUMENT

Every academic argument consists of three basic sections: an opening, the body, and a conclusion. Ideally, all three parts of the paper work together as an organic whole, each making the others more effective. While there are many approaches to writing each section of your argument, you need to choose strategies best suited to your topic and the assignment's rhetorical context. Below are some options you might consider.

Opening and Closing Sections of Arguments

Sometimes the most difficult sections of an argument to write are the opening and closing. Clearly, both play a vital role in making an argument persuasive, but finding just the right way to introduce and wrap up your essay can be challenging. Writing openings and closings for argumentative essays can be a little easier, though, if you understand what each section should accomplish.

Purpose of Opening and Closing Sections in Academic Arguments

The opening section of an argument typically introduces the topic of the essay, states the paper's thesis, and captures reader interest (as noted above, sometimes you may decide to state your thesis later in the essay). The opening section of your essay may consist of one or several paragraphs, depending on which strategy you use to capture reader interest. If you are basing your argument on one or two readings, you may also introduce those source texts in the opening section of your argument by including their titles and the authors' names.

The concluding section of an academic argument usually accomplishes three tasks as well: providing a satisfying sense of closure, wrapping up or reviewing the argument, and reiterating the importance or significance of your thesis. A sense of closure is often accomplished by making direct connections back to the opening of the essay, reemploying the opening strategy to conclude the essay, paraphrasing the thesis, or summarizing the essay's primary assertions.

Common Opening Strategies

Academic writers use many different strategies to open argumentative essays. Some of the most frequently employed are described below. The strategy you choose will likely depend on the topic of your essay, your thesis, your intended audience, and your own preferences.

Overview of the Situation or Background Information

With this strategy, you open your essay by providing some historical background on the topic you are addressing or by summarizing the work of previous researchers who have investigated it. This is an especially effective strategy to use if you believe that your readers need to understand the historical context of your argument or might be unfamiliar with the topic you are addressing.

Interesting Quotation

You can often capture reader interest by quoting another writer at the beginning of your essay. Use this strategy when you think the other writer has stated something in an especially interesting way, if you plan to build on or contradict what that writer states, or if you think that quoting that writer enhances your ethos.

Interesting Fact

As you gather material for your essay, if you uncover some particularly captivating piece of information consider using it to open your paper. Sharing this information could serve as a springboard to your argument—just be sure you connect it clearly to your thesis or the opening section of your essay may appear unfocused.

Interesting Question

Starting your essay with an interesting question works well so long as you answer that question. Opening your argument with an unanswered rhetorical question can be risky—the answer readers come up with, consciously or unconsciously, might not be the one you anticipated. The question itself pulls the reader into your essay; providing the answer can lead them directly to your thesis.

Anecdote

Even in academic writing, some authors open their argument with a story—a hypothetical case, a historical incident, even a relevant personal experience. To work well, the story has to be interesting and concise and must be directly connected to your essay's topic.

Contradiction

To employ this opening strategy, summarize a commonly held position on your essay's topic then contradict or question it: Most people think X about the topic, but Y is actually the case. For this strategy to work, you must present opposing views fairly and respectfully before you critique them and offer your own argument in their place.

Common Closing Strategies

While many writers find introductions difficult to write, others find conclusions even more problematic. Having covered what they wanted to say in their argument, they are left wondering what's left to write. However, you can draw on a range of strategies to help you gracefully and effectively close the arguments you write. Stylistically, try to connect the opening and closing sections of your argument by employing parallel strategies. For example, if you open with a story, come back to it in your conclusion; if you open with a quotation, consider closing your essay with one.

Summary of the Argument

The most commonly employed closing strategy in academic writing is to summarize the argument's primary claims. This strategy is ineffective, however, if it makes your writing too repetitive or mechanical. Merely repeating your thesis *verbatim* at the end of your paper is not a good strategy to employ.

Interesting Quotation

Another strategy is to close your essay with a quotation. If you opened your essay with a quotation, you could return to it at end of your essay but critique it from the new perspective your argument has offered.

Conclusion of Anecdote

If you opened your argument with a story, perhaps come back to it at the end of your paper. If you left the story unfinished at the beginning of your essay, conclude it at the end of your argument. Another strategy is to explain how the story might have turned out differently in light of the position you have advocated in your essay.

Interesting Question

If you opened your essay with a question, answer it in your conclusion. Your answer should arise from the argument you have developed in your essay. You might even show how your argument provides the best answer to that question.

Implications and/or Prediction

Based on what you have argued in your essay, what are the implications if you are correct or if you are wrong, if the course of action you suggest is followed or if it is ignored? Speculations such as these allow you to summarize your primary assertions and leave your readers with something new to think about at the end of your essay.

Something to talk about . . .

With two or three other students in class, review at least five of the readings included in this textbook. Identify which opening and closing strategy each author
employs. As a group, decide which strategies seem more effective than the others.
Be ready to explain your conclusions to the other students in class.

Something to write about . . .

If you are currently working on a paper for class, write three possible opening sections for your essay, each employing a unique strategy. Which do you think is most
effective? Why? If you were to use this opening strategy for your essay, how would
you close your essay? Why?

Organizing the Body of Academic Arguments

Far too often, writers believe that once they begin to write their essays, the paper will
just spontaneously organize itself. More often than not, however, their essays end up
being disorganized and confusing. The better approach is to organize your argument
purposefully, following accepted conventions and paradigms or applying sound
rhetorical principles.

Conventions of Organization in Academic Writing

In some disciplines, convention dictates how writers structure their arguments. These
structural conventions serve important functions in the field. For example, they
ensure that certain types of information are present in every argument—if convention dictates that a discussion of research methods appears in a certain section of the
paper, then writers must include that discussion in their arguments. When writers
in a discipline follow structural conventions, readers can also find the information
they need quickly and efficiently. These structural conventions are usually included
in the research and publication stylebooks members of that discipline follow. As you
move into your major, you will be expected to learn and follow these discipline-
specific conventions when you write papers.

Organizational Paradigms

Paradigms are general formats you can follow when you write an argument.
Teachers often provide paradigms for the papers they assign to help their students gather appropriate material and better organize their thoughts. Sometimes
the paradigms are fairly straightforward. For example, look at this simple paradigm for an argument:

Introduction with thesis
Reason 1
Reason 2
Conclusion

If you were following this paradigm to write your essay, you would begin with an introduction that included your thesis, a thesis you would support with two reasons in the body of your essay before moving to your conclusion. A more complicated paradigm for the same paper might look like this:

Introduction
   Introduce topic
   Capture reader interest
   Provide thesis
Reasons for your position
   Reason 1
   Reason 2
Opposing views
Conclusion

This paradigm indicates that the introduction to your essay should accomplish three goals: introduce the topic of your argument, generate reader interest, and indicate your thesis. The body of your argument will have two primary sections, one in which you lay out the reasons for your position (two of them in this case) and one in which you examine opposing views before you draw your essay to a close.

Many students like paradigms because they lay out exactly how the students can organize the argument they are writing. However, paradigms can also stifle creativity—students may mechanically follow the paradigm even when, given their argument, it would be more effective to organize their work differently. If your teacher assigns a paper and gives you a paradigm to follow, do your best to adhere to it. However, if you think you can organize your argument more effectively using a different organizational strategy, talk to your teacher. Likewise, if you think your paper would be stronger if you modified the paradigm slightly in some way, again get your teacher's approval.

Principles of Organization in Academic Writing

If you are not expected to adhere to a prescribed, conventional structure or follow a particular paradigm when writing an argument, applying certain rhetorical principles can help you effectively organize your essay. You are already likely familiar with many such practices: academic arguments should have effective opening and closing sections, writers should provide a thesis statements that guides the development of the essay, topic sentences should connect each section of the essay with its overarching thesis, and so on. Here are a few more simple yet powerful principles of organization commonly employed by academic writers. They can help you structure most of the academic arguments you write in college.

Start Strong/Finish Strong

After you decide on the reasons you will offer to support your thesis, rank order them strongest to weakest, most convincing to least convincing, in light of the assignment's rhetorical situation. Following the introductory section of your essay, open your argument by examining one of the stronger reasons you have in support of your thesis. Doing so will help you establish your authority and capture your readers' interest. While a strong start is important, so is a strong finish. Readers tend to remember most vividly the first and last sections of the arguments they read. Knowing this, use one of your strongest, most persuasive reasons to close your argument. Finishing on a strong note will help make your argument more persuasive.

Move from Areas of Agreement to Areas of Disagreement

Another commonly employed principle guiding the organization of academic arguments is to consider your readers' likely stance on the topic and move from areas of agreement with them to areas of disagreement. Open your argument by establishing the values you have in common with your readers or by discussing claims your readers are more likely to accept. Then move into areas of possible disagreement and discuss claims they may question or reject. Opening with areas of agreement helps you establish the good will and trust you will need as you move into areas of disagreement.

Old Information to New Information

A final organizing principle you might use is this: open your essay by covering information or arguments that your readers may already be familiar with or by reviewing past research on the topic then move to material that is likely new to your readers. Starting with the old information or arguments helps you place the new information or arguments in context, increasing reader comprehension and making your writing more persuasive than it otherwise would be.

Something to think about . . .

Why do you think the three principles of organization for academic arguments described above are usually effective and so frequently employed? Consider how each principle is related to audience. How does each principle help readers enter into and understand the argument a writer puts forward in his or her essay?

Organizing Academic Arguments around Thesis Statements and Topic Sentences

Whatever organizational strategy or principles you follow, your thesis statement and topic sentences will likely provide the framework for your argument. In a well-written academic argument, the thesis statement and topic sentences guide your readers through your essay, smoothly leading them from one section of your paper to the next, helping them understand the connections you are drawing among your claims and grounds. In the body of your essay, topic sentences introduce each new section of your argument, link it to the previous section of your essay, and tie it back to your overarching thesis.

Suppose you are in an introductory management class. Your teacher has given you a case to study that focuses on a company deciding between two proposals for promoting a new product. Your assignment is to argue in favor of one of these proposals. Your thesis and topic sentences might read something like this:

> Thesis
> **Though the plan proposed by General Advertising would be more cost effective than the plan proposed by United Advertising, the plan put forward by United is more likely to reach the target population group of consumers and offers a better rationale for the expenses associated with promoting the product on television.**
> Topic Sentence #1
> **When comparing the two proposals, clearly General Advertising's plan would be more cost effective than United Advertising's plan.**
> Topic Sentence #2
> **Even though General Advertising's plan is more cost effective than United Advertising's plan, the company should accept United's proposal because it more effectively targets the population groups the company has identified as its primary consumers.**
> Topic Sentence #3
> **Another reason the company should accept United Advertising's proposal instead of General Advertising's proposal involves the rationale United offers to support the large expenditures associated with television advertising.**

This closed thesis statement asserts a central argument (accept United Advertising's proposal), two supporting reasons (because United's plan better targets certain consumers and offers a better cost rational), plus one counter-argument (General Advertising's plan is more cost effective).

Each of these topic sentences introduces a new section of the paper: topic sentence 1 introduces the counter argument while topic sentences 2 and 3 introduce the two primary reasons the writer offers in support of his thesis. The topic sentences also link each of these sections back to the thesis by repeating key terms from the thesis or using synonyms for those key terms. For example, notice how each of the three topic sentences repeats the names of both agencies, because both names are mentioned in the thesis statement. In order to unify the essay, these topic sentences repeat other language or ideas from the thesis as well. For example, topic sentence 1 repeats the phrase "more cost effective"; topic sentence 2 uses "effectively targets the population groups the company has identified as its primary consumers" to echo language found in the thesis; and topic sentence 3 replaces the phrase "a better rationale for the expenses associated with promoting the product on television" used in the thesis with the phrase "the rationale United offers to support the large

> ### Something to write about . . .
>
> Either alone or with a classmate, generate a series of topic sentences that would flow from each of the following thesis statements. Be sure that these topic sentences introduce a new idea, connect back to the thesis, and link to the previous section of the argument.
>
> 1. The increase in comic book sales over the past decade can likely be attributed to the success of so many of comic-inspired movies and the creation of new, relevant heroes.
> 2. One of the best ways to understand a culture is to examine its cuisine, including what people eat, how they prepare it, and how they eat it.
> 3. John Millington Synge became the leading playwright of the Irish Renaissance not so much because of his plays' success but because of the themes he explored and the poetic language he employed.
> 4. The increasing interest in stock car racing can be explained any number of ways.
> 5. For many reasons, *The Wizard of Oz* continues to be a family favorite.
> 6. The definition of the "good life" is not settled—in fact, several competing definitions are commonly found among today's high school students.

expenditures associated with television advertising." As you move from one section of your argument to the next, your topic sentences need to remind readers of the primary claim you are arguing.

Finally, to produce a coherent, unified argument topic sentences should draw connections between each new section of your essay and the one preceding it. To link topic sentence 1 to the thesis, the writer uses the phrase "when comparing the two proposals." Topic sentence 2 uses the transitional phrase "even though General Advertising's proposal is more cost effect than United Advertising's proposal" to remind readers of the counter argument just offered. Finally, topic sentence 3 uses the transition word "another" and the phrase "should accept United Advertising's proposal instead of General Advertising's proposal" to let readers know that a second reason supporting the writer's thesis is coming. Effective topic sentences will make your argument clearer and more unified.

DRAFTING AN ARGUMENT

Every writer develops his or her own unique approach to writing academic essays. In fact, most successful writers actually develop several drafting styles, changing the way they write their essays depending on the nature of the assignment, how much time they have to write the piece, and the rhetorical situation of the task.

Composing Strategies: Three Common Models

Below are descriptions of several commonly employed methods of drafting successful academic arguments based on the research of Linda Flower and John Hayes. No one approach is inherently superior to the others; each has its strengths and limitations. While in college, experiment with them to find which methods work best for you in which situations.

Discovery Draft Writers

To begin the process of writing an argument, discovery draft writers tend to compose the first draft of their essay very quickly and without much planning. In fact, they might not even have a thesis statement in mind when they begin their essay. Instead, they come to discover their thesis as they write their first draft. Writers such as these are comfortable with uncertainty—they don't need to know what they will write or where they will end up before they begin work. They trust that the content, structure, and thesis of their essay will emerge as they write their first draft. They may have spent considerable time thinking about the assignment before they begin to write, but they have not spent time carefully writing out arguments, reasons, or evidence before launching into that first draft. When discovery draft writers finish that first draft, they look it over to determine what their thesis will be, which sections of their paper they would like to develop further, and perhaps even how they might like to structure their next draft. Their writing on subsequent drafts tends to be more organized, but they still look forward to those unexpected insights that emerge as they write their arguments.

Plan, Draft, Revise Writers

These are writers English teachers usually love because they write in ways that match the instruction commonly found in composition textbooks. These writers plan most aspects of their essays before they begin their rough draft. They conduct research, take notes, and perhaps even put together an outline to guide their writing, first paragraph to last. Once they finish that first draft, they go back to the opening and revise the whole essay, beginning to end, as many times as necessary to produce the quality of writing they desire or until time runs out and the assignment is due. While plan, draft, revise writers tend to produce more organized early drafts than discovery draft writers produce, they may cut themselves off from discovering new ideas that emerge as they write: they become so fixated on sticking to the outline they developed before they began to write, that they ignore or too quickly discard new ideas they discover during the drafting process. They can avoid this problem by remaining open to insights that arise as they write, finding ways to incorporate them into their existing plans.

Section-by-Section Writers

These students also like to plan out their entire papers, at least in general terms, before they begin to draft their essays. However, instead of writing the essay straight through, they draft it one section at a time, beginning with the opening paragraph. They keep revising this section of the essay until they are fairly satisfied with the quality of the writing then they move on to the next section. Instead of rewriting the entire essay at one time, they prefer to work on each section separately, believing they have to get it right before they can move on to the next section. Drafting an argument this way demands patience—writers have to delay writing the remainder of their essay as they work on each section sequentially. It also requires the ability to imagine how the section of the essay they are currently working on will lead into the following sections. However, writers who compose essays this way gain a sense of satisfaction and progress as they complete each section of the paper.

Which Approach Is Best for You?

Each model of drafting has its own strengths and weaknesses; no one approach is necessarily better than the others. Instead, you need to be aware of the approach you normally adopt when you write academic papers and decide for yourself how effective it is. If you are efficiently producing the best work possible, then you probably do not need to change how you write papers. However, the composing processes you followed in high school might not serve you well in college. The number and types of papers you write in college may lead you to consider changing the way you write arguments, as might the difficulty or complexity of the assignments themselves. Just know that there are alternatives available—the way you currently write papers for school is not the only option. If you are not sure what your processes are, consider completing the Writing Habit Inventory below.

Writing Habit Inventory

To get a better sense of the way you normally write academic essays, fill out this questionnaire fully and honestly. When you are finished, reflect on your answers. What patterns emerge? What would you say are your strengths and weaknesses as a writer? You might want to compare your answers with other students in class, discussing similarities and differences in your composing processes.

1. When you get a writing assignment, do you begin to work on it right away, do you tend to wait awhile before you begin to work on it, or do you usually wait until the last minute to write it?
2. Do you plan your essay before you write your first draft? If so, what type of planning do you complete: a formal outline, an informal outline, a list, a map?
3. Do you usually write your thesis statement before or after you write the first draft of your essay?
4. When do you write your opening paragraph? When do you write your conclusion?
5. When you write an academic paper that will be graded, how many drafts do you usually complete before turning it in to your teacher?
6. When you revise formal academic papers, what kinds of changes do you tend to make to them?
7. Do you let someone else read your papers before you turn them in for a grade? Who? Why?

(continued)

Writing Habit Inventory . . . *(continued)*

8. If you do let someone else read your work, what types of response do you like to get to your writing? What types of response do you find most helpful as you revise your papers? What types of response do you find least helpful?

9. Do you tend to write your essays straight through, beginning to end, or do you write and revise one section of your essay at a time?

10. Do you tend to write long and have to cut back or do you tend to write short and have to add material to meet length requirements?

11. Do you employ the same basic writing process for most of the papers you write in school or do you adopt different processes for different kinds of assignments? What examples can you think of to illustrate your answer?

12. Where do you do your best writing?

13. What time of day is best for you to write?

14. What are your writing rituals? That is, what do you have to do before you settle in to write a paper (put on comfortable clothes, get something to drink, clean up your work space)?

15. What are your greatest strengths as a writer?

16. What are your primary weaknesses as a writer?

17. If you could change one thing about the way you write academic papers, what would it be?

18. What for you is the hardest part of writing academic papers?

19. What comes easiest for you when writing academic papers?

20. What is the most satisfying aspect of writing for you?

Overcoming Problems That Commonly Arise When Drafting Academic Arguments

Researchers investigating the cognitive processes authors employ when they compose essays (most notably Linda Flower and John Hayes) point out that students frequently encounter four types of problems that cause them to stop writing: problems with content, structure, language, or rhetoric. All writers face these problems at some point. Successful writers have developed strategies for overcoming them, strategies which you can learn and use yourself.

Content Problems

Content problems most frequently occur when you run out of things to say in your paper and the essay is too short or underdeveloped. The best way to address this problem is to engage in additional research, elaborate on the ideas that you have already written in your essay, read your work skeptically and address questions your readers might raise regarding the assertions you make, or provide additional examples to illustrate your assertions.

Structure Problems

Structure problems occur when you do not know how to organize material in your essay. These problems crop up more frequently when you do not take time to plan your argument before you begin your first draft or when you are unsure how to incorporate into your essay ideas or arguments that arise as you draft your paper. The best way to avoid structural problems is to plan out your argument, at least in general terms, before you begin your first draft. You can refer back to this plan when needed to stay on track. Likewise when new ideas or arguments arise as you draft, simply write them down in the margin of the paper or at the bottom of the screen and continue to write. You can decide where they belong later.

Language Problems

Language problems occur when you know what you want to write but can't find the right words to say it. For too many writers, language problems can be completely debilitating. Because they cannot come up with the right word, all composing stops. The best way to address a language problem is simply to leave a blank where that word would go or to write a word that is close to the right word and move on. Circle or otherwise highlight any problematic language and return to it later when you revise your essay.

Rhetoric Problems

Rhetoric problems occur when you face a choice—when there are several words you might use in a sentence and don't know which is best; when there are several directions you might take the paper and don't know which one to choose; when there are two or three claims you might make and don't know which one would be the most persuasive. When you face this type of problem, turn your focus to the rhetorical situation of the assignment. Given your intended audience and purpose, what is the best decision to make?

Something to talk about . . .

Pair up with another student in class. First, individually write out the kinds of problems you typically encounter when you write academic papers. Be as precise as you can. Next, talk with your partner about these problems, explaining what they are and how they inhibit your work. After you both have had a chance to talk, together work out possible solutions to each of the problems you have mentioned, strategies you have or might employ to help you address these difficulties.

REVISING AN ARGUMENT

When you revise any essay as complicated as an academic argument, you usually have to take several passes through the manuscript to make all the necessary changes. Realistically, you can only focus on one or two aspects of an argument at a time when you revise if you hope to do a good job catching errors and improving your prose. Most successful writers will tell you that they are, in fact, successful re-writers—their writing really only improves as they revise draft after draft.

First, once you finish writing your paper, if at all possible let it "rest" for a while before you start to revise it. Taking a break from your essay before you begin to rewrite it and even between revision sessions helps you approach your work with fresh eyes.

Next, adopt a process approach to revision. Following the advice of writer and teacher Donald Murray, first make sure your essay adequately captures what you intended to say. Murray calls this "internal revision," changing the essay until it matches your intention. You may have to write several drafts of the piece until you are satisfied that it's achieving the goals you had in mind. Then revise the essay until it clearly and efficiently communicates your meaning to your readers. Murray calls this "external revision," changing the essay until you are satisfied that your audience will be able to read the piece with ease. Finally, proofread your essay carefully before you turn it in. Be sure all the commas are in the right place, all your documentation is correct, all your words are correctly spelled, and so on.

Below are some questions and directions that can help you revise your argument's content, structure, mechanics, style, use of source material, and documentation. Again, focus on just one or two of these each time you revise your work. Your teacher may have other aspects of the essay he or she would like you to review before turning in your work for a grade.

Revising Content

- How adequately have you supported each of the claims you make?
- How well have you explained each of the claims you make?
- How well have you explained the link between each claim you make and the reasons or evidence you use to support it?
- How clearly have you explained the reasoning that lies behind each claim you make?
- Given the purpose and audience of your paper, what material, ideas, or arguments need the most careful and thorough explanations and support? How successfully have you met this challenge?

Revising Structure

- How clear is your thesis?
- How well does your thesis statement guide the development of your essay?
- Do you deliver on the "promise" you made in your thesis? That is, do you develop your argument in a way that is consistent with the overview your thesis provides?
- Check each of your topic sentences. Does each one (a) introduce a new idea, (b) link back to your thesis, and (c) link back to the previous section of your essay? How well does each of your topic sentences achieve each of these goals?
- How well do the opening and closing sections of your paper accomplish their intended goals?

Revising Mechanics and Style

- Correct any problems with sentence structure and clarity, including wordiness and awkward syntax.
- Correct any punctuation and spelling errors.
- Correct any problems with diction.

- Clarify any vague words or phrases.
- Given the assignment's rhetorical situation, how appropriate and effective is the style of writing you have employed in the argument?
- Where are there any lapses or unintentional shifts in style? How can you fix them?

Revising Quoted and Paraphrased Material

- Check all quoted passages against the original texts and fix any problems with accuracy.
- Review all of your paraphrased passages to be sure they are not too close to the original and represent the author's ideas and arguments fairly.
- Review all quoted and paraphrased passages to ensure they read smoothly.

Revising Documentation

- Review your essay carefully to ensure that all of the material that needs to be documented is documented.
- Review your documentation in the essay to ensure that you have employed the proper form each time.
- Review your bibliography or works cited list. Are all the needed entries present? Are they written correctly? Make the needed additions, deletions, and corrections.

Something to talk about . . .

Why do you think it is important to revise academic arguments in several waves or passes, focusing on just one or two aspects of the text at a time? What makes such a strategy difficult to employ? What are some ways writers can get around these problems?

WRITING DEFINITION ARGUMENTS

WHAT ARE DEFINITION ARGUMENTS?

Definition plays a central role in academic arguments. First, those involved in an academic argument must share common definitions of the terms and ideas under dispute or they will be talking at cross-purposes. In fact, sometimes how to define a term or idea *is* the argument. Still other times writers may argue that redefining a term or idea can help bring about needed change. As a first step in bringing about that change, they argue, key terms or ideas must be reconsidered and redefined. In a definition argument, you present your best case concerning the meaning of a particular word or idea.

If you want to define a word or term, why not just open a dictionary and look it up? In academic writing, dictionary definitions are usually insufficient for arguments. First, dictionaries provide the accepted definitions of words; many academic arguments are written specifically to challenge these accepted definitions. Second, dictionaries offer the most common definitions of words; many academic arguments are written to redefine words or ideas in specific contexts. Dictionaries offer little help settling disputes about definitions that arise from conflicting worldviews or ethical standards. For example, presenting an argument over whether the death penalty is "humane" goes well beyond simple dictionary definitions of the word. Consequently, if you are asked to write a definition argument, do not simply quote a passage from a dictionary.

TYPES OF DEFINITION ARGUMENTS

In academic writing, you are likely to run across two kinds of definition arguments: stipulative and categorical. Stipulative definition arguments tend to focus on new or provisional meanings of words or ideas; categorical definition arguments tend to focus on how we classify words or ideas.

Stipulative Definitions

In a stipulative definition argument, you assert, or stipulate, that a word or idea should be defined in a particular way then defend that claim. Stipulative definition arguments vary in length, from one or two sentences to an entire essay. When they are part of a larger argument, they tend to be brief. If, for example, you are discussing the best way to combat climate change, you might open your essay with a brief stipulative definition of "global warming," explaining how you will be using the term in your essay. If you feel that your audience will accept this definition, you may simply move on with the paper. However, if you believe that this definition might be questioned, then you will need to present an argument explaining and defending it.

Categorical Definitions

In a categorical definition argument, you assert that something should be classified a particular way. For example, if you wanted to argue that cheerleading is a sport, you would first define what a sport is then argue that cheerleading fits that definition. If a sport is defined as an activity that possesses certain characteristics—for instance, that it involves athleticism, physical exertion, and competition—then you would demonstrate that cheerleading possesses the same characteristics and should therefore be classified as a sport. Categorical definition arguments tend to be long and complex, but they can also be very persuasive. Below are a series of questions you could address in categorical definition arguments drawn from a range of fields.

> Was the conflict in Vietnam a just war?
> Is James Joyce a modernist writer?
> Is economics a social science?
> Was the Rodney King beating a hate crime?

Writing on any of these topics would require you to identify the defining characteristics of a broad category (a "just" war, "modernism," "social science," "hate crime"), then analyze a specific case to see if it possesses enough of those characteristics to be included in that category.

Something to talk about . . .

With one or two other students in class, using your own words explain the difference between stipulative and categorical definitions. Once you are satisfied that you have captured the difference, write down your explanations as clearly and succinctly as you can. If asked, give the explanations to your teacher so he or she can review them.

WRITING A STIPULATIVE DEFINITION ARGUMENT

Below are a series of steps you can follow when you write a stipulative definition argument. Remember that these steps are merely suggestive; the assignment you receive or your own composing style may require you follow an alternative process. The key point to remember, though, is to divide the process of writing an argument into a series of manageable steps.

A Model Process for Writing Stipulative Definition Arguments

Step 1: Read and analyze the assignment.

When you receive the assignment, read it carefully. Be sure you understand exactly what the teacher is asking you to write, paying special attention to the assignment's rhetorical situation. Answering the following questions will help you analyze the assignment.

What Is the Topic?

Does the teacher tell you what word or idea to define or is the choice of topic left up to you? If the choice of topics is left open, are there any restrictions? For example, does the teacher need to approve your choice?

Who Is the Intended Audience?

Is a particular audience identified in the assignment? If not, are you writing for a general academic audience? What do you think your readers already know about the word or idea you are defining? On what grounds might readers object to your definition of the word or idea? What questions might they ask about your definition? As you explain your definition, what examples might appeal to or resonate with your readers?

What Is Your Purpose?

You will be expected to argue in support of the definition you offer, but are there any other goals you are expected to achieve? If your goal is to persuade your readers to accept your definition, what appeals might prove especially effective?

What Is the Expected Essay Format?

In practical terms, how long is the paper expected to be? How is it to be formatted? Which documentation style are you expected to use? If this information isn't stated in the assignment, ask your teacher.

What Types of Sources Are You Expected to Use?

Is the content of your essay supposed to come from your own knowledge and experience, course material, outside readings, primary research, or some combination of sources? If secondary research is required, what types of sources are you expected to consult and how many are you expected to include in your essay?

Step 2: Select a topic for your essay.

Developing a topic of your own for a stipulative definition argument can be challenging—there are just too many choices. One way to start, though, is to consider the following questions. The answers you come up with may help you identify an interesting topic. Once you choose a word or idea to define, get your teacher's approval before you begin to work on your argument.

FIGURE 11.1

Stipulative Definition Topic Heuristic

What are some particularly important ideas or terms you have been discussing in class?

What ideas or terms mentioned in class do you find confusing and would like to understand more clearly?

What ideas or terms are frequently mentioned on the news?

What ideas or terms are currently being debated on your campus or in your hometown?

What ideas or terms, when mentioned, tend to upset people?

What ideas or terms have always intrigued you?

What ideas or terms have you heard members of your family debating?

What ideas or terms have your teachers referred to in two or more of the classes you are taking?

What ideas or terms have recently changed meaning?

What ideas or terms do you think people frequently misunderstand or misapply?

What ideas or terms related to a hobby or interest of yours would you would like to investigate?

Step 3: Develop material for your essay.

Once you have a clear understanding of the rhetorical expectations of the assignment and have selected a topic, you can turn your attention to developing material for your essay. Depending on the assignment's requirements, you may use any or all of these methods to gather information for your argument.

Developing Material through Research

Through research, you can discover how the definition of your word or idea has changed over time. You might begin your research by consulting the *Oxford English Dictionary*, which will offer a history of the word's definition. Examine what authorities have to say about the meaning of the word or idea by looking for articles in relevant online data banks and encyclopedias. Through research you can come to understand this ongoing conversation over the term's definition.

Developing Material through Reflection

When developing material for your essay, turn your sight inward as well. What do you think the term means? Ultimately, you will argue in favor of a particular definition of the word or idea, so working through what the term means and has meant to you is a good place to start developing material for your essay. Consider how you have used the term in the past, how others have used the term, and how both you and others have reacted to it in the past. What emotional responses does the word or idea raise in you? If the meaning of the word or idea is in dispute, which side of the debate do you find most compelling? What questions concerning the word or idea do you need to answer before you can stipulate its definition? What features are essential to the term and which are not? Also consider what the word or idea does *not* mean. What other terms are close in meaning to the term you are defining?

Making Connections and Filling Gaps: An Invention Grid

As you recall from Chapter 1, the essential elements of arguments include claims, grounds, explanations, rebuttals, and qualifications. One way to develop material for an argument is to systematically examine each of these elements with your topic in mind. Based on the elements of argument, draw up a grid like the one below and fill in the cells as you generate material through research, reflection, or both (Figure 11.2). Try not to leave a cell blank—the purpose of the grid is to help you think through and generate material for every element of your argument.

To fill out this grid, for each claim indicate one aspect of the term's definition you will examine in your essay. Moving horizontally, note how you plan to support

---

FIGURE 11.2

Sample Invention Grid
Stipulative Definition Argument

Word or idea to be defined: _____

Claim	Grounds	Explanation	Rebuttal	Qualifications

---

each claim, how you will explain the link between that claim and its support, how some might question your claim, how you might address them, and how you might qualify your claim.

Suppose you were working on a stipulative definition of the term "global warming." As you begin to reflect on the term and perhaps engage in some research, a heuristic grid might begin to look like the one presented below (Figure 11.3). Looking at the first horizontal row of the grid, you would argue, in part, that global warming refers to the recent rise in the Earth's temperature. You would plan on supporting this claim with expert testimony, government definitions, and scientific definitions in order to show that many experts define global warming as the recent, post-industrial

FIGURE 11.3

Sample Invention Grid
Stipulative Definition Argument

Word or idea to be defined: **_Global Warming_**

Claim	Grounds	Explanation	Rebuttal	Qualifications
Global warming refers to *recent* rise in Earth temperature	Expert testimony

Government definitions

Scientific definitions | Uniform agreement on time period referred to | Misleading—long cycles of earth warming/cooling in the history | *Today*'s global warming crisis refers to recent rise in Earth's temperature |
| Global warning refers to changes that can be attributed to human activity | Scientific definitions | Human activities and industrialization tied to climate change | There are or can be natural causes | Though may be natural causes, will focus attention only on human ones |
| Global warning does not refer to naturally occurring changes in temperature | Examples of natural vs. man-made sources of global warming | Though natural causes are real, so are human causes | Wrong to limit it to human causes alone | Rate of changes recently can't be linked to natural causes alone |
| Global warming refers to changes in atmosphere, not land mass or water | Expert testimony

Explain cause/effect | Global warming *causes* changes in land and water | If natural causes, can it be linked to the land/earth itself? | No need to qualify |

rise in the Earth's temperature. You know that in rebuttal, someone might point out that over the entire history of the Earth, there have been times of global warming and global cooling. Granting that, you might point out that the current debate over global warming is focused on the cause of recent changes in the Earth's temperature, not the cause of past climate fluctuations.

Step 4: Write your thesis statement.

After you have investigated the word or idea you are going to define, examined its history, considered your understanding of it, identified what it is not, and collected illustrative examples of it, you should be ready to write a thesis statement for your stipulative definition argument. Your thesis can take several forms, from simple to complex. Your first option is just to state your definition.

> **Global warming refers to the recent rise in the Earth's temperature that can be attributed to man-made pollutants in the atmosphere.**

Another option is to indicate something of the debate behind the definition of your term.

> **Though some would argue that global warming refers to a rise in the Earth's temperature that can be attributed to natural or human causes, it most accurately refers only to temperature changes that be can attributed to man-made pollutants in the atmosphere.**

With this second thesis statement, you indicate that in your essay you will discuss two competing definitions of the term, rejecting one and endorsing the other.

Your thesis can also indicate that the term's definition is disputed without indicating the competing conceptions you will discuss in the body of your essay.

> **Though scientists and the popular press disagree about the meaning of the term "global warming," it most accurately refers to the rise in the Earth's temperature that can attributed to man-made pollutants in the atmosphere.**

Whatever form your thesis takes, it needs to state the definition you will argue for in the body of your essay.

Step 5: Organize your argument.

Once you have determined your argument's thesis, you need to consider how to organize your essay. One way to sort through the information you have gathered and to identify areas of your argument that may need further development is to complete a "box outline" of your essay. A box outline is an organizational tool that draws on the work of composition theorist Erika Lindemann, who advises writers to consider how they will structure large "chunks" of text in an essay. Instead of outlining a paper with Roman numerals or the like, Lindemann suggests that writers decide how they will organize various sections of text in their papers, sections that can vary in length from one paragraph to several pages. With a box outline, you divide your argument into various sections or chunks of text, summarize the information you will include in each section, then enclose that material in a box and label it. As you review your plans, you can easily move around large chunks of texts until you are satisfied with the structure.

Figure 11.4 offers a sample box outline for a stipulative definition argument. In the opening section, you would indicate the strategy you plan to employ to capture reader interest and write out your working thesis. You would then fill out a box for each reason you plan to offer to support your thesis. Inside each box, you would write out that reason, summarize how that reason supports your thesis, list any support you have gathered for that reason, and explain the relationship between the reason and its support. If you believe readers might raise some objections or questions concerning your assertions, you would summarize them here as well and indicate how you might address them. The final box would identify the strategy you will use to conclude your argument. You may begin to draft your essay before every box is completely filled out.

FIGURE 11.4	**BOX OUTLINE**

Stipulative Definition Argument

Opening Section
  Strategy you will employ to capture your reader's interest
  Thesis: The stipulative definition you will argue in favor of

Reason 1: First reason you will offer in support of your thesis
  Elaboration: How this reason supports your thesis
  Support: Evidence you will offer in support of this reason
  Explanation: How the evidence supports that reason
  Objections: Objections or questions that might be raised
  Rebuttal: How you would address those objections or questions

Reason 2: The second reason you will offer in support of your thesis
  Elaboration: How this reason supports your thesis
  Support: Evidence you will offer in support of this reason
  Explanation: How the evidence supports that reason
  Objections: Objections or questions that might be raised
  Rebuttal: How you would address those objections or questions

Reason X: The last reason you will offer in support of your thesis
  Elaboration: How this reason supports your thesis
  Support: Evidence you will offer in support of this reason
  Explanation: How the evidence supports that reason
  Objections: Objections or questions that might be raised
  Rebuttal: How you would address those objections or questions

Closing Section
  Strategy you will employ to conclude your argument

Step 6: Write the rough draft.

Opening

The opening section of your essay needs to accomplish several goals: introduce the topic of your argument, state your thesis, and capture your readers' interest. You can employ many different strategies to open your essay, but some of the more common include providing a brief historical overview of various meanings that have been attributed to your term, offering an overview of the current debate over its meaning, providing an explanation of why the term is controversial, and examining why defining the term is important.

Body

When you begin to draft the body of your argument, use the box outline you produced earlier as a guide, understanding that as you compose your essay you may develop new ways to organize your argument. As you develop reasons for your thesis, support them with evidence, explain your line of thought, and continue to keep your readers in mind. Are there terms you need to define? Are there particular claims or reasons that need more explanation than others? If you have a choice of evidence to support a reason, which will your readers find most convincing? Are you basing your argument on assumptions that you need to articulate and defend? Finally, pay attention to your use of source texts. If you quote or paraphrase material from sources, be sure to include the proper documentation in your rough draft. Don't put it off until later. Too frequently that strategy leads to unintentional plagiarism, particularly with paraphrased material.

Conclusion

In the conclusion of your essay, you have two primary goals: draw your argument to a graceful end and remind your readers of your thesis. Simply summarizing your argument and restating your thesis is one way to accomplish these goals, but is usually not the most rhetorically effective strategy to employ. Other commonly employed strategies writers use when closing stipulative definition arguments include indicating how your essay contributes to an ongoing discussion over the definition of the term, noting the significance or utility of the definition you have presented, explaining how your definition addresses particular problems or questions in the field, and pointing out interesting questions your definition raises. Instead of just summarizing your argument at the end of your piece, leave your reader with a sense of what makes your essay significant or important.

Step 7: Revise your argument.

Revise Content and Structure

Start your revision process by making sure the essay meets the assignment's requirements and presents the argument you intended. At this point you may decide to expand certain sections of your argument and cut back others. Make these types of large-scale changes to your essay before you worry too much about spelling or grammar. Address the bigger concerns of content and structure first. Also revise your thesis, topic sentences, and transitions as needed.

Revise for Clarity and Correctness

Once you think you have the argument's content and structure right, pay attention to your writing's clarity and correctness. Scrutinize your writing carefully paragraph by paragraph, examining each sentence to be sure it is clear and grammatically correct. If you have a difficult time catching grammar, spelling, or punctuation errors, consider having someone else read your rough draft to look for these problems. Do not rely on your computer's spelling and grammar programs to edit your paper.

Revise Documentation

Finally, set aside time to check your paper for proper documentation. Be sure all paraphrased and quoted material is correctly documented. If you have to provide a bibliography or works cited list, be sure it is accurate and complete.

Revision Checklist

You will find a revision checklist for categorical definition arguments in Appendix 1 located at the end of this textbook.

Common Errors to Avoid When Writing a Stipulative Definition Argument

A number of errors commonly occur in stipulative definition arguments. Avoiding them will help you produce more effective essays.

Ambiguous Defining Terms

Stipulative definitions should clarify meaning, not confuse it. Students sometimes use vague or ambiguous terms to define the topic of their essay. For example, consider the claim "Bow hunting is not a humane activity because it instills needless suffering and does not serve the public good." What, exactly, is meant by the assertion "does not serve the public good"? Perhaps the writer making this claim could clarify the meaning of this criterion in the body of his or her essay, but as stated, it is ambiguous.

Overly Broad Definitions

Other times, students' stipulative definitions are too broad. The definition applies to not only the topic of the essay but also to many other topics. For example, consider the claim "Marriage is a relationship adults enter into when they love each other." How precise is the criterion "a relationship adults enter into when they love each other"? How many types of relationships can you think of that adults enter into when they love each other that are unrelated to marriage? The claim as written is overly broad.

Circular Definitions

A circular definition defines the topic in terms of itself: A good parent is one who is good. A successful sports team is one that succeeds. An effective economic policy is one that produces an effective economy. Such definitions do little to clarify the meaning of a term. They add nothing to any existing conversations concerning the term's definition.

Assuming Agreement When There Is None

Do not assume that your readers will accept your assertions without adequate support and explanations. Assume you are addressing skeptical readers who expect you to develop and defend your assertions.

Ignoring Controversies

Do not ignore possible opposition to your assertions. If you can identify likely objections to your claims, rebut them in your argument. If you are aware of a controversy concerning the definition of your topic, acknowledge the debate and explain how your argument adds to the conversation.

Sample Stipulative Definition Argument

The following stipulative definition argument examines the term "global warming." The student who wrote this essay, Cassandra Leigh Stemsky, based her argument primarily on her own knowledge and experience. While extensive outside research was not required, the writer was allowed to consult the Internet for information if she wished. Additionally, the assignment asked students to include any necessary documentation in the body of their argument (no works cited list or bibliography was required).

SAMPLE STIPULATIVE DEFINITION ARGUMENT

What Is Global Warming?

Cassandra Leigh Stemsky

Over the past decade, it has been almost impossible to avoid the debate over global warming. The evening newscasts carry stories on it, dire warnings are splashed daily across the headlines of local and national newspapers, even high school science textbooks focus on the phenomena. Though some contend that the debate over global warming is over—that it is a proven scientific fact—others disagree. They either deny that the globe is warming, claim that the dire consequences former Vice President Al Gore and others predict as a result of global warming will not come to pass, or that global warming is a natural, not a man-made phenomena. One of the reasons these debates are so hard to settle, and why it seems that neither side listens to the other, has to do with the various definitions of the term "global warming." Until both sides can agree on a definition, they will not be able to settle their differences and move the debate forward. Given all the research and discussion that has taken place to date, it seems clear that global warming most appropriately refers to recent rises in the Earth's temperature that can be attributed to man-made pollutants in the atmosphere.

First, global warming refers to recent changes in the Earth's temperature, not to past changes. Most scientists agree that the Earth has undergone dramatic shifts in global temperature since it was formed, long ice ages followed by long periods of global warming. According to the University Corporation for Atmospheric Research, "Our climate has been constantly changing since Earth began, with periods of global warming and global cooling long before human beings and their activities began. Modern weather measurements go back only 100 to 150 years" (http://www.ucar. edu/research/climate/past.jsp).

However, when the term "global warming" is used today, it does not refer to those earlier periods of change. Today, the term properly refers to the current rise in the Earth's temperature. That the Earth's temperature is rising or has risen over the past hundred years or so is not under serious dispute. According to the Solar Center at Stanford University:

> Studies indicate that the average global surface temperature has increased by approximately 0.5–1.0°F (0.3–0.6°C) over the last century. This is the largest increase in surface temperature in the last 1,000 years and scientists are predicting an even greater increase over this century. . . .
>   Average global temperatures may increase by 1.4–5.8°C (that's 2.5–10.4° F) by the end of the 21st century. Although the numbers sound small, they can trigger significant changes in climate. (The difference between global temperatures during an Ice Age and an ice-free period is only about 5°C.) (http://solar-center. stanford. edu/sun-on-earth/glob-warm.html).

According to the Public Broadcasting System, most scientists contend that the current wave of global warming began during the industrial revolution (http://www.pbs.org/ now/science/ climatedebate.html). As the term is currently used, global warming refers to these recent changes in the Earth's temperature—ones occurring over the last century.

Second, global warming refers to changes in the Earth's atmosphere that can be attributed to human activity, not to naturally occurring processes. The Earth's temperature has risen and fallen many times through the ages, almost always due to no influence from human beings. Again, the geological and fossil records clearly establish these past changes. However, when someone uses the term "global warming" today, that person is most properly referring to those changes that can be attributed to human activity. According to National Geographic, global warming is caused by greenhouse gasses such as CO_2 released into the atmosphere as a result of human consumption of fossil fuels (http://green. nationalgeographic.com/environment/ global-warming/gw-causes.html).

Some would argue that human activity alone is not responsible for global warming. NASA points out that certain greenhouse gasses occur naturally—from volcanic activity, animal and human digestion, even from plants themselves (http://vathena. arc.nasa.gov/curric/land/global/greenhou.html). Global warming skeptics also note that the Earth is not the only planet in our solar system currently experiencing a rise in temperature. According to the Canadian Broadcasting Company, Mars is heating up as well, which certainly cannot be attributed to human activity (http://www.cbc. ca/technology/story/2007/04/04/science-mars-warming.html). Instead, they contend that the sun is undergoing an unusually intense period of solar activity and flaring which is heating up the entire solar system (http://solar-center.stanford.edu/ sun-on-earth/ FAQ2. html). In fact, researchers at the Max Plank Institute in Germany have found a high correlation between sunspot activity and rises in the Earth's temperature (http://www.hs.uni-hamburg.de/cs13/day1/03_Solanki.ppt).

While these observations appear to be true, they do not affect the definition of global warming. Even though some rise in the Earth's temperature can be credited to natural causes, global warming refers to those causes which can be attributed to *human* activity. For the sake of clarity, when debating global warming it is better to limit the discussion to changes in the Earth's temperature that have resulted or are resulting from human activity, otherwise the term loses precision and those debating the issue end up discussing two different phenomena—one that results from natural causes and one that results from human causes.

Finally, global warming refers to changes in the Earth's atmosphere, not to changes in the temperature of its land or water. Those who believe global warming refers to changes in the Earth's land or water are confusing cause and effect. Changes in the Earth's atmosphere cause rising temperatures on land and sea. When debating global warming, the discussion should be limited to atmospheric changes alone. Any number of factors may cause sea and land temperatures to rise periodically around the globe, but some of those changes can be attributed to global warming. Such changes are a result of global warming which has its origin elsewhere—in the Earth's atmosphere.

The ongoing debates over the cause and consequences of global warming as well as discussion about how best to solve the problem can only move forward if all parties agree on a common definition of the phenomena. Those who believe the term refers to naturally occurring changes in the Earth's temperature due to solar activity will not be open to addressing rises in the Earth's temperature that can be attributed to human activity. As humans, we can do nothing about many natural causes of warming on Earth, but we can act to help curb the effects of global warming that result from our own actions. By reducing man-made pollutants that heat up the Earth's atmosphere we can help alleviate some of the recent increases in temperature and let nature take whatever course it chooses.

Something to write about . . .

After reading "What Is Global Warming," complete the following writing assignments. Your teacher may want you to write them on your own or to work with one or more of your classmates.

1. Write a brief summary of the text.
2. Create a box outline of the text to better understand how it is structured.
3. Critique the text: how convincing or persuasive is it? Why?
4. Write a brief note addressed to the text's author summarizing your response to the argument and offering any suggestions you have for improving the essay. Be sure to explain and defend the suggestions you offer.

WRITING A CATEGORICAL DEFINITION ARGUMENT

When writing a categorical definition argument, you assert that something does or does not fit a particular classification: Cheerleading is or is not a sport. The Vietnam conflict was or was not a just war. Abortion is or is not the termination of a human life. Structurally, categorical definitions are much more complicated than stipulative definitions because they involve two related arguments: one defining the category and another asserting whether the subject of your essay fits that category. Though more complicated to write, a categorical definition argument can be very compelling and persuasive.

A Model Process for Writing Categorical Definition Arguments

Step 1: Read and analyze the assignment.

As with a stipulative definition argument, begin your analysis of the assignment by identifying the elements of its rhetorical situation.

What Is the Topic?

Has the teacher assigned you a particular topic or is it open? If the choice of topics is up to you, are there any restrictions? Do you need your teacher's approval for whatever topic you choose?

Who Is the Intended Audience?

Who are your intended readers? What aspects of your argument might your readers question? What is potentially controversial about your topic? What does your intended audience likely know about the topic of your essay? What feelings or attitudes might they bring to the topic? What aspects of your argument will you need to explain more fully than other aspects?

What Is the Purpose of Your Essay?

What, exactly, is your essay supposed to accomplish? What is the best way to achieve your purpose, given your topic and intended audience?

What Format Are You Expected to Follow?

Is there a format or paradigm for your essay you are expected to follow? Are you supposed to develop an organizational strategy of your own? Which documentation style are you expected to use?

What Types of Sources Are You Expected to Use?

What types and how many sources are you expected to consult as you research the assignment or to incorporate into the final draft of your argument? What types of sources will be most persuasive given your intended audience?

Step 2: Select a topic for your essay.

When they assign categorical arguments, teachers usually prescribe a topic or offer students a list of topics to choose among. However, if you have to develop your own topic, identify a "difficult case" to work with, a person, thing, event, idea, or term that has proven difficult to categorize. "Is basketball a sport" is not a good topic because it is not controversial. Instead, think of a category and then try to identify a subject that might or might not fit. For example, consider these topics:

Is graffiti a form of art?

If you wrote on this topic, you would need to define what you mean by "art" and argue whether graffiti fits that definition.

Can gay couples be truly married?

With this one, you would need to define "marriage" and determine whether that definition can apply to gay couples.

Step 3: Develop material for your essay.

You will likely generate material for your categorical definition argument through both research and reflection.

Developing Material through Research

Researching material for a categorical definition argument can be complicated because there are three distinct areas of research:

1. material to help you define the category;
2. material to support your position on whether the subject of your paper fits the category; and
3. existing arguments concerning whether your subject fits the category.

Suppose you wanted to argue whether men's magazines such as *Maxim* are pornographic. You would first need to research definitions of pornography, identifying what you believe to be the three or four characteristics that make a publication pornographic. Next, you would examine issues of *Maxim* magazine to see if they exhibit those characteristics. If they do, then you would argue that the magazine is pornographic; if they do not, then you would argue that it is not.

Developing Material through Reflection

As you prepare to write your essay, consider what you already know about the subject and category. Even before you begin your research, consider how you would define the category—what are its main defining characteristics? What about your subject would allow it to be placed in that category? What would bar it from being placed in that category? What information or examples do you need to gather to better understand the subject or category you are addressing? Reflection will help you define your category, determine your position, and set a research agenda.

Step 4: Define your category.

To define the category, you will need to answer the following questions.

What Are the Key Defining Features of the Category?

Though the category may contain many features, which ones are central? For example, if a sport is an activity, what features must that activity possess in order to be a sport? Must it involve more than one person? Must competition be involved? Must it require athletic skill to complete successfully? Based on your research and reflection, identify the key defining features of your category.

How Will You Explain and Clarify Each Feature?

Once you develop a list of features that define your category, how will you explain them? Do any of these terms, themselves, need to be defined? If a sport must involve some sort of athletic skill, what does "athletic skill" mean? If asked, how could you explain each feature?

What Examples Can You Provide to Illustrate Each Feature That Are Not Drawn from Your Subject?

In this type of argument, you can offer relevant examples to explain and clarify your categories so long as they do not come from the term you are defining. For example, if you are arguing that cheerleading is a sport and contend that a sport must involve "athletic skill," you can draw illustrative examples from any activity other than cheerleading to explain what you mean.

Which Negative Examples Best Illustrate Your Definition of the Category?

Sometimes the best way to define something is by suggesting what it is not. Are there features people often ascribe to your category that you reject? For example, might some people believe that a sport must always involve teams? If you think that is not true, explain why.

How Have Others Defined Your Category?

How has the category been defined in the past? Your argument should reflect an understanding of prior debates over the category's definition. You may end up accepting and arguing for an existing definition, adopting some features of an existing definition but not others, or completely rejecting prior definitions and proposing your own.

Based on your research and reflection, write out a definition of your category that includes the three or four defining features you have identified. Remember that you are presenting an argument even in this section your essay—you have to assume that your readers will question the way you are defining the category. Therefore, you need to support your definition with clear reasons, examples, counterexamples, expert testimony, and the like. When you write your essay, expect to devote one or more fully developed paragraphs to each of the defining features you decide to include.

Filling out an invention grid will help ensure that you thoroughly considered how you are defining the category. Figure 11.5 presents one version of a grid you might find helpful. Moving horizontally across the grid, you would write down one of the defining features of the category, support for your claim that this is a defining feature, examples you might draw on as you write your essay, any objections readers might raise to your contention, and the strategy you might use to address those objections.

FIGURE 11.5	Invention Grid			
	Defining a Category			
Defining Feature	**Support**	**Illustrative Examples**	**Likely Objections**	**Rebuttals**

Step 5: Determine the fit.

In this section of your paper, you determine whether your subject fits the category as you have just defined it and begin to generate material to defend that assertion.

Assess the Fit

You will likely adopt one of three positions to defend in this section of your argument:

- The subject fits the category
- The subject does not fit the category
- The subject partially fits the category

To argue that the subject fits the category, it must possess, share, or exhibit all of the category's defining features. For example, if you determine that a sport is characterized by four key features and decide that cheerleading possesses all four, you will argue that cheerleading is a sport. If you determine that cheerleading does not possess these features, you will argue that it is not a sport. A more difficult problem occurs if you determine that cheerleading possesses some of those features but not others. If all four features are equally necessary for an activity to be a sport, you will have to argue that cheerleading is not a sport if it lacks one or more of them. If you think certain features are more crucial to determining whether an activity is a sport than others, you might determine that cheerleading is a sport if it possesses those essential features but not the others. As you determine your subject's fit to the category as you have defined it, consider how you will explain or defend your judgments.

Generate Material to Support Your Position through Research

Research can help you determine whether your subject fits the category. First, you might investigate what authorities have to say about your subject and category. Which experts argue in favor of the fit and which argue against it? How do they defend their positions? Over the years, has opinion changed on the question of whether your subject fits your category? Why?

Generate Material to Support Your Position through Reflection

When you finish your research, determine whether and to what degree your subject fits the category you have defined. At this point, you may decide that you need to go back and clarify the definition of your category. Sometimes trying to apply the definition you have developed to the specific subject you are working with will reveal problems, contradictions, or questions you need to address through further research.

Consider Counterpositions

Finally, through research and reflection consider counterarguments to your position. What might others contend if they hold a position different from yours? What are the likely objections to your position? How will you address those objections?

Step 6: Write your thesis statement.

Your thesis for a categorical definition argument can be open or closed. With an open thesis, you indicate whether your subject fits the category.

> **Cheerleading is a sport.**

With a closed thesis, you also indicate how you will define your category and defend your thesis.

> **Because it is an activity that involves physical exertion, athletic skill, and competition, cheerleading is a sport.**

You might also indicate the opposing views you will address in your argument, especially if you find through your research that the position you assume is particularly contentious.

> **Though some have argued that cheerleading is not a sport because it does not involve athletic skill or competition, a careful examination shows that it actually involves both and can therefore be considered a sport.**

Finally, you may believe that your subject possesses some of the features of your category but not others. You can indicate this position in your thesis as well.

> **Though cheerleading does not always involve competition, it can still be considered a sport because it requires athletic skill and physical exertion.**

Step 7: Organize your argument.

You can organize a categorical definition argument using either a block or an alternating format. Using a **block format**, you define the category then argue whether your subject fits it. Using an **alternating format**, you develop and defend your definition of the category one feature at a time and argue that your subject does or does not possess that feature before moving on to the next one.

When employing a block format for a categorical definition argument, a box outline might look like the one offered in Figure 11.6. In the opening section of your argument you would introduce the topic and state your thesis. In the category section, you would state, explain, and defend the category one feature at a time. In the

FIGURE 11.6	BOX OUTLINE

Categorical Definition Argument: Block Format

Opening Section

Strategy you will employ to capture reader interest

Thesis: Whether the subject you are examining fits or matches the category

Category Section

Claim 1: First defining feature of category

Reasons: Reasons justifying first defining feature

Evidence: Support for each reason

Explanation: How the evidence supports each reason

Claim 2: Second defining feature of category

Reasons: Reasons justifying second defining feature

Evidence: Support for the second reason

Explanation: How the evidence supports each reason

Claim X: Last defining feature of category

Reasons: Reasons justifying last defining feature

Evidence: Support for each reason

Explanation: How the evidence supports each reason

Fit Section

Claim 1: Whether subject fits first defining feature of category

Reasons: Reasons subject does or does not fit first defining feature of category

Evidence: Support for each reason

Explanation: How the evidence supports each reason

Claim 2: Whether subject fits second defining feature of category

Reasons: Reasons subject does or does not fit second defining feature of category

Evidence: Support for each reason

Explanation: How the evidence supports each reason

Claim X: Whether subject fits last defining feature of category

Reasons: Reasons subject does or does not fit last defining feature of category

Evidence: Support for each reason

Explanation: How the evidence supports each reason

Closing Section

Strategy you will employ to conclude the essay

fit section, you would claim whether your subject fit that definition one feature at a time. In the final section, you would decide on a strategy for closing your argument.

The block format enables you to define your category in one section of your essay before moving on to the fit or match section. However, you may find yourself repeating information in the second half of your essay as you discuss each feature of the category again.

Figure 11.7 offers a sample outline for a categorical definition argument that follows an alternating format. Notice that with this format you define the category one feature at a time and argue whether your subject possesses, shares in, or demonstrates that feature.

The alternating format is especially good to use if you believe your subject matches some of the features and not others. If you argue that your subject fits the category even though it does not match every feature, begin your essay by discussing those features that do not match so you finish your essay by examining features that do. If you argue that your subject does not fit the category even though it matches one or more of the features but not others, begin your essay by discussing the features it does match so you can finish your essay by examining the features it does not.

Step 8: Write your rough draft.

Once you have generated material for your essay, crafted a working thesis, and devised an organizational plan, you are ready to write your rough draft. The following guidelines will help you compose the introduction, body, and conclusion of your argument.

Writing the Introduction

As with other arguments, the opening section of your essay should introduce the topic of your argument, state your thesis, and capture your readers' interest. A number of strategies work well to capture reader interest in a categorical definition argument: summarizing any ongoing debate over how to categorize the subject of your essay, explaining the importance of categorizing the subject properly, explaining the significance of categorizing the subject the way you recommend in your argument, and offering an anecdote related to the topic or subject of your essay or a relevant personal experience.

Writing the Body of Your Essay

When writing the body of your essay, follow the organizational plan you designed earlier. In the category sections, identify and explain the defining features you work with clearly and anticipate possible objections. When arguing whether your subject possesses those features, carefully explain your reasoning, qualifying your claims as needed and addressing possible questions or objections. Be sure to document all source material as you write your rough draft.

Writing the Conclusion

In the conclusion of your argument, reassert your thesis and provide a graceful end to your argument. If possible, echo the opening strategy you employed: if you started with an anecdote, finish it in your conclusion; if you started by summarizing a debate

FIGURE 11.7 **BOX OUTLINE**

Categorical Definition Argument: Alternating Format

Opening Section

Strategy you will employ to capture reader interest

Thesis: Whether the subject you are examining fits or matches the category

First Category Section

Category Claim 1: First defining feature of category

Reasons: Reasons justifying first defining feature

Evidence: Support for each reason

Explanation: How the evidence supports each reason

Fit Claim: Whether subject fits first defining feature of category

Reasons: Reasons subject does or does not fit first defining feature of category

Evidence: Support for each reason

Explanation: How the evidence supports each reason

Secondary Category Section

Category Claim 2: Second defining feature of category

Reasons: Reasons justifying second defining feature

Evidence: Support for the second reason

Explanation: How the evidence supports each reason

Fit Claim 2: Whether subject fits second defining feature of category

Reasons: Reasons subject does or does not fit second defining feature of category

Evidence: Support for each reason

Explanation: How the evidence supports each reason

X Category Section

Category Claim X: Last defining feature of category

Reasons: Reasons justifying last defining feature

Evidence: Support for each reason

Explanation: How the evidence supports each reason

Fit Claim X: Whether subject fits last defining feature of category

Reasons: Reasons subject does or does not fit last defining feature of category

Evidence: Support for each reason

Explanation: How the evidence supports each reason

Closing Section

Strategy you will employ to conclude the essay

over the definition of your subject, finish by explaining how your essay adds to that conversation.

Step 9: Revise your argument.

Revise Content and Structure

Begin to revise your rough draft by first examining your argument. With your intended audience in mind, decide which assertions need further development, which might be questioned, and which might be unclear then address those problems. Decide if any parts of your paper need further support or explanation.

When reviewing your essay's structure, be sure your thesis accurately forecasts the argument you present—your position may change as you draft your essay, so be sure you revise your thesis accordingly. Next, check whether the transitions you have provided help readers move smoothly through your argument. Your topic sentences should both remind readers of your thesis and introduce the next section of your essay.

Revise for Clarity and Correctness

Review the sentences in each paragraph for clarity and correctness. Consider how your readers will respond to the words and syntax you employ. When you are writing about complex ideas or presenting complicated arguments, your writing needs to be clear and direct—your language and sentence structure should not present obstacles to readers. Finally, check for punctuation errors.

Revise Documentation

If you used source material in your argument, be sure that all paraphrased and quoted material is documented correctly. Check your works cited list or bibliography—have you included all the entries you need to include and employed the correct citation forms?

Revision Checklist

You will find a revision checklist for categorical definition arguments in Appendix 1.

Common Errors to Avoid When Writing a Categorical Definition Argument

A number of errors commonly occur in categorical definition arguments. Knowing that writers frequently make these mistakes can help you avoid them as you develop, draft, and revise your essay.

Poorly Defined Categories

Categorical definition arguments fail if the categories are defined too broadly or too narrowly. If defined too broadly, there will be little argument whether the subject fits the category; if defined too narrowly, only the subject would fit it, again making an argument unnecessary.

Overly Simplified Presentations of the Categories

Too often writers neglect to explain or defend the features they contend define the category, devoting much more attention to other sections of their argument. You need to thoroughly develop all sections of your argument.

Assuming Agreement When There Is None

When you are presenting a categorical definition argument, do not assume that your readers will accept your assertions. Instead, assume you are writing to a skeptical audience, readers you have to persuade with sound reasons, solid evidence, clear reasoning, and effective appeals.

Ignoring Controversies

When generating material for your essay, if you encounter controversies touching on your thesis, do not ignore them. To persuade academic readers, you need to recognize and address opposing views in your essay.

Sample Categorical Definition Argument

The following sample categorical definition argument, written by student Mike Allen, examines whether college cheerleading can be considered a sport.

SAMPLE CATEGORICAL DEFINITION ARGUMENT

Is Cheerleading a Sport? It Depends

Mike Allen

In 1972, Congress passed Title IX of the Education Amendments Act, which required gender equity for boys and girls in all education programs that receive federal funding, including sports. Since then, colleges and universities across the country have tried to ensure that the percentage of students participating in sports conforms to the percentages enrolled at the institution. To achieve this goal, schools have had to increase the number of female athletes participating in recognized sports and/or decrease the number of male athletes participating in them. To achieve Title IX compliance, some colleges have even begun redefining traditional extracurricular activities as varsity sports, especially ones that attract large numbers of female participants, and cheerleading is leading the way. The movement received a boost in 2004 when the University of Maryland became the first Division I school to recognize cheerleading as a varsity sport. Complying with Title IX regulations in this way raises an interesting question: Is cheerleading a sport? Examined carefully, the answer is yes—college cheerleading can indeed be considered a sport if it meets certain requirements.

The Office of Civil Rights (OCR) oversees compliance with Title IX. If a college wants to classify cheerleading as an official varsity sport and include the number of cheerleaders in its compliance reports, it needs OCR approval. Historically, the OCR has not viewed cheerleading as a sport (Orris); however, it does review applications on an individual basis. In reviewing these applications, the OCR "does not rely on a specific definition of a sport. Nor does OCR rely solely on a claim by an institution that the activity in question is a sport. Rather, OCR's practice is to assess each activity on a case-by-case basis" (O'Shea). When the OCR determines whether an activity is a sport, it examines multiple criteria. The ones mentioned most frequently include: (1) whether the primary purpose of the activity is competitive, (2) whether a uniform set of rules or scoring guidelines are used to declare a winner, (3) whether it is administered by the school's athletic department, and (4) whether participants are eligible for scholarships and athletic awards (Orris; O'Shea).

The National Collegiate Athletic Association (NCAA Committee) agrees with the OCR's first criteria—to be a sport, the primary purpose of the activity must be competition. In 2003, the NCAA's Committee on Women's Athletics opened its definition of a sport with the following statement:

> . . . a sport shall be defined as an institutional activity involving physical exertion with the purpose of competition versus other teams or individuals within a collegiate competition structure. Furthermore, a sport includes regularly scheduled team and/or individual, head-to-head competition (at least five) within a defined competitive season(s). . . .

In other words, according to the NCAA, for an activity to be a sport, its participants must compete against other teams or individuals on a regular, scheduled basis. The Women's Sport Federation (WSF) agrees as well, stating that a sport is "a contest or competition against or with an opponent" whose "primary purpose . . . is a comparison of the relative skills of the participants."

The OCR, NCAA, and WSF all agree that an activity is not a sport unless its primary purpose is competition. Under this definition, intramural competitions would not be recognized as a sport because their *primary* purpose is recreation and fitness, not competition. Likewise, dance or drill squads would not be considered sports teams if their primary purpose was entertainment and if they were not involved in competitive matches with other collegiate dance or drill squads.

Additionally, for an activity to be a sport this competition must take place within the context of agreed upon rules or scoring guidelines that determine winners and losers. According to the NCAA, to be a sport, the competition must follow "standardized rules with rating/scoring systems ratified by official regulatory agencies and governing bodies" (NCAA Committee). The OCR also maintains that a set of rules must govern an activity for it to be a sport, while the WSF states that the activity must adhere to "rules which explicitly define the time, space and purpose of the contest and the conditions under which a winner is declared" (Women's Sport Federation). This criterion implies that an activity must be formally organized to be a sport—some organizing body or authority must establish a set of uniform rules and scoring guides.

In colleges and universities, activities like gymnastics and diving, which rely on subjective evaluations to determine a winner, have long been recognized as varsity sports because competition follows established rules and participants are evaluated according to an official scoring system applied by trained judges. According to Idaho State University researchers April Hennefer, Kristina Sowder, Cynthia Lee Pemberton, and Debra Easterly, a sport is a structured physical activity that involves competition based on rules or guidelines (4–5).

While the OCR, NCAA, and WSF agree that a sport must involve competition with winners and losers decided according to prescribed rules and scoring systems, the OCR adds two other criteria that are crucial to determining whether an activity is a sport: it must be administered by the school's athletic department and its participants must be eligible for scholarships and awards (O'Shea). If an activity such an intramural basketball or drill team is not administered by a school's athletic department, then according to the Office of Civil Rights, it is not a sport and its participants cannot be included in Title IX compliance reports. Likewise, those participating on a college sports team must be eligible for awards, such as varsity letter, and athletic scholarships, if they are available. (Athletic scholarships are not always available for college students. For example, Division III institutions offer no athletic scholarships for students participating on their sports teams.)

So, according to all of these criteria, is cheerleading a sport? First, it would have to involve competition. Interestingly, the American Association of Cheerleading Coaches and Advisors denies that cheerleading is a sport specifically because it is not competitive: "The primary purpose is not competition, but that of raising school unity through leading the crowd at athletic functions" (American Association). In their position paper on the issue, the Association acknowledges the difficulties cheerleading programs face when classified merely as an activity and not a sport and advocate adopting a middle ground, classifying it as an "athletic activity" and its participants as "student athletes."

The authors of a *Harvard Law Review* article, "Cheering on Women and Girls in Sports," agree that cheerleading is not competitive and should not be considered a sport, especially when determining whether a school is complying with Title IX requirements: "the cheerleaders at these schools exist in large part to support male athletes. Not only do cheerleaders encourage these athletes' success at individual games, but they also decorate the athletes' lockers, bake them cookies, and perform other supportive functions" (1643). However, the article's overgeneralizations and dismissive tone mask the evolving state of cheerleading.

Few would disagree that cheerleaders do much more than bake cookies and decorate lockers these days. Yet the question of competition persists. While cheerleaders may be athletes, is their activity a sport if they do not regularly compete against other cheerleading teams? Though the Women's Sport Federation denies that cheerleading is currently a sport, they do state that it could be:

> If the primary purpose of . . . cheerleaders is to compete against other . . . cheerleaders on a regular season and post season qualification basis in much the same structure as basketball or gymnastics and if the team conducted regular practices in preparation for such competition while under the supervision of a coach, these activities could be considered sports.

In other words, if the primary purpose of a cheerleading team was competition and if it competed against other cheerleading teams on a regular basis, then cheerleading would be a sport.

When the University of Maryland decided in 2004 to make cheerleading a varsity sport, the school created two cheer squads. One, a female-only squad, became a sports team; the other, which is co-ed, did not. The competition squad competes year-round against other schools and does not perform at games. It is housed in the athletic department, has full-time coaches and trainers, offers scholarships and letters, and adheres to all NCAA requirements covering recruitment and practice schedules (Roenigk). Both the WSF and University of Maryland have recognized that if the primary purpose of a cheerleading team is competition—not supporting other athletes in competition—then it satisfies one of the primary requirements defining a sport.

Most authorities also agree that sports teams compete according to established rules and that their performance is evaluated by standardized criteria. Cheerleading meets both of these qualifications as well. It is governed by rules established by several national bodies, including the Universal Cheering Association and the National Cheerleading Association. At competition, trained judges evaluate routines performed by teams using scoring guidelines that examine the quality of the athletes' jumps, tumbles, stunts, pyramids, and basket tosses; dance techniques; transitions and use of floor space; synchronization and timing; creativity and choreography; showmanship; and overall impression. The rules include mandatory deductions for flaws in the performance and difficulty points added to reward challenging routines (Champions Cup Series). In short, cheering competitions are judged much the way gymnastics and diving are scored.

Finally, to be a sport, cheerleading squads need to be housed by a school's athletic department and its participants need to be eligible for scholarships and awards. Hennefer et al. found that 37% of the schools they surveyed offered cheerleaders at least partial scholarships and 46% of them run cheerleading through their athletic departments (10). As stated earlier, at the University of Maryland, the competitive cheerleading team is maintained by the athletic department and its members can earn scholarships and awards.

The OCR has adopted the best approach to determining whether cheerleading is a sport, deciding the matter on a case-by-case basis. Cheerleading can be a sport if its primary purpose is competition, if during competition it follows established rules and scoring guidelines to determine a winner, if it is housed in the school's athletic department, and if it offers participants scholarships and awards. When a cheerleading team at a school meets these criteria, it ought to be considered a sport and its participants included when evaluating compliance with Title IX requirements.

Works Cited

American Association of Cheerleading Coaches and Advisors. "Addressing the Issue of Cheerleading as a Sport." Web. 12 June 2007.

Champions Cup Series. "2007–2008 Champions Cup Series Cheer Competition Guidelines." Web. 13 June 2007.

"Cheering on Women and Girls in Sports: Using Title IX to Fight Gender Role Oppression." *Harvard Law Review* 110 (1997): 1627–44. Print.

Hennefer, April, Kristina Sowder, Cynthia Lee, A. Pemberton, and Debra M. Easterly. "Dance and Cheerleading as Competitive Sports: Making a Case for OCR Sport Recognition & NCAA Emerging Sport Designation." ERIC Clearinghouse on Teaching and Teacher Education. Aug. 2003. ED 479 762. Print.

NCAA Committee on Women's Athletics. "Definition of Sport." Oct. 2002. Web. 10 June 2007.

Orris, Harry A. "Letter to MHSAA, Cheerleading." 18 Oct. 2001. Web. 10 June 2007. <http://www.ed.gov/print/about/offices/list/ocr/mhsaa-cheer.html>

O'Shea, Mary Francis. "Letter to Stead Re MHSAA." 11 Apr. 2000. Web. 10 June 2007. <http://www.ed.goiv/print/about/offices/list/ocr/stead.html>

Roenigk, Alyssa. "Maryland Trailblazers: A Tale of Two Teams." *American Cheerleader* Oct. 2004. Web. 13 June 2007.

Women's Sports Federation. "Cheerleading, Drill Team, Danceline and Band as Varsity Sports: The Foundation Position." Sept. 2003. Web. 10 June 2007.

Something to write about . . .

After reading "Is Cheerleading a Sport? It Depends," complete the following writing assignments. Again, your teacher may want you to work with one or more of your classmates.

1. Write a brief summary of the text.
2. Create a box outline of the text to better understand how it is organized then explain why you think the author structured the argument this way.
3. Critique the text's argument: how convincing or persuasive is it? Why?
4. Critique the text's sources: are they sufficiently varied and sufficiently academic? How so?
5. Write a brief note addressed to the text's author summarizing your response to the argument and offering any suggestions you have for improving the essay. Be sure to explain and defend the suggestions you offer.

ADDITIONAL READINGS

When I was growing up, I was often told that in polite company one discussed neither politics nor religion. Over the years, I've come to realize how sound that advice can be—few other topics have the potential to ignite such strong, emotional debates. The additional readings at the end of this chapter address an equally touchy topic: spirituality. Both readings first appeared in publications whose primary readers are teachers and other educators.

Both readings address the issue of spirituality in ways that may seem foreign to you, especially if this is the first time you have been exposed to academic studies of the subject. In the first reading, Bruce Speck examines problems related to defining spirituality in higher education: how are college faculty and administrators to understand the term, how are they to understand its relevance to higher education, and how are they to address it in the classroom? In the second reading, renowned educator Alexander W. Astin argues that spirituality—as he defines it—should play a central role in college curricula, given its links to consciousness and creativity.

Before you read these essays, consider your responses to the following questions:

- How would you define spirituality?
- What is the difference, if any, between spirituality and religion?
- What do you think would prove most problematic for writers who are trying to define these terms? Why?
- What kinds of evidence would you find convincing in an argument concerning the definition of spirituality? Why?
- If a writer is addressing the topic of spirituality, what special audience-related concerns or problems might he or she logically anticipate? How might a writer best address these concerns or problems?
- Why might defining spirituality be of interest to college faculty or administrators?

As you read these arguments, consider these questions:

- How does each author attempt to generate reader interest in his argument?
- What opening strategy does each writer employ? How does each conclude his argument?
- What assumptions does each writer seem to make about his readers' knowledge of the topic he is addressing? How do you know?
- How do you think the intended audience of each piece influenced its content, structure, style, and tone?
- Each author discusses competing definitions of spirituality, sometimes at great length. Why do you think the authors pay so much attention to prior thought on the topic?
- What kinds of evidence do the authors offer to support the claims they are making?
- What assumptions about spirituality do the writers leave unexamined or unsupported?

After you finish reading the arguments, consider the following questions:

- How would you assess the quality of writing in each reading? What are the strengths and weaknesses of each reading?
- What makes each of the readings "academic" as opposed to "popular"?
- Which of the readings did you find more interesting than the other? Why?
- If you found reading any of the arguments difficult, what made it hard to follow: its length, its language, its ideas, its structure, its assertions?

- How did any of the readings challenge or expand your understanding of spirituality?
- How are the readings similar in terms of their definitions of spirituality and/or religion? How are they different?

What Is Spirituality?

Bruce W. Speck

Bruce Speck is provost and vice president for academic and student affairs, Austin Peay State University, Clarksville, Tennessee. This essay first appeared in Spirituality in Higher Education: New Directions for Teaching and Learning.

The question posed in this chapter's title cannot be answered with a consensual definition. In fact, literature on spirituality in higher education offers various definitions. As Palmer (2003) says, "'Spirituality' is an elusive word with a variety of definitions—some compelling, some wifty, some downright dangerous" (p. 377). To investigate spirituality, I provide illustrative definitions, explain three points of tension that help explain divergent definitions, and suggest a way to categorize definitions according to the worldview a definition affirms.

Illustrative Examples

Greenstreet (1999) confirms a lack of consensus in defining spirituality when she says, "There are numerous definitions of the concept of spirituality; these vary in their degree of commonality but do not reflect a consensus of thought" (p. 649). Harlos (2000) calls spirituality an "intractably diffuse and deeply personal concept" (p. 614). Hicks (2003), "based on a reading of some one hundred articles on leadership and workplace spirituality," found a variety of terms were used to define spirituality. "In the abstract, few if any of these terms are objectionable," Hicks notes, "but, as abstractions, they provide little more precision than the word spirituality itself does" (p. 55). Like Hicks, others (Johnson, Kristeller, and Sheets, 2004; Laurence, 1999; Lemmer, 2002; Marcic, 2000; Narayanasamy, 1999; Tisdell, 2001), in reviewing literature on spirituality, cite a cacophony of definitions.

The following examples illustrate the definitional dilemma:

- Basically, it [spirituality] is the living out of the organizing story of one's life. In this definition, everyone has a spirituality. The organizing stories of our lives turn around that to which we are ultimately loyal and which we trust for our fulfillment (Bennett, 2003, p. xiii).
- . . . Spirituality is the experience of the transcendent, or the quality of transcendence, something that welcomes, but does not require, religious beliefs (Bento, 2000, p. 653).
- Spirituality is the place in our hearts that holds all of the questions about our purpose in the world and it is reflected in our actions (Campbell, 2003, p. 20).

- *Spirituality* refers to that noncorporal aspect of each human being that is separate from the mind. *Religion* refers to an organized set of doctrines around faith beliefs within an organization (Clark, 2001, p. 38).
- Spirituality can be understood as the ability to experience connections and to create meaning in one's life (Fried, 2001, p. 268).
- Spirituality is the inner experience of the individual when he or she senses a beyond, especially as evidenced by the effect of this experience on his or her behavior when he or she actively attempts to harmonize his or her life with the beyond (Lewis and Geroy, 2000, p. 684).
- By spirituality I mean a sense of compassion, nonviolence, truthfulness, loving kindness, being connected to the whole, and living a simple, peaceful harmonious life (Massoudi, 2003, p. 118).
- Spirituality is the pursuit of a trans-personal and trans-temporal reality that serves as the ontological ground for an ethic of compassion and service (Mayes, 2001, p. 6).
- Spirituality is the eternal human yearning to be connected with something larger than our own egos (Palmer, 2003, p. 377).

Clearly, a consensual definition of spirituality is lacking. To harmonize these definitions would be a herculean task because they point to competing worldviews that are not always fully articulated in the literature, helping explain why the definitions rely on abstractions that, as Hicks (2003) noted, "provide little more precision than the word *spirituality* itself does." We are left with a definitional dilemma.

This dilemma can be explained, in large part, by understanding three points of tension discussed in the literature on spirituality in higher education. How we respond to those three points of tension reveals something about our worldview and shapes the way we define spirituality.

Three Points of Tension

Spirituality, given its large metaphysical sweep, has the potential to posit sundry worldviews, not only because the term itself is an abstraction, open to various interpretations, but also because words with metaphysical import both arise from and inform worldviews. Literature on spirituality in higher education points to at least three points of tension that have helped shape various definitions of spirituality and various worldviews in the United States: separation of church and state, the reigning epistemology of higher education, and lack of faculty education in addressing spirituality.

Separation of Church and State. Despite the seemingly absolute barrier that the word *separation* implies in the phrase "separation of church and state," such is not the case. The Founders never intended to exclude or separate religion from the state; rather, they neither wanted to privilege a particular religious perspective nor to exclude secular perspectives (Mayes, 2001). Thus, the Founders were opposed to establishing a state-endorsed religious perspective and to not allowing freedom of dissent from a secular viewpoint. This attempt to balance competing interests is, of course, a continual walk on a tightrope. The high-wire juggling is complicated because "The authors of the Constitution and the Bill of Rights laid a framework to maintain the legal nonestablishment of religion, but they still assumed an effective cultural establishment of Christianity" (Hicks, 2003, p. 65). When the balancing act tilts toward religious expression, those fearful of the influence of religion on constitutional liberties attempt to redress the balance and vice versa. Marcic (2000) captures the uneasiness of this tension by referring to the obvious "squeamishness . . . in many people when the words *religion* and *God* are used" (p. 629). A like uneasiness accompanies the rhetoric of those who see the culture tilting toward an unabashed endorsement of secularism. Even highly regarded Justice Sandra Day O'Connor acknowledges the difficulty of separating religion from the government: "Speaking broadly about ceremonial prayer and symbols allowed in government buildings, she said, 'It's so hard to draw the line'" (Biskupic, 2005, 2A).

In public higher education, the supposed wall between church and state and the attendant confusion that issues from that misleading metaphor can create a chilling effect, what Lee, Matzkin, and Arthur (2004) describe as "fears of imposing one's so-called 'personal views,' violating laws regarding the separation of church and state." Such fears help explain why "educators have refrained from incorporating religion and spirituality into the[ir] institution[s]" (no page number). Indeed, Collins, Hurst, and Jacobson (1987) say, "The principle of separation of church and state has become so engrained that people say those words and diffuse any interest in the topics of spirituality and religion when nothing needs to be diffused" (p. 275). According to Palmer (2003), students are taught long before they enter academe to resist any questions concerning spiritual issues: ". . . Our students are told from an early age that school is not the place to bring their questions of meaning: take them home, to your religious community, or to your therapist, but do not bring them to school. So students learn, as a matter of survival, to keep their hearts hidden when in the groves of academe" (p. 379). In short, "Religious and spiritual inquiries are not considered to be intellectual endeavors; consequently, they receive little respect and attention in the academy" (Raper, 2001, p. 15).

The definitional dilemma merely adds confusion to an already chilling silence concerning the role of higher education in addressing the relationship between learning, teaching, religion, and spirituality. Indeed, critical terms are blurred, in part, "because of the fuzziness in the distinctions we draw between religion and spirituality" (Fried, 2001, p. 263). Part of the reason for that fuzziness can be attributed to an attempt to solve the separation problem by divorcing spirituality from religion. Thus, literature on spirituality in higher education regularly repeats the refrain "spirituality is not religion." But to make that stratagem work, spirituality is often defined in terms of personal commitment to "something." However, personal commitment does not exactly fit the definitional bill because the *telos* of spirituality, according to those who subscribe to personal commitment to something, cannot result in that something being merely individual fulfillment. A larger goal—generally a goal that encompasses the good of the social order—is introduced to rescue personal spiritual commitment from narcissism. Once rescued, however, the difference between social actions or even personal ethical conduct grounded in spirituality is extremely difficult to distinguish from the social actions or personal ethical conduct many religious people endorse. Little wonder that distinctions between spirituality and religion, despite the refrain that the two are separate, appear to be hazy at best.

Reigning Epistemology of Higher Education. This definitional dilemma is further exacerbated by what Chickering calls "unleavened doses of objectivity and empirical rationality" (2003, p. 41) in higher education. In fact, "Our overwhelming valuation of rational empiricism—a conception of truth as objective and external—and of knowledge as a commodity delegitimizes active public discussions of purpose and meaning, authenticity and identity, or spirituality and spiritual growth" (p. 44). Palmer (1987) calls objectivism in higher education a "seemingly bloodless epistemology" (p. 22). Elsewhere, Palmer (2003) notes that "the bright light of science has been almost exclusively focused on 'objective realities' such as technique, curricula, and cash, rather than on soulful factors such as relational trust" (p. 385). Thus, "the exploration of faith," according to Raper (2001), is seen "as anti-intellectual and politically risky" (p. 21).

As with the separation-between-church-and-state tension, the epistemological tension produces a chilling effect. For example, Zajonc (2003) believes that "formidable barriers block the integration of contemplation and spirituality into higher education" and notes that "the institutional barriers that do exist are mostly informal and take the form of academic peer pressure to eschew approaches involving spiritual or even moral and philosophical analysis [sic] of the disciplines. We should not underestimate the powerful effect this pressure has on the open exploration of important issues within the disciplines, especially by junior faculty. This is all the more ironic, and even tragic, because the academy ostensibly commits itself to completely open inquiry, yet quietly dismisses at the outset certain domains or methodologies as out-of-bounds" (p. 53).

In effect, the "seemingly bloodless epistemology" of higher education prohibits open, frank discussion of spirituality or religion unless, of course, those topics can be shoehorned into the premises of naturalism. Attempts at such shoehorning in literature on spirituality in higher education try to make the concept fit by appealing to personal beliefs. Under the bloodless epistemology, spirituality is tolerated as long as it remains a private concern. As Lindholm (2004) points out, ". . . the structure and culture of academia [have] encouraged faculty to act as if their most deeply held values and beliefs are irrelevant to their work" (p. 13). That is, deeply held values and beliefs that challenge the bloodless epistemology must be kept private and not intrude on serious academic work. Mayes (2001) concurs, citing scholarship that shows a "rather high degree of religious commitment among American scholars, [yet] many of them find that academic culture has constructed a variety of explicit and also tacit constraints against including these commitments in their scholarship." That such constraints "constitute a violation of the very concept of pluralism, which so many of us hold so dear in academic culture" (p. 14) appears to be just another irony of academic life that persists with little regard for its deleterious effect on academic freedom—and integrity.

This irony, however, is parallel to the definitional dilemma produced by the privatization of spirituality under the chilling effect of the separation of church and state. Again, religion has to be greatly marginalized or dismissed to make way for privatized spirituality. Thus, academics may not see themselves as religious but may identify themselves as spiritual. As Johnson, Kristeller, and Sheets (2004) point out, ". . . many social scientists and academics in general show a trend toward dichotomizing or polarizing religion and spirituality; that is, viewing them as opposites. This polarization is accompanied by a tendency to characterize spirituality as good, individualistic, liberating, and mature, while portraying religion as bad, institutionalized, constraining, and childish" (p. 3).

Spirituality, now liberated from religion, needs further to be liberated from the supernatural, a hallmark of religion. Thus, it is not surprising that "the exact role of the supernatural in defining spirituality has been a point of debate, with some authors arguing that a concept of the sacred is essential in defining spirituality . . . while others argue that spirituality can be completely atheistic and separate from any organized religious context" (Johnson, Kristeller, & Sheets, 2004, p. 3). That debate in academe is tilting heavily toward a nonsupernatural point of view, yet a point of view that can include "God terms," if the terms are inclusive. For example, Burrows (2001) affirms, "There is generally a sense of acceptance that God is acknowledged and defined by different individuals and groups in many ways such as the Higher Power, Buddha, Allah, the Force, or the Spirit of the Universe" (pp. 138–139). *God*, Burrows says, is a perfectly acceptable term if by using the term a person means a plurality of names that are assumed to point either to the same entity in the natural realm or to a personal idea divorced from the supernatural. It appears to be of little moment that many of those who bow to Allah, for example, find reprehensible bowing the knee to Buddha—and find it impossible to divorce Allah from a supernatural realm.

Tolerance and diversity are often cited to justify the nonsupernatural view of spirituality that, nonetheless, may be laced with terms carrying metaphysical freight. In the process of trying to separate spirituality from both religion and the supernatural, to ensure that spirituality is a matter of one's heart, individualism is affirmed. But because individualism can become narcissistic, spirituality must be directed toward the social good, if the academy is going to take this private concern with any seriousness.

Palmer (2003) provides a synthesis of the various points of epistemological tension when he concludes, "*What* one names this core of the human being is of no real consequence to me, because no one can claim to know its true name. But *that* one names it is, I believe, crucial. For 'it' is the ontological reality of being human that keeps us from regarding ourselves, our colleagues, or our students as raw material to be molded into whatever form serves the reigning economic or political regime" (pp. 377–378). There's little reason to debate what "it" is, as long as it serves the social good of promoting human dignity. To argue against this noble goal would be to betray humanity. But it remains, ironically, in Palmer's own words, "an elusive word with a variety of definitions" (2003, p. 377) and does not appear to help solve the definitional dilemma.

Lack of Faculty Education in Addressing Spirituality. Because of confusion about the constitutional issues regarding the role of spirituality in higher education and a dominating epistemology that brooks no meaningful discussion about spirituality unless, perhaps, spirituality is a private good, it is little wonder that faculty are unprepared to address what constitutes spirituality when the topic emerges during the educational enterprise. If spirituality is a legitimate academic concern, faculty should be provided insights into addressing the topic with students. Even in disciplines that could make a legitimate claim to helping students address the spiritual needs their future clients or patients will raise, faculty education in spirituality is virtually absent and absent again from the faculty's classrooms.

For example, "Few counselors are exposed to spirituality during their training . . . thus, they risk alienating clients who present with spiritual issues, particularly if the counselor is unaware of his or her own spirituality" (Souza, 2002, p. 213). In addition, "Many studies have highlighted the concern as to whether nurses are prepared to provide spiritual care" (Lemmer, 2002, p. 482). Pesut (2002), in speaking about obstacles to preparing nurses for caring for patients' spiritual needs, notes, "Barriers to integrating spiritual care into the curriculum may include the complexity of defining the concept within a multicultural society; the culture we live in that values secularism and materialism; the resource limitations experienced by many nursing programs; and the lack of models, faculty preparedness, and accountability" (p. 129). In short, "...there has been little thoughtful public recognition by faculty that this concern [supporting students' development of personal and spiritual values] should be addressed as part of their roles and responsibilities" (Stamm, 2003, p. 8).

Related issues, such as proselytizing students (Johnson, Kristeller, & Sheets, 2004; Lindholm, 2004; Mayes, 2001) and addressing students' concerns about their privacy regarding spirituality (Johnson & Mutschelknaus, 2001) are difficult to resolve if spirituality has no legitimate place in the curriculum. In fact, even designing faculty development opportunities requires not only acceptance of spirituality as an appropriate topic for academic discourse but also a narrowing of the definitions of spirituality.

Responding to the Points of Tension: Toward Consensual Definitions of Spirituality

Foundational to any definition of spirituality is the worldview from which the definition arises. Unfortunately, definitions of spirituality, even including the language in texts in which they are embedded, are often not attended by cogent statements that explain a scholar's worldview. Hints of what a scholar's worldview might be are suggestive at best, but worldviews, because they purport to provide a cohesive framework for understanding what exists, by necessity need to address seminal concerns. I suggest three concerns a worldview must address: what exists?, who or what is in charge?, and what is the purpose of existence? A great deal of the definitional dilemma can be solved by applying these three concerns to definitions of spirituality.

What Exists? To answer the question of what exists, two possibilities have to be entertained: the possibility of natural existence only and the possibility of natural and supernatural existence. I recognize that this is a simplistic approach to complex philosophical concepts, but for my present purpose, this rough categorization will do.

One possibility is that all that exists is the natural world, what Sagan (1980) calls the cosmos. If that is the case, spirituality must be defined in terms of the natural order. According to this worldview, no supernatural order exists, and therefore, the natural order is a closed system. Fried (2001) seems to endorse this naturalistic worldview by saying, "We need to discuss spirituality not because God exists, but because we exist and we need to create meaning for ourselves" (p. 277). An implication of

Fried's statement is that recourse to a supernatural order that would provide meaning is not possible.

The other possible way to understand what exists is to posit both a natural and a supernatural realm. The details of the relationship between these two realms vary given particular philosophical or theological traditions, but in virtually all cases, the supernatural realm is ontologically primary. Thus, the natural realm exists because it is derived from and sustained by the supernatural realm.

Who or What Is in Charge? In a naturalistic worldview, who or what is in charge can be answered only by referring to "natural" forces, whether nature or humans or a combination of both. Evolution is typically evoked as the force that causes the cosmos to change. Generally in the literature on spirituality in higher education, humans are the focal point of authority. In fact, "what particularly marks modern spirituality is its tendency toward individual interpretation and idiosyncratic experience" (Mayes, 2001, p. 12). Like Fried, Mayes locates authority in the individual. Individuals have the authority—the right, the responsibility, and the power—to make meaning. The problem of contested authority is difficult to solve when authority is vested in individuals *qua* individuals. The bumper sticker "Question Authority!" is a succinct (albeit undoubtedly unintended) statement of the dilemma of contested authority.

The question of authority when a supernatural realm exists is answered by appealing to the ontological primacy of the supernatural realm. The dependency of the natural realm on the supernatural realm is evidence of the ultimate authority vested in the supernatural realm. This does not mean that people do not have authority of various sorts, but their authority is derivative, and they are accountable to the supernatural realm, whether, for example, that accountability is a last judgment or reincarnation. In sum, "Spirituality may be thought of as being primarily unique to the individual and purely personal, or it may be conceived as having an external referent and normative basis for understanding spiritual truth" (Daniels, Franz, & Wong, 2000, p. 544).

What Is the Purpose of Existence? The question about purpose, under naturalistic presuppositions, cannot include an afterlife, so whatever counts for purpose only counts in relation to the natural order. Under naturalistic worldviews, ethics takes on high importance because how a person relates to the natural order is paramount. Dalton (2001), for example, stresses the ethical dimension of individual spirituality by saying,

> A spiritual quest that focuses primarily on self-definition and self-understanding fails to consider equally serious concerns about relationships with others and the search for transcendence that are central to that quest. If spirituality is regarded as essentially a private and introspective process, a kind of private journey of the soul, in which few if any moral claims are made upon the spiritual traveler, then the claim of spirituality as feel-goodness has some validity . . . but I think we fail as educators if we do not help students link the ethical claims of life and work with others to one's relationship with what is transcendent and sacred. (p. 23)

I take it that Dalton is not using the terms soul, *transcendent*, and sacred as pointing to a supernatural realm. However, by using such terms, Dalton introduces confusion about how his concept of spirituality should be understood. Indeed, the introduction of "God terms" to describe naturalistic worldviews creates confusion. For instance, when a person who espouses a naturalistic worldview uses terms like *sacred, spirit, God, transcendence*, and *spirituality*, the person is not speaking about a supernatural or transcendent order above or over the natural order. Yet, these terms, quite naturally, point to such an order. To qualify spirit as "the vital principle or animating force within living beings; that which constitutes one's unseen intangible being; the real sense or significance of something" (Scott, 1994, p. 64) is apt if no supernatural realm is in view. A definition of spirituality issuing from that definition of spirit should include a clear statement that confines spirituality to the natural order. It is helpful to acknowledge that "spirituality is often connected to things like meaning in life, which can be an entirely secular affair, or meditation, which can also be divorced from any specific religious context" (Johnson, Kristeller, & Sheets, 2004, p. 3). Indeed, definitions of spirituality grounded in a naturalistic worldview should be carefully crafted so that they cannot in good faith be misconstrued as allowing a realm beyond the natural.

The same principle holds true for definitions about spirituality grounded in a natural-supernatural worldview. Definitions that acknowledge the validity of a dualistic worldview should not fudge on either side of the dualism to minimize the other side. "Thus, spirituality is conceptualized as having vertical and horizontal dimensions. The vertical dimension reflects the relationship to God or a supreme being. The horizontal dimension reflects both our connectedness to others and nature, and to our intrapersonal connectedness . . ." (Pesut, 2002, p. 128). As Hicks (2003) warns, "Attempts to translate religiously particular values into common spiritual or secular values are reductionistic at best and inaccurate at worst" (p. 165), a warning that adherents to both worldviews should heed.

Conclusion

In suggesting that definitional dilemmas are rife in the literature on spirituality in higher education, I could be accused of stating the obvious. Unfortunately, the definitional dilemmas tend to undercut the obvious by appealing to tolerance and diversity, hallowed concepts today in the academy, that suggest unanimity is normative. By invoking these concepts, some scholars, it appears, want to erase difficulties that call into question their notions of tolerance and diversity. I assume such attempts to erase differences to establish tolerance and diversity are done with the best of intentions, but in any case the attempts are based on naïve notions of commonality.

Hicks (2003) drives this point home when he says, ". . . the claim that 'spirituality creates common ground' cannot be readily established without undertaking more work at least to address the philosophical and theological difficulties of the term and its definitional components. Authors who make broad and sweeping claims about spirituality should clarify the connections and coherence of their account" (p. 56).

Proponents of spirituality as a legitimate academic subject are asking too much of colleagues who are not warm to such a proposal if they cannot at least provide a coherent definition of spirituality grounded in an explicit, cogent worldview as the focal point of an academic dialogue. I have outlined an approach that provides guidance as we seek to solve the definitional dilemma. It may be that no consensual definition can be fashioned, given the two paradigmatic worldviews I have posited, but it should be the case that definitions of spirituality make explicit the presuppositions on which they are based, providing at least two distinct groups of definitions under the aegis of two paradigmatic worldviews.

References

Bennett, J. B. (2003). *Academic life: Hospitality, ethics, and spirituality.* Bolton, MA.: Anker.

Bento, R. F. (2002). The little inn at the crossroads: A spiritual approach to the design of a leadership course. *Journal of Management Education*, *24*(5), 650–661.

Biskupic, J. (2005, March 5). Commandments cases may hinge on 1 high court justice. *USA Today*, p. 2A.

Burrows, L. T. (2001). Dancing on the edge. In V. M. Miller & M. M. Ryan (Eds.), *Transforming Campus Life: Reflections on Spirituality and Religious Pluralism.* New York: Lang.

Campbell, L. H. (2003, April 21–25). The spiritual lives of artists/teachers. Paper presented at the Annual Meeting of the American Educational Research Association, Chicago.

Chickering, A. W. (2003, January-February). Reclaiming our soul." *Change*, 39–45.

Clark, R. T. (2001). The law and spirituality: How the law supports and limits expression of spirituality on the college campus. In M. A. Jablonski (Ed.), *The Implications of Student Spirituality for Student Affairs Practice.* New Directions for Student Services, no. 95. San Francisco: Jossey-Bass.

Collins, J. R., Hurst, J. C., & Jacobson, J. K. (1987). The blind spot extended: spirituality." *Journal of College Student Personnel, 28*(3), 274–276.

Dalton, J. C. (2001). Career and calling: Finding a place for the spirit in work and community. In M. A. Jablonski (Ed.), *The Implications of Student Spirituality for Student Affairs Practice.* New Directions for Student Services, no. 95. San Francisco: Jossey-Bass.

Daniels, D., Franz, R. S., & Wong, K. (2000). A classroom with a worldview: Making spiritual assumptions explicit in management education. *Journal of Management Education, 24*(5), 540–561.

Fried, J. (2001). Civility and spirituality." In V. M. Miller & M. M. Ryan (Eds.), *Transforming campus life: Reflections on spirituality and religious pluralism.* New York: Lang.

Greenstreet, W. M. (1999). Teaching spirituality in nursing: A literature review." *Nurse Education Today, 19*, 649–658.

Harlos, K. P. (2000). Toward a spiritual pedagogy: Meaning, practice, and applications in management education. *Journal of Management Education, 24*(5), 612–627.

Hicks, D. A. (2003). *Religion and the workplace: Pluralism, spirituality, leadership.* New York: Cambridge.

Johnson, P., & Mutschelknaus, M. (2001, March 14–17). Disembodied spirituality: Conflicts in the writing center. Paper presented at the Annual Meeting of the Conference on College Composition and Communication, Denver.

Johnson, T. J., Kristeller, J., & Sheets, V. L. (2005). Religiousness and spirituality in college students: Separate dimension with unique and common correlates. *Journal of College and Character, 1,* 1–36 [E-journal]. Retrieved from http://www.collegevalues.org/pdfs/Johnson.pdf.

Laurence, P. (1999). Can religion and spirituality find a place in higher education?" *About Campus, 4*(5), 11–16.

Lee, J. J., Matzkin, A., & Arthur, S. (2004). Understanding students' religious and spiritual pursuits: A case study at New York University. *Journal of College and Character, 1,* 1–33 [E-journal]. Retrieved from http://www.collegevalues.org/pdfs/Lee2.pdf.

Lemmer, C. (2002). Teaching the spiritual dimension of nursing care: A survey of U.S. baccalaureate nursing programs. *Journal of Nursing Education, 41*(11), 482–490.

Lewis, J. S., & Geroy, G. D. (2000). Employee spirituality in the workplace: A cross-cultural view for the management of spiritual employees. *Journal of Management Education, 24*(5), 682–694.

Lindholm, J. (2004). The role of faculty in college students' spirituality. *Journal of College and Character, 1* [E-journal]. Retrieved from http://www.collegevalues.org/articles.cfm?id=1221&a=1.

Marcic, D. (2000). God, faith, and management education. *Journal of Management Education, 24*(5), 628–649.

Massoudi, M. (2003). Can scientific writing be creative? *Journal of Science Education and Technology, 12*(2), 115–128.

Mayes, C. (2001). Cultivating spiritual reflectivity in teachers." *Teacher Education Quarterly, 28*(2), 5–22.

Narayanasamy, A. (1999). ASSET: A model for actioning spirituality and spiritual care education and training in nursing. *Nurse Education Today, 19*(4), 274–285.

Palmer, P. (1987). Community, conflict, and ways of knowing: Ways to deepen our educational agenda. *Change, 19*(5), 20–25.

Palmer, P. J. (2003). Teaching with heart and soul: Reflections on spirituality in teacher education. *Journal of Teacher Education, 54*(5), 376–385.

Pesut, B. (2002). The development of nursing students' spirituality and spiritual care-giving. *Nurse Education Today, 22,* 128–135.

Raper, J. (2001). Losing our religion: Are students struggling in silence? In V. M. Miller & M. M. Ryan (Eds.), *Transforming campus life: Reflections on spirituality and religious pluralism.* New York: Lang.

Sagan, C. (1980). *Cosmos.* New York: Random House.

Scott, K. T. (1994). Leadership and spirituality: A quest for reconciliation. In
    J. A. Conger & Associates (Eds.), *Spirit at work: Discovering spirituality in
    leadership.* San Francisco: Jossey-Bass.
Souza, K. Z. (2002). Spirituality in counseling: What do counseling students think
    about it?" *Counseling and Values, 46,* 213–217.
Stamm, L. (2003). Can we bring spirituality back to campus? Higher education's
    re-engagement with values and spirituality. *Journal of College and Character*
    [E-journal]. Retrieved from http://www.collegevalues.org/articles.cfm?
    a=1&id=1075.
Tisdell, E. J. (2001). Spirituality in adult and higher education. Washington, DC:
    Office of Educational Research and Improvement. (ED 459 370)
Zajonc, A. (2003, Winter). Spirituality in higher education: Overcoming the
    divide. *Liberal Education,* 50–58.

ADDITIONAL READING

Why Spirituality Deserves a Central Place in Liberal Education

Alexander W. Astin

Alexander Astin is the director of the Higher Education Research Institute at the University of California, Los Angeles.

Before explaining the assertion put forward in the title of this essay, let me first try to clarify what I mean by "spirituality." Since the term covers a lot of territory and means different things to different people, there's little point in trying to develop a precise definition. Instead, let me simply lay out the general territory and range of things that the word suggests to me.

To begin with, spirituality points to our *interiors,* by which I mean our subjective life, as contrasted to the objective domain of observable behavior and material objects that you can point to and measure directly. In other words, the spiritual domain has to do with human *consciousness*—what we experience privately in our subjective awareness. Second, spirituality involves our qualitative or *affective* experiences at least as much as it does our reasoning or logic. More specifically, spirituality has to do with the values that we hold most dear, our sense of who we are and where we come from, our beliefs about why we are here—the meaning and purpose that we see in our work and our life—and our sense of connectedness to each other and to the world around us. Spirituality can also have to do with aspects of our experience that are not easy to define or talk about, such things as intuition, inspiration, the mysterious, and the mystical. Within this very broad umbrella, virtually everyone qualifies as a spiritual being, and it's my hope that everyone—regardless of their belief systems—can find some personal value and educational relevance in the concept.

Education and human consciousness

One of the most remarkable things about the human consciousness is that each of us has the capacity to *observe* our thoughts and feelings as they arise in our consciousness. Why shouldn't cultivating this ability to observe one's own mind in action—becoming more self-aware or simply more "conscious"—be one of the central purposes of education?

It's difficult to see how most of our contemporary domestic and world problems can ever be resolved without a substantial increase in our individual and collective self-awareness. Self-awareness and self-understanding, of course, are necessary prerequisites to our ability to understand others and to resolve conflicts. This basic truth lies at the heart of our difficulty in dealing effectively with problems of violence, poverty, crime, divorce, substance abuse, and religious and ethnic conflict that continue to plague our country and our world.

Even a cursory look at our educational system makes it clear that the relative amount of attention that higher education devotes to the exterior and interior aspects of our lives has gotten way out of balance. Thus, while we are justifiably proud of our "outer" development in fields such as science, medicine, technology, and commerce, we have increasingly come to neglect our "inner" development—the sphere of values and beliefs, emotional maturity, moral development, spirituality, and self-understanding.

What is most ironic about all of this is that while many of the great literary and philosophical traditions that constitute the core of a liberal education are grounded in the maxim "know thyself," the development of self-awareness receives very little attention in our schools and colleges, and almost no attention in public discourse in general or in the media in particular. If we lack self-understanding—the capacity to see ourselves clearly and honestly and to understand why we feel and act as we do—then how can we ever expect to understand others?

Students, curriculum, and instruction

In exploring the connection between spirituality and higher education, a good way to start is to take a look at the interior lives of our students. If we look at how our students' *values* have been changing during recent decades (Astin, 1998), the good news is they have become strong supporters of both gender and racial equity and of students' rights in general, and most recently they have become much stronger supporters of gay rights. The bad news is that they have become much less engaged both academically and politically, much more focused on making a lot of money, and much *less* likely to concern themselves with "developing a meaningful philosophy of life." These contrasting values—the material and the existential—have literally traded places since the early 1970s, a time when developing a meaningful philosophy of life was the number one value for students. In other words, a focus on the spiritual interior has been replaced by a focus on the material exterior.

Putting more emphasis on students' interior development has enormous implications for how we approach student learning and development. In most institutions today the primary focus is on what students *do*: how well they perform on classroom exercises and examinations, whether they follow the rules and regulations, how many credits they receive, and so on. And while we invest a good deal of our pedagogical effort in developing the student's cognitive, technical, and job skills, we pay little if any attention to the development of "affective" skills such as empathy, cooperation, leadership, interpersonal understanding, and self-understanding. The reality of human consciousness, of course, is not simply that we can think and reason; on the contrary, the essence of being a sentient human is that we can *feel*, that we can experience joy and contentment, frustration and excitement, curiosity and love.

Recently, in connection with a book I've just completed on human consciousness (Astin, 2003), I took on the somewhat daunting task of reading through every word in a medium-sized English dictionary. What I was looking for were all of the different terms that our culture has developed for labeling our affective or feeling states. I eventually came up with a list of more than a thousand different words, which only begins to do justice to the incredibly rich diversity of feeling states that can arise in the human awareness. When you contemplate the different *combinations* of these feeling states that are possible in any given moment of awareness, the numerical possibilities for varying feeling states are staggering.

What was perhaps most surprising in my search for feeling words was the discovery that there are several dozen different affective states that have to do with *thinking*. Let me share just a brief sampling of these terms, and as I run down the list, ask yourself, "Is this something about the students' interior that a classroom teacher should be concerned about?" Surprised, doubtful, focused, reflective, skeptical, comprehending, mindful, astonished, unsure, interested, confused, amazed, curious, and—the feeling state that most frustrates those of us who teach—boredom. Clearly, this list makes it hard to argue that there is any such thing as "pure" cognition that can be studied in isolation from affect; on the contrary, it would appear that our thoughts and our reasoning are almost always taking place in some kind of affective "bed" or context.

Faculty, administrators, and institutions

For many years now I've been interested in educational transformation and reform, and nowhere is the importance of this issue of "the inner versus the outer" more obvious than in the case of our attempts to change institutions. When we talk about educational reform in the academy, for example, we usually focus heavily on exterior "structures" such as programs, policies, curricula, requirements, resources, and facilities. As a consequence, we ordinarily give little attention to the "interior" of the institution, by which I mean the *collective* or *shared* beliefs and values of the faculty that constitute the "culture" of the institution. Our research on institutional change and transformation suggests strongly that any effort to change structures has little chance of success if it ignores our collective interiors or culture. In other words, changing our institutions and programs necessarily requires us to change the academic culture as well.

A similar imbalance can be seen in the way we approach faculty development, where we typically think in terms of external matters such as scholarly activities, teaching techniques, and service to the institution and to the community. The internal aspects of the faculty member's development—values, beliefs, hopes, fears, and frustrations—get relatively little attention. It is probably important to acknowledge at this point that in many respects the way we conduct higher education is simply a reflection of the larger society.

It is probably no exaggeration to say that the modern world, and the United States in particular, has in recent years become increasingly focused on the external aspects of society: economics, acquisitiveness, competitiveness, etc., to the point where the human condition and the quality of life is judged primarily in terms of *things*. Higher education similarly tends to judge itself in materialistic terms: enrollments, funding, the test scores of our students, the publication record of our faculty, and our rankings in popularity polls.

Partly as a response to this external/materialistic emphasis and to the fragmentation that it generates, I see a movement gradually emerging in higher education where many academics find themselves actively searching for meaning and trying to discover ways to make their lives and their institutions more whole. I think this movement reflects a growing concern with recovering a sense of meaning in American society more generally. The particular "spiritual" questions that give rise to these concerns encompass a broad set of issues:

- How do we achieve a greater sense of community and shared purpose in higher education?
- How can we provide greater opportunities for individual and institutional renewal?
- What are the causes of the division and fragmentation that so many academics experience in their institutional and personal lives?
- What does it mean to be authentic, both in the classroom and in our dealings with colleagues?
- What are some of the practices and traditions that make it difficult for us to be authentic in an academic setting?
- What are some of the disconnections that higher education is experiencing in relation to the larger society? How might we better serve the public good?
- How can we help our students achieve a greater sense of meaning and purpose in their academic and personal lives?

Such questions make it clear that "spiritual" issues cover a wide range of questions, and that each person will view his or her spirituality in a unique way. For some academics, religious beliefs may indeed form the core of their spirituality; for others, such beliefs may play little or no part. *How* one defines his or her spirituality or, if you prefer, sense of meaning and purpose in life, is not the issue. The important point is that academia has for far too long encouraged us to lead fragmented and inauthentic lives, where we act either as if we are not spiritual beings, or as if our spiritual side is irrelevant to our vocation or work. Under these conditions, our work becomes divorced from our most deeply felt values and we hesitate to discuss issues of meaning, purpose, authenticity, wholeness, and fragmentation with our colleagues. At the same time, we likewise discourage our students from engaging these same issues among themselves and with us.

The Fetzer dialogues

In recognition of these problems, the Fetzer Institute a few years ago convened a series of retreat meetings where a diverse group of academics was encouraged to explore issues of meaning, purpose, and spirituality in the context of higher education. The steering group for these dialogues—now formally known as The Initiative for Authenticity and Spirituality in Higher Education (IASHE)—recently joined with two other organizations—Education as Transformation (EasT) and The Community for Integrative Learning and Action (CILA)—to form The Consortium on Spirituality in Higher Education. One outcome of our Fetzer dialogues was an in-depth study where we conducted personal interviews with seventy faculty members from four diverse colleges and universities (Astin & Astin, 1999). Our major finding from this study—that college faculty are eager to discuss issues of meaning, purpose, and spirituality—has been strongly reinforced by our experience at several national conferences where sessions have been convened to discuss these same issues.

Inspiration and creativity

If one spends even a little bit of time in serious contemplation of what goes on in one's conscious mind, it quickly becomes obvious that there must be another completely hidden part of the mind that does most of the work. Whatever one prefers to call this "other" mind—the unconscious, the nonconscious mind, the preconscious—its capabilities and its power are nothing short of awesome. It not only serves as a repository for all of our memories, motives, concepts, and beliefs, but it is also the source of our intuition, inspiration, creativity, and spirituality.

When we consider those vitally important human qualities that are implied by words like intuition, inspiration, and creativity, we are coming pretty close to what some people refer to as the "mystical" aspects of human experience. None other than Albert Einstein (2000) has said, "The most beautiful thing we can experience is the mysterious. It is the source of all true Art and Science."

If we academics are really serious when we claim that our institutions are devoted to advancing the arts and sciences, shouldn't we do everything we can to nurture and cultivate that mysterious, nonconscious part of the human psyche from which all of our inspiration and creativity emerges? Intuition is, of course, intimately connected to inspiration and creativity. While doing something creative can sometimes involve a good deal of logical thought or reasoning—a scientist, for example, who is attempting to devise a theory to explain certain observations—many people, especially those in the fine and performing arts, believe that thinking can actually *interfere* with creativity. Indeed, when you read personal accounts of what people experience in their waking consciousness during the creative process (see below), it becomes clear that intuition is almost always a part of that process.

Creativity is basically a process whereby we bring into existence something *new* or *original.* That "something" can be a creative product such as a painting, invention, essay, poem, sculpture, musical composition, dance routine, or theatrical production, but it can also be something less tangible such as a scientific theory, an idea for urban renewal, or a new way of teaching, mentoring, parenting, leading, collaborating, mediating, or serving those in need. Viewed in this way, *creativity is (or should be) central to the goals of liberal learning.* Indeed, *creativity is a fundamental part of human existence* or, as several people have observed, "your life is your own greatest work of art."

That creativity is closely connected to the mystical and the spiritual becomes obvious when we look at verbatim accounts of what people in various fields experience during the process of creating:

- a painter/sculptor: "There's something flowing through you that's not you. To me, the feeling is tangible proof of the existence of spirit: something we can tap into that's beyond ourselves and our senses. The highest goal we can aspire to is to be transmitter of that" (Miller, 1997).
- a writer: "I think creativity is spiritual . . . a synonym for inspiration . . . suddenly it comes clear to me what I need to say and how to say it. I feel awe when this happens, it's an inspiring experience. . . . I'm tempted to say it comes from God. For me this is an experience of divine self-disclosure" (Wakefield, 1996).
- composer Johannes Brahms: "I . . . feel that a higher power is working through me. . . . It cannot be done merely by will power working through the conscious mind . . . I immediately feel vibrations that thrill my whole being. . . . Those vibrations assume the forms of distinct mental images . . . the ideas flow in upon me, directly from God . . . measure by measure the finished product is revealed to me . . . the conscious mind is in temporary abeyance and the subconscious is in control, for it is through the subconscious mind . . . that the inspiration comes. I have to be careful, however, not to lose consciousness, otherwise the ideas fade away" (Abell, 1987).
- composer Richard Strauss: "When in my most inspired moods, I have definite compelling visions, involving a higher selfhood. I feel at such moments that I am tapping the source of Infinite and Eternal energy from which you and I and all things proceed. Religion calls it God" (Abell, 1987).

What are we to make of such accounts? What are the implications of such accounts for higher education? While some academics may be inclined to view the mystical and the spiritual as "irrational," the processes of intuition and creativity are, in fact, more *trans*rational than *ir*rational. The point here is that the mystical or spiritual aspects of our conscious experience are by no means contrary to, or otherwise opposed to, rationality; rather, they *transcend* rationality. Thus, when a composer writes a great piece of music, the inspiration that gives rise to the music is a trans- or nonrational process, but in the process of committing the new music to paper the composer does not therefore ignore all of the rational and logical rules of harmony and theory. In the same way, the painter does not ignore the rational rules of color mixing or perspective, nor does the novelist ignore the rational rules of grammar and sentence structure.

Toward a more spiritual academe

How, then, do we begin to give greater emphasis to these neglected aspects of our conscious experience? As it happens, there are several recent developments in higher education that suggest that we may be ready to pay more attention to our inner lives and those of our students. One of these is the movement to redirect the attention of faculty and staff away from teaching and more in the direction of *learning*. Another closely related trend is the shift in emphasis away from the individual teacher and learner toward learning *communities*. While some of the reformers who have been promoting these changes might wonder at the suggestion that they are advocating a more "spiritual" approach to pedagogy, these innovations are certainly headed in the right direction: to shift our attention away from what we academics do toward a greater concern not only for the interiors of our students, but also toward seeing the entire educational process in a more holistic way. These reforms thus redirect our attention more in the direction of the human *connectedness* that is so basic, not just to the learning process, but also to spirituality. The people involved in these movements are natural allies for those of us who would like to see spiritual issues given a more central place in our institutions.

Another promising trend is the growing popularity of "Freshman 101" courses. In this case, we are encouraging students to look at their education in a more holistic way, and to make deeper connections between their academic work and their sense of meaning and purpose in life.

One final set of potential allies is the growing numbers of academics who are involved in the field of *service learning*. Longitudinal research on students suggests that this unique kind of pedagogy comes closer than anything we've looked at in the past four decades to being a pedagogical panacea: Almost all aspects of the student's academic, personal, and moral development are favorably influenced by participation in service learning, and the teachers themselves are also often transformed by teaching such courses (Astin & Sax, 1998; Astin, Sax, & Avalos, 1999; Astin, Vogelgesang, Ikeda, & Yee, 2000).

Two aspects of the service learning experience appear to be especially relevant to issues of spirituality. First, the entire process is built around *connectedness*, not only between the students and the service recipients but also among the students themselves. Moreover, the pedagogical key to an effective service learning experience appears to be the use of personal *reflection*: What did the service experience mean to you, not only in terms of the academic content of the course, but also in terms of who you are, why you are a student, and what kind of life you want to lead? The most powerful service learning experiences turn out to be those that combine individual reflection—keeping journals, writing integrative essays about the service experience, etc.—with group sessions, where students collectively reflect on the meaning of their service experience.

This growing awareness of the importance of spirituality in higher education was recently underscored by the Templeton Foundation through its award of a $1.9 million grant to UCLA's Higher Education Research Institute to support a large-scale longitudinal study of spiritual development in college undergraduates. A pilot study of 3,700 students enrolled at forty-six colleges and universities was initiated in spring 2003, and a full-scale assessment of 90,000 students enrolling at 150 institutions will be initiated in fall 2004. (See www.spirituality.ucla.edu)

Conclusion

Perhaps the most important thing to keep in mind about spirituality it that is touches directly on our sense of *community*. More than anything else, giving spirituality a central place in our institutions will serve to strengthen our sense of connectedness with each other, our students, and our institutions. This enrichment of our sense of community will not only go a long way toward overcoming the sense of fragmentation and alienation that so many of us now feel, but will also help our students to lead more meaningful lives as engaged citizens, loving partners and parents, and caring neighbors.

References

Abell, A. M. (1987). *Talks with great composers.* New York: Philosophical Library.

Astin, A. W. (1998). The changing American college student: Thirty-year trends, 1966–1996. *The Review of Higher Education, 21*(2), 115–135.

Astin, A. W. (2003). *Mindworks: Becoming more conscious in an unconscious world.* Unpublished manuscript.

Astin, A. W. & Astin, H. S. (1999). *Meaning, purpose and spirituality in the lives of college faculty.* Los Angeles: Higher Education Research Institute.

Astin, A. W. & Sax, L. J. (1998, May/June). How undergraduates are affected by service participation. *Journal of College Student Development, 39*(3),

Astin, A. W., Sax, L. J., & Avalos, J. (1999). Long-term effects of volunteerism during the undergraduate years. *The Review of Higher Education,* Winter, *22*(2), 187–202.

Astin, A. W., Vogelgesang, L. J., Ikeda, E. K., & Yee, J. A. (2000). *How service learning affects students: Executive summary.* Los Angeles: Higher Education Research Institute.

Einstein, A. (2000). What I believe. In A. Calaprice. (Ed.), *The expanded quotable Einstein.* Princeton: Princeton University Press.

Miller, E. P. (1997, April 7). The clear path to creativity: An interview with Dan Wakefield. *The Sun.*

Wakefield, D. (1996). *Creating from the spirit: A path to creative power in art and life.* New York: Ballantine.

Something to write about . . .

1. Using the readings found at the end of this chapter as a starting point, write an argumentative essay on the topic of spirituality. Your teacher may also want you to base your paper on your own knowledge and experience or to conduct additional research.

2. Using the tools for choosing and narrowing a topic develop a proposal for a definition argument you can write in class. This proposal should identify your topic, indicate why it is an important topic worth exploring, and how you will develop your argument. If your teacher accepts your proposal, write that argument using the types of sources your teacher specifies.

3. Identify a current debate over the definition of some term or idea. You may hear about it through the media or through conversations with friends. Briefly summarize this debate and choose one or two aspects of the topic you might want to examine by writing a definition argument. Have your teacher approve your topic before you write the paper.

WRITING CAUSAL ARGUMENTS

WHAT ARE CAUSAL ARGUMENTS?

Why did something happen? Why does it continue to occur? What resulted or is likely to result from some action or condition? These are the kinds of questions you address when you write causal arguments. Questions of cause or effect can be difficult to answer because causes are rarely simple or uncomplicated and effects are hard to define or predict.

Causal arguments assume a range of forms in classes across the curriculum:

- What caused the great dinosaur extinction to occur at the end of the Cretaceous Period?
- What are the primary causes and likely consequences of schoolyard bullying?
- What changes in American culture over the past century might have contributed to the rising number of children diagnosed with depression?
- What has brought about the rise in private home ownership among minority groups in America over the past decade and what does it mean for the country's future?
- Why are horror movies always so popular with American audiences? Are there any negative consequences associated with watching films like these?
- Obesity is a major health problem in many Western countries—why is it occurring and what are the likely consequences?

As you can see, some causal arguments ask you to focus on causes; some ask you focus on effects or consequences; still others ask you to focus on both.

While you might have the knowledge and experience to successfully argue a position on one or more of these questions, chances are you would need to engage in extensive research and reflection to form and persuasively defend a response, especially if you are addressing an academic audience. To write an effective causal argument, you need to know your subject matter well, including facts and opinions that call into question your own thesis.

FORMS OF ARGUMENTS FOCUSING ON CAUSES

Arguments over causes can assume many different forms, but the most common are summarized below.

1. Argue that A caused or will cause B

    With this type of argument, you start with a given situation, phenomena, or event and claim that it has brought about or will bring about a particular result:

    ■ *Overly stringent punishments imposed on Germany following World War I helped bring about World War II.*

    ■ *If current tax breaks for all American citizens are passed, the economy will likely expand, thus actually increasing the total tax revenue taken in by the federal government.*

2. Argue that A, B, and C caused or will cause D

    With this type of argument, instead of investigating a single cause, you examine several, exploring how each contributed to the same effect. You may contend that all of the causes are equally significant or that some are more important than others.

    ■ *While industrial pollution contributes to a decline in polar bear populations, other causes might include solar activity and long-range weather patterns.*

    ■ *Lower interest rates, lower unemployment rates, and a rise in real, after-tax income brought about a rise in consumer confidence.*

3. Argue that A, not B, caused or will cause C

    With this type of claim, you examine several possible causes, arguing in favor of some and against others.

    ■ *Though some have argued that a decline in teen pregnancy rates has caused the recent decrease in juvenile crime rates across America, a more likely cause is the improved economy.*

    ■ *His army's exhausted state did not cause Harold's defeat at Hastings; the loss was actually due to the Normans' superior armaments and leadership skills.*

4. Argue that A caused B which caused C which resulted or will result in D

    In this type of argument, you examine a series of interrelated cause-effect relationships, explaining how this causal chain will bring about or has brought about certain results

    ■ *Global warming will likely cause a decline in polar bear populations across the Artic because as Artic ice recedes, polar bears will lose their natural habitats and food resources, greatly diminishing their chances of survival in the wild.*

    ■ *The invention of the elevator is responsible for the increase in population density that characterizes modern cities: with elevators, multistory buildings became a viable option in city planning, greatly increasing the number of people who could live in a building and the number of buildings that could occupy any given space.*

FORMS OF ARGUMENTS FOCUSING ON EFFECTS

As you might expect, effect arguments are closely related to cause arguments. Instead of arguing that A caused B, in an effect argument, you claim that A resulted from or will result from B. If you are more interested in presenting an argument concerning the results of some action, condition, phenomenon, or situation, you will write an argument that focuses on effects. These arguments can assume a range of forms; below are some of the more common you will encounter in college.

1. Argue that A was or will be a likely effect of B
   In this type of argument, you assert that one thing was or will be a consequence of some other action or condition.
   - *One effect of America's withdrawal from Vietnam in 1975 was a huge increase in the number of "boat people," refugees fleeing the country to avoid Communist persecution and pursue political freedom.*
   - *The number of polar bears living in the Artic will sharply decrease because of environmental changes associated with industrial pollution.*
2. Argue that A, B, and C were or will be likely effects of D
   In this type of argument, you assert that several effects will likely result from a single action or condition.
   - *An increase in the number of boat people seeking freedom, a decrease in American prestige, and a loss of faith in government were all effects of the United States' withdrawal from the Vietnam War.*
   - *The number of polar bears living in the Artic, the amount of food production in the American Midwest, and the acreage of livable shoreline space will all decrease due to environmental changes associated with global warming.*
3. Argue that A, not B, was or will be an effect of C
   If you were working on this type of argument, you would argue in favor of one or more effects and against others.
   - *Though some have argued that the recent decrease in juvenile crime rates across America resulted from a decline in teen pregnancy rates, it is more likely a consequence of an improved economy.*
   - *Harold's defeat at Hastings resulted from the Norman's superior armaments and leadership skills, not from his army's exhaustion.*
4. Argue that A was or will be a likely effect of B, C, and D
   With this final type of effect argument, you would claim that a particular effect is attributable to multiple causes.
   - *The American Civil War was the inevitable consequence of regional economic differences, disputes over states' rights, and the abolitionist movement.*
   - *The quality of health care in America will continue to decline unless more citizens are insured, prenatal care improves, and preventative medical care increases.*

The various forms of cause and effect arguments are summarized in Figure 12.1 below.

TYPES OF CAUSES

As you write causal arguments, consider which causes are immediate and remote and which are necessary and sufficient. Understanding which types of causes you are working with in your essays can help you produce more effective arguments.

FIGURE 12.1

Forms of Arguments Focusing on Causes or Effects

Forms of Arguments Focusing on Causes	Forms of Arguments Focusing on Effects
A caused or will cause B	A was or will be a likely effect of B
A, B, and C caused or will cause D	A, B, and C were or will be likely effects of D
A, not B, caused or will cause C	A, not B, was or will be an effect of C
A caused B which caused C which resulted or will result in D	A was or will be a likely effect of B, C, and D

Immediate and Remote Causes

An immediate cause is closely related to an effect in time and/or space; a remote cause is further removed. While immediate causes may seem easy to identify, be cautious. Do not confuse cause with correlation: just because one thing precedes another in time does not mean that it caused the second thing to occur (logicians have a special name for this type of erroneous reasoning or fallacy: *post hoc ergo propter hoc*—after this therefore on account of this). Immediate causes can also be difficult to identify simply because there may be many to choose among. Remote causes are further removed from the event in time and/or space and are often linked to effects through complicated causal chains—their relationship to an effect may not be immediately clear or easy to determine.

Consider, for example, the cause of World War I. Was it the 1914 assassination of Archduke Franz Ferdinand in Sarajevo? Most historians would say that was the immediate cause of hostilities breaking out between the Entente Powers of France, Russia, and Great Britain and the Central Powers of the Austro-Hungarian, German, Bulgarian, and the Ottoman Empire. However, they would also point out that the underlying, remote causes of the war were much more complex, a set of rivalries and competing political and colonial interests that had been building since at least the time of Napoleon. So to say that Ferdinand's assassination *caused* World War I would be only partially true.

Necessary and Sufficient Causes

A necessary cause must be present for the effect to occur but its mere presence does not guarantee the effect. For example, oxygen is a necessary cause for a fire—without oxygen, no fire will ignite. However, the presence of oxygen alone does not immediately result in a conflagration. Consider possible necessary causes of divorce—adultery, poverty, trauma. Many marriages, however, survive these conditions—adultery, poverty, or trauma alone do not always result in divorce. Sufficient causes are those that in and of themselves can bring about a particular result: decapitation is a sufficient cause of death.

As you identify possible causes for a particular effect, consider which are necessary and which are sufficient. If a cause is necessary, what other conditions must exist for the effect to occur? Answering that question will help you identify a range of causes to consider. When examining sufficient causes, identify what makes it sufficient. In other words, why does it always bring about that particular effect? Answering that question will help you understand differences among sufficient causes and identify those you feel are most significant to the effect you are examining.

WRITING A CAUSAL ARGUMENT
A Model Process for Writing Causal Arguments
Step 1: Analyze the Assignment

First, determine the nature and purpose of the assignment. Are you being asked to develop an argument concerning causes or effects? Are you to argue in support of several causes or effects, to argue in support of some and against others, or to examine several and argue in support of only one or two?

Next, determine the assignment's intended audience. What can you assume about your readers' background, including their knowledge of the topic, interests, and biases? Identifying your intended audience will help you gather appropriate information, choose which causes or effects to examine, form the most persuasive reasons to support your claims, and select the most effective evidence to incorporate into your essay.

Finally, what choice of topics do you have? Is one prescribed or will you develop one on your own? How are you supposed to support your argument—with research or with your own knowledge and experience? If you are to incorporate research into your essay, what types of sources are acceptable and which are not?

Step 2: Select a Topic

When you have a choice of topics, find one that interests you and about which there is some discussion or debate. To find a suitable topic, you can start by answering the questions listed in the heuristic below (Figure 12.2). Answer as many as of these questions as you can; your responses may help you find an interesting topic to write about. Whatever topic you end up choosing to explore, get your teacher's approval before you begin working on your essay.

Step 3: Gather Information

Through some combination of research and reflection, you will need to gather information on both the subject of your argument and its likely causes and/or effects, depending on the assignment.

FIGURE 12.2

Cause/Effect Topic Heuristic

1. Choose any current event covered in the news. What caused it to occur?
2. What caused a particular historical event to occur?
3. What were the event's consequences?
4. Why has some trend become popular?
5. What are the likely consequences of this trend?
6. What are the likely consequences of a particular governmental or school policy?
7. Why was that policy enacted?
8. Has someone assigned a cause to something that you think is incorrect?
9. In a dispute over something's causes or likely effects, which position do you endorse?
10. When have you ever wondered what caused something to happen?

Gather Background Information on the Subject of Your Essay

To write a persuasive causal argument, you may first need to gather information on the subject of your essay. For example, suppose you are required to write an argument concerning the cause of the War of Spanish Succession? You cannot write this essay if you know nothing about the conflict. Before you begin to investigate the war's causes, you will need to research the war itself. Until you have studied the war in some depth, you will not be able to critically evaluate competing claims about its cause.

Gather Information Concerning Causes or Effects

As you investigate the causes or effects of your subject, use these questions to guide your research. Answering them will help you gather the information you need to write your essay.

What do authorities say about the causes or effects of your subject? Consult a range of sources to obtain expert opinion on the causes or effects of your subject. Carefully examine their assertions, support, and reasoning. Because persuasive causal arguments are typically developed by writers who have a thorough understanding of the subject they are addressing, surveying expert opinion is especially helpful when writing this type of essay.

What is the point of contention among competing assertions concerning causes or effects? Causes and effects are rarely simple and uncomplicated, so expect authorities to disagree. Part of your job is to assess these competing arguments and decide which are most informed or persuasive. As you examine what others have written on the topic, identify points of contention. If authorities disagree over the causes or effects of your subject, what is the basis of the disagreement?

How has the debate over the causes or effects of your subject changed over time? Look for trends in the debate over the causes and effects of your subject. Were certain explanations popular at one time only to fall out of favor? Has recent research or thought cast doubt on earlier interpretations or arguments? Have new findings or events caused experts to change their arguments? How so?

What can you add to any ongoing debate concerning the subject's causes or effects? When you write your argument, how will you be advancing the conversation concerning your subject's causes or effects? Are you summarizing the discussion or are you synthesizing existing interpretations in some new way? Are you advancing a position of your own concerning the subject's causes or effects?

Reflect on Causes or Effects

Not every causal argument you write in college will require outside research. At times you will base your argument on your own knowledge and experience or on material you have covered in class. When this is the case, you will generate material for your essay through careful, critical self-reflection. Below are some questions that might aid your reflection.

What do you know about the subject? Causal arguments address the causes and/or effects of some event or phenomena. What do you know about the subject of your essay? What opinions do you hold concerning the subject? On what are your opinions based?

What might be possible causes or effects? Brainstorm possible causes or effects, writing down as many ideas as possible, no matter how silly or outlandish. From this list, you can choose several to consider more carefully and possibly include in your argument. Don't settle for the first causes or effects that come to mind—the best insights usually result from careful, sustained reflection.

Invention Grid

As you gather information for your argument, you might fill out an invention grid such as the one offered below (Figure 12.3). Your goal is to fill in every space on the grid based on information you have gathered through research and/or reflection. Working horizontally, you would first state one possible cause or effect then briefly explain how or why it caused or resulted from the subject. You would then write down any support you have found for the contention that it is a cause or effect. In the final two grids, you would summarize any objections to your claim and indicate how you would address these opposing views.

FIGURE 12.3

Invention Grid
Causal Argument

Subject: _____

	What It Is	Explanation	Support	Objections or Questions	Rebuttal
Cause or Effect 1					
Cause of Effect 2					
Cause of Effect X					

Step 4: Evaluate Possible Causes and Effects

After you have generated a list of possible causes or effects, you need to evaluate them to determine which are clearer, more reasonable, better supported, or more persuasive than others. Answering these questions will help you choose the most effective ones to use in your essay:

- Which causes or effects get mentioned more often than others?
- Which causes or effects seem to be most authoritative and best supported?
- Which causes or effects seem most reasonable or logical?
- Given your intended audience and purpose, which causes or effects would prove most persuasive?
- Which causes are immediate and remote, which are necessary and sufficient?

Step 5: Develop a Thesis

Your thesis statement, will indicate whether you will present an argument concerning causes, effects, or both. If you are arguing about causes, an open thesis statement might read something like this:

> **The most likely cause of global warming today is man-made pollution.**

A closed thesis statement on the same topic might read like this:

> **Both current scientific study of the climate and geological studies of the Earth's past indicate that the most likely cause of global warming today is man-made pollution.**

If you were going to examine counter-arguments as well, an open thesis might read like this:

Though not all scientists agree, the most likely cause of global warming is man-made pollution.

A closed thesis statement along the same lines might read like this:

Though some scientists argue that changes in the polar icecaps and ocean currents are due to naturally occurring cycles of climate change, the most likely cause of these phenomena and others associated with global warming is man-made pollution.

Thesis statements for arguments concerning effects can be just as varied:

- Open thesis
  Banning the private ownership of firearms is likely to result in higher crime rates.

- Closed thesis
  Because criminals will know that their victims are likely unarmed, crimes rates will increase if the government bans the private ownership of firearms.

- Open thesis that includes a counter argument
  Through many suggest that banning the private ownership of firearms will reduce crime, experience shows that just the opposite is true—crime rates will actually increase if such an act is taken.

- Closed thesis that includes counter arguments
  Those wishing to ban the private ownership of firearms are likely correct in their assertion that removing guns from the home will decrease the number of accidental shootings, but are not correct in their assertions that such an act will reduce overall crime rates; in fact, experience shows that just the opposite effect is likely to occur.

Step 6: Organize Your Argument

Once you have chosen the causes or effects you will address in your argument and have drafted a thesis statement, consider how you will organize your essay. If your argument is focusing on one or more possible causes or effects, a block outline of your essay might look something like the one presented in Figure 4.

Following the opening section of you essay, you would present an argument supporting each cause or effect you have decided to include. You would present each cause or effect as a claim and support that assertion with reasons, evidence, and explanations. Finally, you would address likely questions or objections your readers might raise concerning your assertions. You would conclude your argument by reasserting your thesis and again garnering reader interest.

FIGURE 12.4	**BOX OUTLINE**

Causal Argument

One or More Causes or Effects
Opening Section

Strategy you will employ to engender reader interest

Thesis: Your thesis statement concerning the subject's cause(s) or effect(s)

Background Section

Provide your readers with necessary background information on the subject of your essay

Cause or Effect Section

Cause or Effect 1: The first cause or effect you argue in favor of stated as a claim

Reason 1: First reason you offer in support of this claim

  Evidence: Support for first reason

  Explanation: How the evidence supports this reason

Reason X: Last reason you offer in support of this claim

  Evidence: Support for this last reason

  Explanation: How the evidence supports this reason

Objections or Questions

Rebuttals

Cause or Effect X: The last cause or effect you argue in favor of stated as a claim

Reason 1: First reason you offer in support of this claim

Evidence: Support for first reason

Explanation: How the evidence supports this reason

Reason X: Last reason you offer in support of this claim

Evidence: Support for last reason

Explanation: How the evidence supports this reason

Objections or Questions

Rebuttals

Closing Section

Strategy you will employ to conclude the essay

If you plan to examine several causes or effects in your argument, endorsing some and rejecting others, the structure becomes more complicated. You would present your thesis in the opening section of the essay then examine the causes or effects one at a time, beginning with those you plan to reject and ending with the ones you endorse. As you examine a cause or effect you ultimately reject, you would first present an argument in its favor, providing reasons some might offer in its support. However, you would then explain why you reject it, again offering reasons and evidence in support of your assertion. You would also address possible objections to your claims. As you examine a cause or effect you support, you would offer reasons and evidence to back up your assertion and again address likely objections to your claims. Figure 12.5 presents one possible organizational strategy for this type of argument.

FIGURE 12.5	**BOX OUTLINE**

Causal Argument

Endorsing Some Causes/Effects and Rejecting Others
Opening Section

   Strategy you will employ to engender reader interest

   Thesis: Statement indicating which causes/effects you will reject and which ones you will endorse

Background Section

   Provide your readers with necessary background information on the subject of your essay

Possible Causes/Effects Section

   Possible Cause or Effect 1: First cause or effect you examine but ultimately reject stated as a claim

   Supporting Reason 1: First reason you offer in support of this claim
   Evidence: Support for first reason
   Explanation: How the evidence supports this reason
   Supporting Reason X: Last reason you offer in support of this claim
   Evidence: Support for last reason
   Explanation: How the evidence supports this reason
   Opposing Reason 1: First reason you offer opposing the claim
   Evidence: Support for first reason
   Explanation: How the evidence supports this reason

(continued)

⊘ **BOX OUTLINE**

Causal Argument *(continued)*

Opposing Reason X: Last reason you offer opposing the claim

Evidence: Support for last reason

Explanation: How the evidence supports this reason

Objections or Questions

Rebuttals

Possible Cause or Effect X: Last cause or effect you examine but ultimately reject stated as a claim

Supporting Reason 1: First reason you offer in support of this claim

Evidence: Support for first reason

Explanation: How the evidence supports this reason

Supporting Reason X: Last reason you offer in support of this claim

Evidence: Support for last reason

Explanation: How the evidence supports this reason

Opposing Reason 1: First reason you offer opposing the claim

Evidence: Support for first reason

Explanation: How the evidence supports this reason

Opposing Reason X: Last reason you offer opposing the claim

Evidence: Support for last reason

Explanation: How the evidence supports this reason

Objections or Questions

Rebuttals

Actual Causes/Effects Section

Actual Cause or Effect 1: First cause or effect you endorse stated as a claim

Supporting Reason 1: First reason you offer in support of this claim

Evidence: Support for first reason

Explanation: How the evidence supports this reason

Supporting Reason X: Last reason you offer in support of this claim

Evidence: Support for last reason

Explanation: How the evidence supports this reason

Objections or Questions

Rebuttals

Actual Cause or Effect X: Last cause or effect you endorse stated as a claim

Supporting Reason 1: First reason you offer in support of this claim

Evidence: Support for first reason

Explanation: How the evidence supports this reason

Supporting Reason X: Last reason you offer in support of this claim

(continued)

BOX OUTLINE

Causal Argument *(continued)*

Evidence: Support for last reason

Explanation: How the evidence supports this reason

Objections or Questions

Rebuttals

Closing Section

Strategy you will employ to conclude the essay

Step 7: Draft the argument.

Opening Section

In the opening section of your argument, you have several related goals: introduce the topic of your essay, state your thesis, and capture reader interest. To capture reader interest in a causal argument, writers often employ one of these strategies: offer an overview of the current situation, offer an historical overview of the subject, identify a central question in the debate over the cause or effect, offer an interesting quotation, or establish the importance of the topic.

Body

In the body of your essay, provide your readers with background information on the subject of your essay and present your argument concerning its causes or effects. As you prepare to write the background section, ask yourself two questions:

- What do my readers need to know about the subject of my essay in order to understand my discussion of its causes or effects?
- What information regarding my subject can I provide to engage my readers' interest and help them understand the importance of my argument?

Answering these two questions will help you determine what information to include in this section of your essay.

In the next section of your essay, you will examine one cause or effect at a time. As you do, you have several goals: introduce the cause or effect, indicate whether you will argue in favor of or against it, present and support reasons for your position, explain the link between your claims and grounds, and answer likely questions about or possible objections to your position.

Closing Section

You have several goals when crafting a conclusion: bring your argument to a graceful end, remind readers of your primary assertions, and recapture or maintain reader interest. Some of the more common strategies academic writers use to conclude causal arguments include these: restate your thesis and summarize your essay, call for action, stress the importance of your argument, or offer an interesting quotation.

Step 8: Revise your argument.

Don't try to revise every element of your causal argument at once; inevitably, you will miss opportunities to improve your essay if you do.

Revise Content and Structure

First, review the assignment's rhetorical situation: What are you being asked to accomplish in the argument? Next, review your essay focusing only on the argument's content and structure, answering the following questions:

- How well does the essay reflect my intentions? How clearly and effectively does it put forward the argument I want to advance?
- Given my intended audience, what parts of my argument need further elaboration or support?
- Which terms, if any, do I need to explain more clearly? Which lines of reasoning do I need to clarify? Which reasons and what evidence do I need to explain more completely?
- How effectively have I structured my argument? Will readers be able to follow my line of thought?
- How well do my topic sentences guide my readers through my essay and link each new reason or assertion to both my thesis and the preceding section of my essay?
- How can I alter the structure of my essay to aid my argument?

Revise for Clarity and Correctness

Once you have revised your essay for content and structure, turn your attention to your sentences, word choice, and punctuation. Read through your essay again, this time considering the following questions:

- Which sentences can be clearer or more economical?
- Which terms, abbreviations, or technical language might my readers find confusing or problematic? How can I clarify them?
- How correct, clear, and effective are the words I have used?
- How can I improve my argument by revising my sentences?
- How appropriate is my tone in the essay, given my audience and purpose?
- What grammar, usage, and punctuation errors do I need to address?

Revise Documentation

Read through your essay again, this time checking your documentation of the source material. Answer the following questions:

- Have I documented all the material that needs to be documented, including all quoted and paraphrased passages?
- Is the form and format of my documentation correct?
- Is my bibliography or works cited list complete, correctly formatted, and correctly punctuated?

Revision Checklist

You will find a revision checklist for causal arguments in Appendix 1.

Common Errors to Avoid When Writing a Causal Argument

False Cause

Student writers unfamiliar with the subject they are addressing frequently confuse causes with effects when writing causal arguments. Misunderstanding the logic of causation, they assert that one thing caused another when, in fact, both are effects of a single cause or are totally unrelated. For example, consider this claim: Daphne's depression was caused by her anxiety. Perhaps that is the case, but it may be just as likely that both the depression and anxiety have a common cause.

Post-hoc Fallacy

The *post-hoc* fallacy involves the mistaken assumption that just because one thing precedes another in time, it caused that second thing to occur. One of the most common examples of this fallacy is the complaint that it rained because earlier in the day you washed your car. Of course, the two are related only by time and coincidence.

Oversimplification

Avoid the temptation to overly simplify causal arguments. When you write these essays, you are typically examining complex subjects—causes and effects are rarely simple and straightforward. Do not oversimplify the topic in order to make it easier to write about.

Ignoring Opposing Views

Academic audiences usually do not find one-sided arguments persuasive. If you ignore opposing points of view in your essay, your readers may assume that your research was inadequate, that you are ill-informed on the topic, or that you are purposefully misleading your readers. Any of these assumptions will damage your credibility among critical academic readers.

Sample Student Essay: Causal Argument

The following sample causal argument, written by student Carlos Mendez, examines various explanations for the extinction of the dinosaurs 65 million years ago.

SAMPLE CAUSAL ARGUMENT

What Killed Off the Dinosaurs?

Carlos Mendez

Over the past 500 million years of Earth history, five major extinctions have occurred: the Ordovician, the Devonian, the Permian, the Triassic, and the Cretaceous (Merali,

2006). This final mass extinction, which occurred 65 million years ago, marked the end of all nonbird dinosaurs on Earth. When examining layers of rock, dinosaur fossils are common below the Cretaceous-Tertiary (K-T) boundary and disappear above it. According to David Fastovsky (2005), professor of geoscience at the University of Rhode Island, "in the past fifteen years it has become clear that the extinction of the dinosaurs was geologically instantaneous" (p. 52). Scientists do not agree, however, on the cause of this relatively sudden extinction. Some maintain that extreme volcanic activity caused their deaths; others attribute it to severe oceanic and climatic change. For the past twenty years, the most common explanation for the Cretaceous mass extinction has been that a giant meteorite hit the Yucatan Peninsula of Mexico causing global devastation. Recently, however, this theory has been challenged and a new explanation has emerged: severe climate change, extreme volcanic activity, and the effects of a meteorite impact together caused the extinction of dinosaurs on Earth.

Most scientists agree that climate changes contributed to the demise of the dinosaurs. Fossil and geologic evidence at the K-T boundary indicates severe changes in the environment at the end of the Cretaceous period. William Sarjeant (2001) of the University of Saskatchewan and Philip J. Currie (2001) of the Royal Tyrrell Museum of Palaeontology write: "The environmental changes in North America during the Late Cretaceous were considerable. The inland sea, whose margins had provided so congenial a habitation for the big dinosaurs, was gone; . . . the vegetation and the climate were changing drastically" (p. 244). According to Archibald (2005), at the end of the Cretaceous period, around the world sea levels were receding and oceanic currents were changing. These changes brought about a dramatic rise in the Earth's temperature which disrupted the dinosaur's food chain and ultimately caused their extinction.

What brought about these environmental changes is still in dispute, however, with scientists dividing into two groups, those favoring an extraterrestrial cause (a meteorite striking the Earth) and those favoring a terrestrial one (volcanic activity). Scientists who attribute dinosaur extinction to volcanic activity base their theories on history: the Permian extinction, which took place 250 million years ago, is universally attributed to massive volcanic activity in what is now Siberia (Kerr, 2005; Merali, 2006). Evidence of similar volcanic activity can be found today at the K-T boundary, attributed to eruptions in present-day India. Though some scientists have argued that these eruptions were too infrequent to cause the dinosaurs' extinction, more recent studies have found thick layers of lava that built up in only 30,000 years. According to Kate Ravilious (2005) writing in the journal *New Scientist,* "this rapid outpouring is likely to have injected volcanic gases high into the Earth's atmosphere, catastrophically altering the climate and suffocating much of life on earth" (p. 11). Greenhouse gases from the volcanoes would have caused a rapid rise in the Earth's temperature, disrupting the food chain the dinosaurs depended on for their existence and dramatically altering their habitats. The creatures best suited to survive this environment were those living in the sea and smaller animals, such as the early mammals, that could burrow underground (Fastovsky, 2005).

However, not everyone agrees with the theory that volcanic activity killed the dinosaurs. First, they question the claim that recently discovered layers of lava took only 30,000 years to form. Based on a study of magnetic rock in the lava, the layer could have taken up to 500,000 years to form, taking it out of consideration as a cause of the Cretaceous extinction (Ravilious, 2005). Professor G. Keller (2005) of Princeton University's Department of Geosciences agrees that timing is an issue: the main phase of India's volcanic activity occurred too early to cause the extinctions at the end of the Cretaceous period. Instead, Keller contends that the available evidence supports the notion that a meteor impact was primarily responsible for the climatic changes that killed the dinosaurs.

Most scientists who accept the impact theory of dinosaur extinction believe a massive meteorite roughly the size of Manhattan struck the Yucatan Peninsula 65 million years ago creating a massive crater, known as Chicxulub. Exploding on the Earth with the power of 10 trillion megatons of TNT, this meteorite shot billions of tons of debris into the atmosphere (Cowen, 1996). According to David Fastovsky (2005), "such impacts probably have two kinds of dire consequences: dust, smoke, and debris in the atmosphere blocking sunlight for several months, and an instantaneous pulse of thermal energy igniting global fires" (p. 53). Due to the dust and debris in the atmosphere, photosynthesis stopped and the Earth entered a decade of drastic global warming, eliminating the dinosaurs' food supply. Another group of scientists believes that the impact led to a period of global cooling with the same effects on the dinosaurs (Cowen, 1996).

Those who question the role of the Chicxulub meteorite in the K-T extinction raise one primary objection: the meteorite that struck the Yucatan was not big enough to be the sole cause of the dinosaurs' demise. The power of a meteorite is determined by the size of the crater it leaves. However, measuring a crater created 65 million years ago is difficult and inexact due to the effects of weathering. One group of scientists estimates Chicxulub to be 280 km wide; others believe it to be no wider than 180 km. The latest measurements set it between 90 and 170 km (Keller, 2005). Based on the damage done by other meteorites on Earth and on Jupiter, Keller estimates that the mass extinction found at the K-T boundary would only result from a meteorite leaving a crater at least 250–300 km wide. While Keller (2005) agrees that a meteorite impact likely contributed to the dinosaurs' extinction, he concludes that the meteorite that created Chicxulub was not responsible. Given that such a huge crater has never been located, Keller surmises that it might have struck the ocean.

Of the five major extinctions in Earth's history, Keller (2005) concludes that only the Cretaceous is linked to a meteorite impact. Yet it alone did not bring about the end of the dinosaurs. Instead, he endorses a "hybrid hypothesis" (p. 726) to explain the death of the dinosaurs, one that identifies multiple causes of extinction. Writing in the *Canadian Journal of Earth Science*, William Sarjeant and Philip Currie (2001) agree: "the extinction of the dinosaurs . . . must be attributed to more than one cause" (p. 243). J. David Archibald (2005), biology professor at San Diego State University, captures the multiple causes this way:

> Some 65 million years ago, Murphy's Law applied—almost everything that could have gone wrong did: A huge bolide [bright meteor] . . . struck Earth. Globally, the seas receded. Fissures on the Indian subcontinent spewed forth thousands of cubic kilometers of material. All three events took place in

rapid succession, toward the end of the Cretaceous period. Each of them is thought to have been the largest event of its kind in the past 250 million years, and each is thought to have played a role in the demise of the non-bird dinosaurs. (p. 52)

For several reasons, this hybrid hypothesis offers the best explanation for dinosaur extinction.

Scientists disagree over the condition of the dinosaur population on Earth at the time of the Chicxulub impact. David Fastovsky (2005) states flatly that "every published quantitative, field-based stratigraphically refined study addressing this question has concluded that dinosaur diversity was unchanged up to the K-T boundary . . ." (p. 52). Sargeant and Currie (2001) disagree, claiming that fossil evidence demonstrates that prior to the impact, dinosaur populations were in decline, a position endorsed by Cowen (1996), Keller (2005), and Archibald (2005) who writes: "before the time of the boundary is reached, between one-third and one-half of all dinosaur species—mostly such relatively common groups as the duck-billed and horned dinosaurs—had already disappeared" (p. 52).

A combination of climate change, volcanic activity, and meteoric impact seems to have caused the demise of an already stressed dinosaur population about 65 million years ago. Ongoing volcanic activity in India had already spewed deadly amounts of carbon dioxide into the atmosphere, causing massive global warming. At the same time, sea levels were changing and internal seas were drying up. A dinosaur population that was already in decline faced a loss of food supplies and an increasingly hostile environment. (Archibald [2005] even postulated that at about this time, hoofed mammals crossed the Bering Straight and began to compete with dinosaurs for available food supplies.) A meteorite impact sealed the dinosaurs' doom—the terrestrial devastation and long-term climate change the impact brought about made it impossible for the dinosaurs to survive.

Assigning a single cause to the end of the dinosaurs is impossible. Three threats to their existence occurred simultaneously—climate change, volcanic activity, and a meteorite impact. Establishing a cause-effect relationship among these factors is equally complicated. While the impact likely did not cause increased volcanic activity (Keller, 2005), together the two phenomena dramatically affected the climate, exacerbating environmental changes that seem to have been underway for some time. In short, the dinosaurs never had a chance. Non-bird dinosaurs disappear after the Cretaceous period, setting the stage for the rise of mammals as the dominant animals on Earth.

References

Archibald, J. D. (2005). Were dinosaurs the victims of a single catastrophe? No, it only finished them off. *Natural History, 114*(4), 52–53.

Cowen, R. (1996, April). The day the dinosaurs died. *Astronomy*, 34–42.

Fastovsky, D. E. (2005, May). Were dinosaurs the victims of a single catastrophe? Yes, and an asteroid did the deed. *Natural History*, 52–53.

Keller, G. (2005). Impacts, volcanism and mass extinction: Random coincidence or cause and effect? *Australian Journal of Earth Sciences, 52,* 725–757.

Kerr, R. A. (2005, January 21). A prolonged demise. *Science Now.* Retrieved from http://sciencenow. sciencemag. org/cgi/content/full/2005/ 121/2

Merali, Z. (2006, March 1). Climate blamed for mass extinctions. *New Scientist,* 18–21.

Ravilious, K. (2005, August 20). Extreme volcanism doomed the dinosaurs. *New Scientist,* 11.

Sarjeant, W. A. S., and Currie, P. J. (2001). The "great extinction" that never happened: The demise of the dinosaurs considered. *Canadian Journal of Earth Science, 38,* 239–247.

Something to write about . . .

After reading "What Killed Off the Dinosaurs," complete the following writing assignments either individually or with one or two other students in class.

1. Write a brief summary of the essay.
2. Outline the essay, paraphrasing its thesis at the top of a page, then listing each of the essay's major assertions. Beneath each of those assertions, summarize the reasons and/or evidence the author offers as support.
3. Respond to the essay, stating and explaining your reactions to the reading.
4. Critique or evaluate the reading: how persuasive is it? What are its strengths and limitations? How effectively does the author state, support, and explain the essay's primary assertions?

ADDITIONAL READINGS

The additional readings at the end of this chapter both examine the causes and/or effects of bullying. Martín examines how teachers or counselors might effectively intervene to stop bullying while Turkel examines the psychological components of bullying and the differences among girl and boy bullies. Both readings were originally published in academic journals; however, pay attention to how the readings differ from one another, not only in terms of style and voice, but also in terms of coverage and research methodology.

Before you read these arguments, you might want to consider these questions:

- What do you know about the causes and/or effects of bullying?
- Have you ever been the victim of bullying? How did it affect you?
- Have you ever bullied someone else, including a family member? What caused you to behave that way?
- How do you think your behavior affected the person you bullied?
- What, if anything, would you like to learn about the causes and/or effects of bullying?

As you read these arguments, ask yourself the following questions:

- What is each author's thesis?
- What are each author's primary assertions? Would you claim that the purpose of either reading is more informative than argumentative?
- What opening and closing strategies does each author employ?
- Who seems to be the intended audience of each piece?
- What appeals do the writers make to persuade their intended readers that they should care about this topic?
- How does the intended audience influence the content, structure, style, and tone of each reading?
- How would you characterize the reading's style?
- How does the author support her claims in the piece?
- How does the author address opposing views in her argument?
- What makes each of these arguments "academic"?

When you finish reading each essay, ask yourself these questions:

- How effectively did the author present information and arguments in the reading?
- Did you find either of the readings more interesting than the other? What made it more interesting?
- Did you find either of the readings more challenging than the other? Why?
- What are the strengths and limitations of each reading?
- Taken together, how do the readings help you understand the causes and/or effects of bullying?

ADDITIONAL READING

The Causes and Nature of Bullying and Social Exclusion in Schools

Maria el Mar Badia Martín

Maria el Bar Badia Martín is a professor in the Department of Evolutionary Psychology and Education at Universidad Autónoma, Barcelona, Spain. This essay originally appeared in Education Journal.

Bullying is not easy to define. Sometimes it involves hitting or kicking. But threats, teasing, and taunting are more common and can be more damaging. The word "bullying" is used to describe many different types of behaviour ranging from teasing or deliberately leaving an individual out of a social gathering or ignoring them, to serious assaults and abuse. Sometimes it is an individual who is doing the bullying and sometimes it is a group.

The important thing is not the action but the effect on the victim. No one should ever underestimate the fear that a bullied child feels.

Research findings

There is evidence that children who are highly aggressive to their siblings are likely to have problems with peers outside the family, i.e. being more often rejected by peers (Dunn & McGuire, 1992), or to show similar behaviour at school (Berndt & Bulleit, 1985). Bowers, Smith, and Binney (1992, 1994) reported that bullies at school also reported negative relationships with their siblings, whom they viewed as more powerful than themselves. In contrast, victims of bullying reported often positive, even enmeshed, relationships with their siblings. Duncan (1999) reported in a study of 375 seventh and eighth graders that 22 per cent were often hit or pushed around by their siblings and 8.1 per cent reported that they were often beaten by a sibling. Around 40 per cent of children also admitted to bullying their brothers or sisters.

While there was only a moderate association between bullying experience at home and school for those who were identified as bullies or victims at school, bully/victims at school were also most frequently involved in bullying behaviour at home. Sixty per cent of peer bully/victims reported being bullied by their brothers or sisters. In contrast, less than half of the peer victims (38 per cent) and 32 per cent of not-involved children reported bullying by their siblings. Most importantly, those children who were bully/victims at school and involved in bullying at home had the highest levels of psychological pathology (Duncan, 1999). However, despite these apparently high rates of victimisation and the potential influence of these experiences on peer relationships, sibling bullying has been relatively ignored in the literature, perhaps because it is so common (Goodwin & Roscoe, 1990).

Some of the things that researchers have found out about bullying include:

- It happens in all schools.
- It has to be acknowledged as a possible problem before it can be tackled.
- While high profile campaigns at national, local or school level are useful ways of initiating action, on their own they do little or nothing to help.

It has also been found that schools that have taken action have been successful in reducing the level of bullying and that the single most effective thing that any school can do is to develop a policy to which everybody is committed. One way of getting commitment is to work with pupils, teachers and others to find out about the extent of bullying. This raises awareness and signals the school's intention to do something about it.

Characteristics of bully victims

Victims are often targeted because they are considered different—usually those considered overweight, small, with a learning disability or overly sensitive. Many face dirty digital tricks that range from derogatory comments about them online to embarrassing e-mails attributed to them intended to insult friends and crushes.

Boys and girls are both bullies and victims. There is a pattern to their meanness. While girls generally mock others for their physical appearance, boys tend to make more sexually explicit comments.

Boulton and Smith (1994) proposed that bully/victims have irritative tendencies, are often hyperactive in class, often break rules in games, try to join groups in a heavy-handed manner and provoke bullying behaviour from others. Bully/victims have been described as being provocative, physically stronger and more assertive than pure victims (Schwartz, Dodge, Pettit, & Bates, 1997) and have been found to be the least popular children in class (Wolke & Stanford, 1999). The range of behaviours described for these children and their behaviour problems appear to match closely the picture of the rejected aggressive pupil (Coie, Dodge, Terry, & Wright, 1991; Farrington, 1995; Loeber & Hay, 1994; Schwartz et al., 1997; Wolke Woods, Bloomfield, & Karstadt, 2000).

While in primary school bully/victims make up about a third to half of all those others frequently bullied (Wolke et al., 2000; Kumpulainen et al., 1998), they account for about 25 per cent of all children bullying others in secondary school, as shown here and elsewhere (Whitney & Smith, 1993). Thus their proportion within the group of children bullying others appears to reduce with age.

Roles in bullying

Besides the traditional roles of bully, victim, and non-involved, a number of studies have examined the situation of bully/victims or provocative or aggressive victims—children showing characteristics of both bully and victim. Not surprisingly, a number of studies suggest that these children are more at risk than either 'pure bullies' or 'pure victims'.

The work of Salmivalli and colleagues (1996) opened up the dynamics further, by suggesting that bullying children could be considered as either ringleaders (organising a group of bullies and initiating the bullying), followers (who join in the bullying once it is started), and reinforcers (who do not actively join in, but reinforce more passively by watching and laughing or encouraging the bullying). Salmivalli also distinguished outsiders (who are completely non-involved) and defenders (who help the victim, get help, or tell the bullies to stop). Salmivalli's work with adolescents in Finland was based on peer nominations. Sutton and Smith (1999) used a similar procedure with 8- to 11-year-olds in England. Monks, Smith and Swettenham (2003) used a modified cartoon task version with 4- to 5-year-olds, and found that at this age it was mainly just the bully (or aggressor), victim and defender roles that could be elicited reliably.

Types of bullying?

We can define different ways of bullying—physical, verbal and relational—separately: physical bullies (pupils who were involved in physically bullying others frequently but are never or rarely physically victimised); physical victims (frequently victimised but bully others never or rarely); physical bully/victims (pupils who both physically bully others and become physical victims of the two ((a) and (b)) described behaviours frequently); physical neutrals who neither physically bully others nor become physical victims (never or rarely only).

Bullying with mobiles and computers

An Australian mobile phone group is launching a campaign to help combat the increasing trend of schoolyard bullying by text message. A recent study showed 14 per cent of first year high school students in Brisbane had been harassed by SMS. "People who use mobiles think they can get away with it, they believe they were anonymous and they won't get caught, they are wrong on both counts," said Randal Markey from the Australian Mobile Telecommunications Association. "The law is very clear. It's a criminal offence to use a mobile phone to harass, menace or offend someone and almost all calls can be traced. Prevention is always the best way to go and we say be very careful about who you give your number to and also for people to consider using a call ID block. We say don't respond if you get a message, save the message and take a note of the time and date for use as evidence of bullying. Tell your parents."

The incident reflects the latest way technology is altering the social lives of children at an age when they are especially vulnerable to insults. The emergence of cyberbullying has intensified adolescent angst. It allows bullies to unleash put-downs, nasty rumours and humiliating pictures in email and blogs that can strike victims at home and at any time. The damage can be devastating, psychologists say, even as it is not always obvious to parents and teachers. Cyberbullies, mostly ages nine to 14, are using the anonymity of the internet to mete out pain without witnessing the consequences. The problem—aggravated by widespread use of wireless devices such as cellphones and BlackBerrys—is especially prevalent in affluent suburbs, where high-speed internet use is high and kids are technically adept, says Parry Aftab, executive director of WiredSafety.org, an online safety group.

Often, the social cruelties escape the notice of schools, which focus on problems on campus, and of parents, who are unaware of what their kids are doing online. Many victims don't tell their parents, out of fear they'll be barred from using the internet, Aftab and others say.

Several parents agreed to have their children interviewed, but only if their last names were not used and a parent monitored the call. They feared their children would face another round of taunting if they were publicly identified.

Strategies against bullying?

Pupils adopt a variety of coping strategies when bullied. Studies suggest that the success of these varies and is age- and gender-dependent, but non-assertive strategies such as crying are less successful than ignoring or seeking help. The success of seeking help will depend on the school context; and one important part of school context appears to be the existence of peer support systems, which can encourage the 'seeking help' strategy, whether from peer supporters, teachers or others.

There has been growing interest in peer support and mediation as an approach to bullying. These methods hold promise, but more evaluation research is needed. In a review of peer support methods, it is argued that evaluations so far suggest clear benefits for the peer supporters themselves, and general improvement of school climate; but specific benefits for victims of bullying remain to be proven. Evaluations of active listening/counselling-based approaches found that the majority of peer supporters reported benefits arising from the interpersonal skills and teamwork acquired in training; users reported that peer supporters offered helpful interventions; and most pupils and teachers believed that the service was having an impact on the school as a whole. There can also be problems due to some hostility to peer helpers from other pupils; difficulties in recruiting boys as peer supporters; issues of power sharing with staff; and ensuring sufficient time and resources for proper implementation.

Future action

The existing research gives a number of pointers as to how to improve intervention effectiveness in the future. More attention may need to be paid to girls bullying, and rumour-spreading and social exclusion; at present, anti-bullying materials often emphasise the more obvious physical and direct verbal forms. Awareness of different roles may help; peer support schemes can aim to turn 'bystanders' into 'defenders' (Cowie, 2000), and we need to be aware of the clever (though manipulative) social skills of many bullies. Also, since roles take time to get established, starting anti-bullying work early, including, for example, awareness raising and assertiveness training in infant and junior schools, may be important. There is also some debate about the extent to which anti-bullying work should focus on broader school climate issues, and relationships in school, rather than specifically on bullying.

Teachers have good knowledge about some aspects of bullying but do not feel fully equipped to tackle it. Regular inspections of schools by Ofsted address the issue of whether bullying is a problem in a school, and measures taken to combat it. They report on the efforts of secondary schools to tackle bullying and, since 1996, several successful legal actions have been taken by pupils or their parents against schools in which they were persistently bullied. Some schools now have an anti-bullying policy, yet there is no clear evidence that the quality or content of anti-bullying policies, in themselves, predict victimisation rates; one challenge now is to ensure that school policies form a sound base for further action, informed by the continuing research on the issue.

All initiatives and evaluations of the effects of bullying will help us build for the future. Schools have a vital role in reducing bullying, but the impact of the wider society; parenting skills and behaviours; portrayals of violence in the mass media; and attitudes to aggression, bullying and violence in society, the workplace (including among teachers), and the local community all have an influence. The concern with the "systematic abuse of power" in schools has a legitimate and important focus on relationships in school (and even on pupil-pupil relationships primarily), but it is also part of a wider set of relationships and issues in schools, communities and societies that we are still grappling with, and will continue to be doing for the foreseeable future.

Conclusion

All children, whether bullies, victims or bully/victims involved in either physical or verbal (direct) bullying or relational (indirect) bullying at school, had behaviour problems significantly more often than neutral children. Bully/victims in school are found to be at particularly high risk for behaviour problems when compared to pure victims.

The literature shows that there was a clear 'dose response' relationship between participation in an increasing number of bullying types and behaviour problems. More than half of the children involved in all types of bullying (physical, verbal and relational) had behaviour problems in the clinical/borderline range. In the same way, children who were victims at *home*, i.e. were bullied by their siblings, were at a highly increased risk for behaviour problems than children with adaptive sibling relationships even if we allowed for their bullying experiences at school and for socio-demographic factors. Victims at home were much more likely to be involved in bullying at school than children not tormented by their siblings. Being both victimised at home and involved in bullying at school increased the overall risk of clinically significant behaviour problems.

Ethnic differences in bullying involvement and behaviour problems were statistically significant but generally small in effect size.

References

Berndt, T., & Bulleit, T. (1985). Effects of sibling relationships on preschoolers' behaviour at home and at school. *Development Psychology, 21*, 761–767.

Bjorkqvist, K. (1994). Sex differences in physical, verbal and indirect aggression: A review of recent research. *Sex Roles, 30*, 177–188.

Bjorkqvist, K., Lagerspetz, K. M. J., & Kaukiainen, A. (1992). Do girls manipulate and boys fight? Developmental trends in regard to direct and indirect aggression. *Aggressive Behaviour, 18*, 117–127.

Boulton, M. J., & Smith, P. K. (1994). Bully/victim problems in middle-school children: Stability, self-perceived competence, peer perceptions and peer acceptance. *British Journal of Developmental Psychology, 12*, 315–329.

Bowers, L., Smith, P. K., & Binney, V. A. (1992). Cohesion and power in the families of children involved in bully/victim problems at school. *Journal of Family Therapy, 14*, 371–387.

Coie, J. D., Dodge, K. A., Terry, R. R., & Wright, V. (1991). The role of aggression in peer relations: An analysis of aggression episodes in boys' play groups. *Child Development, 62*, 812–826.

Craig, W. M. (1998). The relationship among bullying, victimisation, depression, anxiety and aggression in elementary school children. *Personality and Individual Differences, 24*, 123–130.

Crick, N. R., & Grotpeter, J. K. (1995). Relational aggression, gender and social-psychological adjustment. *Child Development, 66*, 710–722.

Duncan, R. D. (1999). Peer and sibling aggression: An investigation of intra- and extra-familial bullying. *Journal of Interpersonal Violence, 14*, 871–886.

Dunn, J., & McGuire, S. (1992). Sibling and peer relationships in childhood. *Journal of Child Psychology and Psychiatry, 33*, 67–105.

Farrington, D. (1995). The Twelfth Jack Tizard Memorial Lecture: The development of offending and antisocial behaviour from childhood: Key findings from the Cambridge Study in delinquent development. *Journal of Child Psychology and Psychiatry, 36,* 929–964.

Farrington, D. (1993). Understanding and preventing bullying. In M. Tonry (Ed.), *Crime and justice: A review of research* (vol. 17, pp. 381–458). Chicago: University of Chicago Press.

Goodwin, M. P., & Roscoe, B. (1990). Sibling violence and agonistic interactions among middle adolescents. *Adolescence, 25,* 451–467.

Kumpulainen, K., Räsänen, E., Henttonen, I., Almqvist, F., Kresanov, K., Linna, S. L., Moilanen, I., Piha, J., Puura, K., & Tamminen, T. (1998). Bullying and psychiatric symptoms among elementary school-age children. *Child Abuse and Neglect, 22,* 705–717.

Loeber, R., & Hay, D. F. (1994). Developmental approaches to aggression and conduct problems. In M. Rutter & D. F. Hay (Eds.), *Development through life: A handbook for clinicians* (pp. 488–516). Oxford: Blackwell.

Olweus, D. (1991). Bully/victim problems among schoolchildren: Basic facts and effects of a school based intervention program. In D. J. Pepler & K. H. Rubin (Eds.), *The development and treatment of childhood aggression* (pp. 411–448). Hillsdale, NJ: Erlbaum.

Olweus, D. (1993). *Bullying at school: What we know and what we can do.* Oxford: Blackwell.

Olweus, D. & Endresen, I. M. (1998). The importance of sex-of-stimulus object: Age trends and sex differences in empathic responsiveness. *Social Development, 7,* 370–388.

Salmivalli, C., Lagerspetz, K., Björkqvist, K., Österman, K., & Kaukiainen, A. (1996). Bullying as a group process: Participant roles and their relations to social status within the group. *Aggressive Behavior, 22,* 115.

Schwartz, D., Dodge, K. A., Pettit, G. S., & Bates, J. E. (1997). The early socialisation of aggression victims of bullying. *Child Development, 68,* 665–675.

Smith, Peter K. (1991). 'The Silent Nightmare: bullying and victimisation in school peer groups.' *The Psychologist: Bulletin of the British Psychological Society, 4,* 243–248.

Smith, Peter K., Morita, Y., Junger-Tas, J., Olweus, D., Catalano, R., & Slee, P. (1999). *The nature of school bullying: A cross-national perspective.* London: Routledge.

Smith, Peter K., & Thompson, D. (Eds.).(1991). *Practical approaches to bullying.* David Fulton.

Sutton, J., & Smith, P. K. (1999). Bullying as a group process: An adaptation of the participant role approach. *Aggressive Behavior, 25,* 97–111.

Whitney, I. & Smith, P. K. (1993). A survey of the nature and extent of bullying in junior/middle and secondary schools. *Educational Research, 35,* 325.

Wolke, D., & Stanford, K. (1999). Bullying in school children. In D. Messer & S. Millar (Eds.), *Developmental psychology.* London: Arnold.

Wolke, D., Woods, S., Bloomfield, L., & Karstadt, L. (2000). The association between direct and relational bullying and behaviour problems among primary school children. *Journal of Child Psychology and Psychiatry, 8,* 989–1002.

Sugar and Spice and Puppy Dogs' Tails: The Psychodynamics of Bullying

Ann Ruth Turkel

Ann Ruth Turkel is an assistant clinical professor of psychiatry at Columbia University College of Physicians and Surgeons. This article originally appeared in the Journal of the American Academy of Psychoanalysis and Dynamic Psychiatry.

Michael's teasing started with a wisecrack about Robert's sexual orientation. Robert replied with an equally provocative taunt. And then Michael threw a metal chair, striking Robert's face, nearly severing his nose and shattering surrounding bones. Were these two obstreperous adolescents? No, Michael the bully was a New York City fireman, and Robert the victim was his colleague, who was hospitalized and put on a respirator (Healy, 2004).

Mean and vicious taunts are common in firehouses. The tradition being that the verbal abuse inflicted on young firefighters—just as in military service—is necessary to make them tough. But bullying can have a terrible impact on both victims and aggressors, with the latter often becoming increasingly violent.

The massacre at Columbine has served to focus our attention on bullying. Those high school gunmen said that the shootings were retribution for years of teasing because of their unwillingness to conform in action and dress.

In 2003, several female students were involved in a brutal hazing of girls from a suburban Chicago high school. Girls were pushed, kicked, and splattered with garbage and feces. One girl had coffee grounds jammed into her ears, a bucket was put over her head, and someone hammered on the bucket with a baseball bat. She lost consciousness for over two minutes, and was hospitalized. One student had at least ten stitches in her scalp and another had a broken ankle. About 50 girls participated in the incident. Hazing has been a tradition of the Powder Puff football game for girls, but never before on this scale (Meadows & Johnson, 2003).

Studies show that bullies and their victims are more likely to engage in violent behavior than those who have never been involved in bullying. They are at greater risk for more serious violent acts, like carrying weapons, fighting, and being injured in fights. At greatest risk are children who bully, and are themselves bullied. Really, bullying is a sign of potential psychiatric disorder in both bully and victim. Bullies have a high incidence of emotional and physical abuse in their history, and they have a high incidence of conduct and adjustment disorders. Their victims suffer from anxiety and depression.

What are the psychodynamic mechanisms that underlie bullying? As Gonzalez de Rivera (2002) states, psychological abuse is a complex psychosocial syndrome engendered by interaction between the abuser, the victim, and the psychosocial group to which they both belong. All three factors are needed; one of them alone is not sufficient. Together, the dynamics of abuse are activated and reactivated, culminating in a vicious cycle.

In the United States, children and adolescents confront problems which include racism, poverty, pressure to use drugs and alcohol, and to have sex early. So bullying has not been a major public concern, although it is a major problem for 8- to 15-year-olds. A recent American Medical Association report on students in sixth through tenth grades estimated that over 3.2 million youngsters are victims of bullying annually. In its post-Columbine report, the Secret Service stated that nearly three-quarters of perpetrators of deadly school violence reported a history of having been bullied (Viadoro, 2003).

Bullying can occur from the cradle to the grave. It is primarily physical in childhood, becoming relational aggression in adolescence. It continues to be relational in adulthood—where it often appears in the form of sexual harassment—and can be physical and relational at the end of life, where it is not infrequent in nursing homes and by home attendants. This article focuses on bullying in childhood and adolescence, as well as the commonalities between bullying and sexual harassment; the best prophylaxis for prevention in adults and the elderly would be to curtail it in their formative years.

Among Schoolchildren

Bullying is a crime, often committed by children, which can lead to far more serious crimes. The causes of bullying include: the desire to control, revenge, envy, and emotional distress. Although it is rarely noted, bullies have often been bullied, just like child abusers have often been abused. Trigger factors include diversity in race, ethnicity, religion, and language. Even preschoolers can bully by giving other children insulting nicknames, refusing to invite certain children to birthday parties, excluding them from games, extorting toys from them, etc. Their victims are likely to become antisocial and depressed, as well as to be ostracized by classmates.

Other industrialized countries share our problems with bullying. In Japan, *ijime* (bullying) reached new heights in 1985; some victims committed suicide. There were several cases in which nobody noticed that a student had been bullied until his suicide note listed the names of classmates who were his harassers. The cases have been studied from the viewpoint of individual pathology, family dynamics, and environmental factors: academic competitiveness, control-oriented education, and school violence (Kawabata, 2001).

Unpopular children were victimized by both classmates and teachers. Almost daily, newspapers carried stories about children humiliated, ostracized, beaten, and rejected. Thousands of students refused to attend school, and some committed suicide by hanging. And in Japan, where the lightest form of punishment from the teacher is a slap on the face, some children have suffered irreversible brain damage (Horn, 1996).

In the United States, up to 15% of the adolescent population are bullies, and 10% are victims. In the lower grades, more boys than girls are involved, but the gender difference diminishes in the middle and high school years. At that time, there occurs an increase in social bullying, most often in the form of manipulation to impede acceptance into a group. The consequences for the victim can be academic, social, emotional, and legal problems.

A recent study by Twemlow and Fonagy (2005) explored the hypothesis that teachers' attitudes conducive to bullying contribute to behavioral difficulties in children. The higher rates of teacher bullying in schools with more problems suggest either that teachers adjust to the culture of violence in such schools or that predisposed teachers are more inclined to remain in such settings—by choice or by lack of opportunity to transfer. It is not surprising that teachers who were bullied as children grow up to bully students, and are more aware of teachers who bully students. And some teachers may gravitate toward or even contribute to the violent culture of problem schools.

Bullying as a Precursor of Sexual Harassment

Popular attitudes toward aggression exemplify traditional sex role stereotypes, in which men are family protectors and providers, and women are mothers and nurturers—recent social changes notwithstanding. Hence, aggression is the hallmark of masculinity. It allows men to control their livelihoods and their environment. Boys have complete access to rough and tumble play. Indeed, their popularity depends to a large extent on their ability to play rough. They gain the respect of their peers through athletic ability, resisting authority, and acting tough, dominating, confident, and even unruly.

The precursor of peer-to-peer sexual harassment in schools is the bullying behavior which children learn, implement, and/or experience at a young age. Every child knows what a bully is, and both genders have been victims. In the young, much of the bullying is between members of the same sex. Teachers and parents are often unaware of it, or accept it as an unfortunate stage that many children undergo on the road to adolescence and maturity. But if it is not challenged and curtailed, bullying may be one step before sexual harassment.

Even if teachers view bullying and sexual harassment as problems, they are loath to report it. Those boys who have a great interest in dating starting early in middle school, are likely to become sexual harassers by the end of middle school. One-third of teenage girls are subjected to physical, sexual, or emotional abuse from male peers by the end of high school.

My 13-year-old patient Jane recently reported an incident that occurred on a school field trip. A male classmate, Ed, chose to sit next to her on the bus and proceeded to shove his pen into his mouth, making circular motions with it. After this happened twice, the boy across the aisle came to her rescue and told Ed to cut it out. When I asked Jane why she did not report the incident to the driver or to the teacher, she replied, "But students aren't allowed to get out of their seats while the bus is in motion." And when I asked why she had not reported it later, she told me: "I don't want to get Ed in trouble, since he often receives disciplinary action." I gave Jane a brief lesson on handling bullies and encouraged her to relate the incident to her parents. The latter called me and asked what I thought they should do. I suggested they call the dean, which they did—only to learn that the episode had already been reported by the parents of the boy who rescued Jane. This incident demonstrates clearly that both children and adults have a problem coping with bullies.

During early adolescence, dating is a peer group activity, not an intimate relationship. Girls are attracted to more aggressive boys because they are peer group leaders. In addition, the girls are experimenting with different roles and trying out independence from parents, expressing their new positions by becoming involved with these boys.

My own experience, of sexual harassment as a form of bullying, occurred during my first year of medical school when I was 19 years old. I was jeered at every day by one of the three men with whom I shared a cadaver. (The two other women in the class shared a cadaver with two men; the women were lesbian partners.) My antagonist rapidly discovered that I rarely understood the dirty jokes he told daily and he delighted in my discomfort when he insisted on explaining them to me. I didn't know how to stop him and felt both naive and helpless, especially when he escalated to remarks about my personal life, including my being in medical school taking the place of a man because I was looking for a husband.

Eventually I could tolerate his taunts no longer and threatened that if he didn't stop, I was going to hit him. He took my dare. I reached across the table and slapped his face. I had never hit anyone before. An anatomy instructor came running. I was on the verge of tears as I explained. The instructor ordered my tormentor outside. I never knew what transpired between them; all I ever knew was that the jokes and taunts stopped.

Another incident followed but at the time I did not foresee any future consequences because I knew that the prank derived from a longstanding tradition of male medical students: when I performed a splenectomy on a dog in physical anatomy lab, I found the spleen in my locker and could never figure out how it got there.

Shortly before our 25th class reunion, we all received a letter from the class president, who was also president of the state medical society. The letter began: "Dear Colleague, It hardly seems possible that 25 years have elapsed since Jon Smith put a penis (not his) into Ann Turkel's locker." The maturation of years coupled with my active involvement in the women's liberation movement led to a swift response. I fired off a letter to the dean (whom I did not know), as I assumed he would not want to antagonize any alumni and sent copies to the letter writer and to the alumni association president. I began my letter by declaring that I was sorry to learn that the letter writer had not matured since medical school, as he was still denigrating women. I then expounded on gender equity, sexism, and sexual harassment. It took hardly any time for me to receive letters of apology from all of the recipients of my critique. However, I never mentioned bullying; I was not yet fully aware how closely it is related to sexual harassment.

Like sexual harassment, bullying deprives children and adolescents of safety and security. Most states outlaw the practice of hazing in educational institutions, which is defined as the organized practice of induction, usually into a sports team or fraternity through degrading behaviors and/or sexual assault. However, bullying is not illegal and, like sexual harassment, it is often omitted as a formal part of school curriculum.

Bully and Victim: A Brief Summary of the Literature

The primary researcher in the world in the field of bullying is Dan Olweus, a professor of psychology at the University of Bergen, Norway. He has researched this issue for over 25 years. He defines bullying as when someone is "exposed, repeatedly and over time, to negative actions on the part of one or more students" (Olweus, 1978, p. 9). These negative actions may involve threatening, taunting, teasing, name calling, hitting, pushing, kicking, punching, and restraining. Olweus also points out that the negative actions can happen "without the use of words or physical contact, such as by making faces or dirty gestures, intentionally excluding someone from a group, or refusing to comply with another person's wishes" (p. 9). Bullying involves an imbalance of strength. Note that Olweus's definition of bullying matches the definition of sexual harassment. Olweus's significant findings are:

- 15% of children are involved before high school. About 7% are bullies and more than half of the 15% are victims. Boys engage in more direct physical bullying than girls, but the most common type among boys as well as girls, is with words and gestures.
- Girls engage in more indirect bullying such as spreading rumors and manipulation of friendships.
- Boys do 60% of the bullying of girls, and 80% of the bullying of other boys.
- Bullying is at its peak in elementary school and declines steadily thereafter, but much of the bullying is done by older students, especially in the early grades.
- Most bullying occurs in school, in less supervised areas such as the playground, lunchroom, and hallways.
- Parents and teachers are unaware of the intensity and extent of the bullying. Children underreport it due to embarrassment and fear of retaliation.
- Bullies have friends and are popular. Victims are frequently loners.
- For boys, popularity decreases the chance of being bullied; it is very connected to physical strength.
- Size of class or school, and urban versus suburban schools are not significant, but what matters is the attitudes and responses of the adults in the school.

Whitney and Smith (1993) found that most bullying was done primarily by one boy; bullying by several boys came next; then mixed-sex bullying. Bullying by several girls followed, and last was bullying by one girl. Although girls are equally likely to be bullied, they are half as likely to bully others. Boys are bullied almost entirely by other boys, but girls are bullied by both sexes. While boys are rarely bullied by girls, the picture differs for girls. They are bullied by boys until high school, when they are most often bullied by other girls.

Olweus (1993) described risk factors leading to bullying: (1) A lack of parental involvement and warmth; (2) Parents who allow children to be inappropriately aggressive toward their siblings, their peers, and even adults; (3) Parents who use physical punishment and emotional outbursts to discipline their children. He concludes that bullying behavior may be transmitted across generations.

Bullying should be viewed as a continuum between bully and victim. Olweus (1994) differentiated between bullies, passive bullies, passive-submissive victims, and provocative victims along the continuum. Bullies are aggressive, have a positive attitude toward violence, need to dominate, are impulsive, have little anxiety, do not have low self-esteem, and are average or slightly below average in popularity. Passive bullies are followers who participate in bullying (usually in a group), but do not start the abuse. Passive-submissive victims are physically weaker, anxious, and rejected by their peers. When bullied, they do not retaliate. Provocative bullies are anxious, aggressive, and may be hyperactive or have problems concentrating. They retaliate when bullied.

Victims also have unique characteristics. They are likely to express a fear of fighting, do not defend themselves, have a negative attitude toward aggression, are physically weaker than their classmates, and have low self-esteem. The factors that affect the probability of children being habitually abused by peers include influences which are interconnected. Certain family experiences lead children to develop personal problems, such as an anxious style during conflict. Physical weakness is likely to lead to victimization for children lacking friends who can protect them.

Since victims continue to be abused by peers even when environmental changes are made, such as changing classes, teachers, and schools, it seems that victims have relatively stable personal qualities that attract harassment. And although children are often teased for external characteristics such as obesity, visual difficulty, clumsiness, or speech problems, a study by Olweus (1978) showed that chronically victimized children were not more likely than other children to have an obviously stigmatizing physical feature.

More recent research has begun to identify similar links between victimization and parenting practices. For example, children's social withdrawal and running away are connected to being a victim of parental violence. And children who are victimized often have overly supportive and authoritarian parents (Baldry & Farrington, 2000).

Certain types of parent-child relationships predispose children to develop behaviors that contribute to peer harassment. Preschoolers and elementary school students with a history of insecure attachment in infancy, especially anxious, resistant or ambivalent attitudes, are likely to be bullied. These children are easily upset by stress or new situations or separation from a parent, and are not easily soothed when upset.

When they are old enough to join a peer group, they tend to be overtly anxious, explore little, and cry easily. These children have a concept of the self as incompetent, unworthy, and helpless—all risk factors for victimization (Perry, Hodges, & Egan, 2001).

According to Perry et al., at least three types of parental control are linked to being victims. First, the mothers of victimized boys treat their sons as younger than their age, infantilize them, and overly control their free time. The relationship is unusually close. Oversolicitous parenting interferes with behavior such as physical play, exploration, and risk taking. This parenting leaves the child feeling inadequate and weak, and leads him to behave ineffectually and anxiously in peer conflicts. Second, parental control often involves efforts to invalidate, restrict, or manipulate the child's thoughts and feelings. This undermines self-confidence. The parent threatens or actually withdraws love if the child does not conform. The third form of parental control is coercion, which includes bossiness, sarcasm, and direct verbal attacks. All of these undermine the child's feelings of being loved and respected.

When victims try to confront or resist bullies, they meet such increased aggression that they learn, over time, that rapidly submitting leads to the least amount of humiliation and pain. And when bullying continues, peers perceive the victims as lesser and even deserving of the bullying. Thus, the reputations of victims tend to be perpetuated after the victim has changed his behavior or gained new skills.

Thorne (1993) researched the development of gender relationships in elementary school. She found that boys use sexual insults against girls, viewing girls as a group producing contamination. Children who do not conform to this characterization—particularly those who desire to be friends—run the risk of being teased or ostracized. The threat may eliminate such friendships or cause them to be hidden.

Eder (1997) found that children use sexual putdowns toward girls. The girls' use of words like "slut" or "whore" helped maintain a hierarchy with tough, sexually aggressive boys at the top. Girls also tormented boys who were friendly toward them by casting aspersions on their heterosexuality, thus contributing indirectly to male sexual aggression.

R. C. Friedman (2003) has noted that male juvenile-age peer groups are larger than those of girls, more hierarchically organized, and label behaviors they devalue as feminine. Gender role values stem from such groups and influence both the thoughts and actions of many men forever after. The juvenile male peer group can be a major cause of emotional distress for boys on a homosexual developmental track. Boys whose temperaments predispose them to gender role nonconformity are often subjected to gender role abuse by other boys. Those with internalized homophobia have often heard antihomosexual attitudes expressed by family members. Note that gender role bullying can start before middle school years, and is not necessarily noticed by adults. Those who were traumatized feel very ashamed and do not talk about their distress.

Much of the research on bullying and depression has connected victimization to low self-esteem, anxiety, loneliness, social withdrawal, and self-blame. Victims contribute to victimization because of poor social skills. Showing sadness, fear, and social withdrawal invites aggressive behavior from bullies, so a vicious cycle exists that aggravates a child's victim status. Talk about blaming the victim for his own oppression!

Peer Pressure and Sexual Aggression

Peer pressure can be a major factor in bullying as well as in sexual aggression. Peers play a role by either reinforcing the aggressor, failing to intervene to stop him, or allying with the bully. In early adolescence, the importance and function of the peer group changes radically. Searching for autonomy from their parents, adolescents turn to peers to discuss feelings, fears, doubts, and problems. However, this dependence on peers is coupled with increasing pressure to achieve social status.

During adolescence, peer groups become stratified, and popularity and acceptance become more important. Aggressiveness and toughness remain important status symbols for boys, and appearance becomes the major focus for girls. The pressure for status is linked to an increase in ridiculing or name calling.

Peer bystanders play an important role as enablers to bullies. They tend to feel afraid and anxious as they act as reinforcer, assistant, or defendant. Their inaction causes feelings of powerlessness similar to those of victims. The result of their complacent or passive participation is that they rationalize, justify, or undervalue their role. Studies also show that over time, bystanders' empathy for victims decreases, causing them to side with the bully (Olweus, 2001).

There are obvious sex differences in the connection between parenting and victimization. Unduly harsh parenting is conducive to victimization of girls, and the combination of coercive parents or overprotective parents with defiant children produces bullies (Ladd & Ladd, 1998).

Boys are raised with permission to kick and punch to express their negative feelings, and girls are taught to avoid direct confrontation. In our culture, girls and women are expected to appear unaggressive, not to seem bitchy, and to conform to the myth of the kinder, gentler sex. Parents and teachers still discourage direct and physical aggression in girls. From early childhood on, such displays of aggression are frowned upon and often lead to social rejection.

Boys still have more freedom to explore, experiment, and express anger. When boys act "bad," they get excused for sexual and aggressive acts. Unless they bring guns to school or rape another student, adults see their actions as typical. We say, "Boys will be boys." However, many girls are likewise aggressive, and not simply out of frustration, or retaliation, or fear. Many girls have outbursts, or harbor secret injustices that they have done to another that they have never been able to explain to themselves. And many girls want power. They seek it not just for connection, but because they too find power over another pleasurable.

Adolescent aggression is called relational aggression, social cruelty, peer harassment, or relational bullying. It is neither a new phenomenon nor is it limited to girls. It is characterized by both intent and an imbalance of power being directed at another to damage relationships, reputations, or sense of inclusion in a peer group. The strategies include a mixture of easily observable behaviors, such as physical harm, name calling, subtle forms of manipulation, social pressures, threats, or isolation. They may involve verbal threats, spreading rumors maligning someone's reputation, scapegoating, intrigues, and threatening social or romantic relationships. The actions may occur through confrontations or through the use of emissaries (Mullin-Rindler, 2003).

Subtypes of aggression among girls have been identified in addition to direct aggression, such as punching, teasing, or threatening. Relational aggression includes acts that "harm others through damage (or the threat of damage) to relationships or feelings of acceptance, friendship, or group inclusion" (Simmons, 2002, p. 2l). Examples include ostracizing someone socially for revenge, ignoring someone to punish them or to get one's own way, using negative facial expressions or body language, sabotaging another person's relationship, or threatening to end a relationship unless the friend complies with a request. In other words, the perpetrator uses her relationship with the victim as a weapon.

Indirect aggression permits the perpetrator to avoid confronting her target— covert behavior in which there seems no intent to hurt. Other instances of social sabotage include gossip, or use of double entendres. Such actions may be interpreted as clueless or hostile. Girls, just like women, are pros at this type of action.

Margaret Atwood's novel *Cat's Eye* (1989) is replete with examples of relational aggression. It is almost unique in its dear-headed portrayal of girl-to-girl bullying. A childhood victim, now grown up, remembers how her friends turned on her even as she frets about her own daughters:

> This is how it goes. It's the kind of thing girls of this age do to one another, or did then, but I'd had no practice in it. As my daughters approached this age, the age of nine, I watched them anxiously, scrutinized their fingers for bites, their feet, the ends of their hands. I asked leading questions: "Is everything all right, are your friends all right?" And they looked at me as if they had no idea what I was talking about, why I was so anxious. I thought they would give themselves away somehow: nightmares, moping. But there was nothing I could see, which may only have meant they were good at deception, as good as I was. When their friends arrived at our house to play, I scanned their faces for signs of hypocrisy. Standing in the kitchen, I listened to their voices in the other room. . . . Maybe it was worse. Maybe my daughters were doing this sort of thing themselves, to someone else. . . .
>
> Most mothers worry when their daughters reach adolescence, but I was the opposite. I relaxed, I sighed with relief. Little girls are cute and small only to adults. To one another they are not cute. They are life-sized. (p. 124)

While boys frequently bully strangers or acquaintances, girls attack within networks of friends. This, of course, makes their aggression more difficult to identify and deepens damage to their targets. Instead of using knives or fists, girls use relationships and body language. For girls, anger and intimacy are often fused. The intensity of the relationship between girls is important to the understanding of their aggression. Girls love each other long before they love boys.

Girls focus on attachment and continuity, while boys focus on separation and replacement. Boys are encouraged to separate from their mothers and to act masculine by demonstrating emotional restraint. Girls are encouraged to identify with their mothers' nurturing behavior and have unlimited access to intimacy. Boys see aggression as a way of controlling their environment, whereas girls see it as terminating relationships, and they equate conflict with loss. Girls try to avoid being alone, even remaining in abusive friendships out of fear of solitude.

Mothers punish girls for the expression of aggression more than boys. It has been said that girls can be much meaner than boys because they manipulate their social groups. When girls are not permitted the physical expression of aggression, it appears in other forms. They turn it against themselves through being overly self-critical, as well as through self-mutilation, depression, and eating disorders.

When relationships become weapons, friendship is a vehicle of anger. It is painful since the girl knows someone is angry, though she cannot figure out why. For the perpetrator, the silent treatment is a way of avoiding confrontation. But the silence can lead to misunderstandings and heighten the intensity of the conflict (Simmons, 2002).

Certainly the very word "bully" implies the image of an enemy, rather than a close friend. But it is the closest girlfriends who get entrapped in abusive relationships; the perpetrators are often intensely attached to their victims. With this fusion of meanness and friendship, girls may see meanness as an element of friendship, losing their ability to defend themselves from abuse.

Girl bullies are often the most socially adept in a group, more worldly, and more mature, with such charisma that victims are drawn to them. Girls who verbalize issues directly may lead other girls to gang up on them. Thus, a girl learns to internalize her anger and hurt feelings. Ganging up, which Simmons calls alliance building, is the ultimate relational aggression, forcing the target to confront the possible loss of friendship, not only with the bully but with other friends. The victim usually ends up isolated: exactly what she was afraid of.

Alliance building affords girls a chance to belong to a clique. Taking sides demonstrates support, and offers both inclusion and comfort. It is a sign of peer affirmation, implying that you won't be abandoned. If a girl can turn others against a target, they won't turn against her. So alliance building validates the experience of aggression. One-on-one conflict is not acceptable to girls, but alliance building—a plurality—combines aggression with peer approval. Guilt diminishes when responsibility is shared (Simmons, 2002).

A harrowing example of how adolescents become involved with hostile peers is illustrated by the movie *Thirteen* (Hardwicke & Reed, 2003). The film vividly details how Tracy, a smart, well-behaved seventh grade student, is befriended and led astray by Evie, her precocious new best friend. The movie opens with a shocking scene of the two girls, who are high on drugs, smacking each other's face and laughing. In order to maintain the relationship, the previously sweet, sensitive Tracy is bullied into stealing, shoplifting, taking drugs, self-mutilation, and sexual experimentation. It is as though Tracy is being initiated into the sorority from hell. The competition between girls like these two and their friends makes it seem as though the bond that unites them is hate, not love. The girls terrorize each other with stares, put-downs, rebukes, rumors, and rejections. The film makes viewers uncomfortable but needs to be seen in order to help us understand these youngsters.

Conclusions

Gender differences in bullying behavior are like those found in other types of aggression: both the incidence and type of bullying are different in boys and girls. Although males have higher levels of overt aggression, levels of relational aggression are more equal across gender lines. The latter is more common in girls; boys catch up as their verbal skills improve. Over time, verbal bullying becomes common to both genders (Mullin-Rindler, 2003).

Recent studies indicate that beginning with adolescence, students value antisocial behavior more positively, equate popularity with dominance and control, and get more involved with aggressive peers (Mullin-Rindler, 2003). Girls manipulate friendships, gossip, and ostracize others in the competition for social position; boys also spread rumors, threaten isolation, and scapegoat.

Meltz (2003) states that there are two rumors about boys that damage their reputations: to be called gay or to be called a boy slut. The first is spread by other boys as early as sixth grade. By high school, most have been called gay and/or spread rumors about others. The second rumor is spread by high school girls, usually meant as a warning that a boy is casual and cruel in sexual relationships. While this may hinder relationships with girls, it usually adds status with other boys, so that they lie or try to deserve the slur.

A new phenomenon, common among middle and high school students, is cyberbullying. Gossip is now spread not only by web sites, but also on web-based bulletin boards read by teens who can add or reply to comments. They derive their power from both publicity and anonymity. Individual students are extremely vulnerable because the audience can be huge (Guernsey, 2003). Even worse, images of victims are now also posted on web sites.

The new technology permits users to cause pain without seeing its impact. This seems to lead to a deeper level of meanness, particularly because it comes coupled with the typical adolescent lack of impulse control and immature empathy skills. The newest weapons for teenage social cruelty include forwarding personal material to people for whom it was not intended, stealing peers' screen names, sending incendiary messages to friends or crush-objects, and posting negative comments on web journals called blogs. Cyberbullying appeals especially to girls, since they tend to avoid direct confrontation and prefer emotional to physical bullying (Harmon, 2004).

Cultural stereotypes about gender and aggression may interfere with children and adolescents' efforts to make vital connections with their peers. Understanding the development of friendship and empathy augments our understanding of how aggression and bullying can hinder relationships. It is to be hoped that future research will find a link between precocious sexuality and relational aggression in girls. But thus far, most of the research on bullying has focused on boys.

Bullying and the chronic victimization of children and adolescents remains a major problem with far-reaching implications. The recent extensive media coverage of retaliatory violence by children, who believe they have been victimized by their peers, has led to a new awareness and sense of urgency. Aggressive children carry their aggression with them into adulthood. The pervasiveness of such problems underscores our need to study the psychodynamic mechanisms responsible for the maintenance of these social positions. As Sageman (2004) says, it is the role of the analyst to work with patients to foster the development of friendship and empathy instead of aggression so that they are no longer bullies, victims, or bystanders.

Davidson (2003) offered me 10 good rules for children which I shall conclude with, rules made up by a kindergarten class: "Always love your teacher, always read a book to a friend, always play together, always share, always hug a friend, don't stick your tongue out, no fighting, no kicking, no screaming, and no biting."

References

Atwood, M. (1989). *Cat's eye.* New York: Doubleday.

Baldry, A. C., & Farrington, D. P. (2000). Bullies and delinquents: Personal characteristics and parental styles. *Journal of Community and Applied Social Psychology, 10,* 17–31.

Eder, D. (1997). Sexual aggression within the school culture. In B. Bank and P. Hall (Eds.), *Gender, equity, and schooling: Policy and practice.* New York: Garland.

Friedman, R. C. (2003, Fall). Internalized homophobia: Psychodynamics and psychotherapy—plenary lecture summary. *American College of Psychoanalysts Newsletter.*

Gonzalez de Rivera, J. L. (2002). *El maltrato psicologico.* Madrid: Espasa-Calpe.

Guernsey, L. (2003, May 8). Telling tales out of school. *The New York Times.*

Hardwicke, C., & Reed, N. (2003). *Thirteen.* Fox Searchlight Pictures.

Harmon, A. (2004, August 26). Internet gives teenage bullies weapons to wound from afar. *The New York Times.*

Healy, P. (2004, April 12). Expressway argument leads to the arrest of a firefighter. *The New York Times.*

Horn, S. (1996). *Shalom Japan: One woman's journey into the land of sushi, communal baths and hi-tech toilets.* New York: Kensington Books.

Kawabata, N. (2001). Adolescent trauma in Japanese schools: Two case studies of *ijime* (bullying) and school refusal. *Journal of the American Academy of Psychoanalysis, 29*(1), 85–103.

Ladd, G. W., & Ladd, B. K. (1998). Parenting behavior and parent-child relationships: Correlates of peer victimization in kindergarten? *Developmental Psychology, 34,* 145–1458.

Meadows, S., & Johnson, D. (2003, May 19). Girl fight: Savagery in the suburbs. *New York Newsday.*

Meltz, B. (2003, April 3). Boys can have bad reputations, too. *The Boston Globe.*

Mullin-Rindler, N. (2003). *Relational aggression and bullying: It's more than just a girl thing.* (Working Paper No. 408). Wellesley, MA: Wellesley Centers for Research on Women.

Olweus, D. (1978). *Aggression in the schools: Bullies and whipping boys.* Washington, DC: Hemisphere.

Olweus, D. (1993). *Bullying at school: What we know and what we can do.* Cambridge, MA: Blackwell.

Olweus, D. (1994). Bullying at school: Long-term outcomes for the victims and effective school-based intervention program. In L. R. Huesman (Ed.), *Aggressive behavior: Current perspectives* (pp. 97–130). New York: Plenum.

Olweus, D. (2001). Peer harassment: A critical analysis and some important issues. In J. Juvonen & S. Graham (Eds.), *Peer harassment in school: The plight of the vulnerable and victimized* (pp. 3–19). New York: Guilford.

Perry, D. G., Hodges, E. V. F., & Egan, S. K. (2001). Determinants of chronic victimization by peers: A review and new model of family influence. In J. Juvonen & S. Graham (Eds.), *Peer harassment in schools: The plight of the vulnerable and victimized* (pp. 73–104). New York: Guilford.

Simmons, R. (2002). *Odd girl out.* New York: Harcourt.

Thomas, H. E. (1998, April). The shame response to rejection triggers and physical reactions. *Brown University Child and Adolescent Behavior Letter.*

Thone, B. (1993). *Gender play: Girls and boys in school.* New Brunswick, NJ: Rutgers University Press.

Twemlow, S. W., & Fonagy, P. (2005). The prevalence of teachers who bully students in schools with differing levels of behavioral problems. *American Journal of Psychiatry, 162,* 2387–2389.

Viadoro, D. (2003, May 14). Two studies highlight links between violence and bullying by students. *Education Week.*

Whitney, I., and Smith, P .K. (1993). A survey of the nature and extent of bullying in junior (middle) and secondary schools. *Educational Research, 31*(1), 3–25.

Something to write about . . .

1. Using the readings provided at the end of this chapter, write a causal argument on the topic of bullying in school. When writing this essay, you might want to conduct additional research or draw on your own knowledge and experience.

2. Identify some current trend in pop culture that interests you—a style of music, a particular fashion, a way of communicating, a game. Through research and reflection, write an argumentative essay in which you support some assertion concerning the trend's causes and/or effects.

3. Think about an important decision you have made in your life. Write an argumentative essay in which you support some claim concerning the causes and/or effects of that decision.

WRITING PROPOSAL ARGUMENTS

WHAT ARE PROPOSAL ARGUMENTS?

When you write a proposal argument, you support or oppose an existing policy, critique an existing policy, or propose a new policy. Whatever form a proposal argument assumes, your argument should accomplish several goals:

- Identify a problem that needs to be addressed
- Convince your readers that they should be concerned about this problem
- Examine several possible solutions to the problem
- Argue persuasively that one solution or course of action is the best way to address that problem

In your argument, you will explain in detail exactly how the policy or action you advocate will help solve the problem as you have defined it, identify the strengths and weaknesses of the policy or action you support, and persuade your readers that it is preferable to other possible policies or actions.

KEY ELEMENTS OF A PROPOSAL ARGUMENT

Most proposal arguments consist of two parts: a problem section and a solution section. You need to persuade your readers that the problem is serious and worth their consideration and that the solution or solutions you propose can effectively address it.

Establishing the Problem

To persuade your readers that they should be interested in or concerned about the problem you are addressing, you will need to develop answers to the following questions:

What Is the Problem?

Explain the problem as clearly and simply as you can. What makes the problem a problem?

For Whom Is It a Problem?

Who does your problem affect? Does it affect some people more than others? Does it affect all of society? If so, does it affect all parts of society equally or does it impact some parts of society more than others? Is it a problem for all humankind? How so?

How Long Has It Been a Problem?

What is the history of the problem? Is this a recent phenomenon or has it existed for some time? Have there been any changes recently in the nature or severity of the problem? If so, what were these changes? What caused them? Was the problem worse in the past? Why?

Who Has Identified It as a Problem?

Who says it is a problem? Why do they think it is a problem? Do people disagree about whether it is a problem? If so, what is the nature of the disagreement? Have the people defining it as a problem changed their opinions over time?

What or Who Caused the Problem?

What or who caused the problem to occur? Was the problem caused purposefully or accidentally? If purposefully, what were the reasons for causing it? If the problem has occurred periodically throughout history, were its causes the same each time?

What Are the Costs of the Problem?

How does the problem affect people? What are the negative consequences it brings about? What makes these consequences negative? Does it affect people's economic status, safety, sense of security, or pursuit of happiness? Have the costs of the problem changed over time? Are they likely to change in the future?

Identifying Possible Solutions

Once you have established the nature and extent of the problem, you need to investigate possible solutions. In this section of your essay, you will answers questions such as these:

What Are Some Possible Solutions?

What solutions might you consider? What terms need to be defined in order for your readers to understand each solution? Is the relationship between the problem and each solution clear or does it need to be explained?

How Would Each Solution Actually Solve the Problem?

You cannot expect your readers to understand how a solution will work. Instead, you need to explain how each solution you examine would solve the problem as you have defined it in the first part of your paper. How will each solution address each aspect of the problem? What will each solution accomplish? What will each one fail to accomplish?

Evaluating Solutions

Academic readers will want to know the strengths and weaknesses of both the solutions you endorse and the ones you reject. Assuming you are investigating a range of solutions, each of which could solve the problem, what makes one stronger than the others? What are the drawbacks of each solution you examine, even the one you endorse? To identify strengths and weaknesses of solutions, ask these questions:

Is the Solution Practical?

Impractical solutions are likely doomed to failure. As you consider a possible solution to a problem, ask yourself whether it is too complicated or too time-consuming to be implemented effectively. When deciding between two possible solutions, give greater consideration to the one that is less complicated, less time-consuming, and more practical than the other.

Is the Solution Affordable?

Related to the question of whether a solution is practical is the question of whether it is affordable. There may be many reasons to support a particular solution, but if it is too expensive to implement, you may need to reject it. If you feel that readers might object to a solution you endorse because of its cost, propose a way to pay for it.

Would the Solution Have Public Support?

Even if a solution is practical and economically viable, it might not succeed if it lacks public support. Will people accept and act on the proposal you are advocating? Are there significant political, philosophical, religious, or personal reasons your readers might resist or reject the solution you are supporting in your essay? Can you address these concerns?

Has the Solution Been Tried Before?

If the solution has been tried before, what were the results? If the solution succeeded in the past, establish in your essay that the current situation is similar to the previous one, arguing that if the solution you are proposing worked then, it should work now. If the solution failed to adequately solve the problem in the past, establish that the present situation differs in some significant way from the prior situation and argue that these differences make your solution more likely to succeed when employed this time. Perhaps the solution failed because it was not adequately implemented or supported, was not given adequate time to work, or succeeded in solving some but not all aspects of the problem.

What Are the Solution's Drawbacks or Possible Negative Consequences?

What are the weaknesses or negative consequences of every solution you consider? If there are too many limitations or severe negative consequences associated with a solution, is it worth even considering? Even when you identify the solution you think is best—the one you want to support in your essay—consider its shortcomings. What are its limitations and how can you address them?

Is the Solution Ethical?

The most practical, cost-effective solution to a problem might not always be ethical. What ethical questions are raised by each solution you examine? How can you address them in your argument?

What Is the Solution's Possible Impact on Your Readers?

Finally, consider carefully the impact any solution you examine might have on your intended audience. How might each solution impact them? Will the impact be positive, negative, or some combination of the two? How will it influence your readers' attitudes toward your argument? Will they recognize the impact a solution might have on them or do you need to explain it in your essay?

Establishing the Best Solution

Most assignments that require you to examine multiple solutions to a problem also require to you identify which of them you believe is better than the others. The best solution might be one you have not yet discussed in your essay or some combination of those you have already addressed. If it is some combination of solutions you have already examined in your essay, you will need to explain clearly how they would be combined. Your goal in this section of the essay is to persuade your readers that the solution you select is, indeed, the best course of action to follow. To achieve your goals in this section of your argument, consider how you would answer the following questions:

What Makes This the Best Solution?

Any number of factors can make one solution better than others you have examined. Some of the more common criteria are:

- It is best because it is the most comprehensive.
- It is best because it is the most affordable.
- It is best because it is the most ethical.
- It is best because its benefits outweigh its drawbacks.
- It is best because it will be the easiest to implement.

If This Is Such a Good Solution, Why Hasn't It Been Enacted Already?

If the solution you are offering is superior to the alternatives, why isn't it currently being implemented? This question can be difficult to answer, but here are some strategies you might employ:

- It was tried before and failed, but conditions have so significantly changed that it is likely to work now.

- Conditions have changed, so this solution is now more affordable or ethically acceptable.
- The proposal is so new, no one in the past had the opportunity to employ it.

WRITING A PROPOSAL ARGUMENT

A Model Process for Writing Proposal Arguments

Step 1: Analyze the assignment.

As you analyze the assignment, first make sure you understand what kind of proposal argument you are being asked to write. Are you being asked to propose one solution to a problem; to examine several solutions, arguing for one as best; or to analyze and critique an existing policy? Understanding the assignment's intended audience is also crucial. In most cases, you will be expected to persuade your readers to accept or act on your proposal. You will more successfully establish your authority and invoke emotional appeals if you can accurately gauge what your readers know about your topic, how they feel about the problem, and what objections or questions they are likely to raise as they read your argument.

Step 2: Select a topic.

Open topic assignments are fairly common with proposal arguments. Teachers frequently prefer that students investigate topics that interest them. However, the freedom that comes with an open topic can be overwhelming, and students often spend too much time trying to find something to write about. To find a topic, start by answering the questions listed in Figure 13.1 below. Consider how you would explain each problem you identify and how you think it might be solved.

FIGURE 13.1

Proposal Topic Heuristic

A problem facing my community is

_____

A problem facing my country is

_____

A problem I frequently encounter on campus is

_____

A problem I hear my classmates discussing quite a bit is

_____

A problem my parents always face is

_____

A problem people have been trying to solve for years is
_____

A problem that I heard about on the news is
_____

A law that I object to is
_____

A misguided school policy is
_____

A public policy that makes my life more difficult than it needs to be is
_____

A public policy that makes life more difficult for people I know is
_____

A public policy that makes no sense is
_____

A public policy or law that could be improved is
_____

Whatever topic you choose to write about, be sure it interests you: researching and writing a proposal argument takes time, and the quality of your writing will suffer if you are examining a topic that does not capture your imagination. Also, choose a topic about which there is some debate or controversy. Even if you only write about one policy or solution in your essay, you will investigate several, so choose a topic about which experts or authorities disagree.

Step 3: Gather information.

As you gather information for a proposal argument, you need to thoroughly investigate the problem you will address and a range of possible solutions, including the one you will ultimately endorse as best.

Gather Information on the Problem

Through research and reflection, you need to gather information on the nature, scope, history, and cost of the problem you are addressing. Filling out the invention grid found in Figure 13.2 will help you generate helpful material. As you gather information, keep your audience in mind. One of your goals is to persuade your readers that they should care about the problem, that it impacts (or might impact) their lives in some way. What examples, expert testimony, statistics, and the like would they find most persuasive? Likewise, if you are addressing an academic audience, what types of sources are appropriate and which are not? Consider both the type and source of information you generate to establish the problem.

FIGURE 13.2

Invention Grid
Proposal Argument

Investigating the Problem
Problem: _____

What is the problem?

For whom is it a problem?

How long has it been a problem?

Who says it is a problem?

What or who caused the problem?

What are the costs of the problem?

Gather Information on Several Possible Solutions to the Problem

Even if you are required to write about only one solution to a problem, you need to investigate several in order to develop a persuasive argument. The more information you gather on a range of possible actions or policies, the better position you will be in to develop a persuasive argument for your thesis: the more you know about a range of solutions, the easier it will be to formulate an argument for the solution you think is best and anticipate possible objections to or questions about your assertions.

Generate a list of possible solutions to the problem. Keep an open mind and be creative—list as many possible solutions as you can. Once you have generated a list, identify a few solutions you would like to address in your essay, including the one you think is best. Next, evaluate each of the remaining solutions to determine its strengths and limitations. This step may require additional research and reflection. Designing and completing an invention grid such as the one offered in Figure 13.3 will help.

FIGURE 13.3

Invention Grid
Proposal Argument

Evaluating Possible Solutions

Practical Limitations (cost, efficiency, etc.)	Ethical Limitations	Likely Impact on Readers
Possible Solution 1		
Possible Solution 2		
Possible Solution 3		

Gather Material on the Best Solution

You will also need to argue that one solution is better than the others you have examined. To argue persuasively that one solution is best, you need to articulate its strengths and weaknesses and explain why it is better than other policy options. Figure 13.4 offers a tool that might help you identify several reasons you can offer to support your claim that one solution is best.

FIGURE 13.4

Invention Grid
Proposal Argument

Best Solution

Best Solution: _____

How is it more comprehensive than the other possible solutions?
How is it more affordable than the other possible solutions?
How does it avoid the ethical limitations of the other possible solutions?
How do its benefits outweigh its drawbacks?
What makes it easier to implement than the other possible solutions?
Why might the public more readily accept this solution than the others?

Step 4: Form a thesis statement.

Your thesis statement should identify the problem you are addressing and indicate that you are going to propose a solution. In its simplest form, a thesis might read something like this:

> **There is a solution to the problem of teen pregnancy.**
> **Teen pregnancy is a problem that can be solved.**

These open thesis statements tell readers that you will examine one or more solutions to the problem of teen pregnancy. A more specific, closed thesis statement might read like this:

> **Though the recent rise in teen pregnancy rates is troublesome, increasing funds for comprehensive school-based intervention programs is the best way to address the problem.**

Again, the thesis indicates that you will address the problem of teen pregnancy but will argue in favor of one specific solution: increased funding for school-based intervention programs. If you were going to address several solutions to the problem, you might want to list them in your thesis:

> **Though the recent rise in teen pregnancy rates is troublesome, solutions include distributing condoms in school, increasing parental involvement in their children's lives, and increasing funds for comprehensive school-based intervention programs.**

This thesis indicates that you will examine three solutions to the problem of teen pregnancy. Your reader would not know, however, whether you were going to argue that one of these solutions is better than the others. To do that, your thesis might read something like this:

> **Though distributing condoms in school and finding ways to increase parental involvement in students' lives may help address the recent rise in teen pregnancy rates, the best solution to the problem is to increase funding for comprehensive school-based intervention programs.**

Step 5: Organize your argument.

While there are many ways to organize a proposal argument, two of the more common are outlined below: one for a paper that examines a single solution to an existing problem and another that examines multiple solutions to an existing problem, endorsing one as best.

Single Solution to a Problem

If you are writing a proposal argument that will examine a single solution to an existing problem, you might consider following or modifying the outline offered below in Figure 13.5.

FIGURE 13.5	**BOX OUTLINE**

Proposal Argument
Argument Proposing a Single Solution to a Problem

Opening Section

Strategy you will employ to engender reader interest

Thesis: Statement that indicates you will argue in support of a solution to an existing problem.

Problem Section

Claim: Assertion that something is a problem

Reason 1: First reason it is a problem

   Evidence: Support for the first reason

   Explanation: How the evidence supports this reason

Reason X: Last reason it is a problem

   Evidence: Support for the last reason

   Explanation: How the evidence supports this reason

Objections: Possible objections to or questions concerning the claim

Rebuttal: Possible answers to those objections or questions

BOX OUTLINE

Proposal Argument *(continued)*

Solution Section

Claim: Assertion that a proposed course of action will solve the problem

Reason 1: First reason that this solution will work

  Evidence: Support for the first reason

  Explanation: How the evidence supports this reason

Reason X: Last reason that this solution will work

  Evidence: Support for the last reason

  Explanation: How the evidence supports this reason

Objections: Possible objections to or questions concerning the claim

Rebuttal: Possible answers to those objections or questions

Closing Section

Strategy you will employ to conclude your argument

With this organizational strategy, you would include your thesis in the opening section of your argument. You would then examine the problem before you argue in favor of one solution supporting your claim that this course of action will address the problem with reasons, evidence, and explanations. Throughout your argument, you would address questions or objections your readers are likely to raise, as needed.

Multiple Solutions to a Problem

If you are going to examine multiple solutions to a problem before arguing that one is best, you might consider using or modifying the outline provided in Figure 13.6.

FIGURE 13.6   **BOX OUTLINE**

Proposal Argument

Argument Examining Multiple Solutions to a Problem

Opening Section

Strategy you will employ to engender reader interest

Thesis: Statement concerning the problem and solutions

Problem Section

Claim: Assertion that something is a problem

Reason 1: First reason it is a problem

(continued)

BOX OUTLINE

Proposal Argument *(continued)*

Evidence: Support for the first reason

Explanation: How the evidence supports this reason

Reason X: Last reason it is a problem

Evidence: Support for the last reason

Explanation: How the evidence supports this reason

Objections: Possible objections to or questions concerning the claim

Rebuttal: Possible answers to those objections or questions

Solution One Section

Claim: Assertion that this solution might address the problem

Reason 1: First reason that this solution will work

Evidence: Support for the first reason

Explanation: How the evidence supports this reason

Reason X: Last reason that this solution will work

Evidence: Support for the last reason

Explanation: How the evidence supports this reason

Objections: Possible objections to or questions concerning the claim

Rebuttal: Possible answers to those objections or questions

Claim: Assertion that this solution is *not* the best policy to follow

Reason 1: First reason that this solution is not the best one to follow

Evidence: Support for the first reason

Explanation: How the evidence supports this reason

Reason X: Last reason that this solution is not the best one to follow

Evidence: Support for the last reason

Explanation: How the evidence supports this reason

Objections: Possible objections to or questions concerning the claim

Rebuttal: Possible answers to those objections or questions

Solution X Section

Claim: Assertion that this last alternative solution might address the problem

Reason 1: First reason that this solution will work

Evidence: Support for the first reason

Explanation: How the evidence supports this reason

Reason X: Last reason that this solution will work

Evidence: Support for the last reason

Explanation: How the evidence supports this reason

BOX OUTLINE

Proposal Argument *(continued)*

Objections: Possible objections to or questions concerning the claim

Rebuttal: Possible answers to those objections or questions

Claim: Assertion that this solution is *not* the best policy to follow

Reason 1: First reason that this solution is not the best one to follow

    Evidence: Support for the first reason

    Explanation: How the evidence supports this reason

Reason X: Last reason that this solution is not the best one to follow

    Evidence: Support for the last reason

    Explanation: How the evidence supports this reason

Objections: Possible objections to or questions concerning the claim

Rebuttal: Possible answers to those objections or questions

Best Solution Section

Claim: Assertion that this proposed course of action is the best way to solve the problem

Reason 1: First reason that this is the best solution

    Evidence: Support for the first reason

    Explanation: How the evidence supports this reason

Reason X: Last reason that this is the best solution

    Evidence: Support for the last reason

    Explanation: How the evidence supports this reason

Objections: Possible objections to or questions concerning the claim

Rebuttal: Possible answers to those objections or questions

Closing Section

Strategy you will employ to conclude your argument

With this organizational strategy, you would state your thesis in the opening section of your paper. In the problem section, you would provide information that establishes the nature and extent of the problem and employ various appeals to persuade readers to take an active interest in it. You would then examine several possible solutions, one at a time, first arguing that each might solve the problem but is not the best solution possible, supporting your assertions with reasons, evidence, and explanations. As needed, you would address possible questions or objections throughout this section of your argument.

In the next section of your paper, you would present what you believe to be the best solution to the problem. This solution could be one you have not yet discussed in your essay or some combination of the solutions you have already examined. In either case, you would support your claim with reasons, evidence, and explanations and address likely objections to or questions concerning your assertion. The "best solution" should *not* be one you already discussed in your essay. In the conclusion of your essay, you would draw your argument to a satisfying end and make an effort to regain reader interest or motivate action.

Step 6: Draft your argument.

Opening Section

In the opening section of your essay, you should introduce the topic of your argument, state your thesis, and make an effort to capture your readers' interest. Here are some of the more effective strategies you might consider employing to draw your reader into your proposal argument: offer a historical overview of the problem, offer an overview of the current situation, appeal to your readers' emotions, needs, or values, offer an interesting story, pose a provocative question, offer an interesting quotation, or summarize what authorities have written about your topic.

Body

In the body of your essay, follow your outline as you draft each section of your argument, supporting all of your claims with persuasive reasons and evidence. As you move from one section of your essay to the next, pay particular attention to the transitions you employ. In your topic sentences, repeat key words or ideas from your thesis to connect the various sections of your essay and provide transition words or phrases to help readers follow your line of thought. Finally, even as you write your first draft, document any source material you use to avoid problems with plagiarism later in the writing process.

Closing Section

Your conclusion should bring your argument to a logical, satisfying finish, remind readers of your thesis, and maintain reader interest. Some strategies you might consider employing to accomplish these goals include the following: recommend a course of action, suggest what might occur if no action is taken, explain the relationship of your argument to other arguments discussed in your essay, conclude with an interesting story, provide an interesting quotation, or answer a question you raised earlier in your essay.

Step 7: Revise your argument.

Revise Content and Structure

When you revise for content, check your argument one section at a time to be sure you have adequately defined the problem and persuasively supported your claims concerning its solution. As you revise, keep clearly in focus the audience and purpose of your argument—ask yourself whether you have included the most persuasive information, appeals, and arguments possible. When you revise for content, consider the following questions:

- How well will readers understand the argument I am making in this essay?
- How have I attempted to persuade my readers that they should be concerned about the problem I am addressing? How successful is each appeal likely to be?
- How clearly have I explained how each solution I present might solve this problem?
- How clearly have I explained why I reject some of the solutions?
- How clearly have I explained why I believe one solution to be better than the others?
- How successfully have I persuaded my readers that this is the best solution?

When you revise to improve the structure of your essay, consider these questions:

- How well does my thesis guide the development of my essay?
- How well do my topic sentences help guide readers from one section of my essay to the next?
- How well do my topic sentences remind readers of my thesis?
- How well do the transitions in each paragraph help readers follow my argument?

Revise for Clarity and Correctness

As you revise for clarity, pay close attention to word choice and syntax. Do you need to explain any technical terms or allusions? Is your language clear? Are your sentences concise and varied? Carefully check your spelling and punctuation (do not rely on your word processing program's spell-checker to catch errors). If you have a hard time catching sentence-level errors in your own writing, have someone else read your argument and mark any questionable passages.

Revise Documentation

Be sure you have properly documented all of the source material you use in your essay (including all paraphrased passages) and correctly ordered and composed your works cited list or bibliography.

Revision Checklist

You will find a revision checklist for proposal arguments in Appendix 1.

Common Errors to Avoid When Writing a Proposal Argument

Failing to Adequately Establish the Problem

Student writers are often so eager to get to the solution section of their essay that they fail to adequately explain the problem. Be sure you establish that the problem exists and connect it to your readers' lives through appeals to their emotions, needs, and values.

Failing to Explain What Makes the Best Solution Best

At some point in a proposal argument, you will identify what you believe to be the best course of action to follow. Simply asserting that one solution is best will not persuade many academic readers. Instead, you need to support your claim with reasons, evidence, and clear reasoning.

Failing to Acknowledge the Weaknesses of the Best Solution

Whatever solution you ultimately endorse, realize that it is not perfect. Failing to acknowledge and address the limitations or drawbacks of the solution you endorse will weaken your credibility and make your argument less persuasive than it might otherwise be. Academic readers will question your argument if they think it is too one-sided, biased, or uncritical.

Sample Student Essay: Proposal Argument

This sample proposal argument, written by Janelle Jackson, is based on the writer's own knowledge and primary research and addresses a problem at her college—declining student retention.

SAMPLE PROPOSAL ARGUMENT

Improving Student Retention at Mountain University

Janelle Jackson

As a private institution, Mountain University's financial health depends on maintaining enrollment: without enough students paying tuition, Mountain University (MU) will face certain financial crisis. According to Dr. Julia Sanchez, Director of Enrollment Management, a troubling trend has emerged over the past three years. While freshman enrollment has remained strong (about 750 students a year), retention rates have fallen. That is, increasing numbers of students are deciding not to return to Mountain University after their first year of study. These declining retention rates raise two important questions: Why are students dissatisfied with their experience at Mountain University and what can the school do to address the problem? A recent survey of Mountain University students revealed several sources of dissatisfaction. University officials can address these problems by restructuring the institution's financial aid program and increasing entertainment opportunities on campus.

To gain a better understanding of student dissatisfaction at Mountain University, I surveyed 237 first-year and second-year students living in Collins and Melbourne Halls (102 men and 135 women). The survey (Appendix A) asked students to reflect on their first year at Mountain and to identify aspects of campus life that might move them to consider transferring to another school. (See 1 for a summary of the survey results.)

Table 1 Survey Results: What Might Make You Consider Leaving Mountain University?

Reason	Number of Responses
Tuition Costs	131
Lack of Entertainment Options	99
Food Services	72
Housing Options	66
Homesickness	59
Difficulty of Classes	50
Loneliness	20
Quality of Professors/Teaching	12
Lack of Specific Educational Programs, Majors, or Degree Options	7
Quality of Academic Support Services	0
Other	14

Most students mentioned the cost of tuition as a reason they might consider leaving Mountain University, 131 of the 237 students surveyed. However, the survey failed to distinguish between two possible reasons for this response: (1) that tuition costs themselves are too high or (2) that not enough financial aid is available to help students manage tuition costs. Any solution to this problem will have to address both possible reasons.

The second most frequently mentioned reason students cited that might move them to transfer from Mountain had to do with the quality of campus life. In all, 99 students said they were dissatisfied with the availability of entertainment on campus, especially on the weekends. The University provides little programming for students. Since first-year students cannot have cars on campus, going out to shop, see a movie, or catch a concert is difficult if not impossible.

One step Mountain University can take to improve its retention rate would be to change the way it handles tuition costs. According to Samuel Eggers, Assistant Provost for Enrollment Management, tuition plus room and board has increased an average of 4.6% a year for the last 5 years. Though Mountain is still less expensive to attend than comparable universities (Eggers), the survey results show that the increasing cost of attending MU is one of the main reasons students transfer to other schools.

One way to address this problem would be to institute a tuition rebate to all students. Rebating every MU student $500.00 to help pay for books and fees would make attending the university much more affordable for everyone. The problem, however, is that MU currently does not have the financial reserves to enact this policy (Eggers). There is not enough money on hand to afford such a rebate. Another solution to consider would be to offer tuition rebates to students based solely on need. Tony Washington, a senior economics major at MU, believes this policy makes sense: "If you can identify the students that are really facing financial hardships by coming here and give them a little extra help, that might directly aid retention." However,

Sarah Antonelli, President of Mountain's Student Board, sees several problems with this proposal:

> First, will that $500.00 really make a difference if a person is in real financial need? Also, would that really be fair, to offer it to some students and not to others? How would you determine need? What would the cutoff point be? Would a student be in need one year and get the funds and not be in need the next and not get them? Would the funds be guaranteed for four years regardless of how a student's needs change?

Antonelli offered an alternative plan to address the cost-related reasons so many students are leaving Mountain University.

Under Antonelli's proposal, Mountain would increase tuition and fees for all students an additional .5% a year on top of regularly scheduled increases to create a pool of funds that could help students defray the cost of attending MU. The amount of rebate a student receives each year would be determined by need—every student will receive some form of rebate, but those in the most need will receive the most funds. Rebates would be awarded only to those students who request it through an online application process. According to Antonelli, "Overseeing this program would require little additional time from staff in the financial aid office if the application process and rebate calculations could all be handled electronically." This proposal would indeed help solve the problem of cost mentioned by so many students in the survey. Every student would benefit financially, making it fair, and those most in need would benefit most, making it just.

The second problem noted by students in the survey—too little entertainment opportunities on campus—could be addressed by booking additional concerts during the school year, showing additional films in the Student Union, or expanding existing intramural sports and arts groups on campus. Currently, the Student Board sponsors two or three concerts a term. To provide more weekend entertainment, the Board could expand this program and sponsor a concert every other week. However, according to Sarah Antonelli, booking more concerts would be too expensive. Last year the Board lost almost $15,000 on the concerts they sponsored due to poor ticket sales. While booking lesser known local bands would be less expensive than booking better known bands, Antonelli pointed out that if sales were slow for name bands, they may be even worse for bands that are unknown to most students.

An alternative way to increase entertainment opportunities on campus would be to expand the number of movies shown at the Student Union. Currently, the Union shows films on Thursday and Friday nights. DeShay Williams, Director of the Student Union, stated that the movies are usually well attended and was open to the idea of showing films on Saturday and Sunday nights as well. However, Williams noted that the Union's projector and sound system are old and in need of repair. If the Union were to expand its film series, this equipment would need to be replaced, which would cost $30–40 thousand (Williams). Showing films on the weekends would help address one of the problems that makes Mountain University students consider transferring, but the cost would make this option too expensive to implement.

A final solution to student boredom would be to expand the university's intramural sports programs. Athletic Director Dallas Fuquay states that roughly 45% of all MU students participate in intramural sports. Intramural basketball, soccer, fencing, and ultimate Frisbee are some of the more popular programs. A small increase in funding could expand these programs and increase participation. Most of the games and matches occur on the weekends, which would address the concerns students cited on the survey. In addition, expanding the program would improve student health and enhance the social atmosphere of campus. Alice Parkson, a physical education major at MU, stated that she and many of the other students in her program would take advantage of expanded intramural sports programs to gain needed experience coaching or officiating matches and games. Expanding these programs would only require $5–10 thousand, making it a much less expensive option than bringing in more bands or expanding university film programs.

Mountain University is right to be concerned about its student retention rates. The school needs to address this problem. The survey I conducted revealed several sources of dissatisfaction with life at MU that lead students to consider transferring to other schools. Each of these concerns, however, can be solved with a little effort and ingenuity. In its University Bulletin, MU states that it "values each of its students" and offers "a supportive and challenging college experience." Lowering the cost of attending college and improving available extracurricular activities would demonstrate the University's commitment to these ideals.

Works Cited

Antonelli, Sarah. Personal interview. 19 June 2007.
Eggers, Samuel. Personal interview. 25 June 2007.
Fuquay, Dallas. Personal interview. 25 June 2007.
Mountain University Bulletin. August 2005. Web.
Parkson, Alice. Personal interview. 24 June 2007.
Washington, Tony. Personal interview. 24 June 2007.
Williams, DeShay. Telephone interview. 25 June 2007.

Appendix A

What Might Make You Consider Leaving Mountain University?

Based on your experience, what might make you consider leaving Mountain University and transferring to another school? Check all that apply. If you check "other," please specify the reason.

Tuition costs _____
Difficulty of classes _____
Quality of professors/teaching _____
Quality of academic support services _____
Housing options _____
Food services _____
Lack of specific educational programs, majors, or degree options _____
Loneliness _____
Being homesick _____

Lack of entertainment options ——————————————————————————

Other (be specific) ————————————————————————————————

——

——

——

Something to write about . . .

After carefully reading and rereading "Improving Student Retention at Mountain University," complete the following writing assignments.

1. Write a one page summary of the reading.
2. Evaluate the methods the author used to gather information for this argument. How persuasive is the argument given its reliance on interviews and an author-generated survey? As you answer this question, keep in mind the argument's rhetorical situation.
3. Write an essay in which you refute one or more of the solutions to Mountain University's problems offered in the reading.
4. Given what you know about Mountain University's problems, offer your own solution. Be sure you explain what it is, how it might be implemented, and how it might solve the problem. Also, indicate how you might address any limitations to your solution and how you might address likely opposition to your plan.

ADDITIONAL READINGS

Few topics seem to get more attention these days during college orientation programs than does binge drinking. Most college administrators who use the term employ the definition of binge drinking developed by Henry Wechsler, director of the College Alcohol Study at Harvard: five or more drinks for men and four or more drinks for women consumed at one occasion at least once during the last two weeks. While some have called this definition into question (as Alan Berkowitz does in the reading below), many other researchers have explored both the causes and effects of student binge drinking. Not surprisingly, most of these authors also offer suggestions to address the problem. In fact, it is not unusual to find these authors offering definition, proposal, and causal arguments in the same essay. Krohn and Pyc also focus on the reasons some college students drink excessively, examine the range of negative consequences that result from that behavior, and compare the relative effectiveness of two commonly employed solutions: attempts to prohibit alcohol on campus and attempts to moderate its use among students.

Before you read the following essays, ask yourself these questions:

- How would you define "binge drinking"?
- What do you think is the cause of binge drinking among students?
- What do you know about the effects of binge drinking on those who drink and on the people around them?
- What is the best way to address the problem of student binge drinking?

- What difficulties or obstacles would any successful solution to the problem have to overcome? Why?
- What would make someone an expert on the topic of student drinking? What kinds of credentials or background would add to someone's authority on this topic?

As you read these essays, ask yourself these questions:

- Is the primary purpose of each essay informative or argumentative?
- If the purpose is argumentative, what is the thesis in each piece?
- Who is the intended audience of each essay? How might that have influenced the content, structure, and tone of the essay?
- To what extent do these authors agree on the causes and/or effects of binge drinking? How do they differ? How do you account for the differences?
- How do these authors support their claims?

When you finish reading the essays, consider these questions:

- Did the readings give you a better understanding of the causes and/or effects of binge drinking?
- Did reading any of the arguments change your mind concerning the causes and/or effects of binge drinking?
- Which of these authors presents the most compelling argument?
- How do you account for the different styles you find in the readings? Which style is most effective? Why?

ADDITIONAL READING

How Should We Talk about Student Drinking—and What Should We Do about It?

Alan David Berkowitz

Alan David Berkowitz holds a Ph.D. in psychology, serves as an independent consultant on a range of academic and social justice issues, and edits the Report on Social Norms. *This essay originally appeared in the publication* About Campus.

During the course of my twenty-five–year career in higher education I have worked as a counseling center director, program director, faculty member, and director of resident adviser hiring and training. In these capacities I have frequently been asked to train student leaders and colleagues in effective problem-solving skills. One of my goals on these occasions is to pass on the received wisdom that an accurate description of a problem is 90 percent of the solution. This wisdom proves useful when defining alcohol abuse on college campuses today—the subject of this article and of professional and popular debate. How we measure student drinking and the words we use to describe it are more than matters of semantics. They have important and far-reaching implications for our relationships with students and for how effective we are in addressing the problem itself.

There is no debate about whether alcohol abuse is a problem on college campuses. Almost all of our professional associations devote considerable attention to the negative effects of student drinking, and college presidents frequently rate alcohol abuse as the number one problem facing their institutions. Even though only a minority of students abuse alcohol, their behavior has serious negative consequences for themselves and for their peers, the majority of whom behave in a healthy and responsible manner. What, then, do current best practices suggest about how to define alcohol abuse and about how to address it?

Problems with the Binge Drinking Label

One of the most widely used terms to refer to high-risk or problem drinking is *binge drinking*, defined as five or more drinks for men and four or more drinks for women on at least one occasion in the last two weeks. This term has been vigorously advocated by researcher Henry Wechsler, who directs the College Alcohol Study with funding from the Robert Wood Johnson Foundation. With the benefit of a budget of more than one million dollars and a private marketing firm to advertise his research findings, Wechsler has popularized this term and riveted the attention of the media on the statistic that approximately 40 to 45 percent of college students binge drink. Overlooked in the popular press and even in our professional publications is the fact that the binge drinking label has been unanimously rejected by the Inter-Association Task Force on Alcohol Abuse and Other Substance Abuse Issues, a consortium of twenty-one higher education organizations. It is also not endorsed by the National Institute on Alcohol Abuse and Alcoholism and the U.S. Department of Education, or accepted in articles published in the *Journal of Studies on Alcohol*, the premier research journal on alcohol issues. A recent letter to the editor of *About Campus* by Robert Chapman outlined concerns about the binge drinking label. In this article I add my voice to these criticisms, arguing that both the term *binge drinking* and the five/four measure (that is, five drinks for men and four for women on at least one occasion in the past two weeks) are problematic and counter to good professional practice, what we know about students from student development theory, and the recommendations of researchers and experts.

Central to the debate about the binge drinking label are issues such as whether it promotes and fosters a collaborative relationship with students, accurately describes the problem, correctly measures the success or failure of drug prevention programs, or contributes to beneficial solutions. Following a review of these concerns, I present an alternative framework for thinking about and addressing student drinking problems and promoting health on campus.

Our Partnerships with Students. Good educational practice requires that we develop collaborative partnerships with students with the goal of improving the quality of their experience in college. The importance of student involvement and collaboration in successful educational programs was borne out in a recent analysis of effective drug prevention programs published in the *Journal of American College Health*. In this study, researcher Andris Ziemelis and his colleagues found that student involvement and input were among the critical factors distinguishing successful and unsuccessful drug prevention programs.

An important part of this collaboration is agreeing on how to define the problem we are trying to solve. Researchers who study the language used by students to describe drinking have found that most students would not describe four or five drinks once in the past two weeks as a binge, and that they resent being described as binge drinkers if they drink this amount. Ironically, some students who are labeled as binge drinkers may in fact be following the advice of educators who suggest that alcohol use be limited to one drink an hour. In contrast, when the focus is on the negative effects of drinking (regardless of how many drinks one has), there is considerable agreement between students and professionals regarding what constitutes problematic drinking and what institutional sanctions should be imposed.

The five/four definition of *binge drinking* is also at variance with clinical terminology, which uses *binge* to refer to a period of excessive consumption stretching over a few days. Thus, the five/four measure conflicts with clinical practice, student experience, and the recommendations of many authorities.

Using the five/four measure produces very high percentages of college students who are thought to be problem drinkers but who may not be. This has the unintended consequence of providing heavy drinkers of alcohol with a rationale for denying their abuse and also allows them to justify their behavior as normative and as more widespread than it really is. Thus, another problem with the five/four measure is that it serves to enable the misperception of abusers, making it harder to confront and address their problem behavior.

What would be a better term than *binge drinking* as it has been defined? Kate Carey, editor of a recent special issue of the *Psychology of Addictive Behaviors* on binge drinking, acknowledged that the five/four measure can be useful for research purposes but concluded that it is a problematic measure in our work with students and in prevention programs. Among the suggested alternatives were *heavy episodic drinking, heavier drinking, high-risk drinking, risky drinking*, and *at-risk drinking*. I believe that these terms are more acceptable to students, less polarizing, and more accurate in describing the problem we are trying to solve. Thus I use the term *high-risk drinking* in the remainder of this article.

Are Those Defined as Binge Drinkers Problem Drinkers? High-risk drinking can be defined in a number of ways, including how much alcohol is consumed and how often (for example, the five/four measure), motivations for drinking, negative effects of drinking, frequency of intoxication, and blood alcohol level. (Note: blood alcohol concentration, or BAC, is a measure of the amount of alcohol in a person's blood. A BAC equal to or greater than .08 or .10 percent is illegal in every state.) Numerous studies have demonstrated that students who have four or five drinks in a sitting do not necessarily get drunk, may not experience negative consequences, and often have a legal BAC. For example, researchers H. Wesley Perkins, William DeJong, and Jeff Linkenbach demonstrated that 63 percent of young adults who were classified as binge drinkers did not reach a BAC of .10 percent or higher, while 48 percent did not reach a BAC of .08 percent or higher. This finding illustrates some of the problems with the five/four measure—that it does not take into account the period in which the alcohol is consumed, the body weight of the drinker, or the person's drinking history. By using a measure that produces so many false positives, students whose behavior is not problematic are lumped together with their peers who are drinking more dangerously, obscuring the problem we are trying to solve. The unreliability of the five/four binge measure was illustrated in a recent study by Jennifer Bauerle, Cynthia Burwell, and James C. Turner, from the University of Virginia, where extensive drug prevention programming resulted in significant reductions in negative consequences of alcohol use while at the same time the binge rate went up slightly.

Insensitivity to Change. If the University of Virginia program had used the five/four measure, it would have been labeled a failure when the campus had become much safer. In a similar example, drug prevention efforts at another college were followed by a decrease from 20 to 13 percent in the number of students drinking ten or more drinks at a sitting, yet the five/four measure would have revealed no change in the percentage of so-called binge drinkers. These examples suggest that reliance on a dichotomous measure (one that uses a cut-off) to measure change can overlook important outcomes.

An exclusive focus on how many students "binge" can also obscure progress in other ways. For example, a few years ago the Harvard School of Public Health's College Alcohol Study issued alarming press releases about a very slight increase in frequent heavy binge drinking (based on the five/four measure) while downplaying an impressive increase of 20 percent during the same period in the number of students who abstain from alcohol use.

Overemphasizing the Negative. It is human nature to notice extreme visible behavior, remember it, and assume that it is normative. While writing this article, for example, I have frequently had to discipline myself to use language that refers to the problem drinking behavior of some students without attributing it to students in general. While this focus on negative behavior is understandable, we do our students and higher education a disservice when we describe today's collegians as irresponsible and drinking too much when in fact this is true of only a minority. We literally and figuratively pay for this characterization when our state legislatures and other funding sources question our efforts based on this faulty and inaccurate picture of students. As researcher and theorist Jeff Linkenbach has noted, these "cultural cataracts" encourage a distorted view of youth who are seen as problems or as high-risk when in fact most are responsible young adults trying to make their way in a problematic and high-risk world.

Defining the problem in terms of the negative behavior of the minority is also unfair to those students and student groups who drink less and with fewer problems. For example, Latinos, African Americans, Asian Americans, Native Americans, and women all drink less and with fewer problems than Caucasian men, and most Caucasian men drink responsibly. Thus, characterizing all students as part of the problem is unfair and does not acknowledge the range of drinking and nondrinking behaviors common among diverse student cultures and identities.

A Different Way of Thinking about Drinking

What if we instead focus on the positive behavior of the majority at the same time as we address the problem behavior of the minority? Dozens of studies have reported that most students drink seldom if at all and that most of those who drink do so without serious negative consequences. Yet faculty, staff, student leaders, and students may talk about drinking as if most students drink irresponsibly. Research and theory associated with the social norms approach to alcohol use has demonstrated that this overestimation of drinking in fact encourages students to drink more while at the same time allowing irresponsible drinkers to justify their abuse. For example, most students think that their friends, members of their residence halls, and students on their campus drink more than they really do. Correlational and longitudinal studies have demonstrated that when students think their peers drink more than they really do, they drink more. Heavy drinkers also think that other students drink more than they do, allowing them to justify their own behavior. (See Berkowitz's *The Social Norms Approach* for a review of this research.) Furthermore, extensive research and program evaluation have demonstrated that correction of these misperceptions reduces drinking. Countering this misperception requires that we discipline ourselves to acknowledge, reinforce, and appreciate the responsible majority while at the same time responding to the irresponsible behavior of the minority.

Imagine that I am teaching an early morning class and notice that many of the students are tired. In fact, one or two are sleeping! Feeling irritated and insecure, I say to my students, "You all look tired. I bet you were out too late drinking last night." With this one comment I have invalidated the majority who were studying in their rooms or at the library, participating in an organized activity, having fun without drinking, or working at part-time employment. I have reinforced the incorrect belief that drinking is normative for both those who were out drinking and those who weren't.

The use of research and language to identify accurately the scope and nature of the problem is a first step to solving it. A second step is to be informed and to think and speak accurately about students. Advertising and supporting the healthy behavior of the majority is a third step. These three premises are central to the social norms approach, which has successfully lowered high-risk drinking rates and reduced smoking on numerous campuses. Social norms programs have received many best practice awards, and the social norms approach has been recommended by neutral panels of national experts. (Reviews of this literature are available on the Higher Education Center for Alcohol and Other Drug Prevention's Web site, www.edc.org/hec, or in *The Social Norms Approach to Preventing School and College Age Substance Abuse*, edited by H. Wesley Perkins, with contributions by a variety of educators, researchers, and social norms practitioners, published this year by Jossey-Bass.)

The social norms approach provides a means of modifying the larger environment in which drinking takes place—in this case by correcting misperceptions of what is normative in students' social environments. It can be used separately or in combination with other environmental management strategies, such as those that restrict the availability of alcohol and constrain its irresponsible use. This fourth component of effective drug prevention is accomplished through activities such as server training; creating and implementing effective, fair, and consistent policies; developing guidelines for alcohol advertising on campus; and reshaping visible campus events in which alcohol use is prominent. Effective environmental management strategies must be implemented with an awareness of and emphasis on the responsible majority and without exclusively focusing on the irresponsible minority. Many campuses (for instance, Northern Illinois University, Hobart and William Smith Colleges, and Western Washington University) have successfully used social norms interventions to reduce high-risk drinking, and other campuses (for example, the University of Arizona and the University of Missouri at Columbia) have successfully combined social norms with other environmental interventions with similar results.

Recommendations

Here are a few guidelines for drug prevention programs that will accurately define the problem and foster effective solutions.

Always include, listen to, and involve students. Develop policies, procedures, and practices with student input and support. Conduct surveys to determine what students actually do, how they feel about sanctions and policies, what media they find appealing, and what solutions they support. In their analysis of campus drug prevention programs, Ziemelis and his colleagues found that student involvement was one of the strongest predictors of program success. Campuses that use social norms marketing routinely use students to critique, evaluate, and develop social norms media. Student input was also key to the success of a revised alcohol policy at the University of Delaware, where students were surveyed to determine what consequences they thought were appropriate for various policy violations. The fact that most students were in favor of expulsion for multiple violations of the alcohol policy was critical to the success of the revised policy.

Focus on changing the environment in which problem behavior takes place. The most successful drug prevention programs change the physical, social, and legal environment in which drinking takes place and do not focus only on the problem behavior or the problem individual. The University of Arizona, for example, combined a social norms marketing campaign with consistent enforcement of policies regarding alcohol use at homecoming. In addition, the time of the homecoming game was made earlier to allow less time for drinking before the game. These changes in the drinking environment led to dramatic reductions in alcohol problems at homecoming at the same time as the social norms marketing campaign was successful in reducing high-risk drinking. The University of Arizona program has been recently designated by the federal government as a best practice program.

Avoid using the term binge drinking *and be aware of the limitations of the five/four measure.* Employ a variety of measures to gain an accurate understanding of the scope and nature of collegiate drinking, and use language that accurately conveys the complex and nuanced nature of campus drinking and nondrinking cultures.

Focus on high-risk or problematic drinking rather than on alcohol use per se. Clearly our institutions need to respond to illegal behavior such as underage drinking when it is visible. At the same time, a primary emphasis on reducing harm and fostering health is likely to create a broad coalition of support, provide a realistic focus for our efforts, and have the greatest likelihood of increasing the percentage of our students who abstain from alcohol. For example, among the different consequences of alcohol use, some are more harmful to self and others and some are less harmful. It would make sense to focus our efforts first on these more harmful behaviors and design programs to address them rather than direct our efforts toward everyone who drinks.

Utilize strategies that support positive behavior and empower the responsible majority. We must learn to think of education as a process of growing health and wisdom and not only as a process of eliminating problems and ignorance. Most of our students and student communities are resilient, healthy, and full of positive coping mechanisms with respect to alcohol and other issues. Let us commit ourselves to acknowledging, encouraging, and validating this health. For example, when addressing or talking about problem behavior, we can place these problems in context by referring to data that most students engage in healthy behavior that is not problematic.

With parents, trustees, alumni, and the media we can emphasize and describe the positive behavior of the majority while still acknowledging where there are problems. This will in turn encourage our students to act on and express these values in their relationships with one another, bring actions into congruence with values, and create a less hospitable atmosphere for irresponsible behavior. Focusing on the positive behavior of the majority has been shown to "grow" or increase healthy behavior in numerous social norms efforts.

Develop and implement policies that have community support. There will always be times when leaders have to make unpopular decisions. But more often an accurate survey of our community members will demonstrate that they support and agree with the measures we want to take (even when those who support them incorrectly see themselves in the minority).

Target visible events and behaviors that will have the greatest impact. Many of our campuses have traditions and events in which visible and irresponsible alcohol use is common—an important athletic event, a historical tradition, or a particular time of year when excessive alcohol use is visible. These events serve to reinforce the perception that problem behavior is normative. It is important that we reshape these events to deemphasize the role of alcohol and ensure that its use is responsible and legal.

Make a long-term commitment to prevention. Prevention is a process, not an event. There is an ample and growing literature suggesting that social norms and other environmental management strategies can be successfully implemented—independently or together—to reduce problem alcohol use in campus communities. Case studies indicate that this is a long-term and ongoing process that benefits from visible leadership from the top, articulation of a common framework, collection of accurate survey data on a regular basis, collaboration with the local community and important stakeholders on campus, and design of programs that are synergistic and connected, rather that isolated and disconnected from one another. On many campuses, some or all of these components are lacking.

In this article I have outlined a vision of alcohol abuse prevention that is based on an accurate view of the presence or absence of alcohol in our students' lives. This view can engender student support and advocacy because it is consistent with students' own experience, it empowers healthy behavior, and it focuses on harm reduction. It avoids polarizing and inaccurate terminology and measures that oversimplify or distort the problem, and it is based on best practice strategies that have been supported by research and implemented successfully on many campuses.

References

Bauerle, J., Burwell, C., & Turner, J. C. (2002, May 23). Social norms marketing at the University of Virginia. Paper presented at the annual meeting of the American College Health Association, Washington, DC.

Berkowitz, A. D. (2002). Responding to the critics: Answers to common questions and concerns about the social norms approach. *The Report on Social Norms: Working Paper #7*. Little Falls, NJ: PaperClip Communications.

Berkowitz, A. D. (2003). *The social norms approach: Theory, research and annotated bibliography*. Available from Higher Education Center for Alcohol and Other Drug Prevention Web site: http://www.edc.org/hec

Carey, K. B. (2001). Understanding binge drinking: Introduction to the special issue. *Psychology of Addictive Behaviors, 15*(4), 283–286.

Chapman, R. (2002). What Is Binge Drinking? *About Campus, 7*(5), 2–3.

DeJong, W. (2001). Finding common ground for effective campus-based prevention. *Psychology of Addictive Behaviors, 15*(4), 292–296.

Inter-Association Task Force on Alcohol and Other Substance Abuse Issues. (2000). *ITAF proclamation: A position statement from the Inter-Association Task Force on Alcohol and Other Substance Abuse Issues*. Retrieved from http://www/iatf.org/proc1a.htm

Linkenbach, J. (2001). Cultural cataracts: Identifying and correcting misperceptions in the media. *The Report on Social Norms: Working Paper #1*. Little Falls, NJ: PaperClip Communications.

Perkins, H. W. (ed.). (2003). *The social norms approach to preventing school and college age substance abuse: A handbook for educators, counselors, clinicians*. San Francisco: Jossey-Bass.

Perkins, H. W., DeJong, W., & Linkenbach, J. (2001). Estimated blood alcohol levels reached by "binge" and "nonbinge" drinkers: A survey of young adults in Montana. *Psychology of Addictive Behaviors, 15*(4), 317–320.

Ziemelis, A., Bucknam, R. B., & Elfessi, A. M. (2002). Prevention efforts underlying decreases in binge drinking at institutions of higher education. *Journal of American College Health, 50*(5), 238–252.

ADDITIONAL READING

Alcohol Prohibition versus Moderation

Franklin B. Krohn and Brandon M. Pyc

Franklin B. Krohn is a Distinguished Service Professor, and Brandon M. Pyc is a Research Assistant in the Department of Business Administration, State University of New York College at Fredonia.

Introduction

Alcohol has increasingly become a determining factor in the scholastic success and retention rates of college students across the nation (Lall & Schandler, 1991). The abuses associated with alcohol consumption have also triggered many campus organizations to design alcohol awareness programs, which focus on prohibiting and or completely eliminating the use of alcohol on college campuses (Syre, 1992). These goals appear to be unrealistic for the modern college student, who is subjected to the social pressures that exist on campuses. These pressures include (1) conformity, (2) compliance, (3) obedience, and (4) social diversity.

First, conformity occurs when individuals change their attitudes or behavior to follow social norms. Often, college students are expected to consume excessive amounts of alcohol, which alter states of action and integration within the group. Conformity to such risky behavior can be increased by cohesiveness and with the number of people pressuring such actions. Most people conform to the social norms of their group most of the time because of two powerful needs possessed by all human beings: the desire to be liked or accepted by others, and the desire to be right (Deutsch & Gerard, 1955; Insko, 1985). Additionally, cognitive processes lead to viewing conformity as fully justified after it has occurred (Griffin & Buehler, 1993).

The desire to be liked is explained by normative social influence, which is social influence based on individuals' desire to be liked or accepted by other persons. Most people try to appear to be as similar to others as possible. One reason people conform is that they learn that by doing so they can win the approval and acceptance human beings crave.

Second, compliance involves efforts by one or more individuals to change the behaviors of others. In general, people are more willing to comply with requests from friends or from people liked than requests from strangers or people not liked. This principle is referred to as friendship/liking (Cialdini, 1994). Many students comply with excessive drinking patterns because their friends reinforce the behavior. Many fraternities and sororities are guilty of ingratiation: getting others to like them so that they will be more willing to agree to their requests (Jones, 1964; Liden & Mitchell, 1988). Increased liking can in turn lead to greater compliance.

Third, the most direct form of social influence is obedience. Obedience is yielding to direct orders from another person to do something. Obedience is less frequent than conformity or compliance, but deserves attention in social influences of college students. Research findings indicate that people often obey commands from authority figures or upperclassmen even when such people have little or no authority to enforcing the requests (Milgram, 1963, 1965, 1974). Individuals can resist obedience through making a positive choice to decline the command.

Fourth, social diversity involving gender differences in social influence appears not significant in susceptibility to social influence among equal status persons. Early studies on this issue seemed to indicate that women are more susceptible than men (Crutchfield, 1955). Later studies, however, point that there are no significant differences between males and females in this respect (Eagly & Carli, 1981). The reversal occurred because the early studies used materials and tasks more familiar to males, which placed females at a disadvantage to conformity pressure.

There are complex biological, physical, and social characteristics underlying alcohol problems (See Figure 1).

In order to control and punish, there are a number of approaches: (1) current laws increase liabilities for those who serve alcoholic beverages to minors, (2) hold universities liable for not intervening, (3) charge alcohol establishments for violations of intervention, and (4) have reduced the fraternal experience.

First, contributing parties providing alcohol to underage drinkers are held liable for serving alcohol to minors whether it is a bar establishment or a social gathering among friends. This violation is punishable via fines or jail sentencing. Second, a new strategy of reformists is to hold universities liable in cases in which the college did not intervene to subdue the consumption problems. This liability is often invoked at universities that have fraternities and sororities on campus. Third, Dram Shop Laws establish that saloons are liable for contributing to excessive drunkenness. Bar establishments have also lost liquor licenses for serving alcoholic beverages to minors, those under the legal drinking age of 21. Fourth, the social and economic harm of alcohol abuse threatens the survival of the collegiate Greek system in the United States. Poor scholarship, low rush numbers, poor retention of members, personal injuries and property damages are some of the results of excessive drinking patterns. A popular argument made by students is that alcohol prohibition on college campuses hinders the social experience (MacConnell & Clement, 1998). Many students view these radical changes as an infringement of their social life (Cavaretta & Tappon, 1998).

Alcohol Facts

Compulsive drinking in excess has become one of modern society's most serious problems. Many people do not view alcohol as a drug, largely because its uses for religious and social purposes are common, however, the effects depend on the amount consumed at a specific time.

Once alcohol enters the body it is rapidly absorbed into the bloodstream from the small intestine. Alcohol contamination in the blood leads to slower activity in parts of the brain as well as the spinal cord. The drinker's blood alcohol concentration depends on the amount consumed, the drinker's sex, size, and metabolism, and the type and amount of food in the stomach. The effects of alcohol depend on the amount consumed at one time (See Table 1).

Harmful consequences of alcohol consumption vary from person to person, however, the effects remain similar. Drinking heavily over a short period will result in a "hangover," due to poisoning by alcohol and the body's reaction to withdrawal from alcohol. Combining alcohol with other drugs can make

Table 1 *Amount of Alcohol in the Blood and the Effects*

(mg/dL)	Effect
100	Mild Intoxication
	Feeling of warmth, skin flushed; impaired judgment; decreased inhibitions
100	Obvious Intoxication In Most People
	Increased impairment of judgment, inhibition, attention, and control; some impairment of muscular performance; slowing of reflexes
150	Obvious Intoxication In All Normal People
	Staggering gait and other muscular incoordination; slurred speech; double vision; memory and comprehension loss
250	Extreme Intoxication or Stupor
	Reduced response to stimuli; inability to stand; vomiting; incontinence; sleepiness
350	Coma
	Unconsciousness; little response to stimuli; incontinence; low body temperature; poor respiration; fall in blood pressure; clammy skin
500	Death Likely

Source: Addiction Research Foundation

the effects of these other drugs much stronger and more dangerous. Some of these harmful consequences are primary, resulting directly from prolonged exposure to alcohol's toxic effects such as liver disease. Other consequences are secondary. They are indirectly related to chronic alcohol abuse, such as loss of appetite, vitamin deficiencies, and sexual impotence (Addiction Research Foundation, 1971).

Alcohol and the Student

Student drinking is the number one health problem on college and university campuses throughout the country. College students are at a higher risk for alcohol related problems because they have high rates of heavy consumption (binge drinking), tend to drink more recklessly than others, and are heavily targeted by advertising and promotions of the alcoholic beverage industry. Students spend approximately $4.2 billion annually to purchase 430 million gallons of alcoholic beverages. Alcohol is associated with missed classes and poor performance on tests and projects. The number of alcoholic drinks consumed per week is clearly related to lower GPAs (Wells & Presky, 1996).

Campuses throughout the nation have been assisted in combating this pressing problem by the U.S. Drug-Free Schools and Communities Act Amendments of 1989 (Public Law 101-226). It requires that institutions of higher learning receiving

Federal funds attest that they have adopted and implemented a drug prevention program for both students and employees. One example offered to students is peer counseling. Many colleges train peer counselors to educate groups and individuals about the dangers of alcohol use. Some colleges limit or ban alcohol advertising in student newspapers and sponsorship of student events by alcoholic beverage companies. Another solution offered to students is alcohol-free residence halls. An emerging trend is for colleges to establish residence halls where students sign pledges that they will not use alcohol, tobacco, or other drugs. How effective this strategy is has yet to be determined.

Nevertheless, social acceptance of this drug still remains. These laws have neither crippled nor eliminated the problem. The more a behavior is suppressed, often the more it occurs. The alcoholic prohibition experiment in the United States was very revealing about American culture (Norton, Katzman, Escott, Chudacoff, Paterson & Tuttle, 1990).

Prohibition

Attempts to prohibit alcohol usage have been made since colonial times. Temperance movements began to gain sizable support by the public and government. The first national temperance society was formed in 1836. The temperance movement led to the adoption of full prohibition, rather than just temperance alone. Since the major parties of the political sphere refused to take a stance on the prohibition issue, a third party known as the Prohibition Party was formed in 1869. Although the party was never successful, their ideas spread throughout the country.

The prohibition movement reached its peak in the late 19th century, however, it was not until the southwestern states turned to prohibition that the issue gained mass popularity. There were many factors leading to the passage of this ineffective legislation. In order to conserve grain during World War I, federal legislation passed a series of laws to help ration supplies that were needed for the effort. This rationing established the roots for prohibition legislation. The national prohibition amendment was ratified by all but two states on January 16, 1919, and went into effect one year later. Between 1920 and 1933 prohibition was in effect in the United States. Prohibition is the illegality of manufacturing, selling, or transporting any type of alcoholic beverage.

Even though the prohibition amendment was passed by an overwhelming majority in Congress, it soon became evident that the amendment was unenforceable. The enforcement was minimized because the 1920s saw a revolution in social (1) manners, (2) customs, and (3) habits, which led to mass inclination to ignore existing prohibition legislation. "Prohibition did not achieve its goals. Instead, it added to the problems it was intended to solve" (Thorton, 1991 p. 15). Prohibition caused an explosive growth in crime and increased the amount of alcohol consumption. There were also numerous speak-easies which replaced saloons after the start of prohibition. Approximately only five percent of smuggled liquor was hindered from coming into the country in the 1920s.

Furthermore, the illegal liquor business fell under the control of organized gangs, which overpowered most of the law enforcement authorities (Wenburn, 1991). As a result of the lack of enforcement of the Prohibition Act and the creation of an illegal industry, an overall increase in crime transpired. The problems prohibition intended to solve, such as crime, grew worse and they never returned to their preprohibition levels.

The major goal of the 18th Amendment was to abolish the saloon. By outlawing the manufacturing and sale of alcohol only, the patronage of a bootlegger emerged. The Volstead Act was intended to prohibit intoxicating beverages, regulate the manufacture, production and use of spirits other than beverage purposes, and promote scientific research in the development of lawful purposes. Initially, all of these regulations were left for the Treasury Department to oversee. The ineffectiveness in preventing illegal diversions and arresting bootleggers led to the creation of the Prohibition Bureau. This was another incompetent strategy based on the spoils system which filled positions with men who discredited the enforcement efforts.

Prohibition was intended to solve overconsumption of alcohol, but inevitably encouraged consumption. A clause in the Volstead Act made search and seizure virtually unobtainable because any warrant issued was dependent on proof that the liquor was for sale. No matter how much alcohol a person had at home, and no matter how it was obtained or used, agents of the bureau had to have positive evidence that a commercial transaction took place (Aaron & Musto, 1981). This requirement inadvertently promoted home and cottage industry manufacturing of liquor. For example, during the first five years of Prohibition, the acreage of vineyards increased 700 percent, accompanied by insincere warning labeling such as "do not place liquid in bottle away in the cupboard for twenty days, because it would turn into wine" (Binkley, 1930). Although possession of illegally obtained alcohol was prohibited, the act of drinking alcohol was legal. This suggests that even prohibitionists understood the limits of regulating individual behavior.

Data on alcohol prohibition on campuses across the nation have also had little success in solving or finding a solution to this unrelenting problem. One purpose of this paper is to explore whether there is another approach that might be taken to better equip the college student in becoming a responsible alcohol consumer.

Moderation

All societies in which alcohol is consumed employ a range of strategies to minimize the harm associated with its use. The most effective public policies are those that affect the environment of drinking or influence the drinker's demand for alcohol. These include taxation and price policies, controls on access to alcohol such as limiting the condition and time of sale, modifying the drinking environment, a minimum legal drinking age, and countermeasures against drinking in hazardous circumstances such as when driving.

A moderate drinker is defined as one who imbibes one five-ounce glass of wine, one 12-ounce beer, or 1½ shots of liquor daily (O'Connor, 1994). Consuming alcohol above these amounts can be hazardous. However, moderating the amount of alcohol intake can be beneficial. These benefits include (1) health, (2) scholastic performance, and (3) a decline in violence.

First, heavy consumption of alcoholic beverages is linked to many health problems. Excessive use impairs the body's nervous system resulting in a lack of fine motor skills, reaction speed, and visual perception. Alcohol also causes one to tire faster because it weakens the heart's pumping force. The human body recognizes the alcohol as a toxin and metabolizes it before anything else. Thus, the body cannot burn more fuel efficient fats and proteins (Rhodes, 1995). In addition, too much alcohol may cause cirrhosis of the liver, inflammation of the pancreas, damage to the brain and heart, and increased risks for some cancers. Limiting intake of alcohol makes room for foods that provide important nutrients. For all these reasons, drinking alcoholic beverages excessively is not recommended. If students choose to drink them, they should drink them only in moderate amounts or drink alternatives. Alternatives to alcoholic beverages include a mixer or fruit juice, complete with a garnish but without the alcohol.

There have been numerous studies which support the health benefits of moderate drinking. Moderate drinkers tend to have better health and live longer than those who are either abstainers or heavy drinkers (Yuan, 1997). In addition to having fewer heart attacks and strokes, moderate consumers of alcohol are generally less likely to suffer hypertension or high blood pressure, peripheral artery disease, Alzheimer's disease and the common cold (Rimm, 1991; Coate, 1993).

Second, students who consume alcoholic beverages moderately achieve higher scholastic achievement than excessive consumers of alcohol beverages. Alcohol abuse is associated with poor academic performance. According to a national research, 21 percent of binge drinkers fell behind in their studies and 30 percent missed class during the school year (Higher Education Center for Alcohol and Other Drug Prevention, 1997a).

Third, excessive alcohol consumption contributes to violence in multiple ways, chiefly by increasing aggression, particularly when the blood alcohol level rises rapidly (such as with binge drinking). Several studies estimate that between 50 percent and 80 percent of violence on campus is alcohol related. In addition, many students believe intoxication excuses inappropriate and violent behavior (Higher Education Center, 1997b). A study of women who were victims of some type of sexual aggression while in college, from rape to intimidation and illegal restraint found that 68 percent of their male assailants had been drinking at the time of the attack (Higher Education Center, 1997c).

Having control over the amount of alcohol consumption allows people to make better judgments for safety and health purposes. Social drinkers use alcohol in moderate amounts, while alcoholics do not limit their intake. The first step to moderation is practicing safe use of the drug. This means setting boundaries for the amount of alcohol consumed. After establishing a salubrious program, maintenance is the key to continuous moderate use of alcoholic beverages.

Conclusion

There is no simple solution to the alcohol abuse that occurs at colleges and universities across the nation. After examining two opposite methods to control alcohol abuse across college campuses, moderation is a conceivable and attainable goal. Campus administrators should promote moderation as opposed to forbidding the use of alcohol at universities. The acknowledgement of excessive alcohol abuse on campuses is only the first step. Offering alternatives to students, such as moderation lead to solving the problem. It is inconceivable to believe that no calamitous events will occur with both widespread acceptance of alcohol and the heavy promotion by alcohol manufacturers; however, taking the moderation approach is more feasible than outright prohibition.

Table 1 Percentage of past-month male drinkers 18 and older who binge drink by ethnic/racial group

Racial/Ethnic Group	% Currently Drink	Binge Drinkers/Drinkers*
White	59	42
African American	41	49
Hispanic	44	59
Native American	39	71
Asian	41	33

*Binge is defined as five or more drinks on a single occasion.

Source: 2004 National Survey on Drug Use and Health (NSDUH, 2005, table 2.56B)

Table 2 Percentage of males drinking daily, binge drinking, and experiencing adverse consequences in selected countries

Drink Daily	Binge Drinking per Drinking Occasionally	Experiencing Adverse	Consequences
Ireland	2	58	39
Finland	4	29	47
Sweden	3	33	36
UK	9	40	45
Germany	12	14	34
France	21	9	27
Italy	42	13	18

Source: Ramstedt and Hope (2003)

Table 3 Intoxicated 3+ occasions past 30 days, 15- to 16-year-olds, selected countries: 2003 ESPAD

Nation	Percentage
Denmark	26
Ireland	26
United Kingdom	23
Norway	12
Russia	11
Netherlands	7
France	3
Turkey	1

Source: 2003 ESPAD (Hibell et al., 2004)

References

Aaron, P., & Musto, D. (1981). Temperance and prohibition in America: A historical overview. In M. H. Moore & D. R. Gerstein (Eds.), *Alcohol and Public Policy*. Washington, DC: National Academy Press.

Addiction Research Foundation. (1971). Facts about alcohol. Retrieved from http://www.arf.org/isd/pim/Alcohol.html

Binkley, R. C. (1930). *Responsible drinking: A discreet inquiry and a modest proposal*. New York: Vanguard.

Cialdini, R. B. (1994). Interpersonal influence. In S. Shavitt & T. C. Brock (Eds.), *Persuasion* (pp. 195–218). Boston: Allyn & Bacon.

Coate, D. (1993). Moderate drinking and coronary heart disease mortality: Evidence from NHANES I and NHANES I follow-up. *American Journal of Public Health, 83,* 888–890.

Crutchfield, R. A. (1955). Conformity and character. *American Psychologist, 10,* 191–198.

Deutsch, M., & Gerard, H. B. (1955). A study of normative and informational social influences upon individual judgment. *Journal of Abnormal and Social Psychology, 51,* 629–636.

Eagly, A. H., & Carli, L. (1981). Sex of researchers and sex-typed communication as determinants of sex differences in influenceability: A meta-analysis of social influence studies. *Psychological Bulletin, 90,* 1–20.

Griffin, D. W., & Buehler, R. (1993). Role of construal process in conformity and dissent. *Journal of Personality and Social Psychology, 65,* 657–669.

Higher Education Center for Alcohol and Other Drug Prevention. (1997a). College academic performance and alcohol and other drug use. Infofacts Resources. Newton, MA: Author

Higher Education Center for Alcohol and Other Drug Prevention. (1997b). Interpersonal violence and alcohol and other drug use. Infofacts Resources. Newton, MA: Author.

Higher Education Center for Alcohol and Other Drug Prevention. (1997c). Sexual assault and alcohol and other drug use. Infofacts Resources. Newton, MA: Author.

Insko, C. A. (1985). Balance theory, the Jordan paradigm, and the West tetrahedron. In L. Berkowitz (Ed.), *Advances in Experimental Social Psychology*. New York: Academic Press.

Jones, E. E. (1964). *Ingratiation: A social psychology analysis*. New York: Appleton.

Lall, R., & Schandler, S. (1991). Michigan Alcohol Screening Test (MAST) scores and academic performance in college students. *College Student Journal, 25*, 245–251.

Liden, R. C., & Mitchell, T. R. (1988). Ingratiatory behaviors in organizational settings. *Academy of Management Review, 13*, 572–587.

Milgram, S. (1963). Behavior study of obedience. *Journal of Abnormal and Social Psychology, 67*, 371–378.

Milgram, S. (1965). Liberating effects of group pressure. *Journal of Personality and Social Psychology, 1*, 127–134.

Milgram, S. (1974). *Obedience to authority*. New York: Harper.

Moore, M. H., & Gerstein, D. R. (Eds.). (1981). *Alcohol and public policy: Beyond the shadow of prohibition*. Washington, DC: National Academy Press.

Norton, M., Katzman, D., Escott, P., Churdcoff, H., Paterson, T., & Tuttle, W. (1994). *A People and a nation: History of the U.S.* Boston: Houghton Mifflin.

O'Connor, P. (1994). *The facts about alcohol and health*. Madison, CT: Business & Legal Reports.

Rhodes, M. (1995). New thinking about drinking. *Women's Sports & Fitness, 17*(2), 71.

Rimm, E. (1991). Prospective study of alcohol consumption and risk of coronary disease in men. *The Lancet, 338*.

Syre, T. (1992). Alcoholism and Alcoholics Anonymous on campus: Implications for college teachers. *College Student Journal, 26*, 223–230.

Thorton, M. (1991). *Policy analysis: Alcohol prohibition was a failure*. Retrieved from http://www.geocites.Com/Athens/Troy?4399

Wells, W., & Presky, D. (1996). *Consumer Behavior*. New York: Wiley.

Wenburn, N. (1991). *The USA: A chronicle of pictures*. New York: Smithmark.

Yuan, J. M. (1997). Follow up study of moderate alcohol intake and mortality among middle aged men in Shanghai, China. *British Medical Journal, 314*.

Something to write about . . .

1. Using the readings included at the end of this chapter, write a proposal argument on the topic of college drinking. Through reflection and research, you might want to develop additional material for your argument as well.

2. Identify a campus, local, national, or international problem that interests you. Through research and reflection, generate information on two or three possible solutions to that problem and choose one to examine more closely in a fully developed proposal argument. Be sure to clear your topic with your teacher.

3. Choose a problem you would like to investigate but focus your attention on the solutions people have offered to address it. Carefully research each of those solutions. Write an argumentative essay in which you critique each of the solutions you have investigated and argue for one as being best.

WRITING EVALUATION ARGUMENTS

WHAT ARE EVALUATION ARGUMENTS?

How would you answer these questions:

- Who is the better guitarist, Slash or Eddie Van Halen?
- Are the Harry Potter books good literature, just popular, or both?
- Who makes the best mid-size car?
- Which Super Bowl commercial was most effective last year?
- What are the five best television shows of all time?

Evaluation arguments center on disputes over something's quality or value. They are related to definition arguments (Chapter 11), but are more limited in scope. To settle an argument over who the better guitarist is, Slash or Eddie Van Halen, you first need to define your criteria: What makes one guitarist better than another? What skills, aptitudes, or accomplishments do great guitarists possess? You might believe that Slash is more agile and powerful, while Van Halen is more melodic and inventive. However, to settle the question in an argument, you will have to evaluate these musicians according to the same set of criteria and standards.

What about arguments over the best car or the best Super Bowl commercial? From one perspective, these questions seem to be purely matters of taste and personal preference and are therefore not true arguments (see Chapter 1). In informal conversations, that might be the case. However, consumer magazines evaluate and rank automobiles using something more than just personal preference, and marketing companies are paid small fortunes to evaluate and rank commercials that air during the Super Bowl.

In academic settings you will base your evaluations on a set of established criteria and standards, form a judgment that will serve as your thesis, then explain and defend your assertions with reasons and evidence. One important assumption in academic writing is that writers can and will disagree on how they interpret and apply these criteria and standards. Writers can come to quite different conclusions about the quality, value, or worth of the topic they are evaluating even when they use the same criteria and standards. What's important is how well these writers explain and defend their judgments.

TYPES OF EVALUATION ARGUMENTS

In college, expect to evaluate not only people, places, things, and events but also theories, ideologies, and philosophies. Classifying all the evaluation arguments you might encounter in college is difficult, but here are some of the more common types.

Aesthetic Evaluations

In an aesthetic evaluation argument, you assess whether the subject of your essay meets certain artistic standards.

- Which is the better depiction of gangster life, *Goodfellas* or *The Godfather*?
- Which Sibelius symphony best captures the modernist spirit?
- Which poem better communicates Tennyson's moral imperatives, "Ulysses" or "Locksley Hall"?

Functional Evaluations

A functional evaluation argument addresses the question of how well something or someone works or performs.

- Is the new Mazda a good sports car?
- Which is the better home computer: the Dell or the HP?
- Who was more effective at foreign policy, Nixon or Clinton?

Moral Evaluations

Moral and ethical evaluation arguments address questions of whether something, someone, or some action is morally acceptable or ethically sound.

- Is welfare reform fair and humane?
- Is the death penalty just?
- Was the use of atomic weapons at the end of World War II morally acceptable?

Mixed Evaluations

In any evaluation argument, you may find yourself forming and defending claims based on a mixture of functional, aesthetic, or moral criteria. For example, if you are evaluating President Clinton's welfare reforms, you might apply functional criteria (whether they achieved their desired goals) or moral criteria (whether those goals were just or whether the proposals were fair). If you are arguing whether *The Passion of the Christ* is a good movie, you may use moral criteria (whether it depicts Jews fairly) or aesthetic criteria (whether its direction, acting, and cinematography are well done). Unless your teacher specifies otherwise, you can mix criteria so long as you are aware of what you are doing and can explain and defend your decisions.

ELEMENTS OF AN EVALUATION ARGUMENT

The fundamental elements of an evaluation argument include the subject you are writing about and the criteria and standards that you employ to evaluate it.

Topic or Subject

The topic or subject of your argument is the person, place, event, or thing you are evaluating. As you prepare to write an evaluation argument, you need to become thoroughly familiar with the subject of your essay.

Criteria

You will evaluate the subject of your essay using a set of criteria and standards. Criteria are the specific elements or aspects of the subject you examine to reach a judgment. Instead of being idiosyncratic or random, criteria are usually well established in particular fields of study. In fact, as you begin to take classes in your major, you will become increasingly familiar with the criteria experts in your discipline use to make evaluative judgments.

Most students are already familiar with the criteria used in one field of study well before they enter college—film criticism. Movie reviews are essentially evaluation arguments. If you understand how criteria work in movie reviews, you can understand how they work in other fields of study across the curriculum.

When critics evaluate a movie, they focus on certain criteria, or certain elements of the film. Criteria commonly employed by movie critics include acting, direction, writing, lighting, special effects, cinematography, sound, and special effects. Based on certain standards (discussed below), they evaluate these criteria to reach an overall judgment on the quality of the film. However, critics do not write about every feature of a film in their reviews. Instead, they focus only on the criteria that most influence their opinion, the ones they think most significantly contribute to the overall quality of the film. Critics do not have to agree on which criteria to focus on when reviewing a film—one may focus on acting, writing, and special effects while another may focus on direction, theme, and sound. Even if they focus on the same criteria, they may reach different conclusions about the quality of the film—one believing the acting, writing, and special effects were superb and the other finding them weak.

When you write an evaluation argument, you need to decide what criteria will serve as the focus of your essay. In many introductory-level or general education classes, your teachers will tell you what criteria to use when evaluating a subject; other teachers will expect you to develop criteria on your own.

Standards

While criteria are particular features of the subject you are examining, standards are the expectations that form the basis of your judgment, expectations against which you judge each criterion. Once you identify which aspects of your topic you will evaluate (your criteria), you need to determine their relative value, quality, or worth. For example, if you are writing a movie review and decide you will examine the film's acting, what counts as good or bad acting? What makes one performer's acting more effective than another's? When answering these questions, you are identifying the standards you will use in your evaluation.

Again, in most fields of study standards are fairly well established, though some variation is possible. Keeping with film reviews, consider the standards critics might employ to evaluate acting. Most reviewers today would say that good acting is emotional, realistic, convincing, and natural; bad acting is bombastic, flat, overly mannered, or uninvolved. These adjectives—emotional, flat, natural—are the standards critics would use to judge a performer's acting.

One feature of academic writing many students find frustrating is that while the criteria used to determine good arguments remain fairly uniform across the curriculum, standards do not. For example, most teachers across the curriculum would say that in a good argument, claims (a criterion) should be supported by appropriate evidence (a standard). However, what counts as "appropriate" evidence can vary widely across the disciplines.

Mastering both general and discipline-specific criteria and standards takes time and experience. One of the best ways to learn them, however, is through reading—as you study evaluation arguments in class, identify the criteria and standards authors use to form and defend their judgments. Also, pay attention to the way your teachers discuss and critique arguments in class. Through lectures and class discussions, they will demonstrate how to evaluate material using discipline-specific criteria and standards.

Consistent Use of Criteria and Standards

When you are evaluating two or more subjects to decide which is better, more effective, more beautiful, and the like, be sure you employ the same set of criteria and standards when judging each one. Employing a different set with each subject will not allow you to form a thorough, fair evaluation and will undermine your argument.

WRITING AN EVALUATION ARGUMENT
A Model Process for Writing Evaluation Arguments
Step 1: Analyze the assignment.

Be sure you understand the rhetorical situation of any evaluation argument you are required to write, especially the subject, purpose, and audience. You might begin by answering these questions:

- Am I being assigned a topic to write about or do I choose a subject?
- Am I being assigned criteria and standards or am I expected to develop them on my own?
- Who is my intended audience?

■ What can I assume my audience knows or feels about my subject?

■ What is this essay supposed to accomplish?

■ Given the purpose and intended audience, how much research do I need to complete concerning the subject, the criteria, the standards, and the way others have evaluated the subject?

These questions are not exhaustive, but answering them can help you clarify some of the central elements of the assignment's rhetorical situation.

Step 2: Select a topic.

If you are required to choose your own topic, pick one about which there is some controversy concerning its relative value, quality, or worth. Look for topics that invite discussion and debate, topics that people evaluate differently. While these topics may be challenging to write about, both your prose and your argument will likely be stronger and more interesting if you are working with a subject that is open to a range of evaluations. Answering the questions found in Figure 14.1 may help you develop an interesting topic for your evaluation argument. You will find three sets of questions, one set for each type of evaluation argument described above. Be sure the topic you select suits the type of evaluation argument you are being asked to write.

FIGURE 14.1	Evaluation Argument Topic Heuristic	
Aesthetic Evaluations	**Functional Evaluations**	**Moral Evaluations**
What movie would you like to evaluate?	What new technologies would you like to evaluate?	What school or government policy would you like to evaluate?
What novel, poem, or play would you like to evaluate?	What commercial product would you like to evaluate?	What teaching practices would you like to evaluate?
What song, CD, or band would you like to evaluate?	What Web sites would you like to evaluate?	What business practices would you like to evaluate?
What painting, sculpture, or artist would you like to evaluate?	What school policy would you like to evaluate?	What magazine or television ad would you like to evaluate?

Evaluation Argument Topic Heuristic *(continued)*

What famous speech would you like to evaluate?	What government policy would you like to evaluate?	What historical event would you like to evaluate?
What magazine or television ad would you like to evaluate?	What college major would you like to evaluate?	What emerging medical technologies would you like to evaluate?
What building would you like to evaluate?	What magazine or television ad would you like to evaluate?	What philosophical dictum or school of thought would you like to evaluate?
What public space would you like to evaluate?	What parenting practices would you like to evaluate?	What current social trend would you like to evaluate?
What campus structure or space would you like to evaluate?	What workout routines or diets would you like to evaluate?	What Web sites would you like to evaluate?
What clothing style would you like to evaluate?	What research practices would you like to evaluate?	What proposed solutions to a current social problem would you like to evaluate?

Step 3: Gather information.

Evaluation arguments often fail when writers do not thoroughly understand the subject of their essays. Whatever the subject, study it in depth. Also, clarify your own thoughts and feelings about the subject of your essay before and after you conduct any research. Understanding what you know and feel about the subject prior to any research you conduct will help keep your investigation honest and balanced. You want to examine perspectives on the subject you have never considered before or believe to be wrong or misguided. Your goal is to know your subject so well you can anticipate questions or objections readers might raise when they read your argument.

Step 4: Select appropriate evaluative criteria and standards.

Once you have determined your topic, you need to choose appropriate evaluate criteria. Often the criteria are part of the assignment:

> *Using the principles of Toulmin argumentation, critique Martin Luther King's "Letter from Birmingham Jail."*

> *Using the standards Tim O'Brien sets out in "How to Tell a True War Story," is "Sweetheart of the Song Tra Bong" a true war story?*

In the first assignment, you will evaluate King's letter by examining the quality of its claims, grounds, explanations, and rebuttals. In the second, you will use criteria Tim O'Brien establishes in one short story to evaluate another of his stories.

Sometimes evaluation criteria stipulated by an assignment are not clear. Consider this assignment:

> *Evaluate the effectiveness of the argument Plato puts forward in his allegory of the cave.*

The stated criteria here are unclear: Evaluate the effectiveness of Plato's argument in terms of what? Without more guidance from the assignment or the teacher, any of these is a plausible answer:

- in terms of the quality of its claims, grounds, and warrants
- in terms of the quality of its premises and conclusions
- in terms of its ability to persuade readers to respond in a particular way
- in terms of the clarity of its prose
- in terms of the clarity of its central metaphor
- in terms of its relationship to other, related arguments

To complete this assignment, you would need to check with your teacher to see which criteria he or she would like you to use in your argument.

If you are expected to generate them on your own, begin by examining the criteria and standards others have used to evaluate your subject in the past, criteria and standards commonly employed to evaluate material in your class, or criteria and standards provided by a textbook or research guide.

Step 5: Evaluate the topic.

Carefully and systematically evaluate your topic using the criteria and standards you have selected or been assigned. Filling out an invention grid such as the one featured in Figure 14.2 or Figure 14.3 is one way to ensure that you apply the same criteria and standards to each subject you evaluate. Design the grid with a line for every subject you are examining plus the criteria and standards you will be employing. Fill out the grid with your evaluations of each subject. If you are evaluating just one topic, use a grid such as the one found in Figure 14.2; if you are evaluating multiple topics, use a grid like the one in Figure 14.3. What is your judgment concerning each subject if you evaluate it according to each standard of the criteria you are employing? When possible, include in each cell an example drawn from the subject that serves as a basis for or best illustrates your judgment.

FIGURE 14.2

Invention Grid
Evaluation Argument

Evaluating One Topic

Criteria and Standards	Evaluation of Topic by Criterion/Standards
Criterion 1, Standard A	Evaluation
Criterion 1, Standard B	Evaluation
Criterion 2, Standard A	Evaluation
Criterion 2, Standard B	Evaluation
Criterion X, Standard A	Evaluation
Criterion X, Standard B	Evaluation

FIGURE 14.3

Invention Grid
Evaluation Argument

Evaluating More than One Topic

	Criterion 1 Standard A	Criterion 1 Standard B	Criterion 2 Standard A	Criterion 2 Standard B	Criterion X Standard A	Criterion X Standard B
Subject 1						
Subject 2						

Assume you were writing an evaluation argument based on the advertisement for Pearl Izumi trail shoes found on page 000 (Figure 14.7) and are working with two criteria: effective use of copy and product display. Assume you have generated two standards for each of these criteria, outlined below:

Criterion	Effective Use of Copy	Effective Product Display
Standard A	Appropriate appeals for audience	Effective placement of product in ad
Standard B	Appropriate amount of copy	Visual attractiveness of product

Because you are only evaluating one subject, your invention grid might look something like the one displayed in Figure 14.4:

FIGURE 14.4

Invention Grid
Evaluation of Pearl Izumi Advertisement

Criterion and Standard	Pearl Izumi Ad
Effective use of copy; Appropriate appeals	*Appropriate for readers of this magazine—plays on their distain for joggers and their sense of self-worth (they are the real athletes)*
Effective use of copy; Appropriate amount	*Again, effective because it bucks the trend—lots of copy here; it dominates the ad, but it is effective*
Effective product display; Placement on page in ad	*Good placement on page—shoe fills bottom right of page; only thing lit up on page*
Effective product display; Visual attractiveness	*Shoe is dirty and worn—given readers of this magazine, this makes it attractive*

A final word about evaluating a topic as you prepare to write an argument: too often, inexperienced writers rush to judgment when they evaluate their topics, failing to notice contradictions and complications. Be sure to question your own judgments and conclusions as you evaluate the topic of your essay.

Step 6: Develop a thesis statement.

In its simplest form, the thesis statement you use in an evaluation argument will indicate the subject of your essay and your evaluation:

> **Martin Luther King presents an effective case for direct, nonviolent social protest in "Letter from Birmingham Jail."**

This thesis lets readers know the specific argument the writer will put forward in her essay (that King's "Letter from Birmingham Jail" presents an effective argument) but does not indicate the specific criteria she will employ to support that assertion. If the writer were to indicate those criteria, the thesis statement might read something like this:

> **Based on the principles of argumentation established by philosopher Stephen Toulmin, King's "Letter from Birmingham Jail" presents an effective case for direct, nonviolent social protest.**

This thesis tells the reader both the argument the writer will be asserting (that King's "Letter from Birmingham Jail" presents an effective case for direct, nonviolent social protest) and the criteria she will use to support this claim (Toulmin's principles of argumentation).

Step 7: Choose an organizational strategy.

When organizing an evaluation argument, writers frequently use some variation of the formats outlined below. These organizational strategies are offered as guides to help you structure your argument. Modify them as needed when you write your own evaluation arguments.

Evaluation Argument: Block Format

Using a block format (Figure 14.5), following the introductory section of your essay, you define, discuss, and defend your choice of evaluative criteria and standards. In the next section of your essay, you apply these criteria to the topic of your essay, demonstrating how well they match before moving on to your conclusion.

FIGURE 14.5	**BOX OUTLINE**

Evaluation Argument

Block Format

Opening Section
Strategy you will employ to capture reader interest
Thesis: Claim concerning evaluation of subject's quality, value, worth

Criteria Section
Claim 1: First evaluative criterion
Definition: What the criterion is and is not
Standards: Standards that will be used to judge criterion
Reason 1: First reason offered in support of this criterion and these standards
Evidence: Support for the first reason
Explanation: How the evidence supports this reason
Reason X: Last reason offered in support of this criterion and these standards
Evidence: Support for the last reason
Explanation: How the evidence supports this reason

BOX OUTLINE

Evaluation Argument *(continued)*

Objections: Possible objections to or questions concerning your claims

Rebuttals: Possible answers to objections or questions

Claim X: Last evaluative criterion

Definition: What the criterion is and is not

Standards: Standards that will be used to judge criterion

Reason 1: First reason offered in support of this criterion and these standards

Evidence: Support for the first reason

Explanation: How the evidence supports this reason

Reason X: Last reason offered in support of this criterion and these standards

Evidence: Support for the last reason

Explanation: How the evidence supports this reason

Objections: Possible objections or questions concerning to your claims

Rebuttals: Possible answers to objections or questions

Application Section

Claim 1: Whether subject meets first criterion

Reason 1: First reason why subject meets or does not meet this criterion

Evidence: Support for the first reason

Explanation: How the evidence supports this reason

Reason X: Last reason why subject meets or does not meet this criterion

Evidence: Support for the last reason

Explanation: How the evidence supports this reason

Objections: Possible objections or questions concerning to your claims

Rebuttals: Possible answers to objections or questions

Claim X: Whether subject matches last criterion

Reason 1: First reason why subject meets or does not meet this criterion

Evidence: Support for the first reason

Explanation: How the evidence supports this reason

Reason X: Last reason why subject meets or does not meet this criterion

Evidence: Support for the last reason

Explanation: How the evidence supports this reason

Objections: Possible objections or questions concerning to your claims

Rebuttals: Possible answers to objections or questions

Closing Section

Strategy you will employ to conclude your argument

Using a block format, following the introductory section of your essay, you would explain and defend the criteria and standards you will use in your argument then apply them to evaluate the subject of your essay, arguing whether your subject meets each criterion. You would support your assertions with reasons, evidence, and explanations, and address likely objections or questions along the way. Your conclusion would bring your argument to a graceful, satisfying end. (Remember—in a box outline, each box represents one section of your argument, not just one paragraph. It may take you several paragraphs or several pages to cover all of the material outlined in a single box.)

Evaluation Argument: Alternating Format

If you choose instead to employ some type of alternating format for your evaluation argument, following the opening section of your essay, you would examine the first criterion then immediately argue whether your subject meets it. In the next section, you would focus on the second criterion and so on until the end of your essay. In outline form, the structure would resemble the one offered in Figure 14.6.

FIGURE 14.6	**BOX OUTLINE**

Evaluation Argument

Alternating Format

Opening Section
Strategy you will employ to capture reader interest
Thesis: Claim concerning evaluation of subject's quality, value, worth

Criterion One Section
Criterion Claim: First evaluative criterion
Definition: What the criterion is and is not
Standards: Standards that will be used to judge criterion
Reason 1: First reason offered in support of this criterion and these standards
Evidence: Support for the first reason
Explanation: How the evidence supports this reason
Reason X: Last reason offered in support of this criterion and these standards
Evidence: Support for the last reason
Explanation: How the evidence supports this reason
Objections: Possible objections or questions concerning to your claims
Rebuttals: Possible answers to objections or questions
Application Claim: Whether subject meets first criterion
Reason 1: First reason why subject meets or does not meet this criterion

BOX OUTLINE

Evaluation Argument *(continued)*

Evidence: Support for the first reason

Explanation: How the evidence supports this reason

Reason X: Last reason why subject meets or does not meet this criterion

Evidence: Support for the last reason

Explanation: How the evidence supports this reason

Objections: Possible objections or questions concerning to your claims

Rebuttals: Possible answers to objections or questions

Criterion X Section

Criterion Claim: Last evaluative criterion

Definition: What the criterion is and is not

Standards: Standards that will be used to judge criterion

Reason 1: First reason why this is a criterion and why these standards apply

Evidence: Support for the first reason

Explanation: How the evidence supports this reason

Reason X: Last reason why this is a criterion and why these standards apply

Evidence: Support for the last reason

Explanation: How the evidence supports this reason

Objections: Possible objections or questions concerning to your claims

Rebuttals: Possible answers to objections or questions

Application Claim: Whether subject matches last criterion

Reason 1: First reason why subject meets or does not meet this criterion

Evidence: Support for the first reason

Explanation: How the evidence supports this reason

Reason X: Last reason why subject meets or does not meet this criterion

Evidence: Support for the last reason

Explanation: How the evidence supports this reason

Objections: Possible objections or questions concerning to your claims

Rebuttals: Possible answers to objections or questions

Closing Section

Strategy you will employ to conclude your argument

Generally, the longer your essay or the more criteria you use to evaluate the subject, the better it is to use some variation of the alternating format which allows you to apply the criteria and standards to your subject just after you have defined and discussed them.

However, if you think the criteria you plan to use are particularly controversial or build on one another, then you might consider using a block format which allows you to discuss all of the criteria in one section of the essay before you apply them to your subject.

Step 8: Write the rough draft.

Opening Section

In the opening section of your paper, along with stating your thesis, you should also introduce the topic of your essay and capture reader interest. To accomplish these final two goals, you might consider using any of the following strategies: offer historical overview of the subject, summarize any controversy concerning prior or current evaluations, establish the importance of the subject, offer an interesting quotation, or tell an interesting anecdote.

Body

As you work on the body of your essay, follow the outline you developed earlier. Avoid rushing through your argument. Take the time you need to explain each of your criteria thoroughly and to apply each to your topic thoughtfully. In addition, address likely objections to your claims, support your assertions with specific examples and explanations, and cite authorities when you feel it will make your writing more persuasive. As you move through the major sections of your essay, be sure you include effective transitions. Your topic sentences should introduce the new section of your essay, link it to the previous section, and remind readers of your overarching thesis.

Closing Section

In the conclusion of your essay, you again have three primary goals: remind readers of your thesis, bring your essay to a graceful and satisfying close, and maintain your readers' interest and goodwill. Some of the strategies you might use to conclude your essay include mirroring your opening strategy or examining the implications of your argument.

Step 9: Revise the argument.

As with any complex writing assignment, revise your evaluation argument in a series of passes, focusing on just one or two elements of your writing at a time. Revising in waves like this is the best way for you to improve the quality of your writing and strengthen your argument.

Revise Content and Structure

As you revise your essay to improve your argument's content and structure, consider these questions:

- How clearly have I identified each of the criteria?
- How well have I explained and supported each of the criteria?
- How thoroughly have I addressed likely objections to or questions about these criteria?
- How well have I supported and explained each criterion with clarifying examples?

- How well have I explained the standards that apply to each criterion?
- How consistently have I applied these standards when evaluating my topic?
- How well have I addressed likely objections to or questions about these standards?
- How well have I incorporated secondary sources support into my criteria and/or standards?
- How well have I explained how my subject does or does not satisfy or meet each criterion?
- How well have I addressed likely objections to or questions about my assertions?

As you review the structure of your essay, consider these questions:

- How clearly and accurately does my thesis statement forecast the content and structure of my argument?
- Is my thesis statement clear and properly phrased?
- How effective are the topic sentences I've included at the beginning of each major section of my essay?
- How effective are the transitions I've included within each paragraph?
- How effective are the introductory and concluding sections of my argument?

Revise for Clarity and Correctness

As you revise your essay for clarity and correctness, consider the following questions:

- How can I make my sentences clearer and more concise?
- How well do I explain any technical terms or language that might puzzle my readers?
- Have I quoted material correctly?
- Have I punctuated and formatted quoted material correctly?

Revise for Documentation

As with other types of source-based academic arguments, set aside time to review your documentation and works cited list or bibliography. Be sure you have properly documented all quoted and paraphrased material.

Revision Checklist

You will find a revision checklist for evaluation arguments in Appendix 1.

Common Errors to Avoid When Writing an Evaluation Argument

Misunderstanding the Subject

Evaluation arguments often fail because the writer has not fully understood the subject he or she is evaluating. This problem frequently occurs when students are required to evaluate readings. Because they base their evaluation on a misreading of the source text, their criticisms are misguided: they criticize or praise the author for saying something the author does not say or for attempting to do something the author does not attempt to do.

Unclear or Overlapping Criteria

If you develop several criteria against which to evaluate the topic of your essay, be sure they do not overlap. Also, do not assume that your readers define the criteria you employ in your essay the same way you define them. Instead, assume that you need to explain each criterion you examine in your essay.

Failure to State or Explain Standards

Another common problem for writers is failing to explicitly state and, if need be, defend their standards when evaluating a subject. For example, if you are evaluating a reading's claims, you need to state the standards you are using to judge them. Your readers may not understand the standards you are employing if you fail to explain them.

Failure to Explain Evaluations

Too often inexperienced academic writers simply state their conclusions without explicitly explaining the reasoning process that led them to those judgments. You need to explain, in writing, how you reached each of your conclusions, how the application of the criteria and standards you are employing led you to the judgment you are defending.

Sample Student Essay: Evaluation Argument

The following sample evaluation argument, written by student Lilly Boone, is based on an analysis and critique of an ad for Pearl Izumi Seek 2 trail shoes that was published in the August 2007 edition of *Runner's World* magazine (Figure 14.7). The assignment asked students to decide whether the ad was effective given its target audience.

SAMPLE EVALUATION ARGUMENT

Keys to an Effective Shoe Ad

Lilly Boone

"Ever notice how it's always runners who find dead bodies?" That attention-getting question is splashed across the top of an ad for Pearl Izumi Seek 2 trail shoes that appeared in the August 2007 edition of *Runner's World* magazine. In a magazine filled with advertisements targeting running enthusiasts, this particular shoe ad stands out. While most ads in the magazine are bright and colorful, the Pearl Izumi ad is dark and somber which draws a reader's attention. The ad's copy is also very effective, appealing to its intended audience by playing on the distain serious runners hold for casual joggers and by cleverly linking the shoe to today's most popular television shows. The Pearl Izumi ad effectively draws attention to itself through its use of color and its copy's rhetorical appeals.

Against a dark background, the top two-thirds of the ad are filled with white copy. Following the opening question, the copy mocks joggers who never take risks and points out that on popular crime scene investigation television shows (such as *CSI*) off-road runners always discover the victims' bodies. A pair of worn, muddy, unlaced running shoes occupies the lower right-hand corner of the ad, illuminated by a dim light coming in from

Runner's World, August 2007

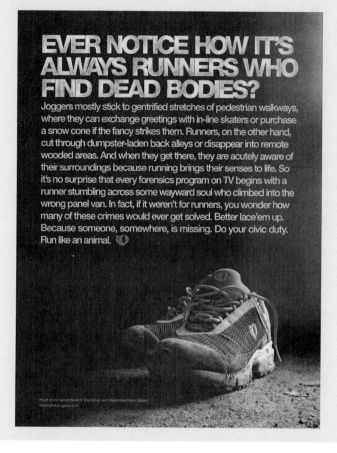

EVER NOTICE HOW IT'S ALWAYS RUNNERS WHO FIND DEAD BODIES?

Joggers mostly stick to gentrified stretches of pedestrian walkways, where they can exchange greetings with in-line skaters or purchase a snow cone if the fancy strikes them. Runners, on the other hand, cut through dumpster-laden back alleys or disappear into remote wooded areas. And when they get there, they are acutely aware of their surroundings because running brings their senses to life. So it's no surprise that every forensics program on TV begins with a runner stumbling across some wayward soul who climbed into the wrong panel van. In fact, if it weren't for runners, you wonder how many of these crimes would ever get solved. Better lace'em up. Because someone, somewhere, is missing. Do your civic duty. Run like an animal.

Pearl Izumi SyncroSeek'2 Trail Shoe with Seamless Race Upper.
WeAreNotJoggers.com

the right. The name of the shoe is located in small type toward the bottom left-hand corner of the ad, along with a URL for more information: WeAreNotJoggers.com.

Generally, advertisers prefer bright, colorful ads over dark, somber ones. Advertisers want readers to associate the products they are selling with the feelings of youth, fresh air, vitality, and sunshine typically associated with bright colors. In fact, *Runner's World* is full of ads like these—colorful shoes displayed against a crisp white background surrounded by multi-colored copy and smiling runners wearing bright multi-colored t-shirts and shorts.

Pearl Izumi takes a completely different approach to using color in its ad. Just leafing through the magazine, this ad catches the reader's eye precisely because it is unique. The ad largely consists of white or off-white copy against a dark background. The opening question is printed in large block letters that are themselves partially covered with dark smudges. Looking at the ad, the reader's eye is drawn to the single source of light in the lower right-hand corner, where the shoes are displayed, the dim light illuminating the shoes apparently being cast by a detective's flashlight as she investigates a night-time crime scene. Though dark and gloomy, the colors used in the Pearl Izumi ad successfully accomplish two goals advertisers clearly hoped to achieve: they arrest the readers' attention and highlight the product.

Most of the Pearl Izumi ad is devoted to copy, again making it different from most other ads in *Runner's World*. The copy, blending references to running and to television, makes several successful rhetorical appeals, playing on the readers' ego, sense of self-worth, and interest in popular culture. The readers of *Runner's World* tend to be serious athletes, enthusiasts of the sport who harbor a deep distain for casual joggers. As runners, they see themselves as serious athletes, not weekend wannabes who jog around the block and call it a day. The magazine's readers tend to be long-distance and cross country runners who like to challenge themselves physically and psychologically, pushing themselves to the limits of human endurance.

The copy in the Pearl Izumi ad appeals directly to these runners' feelings of superiority. Following the opening question, the copy reads: "Joggers mostly stick to gentrified stretches of pedestrian walkways, where they can exchange greetings with in-line skaters or purchase a snow cone if the fancy strikes them." This copy ridicules casual joggers—they are "gentrified" suburban pseudo-athletes who stay on safe and unchallenging sidewalks and bike paths. They have time to exchange greetings with other pseudo-athletes, like in-line skaters, or to purchase a snow cone, like a little child. Their workouts are casual, juvenile, unchallenging, safe, and silly.

The copy then moves on to address real athletes, like the ones who read *Runner's World*: "Runners, on the other hand, cut through dumpster-laden back alleys or disappear into remote wooded areas." Running is adventurous and potentially dangerous. Instead of staying on safe sidewalks, runners cut through back alleys; instead of sharing bike paths with in-line skaters, they plunge alone into "remote wooded areas." Finally, instead of being mind-numbed by jogging, runners are fully alive as they engage in their sport: "they are acutely aware of their surroundings because running brings their senses to life."

The message is clear, if you are a serious runner, not some casual jogger, then these are the shoes for you—you should be wearing the Pearl Izumi Seek 2 trail shoe. Put another way, if you wear the Seek 2, you are a serious runner, someone who is adventurous and daring. If you wear some other shoe, you might as well be a jogger. Again, the readers of *Runner's World* are likely serious runners (or want to be serious runners) so this ad directly targets their sense of superiority and self-worth.

The copy then shifts tone, becoming lighthearted and comic. It points out that "every forensics program on TV begins with a runner stumbling across some wayward soul who climbed into the wrong panel van." Of course, this is an exaggeration; every crime scene investigation show does not begin this way, but so many of them do, readers will recognize the motif. The reference to television is intended to bring a smile to the readers' faces: even Hollywood writers have recognized that serious runners venture off the beaten path. The copy then mocks these crime shows: "In fact, if it weren't for runners, you wonder how many of these crimes would ever get solved." Along with providing humor, this copy shifts the attention of the ad to the readers, addressing them individually as "you." Now the reader is among the serious runners the ad is targeting. The copy closes with a comical admonition: "Better lace 'em up. Because someone, somewhere, is missing. So do your civic duty. Run like an animal." These last few sentences connect the first and second halves of the copy's message: lace on a pair of Pearl Izumi shoes and run like an animal out in the wilderness where you might run across a crime victim.

Currently, the highest rated television shows are those focusing on crime scene investigation, including *CSI* and its many spinoffs. The copy connects Pearl Izumi shoes with these popular television shows, again appealing to the readers' sense of importance and desire to be hip. The message conveyed by the copy is simple: Real runners are like the characters in crime investigation shows who venture off the beaten path. If you, too, want to be a real runner, wear Pearl Izumi shoes and "run like an animal" out in the woods; don't jog along safe city sidewalks.

In sum, the ad's copy effectively appeals to the values and desires of serious runners. It conveys the message that real athletes wear shoes like these, a fact even recognized by Hollywood writers. The ad also relies on humor to convey its message. It mockingly advises runners to "do your civic duty" and start finding bodies like the runners do on TV, offering them another lighthearted reason (or excuse) to devote additional time to their favorite pursuit.

The Pearl Izumi Seek 2 trail shoe ad is effective because its use of color defies expectation and its copy successfully targets the readers of *Runner's World*. The stark black and white motif of the ad makes it stand out in a magazine filled with more colorful advertisements and complements the crime scene theme of the copy. The copy itself appeals to the values, ego, and self-esteem of the magazine's readers—if they purchase and wear this shoe, they will be serious runners like the ones seen on TV's most popular shows. "Ever notice how it's always runners who find dead bodies?" If you have not, you likely will now thanks to this very successful ad.

Something to write about...

Go back and carefully examine the advertisement for the Pearl Izumi Seek 2 trail shoe found on page 000 then reread "Keys to an Effective Shoe Ad" before you complete the following writing assignments. Your teacher might want you to write these assignments on your own, but you might find it beneficial to work with another student in class.

1. Summarize the thesis of "Keys to an Effective Shoe Ad" and the primary reasons the author offers in support of that claim.
2. Evaluate the claims the author offers in the body of the essay. Which are more effective than the others? For example, which are clearer or better supported? Carefully explain your judgments.
3. Write your own evaluation of the Pearl Izumi Seek 2 trail shoe advertisement. Keep in mind the ad's purpose and intended audience.

ADDITIONAL READINGS

Do free speech rights exist on college campuses? Should university administrators have the right to prohibit and punish certain speech? Do faculty and students have the same speech rights on campus? Are college speech codes right, just, or ethical? Are they misguided, unfair, and undemocratic?

Over the past decade, colleges and universities across the country have restricted free speech on campus by enacting speech codes. These codes are usually designed to prohibit and/or punish speech the university administration believes is hateful or demeaning to particular groups of students or individuals. Those favoring campus hate speech restrictions maintain that colleges should offer all students a safe, inviting learning space: hate speech, if allowed, creates a hostile learning environment that can intimidate students and inhibit their education. The two additional readings below address this controversial issue.

In the first reading, Gerald Uelman examines both sides of the debate, offering a summary of the central arguments speech code proponents and opponents frequently offer. Uelman makes clear that the debate often comes down to a question of whether restricting expression through hate speech codes is a practical and/or moral response to actual or potential acts of discrimination or intimidation on campus and whether the right to free expression outweighs the right to an education. Law professor Cass Sunstein offers a lengthy defense of speech codes, basing his argument in part on the purpose of educational institutions, the nature of student learning, the limitations of free speech, and an administration's responsibility to balance competing rights and obligations.

Before you read these essays, consider the following questions:

- What restrictions, if any, do you believe should be placed on the free speech rights of college students and faculty?
- What would it take to change your mind?
- What are the best arguments someone could offer in support of and against campus speech codes?
- What constitutes "speech"? Should speech codes cover things like signs, symbols, or even the writing on someone's clothes?
- On what basis would you evaluate a proposal to restrict campus speech rights? For example, would you examine whether it was legal, practical, or moral? Would you use some other set of criteria?
- Who on a college campus is most likely to support or oppose speech codes? Why?

As you read the essays, consider these questions:

- Does each reading offer an argument? If so, what is its thesis? If not, what is its purpose?
- What evaluative criteria and standards serve as the basis for the authors' judgments?
- What are the primary reasons offered in favor of campus speech codes? What are the primary reasons offered in opposition to them?
- How to the authors support their claims? What kinds of evidence do they provide?
- What is each author's primary audience? How can you tell?
- What types of persuasive appeals do the authors make in each essay? How are these appeals related to the author's intended audience and stated or implied thesis?
- How is each essay structured? How do the authors help readers follow their lines of thought?
- How would you characterize the style of writing found in each reading? Is the style appropriate for an academic essay?

When you finish reading these essays, ask yourself these questions:

- Did any of the readings challenge your previously held beliefs about campus speech codes? How so?
- Have you changed your mind about campus speech codes as a result of reading these essays?
- Which of the essays did you find convincing and which did you find unconvincing? Why?

ADDITIONAL READING

The Price of Free Speech: Campus Hate Speech Codes

Gerald Uelmen

Gerald Uelmen is dean of Santa Clara University School of Law and a fellow of the Center for Applied Ethics. This essay appeared in the journal Issues in Ethics.

At Emory University, certain conduct that is permissible off campus is not allowed on campus. Specifically, some speech and behaviors are prohibited in Emory's version of what are derogatorily labeled "politically correct" codes but are more commonly known as hate speech codes. Emory's code begins with its definition of banned behavior.

Discriminatory harassment includes conduct (oral, written, graphic or physical) directed against any person or group of persons because of their race, color, national origin, religion, sex, sexual orientation, age, disability, or veteran's status and that has the purpose or reasonably foreseeable effect of creating an offensive, demeaning, intimidating, or hostile environment for that person or group of persons.

There were approximately 75 hate speech codes in place at U.S. colleges and universities in 1990; by 1991, the number grew to over 300. School administrators institute codes primarily to foster productive learning environments in the face of rising racially motivated and other offensive incidents on many campuses. According to a recent study, reports of campus harassment increased 400 percent between 1985 and 1990. Moreover, 80 percent of campus harassment incidents go unreported.

Hate speech codes follow several formats. Some codes, including Emory's, prohibit speech or conduct that creates an intimidating, hostile, or offensive educational environment. Others ban behavior that intentionally inflicts emotional distress. Still others outlaw "general harassment and threats," without clarifying what constitutes such conduct. Court rulings have prohibited public (state-run) colleges and universities from enacting codes that restrict the constitutional right to free speech based on content. Private institutions, in contrast, are not subject to these decisions. Emory, for example, as a private university, can ignore public law rulings and draft whatever hate speech policy it chooses.

Hate speech codes raise important ethical questions. When civil liberties are pitted against the right to freedom of speech, which does justice favor? Do the costs of hate speech codes outweigh their benefits? Is the harm that results from hate speech so serious that codes to restrict freedom of speech are morally required?

Arguments Against Campus Hate Speech Codes

The most fundamental argument against hate speech codes rests on the idea that they violate a fundamental human right, freedom of speech. Such a fundamental right, it is argued, should not be limited except to prevent serious harm to others. Libel or shouting "Fire!" in a movie theater, for example, can cause serious harm and, therefore, are legitimately banned. In contrast, what campuses prohibit as "hate speech" is primarily opinion that, while often offensive and unpopular, does not cause serious harm. The fundamental right to free speech should not be restricted merely to prevent hate speech.

Additionally, critics assert that the costs of hate speech codes far outweigh their benefits. Threatened by "politically correct" students who are backed by hate speech codes, students who have reasonable yet nonconforming points of view will be afraid to speak in classes. As a social institution, a university should be open to all opinions, popular and unpopular. As Oliver Wendell Holmes commented, "The very aim and end of our institutions is just this: that we may think what we like and say what we think." Hate speech codes thus inflict a major harm on our social institutions.

Censorship is only one example of how hate speech codes undercut the benefits of higher education. If these codes shield students from dissenting opinions, how will they learn to respond to such opinions after they graduate? Hate speech codes encourage an artificial reality on campus that prevents students from learning effectively to tolerate diversity.

Hate speech codes may obstruct the kind of education that promotes tolerance of diversity in other ways. Over time, the same fervor that brought hate speech codes will bring further restrictions by administrators eager to create egalitarian institutions in a nonegalitarian world.

The law school at the State University of New York, Buffalo, for example, seeks out and asks state bars to deny admission to former students who violate its hate speech code. And following the 1988 passage of the Civil Rights Restoration Act, which denies federal aid to students of private colleges and universities that violate federal anti-discrimination rules, legislators are considering a law that would force private institutions to require courses on racial sensitivity and ethnic history. From defining what specifically constitutes "hate speech" to choosing the manner in which policies are enforced, codes clearly cause or invite more trouble than they are worth.

In Defense of Campus Hate Speech Codes

Those who advocate hate speech codes believe that the harm codes prevent is more important than the freedom they restrict. When hate speech is directed at a student from a protected group, like those listed in Emory University's code, the effect is much more than hurt feelings. The verbal attack is a symptom of an oppressive history of discrimination and subjugation that plagues the harmed student and hinders his or her ability to compete fairly in the academic arena. The resulting harm is clearly significant and, therefore, justifies limiting speech rights.

In addition to minimizing harm, hate speech codes result in other benefits. The university is ideally a forum where views are debated using rational argumentation;

part of a student's education is learning how to derive and rationally defend an opinion. The hate speech that codes target, in contrast, is not presented rationally or used to provoke debate. In fact, hate speech often intends to provoke violence. Hate speech codes emphasize the need to support convictions with facts and reasoning while protecting the rights of potential victims.

As a society we reason that it is in the best interest of the greatest number of citizens to sometimes restrict speech when it conflicts with the primary purpose of an event. A theater owner, for example, has a right to remove a heckler when the heckler's behavior conflicts with the primary purpose of staging a play—to entertain an audience. Therefore, if the primary purpose of an academic institution is to educate students, and hate speech obstructs the educational process by reducing students' abilities to learn, then it is permissible to extend protection from hate speech to students on college or university campuses.

Hate speech codes also solve the conflict between the right to freely speak and the right to an education. A student attending a college or university clearly has such a right. But students exercising their "free speech" right may espouse hateful or intimidating words that impede other students' abilities to learn and thereby destroy their chances to earn an education.

Finally, proponents of hate speech codes see them as morally essential to a just resolution of the conflict between civil rights (e.g., freedom from harmful stigma and humiliation) and civil liberties (e.g., freedom of speech). At the heart of the conflict is the fact that underrepresented students cannot claim fair and equal access to freedom of speech and other rights when there is an imbalance of power between them and students in the majority. If a black student, for example, shouts an epithet at a white student, the white student may become upset or feel enraged, but he or she has little reason to feel terror or intimidation. Yet when a white student directs an epithet toward a black student or a Jewish student, an overt history of subjugation intensifies the verbal attack that humiliates and strikes institutional fear in the victim. History shows that words of hatred are amplified when they come from those in power and abridged when spoken by the powerless.

Discrimination on college and university campuses is a growing problem with an uncertain future. Whether hate speech codes are morally just responses to campus intolerance depends on how society interprets the harms of discriminatory harassment, the benefits and costs of restricting free speech, and the just balance between individual rights and group rights.

ADDITIONAL READING

Liberalism, Speech Codes, and Related Problems

Cass R. Sunstein

Cass R. Sunstein is Karl N. Llewellyn Professor of Jurisprudence at the University of Chicago Law School. He first delivered this essay before a meeting of the American Association of University Professors; it was first published in Academe.

The law has rarely been at odds with academic freedom. In recent years, however, the development of campus "speech codes" has created a range of new controversies. In these remarks, one of my purposes is to defend the constitutionality of narrowly drawn restrictions on hate speech, arguing in the process against the broader versions that have become popular in some institutions. My most general goal is to set the dispute over speech codes in the broader context of the liberal commitment to freedom of speech and academic pluralism. Through this approach it may be possible to overcome the "all or nothing" tone that has dominated much of public and even academic discussion. In the process of defending some narrow restrictions on hate speech, it will be necessary to say a good deal about the principle of neutrality in constitutional law, academic life, and perhaps elsewhere.

The discussion will obviously bear on the subject of academic freedom. The subject is complex in part because no academic institution can avoid making certain controversial substantive judgments; because those judgments will intrude on some forms of freedom; and because those intrusions will interfere with speech. If we understand the hate speech controversy in this light, we will be pushed away from an attractive and commonly held vision of academic freedom—what might be called a neutral or skeptical vision in which all comers are accepted. We might be led to endorse instead a nonneutral, substantive view that embodies three defining commitments: political equality; a mild version of liberal perfectionism; and an insistence on exposure to a wide range of conceptions of the good and the right, so long as all of these are supported by reasons. I will offer some preliminary remarks on the relationship between the "speech code" controversy and these commitments.

1. Low-Value and High-Value Speech

It is almost certainly necessary to distinguish between different forms of speech in terms of their relationship to Constitutional ideals. Current constitutional law does indeed make such distinctions, asking whether speech qualifies as "low-value" or "high-value." Some speech lies at the free speech "core." Such speech may be regulated, if at all, only on the strongest showing of harm. Other speech lies at the periphery or outside of the Constitution altogether. This "low-value" speech may be regulated if the government can show a legitimate, plausible justification.

Ordinary political speech, dealing with governmental matters, unquestionably belongs at the core. Such speech may not be regulated unless there is a clear and present danger, or, in the Supreme Court's words, unless it is "directed to inciting or producing imminent lawless action and is likely to incite or produce such action." Under this standard, a speech containing racial hatred, offered by a member of the Ku Klux Klan, is usually protected; so too with a speech by a member of the Black Panthers, or by neo Nazis during a march in Skokie, Illinois, the home of many survivors of concentration camps.

But much speech falls into the periphery of constitutional concern. Commercial speech, for example, receives some constitutional protection, in the sense that it qualifies as "speech" within the meaning of the First Amendment. Truthful, nondeceptive advertising is generally protected from regulation. But government may regulate commercial advertising if it is false or misleading. There are many other kinds of "low-value" speech.

Consider threats, attempted bribes, perjury, criminal conspiracy, price-fixing, criminal solicitation, private libel, unlicensed medical and legal advice, sexual and racial harassment. All these can be regulated without meeting the ordinary, highly speech-protective standards.

The Supreme Court has not set out anything like a clear theory to explain why and when speech qualifies for the top tier. At times the Court has indicated that speech belongs in the top tier if it is part of the exchange of ideas, or if it bears on the political process. But apart from these ambiguous hints, it has failed to tell us much about its basis for deciding that some forms of expression are different from others.

Is a two-tier First Amendment inevitable or desirable? Some people claim to be free speech absolutists—they think they believe that all speech is protected, or that speech can be regulated only if the government can show overwhelming harm. But it does seem that any well-functioning system of free expression must ultimately distinguish between different kinds of speech by reference to their centrality to the First Amendment guarantee.

Begin with a truly absolutist position: Anyone may say anything at all at any time. A moment's reflection should show that this position could not be seriously maintained. It would not make sense to forbid government from regulating perjury, bribes, threats, fraudulent real estate deals, unlicensed medical and legal advice, willfully false advertising, and many other forms of expression. Realistically speaking, our choices are a range of nonabsolutionist approaches.

It is tempting to resist this conclusion by proposing that the speech that is unprotected is "really" not speech at all, but merely action. When someone attempts to bribe a government official, perhaps he is "acting," or perhaps the regulation of criminal solicitation is "ancillary" or "incidental" to the regulation of conduct. But as stated, I think that this suggestion is unhelpful. Criminal solicitation and attempted bribes are speech, not action. They may lead to action; but by themselves they are simply words: If I tell you that I want you to help me to commit an assault, I have spoken words; if I say that I will give you $10,000 if you vote for me, I have merely talked; if I say "Kill!" to a trained attack dog, I have done something regulable, but I have still just spoken. If these things are to be treated as action—that is, if they are not to be protected as speech—it is because of their distinctive features. This is what must be discussed. The word "action" is simply a placeholder for that unprovided discussion.

So much for the speech-conduct distinction. The only nonabsolutist alternative to an approach that looks at free speech "value" would be this: All speech stands on basically the same footing. We will not look at value at all. The only relevant issue is one of harm. Speech may be regulated if government can make a demonstration that the speech at issue will produce sufficiently bad consequences. Would it not be possible, and desirable, to have a "single tier" first amendment, in the sense that all speech is presumed protected, but we allow government to regulate speech in those rare cases where the harm is "Very great"?

The answer is that it would not be plausible to say that all speech stands on the same footing. For example, courts should not test regulation of campaign speeches under the same standards applied to misleading commercial speech, child pornography, conspiracies, libel of private persons, and threats. If the same standards were applied, one of two results would follow, and both are unacceptable.

The first possible result would be to lower the burden of justification for governmental regulation as a whole, so as to allow for restrictions on misleading commercial speech, private libel, and so forth. If this were the consequence, there would be an unacceptably high threat to political expression. Upon a reasonably persuasive showing of harm, government could regulate misleading campaign statements, just like it can now regulate misleading proxy statements. A generally lowered burden of justification would therefore be intolerable.

The second possible result is that courts would apply the properly stringent standards for regulation of political speech to (for example) conspiracies, criminal solicitation, commercial speech, private libel, and child pornography. The central problem with this approach is that it would ensure that government could not control speech that should be regulated. A system in which the most stringent standards were applied across the board would ensure that government could not regulate criminal solicitation, child pornography, private libel, and false or misleading commercial speech, among others. The harms that justify such regulation are real, but they are insufficient to permit government controls under the extremely high standards applied to regulation of political speech.

If courts are to be honest about the matter, an insistence that "all speech is speech" would mean that they must eliminate many currently unobjectionable and even necessary controls—or more likely that judgments about value, because unavoidable, would continue to be made, but covertly. We will soon see that this claim bears directly on the questions raised by speech codes and by academic freedom generally.

Thus far I have suggested that a workable system of free expression ought to make distinctions between different sorts of speech; but it remains to decide by what standard courts might accomplish this task. To support an emphasis on politics, we need to define the category of political speech. For present purposes I will treat speech as political *when it is both intended and received as a contribution to public deliberation about some issue.* By requiring intent, I do not mean to require a trial on the question of subjective motivation. Generally this issue can be resolved simply on the basis of the nature of the speech at issue. By requiring that the speech be received as a contribution to public deliberation, I do not mean that all listeners or readers must see the substantive content. It is sufficient if some do.

An approach that affords special protection to political speech, thus defined, is justified on numerous grounds. Such an approach receives firm support from history—not only from the constitutional framers' theory of free expression, but also from the development of that principle through the history of American law. There can be little doubt that suppression by the government of political ideas that it disapproved, or found threatening, was the central motivation for the clause. The worst examples of unacceptable censorship involve efforts by government to insulate itself from criticism. Judicial interpretations over the course of time also support a political conception of the First Amendment.

This approach also seems likely to accord fairly well with our initial or considered judgments about particular free speech problems. Any approach to the First Amendment will have to take substantial account of those judgments, and adjust itself accordingly. Of course we are not unanimous in our considered judgments. But it seems clear that such forms of speech as perjury, bribery, threats, misleading or false commercial advertising, criminal solicitation, and libel of private persons—or at least most of these—are not entitled to the highest degree of constitutional protection. No other general approach unifies initial or preliminary judgments about these matters as well as a political conception of the First Amendment.

In addition, an insistence that government's burden is greatest when political speech is at issue responds well to the fact that here government is most likely to be biased. The premise of distrust of government is strongest when politics are at issue. It is far weaker when government is regulating (say) commercial speech, bribery, private libel, or obscenity. In such cases there is less reason to suppose that it is insulating itself from criticism.

Finally, this approach protects speech when regulation is most likely to be harmful. Restrictions on political speech have the distinctive feature of impairing the ordinary channels for political change; such restrictions are especially dangerous. If there are controls on commercial advertising, it always remains possible to argue that such controls should be lifted. If the government bans violent pornography, citizens can continue to argue against the ban. But if the government forecloses political argument, the democratic corrective is unavailable. Controls on nonpolitical speech do not have this uniquely damaging feature.

Taken in concert, these considerations suggest that, in a liberal democracy, government should be under a special burden of justification when it seeks to control speech intended and received as a contribution to public deliberation. This does not mean that government is unconstrained when it attempts to regulate other speech. Recall that government cannot regulate speech because it is persuasive; recall too that offense at ideas is an illegitimate ground for legal controls. Always the government must be able to make a strong showing of harm. For this reason art, literature, and scientific speech will generally be protected from government controls even if some of these fall within the second tier. Of course these statements will leave ambiguities in hard intermediate cases.

II. Liberalism and Speech on Campus

I have tried thus far to set out some of the features of a well-functioning system of free expression. In that system, political speech belongs in the top tier; more speech, not censorship, is the remedy for speech that threatens harm; only an emergency can support suppression. Nonpolitical speech is also protected, but it can be regulated on the basis of a lesser showing of harm. Here too the government must point to something other than persuasiveness or offense at the content of ideas.

We can use this discussion as a basis for exploring the complex problems resulting from recent efforts to regulate hate speech on campus. Some regulations are often associated with alleged efforts to impose an ideological orthodoxy on students and faculty, under the rubric of "political correctness." Perhaps radical left-wing campuses, under pressure from well-organized groups, are silencing people who disagree. Are the campus speech codes constitutional?

To the extent that we are dealing with private universities, the Constitution is not implicated at all, and hence all such restrictions are permissible. This is an exceptionally important point. Private universities can do whatever they like. They can ban all speech by Republicans, by Democrats, or by anyone they want to silence. But many private universities like to follow the Constitution even if they are not required to do so. In any case, public universities are subject to the Constitution, and so it is important to try to establish what the First Amendment means for them.

A. A Provisional Thesis

On the approach provided thus far, we can offer an important provisional conclusion: If campus speech restrictions at public universities cover not merely epithets, but speech that is part of social deliberation, they might well be seen as unconstitutional for that very reason. At least as a presumption, speech that is intended and received as a contribution to social deliberation is constitutionally protected even if it amounts to what is sometimes classified as hate speech—even if it is racist and sexist.

Consider, for example, the University of Michigan's judicially invalidated ban on "[a]ny behavior, verbal or physical, that stigmatizes or victimizes an individual on the basis of race, ethnicity, religion, sex, sexual orientation, creed, national origin, ancestry, age, marital status, handicap, or Vietnam-era veteran status, and that . . . creates an intimidating, hostile, or demeaning environment for educational pursuits. . . ." This broad ban forbids a wide range of statements that are part of the exchange of ideas. It also fails to give people sufficient notice of what statements are allowed. For both reasons, it seems invalid.

In a famous case, Justice Frankfurter, speaking for a 5–4 majority of the Supreme Court, rejected this view. *Beauharnais v. Illinois* upheld an Illinois law making it unlawful to publish or exhibit any publication which "portrays depravity, criminality, unchastity, or lack of virtue of a class of citizens, which [publication] exposes the citizens of any race, color, creed or religion to contempt, derision, or obloquy or which is productive of breach of the peace or riots." The law was applied to ban circulation of a petition urging "the need to prevent the white race from becoming mongrelized by the negro," and complaining of the "aggressions, rapes, robberies, knives, guns, and marijuana of the negro."

In upholding the law, Justice Frankfurter referred to a range of factors. He pointed to the historical exclusion of libel from free speech protection; to the risks to social cohesion created by racial hate speech; and to the need for judicial deference to legislative judgments on these complex matters. Many countries in Europe accept the same analysis and do not afford protection to racial and ethnic hate speech. But most people think that after *New York Times v. Sullivan*, *Beauharnais* is no longer the law. In *New York Times*, the Court indicated that the law of libel must be evaluated in accordance with the constitutional commitment to robust debate on public issues. The conventional view—which the Supreme Court has not directly addressed—is that racial hate speech contains highly political ideas, that it belongs in the free speech "core," and that it may not be suppressed merely because it is offensive or otherwise harmful.

There are real complexities here. In its strongest form, the defense of *Beauharnais* would point toward the contribution of hate speech to the maintenance of a caste system based on race and gender. A principal point here would be the effect of such speech on the self-respect of its victims and also the relationship between such speech and fears of racially-motivated violence. I cannot fully discuss this issue here; but I think that *Beauharnais* was incorrect. No one should deny that distinctive harms are produced by racial hate speech, especially when it is directed against members of minority groups. It is only obtuseness—a failure of perception or empathetic identification—that would enable someone to say that the word "fascist" or "pig" or "communist," or even "honky," produces the same feelings as the word "nigger." In view of our history, invective directed against minority groups, and racist speech in general, create fears of violence and subordination—of second-class citizenship— that are not plausibly described as mere offense. As I have noted, most European countries, including flourishing democracies committed to free speech, make exceptions for such expression. In many countries, including our own, it is possible to think that racial and ethnic hate speech is really *sui generis*, and that it is properly treated differently.

But there are strong counter-arguments. If we were to excise all of what is described as hate speech from political debate, we would severely truncate our discussion of such important matters as civil rights, foreign policy, crime, conscription, abortion, and social welfare policy. Even if speech produces anger or resentment on the basis of race, it might well be thought a legitimate part of the deliberative process, and it bears directly on politics. Foreclosure of such speech would probably accomplish little good, and by stopping people from hearing certain ideas, it could bring about a great deal of harm. These are the most conventional Millian arguments for the protection of speech.

From all this it seems that the University of Michigan ban was far too broad. On the other hand, it should be permissible for colleges and universities to build on the basic case of the epithet in order to regulate certain narrowly defined categories of hate speech. Standing by themselves, or accompanied by little else, epithets are not intended and received as contributions to social deliberation about anything. We are therefore dealing with lower tier speech. The injury to dignity and self-respect is a sufficient harm to allow regulation. (See my discussion below of the Stanford regulation.)

It is now possible to offer a provisional conclusion. A public university should be allowed to regulate hate speech in the form of epithets. But it should be prohibited from reaching very far beyond epithets to forbid the expression of views on public issues, whatever those views may be. I will qualify this conclusion shortly, but it seems like a good place to start.

B. *The Question of Neutrality*

But are restrictions on hate speech impermissibly selective? In *R.A.V. v. St. Paul*, the Court invalidated a law directed against a certain kind of hate speech, principally on the ground that it discriminated on the basis of subject matter. The case involved an act of cross-burning on a private yard. All the justices agreed that the content-neutral trespass law could be applied against that act; the question was whether a special "hate speech" law was constitutional as applied to that act.

As interpreted by the Minnesota Supreme Court, the relevant law banned any so-called "fighting words" that produced anger or resentment on the basis of race, religion, or gender. In invalidating the act, the *R.A.V.* Court emphasized that the law at issue was not a broad or general proscription of fighting words. It reflects a decision to single out a certain category of "fighting words," defined in terms of audience reactions to speech about certain topics. Is this illegitimate? The point bears on almost all efforts to regulate hate speech, on campus and elsewhere.

The Supreme Court's basic idea is this: Whether or not we are dealing with high value speech, government cannot draw lines on a partisan basis. It cannot say, for example, that libel of Democrats will be punished more severely than libel of Republicans, or that obscenity will be regulated only if it makes fun of the president. A law of this sort would be "viewpoint-based," that is, it *makes the viewpoint of the speaker the basis for regulation.* To that extent it is invalid. Moreover, the government is sharply constrained in its ability to limit speech on certain subjects. It could not, for example, ban speech about AIDS. "Subject-matter" restrictions are more neutral than viewpoint-based restrictions. They are not per se invalid, but they are treated with considerable skepticism. For the Supreme Court, the major problem with the Minnesota law was that it was an impermissible subject-matter restriction.

To the distinction between low-value and high-value speech, then, we must add that the First Amendment limits the government's line-drawing power. The government must not be impermissibly selective, even if it is regulating low-value speech. Hence in the *R.A.V.* case, the Court concluded that St. Paul had violated the First Amendment, not because it had regulated constitutionally protected speech, but because it had chosen to regulate only "fighting words" of a certain, governmentally disapproved sort, and allowed the rest to flourish.

In his dissenting opinion, Justice Stevens argued that St. Paul had not made an impermissible distinction, since the harms underlying the regulated speech were sufficiently distinctive. He wrote that "race-based threats may cause more harm to society and to individuals than other threats. Just as the statute prohibiting threats against the president is justifiable because of the place of the president in our social and political order, so a statute prohibiting race-based threats is justifiable because of the place of race in our social and political order." In his view, "[t]hreatening someone because of her race or religious beliefs may cause particularly severe trauma or touch off a riot . . .; such threats may be punished more severely than threats against someone based on, for example, his support of a particular athletic team." Thus there were "legitimate, reasonable, and neutral justifications" for the special rule. But Justice Stevens spoke only for himself, and his view was firmly rejected by the majority.

The question then becomes whether university restrictions on hate speech are impermissibly selective. A university might well, post-*R.A.V.*, be forbidden from singling out for punishment speech that many universities want to control, such as (a) a narrowly defined category of insults toward such specifically enumerated groups as blacks, women, and homosexuals, or (b) a narrowly defined category of insults directed at individuals involving race, sex, and sexual orientation. How would restrictions of this kind be treated?

Under current law, a restriction that involves (a) is viewpoint-based, and to that extent even worse than the restriction in *R.A.V.* itself. On the analysis of the *R.A.V.* Court, restriction (a) tries to silence one side in a debate. A restriction that involves (b) is a subject matter restriction, not based on viewpoint. But it too is impermissibly selective in exactly the same sense as the restriction invalidated in the *R.A.V.* case.

It is possible to say that the conclusions in *R.A.V.* are incorrect in principle, because there are sufficiently neutral grounds for restrictions (a) and (b). Perhaps a university could neutrally decide that epithets directed against blacks, women, and homosexuals cause distinctive harms. But this conclusion is hard to reconcile with the *R.A.V.* decision.

C. The Special Place of the University

Colleges and universities do, however, have some arguments that were unavailable to St. Paul, Minnesota. In order to make the conclusions thus far more than provisional, we have to address those arguments. If *R.A.V.* does not apply to the campus, it might be because public universities can claim a large degree of insulation from judicial supervision. That claim to insulation is closely connected to the idea of academic freedom.

1. *In general.* The largest point here is that colleges and universities are often in the business of controlling speech, and their controls are hardly ever thought to raise free speech problems. Indeed, controlling speech is, in one sense, a defining characteristic of the university. There are at least four different ways in which such controls occur.

First, universities impose major limits on the topics that can be discussed in the classroom. Subject matter restrictions are part of education. Irrelevant discussion is banned. Students cannot discuss the presidential election, or Marx and Mill, if the subject is math. Schools are allowed to impose subject matter restrictions that would be plainly unacceptable if enacted by states or localities.

Second, a teacher can require students to treat each other with at least a minimum of basic respect. It would certainly be legitimate to suspend a student for using consistently abusive or profane language in the classroom. This is so even if that language would receive firm constitutional protection on the street corner. The educational process requires at least a measure of civility. Perhaps it would be unacceptable for universities to ban expressions of anger or intense feeling; the notion of civility should not be a disguise for forbidding irreverence or disagreement. But so long as requirements of civility are both reasonable and neutral with respect to viewpoint, a university may limit abusive or profane comments within the classroom.

The problem goes deeper, for—and this is the third kind of academic control on speech—judgments about quality are pervasive. Such judgments affect admissions, evaluation of students in class and on paper, and evaluation of prospective and actual faculty as well. Academic decisions about quality will of course be based on a conception of appropriate standards of argument and justification. These standards involve judgments about merit or excellence that would of course be unacceptable in the setting of criminal punishment or civil fine, but that are a perfectly and nearly inescapable legitimate part of the educational function. At least this is so if there is no discrimination on the basis of viewpoint, that is, if the person involved in making the assessment offers judgments on the basis of standards of quality that are applied neutrally to everyone (an ambitious aspiration, and one that is conceptually complex).

But there is a fourth and more troublesome way in which universities control speech, and this involves the fact that many academic judgments are viewpoint-based, certainly in practice. In many places, a student who defends fascism or communism is unlikely to receive a good grade. In many economics departments, sharp deviation from the views of Adam Smith may well be punished. History and literature departments have their own conceptions of what sorts of arguments are retrograde or beyond the pale. Viewpoint discrimination is undoubtedly present in practice, and even if we object to it in principle, it is impossible and perhaps undesirable for outsiders to attempt to police it.

Thus far I have mostly been discussing students; but much the same is true for faculty members. Universities can impose on their faculty restrictive rules of decorum and civic participation. A teacher who refuses to teach the subject, fails to allow counter-arguments, treats students contemptuously, or vilifies them in class, can be penalized without offense to the Constitution. The job performance of teachers consists mostly of speech. When that performance is found wanting, it is almost always because of content, including judgments about subject matter and quality, and sometimes because of viewpoint.

It is worthwhile pausing over this point. Initial hirings, tenure, and promotion all involve subject matter restrictions, and sometimes viewpoint discrimination in practice. All this suggests that universities are engaged in regulating speech through content discrimination and at least implicit viewpoint discrimination. The evaluation of students and colleagues cannot occur without resort to content, and it would be most surprising if viewpoint discrimination did not affect many evaluations.

These examples do not by any means compel the conclusion that any and all censorship is acceptable in an academic setting. A university can have a good deal of power over what happens in the classroom, so as to promote the educational enterprise, without also being allowed to decree a political orthodoxy by discriminating on the basis of viewpoint. If a public university were to ban students from defending (say) conservative or liberal causes in political science classes, a serious free speech issue would be raised. There are therefore real limits to permissible viewpoint discrimination within the classroom, even if it is hard to police the relevant boundaries. Certainly the university's permissible limits over the classroom do not extend to the campus in general. We could not allow major restrictions on what students and faculty may say when they are not in class. A university could not say that outside of class, students can talk only about subjects of the university's choice.

From these various propositions, we might adopt a principle: *The university can impose subject matter or other restrictions on speech only to the extent that the restrictions are closely related to its educational mission.* This proposition contains both an authorization to the university and sharp limitations on what it may do. There is a close parallel here with decisions about what to include or exclude from libraries and about how to fund the arts; in all these contexts, certain forms of content discrimination are inescapable. But in cases in which the educational mission is not reasonably at stake, restrictions on speech should be invalidated. Certainly this would be true in cases in which a university attempts to impose a political orthodoxy, whether inside or outside the classroom. We might react to the existence of implicit viewpoint discrimination by saying that it is hard for courts to police, but nonetheless a real offense to both academic aspirations and free speech principles.

2. *Educational requirements and hate speech.* How does this proposition bear on the hate speech issue? Perhaps a university could use its frequently exercised power over speech in order to argue for certain kinds of hate speech codes. Perhaps it could say that when it legitimately controls speech, it does so in order to promote its educational mission, which inevitably entails limits on who may say what. Perhaps a university could be allowed to conclude that its educational mission requires unusually firm controls on hate speech, so as not to compromise the values of education itself.

The university might emphasize in this regard that it has a special obligation to protect all of its students as equal members of the community. This obligation calls for restrictions on what faculty members may say. The university might believe that certain narrowly defined forms of hate speech are highly destructive to the students' chance to learn. It might think that black students and women can be effectively excluded by certain forms of hate speech. Probably a university should be given more leeway to restrict hate speech than a state or locality, precisely because it ought to receive the benefit of the doubt when it invokes concerns of this kind. Surely the educational mission ought to grant the university somewhat greater room to maneuver, especially in light of the complexity and delicacy of the relevant policy questions. Courts might also hesitate before finding viewpoint discrimination or impermissible selectivity. Perhaps there should be a presumption in favor of a university's judgment that narrowly defined hate speech directed at blacks or women produces harm that is especially threatening to the educational enterprise.

This conclusion is buttressed by two additional factors. First, there are numerous colleges and universities. Many students can choose among a range of alternatives, and a restriction in one, two, or more imposes an extremely small incursion into the system of free expression. Colleges that restrict a large amount of speech may find themselves with few students, and in any case other institutions will be available. Second, the Constitution is itself committed to the elimination of second-class citizenship, and this commitment makes it hard to say that an educational judgment opposed to certain forms of hate speech is impermissibly partisan.

3. *Details.* I think that an analysis of this kind would justify two different sorts of approaches to the issue of hate speech on campus. First, a university might regulate hate speech, narrowly defined, as simply a part of its general class of restrictions on speech that is incompatible with the educational mission. On this approach, there

would be no restriction specifically directed against hate speech—no campus "speech code"—but a general, suitably defined requirement of decency and civility, and this requirement would regulate hate speech as well as other forms of abuse. Just as a university might ban the use of profanity in class, or personally abusive behavior on campus, so it might stop racial epithets and similar expressions of hatred or contempt. This is not to say that students and teachers who violate this ban must be expelled or suspended. Generally informal sanctions, involving conversations rather than punishment, are much to be preferred. But the Constitution should not stand as a barrier to approaches of this sort, so long as the university is neutral in this way.

Second, courts should allow narrowly defined hate speech restrictions even if those restrictions are not part of general proscriptions on indecent or uncivil behavior. For example, Stanford University now forbids speech that amounts to "harassment by personal vilification." (Stanford is a private university, free from constitutional restraint, but it has chosen to comply with its understanding of what the First Amendment means as applied to public universities.) Under the Stanford rule, speech qualifies as regulable "harassment" if it (1) is intended to insult or stigmatize an individual or a small number of individuals on the basis of their sex, race, color, handicap, religion, sexual orientation, or national and ethnic origin, (2) is addressed directly to the individual or individuals whom it insults or stigmatizes, and (3) makes use of insulting or "fighting" words or nonverbal symbols. To qualify under (3), the speech must by its "very utterance inflict injury or tend to incite to an immediate breach of the peace," and must be "commonly understood to convey direct and visceral hatred and contempt for human beings" on the basis of one of the grounds enumerated in (2).

The Stanford regulation should not be faulted for excessive breadth. It is quite narrowly defined. If a public university adopted it, the major constitutional problem, fueled by the outcome in *R.A.V.*, would not be breadth but unacceptable selectivity. Why has the university not controlled other forms of "fighting words," like the word "fascist," or "commie," or "bastard"? Does its selectivity show an impermissible motivation? Shouldn't we find its selectivity to be impermissibly partisan? I do not think that we should. A university could reasonably and neutrally decide that the harms caused by the regulated fighting words are, at least in the university setting, more severe than the harms caused by other kinds of fighting words. I conclude that public universities may regulate speech of the sort controlled by the Stanford regulation and probably go somewhat further, and that such restrictions should not be invalidated as impermissibly selective.

We can also use this discussion as a basis for exploring the question of the university's power over employees, arising out of the highly publicized decision of the City University of New York to remove Dr. Leonard Jeffries as chair of the Black Studies department at City College. Jeffries had reportedly made a range of apparently anti-Semitic remarks, blaming rich Jews for the black slave trade, complaining that Russian Jews and "their financial partners, the Mafia, put together a financial system of destruction of black people," and claiming that Jews and Italians had "planned, plotted, and programmed out of Hollywood" to denigrate blacks in films. Could the City University take these remarks as a reason to remove Jeffries from his position as department chair? (We should agree that removal could be justified if, as some say, it was a response to an inadequate record of publication, to poor research, or to low-quality work.)

The answer depends on whether the removal was based on an effort neutrally to promote educational goals, or whether it was instead an effort to punish the expression of a controversial point of view. In the abstract this question is hard to answer, but it can be clarified through examples. Under the First Amendment, a public university could not fire a mathematics professor because he is a Republican, extremely conservative, or a sharp critic of the Supreme Court; such a discharge could not plausibly be connected with legitimate concerns about job performance. Even if the mathematics professor was a department chair, these political convictions are unrelated to job performance.

On the other hand, a university could surely fire the head of an admissions committee who persisted in making invidiously derogatory comments about blacks, women, and Jews. It would be reasonable for the university to say that someone who makes such comments cannot perform his job, which includes attracting good students, male and female, and of various races and religions. The discharge of the admissions head would not really be based on viewpoint: it would be part of a viewpoint-neutral effort to ensure that the head can do what he is supposed to do. Much the same could be said of a university president or many other high-visibility public employees. Consider the fact that the president, or a governor, is freely permitted to fire high-level officials who make statements that compromise job performance, even if those statements are political in nature: if the Secretary of State says publicly that the president is a fool, or even that the president's policy toward Russia is senseless, the president can tell the Secretary to seek employment elsewhere.

It seems to follow that a university could remove a department chair if his comments make him unable successfully to undertake his ordinary duties as chair. The governing principle seems to be this: *A university can penalize speech if and only if it can show that the relevant speech makes it very difficult or impossible for the employee adequately to perform his job.* Whenever a university seeks to punish speech, it should face a large burden to show that it is behaving neutrally, and not trying to punish a disfavored point of view. On this approach, teachers and researchers will almost always be protected. Controversial political statements will not be a sufficient basis for punishment or discharge. A political science professor may criticize (or endorse) the president without becoming less able to perform the job, and most teachers will be able to say whatever they like without subjecting themselves to the possibility of discipline. It follows that the City College could not punish (as it apparently tried to do) a philosophy professor for publishing the view that blacks are, on average, intellectually inferior to whites. It also follows that the City College could not remove Professor Jeffries from his tenured position merely because of actually or apparently anti-Semitic statements.

But we can imagine a range of statements that might make job performance quite difficult, at least for someone in a high-level administrative position—statements, for example, expressing general contempt for students and colleagues, a refusal to participate in the academic enterprise, or hatred directed against people who are part of the university community. Perhaps such statements would not be sufficient to allow discharge from a faculty position: but they could make it hard for the relevant speakers to perform as deans, as admissions officers, or as chairs of departments. In the Jeffries case, the best argument in favor of the City University of New York would be: that it is difficult for someone to succeed as chair of a prominent black studies department if he has made sharply derogatory statements about members of other groups defined in racial, religious, or ethnic terms. This argument would not allow Jeffries to be discharged from his position as professor, but it should allow him to be removed from the position as department chair, which involves a range of distinctive tasks. It follows that on the facts I have assumed, the City College did not violate Jeffries's First Amendment rights. Of course the case would be different if Jeffries could prove that the City College was reacting not to impaired job performance, but to its own disapproval of Jeffries's point of view.

An opposing principle would take the following form. *A university should not be permitted to burden or to deny benefits to an employee on the basis of the employee's point of view, even if the point of view does damage job performance.* On this view, people who disapprove of the point of view—students, other faculty, potential contributors—should not be permitted to enshrine their own views by affecting the university's decisions about employees. We might argue for this principle on the ground that there should no "heckler's veto" against unpopular opinions. We should not have a system in which people who dislike a certain point of view can stop dissenters from assuming prominent positions in the university.

This argument is not without force, but I do not think that it should be adopted. Everyone seems to agree that the president and the governor may make hiring decisions on the basis of viewpoint; it would not make sense to disable the president from ensuring that high-level employees do not try, through speech, to undermine the president's program. Any resulting interference with the system of free expression seems minimal, and the president has a strong need for a loyal staff. Similarly, universities have powerful and legitimate reasons to expect their employees to perform their jobs, especially if those employees are engaged in highly public administrative tasks, and especially if professors who are not performing administrative tasks are realistically not threatened. At least under ordinary circumstances, there will be no substantial interference with the system of free expression if universities are given the narrow authority for which I have argued. I conclude that outside of legitimate judgments about quality and subject matter, universities may punish employees for their speech only in a narrow set of circumstances—almost always involving highly public, administrative positions—in which the relevant speech makes it difficult or impossible for employees to perform their jobs.

It follows from all this that the national government should abandon its efforts to subject private universities to the constraints of the First Amendment. This is an area in which national authorities should proceed with caution. Of course we could imagine experiments that we might deplore. But there is no reason for the federal government to require uniformity on this complex matter.

Conclusion

A system of free expression should be designed to safeguard the exchange of ideas. This understanding calls for protection of much of what might be considered "hate speech"; but it also allows restrictions on speech that amounts to epithets. There are some additional complexities in the academic setting. Universities are pervasively and necessarily engaged in regulation of speech, and this fact complicates many existing claims about hate speech codes. In the end I suggest that the test is whether the restriction on speech is a legitimate part of the institution's educational mission, understanding that ideal by reference to the commitment to liberal education. This mission is not neutral among different conceptions of the good. It embodies a substantive project (though the project is one that allows exposure to a wide range of competing conceptions). This understanding would not permit speech codes to endanger the exchange of ideas, but it would allow for mildly broader restrictions than would be acceptable for states and localities.

Notes

I do not discuss here the issues raised by the claim that academic freedom forbids certain governmental intrusions into the affairs of the university, though some of what I say does bear on those issues.

Brandenburg v. Ohio, 395 U.S. 444 (1969).

New York Times v. Sullivan, 376 U.S. 254 (1964) (invoking democratic goals);
    Chaplinsky v. New Hampshire, 315 U.S. 568 (1942) (invoking exchange of ideas).

See *Doe v. University of Michigan*, 721 F. Supp. 852 (E.D. Mich. 1989); *UWM
    Post, Inc. v. Bd. of Regents*, 774 F. Supp. 1163 (E.D. Wis. 1991).

343 U.S. 250 (1952).

376 U.S. 254 (1964).

See Charles R. Lawrence, "If He Hollers Let Him Go," 1990 Duke L.J. 431; Mari
    Matsuda, "Public Response to Racist Speech," 87 Mich. L. Rev. 2320 (1989);
    Richard Delgado, "Words That Wound," 17 Harv. C.R.-C.L. L. Rev. 133 (1982).

I try to offer an argument to this effect in Cass R. Sunstein, *Democracy and the
    Problem of Free Speech* (forthcoming from The Free Press. September 1993).

Something to write about...

1. Using the readings found at the end of this chapter along with additional material you gather through research and reflection, write an evaluation argument answering one or more of the following question: Are college speech codes beneficial? Are college speech codes ethical?

2. Find a copy of your university's or college's speech code. Write an evaluation argument in which you support a claim concerning the efficacy or ethics of that code. Support your assertions with material you generate through research and reflection.

3. Write a movie or a book review. You can evaluate a current or a classic film or any book you have read. Your teacher may want you to draw material from previously published reviews of that work, or your own analysis and evaluation of the work, or both.

REVISION CHECKLISTS

STIPULATIVE DEFINITION ARGUMENT

1. Have you examined the assignment to determine if you are writing the right kind of definition argument? ☐ Yes ☐ No

2. Have you analyzed the rhetorical situation of the assignment to determine *your* intended audience and purpose? ☐ Yes ☐ No

3. Have you checked to determine the required length of the paper, if any? ☐ Yes ☐ No

4. In the opening section of your essay, do you
   - introduce the topic of your argument? ☐ Yes ☐ No
   - attempt to capture your readers' interest? ☐ Yes ☐ No
   - state your thesis? ☐ Yes ☐ No

5. Does your thesis statement accurately and clearly state your argument's primary assertion? ☐ Yes ☐ No

6. Does your thesis help readers predict how you will develop your argument? ☐ Yes ☐ No

7. Do you explore one criterion at a time in the body of your essay? ☐ Yes ☐ No

8. In developing your argument, do you state, explain, explore, and defend one assertion at a time? ☐ Yes ☐ No

9. Do you support your assertions with sufficient and appropriate evidence and examples? ☐ Yes ☐ No

10. Do you carefully explain how the evidence and examples you supply actually support each of your assertions? ☐ Yes ☐ No

11. Given your intended audience and purpose, have you made the best choice of assertions and support? ☐ Yes ☐ No

12. Have you properly quoted and/or documented all of the source material you have incorporated into your argument? ☐ Yes ☐ No

13. In the concluding section of your argument, do you
    ▪ draw your essay to a graceful, logical end ☐ Yes ☐ No
    ▪ remind your readers of your thesis ☐ Yes ☐ No

14. Have you avoided using ambiguous language in defining your topic? ☐ Yes ☐ No

15. Have you avoided overly broad definitions? ☐ Yes ☐ No

16. Have you avoided circular definitions? ☐ Yes ☐ No

17. Have you addressed possible questions or concerns about your assertions? ☐ Yes ☐ No

18. Have you revised your essay focusing on content and structure? ☐ Yes ☐ No

19. Have you revised your essay focusing on clarity and correctness? ☐ Yes ☐ No

20. Do you follow appropriate conventions regarding form, style, and documentation? ☐ Yes ☐ No

CATEGORICAL DEFINITION ARGUMENT

1. Have you examined the assignment to determine if you are writing the right kind of definition argument? ☐ Yes ☐ No

2. Have you analyzed the rhetorical situation of the assignment to determine *your* intended audience and purpose? ☐ Yes ☐ No

3. Have you adhered to any restrictions regarding your argument's length or format? ☐ Yes ☐ No

4. Have you checked to determine the required length of the paper, if any? ☐ Yes ☐ No

5. In the opening section of your essay, do you
   ▪ introduce the topic of your argument? ☐ Yes ☐ No
   ▪ attempt to capture your readers' interest? ☐ Yes ☐ No
   ▪ state your thesis? ☐ Yes ☐ No

6. Does your thesis indicate whether your subject fits your category? ☐ Yes ☐ No

7. Does your thesis help readers predict the assertions you will make in your argument and/or how you will structure your essay?

8. In the category sections of your argument, do you
   - identify and explain the category one defining feature   ☐ Yes   ☐ No
     at a time?
   - offer reasons in support of each assertion you make?   ☐ Yes   ☐ No
   - illustrate and defend your assertions with sufficient   ☐ Yes   ☐ No
     and appropriate evidence and examples?
   - explain how the evidence and examples you provide   ☐ Yes   ☐ No
     support your assertions?

9. In the fit sections of your argument, do you
   - assert whether your subject does or does not fit each   ☐ Yes   ☐ No
     defining feature one at a time?
   - offer reasons in support of each assertion you make?   ☐ Yes   ☐ No
   - illustrate and defend your assertions with sufficient   ☐ Yes   ☐ No
     and appropriate evidence and examples?
   - explain how the evidence and examples you provide   ☐ Yes   ☐ No
     support your assertions?

10. Given your intended audience and purpose, have you   ☐ Yes   ☐ No
    made the best choice of assertions and support?

11. Have you properly quoted and/or documented all of   ☐ Yes   ☐ No
    the source material you have incorporated into your
    argument?

12. In the concluding section of your argument, do you
    - draw your essay to a graceful, logical end?   ☐ Yes   ☐ No
    - remind readers of your thesis?   ☐ Yes   ☐ No

13. Given your intended audience and purpose, have you   ☐ Yes   ☐ No
    chosen to use the most effective assertions and support?

14. Have you properly quoted and/or documented all   ☐ Yes   ☐ No
    source material?

15. Have you avoided defining your topic too narrowly or   ☐ Yes   ☐ No
    too broadly?

16. Have you avoided oversimplifying your argument?   ☐ Yes   ☐ No

17. Do you address possible questions concerning or   ☐ Yes   ☐ No
    objections to your assertions?

18. Have you revised your essay making all necessary   ☐ Yes   ☐ No
    changes to its content and structure?

19. Have you revised your paper to be sure your writing is   ☐ Yes   ☐ No
    both correct and clear?

20. Do you follow appropriate conventions regarding form,   ☐ Yes   ☐ No
    style, and documentation?

CAUSAL ARGUMENT

1. Have you carefully read the assignment to determine if you are to address your topic's causes, effects, or both? ☐ Yes ☐ No

2. Have you clarified *your* intended audience and purpose? ☐ Yes ☐ No

3. Does your argument conform to any length, format, or topic requirements? ☐ Yes ☐ No

4. In the opening section of your argument, do you
   - introduce the topic of your essay? ☐ Yes ☐ No
   - attempt to capture reader interest ☐ Yes ☐ No
   - state your thesis? ☐ Yes ☐ No

5. Does your thesis indicate whether you will address causes and/or effects in your argument? ☐ Yes ☐ No

6. Does your thesis help readers predict your argument's content and structure? ☐ Yes ☐ No

7. In the body of your essay, do you examine just one cause or effect at a time? ☐ Yes ☐ No

8. Is this cause or effect clearly stated? ☐ Yes ☐ No

9. Do your offer reasons to support your assertions concerning your topic's causes or effects? ☐ Yes ☐ No

10. Do you support your reasons and claims with sufficient and appropriate evidence and examples? ☐ Yes ☐ No

11. Do you explain how the evidence and examples you provide support the assertions you make? ☐ Yes ☐ No

12. Do you address any possible questions concerning or objections to the claims you make? ☐ Yes ☐ No

13. In the conclusion of your essay, do you
    - bring your argument to a satisfying end? ☐ Yes ☐ No
    - reassert or remind readers of your thesis? ☐ Yes ☐ No

14. Do you avoid problems with false causes? ☐ Yes ☐ No

15. Do you avoid problems with the *post-hoc* fallacy? ☐ Yes ☐ No

16. Have you revised your essay to correct any problems with content or structure? ☐ Yes ☐ No

17. Have you revised your essay for clarity and correctness? ☐ Yes ☐ No

18. Do you follow appropriate conventions regarding form, style, and documentation? ☐ Yes ☐ No

PROPOSAL ARGUMENT

1. Have you carefully analyzed the assignment to determine the type of proposal argument you're expected to write? ☐ Yes ☐ No

2. Have you identified your intended audience and purpose? ☐ Yes ☐ No

3. In the opening section of your argument, do you
   - introduce the topic of your essay? ☐ Yes ☐ No
   - attempt to capture reader interest? ☐ Yes ☐ No
   - appeal in some way to your reader's emotions, needs, or values? ☐ Yes ☐ No
   - state your thesis? ☐ Yes ☐ No

4. Does your thesis statement indicate the problem you will focus on in your argument? ☐ Yes ☐ No

5. Does your thesis indicate whether you will examine one or multiple solutions to the problem? ☐ Yes ☐ No

6. Does your thesis statement help readers anticipate the content and structure of your argument? ☐ Yes ☐ No

7. In the problem section of your argument, do you
   - state what the problem is? ☐ Yes ☐ No
   - establish for whom it is a problem? ☐ Yes ☐ No
   - establish how long it has been a problem? ☐ Yes ☐ No
   - establish who or what caused the problem? ☐ Yes ☐ No
   - establish the costs of the problem? ☐ Yes ☐ No
   - examine possible questions concerning or objections to your assertions? ☐ Yes ☐ No
   - support your claims with sufficient and appropriate evidence and examples? ☐ Yes ☐ No
   - explain how the evidence and examples you provide actually support your assertions? ☐ Yes ☐ No

8. In the solution section of your argument, do you
   - examine one solution at a time? ☐ Yes ☐ No
   - explain what the solution is? ☐ Yes ☐ No
   - explain how it would solve the problem? ☐ Yes ☐ No
   - examine the strengths and limitations of each proposed solution? ☐ Yes ☐ No
   - examine and rebut possible objections to your assertions? ☐ Yes ☐ No
   - support your claims with sufficient and appropriate evidence and examples? ☐ Yes ☐ No
   - explain how the evidence and examples you provide actually support your assertions? ☐ Yes ☐ No

9. In the "best solution" section of your argument, do you

    ▩ explain what the best solution is? ☐ Yes ☐ No

    ▩ explain how it will solve the problem? ☐ Yes ☐ No

    ▩ explain what makes it best? ☐ Yes ☐ No

    ▩ examine the limitations of your best solution? ☐ Yes ☐ No

    ▩ examine and rebut possible objections to your assertions? ☐ Yes ☐ No

    ▩ support your claims with sufficient and appropriate evidence and examples? ☐ Yes ☐ No

    ▩ explain how the evidence and examples you provide actually support your assertions? ☐ Yes ☐ No

10. Have your properly quoted and/or documented all source material? ☐ Yes ☐ No

11. In the conclusion of your argument, do you

    ▩ bring your essay to a logical, satisfying, persuasive end? ☐ Yes ☐ No

    ▩ reassert or remind readers of your thesis? ☐ Yes ☐ No

12. Have you revised your argument to address possible problems with its content and structure? ☐ Yes ☐ No

13. Have you revised your argument to fix any problems with its clarity or correctness? ☐ Yes ☐ No

14. Do you follow appropriate conventions regarding form, style, and documentation? ☐ Yes ☐ No

EVALUATION ARGUMENT

1. Have you read the assignment carefully and clarified the type of evaluation argument you are being asked to write? ☐ Yes ☐ No

2. Have you clarified the intended audience and purpose of your argument? ☐ Yes ☐ No

3. Have you clarified any expectations concerning the length or format of your argument? ☐ Yes ☐ No

4. In the opening section of your argument, do you

    ▩ introduce the subject of your argument? ☐ Yes ☐ No

    ▩ attempt to capture your readers' interest? ☐ Yes ☐ No

    ▩ state your thesis? ☐ Yes ☐ No

5. Does your thesis statement indicate the subject of your argument and your overall evaluation of it? ☐ Yes ☐ No

6. Does your thesis statement help readers anticipate the criteria you will use to evaluate your subject? ☐ Yes ☐ No

7. Does your thesis statement help readers anticipate the structure of your argument? ☐ Yes ☐ No

8. In the criteria sections of your argument, do you
   - examine each criterion one at a time? ☐ Yes ☐ No
   - explain what the criterion is? ☐ Yes ☐ No
   - establish the standards you will use to evaluate the subject according to that criterion? ☐ Yes ☐ No
   - offer reasons for your assertions? ☐ Yes ☐ No
   - offer sufficient and appropriate evidence and examples to support the assertions you make? ☐ Yes ☐ No
   - explain how the evidence and examples support your assertions? ☐ Yes ☐ No
   - answer possible objections to or questions concerning your assertions? ☐ Yes ☐ No

9. In the application sections of your argument, do you
   - state whether the subject meets the criterion one at a time? ☐ Yes ☐ No
   - support your assertion with reasons? ☐ Yes ☐ No
   - offer sufficient and appropriate evidence and examples in support of your assertions? ☐ Yes ☐ No
   - explain how you the evidence and examples you offer support your assertions? ☐ Yes ☐ No
   - answer possible objections to or questions concerning your assertions? ☐ Yes ☐ No

10. Have you checked to be sure you do not employ overlapping or redundant criteria? ☐ Yes ☐ No

11. Do you properly quote and/or document all source material? ☐ Yes ☐ No

12. In the concluding section of your argument, do you
    - bring your argument to a satisfying and logical end? ☐ Yes ☐ No
    - reassert your thesis? ☐ Yes ☐ No

13. Have you revised your argument to address any problems with its content or structure? ☐ Yes ☐ No

14. Have you revised your argument to address any problems with clarity or correctness? ☐ Yes ☐ No

15. Do you follow appropriate conventions regarding form, style, and documentation? ☐ Yes ☐ No

ANNOTATED BIBLIOGRAPHIES

ANNOTATED BIBLIOGRAPHIES

Definition and Purpose

An annotated bibliography offers readers a brief overview of or introduction to the resources you consulted as you gathered information for a paper or some other course project. Each entry in an annotated bibliography is composed of two parts—the citation and the annotation. The citation is the bibliographic entry for each source; the annotation is a brief passage summarizing, responding to, or evaluating it. Annotated bibliographies serve several academic purposes. Sometimes teachers include them on their syllabus as a free-standing writing assignment—you complete the annotated bibliography and turn it in for a grade as one of the required essays for the course. Other times, teachers will require you to provide an annotated bibliography as part of a longer research project—they may ask for it when you turn in your essay or as you gather material to write the piece.

The citation you provide should follow the guidelines of whatever stylebook you are using in that particular class. If you normally follow APA documentation guidelines, your citations will adhere to the formats found in that stylebook; if you follow MLA guidelines, they will adhere to those formats. If your teacher voices no preference, choose one and follow it consistently.

The types of annotations you are required to write can vary by length and purpose. You may be asked to summarize each source, summarize and respond to it, or evaluate it. Sometimes teachers will expect you to write your annotations in complete sentences; other times, writing in sentence fragments will be acceptable. When assigned to write an annotated bibliography, if it is not clear, ask your teacher what type of annotations he or she expects, how many sources should be included, how long the annotations should be, and whether you are to use complete sentences when writing the piece.

Qualities of a Good Annotated Bibliography

A good annotated bibliography is formally correct and clears.

Formally Correct

An annotated bibliography entry begins with the bibliographic citation. This citation must adhere to the guidelines established by the stylebook your teacher expects you to follow. Because these citations can be difficult to format correctly, you need to set aside time to proofread them carefully before turning in your final draft. Entries in an annotated bibliography are listed in alphabetical order according to the lead author's last name or by the first key word in the title if there is no author.

Clear

The writing in your annotated bibliography must make sense to someone who has not read the source texts. Explain terms or references you think might confuse your intended audience. If your annotations include responses to or evaluations of the readings, be sure your state your reactions and judgments clearly and explain how you arrived at them.

Writing an Annotated Bibliography

The steps outlined below will help you write an annotated bibliography. Because there is such variety in the types of annotations teachers require across the curriculum, modify these steps as needed to meet the assignment's rhetorical situation and your instructor's expectations.

Step 1: Read and Analyze the Assignment

Be sure you understand the type of annotation you are being asked to write, how many annotations you are to complete, and which documentation guidelines you are expected to follow. If you have any questions concerning any of these matters, be sure to ask your teacher for clarifications.

Step 2: Collect, Read, and Annotate the Source Texts

If you are expected to find the source texts on your own, begin that process as soon as possible. As you locate sources you might include in your bibliography—or receive them from your teacher—read and annotate them according to the demands of the assignment. For example, if in your annotations you are expected to summarize the readings, then carefully summarize each major section of the source text, restating its main ideas, arguments, or findings clearly in your own words. If you are expected to respond to the readings, then jot down your reactions to the text as you read and reread it. If you are supposed to evaluate them, briefly write out your evaluations at then end of each reading, noting passages in the source you could cite, if necessary, to explain and defend your judgments.

Step 3: Write and Revise the Bibliographic Citation

Write the citation for each source text you will include in your bibliography following the models offered in your stylebook. Be sure to include in your citation all the necessary information and follow the proper format.

Step 4: Write and Revise the Annotation

Compose the annotation as directed by the assignment. Follow the teacher's instructions when deciding what information to include in your annotation and what level of diction to employ when composing it.

Sample Annotated Bibliography

The sample annotated bibliography below draws on sources used to write "What Killed Off the Dinosaurs" found on pages [[ref]]–[[ref]]. The bibliographic entries follow MLA guidelines; the annotations are summaries of the readings.

ANNOTATED BIBLIOGRAPHY

Archibald, J. David. "Were Dinosaurs the Victims of a Single Catastrophe? No, It Only Finished Them Off." *Natural History* 111.4 (2005): 52–3.

This article contends that dinosaur extinction was caused by a combination of volcanic activity, sea level change, and asteroid impact. By the end of the Cretaceous period, dinosaur populations were already in decline—somewhere between one-third and one-half of all species were already extinct. The asteroid impact contributed to the dinosaurs' death but can not be cited as the sole cause.

Cowen, Ron. "The Day the Dinosaurs Died." *Astronomy* April 1996: 34–42.

Cowen attributes dinosaur extinction to the impact of a massive asteroid hitting the Yucatan Peninsula. He explains how the impact brought about global warming which resulted in the deaths of dinosaurs whose populations were already stressed due to changes in the environment. Cowen points out that extinction rates were not consistent across the globe; therefore, one single, universal cause of extinction does not exist.

Keller, G. "Impacts, Volcanism and Mass Extinction: Random Coincidence or Cause and Effect?" *Australian Journal of Earth Sciences* 52 (2005): 725–57.

Keller argues that the dinosaurs' extinction can be attributed to extreme volcanism, not to the impact of a large asteroid, such as the one at Chicxulub, Mexico. Caused by shifting tectonic plats, the volcanism resulted in global warming which brought an end to the dinosaurs. Changes in the climate and environment caused the dinosaurs' extinction.

Ravilious, Kate. "Extreme Volcanism Doomed the Dinosaurs." *New Scientist* 20 Aug 2005: 11.

The reading asserts that extreme volcanic activity in the Indian subcontinent doomed the dinosaurs. This volcanic activity emitted enough gas and debris into the Earth's atmosphere to alter the climate and kill most life on earth, including the dinosaurs.

Sarjeant, William A. S., and Philip J. Currie. "The 'Great Extinction' That Never Happened: The Demise of the Dinosaurs Considered." *Canadian Journal of Earthy Science* 38 (2001): 239–47.

Sarjeant and Currie argue that the demise of the great dinosaurs at the end of Cretaceous period was the result of natural causes and not the result of an asteroid hitting the Earth. Though the asteroid may have contributed to the dinosaurs' extinction, other conditions, including climate change and the loss of inland seas, had already weakened them considerably. They also argues that dinosaurs, in fact, are not extinct; they live on as birds.

CREDITS

INDEX